American
Urban Politics

American Urban Politics

The Reader

FOURTH EDITION

EDITED BY

Dennis R. Judd
University of Illinois at Chicago

Paul Kantor
Fordham University

PEARSON
Longman

New York   San Francisco   Boston
London   Toronto   Sydney   Tokyo   Singapore   Madrid
Mexico City   Munich   Paris   Cape Town   Hong Kong   Montreal

Executive Editor: Eric Stano
Supplements Editor: Kristi Olson
Senior Marketing Manager: Elizabeth Fogarty
Production Manager: Eric Jorgensen
Project Coordination, Text Design, and Electronic Page Makeup:
    Electronic Publishing Services Inc., NYC
Cover Design Manager: John Callahan
Cover Designer: Kay Petronio
Cover Images: Left © The Art Archive/Culver Pictures/ Picture Desk, Inc./Kobal
    Collection; Center © Tim Hursley/SuperStock, Inc; Right © age fotostock/
    SuperStock, Inc.
Senior Manufacturing Buyer: Roy L. Pickering, Jr
Printer and Binder: RR Donnelly and Sons Company
Cover Printer: Phoenix Color Corp.

For permission to use copyrighted material, grateful acknowledgment is made to the copyright holders throughout the text, which are hereby made part of this copyright page.

Library of Congress Cataloging-in-Publication Data
American urban politics : the reader / [edited by] Dennis Judd, Paul Kantor.-- 4th ed.
    p. cm.
  Rev. ed. of: The politics of urban America. 3rd ed. 2001.
  Includes bibliographical references.
  ISBN 0-321-12970-9
  1. Urban policy--United States. 2. Municipal government--United States. 3. Metropol-
itan government--United States. 4. Urban renewal--United States. 5. City planning--
United States. I. Judd, Dennis R. II. Kantor, Paul, 1942- III. Title: Politics of urban
America.
HT123.A6663 2006
320.8'5'0973--dc22
                         2005017551

Visit us at http://www.ablongman.com.

ISBN 0-321-12970-9

1 2 3 4 5 6 7 8 9 10 DOC 08 07 06 05

To my grandchildren, Dylan, Miranda, and Jennifer, Jake, Weston, and Wyatt: you make the world go round!

—Dennis R. Judd

To my great brothers, Tony and Conrad, and our Chicago memories.

—Paul Kantor

CONTENTS

PREFACE

The ongoing transformation of cities and urban regions brought about by globalization has prompted scholars to re-examine their approaches to the study of the city. Now, more than ever, the object of our study is a moving target. We have incorporated readings into this fourth edition that capture the historic changes occurring in urban America as a result of globalization: the multiethnic metropolis that has emerged because of recent surges in immigration; the increasing importance of issues connected to race, ethnicity, and inequality; the intense competition among cities in the international marketplace, the fiscal pressures that cities face; new approaches to urban sprawl; and the fear occasioned by terrorism and crime.

Though we highlight new developments, however, we also wish to acknowledge the degree to which many of the "new" urban issues are actually quite old. To accomplish this, we incorporate readings meant to illustrate the continuing themes that have defined urban politics in America through three distinct periods: the first century, when cities spread across the frontier, engaged in a frenetic competition for primacy and power, and coped with the political effects of massive immigration; the twentieth century, when older industrial cities slid into decline, rapid suburbanization eclipsed the central cities, and the federal government withdrew from urban programs; and the global era.

In all three periods, urban leaders have tried to promote local economic prosperity, but they have had to do so within the constraints of democratic processes. The dynamic tension between the two imperatives have shaped cities in the past, and it continues to do so in the global era. This is because the American political order constitutes a merger of capitalism and democracy, or to put it differently, it joins a process in which popular elections and give and take among groups co-exists with private institutions and markets that supply necessary resources in exchange for profit. Local governments and cities are part of this political order.

In Part One we look back at these eras to examine the emergence of timeless themes and forces that continue to shape our local politics. Part Two surveys the emergence of the urban crisis during America's postwar decades, highlighting how racial polarization and suburban development set the stage for many of America's urban dilemmas. The globalization of political, economic and social relations in the metropolis during recent years is the subject of Part Three. These chapters examine the multi-dimensional character of our current urban scene. They describe the immigration and identity issues that now mark political conflict and competition in the new metropolis.

Internationalization of local economies has occurred, redefining how cities engage the marketplace today in a struggle for survival and prosperity. These changes have generated new issues about the use of space, the distribution of income and advantage, as well as race relations in city and suburb alike. Finally, efforts to regulate and cope with conflicts in the new metropolis have precipitated debates over governmental solutions to them. These include a reshaping of federal urban policy as well as attempts to employ new forms of regional political cooperation in order to respond to sprawl and other problems that spill over the borders of any one political jurisdiction.

The Internet and electronic libraries provide ready access to information about urban politics, and yet students often find these sources overwhelming or lacking in selectivity and context. This volume overcomes these deficiencies. We bring together a selection of readings that represent some of the most important trends and topics in urban scholarship today. These are placed in context by means of editors' essays that explain how each reading fits into past and contemporary developments in the study of urban politics. We survey the grand themes that have dominated urban politics since the beginning of the Republic to the present day in an introductory essay. The readings in subsequent chapters are introduced and discussed by the editors in order to place them into thematic context and to highlight particularly important insights. This book is a suitable companion for any good urban politics text, but its organization and themes fit particularly well with Dennis R. Judd and Todd Swanstrom's *City Politics*, a textbook also published by Longman Publishers.

Although we have attempted to provide both depth and scope in surveying urban America through the work of some of our nation's leading scholars, not every area of importance could be included. For example, the noble efforts of neighborhood and community organizations in responding to the dilemmas of the new metropolis had to be neglected. Nevertheless, we believe this Fourth Edition of *American Urban Politics: The Reader* will provide a worthy profile of the new and old political dynamics that shape the politics of America's cities.

We wish to thank Eric Stano, our Longman political science editor, for championing this book. His interest, ideas, and encouragement were essential to this enterprise.

DENNIS R. JUDD
PAUL KANTOR

INTRODUCTORY ESSAY

THE EVOLUTION OF URBAN POLITICS IN AMERICA

The politics of cities in the global age do not constitute a clean rupture from the past. Continuities are more striking than differences, considerable though they may be. The governance of American cities has always required urban leaders to nurture and promote local prosperity and at the same time to manage the conflicts that inevitably arise from the racial, ethnic, and social diversity. These two imperatives have always constituted the mainsprings of American politics, and they explain why the big issues have been so enduring. This volume highlights these continuities in our history as well as the exploding new forces of our global era.

There is an economic and a political logic in America's urban politics. The logic of the marketplace treats cities solely as locations for private economic activity—commerce, industry, finance, land investment, jobs. The economic behavior of business and entrepreneurs is rarely, if ever, influenced significantly by a concern for the public at large because the discipline of the market does not reward—and may actually penalize—business for doing so. Aside from occasional philanthropy, citizens do not look to the marketplace and business to address the problems of society; ultimately, the business of business is to make profits. By contrast, the political logic of democratic institutions motivates public officials to maintain and expand political support for what they do; otherwise, they do not remain in office for long. Political logic requires elected officials to pay attention not only to issues of prosperity, but also to *governance*. They are motivated to represent interests and resolve conflicts that the logic of the marketplace usually ignores. How economic and political logic interact in the urban governance process changes over time, but the fundamentals of the urban political economy have remained the same.

The principle defining feature of the global era is the speed with which capital and people are able to move. This geographic mobility has had profound consequences for cities. First, cities have been thrown into an intense competition for business and investment of every kind. In the 1980s, gleaming office towers, luxury hotels, and tourism and entertainment facilities sprang up in central cities all across the nation. Much of this activity could be tied to public leadership and public subsidies. It may sometimes appear that all politics revolves around efforts to regenerate the local economy. Cities and other units of government provide subsidies and incur long-term debt to build new sports stadiums and convention centers, to restore waterfronts and historic buildings, and to lure big-box stores and build office buildings. Such activities draw critical comments in the letters sections of local newspapers precisely because they are so ubiquitous.

The other defining feature of the global age is the accelerated movements of populations across national borders and within nations. In the last two decades of the twentieth century the American metropolis was changing into a complex mosaic. New immigrants—first Latinos and Asians, then people from all over the globe—moved to the suburbs as well as the cities. The old urban pattern that had sharply divided central cities from suburbs has begun to break down, replaced by a new reality that is more complex and less predictable. Like the cities, the suburbs are becoming home to the affluent and the poor alike, to native-born and immigrant, and to every racial and ethnic group.

The multiethnic metropolis places a premium upon effective governance. In recent decades minorities have become increasingly incorporated into local politics. This is a historic development because it helps to channel demands and grievances into the political system and away from the streets. But it will have limited effects if the metropolis becomes fragmented into a patchwork of inequality. The fragmentation of governments in urban regions tends to mirror residential patterns, making it impossible to speak of a metropolitan community. There are many communities. One of the great challenges of the global era is the question of how to effectively govern metropolitan regions that are so politically divided.

The readings that make up the chapters of Part One serve as useful reminders that these themes are timeless. From the nation's founding until the 1880s (and in many cities much longer), patricians and commercial elites governed the cities with one transcendent purpose in mind: to promote local economic growth. As the readings making up Chapter 2 illustrate, the coalitions that governed cities regarded them as instruments to promote private opportunity and little else. In the nineteenth century, the fate of individual cities—and the prospects of the individuals within them—depended upon their ability to tie into a national and international system of trade and commerce. As a consequence, urban elites engaged in an intense interurban competition; in addition to extolling their city's alleged economic and cultural advantages, they invested heavily in canals, railroads, and an infrastructure to support local commerce today, equivalent activities include such projects as sports stadiums, waterfront developments, and casinos.

By the late nineteenth century the imperative of governance began to supplant the imperative of growth. Because a stable urban hierarchy of cities began to emerge in the industrial age, the mad scramble for supremacy gave way to the much different task of managing the political tensions of the industrial city. After the Civil War, industrialization led to explosive urban growth. Lured by jobs in the factories, foreign immigrants poured into the cities by the millions. Universal suffrage for white males meant that the immigrants possessed a significant resource that could be used to transform politics. The readings in Chapter 3 shed light on the political struggles that the immigrants' entry into politics ignited. A new generation of politicians mobilized the Irish and other ethnic voters by distributing petty favors to needy constituents and by manipulating the symbols of ethnic solidarity. City hall typically became the forum for making deals, large and small. This style of politics prompted a reaction by upper- and middle-class people who objected to the free-wheeling and often corrupt practices of the immigrant politicians. The reformers pressed for election reforms, and succeeded in instituting such reforms as voting registration, secret balloting, at-large elections, and nonpartisan elections. In part they sought to make elections honest, but many of their proposals also were designed to reduce the influence of immigrant voters.

Part Two is composed of readings that trace the most significant developments in the urban crisis of the twentieth century: racial conflict, the decline of the central cities, and white flight to the suburbs. In the twentieth century, the divide between the central cities and the suburbs became a defining feature of America's political consciousness. A new phrase, "the urban crisis", was coined as a shorthand way to refer to the racial divide in American society. The phrase conjured up stark images of "the black ghetto" of concentrated poverty, which appeared in bold relief when juxtaposed against a powerful cultural stereotype: the American dream in the suburbs.

All through the century, the cities continued to serve as magnets for people escaping oppression and poverty and searching for jobs and opportunity. Before, then after, the Great Depression and again after World War II, blacks left the South by the millions and poured into the cities of the North. Between 1940 and 1970, five million blacks moved from the South to northern cities. At the same time, white middle-class families fled the cities to low-density, single-family homes in suburban subdivisions. By the 1970 census, for the first time, more Americans lived in suburbs than lived either in cities or in small towns and rural areas. During the 1980s and 1990s, population continued to sprawl in ever-widening suburban arcs around the core cities.

These developments exerted a tremendously negative impact on the central cities. In the past the cities had been the engines of the national economy; now it seemed they were losing all economic vitality and becoming the repository for the nation's social problems. The readings in Chapter 4 comment on the decline of downtown; the readings in Chapter 5 focus on the attempts by suburban residents to insulate themselves from the problems of the cities.

The chapters making up Part Three present selections about the consequences of globalization for the politics of cities and urban regions. Since the early 1990s, the divide between the cities and the suburbs has been giving way to a radically fractured metropolis. Since the mid-1960s, the United States has been experiencing one of the heaviest periods of immigration in the nation's history. New ethnic groups from Asia, Latin America, the Caribbean, and Eastern and Central Europe now constitute a substantial and growing proportion of the residents of America's cities. The political consequences of this development are far-reaching. For decades, the urban crisis was defined as the segregation between blacks in the central cities and whites in the suburbs. The difference now is that the tensions of urban society not only stir within these minority communities, but also have spread to the suburbs; conflicts over race and ethnicity are no longer located primarily in central cities. In the twenty-first century, the suburb/city dichotomy may become a thing of the past, replaced by metropolitan areas fractured into a mosaic of interethnic enclaves.

In the global era as in the past, issues of urban politics spring from the imperatives of growth and governance. Businesses and investors often can go wherever they please, while cities must compete vigorously for their jobs and dollars; nothing can be left to chance. The public sector is closely involved in making sure that the global city is a place attractive to corporations and to the people who work within them. Yet this is not entirely new. The parallel with the politics of growth in the nineteenth century is striking. Just as in that era, civic boosters are fired with the conviction that the fate of their cities hangs in the balance. This time, however, cities are pursuing corporate and service workers, tourists, and suburban visitors.

As in the past, the imperative of governance compels urban political leaders to seek popular consent while confronting complex social problems. As the ethnic and racial character of contemporary cities and suburbs changes, urban political agendas are also bound to change. Immigration is already altering the dominant issues and political conflicts of central cities. This is because immigrant groups have distinct priorities and are beginning to mobilize in support of strategies that will give them a share of power. These kinds of governance issues have also emerged in the past, as the readings in Part One suggest. To understand the politics of cities today, it is helpful to make comparisons with the past.

In the remainder of this essay we provide a context for understanding how urban politics in the global era has evolved from America's urban past. The similarities over time are striking, but each era also has its own distinct signature. Detailed comments on the individual selections are contained within the brief essays that introduce the selections making up each chapter.

Part One: From Competition to Governance: City Politics in the First Century

Entrepreneurial Cities and the Economic Imperative

For much of the nineteenth century an intense interurban competition provided the main dynamic of urban politics. Before the industrial revolution, the nation's cities prospered by presiding over an economic system that relied on the exchange of agriculture and extractive products for goods shipped from abroad or produced by craft shops located mostly in cities. The fortunes of individual cities were determined partly by the proximity to harbors, navigable rivers, or natural resources. But civic leaders were not willing to rely on luck and circumstance. Local elites actively promoted town growth and shaped their circumstances. They were indefatigable promoters of local growth because they instinctively understood that some cities—but not all—would prosper in the new market system that was in formation. Initially, the major obstacles to local economic growth were physical barriers that impeded the exchange of goods between a rural hinterland and the city, and between the city and other commercial centers. The building of the Erie Canal was a landmark event that precipitated several decades of interurban rivalry. Prodded by entrepreneurs in New York City, in 1817 the state of New York authorized construction of the 364-mile waterway to connect the Hudson River with Lake Erie. After completion of the canal in 1825, New York City gained access to the vast agricultural hinterland of the old Northwest (now the upper Midwest). The dramatic payoff from the construction of the Erie Canal encouraged other cities and states to begin their own somewhat more modest projects.

With the coming of railroads in the industrial age, the competition became, if anything, more fierce and expensive. Railroad building transformed the economic competition among cities into a truly national phenomenon. Cities everywhere, big and small, new and old, could use railroad lines to penetrate their hinterland in the expectation that they could gather up the trade of the back country and channel it through to their own commercial streets. Individual cities, as public corporations, provided massive assistance to railroad companies that agreed to build the necessary connections. By 1870, cities supplied an estimated one-fifth of the construction costs for the railroad lines then in existence (Taylor, 1951: 92).

Such a profligate use of municipal resources could only have occurred behind a strong, united leadership that shared a singular vision of the city's purpose. The economic interests of the governing elites were tied so closely to the growth of their cities that it drove them to close ranks and unite behind even the most ambitious and risky schemes to promote local development. Local political leadership became virtually defined as the task of convincing all the factions in the community that it was in everybody's interest to support or contribute to some specific public works project, canal project, or railway venture. Most voters followed the lead of the governing class; they generally shared the belief that a growing economy would, indeed, benefit everyone. Such claims will ring familiar to many urban residents today when they hear claims that a sports team will make a city a "big league" player.

Machines, Reform, and the Political Imperative

The industrial revolution and the development of mass democratic institutions transformed the politics of cities. Eventually, a rapidly expanding urban electorate became an enduring fixture in the politics of cities, challenging those who saw local politics as only a means of promoting growth. This was bound to change the entire complexion of local politics. By the 1840s property qualifications to vote were abolished almost everywhere, enfranchising mass electorates. After the Civil War, city populations exploded when waves of immigrants from abroad and migrants from rural areas came in search of jobs in the factories. Wide-open political struggles began to replace oligarchic control by business elites. A new generation of politicians learned how to mobilize the urban electorate. These professional politicians were often motivated by little more than a desire to use the political system for personal advancement. Public officials and those seeking favorable governmental action became accustomed to buying loyalty and favors with cash, jobs, contracts and other material inducements.

In many cities, this style of politics became structured and regularized. By the turn of the century several cities were governed by party machines that gathered the reins of power into the hands of a boss or a few ward politicians. The survival of this system was closely tied to two constituencies: voters and business. Machine politicians distributed jobs and favors to gain the loyalty of ethnic voters, and they also traded on the symbols of ethnic identity and solidarity. At the same time they made themselves useful—at a price, of course—to business entrepreneurs who benefited from stable, reliable relationships with politicians who could manipulate the powers of city government. Government officials routinely made important decisions granting franchises and setting utility rates; they approved contracts for the installation of street lights, gas, telephones, and trolley lines. Exclusive contracts for these services made fortunes; the politicians might receive bribes, but business entrepreneurs could make millions. The machines enabled business to operate freely in its own sphere; the politicians expected in exchange that they would be allowed to operate freely within theirs. For this reason, urban businessmen were sometimes the main supporters and beneficiaries of machine governments.

Machine politicians created their own opposition because they were often remarkably exclusionary. They represented some immigrant groups, but not others, and they were useful to only that fraction of the local business community that was willing or able to engage in deal-making and privilege-buying. Machine politicians often affronted middle- and upper-class sensibilities. The fledgling reform efforts that arose during the last years of the nineteenth century were mostly met with failure because they did not succeed at articulating a vision of the city that could unite enough groups behind a compelling cause. During the Progressive Era, however, a national movement coalesced behind the cause of municipal reform.

The system of boss politics found its most potent challenge in a municipal reform movement that became increasingly well-coordinated at the national level after the turn of the century. When national business corporations and organizations lined up behind the banner of municipal reform, the movement gained real strength. In principle, the reformers could have challenged the machines by destroying the machines' social base of support through appeals and programs designed to attract immigrants away from the machines. For instance, relief and housing programs could have competed with the bosses' unreliable dispensing of favors; taxes could have been imposed on businesses and the wealthy to pay for such programs. In reality, however, those who dominated municipal reform sought not only to limit the influence of bosses but also of the immigrants. They certainly did not imagine that the role of city government was to redistribute political power downward.

Quite the opposite was true. Most reformers wanted to use local government for their own purposes, and they wanted to gain firm control of municipal authority. They artfully obfuscated their agenda behind a rhetoric of "good government," in which they proposed that the public interest could be objectively defined, and that this interest dictated only one objective: the delivery of basic city services at the lowest possible cost. This theory was directly related to local democratic politics in the reformers' assertion that elections and representation should be strictly separated from the day-to-day administration of services. To protect municipal government from politics, the reformers said that experts with

training, experience, and ability should run the public's business. In sum, the reformers asserted that urban politics was not about governance, that is, the task of
brokering among various political interests. Rather, city government was merely a
matter of the proper mechanics—administration, not politics. "There is no Republican or Democratic way to pave the streets!" went the reform campaign slogan. Consistent with such a belief, the reformers fought to replace mayors with
city managers, partisan elections with the non partisan ballot, and wards with at-
large election systems. Despite all of their attempts to return power to the better
classes, however, the reformers could not return to the halcyon days when patricians and businessmen ran city affairs. There were simply too many claimants to
power to remove politics from the governance of the industrial city.

Part Two: City vs. Suburb: The Political Economy of the Urban Crisis

It was inevitable that race would become an ascendant issue in the politics of
central cities during the twentieth century. Since early in the century black populations in older cities had been increasing. By the 1960s conflicts over race affected virtually all the social institutions located in cities—from schools to neighborhoods to city halls. After World War II, the migration of blacks to cities
prompted a massive process of white flight to the suburbs. When businesses and
retailers followed suit, downtown districts began an alarming slide—one that began to moderate only in the global era with the growth of a new service sector
and visitor economy in central cities.

Images of race, poverty, crime, and slums came to symbolize the inner cities
in the twentieth century, while at the same time the suburbs became identified, in
the popular imagination, with tranquil subdivisions with cul-de-sacs and green
expanses of lawn. When racial animosities became a defining feature of the political and social life of metropolitan areas in the twentieth century, the suburbs became even more defensive of their separate status.

It is impossible to understand the issues and controversies that defined urban
politics in twentieth-century America without reference to the great central
city/suburban divide. People had begun to spill beyond the boundaries of the
cities even in the nineteenth century, and by the decade of the 1920s, the street-
car and the first auto suburbs began proliferating. For a time the suburban movement was stalled by the Great Depression and World War II. When prosperity returned in the postwar years, the floodgates were flung open. The suburbs grew by
35 million people in just the two decades from 1950 to 1960. Where people
went, business followed. By the 1960s shopping centers began to spring up in the
suburbs, and soon other businesses followed suit. Since World War II, older industrial cities have been faced with a steady erosion of populations and jobs.

Reflecting the stark differences between them, the politics of the suburbs and
the central cities diverged sharply. Relatively affluent, white suburban governments rapidly proliferated as suburbanites formed new towns and cities beyond
the boundaries of older core cities. Political separation allowed upper-income

and middle-class whites to segregate themselves from the people and problems of the central cities and to maintain low taxes, high property values, and amenities not available elsewhere.

National governmental policies encouraged and even subsidized the dispersal of people to suburbia. Federal mortgage insurance programs only financed new homes in white areas and excluded older housing in inner city neighborhoods. The federal interstate highway program, launched in the 1950s, cut new paths to suburban subdivisions, thus subsidizing a process of population deconcentration that is still occurring today. The public housing programs that Congress passed to help the cities actually disadvantaged blacks by increasing the number living in poverty neighborhoods even more than before; at the same time, urban renewal programs became one way of destroying the neighborhoods inhabited by blacks and the poor. Only when widespread social unrest and agitation precipitated a political crisis of national proportions in the 1960s did federal urban policies begin to target the housing, educational, and health ills of the inner cities.

By the late 1970s, a coalition of Sunbelt conservatives and probusiness interests were brought together under the Republican Party banner in a national political party realignment. This coalition opposed an activist federal role in the cities, leading to the elimination of most federal urban programs. By the 1980s cities became marginalized in national electoral politics.

Part Three: The Multiethnic Metropolis: The Metropolis in the Global Era

By the late twentieth century, new political issues began to emerge in metropolitan areas. The increased mobility of capital and new waves of immigration unleashed political struggles over urban space and fueled an anxiety about the local economy that has interesting parallels to the nineteenth century. As in that era, cities today cannot look to the federal government for help. Left increasingly to their own resources, cities and suburbs compete for wealth and residents in an economy that is marked by dependence on large, transnational corporations with little or no stake in any particular locale.

At the same time, political leaders struggle to obtain popular consent in a multiethnic metropolis. New immigrants are competing with older ethnic and racial minorities for jobs, space, and power. The old patterns of race relations have begun to break down, replaced by a new reality that is more complex and less predictable. The suburbs are becoming home to the affluent and the poor alike, to native-born and immigrant, and to every racial and ethnic group. At the same time, affluent empty-nesters and young professionals are moving back downtown. Central cities are once again becoming hot spots for culture, nightlife, and fun.

The Multiethnic Metropolis

Issues of race and ethnicity became contentious, even explosive, issues in the 1960s, and they have remained crucially important ever since. In the 1960s and

1970s mayors looked to Washington in the hope that social and urban programs could help them to cope with the racial tensions and social problems that confronted them. Since the withdrawal of the federal government from the cities, their task has been challenging, to say the least. On the one hand, mayors have been forced into strategies to rebuild downtown economies. On the other hand, they must also try to maintain some minimal degree of social cohesion, a task made even more difficult in those cities that have received waves of new immigrants coming from countries in Asia, Latin America, and the Caribbean. The decade of the 1980s saw the second-largest flow of legal immigration in American history, exceeding even the flood tide of 1900–1910. As a result, the urban politics of the 1990s and beyond is likely to revolve around interracial and interethnic rivalries.

As their presence and political activism grew from the 1960s to the 1990s, African Americans and Latinos began to capture roles as major power brokers in the big cities. By 1990 there were 7,935 black elected officials in the United States. Significantly, most of the increase in black representation occurred in central cities (Kantor, 1995: 83). The number of Latino officials has also grown, particularly in the cities. The ability of urban officials to leverage their access to government into tangible gains for inner-city populations is, however, constrained by the fact that the cities they govern lack the fiscal resources to do very much. For this reason, minority mayors who talk a language of social reform are elected, but they typically end up pursuing policies designed to promote private investment (Reed, 1987; Judd, 1986). Faced with such limited resources, city hall has embraced the rhetoric of neighborhood and community self-help. Empowerment and city participation are the new code words of the 1990s. They carry a promise that since government cannot do as much as before, communities should work with government and non profits to solve their own problems. It remains to be seen whether the cities can ultimately be governed in this way.

The breakup of the old urban pattern does not guarantee that the racial and ethnic segregation that has long characterized urban America will become a thing of the past. Within cities, affluent downtown and gentrified neighborhoods are sharply separated from the neighborhoods inhabited by the urban poor. This pattern shows up most starkly in the global cities and, in fact, in all cities that have attracted highly paid workers connected to the global economy. High-rise condominium and townhouse developments sometimes sit only a block or two from neighborhoods with extremely high levels of poverty. Something similar may be happening in the suburbs. Though the suburbs are becoming multiethnic, like the central cities they seem to be breaking into enclaves that separate minorities and lower-income residents from the middle-class residents of gated communities. The incorporation of these new interests into urban political systems is a complex process that is changing the stakes, players, and rewards of local governance.

Cities in the International Marketplace

Urban leaders have little choice; in the global era they must compete vigorously for private investment. What began as the movement of manufacturing, wholesaling, and retailing firms from older cities in the 1970s has matured into an economic reality in which many firms easily move from one city or region to another, or even outside the United States entirely. In recent decades, cities (and even nations) have been forced to compete with one another for investment in innovative ways. In the environment of a globalized economy, most cities are now fighting for a niche in the new urban hierarchy. All of the older industrial cities have joined a fierce competition for corporate jobs and professional services and for entertainment, leisure, and tourism. Devising strategies to make the local economy competitive while also addressing the political claims of various ethnic groups turns city politics into a delicate balancing act.

Rising inequality is occurring throughout American society, but the consequences are amplified in cities. Since the early 1980s inequality has risen sharply in the United States. In 1980, the bottom one-fifth of the population earned 4.3 percent of all earned income. Only a few years later, in 1998, the poorest fifth of wage earners accounted for just 3.6 percent. Meanwhile, from 1980 to 1998 the richest fifth increased its share from 44 percent to 49.2 percent. Perhaps even more telling, the top five percent of wage earners had increased its share of earnings in the same period from 16 percent to 21.4 percent (U.S. Bureau of the Census, 2000).

Differences between the downtown professional class and the residents of minority neighborhoods have become especially obvious in the global era. This kind of social polarization is particularly prominent in cities tied closely to the global economy. Global cities have attracted a more diverse profile of immigrants than any other cities (Abrahamson, 2004). Jobs are the lure. The concentration of multinational businesses, financial service corporations, and the businesses connected to them draw highly educated workers from all over the globe. But the greatest demand for jobs (at least expressed in numbers) is found at the other end of the labor market. Lower-status service workers are indispensable to the working of a global city. Clerical workers, janitors and cashiers, nannies, cooks and busboys, maintenance and security workers, hotel maids, and a multitude of personal-service specialists from masseuses, personal shoppers, and dog-walkers—these jobs are taken by immigrants and minorities disproportionately.

Defended Space and the Politics of Fear

The geography and politics of cities in the twenty-first century is being powerfully shaped by perceptions of safety and security. Neighborhoods and the downtowns of large cities are often demarcated and defended from surrounding land uses that might seem threatening (Davis, 1990; Judd, 1996). The barriers that protect downtowns come in various forms, such as shopping centers, entertainment districts, and tourist enclaves. Perhaps the most comprehensive barriers have been built in Atlanta and Detroit, where a large proportion of downtown office workers commute to the sealed realms of the Peachtree Center and the Renaissance Center. In both these structures, workers drive into parking garages and then enter a city-within-a-city where they can work, shop, eat lunch, and find a variety of diversions after work. They never have to set foot in the rest of the city. In other cities, the downtown enclosure may be less extreme, but for visitors the experience of the city may not be much different. Tourists and visitors who visit central cities now commonly fly into an airport, take a taxi or a light rail to a downtown hotel, and stay within the well-defined tourist area, never seeing or even becoming aware of the larger city around them.

Protected enclaves have proliferated in suburbs just as they have in central cities. A large proportion of urban residents commute from subdivisions, gated communities, townhouse developments, or condominium complexes to high-rise downtown office buildings or suburban office parks, and they drive to enclosed malls or mall complexes for shopping and commute to tourist bubbles to enjoy themselves (Judd, 1996). By 2002, an estimated 50 million Americans lived in common interest developments with private governments, compared to 32 million only one decade before (*Realty Times,* 2002; McKenzie, 1994). For many, the urban experience has turned into a series of enclosures, each connected by a transportation corridor.

If people feel secure, urban areas will gradually open up. Neighborhoods will become less segregated and racial and ethnic differences will lose their divisive force. If, on the other hand, people do not feel secure, the lessons from the past are clear. In the twentieth century, affluent citizens escaped the problems of the city by moving to the suburbs. In the twenty-first century, an escape from urban problems will be expressed in a different way. In city and in suburb, people will move into walled-off spaces such as gated communities, condominium towers, and fortress office buildings.

Federal Policy

For half a century, Congress enacted legislation designed to help the cities with mixed results. As the federal presence in our cities shrank and central-city voters no longer played a decisive role in national politics, a politics of devolution has engaged the cities. For a few years federal programs helped the cities stave off the consequences of economic decline. When Republicans won the White House in 1980, the cities' biggest source of new revenue since the early 1960s—federal dollars—dried up quickly. Federal policy went in a new direction; the devolution of powers and responsibilities to states and localities became the new guiding principle. Cities have been forced to do more with less, and innovate on their own. Not surprisingly, urban management issues have become more prominent and state governments have come to play a large role in urban policy.

Sprawl and the New Regionalism

Globalization is redefining the relations between city and suburb. Sprawl now characterizes metropolitan areas after decades of population dispersal. These areas are also fragmented into scores or even hundreds of governmental jurisdictions. Yet these far-flung communities are in fact often quite interdependent and, according to some, must compete as regions in order to prosper in the new economy. Further, attempts to achieve equitable and effective governance in urban America will have limited effects if the metropolis becomes fragmented into a patchwork of inequality.

The fragmentation of governments within urban regions tends to mirror residential patterns, making it impossible to speak of a metropolitan community. There are many communities. Can they cooperate to address common problems? The quality of life in the multiethnic metropolis of the twenty-first century will be determined not only by how effectively individual municipalities are governed, but also by how well they work with one another.

References

Abrahamson, Mark. *Global Cities.* New York: Oxford University Press, 2004.

Beauregard, Robert A. *Voice of Decline: The Postwar Fate of U.S. Cities.* New York: Blackwell, 1993.

Davis, Mike. *City of Quartz.* New York: Vintage, 1990.

Downs, Anthony. *New Visions for Metropolitan America.* Washington, D.C.: Brookings Institution, 1994.

Edsall, Thomas Byrne, and Mary D. Edsall. *Chain Reaction: The Impact of Race, Rights, and Taxes on American Politics.* New York: W.W. Norton & Co, 1991.

Garreau, Joel. *Edge City: Life on the New Frontier.* New York: Doubleday, 1991.

Glabb, Charles N., and A. Theodore Brown. *A History of Urban America.* New York: Macmillan, 1967.

Goodrich, Carter. *Government Promotion of American Canals and Railroads, 1800–1890.* New York: Columbia University Press, 1960.

Goodrich, Carter, ed. *Canals and American Economic Development.* New York: Columbia University Press, 1961.

"Homeowner Associations—General Housing." *Realty Times,* (June 28, 2002).

Judd, Dennis R. "Electoral Coalitions, Minority Mayors, and the Contradictions in the Municipal Policy Agenda." pp. 145–170 in *Cities in Stress: A New Look at the Urban Crisis,* ed. M. Gottdiener, Sage Publications, 1986.

———. "Enclosure, Community, and Public Life," pp. 217–238 in *Research in Community Sociology: New Communities in a Changing World,* Dan A. Chekki, ed. Greenwich, Conn. and London: JAI Press, 1996.

Kantor, Paul. *The Dependent City Revisited. The Political Economy of Urban Development and Social Policy.* Boulder, Colo.: Westview Press, 1995.

———. "The Dual City as Political Choice." *Journal of Urban Affairs,* 15 (3), (1993): 231–244.

McKenzie, Evan. *Privatopia: Homeowner Associations and the Rise of Residential Private Government.* New Haven, Conn.: Yale University Press, 1994.

Pomper, Gerald. "The Presidential Election." in *The Election of 1984: Reports and Interpretations,* ed. Pomper, Chatham, N.J.: Chatham House, 1985.

Reed, Adolph, Jr. "A Critique of Neo-Progressivism in Theorizing About Local Development Policy: A Case of Atlanta." pp. 199–215 in *The Politics of Urban Development,* Clarence N. Stone and Heywood T. Sanders, ed. Lawrence: University Press of Kansas, 1987.

Sassen, Saskia. *The Global City.* Princeton, N.J.: Princeton University Press, 1991.

Shefter, Martin. *Political Crisis, Fiscal Crisis* New York: Basic Books, 1985.

Stone, Clarence N. *Regime Politics: Governing Atlanta.* Lawrence: University Press of Kansas, 1989.

Swanstrom, Todd. "Semi-sovereign Cities: The Politics of Urban Development," *Polity* 21, no. 1 (Fall 1989): 83–110.

Taylor, George Rogers. *The Transportation Revolution: 1815–1860.* New York: Rinehart, 1951.

U.S. Bureau of the Census. *The Changing Shape of the Nation's Income Distribution, 1947–1998.* Table 1, p. 3, June 2000. *http://www.census.gov/prod/2000.*

CHAPTER 1

THE POLITICAL ECONOMY
OF CITIES

The Nature of Urban Governance

Urban scholars and policymakers frequently speak of cities as if they were people, capable of independent action and thought. Such a construction is more than a mere rhetorical flourish because, in fact, cites are public corporations that take significant actions every day. As Paul E. Peterson points out in Essay 1, there are constant debates about the public interest that cities ought to pursue. Some people might demand that cities spend their resources on redistributive policies designed to help those most in need. Others might promote the view that city government should do little more than provide the services necessary to keep the city a healthy and functioning environment. Peterson's view is that cities must at all costs avoid redistributive services, provide basic services at an adequate level, and place the greatest possible emphasis upon policies that will stimulate economic growth. Such policies, he says, respond to a "unitary interest . . . to help sustain a high-quality local infrastructure generally attractive to all commerce and industry." Even the social health of a city, he argues, depends on its economic prosperity: when the economy is growing, "tax revenues increase, city services can be improved, donations to charitable organizations become more generous, and the social and cultural life of the city is enhanced."

In Peterson's view, local civic leaders cannot leave economic growth to chance because cities compete with one another. City governments are unable to control the movement of capital and labor across borders. Unlike the national government, they lack the authority to regulate immigration, currency, or to regulate the import or export of goods and services. Cities occupy a specific space; if the local business environment is not pleasing to them, investors and businesses can (and often do) go elsewhere. This logic drives cities to minimize taxes, avoid expensive regulations, and offer a variety of subsidies to business. Put simply, Peterson's logic would lead politicians to resist the clamor of all political interests that might compromise the preferences of business in any way.

The book from which the Peterson selection is taken ignited a controversy among urban scholars—a controversy that has not died down completely even after more than two decades (Peterson's book was published in 1981). Many scholars took Peterson to task for his assertion that growth benefits everyone. Others accused him of ignoring the complexities of urban politics by pointing out that the mix of local policies differs substantially from city to city depending upon the population demographics, the political organization of various groups, the degree of political participation, and governmental structures. The importance of local prosperity is likely to always be on the agenda, but politicians must also mobilize sufficient political support to remain in office; in other words, they must win elections. A new literature on urban regimes provided a way of understanding the specific mechanisms by which the tensions between the marketplace and local democracy are managed. As described by Clarence N. Stone in Essay 2, the two most powerful components of urban regimes include city hall—the officals who are most motivated by electoral concerns—and the city's business elites. Governmental officials lack the resources to do much on their own. Likewise, the business community requires government to help create and maintain the city as an environment for both investment and political stability. Thus, in Stone's account of politics in Atlanta, he notes that, "What makes governance in Atlanta effective is not the formal machinery of government, but rather the informal partnership between city hall and the downtown business elites. This informal partnership and the way it operates constitute the city's regime; it is the same means through which major policy decisions are made." Note that Stone's use of the word "partnership" suggests cooperation rather than control. If regime participants learn to work together to accomplish mutual goals, all are empowered in the sense that each of them can accomplish things that none of them working alone can accomplish.

With few exceptions, urban scholars have embraced Stone's premise that urban politics and policymaking involve a close cooperation between governmental and nongovernmental actors. His claim, however, that a city-hall business coalition normally constitutes the core of urban governance has been questioned. Issues connected to race and ethnicity have always been crucial features of urban politics in America. As the selection by Elaine B. Sharp demonstrates, just as the culture wars over social issues have become increasingly important in national politics, they also have penetrated into local communities. Accordingly, urban governments often wrestle with contentious issues such as gay rights, pornography, the operation of abortion clinics, hate-group activity, and judicial decisions regarding sexual assault. Sometimes local officials instigate controversy to press their own agendas. Sharp's point is important because it shows that local governments can sometimes become just as preoccupied with the task of maintaining social order as with other priorities.

1

Paul E. Peterson

THE INTERESTS OF THE LIMITED CITY

Like all social structures, cities have interests. Just as we can speak of union interests, judicial interests, and the interests of politicians, so we can speak of the interests of that structured system of social interactions we call a city. Citizens, politicians, and academics are all quite correct in speaking freely of the interests of cities.[1]

Defining the City Interest

By a city's interest, I do not mean the sum total of the interests of those individuals living in the city. For one thing, these are seldom, if ever, known. The wants, needs, and preferences of residents continually change, and few surveys of public opinion in particular cities have ever been taken. Moreover, the residents of a city often have discordant interests. Some want more parkland and better schools; others want better police protection and lower taxes. Some want an elaborated highway system; others wish to keep cars out of their neighborhood. Some want more inexpensive, publicly subsidized housing; others wish to remove the public housing that exists. Some citizens want improved welfare assistance for the unemployed and dependent; others wish to cut drastically all such programs of public aid. Some citizens want rough-tongued ethnic politicians in public office; others wish that municipal administration were a gentleman's calling. Especially in large cities, the cacophony of competing claims by diverse class, race, ethnic, and occupational groups makes impossible the determination of any overall city interest—any public interest, if you like—by compiling all the demands and desires of individual city residents.

Some political scientists have attempted to discover the overall urban public interest by summing up the wide variety of individual interests. The earlier work of Edward Banfield, still worth examination, is perhaps the most persuasive effort of this kind.[2] He argued that urban political processes—or at least those in Chicago—allowed for the expression of nearly all the particular interests within the city. Every significant interest was represented by some economic firm or voluntary association, which had a stake in trying to influence those public policies that touched its vested interests. After these various groups and firms had debated and contended, the political leader searched for a compromise that took into account the vital interests of each, and worked out a solution all could accept with some satisfaction. The leader's own interest in sustaining his political power dictated such a strategy.

Banfield's argument is intriguing, but few people would identify public policies as being in the interest of the city simply because they have been formulated according to certain procedures. The political leader might err in his judgment; the interests of important but politically impotent groups might never get expressed; or the consequences of a policy might in the long run be disastrous for the city. Moreover, most urban policies are not hammered out after great controversy, but are the quiet product of routine decision making. How does one evaluate which of these are in the public interest? Above all, this mechanism for determining the city's interest provides no standpoint for evaluating the substantive worth of urban policies. Within Banfield's framework, whatever urban governments do is said to be in the interest of their communities. But the concept of city interest is used most persuasively when there are calls for reform or innovation. It is a term used to evaluate existing programs and to discriminate between promising and undesirable new ones. To equate the interests of cities with what cities are doing is to so impoverish the term as to make it quite worthless.

The economist Charles Tiebout employs a second approach to the identification of city interests.[3] Unlike Banfield, he does not see the city's interests as a mere summation of individual interests but as something which can be ascribed to the entity, taken as a whole. As an economist, Tiebout is hardly embarrassed by such an enterprise, because in ascribing interests to cities his work parallels both those orthodox economists who state that firms have an interest in maximizing profits and those welfare economists who claim that politicians have an interest in maximizing votes. Of course, they state only that their model will assume that firms and politicians behave in such a way, but insofar as they believe their model has empirical validity, they in fact assert that those constrained by the businessman's or politician's role must pursue certain interests. And so does Tiebout when he says that communities seek to attain the optimum size for the efficient delivery of the bundle of services the local government produces. In his words, "Communities below the optimum size seek to attract new residents to lower average costs. Those above optimum size do just the opposite. Those at an optimum try to keep their populations constant."[4]

Tiebout's approach is in many ways very attractive. By asserting a strategic objective that the city is trying to maximize—optimum size—Tiebout identifies an overriding interest which can account for specific policies the city adopts. He provides a simple analytical tool that will account for the choices cities make, without requiring complex investigations into citizen preferences and political mechanisms for identifying and amalgamating the same. Moreover, he provides a criterion for determining whether a specific policy is in the interest of the city—does it help achieve optimum size? Will it help the too small city grow? Will it help the too big city contract? Will it keep the optimally sized city in equilibrium? Even though the exact determination of the optimum size cannot presently be scientifically determined in all cases, the criterion does provide a useful guide for prudential decision making.

The difficulty with Tiebout's assumption is that he does not give very good reasons for its having any plausibility. When most economists posit a certain form of maximizing behavior, there is usually a good commonsense reason for believing the person in that role will have an interest in pursuing this strategic objective. When orthodox economists say that businessmen maximize profits, it squares with our understanding in everyday life that people engage in commercial enterprises for monetary gain. The more they make, the better they like it. The same can be said of those welfare economists who say politicians maximize votes. The assumption, though cynical, is in accord with popular belief— and therefore once again has a certain plausibility.

By contrast, Tiebout's optimum size thesis diverges from what most people think cities are trying to do. Of course, smaller communities are often seeking to expand—boosterism may be the quintessential characteristic of small-town America. Yet Tiebout takes optimum size, not growth or maximum size, as the strategic objective. And when Tiebout discusses the big city that wishes to shrink to optimum size, his cryptic language is quite unconvincing. "The case of the city that is too large and tries to get rid of residents is more difficult to imagine," he confesses. Even more, he concedes that "no alderman in his right political mind would ever admit that the city is too big." "Nevertheless," he continues, "economic forces are at work to push people out of it. Every resident who moves to the suburbs to find better schools, more parks, and so forth, is reacting, in part, against the pattern the city has to offer."[5] In this crucial passage Tiebout speaks neither of local officials nor of local public policies. Instead, he refers to "economic forces" that may be beyond the control of the city and of "every resident," each of whom may be pursuing his own interests, not that of the community at large.

The one reason Tiebout gives for expecting cities to pursue optimum size is to lower the average cost of public goods. If public goods can be delivered most efficiently at some optimum size, then migration of residents will occur until that size has been reached. In one respect Tiebout is quite correct: local governments must concern themselves with operating local services as efficiently as possible in order to protect the city's economic interests. But there is little evidence that there is an optimum size at which services can be delivered with greatest efficiency. And even if such an optimum did exist, it could be realized only if migration occurred among residents who paid equal amounts in local taxes. In the more likely situation, residents pay variable prices for public services (for example, the amount paid in local property taxes varies by the value of the property). Under these circumstances, increasing size to the optimum does not reduce costs to residents unless newcomers pay at least as much in taxes as the marginal increase in costs their arrival imposes on city government.[6]

Conversely, if a city needs to lose population to reach the optimum, costs to residents will not decline unless the exiting population paid less in taxes than was the marginal cost of providing them government services. In most big cities losing population, exactly the opposite is occurring. Those who pay more in taxes than they receive in services are the emigrants. Tiebout's identification of city interests with optimum size, while suggestive, fails to take into account the quality as well as the quantity of the local population.

The interests of cities are neither a summation of individual interests nor the pursuit of optimum size. Instead, policies and programs can be said to be in the interest of cities whenever the policies maintain or enhance the economic position, social prestige, or political power of the city, taken as a whole.[7]

Cities have these interests because cities consist of a set of social interactions structured by their location in a particular territorial space. Any time that social interactions come to be structured into recurring patterns, the structure thus formed develops an interest in its own maintenance and enhancement. It is in that sense that we speak of the interests of an organization, the interests of the system, and the like. To be sure, within cities, as within any other structure, one can find diverse social roles, each with its own set of interests. But these varying role interests, as divergent and competing as they may be, do not distract us from speaking of the overall interests of the larger structural entity.[8]

The point can be made less abstractly. A school system is a structured form of social action, and therefore it has an interest in maintaining and improving its material resources, its prestige, and its political power. Those policies or events which have such positive effects are said to be in the interest of the school system. An increase in state financial aid or the winning of the basketball tournament are events that, respectively, enhance the material well-being and the prestige of a school system and are therefore in its interest. In ordinary speech this is taken for granted, even when we also recognize that teachers, pupils, principals, and board members may have contrasting interests as members of differing role-groups within the school.

Although social roles performed within cities are numerous and conflicting, all are structured by the fact that they take place in a specific spatial location that falls within the jurisdiction of some local government. All members of the city thus come to share an interest in policies that affect the well-being of that territory. Policies which enhance the desirability or attractiveness of the territory are in the city's interest, because they benefit all residents—in their role as residents of the community. Of course, in any of their other social roles, residents of the city may be adversely affected by the policy. The Los Angeles dope peddler—in his role as peddler—hardly benefits from a successful drive to remove hard drugs from the city. On the other hand, as a resident of the city, he benefits from a policy that enhances the attractiveness of the city as a locale in which to live and work. In determining whether a policy is in the interest of a city, therefore, one does not consider whether it has a positive or negative effect on the total range of social interactions of each and every individual. That is an impossible task. To know whether a policy is in a city's interest, one has to consider only the impact on social relationships insofar as they are structured by their taking place within the city's boundaries.

An illustration from recent policy debates over the future of our cities reveals that it is exactly with this meaning that the notion of a city's interest is typically used. The tax deduction that homeowners take on their mortgage interest payments should be eliminated, some urbanists have argued. The deduction has not served the interests of central cities, because it has provided a public subsidy for families who purchase suburban homes. Quite clearly, elimination of this tax deduction is not in the interest of those central city residents who wish to purchase a home in the suburbs. It is not in the interest of those central city homeowners (which in some cities may even form a majority of the voting population), who would then be called upon to pay higher federal taxes. But the policy might very well improve the rental market in the central city, thereby stimulating its economy—and it is for this reason that the proposal has been defended as being in the interest of central cities.

To say that people understand what, generally, is in the interest of cities does not eliminate debate over policy alternatives in specific instances. The notion of city interest can be extremely useful, even though its precise application in specific contexts may be quite problematic. In any policy context one cannot easily assert that one "knows" what is in the interest of cities, whether or not the residents of the city agree. But city residents do know the kind of evidence that must be advanced and the kinds of reasons that must be adduced in order to build a persuasive case that a policy is in the interest of cities. And so do community leaders, mayors, and administrative elites.

Economic Interests

Cities, like all structured social systems, seek to improve their position in all three of the systems of stratification—economic, social, and political—characteristic of industrial societies. In most cases, improved standing in any one of these systems helps enhance a city's position in the other two. In the short run, to be sure, cities may have to choose among economic gains, social prestige, and political weight. And because different cities may choose alternative objectives, one cannot state any one overarching objective—such as improved property values—that is always the paramount interest of the city. But inasmuch as improved economic or market standing seems to be an objective of great importance to most cities, I shall concentrate on this interest and only discuss in passing the significance of social status and political power.

Cities constantly seek to upgrade their economic standing. Following Weber, I mean by this that cities seek to improve their market position, their attractiveness as a locale for economic activity. In the market economy that characterizes Western society, an advantageous economic position means a competitive edge in the production and distribution of desired commodities relative to other localities. When this is present, cities can export goods and/or services to those outside the boundaries of the community.

Some regional economists have gone so far as to suggest that the welfare of a city is identical to the welfare of its export industry.[9] As exporters expand, the city grows. As they contract, the city declines and decays. The economic reasoning supporting such a conclusion is quite straightforward. When cities produce a good that can be sold in an external market, labor and capital flow into the city to help increase the production of that good. They continue to do so until the external market is saturated—that is, until the marginal cost of production within the city exceeds the marginal value of the good external to the city. Those engaged in the production of the exported good will themselves consume a variety of other goods and services, which other businesses will provide. In addition, subsidiary industries locate in the city either because they help supply the exporting industry, because they can utilize some of its by-products, or because they benefit by some economies of scale provided by its presence. Already, the familiar multiplier is at work. With every increase in the sale of exported commodities, there may be as much as a four- or fivefold increase in local economic activity.

The impact of Boeing Aircraft's market prospects on the economy of the Seattle metropolitan area illustrates the importance of export to regional economies. In the late sixties defense and commercial aircraft contracts declined. Boeing laid off thousands of workmen, the economy of the Pacific Northwest slumped, the unemployed moved elsewhere, and Seattle land values dropped sharply. More recently, Boeing has more than recovered its former position. With rapidly expanding production at Boeing, the metropolitan area is enjoying low unemployment, rapid growth, and dramatically increasing land values.

The same multiplier effect is not at work in the case of goods and services produced for domestic consumption within the territory. What is gained by a producer within the community is expended by other community residents. Residents, in effect, are simply taking in one another's laundry. Unless productivity increases, there is no capacity for expansion.

If this economic analysis is correct, it is only a modest oversimplification to equate the interests of cities with the interests of their export industries. Whatever helps them prosper redounds to the benefit of the community as a whole—perhaps four and five times over. And it is just such an economic analysis that has influenced many local government policies. Especially the smaller towns and cities may provide free land, tax concessions, and favorable utility rates to incoming industries.

The smaller the territory and the more primitive its level of economic development, the more persuasive is this simple export thesis. But other economists have elaborated an alternative growth thesis that is in many ways more persuasive, especially as it relates to larger urban areas. In their view a sophisticated local network of public and private services is the key to long-range economic growth. Since the world economy is constantly changing, the economic viability of any particular export industry is highly variable. As a result, a community dependent on any particular set of export industries will have only an episodic economic future. But with a well-developed infrastructure of services, the city becomes an attractive locale for a wide variety of export industries. As older exporters fade, new exporters take their place and the community continues to prosper. It is in the city's interest, therefore, to help sustain a high-quality local infrastructure generally attractive to all commerce and industry.

I have no way of evaluating the merits of these contrasting economic arguments. What is important in this context is that both see exports as being of great importance to the well-being of a city. One view suggests a need for direct support of the export industry; the other suggests a need only for maintaining a service infrastructure, allowing the market to determine which particular export industry locates in the community. Either one could be the more correct diagnosis for a particular community, at least in the short run. Yet both recognize that the future of the city depends upon exporting local products. When a city is able to export its products, service industries prosper, labor is in greater demand, wages increase, promotional opportunities widen, land values rise, tax revenues increase, city services can be improved, donations to charitable organizations become more generous, and the social and cultural life of the city is enhanced.

To export successfully, cities must make efficient use of the three main factors of production: land, labor, and capital.[10]

Land

Land is the factor of production that cities control. Yet land is the factor to which cities are bound. It is the fact that cities are spatially defined units whose boundaries seldom change that gives permanence to their interests. City residents come and go, are born and die, and change their tastes and preferences. But the city remains wedded to the land area with which it is blessed (or cursed). And unless it can alter that land area, through annexation or consolidation, it is the long-range value of that land which the city must secure—and which gives a good approximation of how well it is achieving its interests.

Land is an economic resource. Production cannot occur except within some spatial location. And because land varies in its economic potential, so do the economic futures of cities. Historically, the most important variable affecting urban growth has been an area's relationship to land and water routes.

On the eastern coast of the United States, all the great cities had natural harbors that facilitated commercial relations with Europe and other coastal communities. Inland, the great industrial cities all were located on either the Great Lakes or the Ohio River–Mississippi River system. The cities of the West, as Elazar has shown, prospered according to their proximity to East-West trade flows.[11] Denver became the predominant city of the mountain states because it sat at the crossroads of land routes through the Rocky Mountains. Duluth,

Minnesota, had only limited potential, even with its Great Lakes location, because it lay north of all major routes to the West.

Access to waterways and other trade routes is not the only way a city's life is structured by its location. Its climate determines the cost and desirability of habitation; its soil affects food production in the surrounding area; its terrain affects drainage, rates of air pollution, and scenic beauty. Of course, the qualities of landscape do not permanently fix a city's fate—it is the intersection of that land and location with the larger national and world economy that is critical. For example, cities controlling access to waterways by straddling natural harbors at one time monopolized the most valuable land in the region, and from that position they dominated their hinterland. But since land and air transport have begun to supplant, not just supplement, water transport, the dominance of these once favored cities has rapidly diminished.

Although the economic future of a city is very much influenced by external forces affecting the value of its land, the fact that a city has control over the use of its land gives it some capacity for influencing that future. Although there are constitutional limits to its authority, the discretion available to a local government in determining land use remains the greatest arena for the exercise of local autonomy. Cities can plan the use of local space; cities have the power of eminent domain; through zoning laws cities can restrict all sorts of land uses; and cities can regulate the size, content, and purpose of buildings constructed within their boundaries. Moreover, cities can provide public services in such a way as to encourage certain kinds of land use. Sewers, gas lines, roads, bridges, tunnels, playgrounds, schools, and parks all impinge on the use of land in the surrounding area. Urban politics is above all the politics of land use, and it is easy to see why. Land is the factor of production over which cities exercise the greatest control.

Labor

To its land area the city must attract not only capital but productive labor. Yet local governments in the United States are very limited in their capacities to control the flow of these factors. Lacking the more direct controls of nation-states, they are all the more constrained to pursue their economic interests in those areas where they do exercise authority.

Labor is an obvious case in point. Since nation-states control migration across their boundaries, the industrially more advanced have formally legislated that only limited numbers of outsiders—for example, relatives of citizens or those with skills needed by the host country—can enter. In a world where it is economically feasible for great masses of the population to migrate long distances, this kind of restrictive legislation seems essential for keeping the nation's social and economic integrity intact. Certainly, the wage levels and welfare assistance programs characteristic of advanced industrial societies could not be sustained were transnational migration unencumbered.

Unlike nation-states, cities cannot control movement across their boundaries. They no longer have walls, guarded and defended by their inhabitants. And as Weber correctly noted, without walls cities no longer have the independence to make significant choices in the way medieval cities once did.[12] It is true that local governments often try to keep vagrants, bums, paupers, and racial minorities out of their territory. They are harassed, arrested, thrown out of town, and generally discriminated against. But in most of these cases local governments act unconstitutionally, and even this illegal use of the police power does not control migration very efficiently.

Although limited in its powers, the city seeks to obtain an appropriately skilled labor force at wages lower than its competitors so that it can profitably export commodities. In larger cities a diverse work force is desirable. The service industry, which provides the infrastructure for exporters, recruits large numbers of unskilled workers, and many manufacturing industries need only semiskilled workers. When shortages in these skill levels appear, cities may assist industry in advertising the work and living opportunities of the region. In the nineteenth century when unskilled labor was in short supply, frontier cities made extravagant claims to gain a competitive edge in the supply of ordinary labor.

Certain sparsely populated areas, such as Alaska, occasionally advertise for unskilled labor even today. However, competition among most cities is now for highly skilled workers and especially for professional and managerial talent. In a less than full-employment economy, most communities have a surplus of semiskilled and unskilled labor. Increases in the supply of unskilled workers increase the cost of the community's social services. Since national wage laws preclude a decline in wages below a certain minimum, the increases in the cost of social services are seldom offset by lower wages for unskilled labor in those areas where the unemployed concentrate. But even with high levels of unemployment, there remains a shortage of highly skilled technicians and various types of white collar workers. Where shortages develop, the prices these workers can command in the labor market may climb to a level where local exports are no longer competitive with goods produced elsewhere. The economic health of a community is therefore importantly affected by the availability of professional and managerial talent and of highly skilled technicians.

When successfully pursuing their economic interests, cities develop a set of policies that will attract the more skilled and white collar workers without at the same time attracting unemployables. Of course, there are limits on the number of things cities can do. In contrast to nation-states, they cannot simply forbid entry to all but the highly talented whose skills they desire. But through zoning laws, they can ensure that adequate land is available for middle-class residences. They can provide parks, recreation areas, and good-quality schools in areas where the economically most productive live. They can keep the cost of social services, little utilized by the middle class, to a minimum, thereby keeping local taxes relatively low. In general, they can try to ensure that the benefits of public service outweigh their costs to those highly skilled workers, managers, and professionals who are vital for sustaining the community's economic growth.

Capital

Capital is the second factor of production that must be attracted to an economically productive territory. Accordingly, nation-states place powerful controls on the flow of capital across their boundaries. Many nations strictly regulate the amount of national currency that can be taken out of the country. They place quotas and tariffs on imported goods. They regulate the rate at which national currency can be exchanged with foreign currency. They regulate the money supply, increasing interest rates when growth is too rapid, lowering interest rates when growth slows down. Debt financing also allows a nation-state to undertake capital expenditures and to encourage growth in the private market. At present the powers of nation-states to control capital flow are being used more sparingly and new supranational institutions are developing in their place. Market forces now seem more powerful than official policies in establishing rates of currency exchange among major industrial societies. Tariffs and other restrictions on trade are subject to retaliation by other countries, and so they must be used sparingly. The economies of industrialized nations are becoming so interdependent that significant changes in the international political economy seem imminent, signaled by numerous international conferences to determine worldwide growth rates, rates of inflation, and levels of unemployment. If these trends continue, nation-states may come to look increasingly like local governments.

But these developments at the national level have only begun to emerge. At the local level in the United States, cities are much less able to control capital flows. In the first place, the Constitution has been interpreted to mean that states cannot hinder the free flow of goods and monies across their boundaries. And what is true of states is true of their subsidiary jurisdictions as well. In the second place, states and localities cannot regulate the money supply. If unemployment is low, they cannot stimulate the economy by increasing the monetary flow. If inflationary pressures adversely affect their competitive edge in the export market, localities can neither restrict the money supply nor directly control prices and wages. All of these powers are reserved for national governments. In the third place, local governments cannot spend more than they receive in tax revenues without damaging their credit or even running the risk of bankruptcy. Pump priming, sometimes a national disease, is certainly a national prerogative.

Local governments are left with a number of devices for enticing capital into the area. They can minimize their tax on capital and on profits from capital investment. They can reduce the costs of capital investment by providing low-cost public utilities, such as roads, sewers, lights, and police and fire protection. They can even offer public land free of charge or at greatly reduced prices to those investors they are particularly anxious to attract. They can provide a context for business operations free of undue harassment or regulation. For example, they can ignore various external costs of production, such as air pollution, water pollution, and the despoliation of trees, grass, and other features of the landscape. Finally, they can discourage labor from unionizing so as to keep industrial labor costs competitive.

This does not mean it behooves cities to allow any and all profit-maximizing action on the part of an industrial plant. Insofar as the city desires diversified economic growth, no single company can be allowed to pursue policies that seriously detract from the area's overall attractiveness to capital or productive labor. Taxes cannot be so low that government fails to supply residents with as attractive a package of services as can be found in competitive jurisdictions. Regulation of any particular industry cannot fall so far below nationwide standards that other industries must bear external costs not encountered in other places. The city's interest in attracting capital does not mean utter subservience to any particular corporation, but a sensitivity to the need for establishing an overall favorable climate.

In sum, cities, like private firms, compete with one another so as to maximize their economic position. To achieve this objective, the city must use the resources its land area provides by attracting as much capital and as high a quality labor force as is possible. Like a private firm, the city must entice labor and capital resources by offering appropriate inducements. Unlike the nation-state, the American city does not have regulatory powers to control labor and capital flows. The lack thereof sharply limits what cities can do to control their economic development, but at the same time the attempt by cities to maximize their interests within these limits shapes policy choice.

Local Government and the Interests of Cities

Local government leaders are likely to be sensitive to the economic interests of their communities. First, economic prosperity is necessary for protecting the fiscal base of a local government. In the United States, taxes on local sources and charges for local services remain important components of local government revenues. Although transfers of revenue to local units from the federal and state governments increased throughout the postwar period, as late as 1975–76 local governments still were raising almost 59 percent of their own revenue.[13] Raising revenue from one's own economic resources requires continuing local economic prosperity. Second, good government is good politics. By pursuing policies which contribute to the economic prosperity of the local community, the local politician selects policies that redound to his own political advantage. Local politicians, eager for relief from the cross-pressures of local politics, assiduously promote goals that have widespread benefits. And few policies are more popular than economic growth and prosperity. Third, and most important, local officials usually have a sense of community responsibility. They know that, unless the economic well-being of the community can be maintained, local business will suffer, workers will lose employment opportunities, cultural life will decline, and city land values will fall. To avoid such a dismal future, public officials try to develop policies that assist the prosperity of their community—or, at the very least, that do not seriously detract from it. Quite apart from any effects of economic prosperity on government revenues or local voting behavior, it is quite reasonable to posit that local governments are primarily interested in maintaining the economic vitality of the area for which they are responsible.

Accordingly, governments can be expected to attempt to maximize this particular goal—within the numerous environmental constraints with which they must contend. As policy alternatives are proposed, each is evaluated according to how well it will help to achieve this objective. Although information is imperfect and local governments cannot be expected to select the one best alternative on every occasion, policy choices over time will be limited to those few which can plausibly be shown to be conducive to the community's economic prosperity. Internal disputes and disagreements may affect policy on the margins, but the major contours of local revenue policy will be determined by this strategic objective.

Notes

1. Flathman, R. E. 1966. *The public interest* (New York: John Wiley).
2. Banfield, E. C. 1961. *Political influence* (Glencoe, Illinois: Free Press). Ch. 12.
3. Tiebout, C. M. 1956. A pure theory of local expenditures. *Journal of Political Economy* 64: 416–424.
4. Ibid., p. 419.
5. Ibid., p. 420.
6. Bruce Hamilton, "Property Taxes and the Tiebout Hypothesis: Some Empirical Evidence," and Michelle J. White, "Fiscal Zoning in Fragmented Metropolitan Areas," in Mills, E. S., and Oates, W. E. 1975. *Fiscal zoning and land use controls* (Lexington, Massachusetts: Lexington Books). Chs. 2 and 3.
7. See Weber, "Class, Status, and Power," in Gerth, H. H., and Mills, C. W., trans. 1946. *From Max Weber* (New York: Oxford University Press).
8. For a more complete discussion of roles, structures, and interests, see Greenstone, J. D., and Peterson, P. E. 1976. *Race and authority in urban politics.* Phoenix edition (Chicago: University of Chicago Press). Ch. 2.
9. Cf. Thompson, W. R. 1965. *A preface to urban economics* (Baltimore, Maryland: Johns Hopkins University Press).
10. I treat entrepreneurial skill as simply another form of labor, even though it is a form in short supply.
11. Elazar, D. J. 1976. *Cities of the prairie* (New York: Basic Books).
12. Weber, M. 1921. *The city* (New York: Collier Books).
13. United States Department of Commerce, Bureau of the Census. 1977. *Local government finances in selected metropolitan areas and large counties: 1975–76.* Government finances: GF 76, no. 6.

2

Clarence N. Stone

URBAN REGIMES: A RESEARCH PERSPECTIVE

What makes governance in Atlanta effective is not the formal machinery of government, but rather the informal partnership between city hall and the downtown business elite. This informal partnership and the way it operates constitute the city's regime; it is the means through which major policy decisions are made.

The word "regime" connotes different things to different people, but in this [selection] regime is specifically about the *informal arrangements* that surround and complement the formal workings of governmental authority. All governmental authority in the United States is greatly limited—limited by the Constitution, limited perhaps even more by the nation's political tradition, and limited structurally by the autonomy of privately owned business enterprise. The exercise of public authority is thus never a simple matter; it is almost always enhanced by extraformal considerations. Because local governmental authority is by law and tradition even more limited than authority at the state and national level, informal arrangements assume special importance in urban politics. But we should begin our understanding of regimes by realizing that informal arrangements are by no means peculiar to cities or, for that matter, to government.

Even narrowly bounded organizations, those with highly specific functional responsibilities, develop informal governing coalitions.[1] As Chester Barnard argued many years ago, formal goals and formal lines of authority are insufficient by themselves to bring about coordinated action with sufficient energy to accomplish organizational purposes,[2] commitment and cooperation do not just spring up from the lines of an organization chart. Because every formal organization gives rise to an informal one, Barnard concluded, successful executives must master the skill of shaping and using informal organization for their purposes.

Attention to informal arrangements takes various forms. In the analysis of business firms, the school of thought labeled "transaction cost economics" has given systematic attention to how things actually get done in a world full of social friction—basically the same question that Chester Barnard considered. A leading proponent of this approach, Oliver Williamson,[3] finds that what he terms "private orderings" (as opposed to formal and legal agreements) are enormously important in the running of business affairs. For many transactions, mutual and tacit understanding is a more efficient way of conducting relations than are legal agreements and formal contracts. Williamson quotes a business executive as saying, "You can settle any dispute if you keep the lawyers and accountants out of it. They just do not understand the give-and-take needed in business."[4] Because informal understandings and arrangements provide needed flexibility to cope with nonroutine matters, they facilitate cooperation to a degree that formally defined relationships do not. People who know one another, who have worked together in the past, who have shared in the achievement of a task, and who perhaps have experienced the same crisis are especially likely to develop tacit understandings. If they interact on a continuing basis, they can learn to trust one another and to expect dependability from one another. It can be argued, then, that transactions flow more smoothly and business is conducted more efficiently when a core of insiders form and develop an ongoing relationship.

A regime thus involves not just any informal group that comes together to make a decision but an informal yet relatively stable group *with access to institutional resources* that enable it to have a sustained role in making governing decisions. What makes the group informal is not a lack of institutional connections, but the fact that the group, *as a group,* brings together institutional connections by an informal mode of cooperation. There is no all-encompassing structure of command that guides and synchronizes everyone's behavior. There is a purposive coordination of efforts, but it comes about informally, in ways that often depend heavily on tacit understandings.

If there is no overarching command structure, what gives a regime coherence? What makes it more than an "ecology of games"?[5] The answer is that the regime is purposive, created and maintained as a way of facilitating action. In a very important sense, *a regime is empowering.* Its supporters see it as a means for achieving coordinated efforts that might not otherwise be realized. A regime, however, is not created or redirected at will. Organizational analysis teaches us that cognition is limited, existing arrangements have staying power, and implementation is profoundly shaped by procedures in place.[6] Shrewd and determined leaders can effect purposive change, but only by being attentive to the ways in which existing forms of coordination can be altered or amplified.[7]

We can think of cities as organizations that lack a conjoining structure of command. There are institutional sectors within which the power of command may be much in evidence, but the sectors are independent of one another.[8] Because localities have only weak formal means through which coordination can be achieved, informal arrangements to promote cooperation are especially useful. *These informal modes of coordinating efforts across institutional boundaries are what I call "civic cooperation."* In a system of weak formal authority, it holds special importance. Integrated with the formal structure of authority into a suprainstitutional capacity to take action, any informal basis of cooperation is empowering. It enables community actors to achieve cooperation beyond what could be formally commanded.

Consider the case of local political machines. When ward politicians learned to coordinate informally what otherwise was mired in institutional fragmentation and personal opportunism, the urban political machine was created and proved to have enormous staying power.[9] "Loyalty" is the shorthand that machine politicians used to describe the code that bound them into a cohesive group.[10] The political machine is in many ways the exemplar of governance in which informal arrangements are vital complements to the formal organization of government. The classic urban machines brought together various elements of the community in an informal scheme of exchange and cooperation that was the real governing system of the community.

The urban machine, of course, represents only one form of regime. In considering Atlanta, I am examining the governing coalition in a nonmachine city. The term "governing coalition" is a way of making the notion of regime concrete. It makes us face the fact that informal arrangements are held together by a core group—typically a body of insiders—who come together repeatedly in making important decisions. Thus, when I refer to the governing coalition in Atlanta, I mean the core group at the center of the workings of the regime.

To talk about a core group is not to suggest that they are of one mind or that they all represent identical interests—far from it. "Coalition" is the word I use to emphasize that a regime involves bringing together various elements of the community and the different institutional capacities they control. "Governing," as used in "governing coalition," I must stress, does not mean rule in command-and-control fashion. Governance through informal arrangements is about how some forms of coordination of effort prevail over others. It is about mobilizing efforts to cope and to adapt; it is not about absolute control. Informal arrangements are a way of bolstering (and guiding) the formal capacity to act, but even this enhanced capacity remains quite limited.

Having argued that informal arrangements are important in a range of circumstances, not just in cities, let me return to the specifics of the city setting. After all, the important point is not simply that there are informal arrangements; it is the particular features of urban regimes that provide the lenses through which we see the Atlanta experience. For cities, two questions face us: (1) Who makes up the governing coalition—who has to come together to make governance possible? (2) How is the coming together accomplished? These two questions imply a third: What are the consequences of the *who* and *how?* Urban regimes are not neutral mechanisms through which policy is made; they shape policy. To be sure, they do not do so on terms solely of the governing coalition's own choosing. But regimes are the mediating agents between the ill-defined pressures of an urban environment and the making of community policy. The *who* and *how* of urban regimes matter, thus giving rise to the further question of *with what consequences*. These three questions will guide my analysis of Atlanta.

Urban Regimes

As indicated above, an urban regime refers to the set of arrangements by which a community is actually governed. Even though the institutions of local government bear most of the formal responsibility for governing, they lack the resources and the scope of authority to govern without the active support and cooperation of significant private interests. An urban regime may thus be defined as the *informal arrangements by which public bodies and private interests function together in order to be able to make and carry out governing decisions.* These governing decisions, I want to emphasize, are not a matter of running or controlling everything. They have to do with *managing conflict* and *making adaptive responses* to social change. The informal arrangements through which governing decisions are made differ from community to community, but everywhere they are driven by two needs: (1) institutional scope (that is, the need to encompass a wide enough scope of institutions to mobilize the resources required to make and implement governing decisions) and (2) cooperation (that is, the need to promote enough cooperation and coordination for the diverse participants to reach decisions and sustain action in support of those decisions).

The mix of participants varies by community, but that mix is itself constrained by the accommodation of two basic institutional principles of the American political economy: (1) popular control of the formal machinery of government and (2) private ownership of business enterprise.[11] Neither of these principles is pristine. Popular control is modified and compromised in various ways, but nevertheless remains as the basic principle of government. Private ownership is less than universal, as governments do own and operate various auxiliary enterprises from mass transit to convention centers. Even so, governmental conduct is constrained by the need to promote investment activity in an economic arena dominated by private ownership. This political-economy insight is the foundation for a theory of urban regimes.[12]

In defining an urban regime as the informal arrangements through which public bodies and private interests function together to make and carry out governing decisions, bear in mind that I did not specify that the private interests are business interests. Indeed, in practice, private interests are not confined to business figures. Labor-union officials, party functionaries, officers in nonprofit organizations or foundations, and church leaders may also be involved.[13]

Why, then, pay particular attention to business interests? One reason is the now well-understood need to encourage business investment in order to have an economically thriving community. A second reason is the sometimes overlooked factor that businesses control politically important resources and are rarely absent totally from the scene. They may work through intermediaries, or some businesses may even be passive because others represent their interests as property holders, but a business presence is always part of the urban political scene. Although the nature of business involvement extends from the direct and extensive to the indirect and limited, the economic role of businesses *and the resources they control* are too important for these enterprises to be left out completely.

With revived interest in political economy, the regime's need for an adequate institutional scope (including typically some degree of business involvement) has received significant attention. However, less has been said about the regime's need for cooperation—and the various ways to meet it.[14] Perhaps some take for granted that, when cooperation is called for, it will be forthcoming. But careful reflection reminds us that cooperation does not occur simply because it is useful.

Robert Wiebe analyzed machine politics in a way that illustrates an important point: "The ward politician . . . required wider connections in order to manage many of his clients' problems. . . . Therefore clusters of these men allied to increase their bargaining power in city affairs. But if logic led to an integrated city-wide organization, the instinct of self-preservation did not. The more elaborate the structure, the more independence the ward bosses and area chieftains lost."[15] Cooperation can thus never be taken as a given; it must be achieved and at significant costs. Some of the costs are visible resources expended in promoting cooperation—favors and benefits distributed to curry reciprocity, the effort required to establish and maintain channels of communication, and responsibilities borne to knit activities together are a few examples. But, as Wiebe's observation reminds us, there are less visible costs. Achieving cooperation entails commitment to a set of relationships, and these relationships limit independence of action. If relationships are to be ongoing, they cannot be neglected; they may even call for sacrifices to prevent alienating allies. Forming wider connections is thus not a cost-free step, and it is not a step that community actors are always eager to take.

Because centrifugal tendencies are always strong, achieving cooperation is a major accomplishment and requires constant effort. Cooperation can be brought about in various ways. It can be induced if there is an actor powerful enough to coerce others into it, but that is a rare occurrence, because power is not usually so concentrated. More often, cooperation is achieved by some degree of reciprocity.

The literature on collective action focuses on the problem of cooperation in the absence of a system of command. For example, the "prisoner's dilemma" game instructs us that noncooperation may be invited by a number of situations.[16] In the same vein, Mancur Olson's classic analysis highlights the free-rider problem and the importance of selective incentives in inducing cooperation.[17] Alternatively, repeated interactions permit people to see the shortcomings of mutual noncooperation and to learn norms of cooperation.[18] Moreover, although Robert Axelrod's experiments with TIT FOR TAT computer programs indicate that cooperation can be instrumentally rational under some conditions, the process is not purely mechanical.[19] Students of culture point to the importance of common identity and language in facilitating interaction and promoting trust.[20] Size of group is also a consideration, affecting the ease of communication and bargaining among members; Michael Taylor, for example, emphasizes the increased difficulty of conditional cooperation in larger groups.[21]

What we can surmise about the urban community is thus twofold: (1) cooperation across institutional lines is valuable but far from automatic; and (2) cooperation is more likely to grow under some circumstances than others. This conclusion has wide implications for the study of urban politics. For example, much of the literature on community power has centered on the question of control, its possibilities and limitations: to what extent is domination by a command center possible and how is the cost of social control worked out. The long-standing elitist-pluralist debate centers on such questions. However, my line of argument here points to another way of viewing urban communities; it points to the need to think about cooperation, its possibilities and limitations—not just any cooperation, but cooperation of the kind that can bring together people based in different sectors of a community's institutional life and that enables a coalition of actors to make and support a set of governing decisions.

If the conventional model of urban politics is one of social control (with both elitist and pluralist variants), then the one proposed here might be called "the social-production model." It is based on the question of how, in a world of limited and dispersed authority, actors work together across institutional lines to produce a capacity to govern and to bring about publicly significant results.

To be sure, the development of a system of cooperation for governing is something that arises, not from an unformed mass, but rather within a structured set of relationships. Following Stephen Elkin, I described above the basic configuration in political-economy terms: popular control of governmental authority and private ownership of business activity. However, both of these elements are subject to variation. Populations vary in characteristics and in type of political organization; hence, popular control comes in many forms. The economic sector itself varies by the types of businesses that compose it and by the way in which it is organized formally and informally. Hence there is no one formula for bringing institutional sectors into an arrangement for cooperation, and the whole process is imbued with uncertainty. Cooperation is always somewhat tenuous, and it is made more so as conditions change and new actors enter the scene.

The study of urban regimes is thus a study of who cooperates and how their cooperation is achieved across institutional sectors of community life. Further, it is an examination of how that cooperation is maintained when confronted with an ongoing process of social change, a continuing influx of new actors, and potential break-downs through conflict or indifference.

Regimes are dynamic, not static, and regime dynamics concern the ways in which forces for change and forces for continuity play against one another. For example, Atlanta's governing coalition has displayed remarkable continuity in the post-World War II period, and it has done so despite deep-seated forces of social change. Understanding Atlanta's urban regime involves understanding how cooperation can be maintained and continuity can prevail in the face of so many possibilities for conflict.

Structure, Action, and Structuring

Because of the interplay of change and continuity, urban regimes are perhaps best studied over time. Let us, then, take a closer look at historical analysis. Scholars make sense out of the particulars of political and social life by thinking mainly in terms of abstract structures such as democracy and capitalism.

Although these are useful as shorthand, the danger in abstractions is that they never capture the full complexity and contingency of the world. Furthermore, "structure" suggests something solid and unchanging, yet political and social life is riddled with contradictions and uncertainties that give rise to an ongoing process of change and adjustment. Much of the change that occurs is at the margins of basic and enduring relationships, making it easy to think in terms of order and stability. Incrementalists remind us that the present is the best predictor of the near future. But students of history, especially those accustomed to looking at longer periods of time, offer a different perspective. They see a world undergoing change, in which various actors struggle over what the terms of that change will be. It is a world shaped and reshaped by human efforts, a world that never quite forms a unified whole.

In historical light, social structures are less solid and less fixed than social scientists have sometimes assumed. Charles Tilly has argued that there is no single social structure. Instead, he urges us to think in terms of multiple structures, which "consist of shifting, constructed social relations among limited numbers of actors."[22] Philip Abrams also sees structures as relationships, relationships that are socially fabricated and subject to purposive modification.[23]

Structures are real but not fixed. Action does not simply occur within the bounds set by structures but is sometimes aimed at the structures themselves, so that a process of reshaping is taking place at all times. Abrams thus argues that events have a two-sided character, involving both structure and action in such a way that action shapes structures and structures shape actions. Abrams calls for the study of a process he labels as "structuring," by which he means that events occur in a structured context and that events help reshape structure.[24]

Abrams therefore offers a perspective on the interplay of change and continuity. This continuity is not so much a matter of resisting change as coping with it. Because the potential for change is ever present, regime continuity is a remarkable outcome. Any event contains regime-altering potential—perhaps not in sudden realignment, but in opening up a new path along which subsequent events can cumulatively bring about fundamental change.[25] The absence of regime alteration is thus an outcome to be explained, and it must be explained in terms of a capacity to adapt and reinforce existing structures. Events are the arena in which the struggle between change and continuity is played out, but they are neither self-defining nor free-formed phenomena. They become events in our minds because they have some bearing on structures that help shape future occurrences. It is the interplay of event and structure that is especially worthy of study. To identify events, one therefore needs to have some conception of structure. In this way, the researcher can focus attention, relieved of the impossible task of studying everything.

There is no escaping the necessity of the scholar's imposing some form of analysis on research. The past becomes known through the concepts we apply. Abrams sees this as the heart of historical sociology: "The reality of the past is just not 'there' waiting to be observed by the resurrectionist historian. It is to be known if at all through strenuous theoretical alienation."[26] He also reminds us that many aspects of an event cannot be observed in a direct sense; too much is implicit at any given moment.[27] That is why the process, or the flow of events over time, is so important to examine. That is also why events are not necessarily most significant for their immediate impact; they may be more significant for their bearing on subsequent events, thus giving rise to modifications in structure.

Prologue to the Atlanta Narrative

Structuring in Atlanta is a story in which race is central. If regimes are about who cooperates, how, and with what consequences, one of the remarkable features of Atlanta's urban regime is its biracial character. How has cooperation been achieved across racial lines, particularly since race is often a chasm rather than a bridge? Atlanta has been governed by a biracial coalition for so long that it is tempting to believe that nothing else was possible. Yet other cities followed a different pattern. At a time when Atlanta prided itself on being "the city too busy to hate," Little Rock, Birmingham, and New Orleans pursued die-hard segregation and were caught up in racial violence and turmoil. The experience of these cities reminds us that Atlanta's regime is not simply an informal arrangement through which popular elections and private ownership are reconciled, but is deeply intertwined with race relations, with some actors on the Atlanta scene able to overcome the divisive character of race sufficiently to achieve cooperation.

Atlanta's earlier history is itself a mixed experience, offering no clear indication that biracial cooperation would emerge and prevail in the years after World War II. In 1906, the city was the site of a violent race riot apparently precipitated by inflammatory antiblack newspaper rhetoric.[28] The incident hastened the city's move toward the economic exclusion and residential segregation of blacks, their disenfranchisement, and enforcement of social subordination; and the years after 1906 saw the Jim Crow system fastened into place. Still, the riot was followed by modest efforts to promote biracial understanding, culminating in the formation in 1919 of the Commission on Interracial Cooperation.

Atlanta, however, also became the headquarters city for a revived Ku Klux Klan. During the 1920s, the Klan enjoyed wide support and was a significant influence in city elections. At this time, it gained a strong foothold in city government and a lasting one in the police department.[29] In 1930, faced with rising unemployment, some white Atlantans also founded the Order of Black Shirts for the express purpose of driving blacks out of even menial jobs and replacing them with whites. Black Shirt protests had an impact, and opportunities for blacks once again were constricted. At the end of World War II, with Atlanta's black population expanding beyond a number that could be contained in the city's traditionally defined black neighborhoods, another klanlike organization, the Columbians, sought to use terror tactics to prevent black expansion into previously all-white areas. All of this occurred against a background of state and regional politics devoted to the subordination of blacks to whites—a setting that did not change much until the 1960s.

Nevertheless, other patterns surfaced briefly from time to time. In 1932, Angelo Herndon, a black Communist organizer, led a mass demonstration of white and black unemployed protesting a cutoff of work relief. Herndon was arrested, and the biracial following he led proved short-lived. Still, the event had occurred, and Atlanta's city council did in fact accede to the demand for continued relief.[30] In the immediate postwar period, a progressive biracial coalition formed around the successful candidacy of Helen Douglas Mankin for a congressional seat representing Georgia's fifth district. That, too, was short-lived, as ultra-conservative Talmadge forces maneuvered to reinstitute Georgia's county-unit system for the fifth district and defeat Mankin with a minority of the popular vote.[31]

It is tempting to see the flow of history as flux, and one could easily dwell on the mutable character of political alignments. The Atlanta experience suggests that coalitions often give expression to instability. Centrifugal forces are strong, and in some ways disorder is a natural state. What conflict does not tear asunder, indifference is fully capable of wearing away.

The political incorporation of blacks into Atlanta's urban regime in tight coalition with the city's white business elite is thus not a story of how popular control and private capital came inevitably to live together in peace and harmony. It is an account of struggle and conflict—bringing together a biracial governing coalition at the outset, and then allowing each of the coalition partners to secure for itself an advantageous position within the coalition. In the first instance, struggle involved efforts to see that the coalition between white business interests and the black middle class prevailed over other possible alignments. In the second instance, there was struggle over the terms of coalition between the partners; thus political conflict is not confined to "ins" versus "outs." Those on the inside engage in significant struggle with one another over the terms on which cooperation will be maintained, which is one reason governing arrangements should never be taken for granted.

Atlanta's urban regime therefore appears to be the creature of purposive struggle, and both its establishment and its maintenance call for a political explanation. The shape of the regime was far from inevitable, but rather came about through the actions of human agents making political choices. Without extraeconomic efforts by the city's business leadership, Atlanta would have been governed in a much different manner, and Atlanta's urban regime and the policies furthered by that regime might well have diverged from the path taken. History, perhaps, is as much about alternatives not pursued as about those that were. . . .

The Political Ramifications of Unequal Resources

From Aristotle to Tocqueville to the present, keen political observers have understood that politics evolves from and reflects the associational life of a community. How people are grouped is important—so much so that, as the authors of the *Federalist* essays understood, the formation and reformation of coalitions [are] at the heart of political activity. Democracy should be viewed within that context; i.e., realizing that people do not act together simply because they share preferences on some particular issue.

Overlooking that long-standing lesson, many public-choice economists regard democracy with suspicion. They fear that popular majorities will insist on an egalitarian redistribution of benefits and thereby interfere with economic productivity. As worded by one economist, "The majority (the poor) will always vote for taxing the minority (the rich), at least until the opportunities for benefiting from redistribution run out."[32] In other words, majority rule will overturn an unequal distribution of goods and resources. This reasoning, however, involves the simple-minded premise that formal governmental authority confers a capacity to redistribute at the will of those who hold office by virtue of popular election. The social-production model of politics employed here offers a contrasting view. Starting from an assumption about the costliness of civic cooperation, the social production model suggests that an unequal distribution of goods and resources substantially modifies majority rule.

In operation, democracy is a great deal more complicated than counting votes and sorting through the wants of rational egoists. In response to those who regard democracy as a process of aggregating preferences within a system characterized by formal equality, a good antidote is Stein Rokkan's aphorism, "Votes count but resources decide."[33] Voting power is certainly not insignificant, but policies are decided mainly by those who control important concentrations of resources. Hence, governing is never simply a matter of aggregating numbers, whether for redistribution or other purposes. . . .

Of course, the election of key public officials provides a channel of popular expression. Since democracy rests on the principle of equal voting power, it would seem that all groups do share in the capacity to become part of the governing regime. Certainly the vote played a major role in the turnaround of the position of blacks in Atlanta. Popular control, however, is not a simple and straightforward process. Much depends on how the populace is organized to participate in a community's civic life. Machine politics, for example, promotes a search for personal favors. With electoral mobilization dependent upon an organizational network oriented toward patronage and related considerations, other kinds of popular concerns may have difficulty gaining expression.[34] The political machine thus enjoys a type of preemptive power, though the party organization is only one aspect of the overall governing regime.

On the surface, Atlanta represents a situation quite different from machine politics. Nonpartisan elections and an absence of mass patronage have characterized the city throughout the post-World War II era. Yet it would hardly be accurate to describe civic life in Atlanta as open and fluid. Nonpartisanship has heightened the role of organizations connected to business, and the newspapers have held an important position in policy debate. At the same time, working-class organizations and nonprofit groups unsupported by business are not major players in city politics.

Within Atlanta's civic sector, activities serve to piece together concerns across the institutional lines of the community, connecting government with business and each with a variety of nonprofit entities. The downtown elite has been especially adept at building alliances in that sector and, in doing so, has extended its resource advantage well beyond the control of strictly economic functions. Responding to its own weakness in numbers, the business elite has crafted a network through which cooperation can be advanced and potential cleavages between haves and have-nots redirected.

Consider what Atlanta's postwar regime represents. In 1946, the central element in the governing coalition was a downtown business elite organized for and committed to an active program of redevelopment that would transform the character of the business district and, in the process, displace a largely black population to the south and east of the district. At the same time, with the end of the white primary that same year, a middle-class black population, long excluded from power, mobilized its electoral strength to begin an assault on a firmly entrenched Jim Crow system. Knowing only those facts, one might well have predicted in 1946 that these two groups would be political antagonists. They were not. Both committed to an agenda of change, they worked out an accommodation and became the city's governing coalition. The alliance has had its tensions and even temporary ruptures, but it has held and demonstrated remarkable strength in making and carrying out policy decisions.

To understand the process, the Atlanta experience indicates that one must appreciate institutional capacities and the resources that various groups control. That is why simple preference aggregation is no guide to how coalitions are built. The downtown elite and the black middle class had complementary needs that could be met by forming an alliance, and the business elite in particular had the kind and amount of resources to knit the alliance together.

Politics in Atlanta, then, is not organized around an overriding division between haves and have-nots. Instead, unequally distributed resources serve to destabilize opposition and encourage alliances around small opportunities. Without command of a capacity to govern, elected leaders have difficulty building support around popular discontent. That is why Rokkan's phrase, "Votes count but resources decide," is so apt.

Unequal Resources and Urban Regimes

Regimes, I have suggested, are to be understood in terms of (1) who makes up the governing coalition and (2) how the coalition achieves cooperation. Both points illustrate how the unequal distribution of resources affects politics and what differences the formation of a regime makes. That the downtown elite is a central partner in the Atlanta regime shapes the priorities set and the trade-offs made. Hence, investor prerogative is protected practice in Atlanta, under the substantial influence of the business elite *within* the governing coalition. At the same time, the fact that the downtown elite is part of a governing coalition prevents business isolation from community affairs. Yet, although "corporate responsibility" promotes business involvement, it does so in a way that enhances business as patron and promoter of small opportunities.

Similarly, the incorporation of the black middle class into the mainstream civic and economic life of Atlanta is testimony to its ability to use electoral leverage to help set community priorities. The importance of the mode of cooperation is also evident. Although much of what the regime has done has generated popular resistance, the black middle class has been persuaded to go along by a combination of selective incentives and small opportunities. Alliance with the business elite enabled the black middle class to achieve particular objectives not readily available by other means. This kind of enabling capacity is what gives concentrated resources its gravitational force.

The pattern thus represents something more than individual cooptation. The black middle class as a group benefited from new housing areas in the early postwar years and from employment and business opportunities in recent years. Some of the beneficiaries have been institutional—colleges in the Atlanta University system and a financially troubled bank, for example. Because the term "selective incentives" implies individual benefits (and these have been important), the more inclusive term "small opportunities" provides a useful complement. In both cases, the business elite is a primary source; they can make things happen, provide needed assistance, and open up opportunities. At the same time, since the downtown elite needs the cooperation of local government and various community groups, the elite itself is drawn toward a broad community-leadership role. Although its bottom-line economic interests are narrow, its community role can involve it in wider concerns. Selective incentives, however, enable the elite to muffle some of the pressure that might otherwise come from the larger community.

Once we focus on the regime and the importance of informally achieved cooperation, we can appreciate better the complex way in which local politics actually functions. Public-choice economists, fearful that democracy will lead to redistribution, misunderstand the process and treat politics as a causal force operating in isolation from resources other than the vote. That clearly is unwarranted. Atlanta's business elite possesses substantial slack resources that can be and are devoted to policy. Some devotion of resources to political purposes is direct, in the form of campaign funds, but much is indirect; it takes on the character of facilitating civic cooperation of those efforts deemed worthy.

The business elite is small and homogeneous enough to use the norms of class unity and corporate responsibility to maintain its cohesion internally. In interacting with allies, the prevailing mode of operation is reciprocity, reinforced in many cases by years of trust built from past exchanges. The biracial insiders have also been at their tasks long enough to experience a sense of pride in the community role they play. Even so, the coalition is centered around a combination of explicit and tacit deals. Reciprocity is thus the hallmark of Atlanta's regime, and reciprocity hinges on what one actor can do for another. Instead of promoting redistribution toward equality, such a system perpetuates inequality.

Reciprocity, of course, occurs in a context, and in Atlanta, it is interwoven with a complex set of conditions. The slack resources controlled by business corporations give them an extraordinary opportunity to promote civic cooperation. Where there is a compelling mutual interest, as within Atlanta's downtown elite, businesses have the means to solve their own collective-action problem and unite behind a program of action. Their resources also enable them to create a network of cooperation that extends across lines of institutional division, which makes them attractive to public officials and other results-oriented community groups. In becoming an integral part of a system of civic cooperation, Atlanta's business elite has used its resource advantage to shape community policy and protect a privileged position. Because the elite is useful to others, it attracts and holds a variety of allies in its web of reciprocity. The concentration of resources it has gathered thus enables the elite to counter demands for greater equality.

Social Learning versus Privilege

Instead of understanding democratic politics as an instance of the equality (redistribution)/efficiency (productivity) trade-off. I suggest an alternative. Policy actions (and inactions) have extensive repercussions and involve significant issues that do not fit neatly into an equality-versus-efficiency mold. There is a need, then, for members of the governing coalition to be widely informed about a community's problems, and not to be indifferent about the information. That is what representative democracy is about.

For their part, in order to be productive, business enterprises need a degree of autonomy and a supply of slack resources. It is also appropriate that they participate in politics. However, there are dangers involved in the ability of high-resource groups, like Atlanta's business elite, to secure for themselves a place in the governing coalition and then use that inside position along with their own ample resources to shape the regime on their terms. Elsewhere I have called this "preemptive power,"[35] and have suggested that it enables a group to protect a privileged position. The ability to parcel out selective incentives and other small opportunities permits Atlanta's business elite to enforce discipline on behalf of civic cooperation by vesting others with lesser privileges—privileges perhaps contingently held in return for "going along."

The flip side of discipline through selective incentives is a set of contingent privileges that restrict the questions asked and curtail social learning. Thus, one of the trade-offs in local politics can be phrased as social learning versus privilege. Some degree of privilege for business may be necessary to encourage investment, but the greater the privilege being protected, the less the incentive to understand and act on behalf of the community in its entirety.

The political challenge illustrated by the Atlanta case is how to reconstitute the regime so that both social learning and civic cooperation occur. The risk in the present situation is that those who govern have only a limited comprehension of the consequences of their actions. Steps taken to correct one problem may create or aggravate another while leaving still others unaddressed. Those who govern can discover that only, it seems, through wide representation of the affected groups. Otherwise, choices are limited by an inability to understand the city's full situation.

No governing coalition has an inclination to expand the difficulties of making and carrying out decisions. Still, coalitions can be induced to attempt the difficult. For example, Atlanta's regime has been centrally involved in race relations, perhaps the community's most difficult and volatile issue. Relationships within the governing coalition have been fraught with tension; friction was unavoidable. Yet the coalition achieved a cooperative working relationship between the black middle class and the white business elite. In a rare but telling incident, black leaders insisted successfully that a 1971 pledge to build a MARTA spur to a black public-housing area not be repudiated. The newspaper opined that trust within the coalition was too important to be sacrificed on the altar of economizing. Thus the task of the governing regime was expanded beyond the narrow issue of serving downtown in the least expensive manner possible; concerns *can* be broadened.

Although no regime is likely to be totally inclusive, most regimes can be made more inclusive. Just as Atlanta's regime was drawn into dealing with race relations, others can become sensitive to the situations of a larger set of groups. Greater inclusiveness will not come automatically nor from the vote alone. Pressures to narrow the governing coalition are strong and recurring. Yet, if civic cooperation is the key to the terms on which economic and electoral power are accommodated, then more inclusive urban regimes can be encouraged through an associational life at the community level that reflects a broad range of perspectives. The problem is not an absence of associational life at that level but how to lessen its dependence on business sponsorship, how to free participation in civic activity from an overriding concern with protecting insider privileges, and how to enrich associational life so that nonprofit and other groups can function together as they express encompassing community concerns.

This step is one in which federal policy could make a fundamental difference. In the past, starting with the urban-redevelopment provision in the 1949 housing act and continuing through the Carter administration's UDAG program, cities have been strongly encouraged to devise partnerships with private, for-profit developers, thus intensifying already strong leanings in that direction. Since these were matters of legislative choice, it seems fully possible for the federal government to move in another direction and encourage nonprofit organizations. The federal government could, for example, establish a program of large-scale assistance to community development corporations and other nonprofit groups. Some foundations now support such programs, but their modest efforts could be augmented. Programs of community service required by high schools and colleges or spawned by a national-level service requirement could increase voluntary participation and alter the character of civic life in local communities. It is noteworthy that neighborhood mobilization in Atlanta was partly initiated by VISTA (Volunteers in Service to America) workers in the 1960s and continued by those who stayed in the city after completing service with VISTA. This, however, is not the place to prescribe a full set of remedies; my aim is only to indicate that change is possible but will probably require a stimulus external to the local community.

Summing Up

If the slack resources of business help to set the terms on which urban governance occurs, then we need to be aware of what this imbalance means. The Atlanta case suggests that the more uneven the distribution of resources, the greater the tendency of the regime to become concerned with protecting privilege. Concurrently, there is a narrowing of the regime's willingness to engage in "information seeking" (or social learning). Imbalances in the civic sector thus lead to biases in policy, biases that electoral politics alone is unable to correct.

A genuinely effective regime is not only adept at promoting cooperation in the execution of complex and nonroutine projects, but is also able to comprehend the consequences of its actions and inactions for a diverse citizenry. The promotion of this broad comprehension is, after all, a major aim of democracy. Even if democratic politics were removed from the complexities of coordination for social production, it still could not be reduced to a set of decision rules. Arrow's theorem shows that majority choices cannot be neutrally aggregated when preference structures are complex,[36] as indeed they are bound to be in modern societies.

Democracy, then, is not simply a decision rule for registering choices; it has to operate with a commitment to inclusiveness. Permanent or excluded minorities are inconsistent with the basic idea of equality that underpins democracy. That is why some notion of social learning is an essential part of the democratic process; all are entitled to have their situations understood. Thus, to the extent that urban regimes safeguard special privileges at the expense of social learning, democracy is weakened.

Those fearful that too much community participation will lead to unproductive policies should widen their own understanding and consider other dangers on the political landscape. Particularly under conditions of an imbalance in civically useful resources, the political challenge is one of preventing government from being harnessed to the protection of special privilege. The social-production model reminds us that only a segment of society's institutions are under the sway of majority rule; hence, actual governance is never simply a matter of registering the preferences of citizens as individuals.

The character of local politics depends greatly on the nature of a community's associational life, which in turn depends greatly on the distribution of resources other than the vote. Of course, the vote is significant, but equality in the right to vote is an inadequate guarantee against the diversion of politics into the protection of privilege. If broad social learning is to occur, then other considerations must enter the picture. "One person, one vote" is not enough.

Notes

1. James G. March, "The Business Firm as a Political Coalition," *Journal of Politics* 24 (November 1962): 662–678.
2. Chester I. Barnard, *The Functions of the Executive* (Cambridge, Mass.: Harvard University Press, 1968).
3. Oliver E. Williamson, *The Economic Institutions of Capitalism* (New York: Free Press, 1985).
4. Ibid., 10.
5. See Norton E. Long, "The Local Community as an Ecology of Games," *American Journal of Sociology* 64 (November 1958): 251–261.
6. Cf. Graham T. Allison, *Essence of Decision* (Boston: Little, Brown, 1971).
7. See Philip Selznick, *Leadership in Administration* (New York: Harper & Row, 1957).
8. Cf. Bryan D. Jones and Lynn W. Bachelor, *The Sustaining Hand* (Lawrence: University of Kansas Press, 1986).
9. See especially Martin Shefter, "The Emergence of the Political Machine: An Alternative View," in *Theoretical Perspectives on Urban Politics,* by Willis D. Hawley and others (Englewood Cliffs, N.J.: Prentice-Hall, 1976).
10. Clarence N. Stone, Robert K. Whelan, and William J. Murin. *Urban Policy and Politics in a Bureaucratic Age,* 2d ed. (Englewood Cliffs, N.J.: Prentice-Hall, 1986, 104).
11. Stephen L. Elkin, *City and Regime in the American Republic* (Chicago: University of Chicago Press, 1987).
12. See ibid.
13. Cf. Jones and Bachelor, *The Sustaining Hand,* 214–215.
14. But see Elkin, *City and Regime;* Martin Shefter, *Political Crisis/Fiscal Crisis: The Collapse and Revival of New York City* (New York: Basic Books, 1985): and Todd Swanstrom, *The Crisis of Growth Politics* (Philadelphia: Temple University Press, 1985).
15. Robert H. Wiebe, *The Search for Order, 1877–1920* (New York: Hill and Wang, 1967), 10.
16. Russell Hardin, *Collective Action* (Baltimore: Johns Hopkins University Press, 1982); and Michael Taylor, *The Possibility of Cooperation* (Cambridge, Mass.: Cambridge University Press, 1987).
17. Mancur Olson, Jr., *The Logic of Collective Action* (Cambridge, Mass.: Harvard University Press, 1965).
18. Hardin, *Collective Action.*
19. Robert Axelrod, *The Evolution of Cooperation* (New York: Basic Books, 1984).
20. Hardin, *Collective Action;* and David D. Laitin, *Hegemony and Culture* (Chicago: University of Chicago Press, 1986).
21. Taylor, *Possibility of Cooperation.*
22. Charles Tilly, *Big Structures, Large Processes, Huge Comparisons* (New York: Russell Sage Foundation, 1984), 27.
23. Philip Abrams, *Historical Sociology* (Ithaca, N.Y.: Cornell University Press, 1982). For a similar understanding applied to urban politics, see John R. Logan and Harvey L. Molotch, *Urban Fortunes* (Berkeley and Los Angeles: University of California Press, 1987).
24. Cf. Anthony Giddens, *Central Problems in Social Theory* (Berkeley and Los Angeles: University of California Press, 1979).
25. Cf. James G. March and Johan P. Olsen, "The New Institutionalism," *American Political Science Review* 78 (September 1984): 734–749.
26. Abrams, *Historical Sociology,* 331.
27. Ibid.

28. Michael L. Porter, "Black Atlanta: An Interdisciplinary Study of Blacks on the East Side of Atlanta, 1890–1930" (Ph.D. diss., Emory University, 1974); Walter White, *A Man Called White* (New York: Arno Press and the New York Times, 1969); and Dana F. White, "The Black Sides of Atlanta," *Atlanta Historical Journal* 26 (Summer/Fall 1982): 199–225.

29. Kenneth T. Jackson, *The Ku Klux Klan in the City 1915–1930* (New York: Oxford University Press, 1967); and Herbert T. Jenkins, *Forty Years on the Force: 1932–1972* (Atlanta: Center for Research in Social Change, Emory University, 1973).

30. Charles H. Martin, *The Angelo Herndon Case and Southern Justice* (Baton Rouge: Louisiana State University Press, 1976); Kenneth Coleman, ed., *A History of Georgia* (Athens: University of Georgia Press, 1977), 294; and Writer's Program of the Works Progress Administration, *Atlanta: A City of the Modern South* (St. Clairshores, Mich.: Somerset Publishers, 1973), 69.

31. Lorraine N. Spritzer, *The Belle of Ashby Street: Helen Douglas Mankin and Georgia Politics* (Athens: University of Georgia Press, 1982).

32. John Bonner, *Introduction to the Theory of Social Choice* (Baltimore: Johns Hopkins University Press, 1986), 34.

33. Stein Rokkan, "Norway: Numerical Democracy and Corporate Pluralism," in *Political Oppositions in Western Democracies,* ed. Robert A. Dahl (New Haven, Conn.: Yale University Press, 1966), 105; see also [Steven Erie, *Rainbow's End: Irish-Americans and the Dilemmas of Urban Machine Politics, 1840–1985* (Berkeley: University of California Press, 1988)].

34. Matthew A. Crenson, *The Un-Politics of Air Pollution* (Baltimore: Johns Hopkins University Press, 1971); see also Edwin H. Rhyne, "Political Parties and Decision Making in Three Southern Counties," *American Political Science Review* 52 (December 1958): 1091–1107.

35. Clarence N. Stone, "Preemptive Power: Floyd Hunter's 'Community Power Structure' Reconsidered," *American Journal of Political Science* 32 (February 1988): 82–104.

36. Norman Frohlich and Joe A. Oppenheimer, *Modern Political Economy* (Englewood Cliffs, N.J.: Prentice-Hall, 1978), 19–31.

3

Elaine B. Sharp

CULTURE WARS AND CITY POLITICS
Local Government's Role in Social Conflict

In communities across the United States, strident social conflicts are posing thorny problems for local governance. In some communities, these stem from controversy over abortion and the efforts of the pro-life movement to disrupt the functioning of abortion clinics. In other communities, controversy surrounds gay rights initiatives as struggles emerge over ordinances to provide civil rights protections for gays or efforts to ban such protections. In still other

"Culture Wars and City Politics," by Elaine B. Sharp, in *Urban Affairs Review,* Vol. 31, No. 6, July 1996, pp. 738–758.

communities, episodes over book banning and antipornography crusades, sometimes spearheaded by public officials, have sparked controversy over free speech, women's civil rights, and the community's efforts to enforce moral standards. And, in a number of communities, the efforts of authorities to deal with the emergence of neo-Nazi groups or with particular hate crimes directed at religious minorities have been embedded in controversy. In contemporary America, such controversies reflect a new era of conflict, and they have, on many occasions, placed city governments in the eye of a firestorm.

These various conflicts and controversies exemplify what Hunter (1991) called *culture wars* or what others have variously referred to as the politics of *social regulatory policy* (Tatalovich and Daynes 1988). They involve strident social conflict over issues of morality. Treatments of this category of issues emphasize the intensity and persistence of the controversies that they evoke (Tatalovich and Daynes 1988, 3) and their potential for violence (Hunter 1994).

Several social theorists offer insights into the reasons for the spate of contemporary culture wars. Bellah et al. (1985), for example, treated culture wars as manifestations of an ongoing tension between four discrete themes or strands in our cultural heritage: the biblical strand, with its emphasis upon the shared building of a "community in which a genuinely ethical and spiritual life could be lived" (p. 29); the republican strand, with its emphasis upon participation in a politically egalitarian community; the strand of utilitarian individualism, with its emphases on individual self-improvement and material advancement through pragmatism and industry; and the strand of expressive individualism, with its emphasis upon the freedom to realize goals that transcend materialism—goals of self-actualization and personal fulfillment through emotional expression. Bellah and colleagues argued that the biblical and republican strands have been partly supplanted by utilitarian and then expressive individualism as a result of industrialization followed by the rise of postwar technological affluence. By the same token, they suggested that there are remaining currents of all four themes in American life and that challenges to the newest cultural themes "have arisen from a variety of quarters, from those left out of that prosperity, as well as from those who, while its beneficiaries, criticize it for moral defects" (p. 50).

Hunter (1991) portrayed culture wars as the manifestations of tensions between orthodox, denominationally grounded religion and progressive, ecumenical religious forces. In this characterization, competing moral visions give rise to strident disagreement across an array of policy issues because orthodox forces, or cultural conservatives, "tend to define freedom economically (as individual economic initiative) and justice socially (as righteous living)," and "progressives tend to define freedom socially (as individual rights) and justice economically (as equity)" (p. 115).

In his analysis, Inglehart (1990) posited an intergenerational culture shift, premised upon the fact that those who have come of age after World War II have been socialized in an era of relative economic security. Unlike older generations, whose materialist values are rooted in scarcity and the priorities of ensuring physical sustenance and safety, the post-World War II generation takes economic security more for granted and places a "heavier emphasis on belonging, self-expression, and the quality of life" (p. 66). Furthermore, Inglehart suggested that postmaterialists are also less likely to adhere to traditional sexual norms or to be strongly religious than those with materialist values, because "it is precisely those who experience the least economic security in their lives who have the greatest need for the guidance and reassurance that familiar cultural norms and absolute religious beliefs provide" (p. 185).

These various analyses offer differing interpretations of the roots of contemporary culture wars, but there are important commonalities as well. Hunter's (1991) orthodox religious forces, like the materialists in Inglehart's (1990) analysis, are characterized by an emphasis upon what Bellah et al. (1985) referred to as the biblical strand in American culture. And the importance of participation and self-expression for Inglehart's postmaterialists makes that category quite consistent with the expressive individualist category of Bellah and colleagues. For the purposes of this article, however, neither a synthesis of these approaches nor an extended critical comparison is necessary. The important point is that each of these interpretations highlights cultural fault lines that inevitably lead to strident political conflicts, conflicts that are not a simple function of economic cleavages.

This is not to say that economic conditions are irrelevant. As these theorists have acknowledged, they are part of the context for the emergence of cultural tensions. Hunter (1991, 62), for example, noted that the struggle between orthodox and traditional forces rises to the surface at times of societal transition, such as the economic transformation to a postindustrial society in recent decades. He also acknowledged that the progressive side of the religious divide is more likely to be populated by the better-educated and professionalized upper-middle classes and that orthodox forces are composed more heavily of lower-middle and working-class individuals (p. 63). Inglehart (1990) was even more explicitly concerned with economic conditions because of the contextual importance in his theory of economic security versus economic scarcity. But Bellah et al. (1985), Inglehart, and Hunter are distinctively theorists of *cultural* conflict. They emphasized the ways in which traditional left-right distinctions are not adequate to understand the new social movements (Inglehart 1990) and the ways in which contemporary culture wars simply are not reducible to class or economic conflicts (Hunter 1991, 118).

Urban Scholarship and Culture Wars

Scholars of urban politics have largely overlooked this category of conflict. There are exceptions, of course. There are some relevant case studies, several of which will be referred to often in this article. However, relatively few of these case studies are written by urban scholars or approached with a focus on local government's role in the controversy. There is also a substantial body of work on racial and ethnic conflict and protest activity in U.S. cities. However, the culture wars that are the focus of this analysis are arguably distinct from racial and ethnic conflict, even if there are some important commonalities between the two.[1] And, if anything, contemporary treatments of protest over racial issues are moving toward rational self-interest explanations rather than explanations that emphasize the cultural bases and nonmaterial stakes that underlie the controversies of interest in this article (Green and Cowden 1992).

There are several likely reasons for urban scholars' lack of attention to the sorts of social conflict at issue here. For one thing, police, prosecutors, and the local judiciary are likely to play a relatively central role in these controversies because decisions are made about parade permits, arrest tactics for protesters, enforcement of hate-crimes statutes, changes in human rights ordinances; yet changes to and prosecutions stemming from pornography laws, and the like, yet these institutions are among the least well integrated into mainstream theories of urban politics and are less often incorporated in urban research.

Lack of attention may also stem from the ideological complexity of the issues in contemporary culture wars. In the 1960s, activism was associated with the Left, and studies of social protest and civil rights agitation attracted the research interest of sympathetic intellectuals (Hunter 1991, 161). However, the *status quo challengers*[2] in contemporary culture-war controversies include activists such as abortion clinic protesters and pornography crusaders (representing Hunter's category of orthodox forces) as well as gay rights activists and feminists (better fitting Hunter's category of progressive forces).

The character of this issue domain is an obstacle to scholarly attention in another way as well. The elevation of *interests* over *values* as the focus of inquiry in political science leaves the matter of morals-based social conflict on the periphery of the intellectual enterprise. For example, there has long been an assumption that groups based on expressive and solidary values are unstable and less likely to be of relevance to policy formation than are materially based interest groups (Salisbury 1969, 18–19), and the groups at issue in these culture wars are expressive and solidary groups par excellence. Furthermore, the very intensity that makes these conflicts attractive to the media marginalizes them as a topic for urban scholarship:

> The events themselves tend to be presented as flashes of political insanity—spasmodic symptoms of civic maladjustment—against the routine conduct of public affairs. Such events are rarely related to one another, but appear to be merely "disparate" outbursts by disparate (and sometimes "desperate") individuals and groups. Commentators make little effort to explain and interpret these stories and the issues that underlie them, to place them in a broader frame of reference. (Hunter 1991, 33).

To the extent that the social conflicts emerging from contemporary culture wars are viewed as irrational flashes of political insanity on the fringes of the normal life of the community, they are also distanced from the mainstream of urban political theory in particular. To a large extent, theories of urban politics are theories in the political-economy tradition: They emphasize the material stakes that various organizations and interests have in the life of the city. This is most clearly true of Peterson's (1981) theoretical formulation, with its emphasis on the unitary interests of cities in fostering a competitive economy, the implications that this has for the *unpolitics* of redistribution, and the materially based distributional conflicts that are the heart of the politics of allocation. Although Stone's (1989) work on regime theory differs markedly from Peterson's approach in many respects, like Peterson's, it is essentially based in political economy. Regime theory focuses on the building of coalitions for urban governance—that is, a social production model that emphasizes the assembling of resources for problem solving. Although this theory reasserts the value of the political side of political economy, it emphasizes divisible benefits and assemble-able resources. But the symbolic politics and morality issues that are at the heart of local culture wars are not readily treated as divisible benefits, and the compromise and coalition building that are central to regime theory are less relevant for understanding the uncompromising social conflicts of interest here. The gap between theories of urban politics and the character of social conflicts of the culture-war variety stands as yet another reason why these conflicts tend to be overlooked by urban scholars.

Some may be inclined to argue that culture-war conflicts have also been marginalized in the study of urban politics because they are not properly viewed as issues for urban government. Important as they are, some might claim that the conflicts that constitute the contemporary culture wars occur essentially at the national level. From such a perspective, community controversies over cultural issues are local manifestations of broader social tensions. Local government is not as relevant for the development of these controversies as are the federal courts, politicians at the federal level, and nationally based interest groups, nor does understanding the unfolding of these controversies in local communities have the potential to contribute to fundamental knowledge about urban governance.

Culture-war conflicts are critical aspects of urban governance, however, for several reasons. Although Congress, the federal courts, and state governments are significant institutions in the ongoing development of policy regarding abortion, pornography, hate crimes, and the like, city governments are critical to the policy process as well, in initiating policy change and in implementing federal and state policy. With respect to policy initiation, for example, a number of cities have enacted local ordinances that offer civil rights protections for homosexuals, and others are grappling with the issue. City governments have also been on the front line in attempting to deal with the potential, and in some cases the reality, of violence around abortion clinics. The concept of a buffer zone around abortion clinics clearly emerged from the difficulties that local police experienced in handling this potential for violence—experience that led to congressional passage of the Freedom of Access to Clinic Entrances Act (1993).

It is important to note that social conflict and the implementation of policies addressing it involve local government in a web of intergovernmental relations that are at least as important, and as complex, as are intergovernmental relations surrounding policies with material stakes. The rights-based federal laws that are at issue in the social regulatory realm affect large numbers of individuals, often receive minimal federal enforcement attention, and often are implemented by state and local authorities "who are permitted much discretion" (Tatalovich and Daynes 1988, 224–25). In the case of pornography, the primary regulatory is "state and local government with the principal emphasis at the municipal level" because of the Supreme Court's ruling that "community values" must shape the regulation of pornography (Hawkins and Zimring 1991, 210–11).

Culture-war controversies are also important phenomena from the local government perspective because of the substantial consequences that such controversies can have for local officials and the communities they serve. The dollar costs of maintaining social order in the face of strident social conflicts can be quite high, and the outcomes of local elections can turn on the dynamics of these culture-war issues. Furthermore, because the emergence of these explosive issues often draws national media attention, local governments find themselves in the spotlight, with the reputation and image of the community at stake. To the subtleties of image, one can add the realities of lives saved or lost, and injuries and property damage suffered or averted, depending upon local government's handling of the explosive issues in the culture-war domain.

Case Selection

The purpose of this article is to explore the various roles, both proactive and reactive, that city governments may play in emergent social conflicts. Ultimately, theoretical development in this area will require explanation of variation in city government responses. Because of the limited attention that these conflicts have received and because of the lack of urban theory concerning them, however, my goal here is more modest—that is, to develop a theoretically rich typology of city government roles in such conflicts. To enhance its theoretical potential, the typology will be based in part on application of concepts from social-movements, political-entrepreneurship, and agenda-setting theory.

However, the typology should also be empirically grounded. In this analysis, that empirical grounding consists of analyzing cases of community controversy involving abortion clinic protest, gay rights, regulation of pornography, protests against judicial handling of sexual assault, and controversy over neo-Nazis. Table 1.1 lists the cases that will be used. The cases were chosen based upon the availability of published accounts of community controversies and because they most clearly epitomize the issues of sexual morality and religion that are at the heart of contemporary culture wars.[3] The cases constitute a convenience sample rather than a representative random sample. However, the purpose of the analysis is not hypothesis testing and generalization but exploration of the potential diversity of city government roles in social conflicts. Fortunately for this purpose, not only were there cases in each issue area, but the cases involve large and small communities and conservative and liberal-progressive communities; there were cases that received national attention, and cases that did not. The time frames for the cases vary as well, in line with the cycles of activism that have occurred in each issue area.

Table 1.1 Cases of Community Conflict over Culture War Issues

Issue Area	Case Coverage	Source(s)
Abortion clinic protest	Conflict concerning Operation Rescue activities in Brookline, Massachusetts, late 1980s	Hertz (1991)
Abortion clinic protest	Controversy concerning an abortion clinic in Fargo, North Dakota, 1980s	Ginsburg (1989)
Pornography regulation	Conflict concerning an antipornography ordinance with a feminist, civil rights orientation, Minneapolis, Minnesota, 1983	Downs (1989)
Pornography regulation	Events concerning the city's adoption of an antipornography ordinance with a feminist, civil rights orientation, Indianapolis, Indiana, 1984	Downs (1989)
Gay rights	Conflict concerning a drive for gay rights legislation in New York City, 1970–1971	Marotta (1981)
Gay rights	Conflict concerning the adoption of a gay rights ordinance in Wichita, Kansas, 1977	Various journalistic accounts, assembled by the author
Gay rights	Emergence of a politically mobilized gay community in San Francisco (1960s) and the adoption of a gay rights ordinance in 1977	D'Emilio (1983) and Shilts (1982)
Hate-group regulation	Conflict concerning plans by a Chicago-based Nazi group to march in Skokie, Illinois, 1977	Downs (1985)
Judicial handling of rape	Effort to recall Judge Simonson, Madison, Wisconsin, after his bench comments during a rape case, 1977	Woliver (1993)
Judicial handling of sexual assault	Effort to recall Judge Reinecke, Grant County, Wisconsin, after his bench comments concerning the sexual promiscuity of a five-year-old sexual-assault victim	Woliver (1993)

Finally, there is variation both across the cases and within the cases (i.e., across the various phases of each case) in the amount of conflict and controversy evoked by the issue. Brief descriptions of each of the cases illustrate these variations in level of conflict. In the case of abortion clinic protests in Brookline, Massachusetts, there were disruptions over several months as Operation Rescue repeatedly descended upon local abortion clinics, blocking entry when possible and attracting street-side shouting matches between rescuers and pro-choice opponents. Local police were forced to provide extra coverage at a cost of at least $17,000 per day in overtime pay (Hertz 1991, 12). In the Fargo, North Dakota, case, controversy over the scheduled opening of the community's first abortion clinic was initially confined to low-key prayer vigils; then a new pro-life group emerged, which "introduced a confrontational style" (Ginsburg 1989, 115) of protest, bringing ABC television coverage of the activities of the militant group, and a local reaction to the group, culminating in a variety of legal actions against them (pp. 95, 115–119).

In Minneapolis, Minnesota, the city council passed a controversial ordinance that prohibited "discrimination [against women] by trafficking in pornography" and allowed a woman to sue for damages against the purveyors of pornography if she could show a causal link between an assault she suffered and a particular piece of pornography (Downs 1989, 43, 46–47). The ordinance was vetoed by the mayor, but a revised version was enacted at a meeting featuring the arrest of 24 women "for disrupting the council's proceedings" (pp. 62, 65). In Indianapolis, Indiana, an antipornography ordinance modeled on that of Minneapolis was enacted with much less controversy, despite opposition from the Indianapolis Civil Liberties Union, the city's Urban League, its equal opportunity board, and its legal staff (pp. 117–120).

In Madison, Wisconsin, Judge Archie Simonson's comments about the dress of women clashed with the rape reform efforts of women's groups attempting "to change the public's perception of rape from a crime of passion to a crime of violence" (Woliver 1993, 29) and evoked protests and a campaign to recall Simonson. With the support of many governmental organizations, politicians, and groups, Simonson was successfully recalled from the bench (pp. 52, 32). In the Grant County, Wisconsin, case, parents organized to recall Judge Reinecke after his bench comments about the sexual permissiveness or promiscuity of a five-year-old victim of sexual assault. This recall effort was more divisive than that involving Judge Simonson, because law enforcement officers, the county prosecutor, the local bar, and local newspapers rallied to support Judge Reinecke. In a recall election, Reinecke retained his judgeship, capturing 51% of the vote.

Of the cases involving proposed gay rights legislation, two exhibited considerable controversy. The New York City case featured a series of high-profile protest actions by the Gay Activists' Alliance, at least one of which turned into a melee between local police officers and gay activists. The proposed gay rights ordinance ultimately stalled in committee (D'Emilio 1983). In Wichita, Kansas, the proposal for a gay rights ordinance split the community and the city council, which, after heated hearings, passed the ordinance on a split vote. With the support of the local district attorney, a petition drive was mounted to force the ordinance to a referendum, in which it was defeated overwhelmingly. By contrast, a gay rights ordinance was enacted in San Francisco in 1977 on a 10-1 city council vote with only minimal criticism. The ordinance, the "pet project" of Harvey Milk, the first openly gay municipal official in the United States, reflected the substantial electoral muscle of the gay community (Shilts 1982, 199). The sole vote against the ordinance came from Councilman Dan White in an ongoing feud with Milk that culminated in White's assassination of both Milk and Mayor Moscone (Shilts 1982, 199).

In the Skokie, Illinois case, the National Socialist Party of America (NSPA) planned a march in the community, home to large numbers of Holocaust survivors, after the Chicago Park District prevented their demonstration in Marquette Park. In response to threatened violence by the Holocaust survivor community, Skokie officials got an injunction to prevent the march and enacted a series of ordinances to deter the activities of such organizations. With help from the American Civil Liberties Union, the NSPA filed several suits, which were eventually decided against Skokie.

A Taxonomy of Local Government Roles in Social Controversies

Exploration of these cases yields evidence of a variety of different roles that local governments play in social controversies. This section delineates six distinctive roles that were so identified: evasion, repression, hyperactive responsiveness, responsiveness, entrepreneurial instigation, and unintentional instigation.

Initially, it might be expected that local politicians would avoid the volatile issues that evoke culture wars or, when they are raised by citizen activists, evade them as much as possible by referring them to task forces or using other responses that provide access or agenda responsiveness while evading policy responsiveness (Schumaker 1975, 494). After all, the intense minorities that are typically involved in culture-war conflicts can pose problems for political officials, whose constituencies may be alienated by extremist actions or policies that evoke strident protest from opposing single-issue groups. The evasion approach is indeed evident in several of the cases. Skokie officials initially planned to allow the Nazi march, reasoning that it would be best to keep it routine and hope that the event would pass unnoticed and without disturbance. This was precisely the meaning of the "quarantine" policy that major Jewish organizations espoused as a way of preventing anti-Semitic groups from attaining the publicity that they desired (Downs 1985, 23). As I will discuss later, this intentionally low-key approach ultimately backfired for Skokie officials. Evasion also characterizes the response of key New York officials in the case of the failed drive for gay rights legislation in New York in 1971. Although a bill was introduced and many council members gave encouraging responses to activists pressing for the legislation, then-Mayor Lindsay delayed making a public announcement in favor of the ordinance, and without his public support, the legislation remained bottled up in council committee.

Evasion is characterized by symbolic politics and other low-key efforts to maintain the status quo. But, at other times, local governments take more overt and aggressive action to maintain the status quo in the face of challengers. During an intense culture controversy, especially one that imposes substantial costs on local government, local officials may respond in ways that approximate Tarrow's (1994, 95) definition of repression—that is, action to "either depress collective action or raise the cost of its two main preconditions— the organization and mobilization of opinion." In Brookline, for example, city officials filed suit against Operation Rescue under the provisions of the Racketeer Influenced and Corrupt Organizations Act (RICO), ostensibly to recover the roughly $75,000 in police overtime costs that had resulted from the organization's "rescue" effort (Hertz 1991, 46). However, the repressive purpose of filing the suit is clear from the case. None of the Operation Rescue leaders had monetary resources that the town could have recaptured, and the town counsel did not pursue the litigation once suit was filed. However, the chair of the town council explained that "the RICO suit had done its job, that it had scared off potential rescuers and was largely responsible for the group's dwindling numbers" (p. 227).

Concerned Citizens for Children in Grant County also found itself subject to repression. Judge Reinecke's supporters included law enforcement officials, and the husband of an activist was nearly run off the road by a county police officer in what was considered a "life-threatening situation" (Woliver 1993, 133). There was also a more subtle form of tacit repression, as Woliver (p. 140) explained: "People active in the recall recounted their fears for their families, businesses and futures in Grant County because of their involvement in a controversy against one of only two local judges."

In Fargo, court decisions and city council action generated repressive responses to a relatively militant pro-life group, Save-A-Baby, especially when that group received national television attention. The group, which had established a women's clinic to compete with the community's abortion clinic, had been sued by the abortion clinic for using an imitative clinic name and false advertising to lure women with unwanted pregnancies who presumably had been seeking abortion services. The district court issued a preliminary injunction against the pro-life center, mandating "that they change their name and publicity, and inform callers that they do not perform abortions" (Ginsburg 1989, 120). Ultimately, a county district court jury assessed $23,000 in special damages against the pro-life clinic. The abortion clinic had also sued a leader of the Save-A-Baby group for harassment after he went into the abortion clinic dressed as Santa Claus. The Court ruled in the abortion clinic's favor on this as well, sentencing the Save-A-Baby leader to "two days in jail, a $200 fine, and a year on probation during which he could not be near the abortion clinic" (p. 120). Meanwhile, the city council passed a ban on the picketing of private residences in direct response to the activities of the Save-A-Baby group. Ginsburg (p. 121) argued that these official responses "drew authoritative limits to the range of acceptable behaviors that would be tolerated in the battle over the abortion clinic."

Tarrow (1994) argued that even relatively low-level action, such as a requirement for parade permits, should be conceptualized as a form of repression, because "it gives officials an easy way to keep tabs on their [protestors'] organization and encourages them to resort to legal means" (p. 96). By such standards, the Chicago Park District's requirement that the Nazis obtain

$250,000 in liability insurance before being allowed to demonstrate in any Chicago park is clearly an example of repression, as were the Skokie ordinances banning the distribution of hate literature or the wearing of military regalia and the Skokie government's effort to get an injunction barring the neo-Nazis from demonstrating in the community. These efforts to repress an organization whose hate message was offensive to the community were all declared unconstitutional by either the Illinois Supreme Court or the federal district and appeals courts.

There are, in short, substantial legal constraints on the repressive responses that local governments can use, even in dealing with the most disruptive culture-war situations. However, there has also been a wave of innovation in the use of the law in these situations, especially as an instrument to repress hate groups. City governments may, for example, take a cue from civil rights attorney Morris Dees, who pioneered in "bankrupting white extremist groups with extraordinary civil judgments" (Hamm 1993, 210).

But local governments do not necessarily act in ways opposed to the challengers of the status quo. Even when vocal minorities are promoting relatively radical changes, local governments can and do play several kinds of roles in support of status quo challengers; and, sometimes, local officials initiate the movement for radical change.

A number of the cases provide evidence of overt and aggressive action in support of status quo challengers. The hyperactive responsiveness to the agenda of an intense minority is a far cry from the stereotype of local officials studiously hiding from the explosiveness of culture-war issues. Characterizing a response as hyperactive is, of course, a normative judgment, suggesting that officials have gone too far or acted rashly. In several of the case studies, however, evidence is presented to suggest such a characterization—evidence suggesting official action that (a) was relatively precipitous, (b) bypassed normal procedures, (c) disregarded obvious legal or constitutional issues, or (d) was some combination of these. For both the Minneapolis and the Indianapolis cases, Downs (1989) provides evidence that antipornography ordinances were rushed to enactment, some normal procedures that would have provided input from a broader array of stakeholders were bypassed, decision making was swayed by emotional, one-sided hearings, and the constitutional concerns of city legal staff were overlooked. As a result, Downs' interpretation is that the two cases represent "something all too common in political life—the reluctance of elected officials to be found on the wrong side of an emotionally charged issue which partisans have framed as a matter of good versus evil" (p. 91).

The case of abortion clinic protest in Fargo presents another example of government officials making a relatively precipitous decision, apparently as a result of being swept up in the intense emotions of the issue, without due consideration of constitutional issues, at least until their hyperactive responsiveness was reversed by the action of another official. Shortly before the city's first abortion clinic was to open, a local pro-life organization tried to block the clinic's opening by petitioning the city council to revoke its building permit. With the mayor out of town, the remaining city commission members hurried a vote in favor of the petition, but upon his return, the permit was reinstated by the mayor, who declared that the clinic was a legal enterprise and that the use of local regulations to discriminate against it would embroil the city in pointless litigation (Ginsburg 1989, 88).

Local politicians can be responsive to the policy demands of status quo challengers without being hyperactive. This straightforward form of responsiveness is nowhere better illustrated than in the case of Wichita, where the city council passed a gay rights ordinance in 1977. In contrast to the precipitousness, disregard of constitutional issues, and short circuiting of normal procedure that characterize hyperactive responsiveness, city officials in this case took excruciating pains over the ordinance. Before passing the ordinance, Wichita council members heard public comment from both sides at a council meeting, delayed action for a month in order to obtain an opinion from the Kansas attorney general stipulating that the ordinance would not conflict with state law (Stinson 1977), and had nearly seven hours of hearings on the issue before voting 3-2 in favor ("Wichita, Kansas Bans Bias" 1977). After the positive vote on first reading (in Wichita, an ordinance must be endorsed twice), council delayed action on the second reading to get another ruling on the issue of whether the ordinance would affect the school board and other governmental units ("Gay Rights Foes" 1977).

Local politicians are, of course, not limited to responding to culture-war-style conflicts. They can, and sometimes do, play a role in instigating the conflicts, in one of two ways. Conflict can be intentionally instigated if public officials take on the role of issue entrepreneurs, mobilizing the public on symbolic or morals issues. This entrepreneurial instigation is especially evident in the cases involving pornography crusades. In Minneapolis, a veteran city council member, Charlee Hoyt, served as an entrepreneur for the issue of fighting pornography by using the new weapon of an ordinance defining pornography as a violation of women's civil rights (Downs 1989, 57)—an innovative approach that was being promulgated by feminist theorists Andrea Dworkin and Catharine MacKinnon. In Indianapolis, both Mayor Hudnut and the local prosecutor, Steven Goldsmith, were issue entrepreneurs for the city's crusade against pornography. Goldsmith had won the prosecutor's office in 1979 on a campaign emphasizing pornography problems and had immediately initiated pornography raids on local establishments. In the early 1980s, Mayor Hudnut pushed the antipornography issue and directed the local police to escalate their crackdown (p. 99). When Hudnut learned of the innovative ordinance with which Minneapolis had experimented, he established communication between the Indianapolis council and the city council member in Minneapolis who had championed the issue, and he maintained visible and vocal support for passage of the ordinance in Indianapolis (pp. 107–112).

Entrepreneurial instigation sometimes occurs when local officials, who are elected on platforms stressing pornography, gay rights, or abortion-related issues, follow through with policy initiatives in the culture-war genre. In the Indianapolis pornography case just described, for example, electoral politics positioned prosecutor Goldsmith for a role in promoting an aggressive response to pornography. With respect to gay rights, the same is true of Milk, who won election to a San Francisco council seat as a champion of the gay community and made a ban on gay discrimination his first legislative initiative (Shilts 1982, 190).

The category entrepreneurial instigation is meant to be reserved for those instances in which public officials serve as the initial promoters of a culture-war issue, in the process mobilizing citizen groups behind the issue. In practice, it may be difficult to distinguish entrepreneurial instigation from another familiar category—co-optation. Although the term is commonly used to refer to the neutralization of the independent agenda of citizen groups by government, McCarthy and Wolfson (1992, 274) emphasized the possibility that the apparatus of the state can be co-opted by a social movement. The example of entrepreneurial instigation in the Minneapolis case could be interpreted as co-optation of the state by nonstate activists, in this case, Dworkin and MacKinnon. Although there was a history of antipornography efforts in the community, the radical legal departure represented by Dworkin and MacKinnon's ordinance was made possible when Councilwoman Hoyt "opened her office and all its resources to Dworkin, MacKinnon, and their followers" (Downs 1989, 57)—a relatively clear-cut statement of co-optation of a segment of the state. Although it may be empirically difficult to make a clear distinction between issue entrepreneurship that is literally initiated by public officials and issue entrepreneurship that public officials take up as a result of being co-opted by activists within a social movement, the distinction itself may not be conceptually important, because both involve entrepreneurial instigation. As Tarrow (1994, 98) argued, "protesting groups create political opportunities for elites . . . when opportunistic politicians seize the opportunity created by challengers to proclaim themselves tribunes of the people."

At other times, local officials appear to instigate controversy unintentionally—typically by taking actions that spark the emergence of local protest groups and frame a heretofore nonissue in rights-oriented terms. This unintentional instigation is especially apparent in the early history of the gay rights movement. In San Francisco in the 1960s, the emergence of a politically mobilized gay community was in large part the unintended consequence of aggressive police action against the gay community. The San Francisco police "had a long history of harassing gay bars" (D'Emilio 1983, 182–183), and a major scandal in 1959 had revealed that the police had been shaking down a number of gay bar owners for payments, in exchange for which they would be allowed to continue to operate (pp. 182–183). Aggressive police crackdowns on gay bars continued even after this "gayola" episode, and when a group of Protestant clergy instituted a new organization to work with the gay community, local police attempted to force the cancellation of a benefit dance organized by the group. Failing to stop the dance, the police made an aggressive show of force outside the dance and arrested lawyers for the organization who were challenging the police action (pp. 193–194). But the ministers and lawyers "provided a legitimacy to the charges of police harassment that the word of a homosexual lacked" (p. 194). More generally, political agitating for gay rights in

San Francisco "came alive through the attacks mounted against it by a hostile city administration and police force" (pp. 195–196).

The case of Judge Simonson's recall in Madison provides yet another example of unintentional instigation if one is willing to construe the concept to include catalytic action for a social movement that is already organized. That is precisely the interpretation offered by Woliver (1993, 45), who noted that "A critical mobilizing event, like Simonson's remarks, can actually help an incipient social movement. Whether mobilization occurs, though, also often depends on the facilitation provided by a preexisting social movement."

Yet another version of unintentional instigation is exemplified by the dilemma of Skokie officials, whose choice of a minimalist strategy in response to a planned Nazi march turned out to be a miscalculation. Skokie officials had not understood how strong the response of Holocaust survivors would be. Their anger and threats of violence placed officials unexpectedly in the eye of a firestorm, even though evasion was intended to prevent just such controversy (Downs 1985, 44).

This transformation of our interpretation of Skokie's response from one of evasion to unintentional instigation suggests a problem with the typology. If a single behavior or set of behaviors, such as Skokie officials' adoption of a quarantine policy, can be classified in one of two different categories, the typology is not mutually exclusive. The answer to this dilemma lies in recognizing the fact that Skokie officials' unintentional instigation of controversy hinges upon the reaction of nongovernmental groups to local government's action. Similarly, it may be that some local government efforts at repression may instead turn out to be unintentional instigation—for example, if overly aggressive efforts to prevent protest activity by pro-life groups actually sparked a determination on the part of such groups to target the city for high-profile activity. In short, the typology of local government's role in local culture wars perhaps should be conceptualized as including both first-order and second-order responses (see Table 1.2). First-order responses, such as repression, evasion, responsiveness, and intentional instigation, are primarily based upon the intent of the local decision makers who take the action. A second-order response, such as unintentional instigation, hinges upon the interactive effects of governmental actions and the actions of nongovernmental groups that are a party to the controversial issue. As the foregoing examples suggest,

Table 1.2 A Typology of Local Government's Role in Culture Wars

	Supportive of Status Quo Challengers	Not Supportive of Status Quo Challengers
First order	Hyperactive responsiveness Responsiveness Entrepreneurial instigation	Evasion Repression
Second order	Unintentional instigation	Unintentional instigation

unintentional instigation can either be supportive or nonsupportive of status-quo challengers depending upon who is inadvertently mobilized by governmental action.

Local Governments and Social Controversy

The development of this taxonomy of local government roles in controversies over culture-war issues is only the first step in theory building. Nevertheless, it is a critical first step because existing theories of governmental links to social movements and protest groups are not fully developed for the task and because existing case studies, typically focusing on only one or two cases at a time, have not explored the full range of governmental roles. In this article, my consideration of a varied set of cases of local culture wars yields a taxonomy of local government roles that dovetails with, but that is more wide-ranging than, existing typologies of local governmental responsiveness to social movements.

The cases show that local governments can, like national governments, opt for repressive responses to status quo challengers. Although the specific tactics used for repression may be distinctive for local government, there is a substantial collection of such tactics, ranging from parade permit requirements to disorderly conduct arrests to legal action intended to financially cripple mobilized organizations. For this reason, any theory of local government's role in local culture wars must be anchored at one extreme by the realities of repression—an insight that has been somewhat submerged in recent urban scholarship because of its emphasis upon service delivery or development issues, issue arenas for which the concept of repression is less relevant.

The analysis also suggests that existing typologies of policy responsiveness are limited because they do not include the possibility of hyperactive responsiveness. Indeed, treatments of the extent and character of local government responsiveness to citizen groups have traditionally conceptualized *lack* of responsiveness and co-optation as the only problematic aspects of the responsiveness continuum (Schumaker 1975; Gittell 1980). When emotional, culture-war-style issues are at stake, however, public officials can sometimes be overwhelmed by intense special interest minorities or themselves committed to moral crusades. The resulting rush to policy, in processes that override procedural safeguards, squelch dissent, and ignore constitutional viability, can be problematic. The concept of hyperactive responsiveness may not be as relevant for the discussion of issues in other policy domains, in which there are material stakes and compromise and coalition building are the key phenomena. To understand governmental responses to culture wars, however, it is necessary to consider the possibility of too much responsiveness.

Theorists of agenda setting have long noted that an *outside initiative* is not the only path for issues to attain agenda status; instead of reacting to popular demands, government officials can be instrumental in mobilizing the public behind issues (Cobb, Keith-Ross, and Ross 1976). When the intense issues that characterize the culture-war domain are at stake, officials who engage in such mobilization are perhaps playing with fire. Strident controversies over abortion, gay rights, pornography, and the like can impose substantial costs on the community, in the form of violence, law enforcement costs, disruptive action, and threats to the community's image nationally. Yet, these cases suggest that public officials do sometimes mobilize the community on culture-war issues. There are at least two reasons for this. Officials may have their own strongly held views about pornography, gay rights, or abortion and may even have won office based upon those views. From a more cynical standpoint, it must be acknowledged that culture-war issues can be excellent raw material for the game of symbolic politics, with its potential advantages for public officials who are skillful players (Edelman 1977).

The intensely held views that are the essence of culture-war issues make yet another form of governmental involvement more important than it would be in other policy domains. As this article has shown, public officials can inadvertently bring about the mobilization of a social movement, either through words or actions that crystallize a grievance, attempts at repression that spark resistance, or any number of other symbolic miscalculations. Unlike the other forms of governmental involvement, however, unintentional instigation is conceptualized here as a second-order phenomenon—that is, the result of reactions to governmental action, regardless of the intent of those actions.

Acknowledgment of this fact suggests yet another possibility: Local government's role in any given culture-war controversy may change several times over the course of the controversy. Perhaps the sequencing of these roles would be of as much interest as are the individual responses or actions that form the building blocks for sequences. Perhaps evasion, for example, is characteristically followed by responsiveness under other circumstances. Perhaps yet another prototypical sequence would involve hyperactive responsiveness after unintentional instigation, as some political leaders take advantage of opportunities inadvertently created by the miscalculation of others. Stated another way, further inquiry into local culture wars may need to take account of various stages in the development of the controversy, from initial agenda setting to the unintended consequences of the policy strategy chosen.

A theory of local government's role in social controversy will, of course, require propositions to account for variation in city governments' adoption of one or the other actions defined here. Variation in institutional arrangements for governance, in the social composition of the community, and many other factors that have long been incorporated into explanations for variation in other spheres of city policy need to be adapted to the task of explaining local governments' role in culture-war issues. For example, the structural arrangements of local government that have been so heavily investigated with respect to their role in shaping economic development policy and service delivery might also be expected to shape local government's role in culture-war controversies. Recent investigations have examined the impact of strong mayors, city managers' offices, and district elections in accounting for the emergence of progrowth and antigrowth entrepreneurs (Schneider and Teske 1993a, 1993b).

Similar exploration of the role of these institutional arrangements in the entrepreneurial instigation of culture wars is called for.

Differences in *political* subculture (Elazar 1970) may be significant in explaining the propensity of local governments to engage in hyperactive responsiveness because of the differing expectations of the role of government that are
embedded in those subcultural differences. The size and homogeneity of the
community may be important predictors of the likelihood of repressive action
because smaller, more homogeneous communities may have a stronger sense
of community norms being broached by status quo challengers. And Lieske
(1993) has recently charted, at a quite localized level, cultural variables that
might be used to operationalize broader cultural cleavages between orthodox
and progressive (Hunter 1991), materialist and postmaterialist (Inglehart 1990),
or biblical and expressive individualist (Bellah et al. 1985) areas. The degree to
which these cultural cleavages exist within communities, or perhaps the degree
to which a community exhibits a cultural strand that is declining nationally,
may be predictive of entrepreneurial instigation because of either status discontents or moral outrages (Wallis 1979, 92–102) that such cleavages provide as
the raw material for entrepreneurial instigation.

These are preliminary suggestions of the directions that may be fruitful in
the next phase of theory building—the development of propositions to account
for variation in local government roles in culture wars. But urban scholars will
collectively take up that task only if the phenomenon to be explained is viewed
as important and interestingly variegated. It has been the task of this article to
contribute to that acknowledgment.

Notes

1. Racial and ethnic conflict is distinctive in that it has a longer history in the United States
   and played a major role in shaping partisan alignments and other features of national and
   local politics.
2. In this article, the term *status quo challengers* is used to refer to gay rights activists, abortion clinic protesters, pornography crusaders, feminists critical of judicial permissiveness
   about rape, and neo-Nazi groups. For the cases and time periods of interest here, those on
   these sides of various culture-war issues were opposed to the status quo. The status quo
   for most communities, then and now, is lack of explicit gay rights protections; the existence, or at least the legality, of abortion services; substantial constitutional constraints on
   the regulation of pornography; and community opposition to and laws limiting the activities of hate groups. Treating feminist groups dealing with judicial treatment of rape as status quo challengers is somewhat less definitive. However, for the cases at issue in this regard, Woliver (1993, 29) argued convincingly that feminist critiques are part of an
   as-yet-incomplete effort to change prevailing attitudes toward rape.
3. Other controversies, such as those pitting progrowth against antigrowth activists over locational decisions, or conflicts emanating from the environmental justice movement,
   clearly do involve value conflicts, and just as environmentalism is a component of post-
   materialism in Inglehart's (1990) analysis, these growth- and environment-based conflicts

arguably are rooted in cultural differences. However, development and land-use conflicts such as these also have features that make them less clearly distinct from the traditional realm of political economy and, hence, less clearly seated in a distinctive realm of cultural conflict. In particular, growth controls, not-in-my-backyard siting, and similar controversies involve substantial material stakes and cultural values for status quo challengers. And, in principle if not in practice, the divisible outcomes at stake in these issues lend themselves to compromise and the politics of coalition formation around compromise solutions (as, for example, around questions of the share of environmental hazards that each neighborhood should bear or the amount of growth that is tolerable). Development, land-use, and environmental issues do not, in this sense, share the uncompromising, all-or-nothing character of culture-war issues such as abortion (i.e., pro-life forces view the occurrence of any abortions as unacceptable).

Bibliography

Bellah, R., R. Madsen, W. Sullivan, A. Swidler, and S. Tipton. 1985. *Habits of the heart.* Berkeley: University of California Press.

Cobb, R., J. Keith-Ross, and M. H. Ross. 1976. Agenda building as a comparative political process. *American Political Science Review* 70:126–38.

D'Emillo, J. 1983. *Sexual politics, sexual communities.* Chicago: University of Chicago Press.

Downs, D. 1985. *Nazis in Skokie: Freedom, community, and the First Amendment.* Notre Dame, IN: University of Notre Dame Press.

———. 1989. *The new politics of pornography.* Chicago: University of Chicago Press.

Edelman, M. 1977. *Political language.* New York: Academic Press.

Elazar, D. 1970. *Cities of the prairie.* New York: Basic Books.

Gay rights foes reject Miami aid. 1977. *Wichita Eagle,* 15 September, C3.

Ginsburg. F. 1989. *Contested lives: The abortion debate in an American community.* Berkeley: University of California Press.

Gittell, M. 1980. *Limits to citizen participation.* Beverly Hills, CA: Sage Publications.

Green, D. P., and J. A. Cowden, 1992. Who protests: Self-interest and white opposition to busing. *Journal of Politics* 54:471–496.

Hamm, M. 1993. *American skinheads: The criminology and control of hate crime.* Westport, CT: Praeger.

Hawkins, G., and F. Zimring. 1991. *Pornography in a free society.* Cambridge, UK: Cambridge University Press.

Hertz, S. 1991. *Caught in the crossfire.* New York: Prentice Hall.

Hunter, J. D. 1991. *Culture wars.* New York: Basic Books.

——— 1994. *Before the shooting begins.* New York: Free Press.

Inglehart, R. 1990. *Culture shift.* Princeton, NJ: Princeton University Press.

Lieske, J. 1993. Regional subcultures of the United States. *Journal of Politics* 55 (November): 888–913.

Marotta, T. 1981. *The politics of homosexuality.* Boston: Houghton Mifflin.

McCarthy, J. D., and M. Wolfson. 1992. Consensus movements, conflict movements, and the cooptation of civic and state infrastructures. In *Frontiers in social movement theory,* edited by A. Morris and C. M. Mueller, 273–97. New Haven, CT: Yale University Press.

Peterson, P. 1981. *City limits.* Chicago: University of Chicago Press.

Salisbury, R. 1969. An exchange theory of interest groups. *Midwest Journal of Political Science* 13 (February): 1–32.

Schneider, M., and P. Teske. 1993a. The antigrowth entrepreneur: Challenging the "equilibrium" of the growth machine. *Journal of Politics* 55 (August): 720–736.

———. 1993b. The progrowth entrepreneur in local government. *Urban Affairs Quarterly* 29 (December): 316–327.

Schumaker, P. 1975. Policy responsiveness to protest-group demands. *Journal of Politics* 37:488–521.

Shilts, R. 1982. *The mayor of Castro street,* New York: St. Martin's.

Stinson, J. 1977. Gay forces win as city OK's law. *Wichita Eagle,* 7 September, C1, C4.

Stone, C. 1989. *Regime politic.* Lawrence: University of Kansas Press.

Tarrow, S. 1994. *Power in movement: Social movements, collective actions and politics.* Cambridge, UK: Cambridge University Press.

Tatalovich, R., and B. Daynes. 1988. *Social regulatory policy: Moral controversies in American politics.* Boulder, CO: Westview.

Wallis, R. 1979. *Salvation and protest.* London: Frances Pinter.

Wichita, Kansas bans bias against homosexuals. 1977. *The New York Times,* 8 September, A18.

Woliver, L. 1993. *From outrage to action: The politics of grass-roots dissent.* Urbana: University of Illinois Press.

CHAPTER 2

ENTREPRENEURIAL CITIES: THE ECONOMIC IMPERATIVE

The Economic Imperative

Founded originally as centers of trade and commerce, the nation's cities and towns came into being as places where people could make money. The aristocrats and businessmen who ran them recognized that in order to ensure their mutual success, they had to take steps to promote their city. This economic imperative became deeply embedded in politics because there was no separation between economic and political leadership—and because the urban population generally believed it too.

These circumstances helped to establish what Sam Bass Warner describes as a "culture of privatism" that favored individual wealth-making above all other goals. By espousing the notion that cities mainly existed to serve private economic activities, urban leaders permitted the agenda of local political and even the physical character of cities to be driven primarily by the market decisions of traders, builders, land speculators, and investors. Warner maintains that the culture of privatism made it difficult for public authorities to respond with much effectiveness to the problems of cities as they grew in size and became complex social and political entities. As a way of making this argument he describes the frustrations that Philadelphia civic leaders faced in their efforts to improve the city's water supply. Although the health of its citizens and even its continued economic prosperity made a safe and clean supply of water a necessity, the city's leaders struggled with the notion that the public provisions of water should become the norm.

Cities could prosper only by gaining a competitive advantage over other cities as trading centers. Consequently, urban leaders launched what we would now recognize as marketing campaigns. They boasted about local culture—music societies, libraries, and universities. And they went further than boasting; they used the powers of city governments to promote local prosperity. These entrepreneurs were aware that they were participating in a race that some cities would win and others would lose. As the city went, so went their own prospects.

The spirit of this intercity rivalry is captured by Richard C. Wade, who portrays the commercial struggles among frontier cities in the first decades of the nineteenth century. In this selection Wade notes that in these contests, the rewards for winning might be considerable, and the penalties for losing could be devastating: "the economically strongest survived and flourished . . . [while] smaller places were trampled in the process, some being swallowed up by ambitious neighbors, others being overwhelmed before they could attain a challenging position." This kind of interurban competition continues to be an important feature of urban politics even today.

4

Sam Bass Warner, Jr.

THE ENVIRONMENT OF PRIVATE OPPORTUNITY

American cities have grown with the general culture of the nation, not apart from it. Late eighteenth-century Philadelphia was no exception. Its citizens, formerly the first wave of a Holy Experiment, had been swept up in the tides of secularization and borne on by steady prosperity to a modern view of the world. Like the Puritans of Massachusetts and Connecticut, the Quakers of Pennsylvania had proved unable to sustain the primacy of religion against the solvents of cheap land and private opportunity. Quaker, Anglican, Presbyterian, Methodist, Pietist—each label had its social and political implications—but all congregations shared in the general American secular culture of privatism.[1]

Already by the time of the Revolution privatism had become the American tradition. Its essence lay in its concentration upon the individual and the individual's search for wealth. Psychologically, privatism meant that the individual should seek happiness in personal independence and in the search for wealth; socially, privatism meant that the individual should see his first loyalty as his immediate family, and that a community should be a union of such money-making, accumulating families; politically, privatism meant that the community should keep the peace among individual money-makers, and, if possible, help to create an open and thriving setting where each citizen would have some substantial opportunity to prosper.

To describe the American tradition of privatism is not to summarize the entire American cultural tradition. Privatism lies at the core of many modern cultures; privatism alone will not distinguish the experience of America from that of other nations. The tradition of privatism is, however, the most important element of our culture for understanding the development of cities. The tradition of privatism has always meant that the cities of the United States depended for their wages, employment, and general prosperity upon the aggregate successes and failures of thousands of individual enterprises, not upon community action. It has also meant that the physical forms of American cities, their lots, houses, factories, and streets, have been the outcome of a real estate market of profit-seeking builders, land speculators, and large investors. Finally, the tradition of privatism has meant that the local politics of American cities have depended for their actors, and for a good deal of their subject matter, on the changing focus of men's private economic activities.[2]

In the eighteenth century the tradition of privatism and the social and economic environment of colonial towns nicely complemented each other. Later as towns grew to big cities, and big cities grew to metropolises, the tradition became more and more ill-suited to the realities of urban life. The tradition assumed that there would be no major conflict between private interest, honestly and liberally viewed, and the public welfare. The modes of eighteenth-century town life encouraged this expectation that if each man would look to his own prosperity the entire town would prosper. . . .

The goals of the nineteenth-century municipality remained those of the Revolutionary era. The city was to be an environment for private money-making, and its government was to encourage private business. At the same time the city was to be an equalitarian society; its government should endeavor to maintain an open society where every citizen would have some chance, if not an equal chance, in the race for private wealth. These traditional goals worked upon the settled forms of the municipal corporation; they set the framework of the new municipal institutions, and they directed the attention and the efforts of the city's leaders, both the merchant amateurs and the new professionals.

The enduring effects of the interaction of these traditional goals with the demands of big city life can be summarized in the history of . . . the municipal corporation [and] the waterworks. . . . The history of the municipal corporation is best known and therefore can be sketched briefly. The story of Philadelphia's pioneer municipal waterworks demands more attention since it shows the permanent constraints that the city's tradition of privatism placed upon what was to be a universal public health program. . . .

Municipal Corporation

The Philadelphia municipal corporation grew directly out of the Revolution. The moderate merchant-artisan faction which had resumed control of the city and state at the end of the Revolution wrote the 1789 Philadelphia city charter, the first since independence was gained. It blended the traditional offices of colonial municipal government with the federalist fashion for bicameral legislatures. The taxpayer franchise established in 1776 by the radicals for all of Pennsylvania remained the electoral base of the city. The taxpayers of the city elected at-large both select and common councils which, together, voted appropriations, levied taxes, and enacted local ordinances. The mayor, not popularly elected, but chosen by the councils, as in colonial times, was the chief executive officer. With the approval of the councils he appointed a board of commission-ers and together the mayor and the board carried on the executive business of the city government.

Despite domination by merchants, in the years following the 1789 charter, the demands of radical equalitarianism continued to press upon Philadelphia's corporation and thereby to hold it to a weak executive, to increase local control, and to expand both the franchise and the number of elected offices.[3] Philadel-phia's municipal history, thus, ran directly counter to the trends of centraliza-tion and large-scale activity which characterized the contemporaneous indus-trialization of the city.

The radical fears of strong executives, inherited from the conflicts of the Revolution and continued by the Jacksonians in the nineteenth century, pre-vented the mayor and commissioners of the Philadelphia corporation from exercising much independence of action. When new municipal functions were added, like responsibilities for municipal water and gas, the councils created independent committees which did not report to the mayor but to the councils themselves. The patronage of the new activities, thus, fell to the councilors, not the mayor, and therefore the effectiveness of the municipal corporation throughout the first half of the nineteenth century depended on the quality of the elected councilors and the volunteers who served on the council's committees.

Localism also gained with successive reforms of the post-Revolutionary Philadelphia and Pennsylvania governments. In 1834, when the basic public school statute for Pennsylvania was enacted it stipulated that three citizens be elected from each ward of Philadelphia to serve as school directors. The colo-nial tradition of having resident tax collectors and assessors in each ward was continued on an elected basis until just before the Civil War. The pressures of neighborhood partisan politics upon these officials produced widely fluctuat-ing assessments and ultimately great confusion in the tax rolls. In 1854, when all the boroughs and districts of Philadelphia County joined into one consoli-dated city, to preserve the strength of past localisms, the select and common councillors were hereafter chosen on a ward basis, not at-large as formerly.

State and municipal election reforms expanded the number of voters and the number of elected offices. In 1838, state judges became elected officials. At the same time the franchise, which had been restricted to all taxpayers, was re-defined to include all white males who had reached the age of twenty-one. This franchise reform, one of the few genuinely popular accomplishments in a deeply divided constitutional convention (1837–1838), reflected an important current in American equalitarianism: an enthusiasm for the uniform political status of whites was often accompanied by a heavy prejudice against Negroes. By the time the state constitutional convention convened in Philadelphia the city had already experienced its first major race riot. In 1841 the mayorality be-came a popularly elected office, while the ballot for Philadelphia county posi-tions grew steadily longer.[4]

By mid-century the city of Philadelphia had grown to a big city and the functions of its government had kept pace with this growth. The cost of half a century of political change which ran against the trends of the city's industrialization now stood out clearly. The committee system of the councils, the extreme localism of politics, and the large number of elected offices appeared as handicaps to effective government. The consolidation of all the county into one municipal corporation in 1854 brought unity of management to the major functions of government, but it did not bring with it imagination or high quality of service.

The authors of the 1854 consolidation charter had voiced concern for effective control over municipal departments and sought devices for protecting the corporation from looting by predatory local political groups. To these ends they considerably enlarged the powers of the mayor at the expense of the councils' committees, and they created new executives in the offices of comptroller and receiver of taxes. So strong was the tradition of elected officials, however, that both these new executives had to be elected, not appointed by the mayor. Altogether, the reforms of 1854 could make but little progress. Bigness and industrialization had already destroyed both the source of competent leadership and the informed community which would have been necessary for the city to have enjoyed a future of strong, efficient, and imaginative government. Instead, a century of weakness and corruption lay ahead.[5]

Development of Waterworks

Philadelphia pioneered in building America's first municipal waterworks and thus operated for forty years an experimental water supply project for all other large cities in the nation. The success of Philadelphia's water program stands as a tribute to its old merchant-led committee system of government. Indeed, in the beginning, its success was as much a product of an aggressive committee as it was the result of sponsorship by the municipal corporation.[6]

The yellow fever epidemic of 1793 forced Philadelphians into their pioneering public water system. In that epidemic, the city's first major plague, one in twelve Philadelphians perished. More than 23,000 persons fled the city, and all business with the outside world ceased for a month.[7] It was clear to those who tasted the well water of different neighborhoods that in crowded blocks the contents of privies penetrated the wells.[8] Although doctors debated repeatedly the causes of the fever, all sides agreed that the cleansing of the streets, yards, and houses of filth and an abundant supply of cool, clear water for drinking were essential requirements if the city was to be preserved.

During these years a private company was digging a canal to connect the Schuylkill River to the Delaware River. It therefore seemed reasonable to add to these transportation plans a branch water supply canal through the center of the city. The canal company, however, soon went bankrupt. In 1797 another serious epidemic of yellow fever struck the city and carried away over 3,000 citizens. Extended negotiations between the canal company and the city were renewed, but satisfactory financial arrangements could not be worked out. The issue then moved to the state legislature, where the company proved a more powerful lobbyist than the municipal corporation. The fever returned in 1798.

In 1799 the immigrant English engineer and architect, Benjamin Latrobe (1764–1820), visited Philadelphia on a commission to design the Bank of Pennsylvania. While in town he heard of the problem and published a pamphlet proposing a quick solution. He suggested, as an alternative to the slow and expensive program of a dam and canals, that the city build two steam pumps, a culvert from the Schuylkill to the edge of the city's dense settlement (then Pennsylvania Square), and a distribution system of wooden pipes and street hydrants. To capture popular support he added the provision of free water to the poor at the street hydrants. The cost of construction and operation of the system, Latrobe maintained, could be met by rents charged to businesses and private homes that were directly connected to the system. Although there had been a steam engine in Philadelphia before the Revolution, Latrobe's scheme was a bold innovation.[9]

At this point, as in the later expansion of Fairmount Dam, the strength of the city's merchant-led committee system of government proved itself. During the years from 1799 to 1837 very able leaders of the city served on the Watering Committee of the City Councils. Henry Drinker, Jr. (1757–1822), son of the well-known Quaker merchant and himself cashier of the Bank of North America, Thomas P. Cope (1768–1854), then at the beginning of his successful merchant career, and Samuel M. Fox (1763–1808) of the Bank of Pennsylvania led the campaign for the Latrobe plan. In subsequent years William Rush (1766–1833), the famous sculptor; Joseph S. Lewis (1778–1836), prominent attorney and son of a wealthy China merchant; and John P. Wetherill (1794–1853), of the old Philadelphia paint manufacturing company Wetherill and Brother, all served on the Watering Committee and directed its aggressive policies.[10]

The city councils and their watering committee fought free of the canal interests and arranged their own financing without state aid. Despite setbacks in construction and periodic shortages of funds which the committee sometimes met by the members' advancing money out of their own pockets, they pushed the project through to completion by 1801. Henceforth Philadelphians enjoyed a reasonably adequate supply of water to cleanse themselves and to fight fires. The trials of the watering committee, however, did not cease. It continued to suffer all the pains of innovation. Engineering problems hampered the Committee until the twenties, financial problems until the thirties. The steam engines for the pumps, though good examples of Watt's low-pressure engine, broke down frequently and consumed mountains of cordwood. After sixteen years of difficulty they were replaced with high-pressure engines but these, though steady and powerful, used even more fuel. The original hydrants rarely shut off completely and in the winter froze solid. After two seasons the hydrants had to be entirely replaced by a new design. The hollow wooden logs used to distribute the water from the tank above the second pump leaked badly and after a few years a program of replacement by cast iron pipe was instituted.[11]

The original Latrobe scheme for financing the works was based on the assumption that many families would want direct water connections to their houses and that these private subscriptions would carry the cost of building and operating the system. Except for the boldest thinkers, however, Philadelphians in 1801 used water sparingly. By 1811 only 2,127 Philadelphians subscribed for water. Most of the city's 54,000 residents (city proper in 1810) depended for water on street hydrants or private wells. There were only two bath-houses in the entire city. As for home bathrooms, American inventors did not turn their attention to sanitary appliances until the 1830's. Thus over the first three decades of operation the watering committee struggled against heavy deficits while continuing to supply its product at a loss in advance of popular usage, for public health reasons.

Having established abundant clear water as part of the city's health services, the watering committee could not turn back even in the face of heavy financial deficits. During the second decade of the nineteenth century the city grew at the rate of about 2,200 persons per year. By 1820 Philadelphia and its immediate environs held a population of 114,000. The lawyer Joseph S. Lewis led the committee to seek a lasting solution to its problems of high operating costs and inadequate supply for the enlarging city. In 1819, in the midst of a severe depression, he proposed, and the City Councils accepted, a plan to invest another $400,000, this time in a dam across the Schuylkill and a series of water-powered pumps to raise the water to adjacent Fairmount Hill, where large reservoirs for a gravity-fed system could be built. The water-powered pumps would cut the operating costs to a mere fraction of the former steam costs. Also, the dam was to be constructed for eight water wheels, although only three would be needed immediately. Thus it was hoped that the Fairmount scheme afforded enough surplus capacity for years to come. Within four years the works were completed.

The Fairmount works met every economic and engineering expectation. They also stand as a lasting memorial to the era of Philadelphia's merchant-led committee government. The watering committee had sufficient taste, standing in the city, and pride in its accomplishment to finish the works and lay out the grounds as a beautiful park. Although only a beginning, like the works themselves, the park was an extremely valuable project. With its 1844 additions, it became the first large urban park in America, and, as such, was an essential link in the chain of outstanding landscapes that included Boston's Mt. Auburn Cemetery, New York's Central Park, and Chicago's lake front. Over the years Philadelphians expanded the original waterworks layout to create the greatest civic monument of Philadelphia, the Fairmount Park system.[12]

The excess capacity of the Fairmount works soon disappeared. Since public waterworks with their abundant supply of water for domestic and commercial users offered a novel product, there was no way to predict its future use. The growth of Philadelphia during the years 1830–1850 exceeded its rate for any other period (1820–1830 38 percent, 1830–1840 37 percent, 1840–1850 58 percent, Philadelphia only). Such a pace of growth, occurring for the first time in large American cities, likewise could not be expected to yield reliable future estimates. Both the sustained, rapid growth in Philadelphia's population and the increase in per capita consumption of water must have surprised contemporaries.[13]

In 1837 the committee issued a triumphant report. It had $100,000 in the bank, six wheels running at the dam, and the number of paying customers had jumped to 20,000. Of equal significance, consumption had begun its rise toward modern levels; doubling since 1823, it now equaled twenty gallons per person per day. The system as a whole—street hydrants, house and commercial connections—served a total population of 196,000. The report noted that 1,500 Philadelphians had installed bathrooms with running water. That critical moment in the history of any social innovation, the time when a fashion of the rich becomes an imperative for the middle class, seemed to have arrived.[14]

Though public enthusiasm for bathing and water closets grew apace, after 1837 the watering committee began to lose the imagination and largeness of view which had characterized its early performance. It seems reasonable to detect in this falling off of the quality of the committee the beginning of the decline in the quality of Philadelphia's municipal officers and a weakening of the committee system of government. Perhaps the very triumph of the Fairmount works in routinizing the water supply of the city, at least for a few years, made the watering committee unattractive to the most imaginative city leaders. Whatever the cause, the committee began to falter and in one way or another failed to keep pace with the growing needs of the city.

During the 1840's, spurred by immigration and industrial expansion, Philadelphia filled up rapidly and the towns and districts outside its boundaries grew at unprecedented rates. Spring Garden, Kensington, and Northern Liberties, districts which had joined the Philadelphia system, now used water in enormous amounts and demanded an equalization of their rates with those of Philadelphia customers. In addition, Spring Garden requested a high-pressure reservoir to give more adequate service on its hills. The watering committee, forgetting the essential public health purpose of its undertaking, now responded like a short-sighted monopolist by refusing to lower its rates. Spring Garden countered by securing legislative authorization to build its own works. Negotiations continued for a time, and ultimately the rates were conceded by the watering committee, but no satisfactory long-term contract could be worked out among Philadelphia and its neighbors. Spring Garden, Northern Liberties, and Kensington joined together to build their own pumping station in 1844. Ironically, they drew their water from behind the Fairmount Dam. In 1850 Kensington set up its own station, drawing from the Delaware River.

By 1850 only Southwark remained connected to the Philadelphia system. Yet such had been the decade's increase in per capita consumption that with all eight wheels working at the dam, and all the reservoirs filled, only three day's supply of water could be stored. In the summer 160,000 people drew forty-four gallons per person per day. Fifteen thousand houses had water closets, and 3,500 had baths. Clearly, the middle class of Philadelphia had adopted modern plumbing as an essential in its standard of living. The modern urban rate of water usage had arrived.

The subsequent history of the Philadelphia Water Works is inglorious. In 1851 inadequate capacity forced the watering committee to refuse West Philadelphia's request for service. The consolidation of all Philadelphia County into one city government in 1854 reunited all the water systems of the city, but union did not revive the old policy of aggressive building to meet future needs and to popularize higher standards of consumption. In the 1870's the city erected new steam pumping stations, but droughts brought shortages. Increasing pollution of the Schuylkill and Delaware rivers destroyed the former quality of the water. Such were the popular priorities of the city that the citizens taxed themselves with disease and dirty drinking water in order to allow private pollution of the rivers to continue unabated. In the years from 1880 to 1910 the typhoid fever rate in Philadelphia exceeded that of New York and Boston. Though filter systems had been demonstrated for over a decade, Philadelphia purchased its filters late and proceeded slowly. As late as 1906, 1,063 persons died of typhoid in Philadelphia in one season. In 1910–1911 filters and chlorine brought relief from these recurrent epidemics.[15]

The early history of Philadelphia's waterworks does more than help to date the mid-nineteenth-century decline in the effectiveness of its municipal government. Its history shows how the city's general culture of privatism stopped a universal public health program short of full realization. Fear of epidemics had created the water system, but once this fear had abated, little or no public support remained to bring the benefits of the new technology to those who could not afford them. The popular goal of the private city was a goal to make Philadelphia a moderately safe place for ordinary men and women to go about conducting their own business; the goal was never to help raise the level of living of the poor.

Notes

1. Quaker historians agree that the Holy Experiment died from materialism and secularization during the eighteenth century, Frederick B. Tolles, *Meeting House and Counting House* (Chapel Hill, 1948), 240–243; Sydney V. James, *A People Among Peoples* (Cambridge, 1963), 37–43, 211–215; and see the charges against his contemporaries in John Woolman, *The Journal of John Woolman* (F. B. Tolles, Introduction, New York, 1961).

2. Howard Mumford Jones, *O Strange New World* (New York, 1964), 194–272, treats with this tradition as a blend of Christian and classical ideas.

3. Philadelphia's experience in these years appears to have been part of a general national trend. Ernest S. Griffith, *Modern Development of City Government in the United Kingdom and the United States* (London, 1927), 1, 3–29.

4. The history of the municipal corporation is taken from Edward P. Allinson and Boies Penrose, *City Government of Philadelphia (Johns Hopkins Studies in Historical and Political Science,* Fifth Series, 1–11, Baltimore, 1887), 33–61; J. Thomas Scharf and Thompson Westcott, *History of Philadelphia 1606–1884* (Philadelphia, 1884), III, 1703, 1737, 1936.

5. Eli K. Price, *The History of the Consolidation of the City of Philadelphia* (Philadelphia, 1873), 82–89. Compare with Lincoln Steffens, "Philadelphia: Corrupt and Contented," *The Shame of Cities* (New York, 1904, 1957 ed.), 134–161.

6. Public water supplies were established in Philadelphia in 1801, in New York in 1842, Boston 1848, Baltimore, a small private system in 1808, expanded in 1838, and a full public system in 1857.

7. The first U.S. Census returned 44,096 persons for Philadelphia, the Liberties, and Southwark. Therefore the population of the city on the eve of the plague must have been about 48,000. The epidemic is recounted in detail in John H. Powell, *Bring Out Your Dead: The Great Plague of Yellow Fever in Philadelphia in 1793* (Philadelphia, 1949).

8. [Benjamin] Latrobe noted the seepage of wastes through the Philadelphia sand in his journal. Talbot Hamlin, *Benjamin Henry Latrobe* (New York, 1955), 157.

9. Hamlin, Latrobe, 134–135, 157–167; John A. Kouwenhoven, *Made in America* (New York, 1948), 41.

10. For the narrative of the Philadelphia waterworks I have relied on Nelson M. Blake, *Water for the Cities* (Syracuse, 1956), Ch. II, V.

11. There is some evidence that the Philadelphia waterworks may be a case of provincial technological backwardness caused by the imperfect communication of engineering technique in the Atlantic world. W. H. Chaloner, "John Wilkinson, Ironmaster," *History Today*, I (May, 1951), 67, reports shipments of cast iron water pipe from England to Paris in 1780–1781 but does not indicate whether these pipes were for a Paris waterworks or for the Versailles fountain system. Whichever the case it would seem that French engineering and specifications would have saved Philadelphia the grief it experienced with faulty hydrants and fittings. The changeover to cast iron pipe went slowly. Scharf and Westcott claim replacement did not begin until 1818 and that in 1822 there were still thirty-two miles of wooden pipe in the city, *History of Philadelphia* I, 605.

12. Commissioners of Fairmount Park, *First Annual Report* (Philadelphia, 1869), 6–12; George B. Tatum, "The Origins of Fairmount Park," *Antiques* LXXXII (November, 1962), 502–507.

13. Today planners struggle with the identical problem which faced the Philadelphia Watering Committee. How much extra capacity should be built into the works in the case when capital is in short supply and a city is growing at an indeterminate pace? The size of the Fairmount works, and hence the amount of extra capacity for the entire system, was set by a combination of engineering considerations and prior private property rights. The design of the dam and its wheels followed the plans of an English engineer who had formerly built mills along the nearby Brandywine River. He estimated the possible height of the dam and hence the available power at the site on the basis of contemporary rules of thumb. To guard against an underestimate on his part of the efficiency of the pumps, the Watering Committee purchased additional upstream riparian rights so that the height of the dam could be raised to carry its lake to the Manayunk mills upstream. No further height was possible since to purchase the Manayunk mill rights would have been enormously expensive. Thus the efficiency of the overshot wheels at the Fairmount Dam and the presence of the Manayunk mills determined the capacity of the Philadelphia system for the next thirty years. Thomas Gilpin, "Fairmount Dam and Waterworks, Philadelphia," *Pennsylvania Magazine* XXXVII (October, 1913), 471–479; Select and Common Councils of Philadelphia, *Report of the Watering Committee on the Propriety of Raising the Dam at Fair Mount* (Philadelphia, 1820), 4–6.

14. A great enthusiasm for bathing seized the public at this moment and even suggested to an editorial writer that public bathhouses would improve the moral habits of the poor by lessening the jealousy between classes. *Public Ledger,* July 10, 1838. Purity of the water had not been entirely satisfactory. The same paper complained that the hydrant system meant impure water. It reported an "animal, like a centipede," in a glass of hydrant water. *Public Ledger,* October 6, 1836.

15. Philadelphia Bureau of Water, *Description of the Filtration Works and History of Water Supply 1789–1900* (Philadelphia, 1909), 3–4, 50–51, 70–71; City of Philadelphia, *Third Annual Message of Mayor Harry A. Mackey* (Philadelphia, 1931), 388; Blake, *Water for the Cities,* 97–98, 255–256, 259–261.

5

Richard C. Wade

THE URBAN FRONTIER

Part of Philadelphia's appeal to towndwellers was its leadership among the nation's cities, for nearly every young metropolis . . . coveted a similar primacy in the West. Indeed, one of the most striking characteristics of this period was the development of an urban imperialism which saw rising young giants seek to spread their power and influence over the entire new country. The drive for supremacy, furthermore, was quite conscious, infusing an extraordinary dynamic into city growth, but also breeding bitter rivalries among the claimants. In the ensuing struggles, the economically strongest survived and flourished, while the less successful fell behind. Smaller places were trampled in the process, some being swallowed up by ambitious neighbors, others being overwhelmed before they could attain a challenging position. The contest, however, produced no final victor. In fact, the lead changed three times, and though Cincinnati commanded the field in 1830, Pittsburgh, Louisville, and St. Louis were still in the running.

The rivalries developed very early. Lexington jumped off to a quick start, but by 1810 Pittsburgh, enjoying a commercial and manufacturing boom, forged ahead. The postwar depression undermined its leadership, however, and Cincinnati moved forward to take its place. The fierce competition led to widespread speculation about the outcome. Most of the prophecy was wishful, stemming from the hopes of boosters and involving doubtful calculations. In 1816, for instance, a Pittsburgher summed up many of the elements of this competition in a table (with ratings presumably on a scale of excellence from one to ten) designed to illustrate the inevitability of the Iron City's supremacy.[1] Not only did the author work out the estimates in scientific detail, but he also predicted that the totals represented the population (in thousands) which each would reach in 1830.

	Pittsburgh	Lexington	Cincinnati
Situation for inland trade and navigation	9	2	6
Adaptness for manufacturers	9	3	5
Fertility of surrounding soil	2	7	4
Salubrity	9	7	5
Pleasantness and beauty	.3	1	.6
Elegance of scite [*sic*] and environs	1	.3	.6
	30.3	20.3	21.2

Reprinted by permission of the publisher from *The Urban Frontier: The Rise of Western Cities,* by Richard C. Wade. Cambridge, Mass.: Harvard University Press. Copyright © 1959 by the President of the Fellows of Harvard College.

Before a city could hope to enter the urban sweepstake for the largest prize, it had to eliminate whatever rivals arose in its own area. In many instances the odds in these battles were so uneven that smaller places gave in quickly. In others, a decision came only after a bitter and prolonged struggle. Edwardsville, Illinois, fell easily before St. Louis, but Wheeling's submission to Pittsburgh followed a decade of acrimony. Sometimes defeat meant the end of independence for a town. Louisville, for example, ultimately annexed Shippingport and Portland, while Pittsburgh reached across the river to take in Allegheny. In other cases, the penalty for failure was the lessening of power and prestige. Steubenville and Wheeling, unable to sustain their position against Pittsburgh in the Upper Ohio, had to settle for a much reduced pace of development. The same fate befell Ste. Genevieve, an early challenger of St. Louis's domination of the Mississippi and Missouri. Occasionally a victor reduced its competitor to a mere economic appendage. This is what happened to Jeffersonville and New Albany, Indiana, after Louisville captured the trade of the Falls.

Though struggles for regional primacy characterized the urban growth of the entire West, the most celebrated was Pittsburgh's duel with Wheeling. Both were situated on the Ohio and both hoped to capture its flourishing commerce. Wheeling's great advantage lay in its down-river position, where it outflanked the shoals and rapids which dominated the approach to Pittsburgh. During the late summer, low water made navigation difficult and at times impossible, inducing some merchants to use the Virginia town as a transshipment point to the East. This fact alone made Wheeling a competitor, for in no other department could it match the Iron City. Pittsburgh's detractors saw this situation as early as 1793, when the Army considered establishing a post at Wheeling. Isaac Craig complained that "this new arrangement, . . . has Originated in the Brain of the Gentlemen in Washington who envy Pittsburgh, and . . . have represented to General Knox, that Navigation is practicable from Wheeling in the dry season."[2] The same consideration made Wheeling a stop in the mail route to the West and the Ohio River terminus of the National Road.

Despite these advantages, Wheeling's population barely reached 1,000 by 1815, while Pittsburgh had become the new country's leading metropolis. A serious rivalry seemed almost ridiculous. But the postwar depression, felling the Iron City, gave its smaller neighbor the hope of rising on the ruins. This prospect brightened in 1816, when, after many abortive attempts to change the terminus, the National Road was completed to Wheeling. Optimism about the town's future abounded throughout the valley. A Steubenville editor caught the spirit in verse:

Wheeling has secured her roads,
Come waggoners, come and bring your loads.
Emigrants, come hither, and build a town,
And make Wheeling a place of renown.

By 1822, 5,000 wagons were arriving annually in the booming settlement. "Wheeling is a thriving place," a traveler observed; "it bids fair to rival Pittsburgh in the trade of the Western country."[3]

The Iron City, troubled by a stagnant economy and worried about its future, warily watched the progress of this upstart. Actually, Wheeling's challenge was only a small part of Pittsburgh's total problem, but its very ludicrousness made the situation all the more intolerable. "A miserable Virginia country town, which can never be more than two hundred yards wide, having the mere advantage of a free turnpike road and a warehouse or two, to become rivals of this *Emporium* of the West!" exclaimed the incredulous editor of the *Statesman*. As Wheeling continued to prosper, Pittsburgh accused its competitor of unfair practices, particularly of circulating the rumor that ships could not go up the river to "the Point." "They have taken to lying," the *Statesman* snapped. "We cannot believe this report," the *Gazette* asserted with more charity; "the citizens with whom we are acquainted in that place, are too honorable to countenance such childish, hurtless falsehood," especially since "everybody acquainted with the river knows that the water is as good if not better above than for 100 miles below."[4]

Civic leaders in Wheeling, feeling their oats and certain that the National Road provided a secure base for unlimited growth, continually goaded the stricken giant. "Strange that a 'miserable Virginia Country Town,' a 'mere village,' should have attracted so much attention at the 'emporium of the West,'" the *Northwestern Gazette* observed. Moreover, it asserted that the difficulty of navigation on the Upper Ohio was not mere rumor. "During the drier part of the season the greater part of the Western Merchants order their goods to Wheeling and *not* to Pittsburgh. This fact is a stubborn and decisive one. It speaks volumes. It is a demonstration." A patronizing condescension expressed an increasing confidence. "Pittsburgh may, if she will, be a large and respectable manufacturing town. She may also retain a portion of the carrying trade," the same source graciously conceded. There seemed no limit to Wheeling's assurance. Travelers reported that its residents were "actually doing nothing but walking about on stilts, and stroking their chins with utmost self-complacency. Every man who is so fortunate as to own about 60 feet front and 120 feet back, considers himself . . . snug."[5]

The next few years demonstrated, however, that history was only teasing. Wheeling's hopes for greatness were soon dashed. The National Road proved disappointing as a freight carrier, and Pittsburgh recovered from its depression, once again becoming the urban focus of the Upper Ohio. Though the Virginia town could boast over 5,000 inhabitants in 1830, its rate of growth lagged and its future prospects dimmed. To some shrewd observers the outcome was not unexpected. A Steubenville editor, consoling his readers in 1816 after their efforts to get the National Road had failed, asserted that cities could not be reared on mere highway traffic. "Rely on agriculture and manufactures," he counseled," and you will do well without the mail or the turnpike bubble—it is not the sound of the coachman's horn that will make a town flourish."[6]

Though Pittsburgh beat back Wheeling's challenge, it could not maintain its Western leadership. Cincinnati, less affected by the postwar collapse, surged by the Iron City and established its primacy throughout the new country. It was not content, however, to win its supremacy by another's injury. Rather it developed its own positive program to widen its commercial opportunities and spread its influence. In fact, the city was so alive with ideas that one visitor referred to it as "that hot bed of projects," and another observed "great plans on foot; whenever two or three meet at a corner nothing is heard but schemes." In broad terms the object of Cincinnati's statesmanship was threefold: to tap the growing trade on the Great Lakes by water links to the Ohio, to facilitate traffic on the river by a canal around the Falls, and to reach into the hinterland with improved roads. Later another canal—this time down the Licking "into the heart of Kentucky"—a bridge across the Ohio, and a railway to Lexington were added.[7] Success would have made the entire valley dependent upon this urban center, and given the Ohio metropolis command of the strategic routes of trade and travel.

This ambitious program caused great concern in Pittsburgh. "We honestly confess," the *Gazette* admitted, that "a canal from the lakes either into the Ohio or the Great Miami . . . adds another item to the amount of our present uneasiness." By tipping the commerce of the valley northward, Cincinnati would substantially reduce the Iron City's importance as the central station between East and West. "Without this trade," the *Statesman* warned, "what can Philadelphia and Pittsburgh become but deserted villages, compared with their great rivals?"[8] Pennsylvania responded to this threat by improving the turnpike between its urban centers and ultimately constructing an elaborate canal across the mountains. In addition, Pittsburgh proposed to head off Cincinnati by building a water route to Lake Erie or tying into the Ohio system below Cleveland.

The challenge to Cincinnati's supremacy, however, came not only from a resurgent Pittsburgh, but also from a booming downriver neighbor, Louisville. As early as 1819 a visitor noted this two-front war. "I discovered two ruling passions in Cincinnati; enmity against Pittsburgh and jealousy of Louisville." In one regard the Falls City was the more serious rival, because as a commercial center it competed directly with the Ohio emporium. In fact, guerilla warfare between the two towns for advantage in the rural market began early in the century.[9] But the great object of contention was the control and traffic on the river—the West's central commercial artery.

In this contest Louisville held one key advantage. Its strategic position at the Falls gave it command of both parts of the Ohio. All passengers and goods had to pass through the town, except during the few months of high water when even large vessels could move safely over the rapids. It was a clumsy system, and from the earliest days many people envisaged a canal around the chutes. Nothing came of these plans until the coming of the steamboat immensely expanded traffic and made the interruption seem intolerable. Though nearly every shipper favored a canal, it was not until Cincinnati, anxious both to loosen river commerce and weaken a rival city, put its weight behind the improvement that any real activity developed.

Cincinnati had a deep stake in this project. A canal would not only aid the town generally but also advance the interests of some powerful groups. The mercantile community was anxious to get freer trade, and many residents had large investments in companies which hoped to dig on either the Kentucky or

Indiana side of the Falls.[10] Others owned real estate in the area. William Lytle, for example, had large holdings around Portland of an estimated value of between $100,000 and $500,000.[11] Moreover, ordinary Cincinnatians had come to the conclusion that a canal would serve a broad public purpose. Hence in 1817 a town meeting was called to discuss the issue. An editor provided the backdrop: "No question was ever agitated here that involved more important consequences to this town." And from the beginning Louisville was cast as the villain of the piece. *Liberty Hall* referred to it as "a little town" trying to make "all the upper country tributary to it, by compelling us to deposit our goods in its warehouses and pay extravagant prices for transportation around or over the Falls."[12]

Since the Falls City could frustrate any project on Kentucky soil, Cincinnati's first move was to build on the opposite side. The Indiana legislature incorporated the Jeffersonville Ohio Canal Company in 1817, empowering it to sell 20,000 shares of stock at $50 apiece, and authorizing a lottery for $100,000 more. From the outset it was clear that the scheme stemmed from the Queen City. Not only did that town provide more than half the concern's directors, but also the campaign for funds emphasized its role. "The public may be assured that the wealth, influence, enterprise and talents of Cincinnati are at the head of this measure," *Liberty Hall* declared in 1818. Moreover, advocates underlined the stake of the Ohio metropolis, warning residents that if they did not support the drive they "deserved to be hewers of wood and drawers of water" for Louisville. In May 1819 a prominent Cincinnatian gave the ceremonial address as digging began on the Indiana side.[13]

Louisville hesitated to support any canal. The city had flourished on the transportation break, and many inhabitants felt that facilitating travel over the rapids would destroy the very *raison d'être* of the place. That view was probably extreme, but in the short run no one could deny that certain interests were jeopardized. "It must be admitted that the business of a portion of our population would be affected," the *Public Advertiser* confessed. "The storage and forwarding business would probably be diminished—and there might be less use for hacks and drays."[14] Tavern and hotel owners shared this anxiety, while the pilots who guided the ships through the chutes faced almost certain unemployment.

Unwilling to sacrifice these interests and uneasy about the town's future, Louisville leaders tried to deflect the mounting enthusiasm for a canal. Their first strategy was to suggest a small cut around the Falls which would accommodate keelboats and lesser craft. This expedient found few supporters, and Louisville next tried to reduce the pressure by paving the road to Portland and Shippingport, thus, facilitating the transshipment process.[15] But this, too, was inadequate, and within a few years the clamor for a canal became irresistible.

Yet the city still hoped to salvage something out of defeat, to find some compensation for the loss of its strategic position. In 1824 a local editor laid down the conditions. "It is true that we could feel but little interest in opening a canal merely for the purpose of navigation," he conceded. "A canal to be useful . . . should be constructed to give us ample water power, for various and extensive manufacturing establishments; and a sufficient number of dry docks for the building and . . . repair of nearly all the steamboats employed on western waters, should be constructed as necessary appendages." If the project included these items, he declared, then "the citizens of Louisville will be found among its most zealous advocates."[16]

The Falls City could afford to take its pound of flesh, because building on the Indiana side was much less feasible than the Kentucky route. The engineering problems were immensely more complicated, and the cost was nearly three times as great. In 1819 an official committee, comprised of delegates from Virginia, Pennsylvania, Ohio, and Kentucky, estimated the expense of the northern plan at $1,100,000 and the southern one at $350,000.[17] Hence few people acquainted with the situation took seriously the Jeffersonville Ohio Canal Company's enterprise. Yet the disadvantages of the Indiana route were not insurmountable, and Louisvillians realized that in the long run the Falls would be skirted on one side or the other. If they dragged their feet too much, their opponents would press for action regardless of the cost or difficulty. This possibility ultimately brought the Kentucky emporium to its knees.[18]

While Louisville reluctantly yielded at the Falls, Cincinnati pursued the rest of its expansion program. By 1822 the Miami Canal to Dayton was open, and work had begun on the state system which ultimately connected the Great Lakes with the Ohio River. Though the Queen City could claim less success in the Kentucky area, its economic supremacy in the West was not questioned. The new country's largest urban center, it had corralled the bulk of the region's mounting commerce and become the nexus of trade lines that reached from the Atlantic Ocean to the Gulf of Mexico.

Cincinnati's economic primacy, however, did not yet carry with it cultural leadership. This honor still belonged to Lexington, whose polish and sophistication were the envy of every transmontane town. "Cincinnati may be the Tyre, but Lexington is unquestionably the Athens of the West," *Liberty Hall* conceded in 1820. This admission reflected a sense of inadequacy which constantly shadowed the Queen City and compromised its claim to total supremacy. One resident suggested an ambitious lecture program to overcome the deficiency and "convince those persons at a distance who pronounce us as a *Commercial* people alone, that we have here, both the *Tyre* and the *Athens* of the West." Another observer, though not armed with a remedy, made the same point. "It may be well for us," he counseled, "when we can catch a moment from the grovelling pursuits of commercial operations, to cull and admire the varied sweets of those literary and scientific effusions, which have stamped Lexington as the headquarters of *Science and Letters* in the Western country."[19]

The establishment and success of Transylvania University [in Lexington] aggravated this inferiority complex. Not only did it lend prestige to another place, but it also lured local youths to its classrooms. The *Western Spy* admitted that it was "particularly mortifying to see the College of a neighboring state attract both Students and Professors" from the Ohio metropolis. In the early twenties Cincinnati countered with a medical school which it hoped would become a "powerful rival" and "ultimately go beyond" the Kentucky institution.[20] But it was not until financial difficulties and fire brought down Transylvania that the Queen City could claim cultural parity with its Blue Grass rival.

Lexington's position also bred jealousy in Louisville. Though the larger and more prosperous of the two by 1825, the Falls City had to concede that intellectual primacy rested with its Kentucky neighbor. This admission was not easy to make, because the two towns had been bitter foes for many years. They contended for political leadership in the state; earlier, in fact, each had hoped to become its capital. Moreover, their economic interests often collided, with Lexington depending upon manufacturing and protection and Louisville emphasizing commerce and wanting freer trade. Neither yielded readily to the other on any issue. Yet the cultural leadership of the Blue Grass town was too obvious to be denied, and, from the Falls City viewpoint, it was certainly too important to be permanently surrendered.

There was, however, something of a family quarrel about this rivalry. Despite their differences, both professed love for mother Kentucky, and occasionally one deferred to the other out of filial pride. In 1820, for example, Louisville's *Public Advertiser* supported state aid to Transylvania, explaining that "distinguished institutions of learning in our own state, where education from its cheapness, shall be within the reach of the poor, is the *pivot* on which the grandeur of the state depends." In addition, the Falls City stood to gain by its success. "Louisville cannot be jealous of Lexington," the same newspaper declared; "her future interest is measurably blended with that of Transylvania University; for as that flourishes Lexington will become a more extensive and important customer to her in a commercial point of view." Likewise, when Lexington tried to get money for a hospital, its old foe offered support, but for perhaps less elevated reasons. If the Blue Grass got such an institution, "one of the same kind at this place cannot, consistently, be refused," the editor observed.[21]

And nothing forced the two to discover common interests more quickly than the appearance of a hostile outsider. When Cincinnati planned a medical school to compete with Transylvania, Louisville stood behind the testimony of the university, whose spokesman urged the state to give additional money to the institution. Otherwise, he warned, "in the struggle that must ensue, we of Transylvania will be compelled to enter the lists naked and defenceless, our opponents of Cincinnati being . . . armed. The issue of such a conflict cannot be doubted. We shall certainly be vanquished and your young men will . . . repair to the eastern schools for medical education, or Kentucky must become tributary to the state of Ohio."[22] Lexington reciprocated when the Queen City threatened a canal on the Indiana side of the river.

Kind words were few, however, and mutual aid sporadic. Usually the two communities did little to conceal their animosity. In fact, Louisville had no sooner supported Transylvania's expansion than it began again its vicious barrage on the school and its town. The attack stemmed from a mixture of political, economic, and urban motives, but it centered on the university because it was at once the symbol of Lexington's importance and its most vulnerable spot. The city's economy never recovered from the postwar depression and only its cultural renaissance kept stores and shops open. If the college failed, all failed. This was understood in the Falls City. Indeed, the *Public Advertiser* noted that the "ablest and best citizens" of the Blue Grass metropolis had tried to give a "new impetus" to the place by the encouragement of its "literary establishments."[23] Knowingly, then, Louisville struck at Lexington where it would hurt most.

Nor was there anything gentle about the tactics. In 1816, during the first debate over state assistance to Transylvania, John Rowan from the Falls City argued that the institution ought to be moved elsewhere to keep it from "improper influence" and the "many means of corrupting the morals of youth," which existed in the town. Four years later the criticism had become more barbed. "If you wish to jeopardize every amiable trait in the private character of your son, send him to Lexington," the *Public Advertiser* contended, linking the college to radical politics. "If you wish him to become a Robespierre or a Murat, send him to Lexington to learn the rudiments of Jacobinism and disorganization." By 1829 a Louisville editor was warning parents that at the university their children would be "surrounded by political desperadoes" and that "the very atmosphere of the place has been calculated to pollute the morals and principles of the youth attending it.[24]

Lexington, though an old veteran of urban rivalries, had not anticipated this bitterness. "We thought of all our institutions, it was the pride and boast of the town; and the least calculated to excite the envy, and stir up the opposition of any individual or section of the country." But the assault threatened the city's very life, and it fought back. The defense was generally constructive, detailing the achievements of Transylvania and extolling its influence on students and the new country. Graduates wrote testimonials and local citizens publicized the healthfulness and "literary atmosphere" of the community, while officials dispelled rumors about the snobbery of the college.[25]

The case was good, but Lexington strategists bungled in several respects. In 1829 not a single Jacksonian was appointed to the Board of Trustees, and not enough was done to quiet the uneasiness of either the farmers or the highly religious.[26] As a result, when Transylvania needed support most, it was almost friendless. By 1830 the campaign instituted by Louisville had destroyed Kentucky's brightest ornament and pulled the most substantial prop from Lexington's economy.

Even before Transylvania's demise Lexington felt itself slipping economically, and it tried to steady itself by better connections with the trade of the Ohio River. Canals and roads proved either impractical or inadequate, and in 1829 civic leaders planned a railroad. The act of incorporation in the next year left the northern terminus undecided, with the understanding that it would be either Louisville or Cincinnati. The uncertainty set off a curious kind of competition between those two cities. Neither could foresee the impact that a railroad might have on its own importance, yet they equally feared that it would give their rival a substantial advantage.

Louisville was especially wary. This looked like the canal issue in another form, and many people thought it wise to wait for the results of the first project. Moreover, some of the same local interests seemed to be threatened. The hack and dray owners protested that their $125,000 business would be jeopardized. And since the railroad would pass through the city and continue on to Portland, others feared the growth of a "rival town" on the western end of the Falls. The city council, walking gingerly because of this opposition, appointed a committee to look into the question, and called a public hearing to sound out local opinion. The meeting attracted over three hundred people, and after a lively debate, it voted to keep the tracks out of Louisville.[27]

Very quickly, however, civic leaders realized that any alternative terminus was more perilous to the Falls City than the possible dislocations occasioned by accepting the railroad. Thus "S" wrote that if "we are to have a rival town, the nearer to us the less dangerous," and a "Gentleman in Lexington" warned that its "great rival, Cincinnati," was "straining every nerve" to induce the company to build in that direction. By December 1830 the tide had turned, and the council invited the Lexington and Ohio Railroad to come to Louisville.[28]

Cincinnati, despite its official policy, had many qualms about a railroad from Lexington. "Why should the citizens of Cincinnati be so anxious to create a rival town across the river?" asked the editor of the *Advertiser*. Yet the same logic which drove Louisville to change its mind sustained the Queen City's original decision. On December 7, 1830, a public meeting declared that the project "would conduce to the prosperity of this city, in an eminent degree," and a committee of prominent civic leaders invited the company's directors to come to Cincinnati to discuss details.[29] These events, coupled with Louisville's acceptance, brought great rejoicing to Lexington, for it now looked as though the railroad would bring it a share of the Ohio's commerce and arrest at last the economic decay which had brought the "Athens of the West" to the very brink of disaster.

The struggle for primacy and power—and occasionally survival—was one of the most persistent and striking characteristics of the early urban history of the West. Like imperial states, cities carved out extensive dependencies, extended their influence over the economic and political life of the hinterland, and fought with contending places over strategic trade routes. Nor was the contest limited to the young giants, for smaller towns joined the scramble. Cleveland and Sandusky, for example, clashed over the location of the northern terminus of the Ohio canal, the stakes being nothing less than the burgeoning commerce between the river and the lakes. And their instinct to fight was sound, for the outcome shaped the future of both.

Like most imperialisms, the struggle among Western cities left a record of damage and achievement. It trampled new villages, smothered promising towns, and even brought down established metropolises. Conflicting ambitions infused increasing bitterness into the intercourse of rivals, and made suspicion, jealousy, and vindictiveness a normal part of urban relationships. Yet competition also brought rapid expansion. The fear of failure was a dynamic force, pushing civic leaders into improvements long before they thought them necessary. The constant search for new markets furnished an invaluable stimulus to commercial and industrial enterprise. And, at its best, urban imperialism bred a strong pride in community accomplishment. As one resident put it, "there exists in our city a spirit . . . which may render any man proud to being called a Cincinnatian."[30]

Notes

1. *Pittsburgh Mercury,* February 3, 1816.
2. I. Craig to J. O'Hara, June 15, 1793, MS, Isaac Craig Papers, Carnegie Library of Pittsburgh.
3. C. B. Smith, "The Terminus of the Cumberland Road on the Ohio River" (M.A. Thesis, University of Pittsburgh, 1951), 69; *Western Herald* (Steubenville), April 12, 1816; Smith, "Cumberland Road," 71; Woods, *Illinois Country,* 75.
4. *Pittsburgh Statesman,* June 2, 1821; *Pittsburgh Gazette,* May 4, 1821.
5. *Northwestern Gazette* (Wheeling), June 16, 1821; *Pittsburgh Gazette,* December 18, 1818.
6. Smith, "Cumberland Road," 69; *Western Herald* (Steubenville), September 20, 1816.
7. *Pittsburgh Gazette,* January 22, 1819; February 5, 1819; *Liberty Hall* (Cincinnati), January 21, 1823; November 25, 1825.
8. *Pittsburgh Gazette,* January 22, 1819; *Pittsburgh Statesman,* November 26, 1818.
9. *Pittsburgh Gazette,* February 5, 1819; *Louisville Public Advertiser,* June 21, 1820.
10. For example, see the account of the Ohio Canal Company in *Liberty Hall* (Cincinnati), March 24, 1817.
11. The William Lytle Collection in the Historical and Philosophical Society of Ohio library includes a series of letters which explain his stake in the canal. He owned most of the land in the Portland area through which the canal ultimately passed. For a statement of its value, see D. McClellan to W. Lytle, October 21, 1817. Lytle Collection.
12. *Liberty Hall* (Cincinnati), December 29, 1817; March 26, 1817.
13. *Liberty Hall* (Cincinnati), June 5, 1818; February 26, 1818; May 20, 1818; May 6, 1818; May 14, 1819.
14. *Louisville Public Advertiser,* February 7, 1824.
15. *Liberty Hall* (Cincinnati), March 18, 1816; *Louisville Public Advertiser,* October 16, 1819.
16. *Louisville Public Advertiser,* January 21, 1824.
17. *Louisville Public Advertiser,* November 17, 1819.
18. *Louisville Public Advertiser,* February 7, 1824.
19. *Liberty Hall* (Cincinnati), May 27, 1820; December 17, 1819; May 27, 1820.
20. *Western Spy* (Cincinnati), October 13, 1817; *Liberty Hall* (Cincinnati), January 14, 1823.
21. *Louisville Public Advertiser,* September 20, 1820; September 27, 1820; December 20, 1820.
22. *Louisville Public Advertiser,* November 27, 1820.
23. *Louisville Public Advertiser,* August 23, 1820.
24. *Kentucky Reporter,* February 14, 1816; *Louisville Public Advertiser,* September 9, 1820; October 13, 1829.
25. *Kentucky Reporter,* March 7, 1827; March 10, 1823; February 21, 1827; September 8, 1828.
26. For these problems see, for example, *Louisville Public Advertiser,* October 29, 1829.
27. *Louisville Public Advertiser,* December 8, 1830; November 2, 1830; Louisville, City Journal, October 20, 1830; October 29, 1830; *Louisville Public Advertiser,* November 4, 1830.
28. *Louisville Public Advertiser,* November 3, 1830; November 5, 1830; Louisville, City Journal, December 3, 1830.
29. *Cincinnati Advertiser,* December 11, 1830; *Liberty Hall* (Cincinnati), December 10, 1830.
30. *Liberty Hall* (Cincinnati), January 9, 1829.

CHAPTER 3

MACHINES, REFORM, AND THE POLITICAL IMPERATIVE

The Political Imperative

The logic of governance requires that city governments negotiate the differences among the groups and political interests that make up the city. Although the specific interests have changed over time, there are constants, too. American cities have always experienced ethnic, racial, and neighborhood rivalries. During the nineteenth century and the early twentieth century, cities attracted waves of immigrants, first from England, Ireland, and Germany, then from Italy and eastern Europe. The successive waves of immigrants held the potential for utterly rending the urban fabric. In the 1840s several antiIrish riots broke out. These, however, were small when compared to the several weeks of riots that swept New York City in 1863, an upheaval that killed as approximately 3,000 people (an event portrayed in the popular film *Gangs of New York*). Against this background it can safely be said that there was a political imperative to achieve an acceptable level of peace in the governance of cities.

An emerging system of machine-style politics based in the ethnic wards broke the iron grip that aristocrats and businessmen had long maintained on city politics. By the late nineteenth century, well-organized party machines that relied on ethnic solidarity and the distribution of material benefits became the dominant mode of governance in many industrial cities. Machine organizations came together as alliances among politicians from the ethnic wards. Individual politicians could deliver the vote because they had come to know their constituents as friends and neighbors. By cooperating with one another, each of these entrepreneur-politicians could gain control of the levers of power that make cities work. But the ethnic voters comprised only the electoral portion of the system. Machine politicians made themselves useful to business by exacting payoffs in exchange for a host of favors ranging from business licenses to construction contracts to monopoly control over streetcars and utilities. Whether what was on offer from this system added up to constituency service or graft and corruption was in the eye of the beholder.

This style of politics is colorfully rendered by George Washington Plunkett (the subject of William Riordan's book, *Plunkitt of Tammany Hall*), who climbed out of poverty to become a millionaire during his forty years of service in the famous (or infamous) Tammany Hall machine in New York City. Note that Plunkett's secret for political success did not depend on winning the minds or appealing to the ideals of the voters, but in gaining the voters' loyalty through petty favors or, when necessary, giving them jobs. Conveying lovable cynicism, Plunkett even saw how it was possible to convert treats to little children into votes on election day!

The United States stands virtually alone among western industrial democracies in producing machine-style politics. Why did such organizations arise in American cities? Who really benefited? Machine politicians clearly thought that the services they provided to their constituents were valuable and much needed. But in a selection from his book, *Rainbow's End,* Steve Erie gives a different point of view. In his account, the small favors actually impeded the assimilation and upward mobility of their immigrant followers. Party bosses were inclined to spread patronage as thinly as possible as a way of maximizing the size of their electoral coalitions. This logic led them to create a multitude of blue-collar and poorly paid public jobs that had no future. To get ahead, an immigrant worker would have been well-advised to seek employment in the private sector.

Erie also shows that, in any case, most immigrants had no access to whatever largesse the machines handed out. Nearly all party machines that Erie studied were dominated by Irish politicians who favored the Irish over other groups in the distribution of jobs, contracts and other rewards. In cities where Irish bosses had secure power bases, they found it advantageous to exclude newer immigrant groups from participating in the machine. Erie thinks that the lessons of the Irish machines should give pause to any of today's minority politicians who might be tempted to believe that a strategy of machinelike politics offers their constituents an effective means of political advancement.

Who governs the city substantially determines what it does; this is why governance often involves momentous political struggles. By the late nineteenth century, the machine politics that were prevalent in most cities began to provoke opposition from better educated, upper- and middle-class citizens. At first, the fledgling reform efforts mostly met with failure because they did not successfully articulate a vision of the city that could unite enough groups. During the Progressive Era, however, the agenda that defined municipal reform became well articulated within a national movement. Though the reformers often attacked the machines by claiming that "boss politics" undermined democracy, they were less interested in improving democracy than in undermining the electoral influence of immigrant voters.

The spirit and substance of the reformers' objectives was stated in an unusually candid way in a magazine article reprinted here, which was published in 1890 by Andrew D. White, the first president of Cornell University. White believed that cities could be run just like a business and that its affairs were nonpartisan in character, having nothing to do with politics. Note that White's advocacy of nonpartisanship was intimately linked to his belief that removing the party label from election ballots could help remove local government from the influence of immigrant voters. The reformers said that they wanted to make local government more efficient, but this claim often served as a useful cover for an antidemocratic attack on poor immigrants.

According to the selection by the urban historian Samuel P. Hays, business leaders and the upper class spearheaded reform. The reformers shared a conviction that only they were capable of properly managing the affairs of government. Reformers claimed that they were merely protecting municipal government from corruption, but the reforms they advocated ushered in a centralized style of politics that made it more difficult for all but the most influential and educated of citizens to exert much influence. It was the birth of governance by bureaucracy that still bothers many people today.

6

William L. Riordon

"TO HOLD YOUR DISTRICT: STUDY HUMAN NATURE AND ACT ACCORDIN' "

There's only one way to hold a district: you must study human nature and act accordin'. You can't study human nature in books. Books is a hindrance more than anything else. If you have been to college, so much the worse for you. You'll have to unlearn all you learned before you can get right down to human nature, and unlearnin' takes a lot of time. Some men can never forget what they learned at college. Such men may get to be district leaders by a fluke, but they never last.

To learn real human nature you have to go among the people, see them and be seen. I know every man, woman, and child in the Fifteenth District, except them that's been born this summer—and I know some of them, too. I know what they like and what they don't like, what they are strong at and what they are weak in, and I reach them by approachin' at the right side.

For instance, here's how I gather in the young men. I hear of a young feller that's proud of his voice, thinks that he can sing fine. I ask him to come around to Washington Hall and join our Glee Club. He comes and sings, and he's a follower of Plunkitt for life. Another young feller gains a reputation as a baseball player in a vacant lot. I bring him into our baseball club. That fixes him. You'll find him workin' for my ticket at the polls next election day. Then there's the feller that likes rowin' on the river, the young feller that makes a name as a waltzer on his block, the young feller that's handy with his dukes—I rope them

---

In this selection, Riordon is interviewing Plunkitt—Ed.

"To Hold Your District: Study Human Nature and Act Accordin'," from *Plunkitt of Tammany Hall* by William L. Riordon, introduction by Arthur Mann, pp. 25–28. Copyright © 1963 by E.P. Dutton and Co., Inc., renewed 1991 by Penguin Books USA, Inc. Used by permission of Dutton Signet, a division of Penguin Books USA, Inc.

all in by givin' them opportunities to show themselves off. I don't trouble them with political arguments. I just study human nature and act accordin'.

But you may say this game won't work with the hightoned fellers, the fellers that go through college and then join the Citizens' Union. Of course it wouldn't work. I have a special treatment for them. I ain't like the patent medicine man that gives the same medicine for all diseases. The Citizens' Union kind of a young man! I love him! He's the daintiest morsel of the lot, and he don't often escape me.

Before telling you how I catch him, let me mention that before the election last year, the Citizens' Union said they had four hundred or five hundred enrolled voters in my district. They had a lovely headquarters, too, beautiful roll top desks and the cutest rugs in the world. If I was accused of havin' contributed to fix up the nest for them, I wouldn't deny it under oath. What do I mean by that? Never mind. You can guess from the sequel, if you're sharp.

Well, election day came. The Citizens' Union's candidate for Senator, who ran against me, just polled five votes in the district, while I polled something more than 14,000 votes. What became of the 400 or 500 Citizens' Union enrolled voters in my district? Some people guessed that many of them were good Plunkitt men all along and worked with the Cits just to bring them into the Plunkitt camp by election day. You can guess that way, too, if you want to. I never contradict stories about me, especially in hot weather. I just call your attention to the fact that on last election day 395 Citizens' Union enrolled voters in my district were missin' and unaccounted for.

I tell you frankly, though, how I have captured some of the Citizens' Union's young men. I have a plan that never fails. I watch the City Record to see when there's civil service examinations for good things. Then I take my young Cit in hand, tell him all about the good thing and get him worked up till he goes and takes an examination. I don't bother about him any more. It's a cinch that he comes back to me in a few days and asks to join Tammany Hall. Come over to Washington Hall some night and I'll show you a list of names on our rolls marked "C.S." which means, "bucked up against civil service."

As to the older voters, I reach them, too. No, I don't send them campaign literature. That's rot. People can get all the political stuff they want to read— and a good deal more, too—in the papers. Who reads speeches, nowadays, anyhow? It's bad enough to listen to them. You ain't goin' to gain any votes by stuffin' the letter boxes with campaign documents. Like as not you'll lose votes, for there's nothin' a man hates more than to hear the letter carrier ring his bell and go to the letter box expectin' to find a letter he was lookin' for, and find only a lot of printed politics. I met a man this very mornin' who told me he voted the Democratic State ticket last year just because the Republicans kept crammin' his letter box with campaign documents.

What tells in holdin' your grip on your district is to go right down among the poor families and help them in the different ways they need help. I've got a regular system for this. If there's a fire in Ninth, Tenth, or Eleventh Avenue, for example, any hour of the day or night, I'm usually there with some of my election district captains as soon as the fire engines. If a family is burned out I don't ask whether they are Republicans or Democrats, and I don't refer them to the Charity Organization Society, which would investigate their case in a month or two and decide they were worthy of help about the time they are dead from starvation. I just get quarters for them, buy clothes for them if their clothes were burned up, and fix them up till they get things runnin' again. It's philanthropy, but it's politics, too—mighty good politics. Who can tell how many votes one of these fires bring me? The poor are the most grateful people in the world, and, let me tell you, they have more friends in their neighborhoods than the rich have in theirs.

If there's a family in my district in want I know it before the charitable societies do, and me and my men are first on the ground. I have a special corps to look up such cases. The consequence is that the poor look up to George W. Plunkitt as a father, come to him in trouble—and don't forget him on election day.

Another thing, I can always get a job for a deservin' man. I make it a point to keep on the track of jobs, and it seldom happens that I don't have a few up my sleeve ready for use. I know every big employer in the district and in the whole city, for that matter, and they ain't in the habit of sayin' no to me when I ask them for a job.

And the children—the little roses of the district! Do I forget them? Oh, no! They know me, every one of them, and they know that a sight of Uncle George and candy means the same thing. Some of them are the best kind of vote-getters. I'll tell you a case. Last year a little Eleventh Avenue rosebud, whose father is a Republican, caught hold of his whiskers on election day and said she wouldn't let go till he'd promise to vote for me. And she didn't.

7

Steven P. Erie

BIG-CITY RAINBOW POLITICS: MACHINES REVIVIDUS?

Machines and Ethnic Assimilation

The Pluralist Approach

In the postwar era, social scientists eulogized the dying and much-maligned machine. In the 1940s and 1950s, a new generation of empirically trained sociologists such as William Foote Whyte, Robert K. Merton, and Daniel Bell used the machine as a test case to critique the middle-class Protestant value orientation that had dominated social analysis. Buttressing their claims for a value-neutral, functional approach to social science, the Young Turks argued that the censorious view of machine politics ignored the positive functions performed by lower-class ethnic institutions offering unconventional mobility routes. Finding their career opportunities blocked in the Protestant-controlled business world, the Irish had turned to the machine; the Italians, to the mob. Because it served the material needs of the immigrant working class, machine politics persisted, despite middle-class Protestant opposition.[1]

By the 1960s, political scientists such as [Robert] Dahl, Fred Greenstein, Elmer Cornwell, and Edgar Litt had joined the chorus of machine defenders, arguing that the big-city party bosses had been both ethnic integrators and system stabilizers-transformers.[2] In the hands of the pluralists, the machine became a local precursor to the New Deal ethnic coalition and the welfare state; the boss, a new paradigm of democratic leadership and mass politics.

The pluralist locus classicus was *Who Governs?*, Robert Dahl's 1961 survey of New Haven's political development over two centuries. Dahl's treatment of the Irish party bosses represented part of a larger analysis of successful regime transformation. In nineteenth-century New Haven, an oligarchic system of cumulative inequalities and overlapping privileges (the same hands holding wealth, social standing, and power) gradually and peacefully gave way to a pluralist system of dispersed inequalities and advantages (in which different people controlled different resources).[3]

By the mid-nineteenth century, a new breed of Yankee businessmen-politicians had displaced the "Old Standing Order" of leading Federalist and Congregationalist families. From humble origins, the new self-made entrepreneurs fought to end property restrictions on voting in order to mobilize a new electoral majority of native-born artisans and laborers. But this insurgent elite's primary weapon of victory—the vote—would soon be turned against them. Successfully challenging Yankee leadership at century's end, Irish Democratic politicians naturalized, registered, and claimed the votes of their countrymen in order to forge a new electoral majority.[4]

The Irish bosses then turned to the task of group economic uplift. According to Dahl, politics and city jobs served as "major springboards" for the Irish into the middle class. Controlling the levers of urban power, the Irish traded votes for patronage, accelerating their movement out of the laboring classes. The early machine's patronage cache awaiting capture appeared sizable indeed. In the pre-New Deal era, the big-city machines controlled thousands of public sector and private sector patronage jobs. Tammany Hall, for example, had more than 40,000 patronage jobs at its disposal in the late 1880s. Furthermore, the public sector offered greater social mobility opportunities than did the private sector. In San Francisco at the turn of the century, nearly one-quarter of all public employees were in professional and managerial positions compared with only 6 percent of the privately employed workforce.[5]

Using machine patronage, the Irish supposedly built a middle class with surprising rapidity considering their meager job skills and the discrimination they encountered. In the big cities, the proportion of first- and second-generation Irish in white-collar jobs rose from 12 percent to 27 percent between 1870 and 1900. Among the non-Irish, the white-collar increase was smaller, from 27 percent to 34 percent. As Andrew Greeley has shown, Irish-Americans are now the most affluent of the country's non-Jewish ethnic groups, having translated their apparently early white-collar job gains into a solid middle and upper middle class anchored in business and the professions in the post–World War II era.[6]

Dahl's account of the rise of the Irish "ex-plebes" and the accompanying systemic shift from cumulative to dispersed inequalities is central to a larger pluralist theory of American politics. Placing himself in an Aristotelian-Machiavellian tradition, Dahl highlighted the creative role of political elites such as the Irish party bosses in promoting both change and stability in the modern city-state. In the hands of gifted leaders, the mechanisms of political equality— popular sovereignty, universal suffrage, competitive parties, and the patronage system—could be used to reduce social and economic inequalities.

Our case studies support the pluralist argument regarding the machine's *political* assimilation of the Irish. The English-speaking famine Irish arrived as the competitive second party system was entering its modern or mobilization phase. As the Irish allegiance to the Democratic party solidified, the embryonic machines actively worked to naturalize and enroll Irish voters. Group mobilization allowed the Irish to infiltrate and take over the helm of the big-city Democratic machines.

Yet the machine's *economic* assimilation of the Irish—and its redistributional potential generally—was smaller than pluralists allow. For one thing, early Irish economic progress was slower and more uneven than the growth in white-collar jobholders indicates. As Stephan Thernstrom has carefully shown for Boston, many middle-class gains by first- and second-generation Irish were marginal at best, signaling entry into poorly paid clerical and sales work rather than into business and the professions.[7]

Thernstrom also cautions that it is misleading to compare Irish economic progress with the sluggish performance of the new immigrants. The new immigration was made up of successive waves of impoverished Southern and Eastern Europeans. More instructive is his comparison of the progress of the politically powerful Irish in Boston's labor market relative to that of other early-arriving but politically weaker immigrant groups. First- and second-generation Germans, Scandinavians, and English all climbed the economic ladder more quickly than did their Irish counterparts.

Our case studies of the classic Irish machines suggest that the pluralist model overestimates the magnitude of machine resources and the Irish ability to use them for sizable group economic gain. The Democratic machines of the late nineteenth century offered impressive channels of advancement for *individual* Irish politicians and contractors. But the early machines could do only so much for Irish *group* mobility.

Political and class constraints hampered the early bosses in their search for greater resources. Middle-class Yankee Republicans had not yet migrated to the suburbs. They vigorously contested local elections, demanding fiscal retrenchment. The early Irish bosses like John Kelly also had to contend with opponents in their own ranks: Democratic businessmen-reformers advocating "tight-fisted" economic policies. This bipartisan conservative coalition forced the nascent Celtic machines to pursue cautious fiscal policies, limiting their patronage take.

Republicans dominated state politics during much of this era, reinforcing the fiscal conservatism of the early Irish machines. Republican governors and legislators imposed constitutional restrictions, severely limiting the bosses' ability to raise taxes, increase municipal debts, and reward their working-class ethnic followers. Consequently, . . . only a small minority of the Irish working class in the late nineteenth century could crowd into the machine's patronage enclave.

The twentieth-century machines did a better job of economically aiding the Irish. Political and legal constraints on the bosses' ability to raise and spend money—and thus to create patronage jobs—began to ease as the machine's middle-class Republican and reform opponents moved to the suburbs, as home rule lifted state fiscal restraints, and as the millions of Southern and Eastern Europeans filling the cities demanded new services. Machines directly and indirectly controlled more than 20 percent of post-1900 urban job growth, double their pre-1900 share. In the Irish-run machine cities of New York, Jersey City, and Albany, the Irish were rewarded with more than 60 percent of this newly created patronage. As a result, on the eve of the Depression, at least one-third of the Irish-stock workforce toiled in machine-sponsored jobs.

The second-generation machine's patronage policies appear to support the pluralist argument that politics served as an important conduit of Irish economic advancement. Compared with Yankees, Germans, and Jews, though, the Irish were slow to build a middle class in business and the professions. Today's Irish affluence was latecoming, postdating the heyday of the machine. As even Greeley admits, the Irish middle class was only emerging on the eve of the Depression; its arrival would not occur until after World War II.[8]

In light of Irish political success, why was Irish middle-class status so slow in coming? Was there an *inverse* relation between political success and economic advancement? The Irish crowded into the largely blue-collar urban public sector in the late nineteenth and early twentieth centuries. Yet as low-paid policemen, firemen, and city clerks, the Irish were solidly lower-middle-rather than middle-class. The relative security of blue-collar jobs in public works, police, and fire departments may have hindered the building of an Irish middle class by encouraging long tenure in poorly paid bureaucratic positions. The pluralist machine's apparent cornucopia of resources could turn into a blue-collar cul-de-sac.[9]

It can be argued that by channeling so much of their economic energy into the public sector, the Irish forsook opportunities in the private sector save for industries such as construction that depended on political connections. As Moynihan has accurately observed, the economic rewards of America have gone to entrepreneurs, not to functionaries. Moreover, the Irish public sector job gains were fragile. The Depression forced the cities to cut their payrolls. The 1930s also witnessed the long-awaited revolt of the Southern and Eastern Europeans against their Irish overlords. Thousands of Irish-American payrollers lost their jobs as a result of retrenchment and machine overthrow. Only with lessened job dependence on the machine in the prosperous post-World War II era were the third- and fourth-generation Irish able to move rapidly into business and the professions.

The puzzling question is why the Irish embraced the machine's blue-collar patronage system with such enthusiasm. Dahl has advanced a "blocked mobility" explanation. In his account, the Irish quickly assimilated the American value of upward mobility. However, limited job skills and anti-Catholicism blocked Irish advancement in the private sector. Thus, the Irish, in Dahl's words, "eagerly grabbed the 'dangling rope' [of politics] up the formidable economic slope."[10]

If the Irish so easily assimilated the American success ethic, why did they allow the dangling rope of politics to become a noose? There are both cultural and resource explanations for the Irish overreliance on the patronage system. Moynihan has taken issue with Dahl, arguing that the Irish displayed a "distaste for commerce," valuing security over entrepreneurial success. Seeking safe bureaucratic havens, the Irish settled for marginal advancement through politics.[11]

Borrowing a page from Max Weber, Edward Levine similarly argues that the Irish working class consciously rejected the middle-class Protestant value of economic achievement. Alienated from Protestant values and institutions, the Irish constructed the Democratic party and the Catholic church as mutually reinforcing institutions rooted in working-class Irish Catholic values. For the Irish, power and security, not money or status, represented the highest values. In this scheme of things, social and geographical mobility meant apostasy. Reinforcing their separateness from the Protestant mainstream, politics enveloped the Irish, becoming *the* approved secular career. As the machines have declined, however, the Irish have gradually replaced the values of power and security with those of money and status.[12]

A resource explanation for limited Irish patronage mobility looks to the machine's maintenance needs. To win the jurisdictional battles for working-class support, machines quickly realized the potency of economic appeals. Yet scarce economic benefits had to be spread as widely as possible to realize their full vote-getting value. Thus the Irish bosses stretched patronage, creating large numbers of poorly paid blue-collar positions to maximize the number of working-class voters rewarded. The machine's job growth strategy created ever more blue-collar public employment for the Irish at a time when the cities were moving from a manufacturing to a service economy and when the greatest increases in private sector employment occurred in white-collar ranks.

The party's maintenance needs conflicted with the long-run goal of Irish prosperity. But patronage had short-run economic advantages. The machine's job system allowed unskilled and semiskilled Irish workers to move to the next rung above the working class. In fact, the ready availability of blue-collar patronage helped to *shape* Irish economic horizons, encouraging the values of security, seniority, and slow bureaucratic advancement.

The pluralist view of the machine as an integrator of the immigrants has been applied to the Southern and Eastern Europeans. Elmer Cornwell, for example, argues that the Irish bosses in the northern cities were forced to politically assimilate the second-wave immigrants in order to continue to win elections.[13] Competitive electoral pressures encouraged the Irish bosses to naturalize and register the newer arrivals. Our survey of the classic Irish machines found that the machine's invisible hand did not automatically embrace the newcomers. Mature machines were one-party regimes lacking the political incentive to mobilize the second-wave immigrants. The Irish Democratic bosses had already constructed winning electoral coalitions among early-arriving ethnic groups. The newcomers' political assimilation would only encourage demands for a redistribution of power and patronage.

In entrenched machine cities like New York and Jersey City, naturalization and voter registration rates for the Southern and Eastern Europeans remained quite low until the late 1920s. Electoral participation rates for the second-wave immigrants increased thereafter in response to national candidates and issues rather than to sponsorship by local party bosses.

In competitive party cities, however, the Irish party chieftains worked energetically to mobilize the Southern and Eastern Europeans. The fledgling Democratic machines of Chicago and Pittsburgh most successfully mobilized the newcomers. As the minority party in these cities in the 1920s, the Democrats were forced into actively courting the new ethnics. Chicago's Democratic precinct captains naturalized and registered the new immigrants far more quickly than did their counterparts in one-party New York, Jersey City, and Boston.

Entrenched machines did little to further economic assimilation among the Southern and Eastern Europeans before the latter mobilized in the 1930s. With so much of Irish well-being and group identity dependent on continued control of the machines, Irish politicos were understandably loath to share power and patronage. To preserve their hegemony, the Irish accommodated the slowly mobilizing newcomers in parsimonious fashion, dispensing social services, symbolic recognition, and collective benefits rather than the organization's core resources of power and patronage.

At critical moments the Irish were forced by electoral pressures to enter tactical alliances with some groups for a greater share of the machine's jealously guarded core resources. As Jews flexed their political muscle in New York in the 1920s, the Irish offered them minor offices and a greater share of municipal employment, particularly in the rapidly expanding school system. The Celtic bosses worked as actively to reduce Italian influence by gerrymandering Italian neighborhoods.

Postwar machines such as the Daley organization accommodated the Southern and Eastern Europeans in different and less costly ways than those in which the prewar machines had rewarded the Irish. Wartime and postwar prosperity benefited the second-wave immigrants and their children, propelling large numbers into the property-owning middle class. As homeowners, white ethnics objected to high property taxes to pay for patronage jobs they did not need. The Southern and Eastern Europeans demand a different set of machine policies: low property taxes, the preservation of property values and white neighborhoods, and homeowner rather than welfare services. The postwar Irish-led machines accommodated these taxation and service demands—as long as the Irish maintained control over key party positions and those city offices with major policy-making and patronage-dispensing responsibilities.

Machines did little to assimilate blacks and Hispanics. In the pre-1960 period, black sub-machines to the white machines had emerged in cities such as Chicago and Pittsburgh. Congressman William Dawson, the only black in the Daley machine's inner circle, ran the black sub-machine in the South Side ghetto. To counter the threat of Polish insurgency, Dawson and his lieutenants mobilized the minority vote for Mayor Daley. As the threat of white revolt diminished in the 1960s, the threat of black revolt grew. Using welfare-state benefits, the machine systematically demobilized the black vote.

Contrary to pluralist theory, the big-city machine's political and economic incorporation of ethnic groups was limited. The Irish represent the theory's par excellence case. The nascent Democratic machines actively assisted the Irish in acquiring citizenship, in voting, and in securing patronage jobs. Yet pluralist theory exaggerates the ability of the Irish to turn political into economic success. The economic disadvantages suffered by the Irish could not readily be overcome by politics; they may even have been aggravated. Celtic economic success came *after* the machine's heyday. Failing to consider the class and political constraints on the machine's creation and distribution of resources, pluralists overestimate the old-style party organization's redistributional capacity.

The pluralist case is further weakened when we consider the machine's limited assimilation of other ethnic groups. The entrenched Democratic machines did little to mobilize and reward the new arrivals from Southern and Eastern Europe, the South, the Caribbean, and Latin America. Deprived of machine sponsorship, the newcomers would have to rely on internal group resources to contest urban power. . . .

Today's Big-City Rainbow Politics: Machines Revividus?

In the past twenty years the baton of urban power has slowly been passed to the third- and fourth-generation ethnic arrivals—blacks, Hispanics, and Asians. Black mayors have been elected in Los Angeles, Chicago, Philadelphia, Detroit, Atlanta, Washington, Cleveland, Gary, Newark, and New Orleans. Blacks have also been elected in large numbers to city councils and school boards. The new black power is bureaucratic as well as electoral. In the big cities, black administrators have been appointed to such top policy-making positions as city manager, police chief, and school superintendent.[14]

In the Sunbelt, Hispanics and Asians are beginning to transform urban political life. San Antonio's voters in 1981 elected Henry Cisneros as the first Mexican-American mayor of a major U.S. city. Miami has a Cuban-American mayor and a Hispanic majority on the city council. Reversing a century-old legacy of racism and discrimination against Asians, California's cities are witnessing the first stirrings of Asian-American power. Los Angeles's voters elected Michael Woo to the city council, and San Francisco Mayor Dianne Feinstein appointed Thomas Hsieh to the city's Board of Supervisors.[15]

As the new minorities mobilize, particularly the black and Mexican-American communities with large lower-class populations, they have searched for strategies of group uplift. The viability of the machine model was problematic for the new groups. Before the 1960s, minorities were deliberately kept out of the established system of "city trenches." Except for a few independent politicians such as New York's Adam Clayton Powell, the legacy of the machine era for blacks was "plantation politics" Chicago-style. When the minority assault finally came, the old-style party organizations were in the last stages of decline.[16]

In the postmachine era, the prizes of urban politics seemed hollow indeed. The northern cities where blacks had migrated in massive numbers had experienced economic decline, their treasuries nearing bankruptcy. The rapidly growing Sunbelt cities had small, lean public sectors (the legacy of conservative reformers), limiting government job opportunities. To make matters worse, white civil service commissioners and municipal union stewards zealously guarded the prerogatives of the heavily white public sector workforce, making it difficult for minorities to translate political gains into economic advancement.[17]

Even the means of ethnic capture were more difficult. The new minorities were the victims of reform. In the process of wresting power from the Irish, the Southern and Eastern Europeans had created additional barriers for later-arriving groups. The second-wave ethnics joined Yankee reformers in bringing to the eastern cities the reforms first implemented by progressives in the West and South: at-large city council elections, nonpartisanship, educational requirements for public employment, and expanded civil service coverage. At-large electoral systems, in particular, made it harder for blacks to gain representation on city councils. Designed to prevent the machine's reemergence, reforms also made it more difficult for working-class blacks and Hispanics to gain group influence and benefits.[18]

In this bleak age of reform, a possible return to machine politics didn't seem so bad after all. Black politicians in particular called for the machine's resurrection in part or in toto. During the 1960s, black moderates committed to "working within the system" had embraced the Irish model of group electoral politics to counter radical separatist demands. The radical rhetoric of militant nationalism and community control ultimately proved an empty threat, revealing an incrementalist and patronage core that could be accommodated as the emerging black bourgeoisie took over such community institutions as schools and health clinics. By the 1970s, blacks of diverse ideological inclinations had moved "from protest to politics," emulating the strategy of ethnic group mobilization—registration, turnout, and bloc voting en masse—first perfected by the Irish.[19]

To appeal to both militants and moderates in the minority community, contemporary black politicians disingenuously coupled radical-reformist rhetoric with venerable machine-building techniques designed to enhance group influence and payoffs. Claiming that at-large electoral systems discriminated against racial minorities, followers of rainbow "reformer" Jesse Jackson in cities such as Pittsburgh and Cincinnati have pursued the machine gambit of reviving the ward system. Chicago's "antimachine" Mayor Harold Washington ransacked city hall and special district governments for additional patronage to pay off his supporters and consolidate power. Reformer Washington also vigorously opposed a move to make the city's elections nonpartisan.[20]

Are black politicians correct in looking to the machine past? What lessons could the departed Irish bosses offer today's minorities about group influence, electoral coalition building, and economic advancement through local politics? Moynihan has argued that the twentieth-century black experience needs to be understood in terms of a critical comparison with the nineteenth-century Irish experience.[21]

Both groups have tried their hand at public sector politics, seeking governmental channels of group mobility. The Irish political experience cannot fully be emulated by blacks because the big-city machines—centralized party structures—are unlikely to be revived in anything like their historical form. Yet machine politics—the trading in divisible benefits—has staying power in local politics. The Irish bosses were the undisputed masters of this game. Can their example educate today's minority power brokers about both the possibilities and the limits of ethnic politics?

On the positive side, the Irish experience demonstrates some potential for group economic uplift through the local political process. The votes of the Irish working class could be translated into group power and a major share of city jobs and services. The twentieth-century Celtic municipal engines served as modest redistributional devices, reallocating economic burdens and benefits within the middle of the class structure. To the extent that the Irish bosses were Robin Hoods, they were selective about their victims and beneficiaries. Rather than taking from the very rich and giving to the very poor, the Irish politicos took from the Yankee middle class and gave to the lower-middle-class payroll Irish.

On the negative side, the Irish machines were as much instruments of social control as of economic reward. The nineteenth-century Irish bosses imposed retrenchment on their followers as the price of keeping power. Black mayors are under the same fiscal constraints today. Retrenchment produced ideological-class schisms among the Irish in the 1880s and is doing the same for blacks in the 1980s. The conflict between Tammany's conservative "long-hair" Irish faction and the militant working-class "short-hairs" finds contemporary expression in the tensions between moderate black mayors and militant followers of the Jacksonian rainbow.

The early Irish bosses parsimoniously accommodated later arrivals on the rainbow bandwagon. With limited resources and pressing group demands, black politicians may have to do the same with Hispanics and Asians. The down-side risk of today's slow-growth politics is that the new rainbow coalition may produce a small pot of gold for the black political elite, while browns, yellows, and even the black underclass are left chasing the mirage.

Concluding the Irish-black comparison on an even more pessimistic note, what will urban politics look like at century's end if present trends in conservative national politics and uneven regional economic development continue? Will big-city minority politicians in declining Frostbelt cities be called on to implement an updated "System of '96"—for 1996? Will black leaders soothe the "mixed multitudes" with populist rhetoric while cutting deals with conservative national politicians? And will federally funded "urban enterprise zones" prove to be the newest species of "plantation politics" designed to discipline the have-nots? Big-city minority politicians might have to take a lesson from the Christian Democratic party bosses of stagnant Palermo after all.

Blacks are now emulating the Irish by using political strategies of group uplift. The means employed, however, are different. The Irish used the big-city party organizations; blacks use local and national bureaucracies. The locus of urban power has shifted from political machines to independent and semiautonomous bureaucracies, organized along functional lines. Furthermore, urban politics has been nationalized. In the post–New Deal era, the political access and economic distribution functions once monopolized by local machines now are nationally performed by the Democratic party and federal welfare-state bureaucracies.[22]

Peter Eisinger finds black mayors pursuing a dual strategy of group advancement in this new arena of urban politics. The first prong consists of the politics of public sector bureaucracies. Black leaders in cities such as Detroit and Atlanta have used their appointment powers to name minorities to head city personnel departments and other major agencies. Minority administrators, in turn, have launched aggressive affirmative action programs, producing a dramatic increase in the minority share of public employment. Black mayors are also using affirmative action to award city contracts to minority businesses. Newark's former Mayor Kenneth Gibson, for example, set aside 25 percent of all federal public works project monies for minority contractors.[23]

The second prong consists of a strategy of "trickle down" from private sector economic growth. Black mayors in Los Angeles, Chicago, Detroit, Washington, Atlanta, and Newark have formed alliances with the white business community to promote downtown redevelopment, hoping to create private sector job opportunities for minorities.

The Irish experience suggests the limits of this dual strategy. On the public sector side, the approach has a major down-side risk—retrenchment. The Irish were the principal beneficiaries of city payroll growth from 1900 to 1929; after 1929, however, they were also the victims of retrenchment. Blacks clearly benefited from the halcyon municipal employment growth of the 1960s and early 1970s. The late 1970s, however, brought municipal austerity, threatening to reverse black city payroll gains. As the last hired, minorities were frequently the first victims of budgetary cutbacks. Detroit's black Mayor Coleman Young, for example, was forced by budget-balancing pressures to fire hundreds of minority police, undoing in a single afternoon ten years of hard-fought affirmative action in police hiring.

Black politicians and civil servants may also face a political challenge to their power and prerogatives. In the 1930s and 1940s, the Irish machine's jerry-built rainbow coalition unraveled as the new immigrants countermobilized, jeopardizing the jobs of thousands of Irish payrollers. In the 1990s, Asian-Americans and Hispanics could challenge blacks for control of the big cities, particularly if black politicians are unable or unwilling to share power and patronage. With a large and prosperous middle class, Asian-Americans in particular might assume the broker role, financing and leading an Asian-Hispanic coalition that could threaten today's black municipal workers.

The Irish experience also suggests caution regarding the extent of "trickledown" to the black masses from publicly subsidized private sector growth. Public investment in urban infrastructure was the early equivalent of today's publicly assisted downtown redevelopment projects. Public works contracts benefited individual Irish contractors while providing temporary low-wage employment for the masses of unskilled and semiskilled Irish workers.

Today, black mayors offer public seed money, tax and zoning abatements, and lease-back arrangements to downtown developers. Ambitious redevelopment projects like Detroit's Renaissance Center and Atlanta's Peachtree Plaza are sold to minorities and the poor on the premise that economic benefits—primarily in the form of job opportunities—will filter down to them. But new convention centers, hotels, and shopping centers are not a viable vehicle of group uplift. Too few jobs are created to make an appreciable dent in inner-city poverty. The limited pool of high-paying professional and managerial positions disproportionately goes to upper-middle-class white suburbanites. Minority "trickle down" has primarily taken the form of a limited number of low-wage service jobs.[24]

There is a vital third element to today's black advancement strategy—federal social programs. Both Irish and black politicians have used the expanding welfare state to consolidate power. The nascent Irish Democratic machines of the 1930s fused with New Deal programs. A generation later, the Great Society served as a catalyst for black power. Studying minority politics in ten northern California cities, Rufus Browning, Dale Marshall, and David Tabb argue that the Great Society programs "provided the functional equivalent of earlier forms of patronage." In the Bay Area cities, federal social initiatives encouraged minority political mobilization, promoted their incorporation into local governing coalitions, and secured greater local governmental responsiveness to minority job and service demands.[25]

The expanding welfare state was more than a vehicle for black assimilation into local politics. It was a primary route of group *economic* advancement. Where the Irish had used machine patronage, blacks now relied on federally funded social programs. In the 1960s and early 1970s, the new black middle class found jobs in the expanding federally funded human services sector—health, education, and welfare. By the late 1970s, nearly half of all black professionals and managers worked in the social welfare sector, compared with less than one-quarter of comparably situated whites.[26]

The welfare state meant more than jobs for the black middle class; it also represented cash and in-kind welfare payments for the underclass. From the mid-1960s onward, the black poor increasingly relied on transfer payments. Two-thirds of poor black families received welfare in the late 1970s, up from one-third in the late 1960s. Economically, blacks were more integrated into the public sector in the late 1970s than the Irish had been during the machine's heyday—but under *federal* and *bureaucratic* auspices.[27]

But black politicians lack integrating mechanisms like the machine that can fuse together the disparate elements of today's urban politics—national versus local, bureaucratic versus electoral. As a result, big-city and minority politics reflect their unreconciled imperatives. The continued flow of welfare-state jobs, transfer payments, and social services, which sustain the black middle class and underclass, depend on group influence and alliance building at the national and state levels where social policy is made and funded. Blacks, however, are not as well organized to press their claims outside the local political arena.

In the absence of local machines capable of mobilizing voters, bureaucratic politics has acted as a depressant on electoral participation. The relationship between the bureaucratic service provider and the recipient differs from the relationship between the party cadre and the voter. Precinct workers are encouraged to mobilize loyal voters on election day. Human service workers, however, have little incentive to politically mobilize their clientele—as long as social programs and budgets grow. In the 1970s, minority service providers increasingly involved themselves in bureaucratic politics within the intergovernmental grant system rather than in mobilizing their clientele in local electoral politics. The expansion of means-tested programs such as AFDC depoliticized welfare recipients by isolating them from the work experiences encouraging political participation.[28]

Whatever the Great Society's initial mobilization effect, it soon acted as a brake on black voter turnout. During the period of welfare-state expansion, from 1964 to 1976, the mass electoral base of black politics in the northern cities eroded. The voting rate for young urban blacks plummeted, from 56 percent to 29 percent, while the rate for unemployed blacks dropped nearly as sharply, from 62 percent to 37 percent. Low turnout hurt big-city black politicians seeking to challenge white-controlled machine and reform regimes.[29]

Welfare-state contraction in the 1980s, however, reversed the bureaucratic expansion–electoral decline cycle. Threatened with job and benefit loss by the Reagan cutbacks, minority social service providers and recipients quickly rediscovered the value of electoral politics. Though primarily generated by national forces, the remobilization drive could be used in local politics. In machine Chicago and reform Philadelphia, black mayoral candidates rode the electoral surge to victory.

It is ironic that the policies of a president who points to his Irish ancestry during campaigns helped to produce the last hurrah for the Irish Democratic machines. Black mayors have ridden the turbulent waves of Reaganite austerity into office. Yet the practitioners of the new ethnic politics are trying to consolidate power with limited local resources and diminished welfare-state largesse. Lacking the tangible benefits demanded by their supporters, the new minority power brokers may discover what was learned the hard way by the now-departed Irish bosses: the real lessons at rainbow's end.

Notes

1. William Foote Whyte, "Social Organization in the Slums," pp. 34–39; William Foote Whyte, *Street Corner Society: The Social Structure of an Italian Slum,* pp. 194–252; Robert K. Merton, *Social Theory and Social Structure,* pp. 125–136; Daniel Bell, "Crime as an American Way of Life," pp. 131–154; Jerome K. Myers, "Assimilation in the Political Community," pp. 175–182.

2. Fred I. Greenstein, "The Changing Pattern of Urban Party Politics," pp. 1–13; Elmer E. Cornwell, "Party Absorption of Ethnic Groups: The Case of Providence, Rhode Island," pp. 87–98; Elmer E. Cornwell, "Bosses, Machines, and Ethnic Groups," pp. 27–39; Edgar Litt, *Beyond Pluralism: Ethnic Politics in America,* esp. pp. 60–74, 155–168.

3. Robert A. Dahl, *Who Governs? Democracy and Power in an American City,* pp. 2–86.

4. Ibid., pp. 11–31. In support of his "springboard" thesis, Dahl cites a 1933 sample survey of 1,600 New Haven families conducted by Yale's Institute of Human Relations. Constituting 13 percent of the sample, Irish-Americans held nearly half of the public service jobs. Yet the city's public sector constituted only 5 percent of the local economy and employed only 15 percent of the Irish-stock workforce. The 1930 census reports that blue-collar jobs accounted for nearly half of all public employment. See John W. McConnell, *The Evolution of Social Classes,* pp. 84–85; and U.S. Bureau of the Census. *Fifteenth Census of the United States, 1930,* vol. 4, Table 12, pp. 280–283.

5. Dahl, *Who Governs?* pp. 40–44; Eric L. McKitrick, "The Study of Corruption," pp. 502–514; Steven P. Erie, "Two Faces of Ethnic Power," pp. 262–263.

6. U.S. Census Office, *Ninth Census, 1870,* vol. 1, Tables 29, 32; U.S. Bureau of the Census, *Special Reports: Occupations at the Twelfth Census,* Tables 41, 43; Andrew Greeley, *That Most Distressful Nation: The Taming of the American Irish,* pp. 122–128; Andrew Greeley, *Ethnicity, Denomination, and Inequality,* pp. 54–55.

7. Stephan Thernstrom, *The Other Bostonians,* pp. 132–133, 232.

8. Greeley, *That Most Distressful Nation,* pp. 122–128; Greeley, *Ethnicity,* pp. 54–55.

9. Dennis P. Ryan, *Beyond the Ballot Box: A Social History of the Boston Irish, 1845–1917,* pp. 106, 149.

10. Dahl, *Who Governs?* pp. 33–34, 40–41. Oscar Handlin argues that the acculturated second-generation Irish, not the transplanted first generation, saw politics as a route of personal and group advancement; see Handlin, *The Uprooted,* pp. 201–216.

11. Daniel Patrick Moynihan, "The Irish," in Nathan Glazer and Daniel Patrick Moynihan, *Beyond the Melting Pot,* pp. 229, 259–260.

12. Edward M. Levine, *The Irish and Irish Politicians: A Study of Cultural and Social Alienation,* pp. 134–138.

13. Cornwell, "Bosses."

14. Regarding urban black politics, see Leonard A. Cole, *Blacks in Power: A Comparative Study of Black and White Elected Officials;* William E. Nelson, Jr., and Philip J. Meranto, *Electing Black Mayors: Political Action in the Black Community;* John R. Howard and Robert C. Smith, eds., "Urban Black Politics," pp. 1–150; Peter K. Eisinger, *The Politics of Displacement: Racial and Ethnic Transition in Three American Cities;* Albert Karnig and

Susan Welch, *Black Representation and Urban Policy;* and Michael B. Preston et al., eds., *The New Black Politics: The Search for Political Power.*

15. On Hispanic and Asian-American politics, see F. Chris Garcia and Rudolpho de la Garza, *The Chicano Political Experience: Three Perspectives;* Raymond A. Mohl, "Miami: The Ethnic Cauldron," in Richard M. Bernard and Bradley R. Rice, eds., *Sunbelt Cities: Politics and Growth Since World War Two,* pp. 58–99; David L. Clark, "Los Angeles: Improbable Los Angeles," in Bernard and Rice, eds., *Sunbelt Cities,* pp. 268–308; Joan Moore and Harry Pachon, *Hispanics in the United States;* Bruce E. Cain and D. Roderick Kiewiet, *Minorities in California;* and Judy Tachibana, "California's Asians: Power from a Growing Population," pp. 534–543.

16. Martin Kilson, "Political Change in the Negro Ghetto, 1900–1940s," in Nathan Huggins et al., eds., *Key Issues in the Afro-American Experience,* pp. 182–189; Hanes Walton, Jr., *Black Politics: A Theoretical and Structural Analysis,* pp. 56–69.

17. Roger E. Alcaly and David Merrnelstein, eds., *The Fiscal Crisis of American Cities;* George Sternlieb and James W. Hughes, "The Uncertain Future of the Center City," pp. 455–572; Marilyn Gittell, "Public Employment and the Public Service," in Alan Gartner et al., eds., *Public Service Employment: An Analysis of Its History, Problems, and Prospects,* pp. 121–142.

18. Leonard Sloan, "Good Government and the Politics of Race," pp. 171–174; Albert Karnig, "Black Representation on City Councils: The Impact of District Elections and Socioeconomic Factors," pp. 223–242; Theodore P. Robinson and Thomas R. Dye, "Reformism and Black Representation on City Councils," pp. 133–142; Richard L. Engstrom and Michael D. McDonald, "The Election of Blacks to City Councils: Clarifying the Impact of Electoral Arrangements on the Seats/Population Relationship," pp. 344–354; Peggy Heilig and Robert J. Mundt, "Changes in Representational Equity: The Effect of Adopting Districts," pp. 393–397.

19. Joyce Gelb, "Blacks, Blocs, and Ballots: The Relevance of Party Politics to the Negro," pp. 44–69; Charles V. Hamilton, "Blacks and the Crisis of Political Participation," pp. 191–193; Robert C. Smith, "The Changing Shape of Urban Black Politics: 1960–1970," pp. 16–28.

20. Linda M. Watkins, "Pittsburgh Blacks' Paucity of Political Clout Stirs Struggle over the City's At-Large Election System," p. 58; Marty Willis, "Jan. 6 Demonstration to Greet All-White City Council," pp. A-1, A-4; Gilbert Price, "Skirmish Begins 'At Large' Battle" [Cincinnati], p. H-8; Larry Green, "Chicago's Mayor Finally Grasps Power and Spoils," pp. 1, 18; Chinta Strausberg, "Mayor Seizes Control of Park Board," pp. 1, 18; Robert Davis and Joseph Tybor, "Mayor Wins Election Ruling," pp. 1, 10.

21. Daniel Patrick Moynihan, "Foreword" to Greeley, *That Most Distressful Nation,* p. xi.

22. Ira Katznelson, "The Crisis of the Capitalist City: Urban Politics and Social Control," in Willis D. Hawley et al., eds., *Theoretical Perspectives on Urban Politics,* pp. 223–226.

23. Peter K. Eisinger, "Black Employment in Municipal Jobs: The Impact of Black Political Power," pp. 380–392; Peter K. Eisinger, "The Economic Conditions of Black Employment in Municipal Bureaucracy," pp. 754–771; Peter K. Eisinger, "Black Mayors and the Politics of Racial Economic Advancement," in William C. McReady, ed., *Culture, Ethnicity, and Identity,* pp. 95–109; John J. Harrigan, *Political Change in the Metropolis,* pp. 129–139. For evidence that minority gains in elective office have not been translated into significant minority policy payoffs, see Susan Welch and Albert Karnig, "The Impact of Black Elected Officials on Urban Social Expenditures," pp. 707–714; and Edmond J. Keller, "The Impact of Black Mayors on Urban Policy," pp. 40–52.

24. Clarence N. Stone, *Economic Growth and Neighborhood Discontent: System Bias in the Urban Renewal Program of Atlanta,* pp. 90–185; Clarence N. Stone, "Atlanta: Protest and

Elections Are Not Enough," in Rufus P. Browning and Dale Rogers Marshall, eds., "Black and Hispanic Power in City Politics: A Forum," pp. 618–625; Dennis R. Judd, *The Politics of American Cities: Private Power and Public Policy,* pp. 373–407; John Helyar and Robert Johnson, "Tale of Two Cities: Chicago's Busy Center Masks a Loss of Jobs in Its Outlying Areas," pp. 1, 22.

25. Rufus P. Browning et al., *Protest is Not Enough: The Struggle of Blacks and Hispanics for Equality in Urban Politics,* pp. 207–238 (quote at p. 214).

26. Michael K. Brown and Steven P. Erie, "Blacks and the Legacy of the Great Society: The Economic and Political Impact of Federal Social Policy," pp. 302–309, esp. Table 3, p. 308; U.S. Equal Employment Opportunity Commission, *Minorities and Women in State and Local Government, 1977,* vol. 1; U.S. Civil Service Commission, *Minority Group Employment in the Federal Government,* 1975.

27. Steven P. Erie, "Public Policy and Black Economic Polarization," pp. 311–315, esp. Table 1, p. 313.

28. Charles V. Hamilton, "Public Policy and Some Political Consequences," in Marguerite R. Barnett and James A. Hefner, eds., *Public Policy for the Black Community,* p. 245; and Charles V. Hamilton, "The Patron-Recipient Relationship and Minority Politics in New York City," p. 224.

29. U.S. Bureau of the Census, *Voter Participation in the National Election, November, 1964,* pp. 11–13, 21–22; U.S. Bureau of the Census. *Voting and Registration in the Election of November, 1976,* pp. 14–23, 61–62.

Bibliography

Alcaly, Roger E., and David Mermelstein, eds. *The Fiscal Crisis of American Cities.* New York: Vintage Books, 1977.

Bell, Daniel. "Crime as an American Way of Life." *Antioch Review* 13 (Summer 1953): 131–154.

Brown, Michael K., and Steven P. Erie. "Blacks and the Legacy of the Great Society: The Economic and Political Impact of Federal Social Policy." *Public Policy* 29, no. 3 (Summer 1981): 299–330.

Browning, Rufus P., Dale Rogers Marshall, and David H. Tabb. *Protest Is Not Enough: The Struggle of Blacks and Hispanics for Equality in Urban Politics.* Berkeley and Los Angeles: University of California Press, 1984.

Cain, Bruce E., and D. Roderick Kiewiet. *Minorities in California.* Pasadena, Ca.: California Institute of Technology, 1986.

Clark, David, L. "Los Angeles: Improbable Los Angeles." In *Sunbelt Cities: Politics and Growth Since World War Two,* edited by Richard M. Bernard and Bradley R. Rice, pp. 268–308. Austin: University of Texas Press, 1983.

Cole, Leonard A. *Blacks in Power: A Comparative Study of Black and White Elected Officials.* Princeton: Princeton University Press, 1976.

Cornwell, Elmer E. "Party Absorption of Ethnic Groups: The Case of Providence, Rhode Island." *Social Forces* 38 (March 1960): 205–210.

———. "Bosses, Machines, and Ethnic Groups." *Annals* 353 (May 1964): 27–39.

Dahl, Robert A. *Who Governs? Democracy and Power in an American City.* New Haven: Yale University Press, 1961.

Davis, Robert, and Joseph Tybor. "Mayor Wins Election Ruling." *Chicago Tribune,* September 3, 1986, pp. 1, 10.

Eisinger, Peter K. *The Politics of Displacement: Racial and Ethnic Transition in Three American Cities.* New York: Academic Press, 1980.

———. "Black Employment in Municipal Jobs: The Impact of Black Political Power." *American Political Science Review* 76, no. 2 (June 1982): 380–392.

————. "The Economic Conditions of Black Employment in Municipal Bureaucracy." *American Journal of Political Science* 26, no. 4 (November 1982): 754–771.

————. "Black Mayors and the Politics of Racial Economic Advancement." In *Culture, Ethnicity, and Identity,* edited by William C. McReady, pp. 95–109. New York: Academic Press, 1983.

Engstrom, Richard L., and Michael D. McDonald. "The Election of Blacks to City Councils: Clarifying the Impact of Electoral Arrangements of the Seats/Population Relationship." *American Political Science Review,* 75, no. 2 (June 1981): 344–354.

Erie, Steven P. "Public Policy and Black Economic Polarization." *Policy Analysis* 6, no. 3 (Summer 1980): 305–317.

————. "Two Faces of Ethnic Power: Comparing the Irish and Black Experiences." *Polity,* 13, no. 2 (Winter 1980): 261–284.

Garcia, F. Chris, and Rudolpho de la Garza. *The Chicano Political Experience: Three Perspectives.* North Scituate, Mass.: Duxbury Press, 1977.

Gelb, Joyce. "Blacks, Blocs, and Ballots: The Relevance of Party Politics to the Negro." *Polity* 3, no. 1 (Fall 1970): 44–69.

Gittell, Marilyn. "Public Employment and the Public Service." In *Public Service Employment: An Analysis of Its History, Problems, and Prospects,* edited by Alan Gartner et al., pp. 121–142. New York: Praeger, 1973.

Glazer, Nathan, and Daniel Patrick Moynihan. *Beyond the Melting Pot.* Cambridge, Mass.: MIT Press, 1964.

Greeley, Andrew. *That Most Distressful Nation: The Taming of the American Irish.* Chicago: Quadrangle, 1972.

————. *Ethnicity, Denomination, and Inequality.* Beverly Hills, Ca.: Sage Publications, 1976.

Green, Larry. "Chicago's Mayor Finally Grasps Power and Spoils." *Los Angeles Times,* August 2, 1986, pt. 1, pp. 1, 18.

Greenstein, Fred I. "The Changing Pattern of Urban Party Politics." *Annals* 353 (May 1964): 1–13.

Hamilton, Charles V. "Blacks and the Crisis of Political Participation." *Public Interest* 34 (Winter 1974): 185–210.

————. "Public Policy and Some Political Consequences." In *Public Policy for the Black Community,* edited by Marguerite R. Barnett and James A. Hefner, pp. 239–255. New York: Alfred Publishing, 1976.

————. "The Patron-Recipient Relationship and Minority Politics in New York City." *Political Science Quarterly* 95 (Summer 1979): 211–227.

Hamilton, Fred. *Rizzo.* New York: Viking Press, 1973.

Handlin, Oscar. *The Uprooted.* New York: Crosset and Dunlap, 1951.

————. *Boston's Immigrants: A Study in Acculturation.* Rev. ed. New York: Atheneum, 1970. Originally published in 1941.

Harrigan, John J. *Political Change in the Metropolis.* Boston, Little, Brown, 1985.

Heilig, Peggy, and Robert J. Mundt. "Changes in Representational Equity: The Effect of Adopting Districts," *Social Science Quarterly* 64, no. 1 (June 1983): 393–397.

Helyar, John, and Robert Johnson. "Tale of Two Cities: Chicago's Busy Center Masks a Loss on Jobs in its Outlying Areas." *Wall Street Journal,* April 16, 1986, pp. 1, 22.

Howard, John R., and Robert C., Smith, eds. "Urban Black Politics." *Annals* 439 (September 1978): 1–150.

Judd, Dennis R. *The Politics of American Cities: Private Power and Public Policy.* 2d. ed. Boston: Little, Brown, 1984.

Karnig, Albert. "Black Representation on City Councils: The Impact of District Elections and Socioeconomic Factors." *Urban Affairs Quarterly* 12, no. 2 (December 1976): 223–242.

Katznelson, Ira. "The Crisis of the Capitalist City: Urban Politics and Social Control." In *Theoretical Perspectives on Urban Politics,* edited by Willis D. Hawley et al., pp. 214–229. Englewood Cliffs, N.J.: Prentice-Hall, 1976.

Keller, Edmond J. "The Impact of Black Mayors on Urban Policy." *Annals* 439 (September 1979): 40–52.

Kilson, Martin, "Political Change in the Negro Ghetto, 1900–1940s." In *Key Issues in the Afro-American Experience,* edited by Nathan I. Hugins, Martin Kilson, and Daniel M. Fox, pp. 182–189. New York: Harcourt Brace Jovanovich, 1971.

Levine, Edward M. *The Irish and Irish Politicians: A Study of Cultural and Social Alienation.* Notre Dame, Ind.: University of Notre Dame Press, 1966.

Litt, Edgar. *Beyond Pluralism: Ethnic Politics in America.* Glenview, Ill.: Scott, Foresman, 1970.

McConnell, John W. *The Evolution of Social Classes.* Washington, D.C.: American Council on Public Affairs, 1942.

McKitrick, Eric L. "The Study of Corruption." *Political Science Quarterly* 72 (December 1957): 502–514.

Merton, Robert K. *Social Theory and Social Structure.* Rev. ed. New York: Free Press, 1968. Originally published in 1949.

Mohl, Raymond A. "Miami: The Ethnic Cauldron." In *Sunbelt Cities: Politics and Growth Since World War Two,* edited by Richard M. Bernard and Bradley R. Rice, pp. 58–99. Austin: University of Texas Press, 1983.

Moore, Joan, and Harry Pachon. *Hispanics in the United States.* Englewood Cliffs, N.J.: Prentice-Hall, 1985.

Moynihan, Daniel Patrick. "The Irish." In *Beyond the Melting Pot,* by Nathan Glazer and Daniel Patrick Moynihan, pp. 217–287. Cambridge, Mass.: MIT Press, 1964.

Myers, Jerome K. "Assimilation in the Political Community." *Sociology and Social Research* 35 (January–February 1951): 175–182.

Nelson, William E., Jr., and Philip J. Meranto. *Electing Black Mayors: Political Action in the Black Community.* Columbus: Ohio State University Press, 1977.

Preston, Michael B., Lenneal J. Henderson, Jr., and Paul Puryear, eds. *The New Black Politics: The Search for Political Power.* New York: Longman, 1982.

Price, Gilbert. "Skirmish Begins 'At Large' Battle." *Cleveland Call and Post,* February 13, 1986, p. H8.

Robinson, Theodore P., and Thomas R. Dye, "Reformism and Black Representation on City Councils." *Social Science Quarterly* 59, no. 1 (June 1978): 133–142.

Ryan, Dennis P. *Beyond the Ballot Box: A Social History of the Boston Irish, 1845–1917.* Rutherford, N.J.: Fairleigh Dickinson University Press, 1983.

Sloan, Leonard. "Good Government and the Politics of Race." *Social Problems* 17 (Fall 1969): 171–174.

Smith, Robert C. "The Changing Shape of Urban Black Politics: 1960–1970." *Annals* 439 (September 1978): 16–28.

Sternlieb, George, and James W. Huges. "The Uncertain Future of the Center City." *Urban Affairs Quarterly* 18, no. 4 (June 1983): 455–472.

Stone, Clarence N. *Economic Growth and Neighborhood Discontent: System Bias in the Urban Renewal Program of Atlanta.* Chapel Hill: University of North Carolina Press, 1976.

———. "Atlanta: Protest and Elections Are Not Enough." In "Black and Hispanic: Power in City Politics: A Forum," edited by Rufus P. Browning and Dale Rogers Marshall. *PS* 19, no. 3 (Summer 1986): 618–625.

Strausberg, Chinta. "Humes, Stroger Trade Blows." *Chicago Defender,* June 3, 1986.

———. "Mayor Seizes Control of Park Board." *Chicago Defender,* June 17, 1986. pp. 1, 18.

Tachibana, Judy. "California's Asians: Power from a Growing Population." *California Journal* 17, no. 11 (November 1986): 534–543.

Thernstrom, Stephan. *The Other Bostonians: Poverty and Progress in the American Metropolis, 1880–1970,* Cambridge, Mass.: Harvard University Press, 1973.

U.S. Bureau of the Census. *Special Reports: Occupations at the Twelfth Census.* Washington, D.C.: Government Printing Office, 1904.

———. *Fifteenth Census of the United States, 1930.* Washington, D.C.: Government Printing Office, 1933.

———. *Voter Participation in the National Election, November, 1964.* Washington, D.C.: Government Printing Office, 1965.

———. *Voting and Registration in the Election of November, 1976,* Washington, D.C.: Government Printing Office, 1977.

U.S. Census Office. *Ninth Census, 1870.* Washington, D.C.: Government Printing Office, 1872.

U.S. Civil Service Commission. *Minority Group Employment in the Federal Government,* 1975. Washington, D.C.: Government Printing Office, 1977.

U.S. Equal Employment Opportunity Commission. *Minorities and Women in State and Local Government, 1977.* Washington, D.C.: Government Printing Office, 1977.

Walton, Hanes, Jr. *Black Politics: A Theoretical and Structural Analysis.* Philadelphia: J. B. Lippincott, 1972.

Watkins, Linda M. "Pittsburgh Blacks' Paucity of Political Clout Stirs Struggle over the City's At-Large Election System." *Wall Street Journal,* April 1, 1986, p. 58.

Welch, Susan, and Albert Karnig. "The Impact of Black Elected Officials on Urban Social Expenditures." *Policy Studies Journal 7* (Summer 1979): 707–714.

Whyte, William Foote. "Social Organization in the Slums." *American Sociological Review* 8, no. 1 (February 1943): 34–39.

———. *Street Corner Society: The Social Structure of an Italian Slum.* Chicago: University of Chicago Press, 1955. Originally published in 1943.

Willis, Marty. "Jan. 6 Demonstration to Greet All-White City Council," *Pittsburgh Courier,* January 11, 1986, pp. A-1, A-4.

8

Andrew D. White

CITY AFFAIRS ARE NOT POLITICAL

Without the slightest exaggeration we may assert that, with very few exceptions, the city governments of the United States are the worst in Christendom—the most expensive, the most inefficient, and the most corrupt. No one who has any considerable knowledge of our own country and of other countries can deny this. . . .

What is the cause of the difference between municipalities in the old world and in the new? I do not allow that their populations are better than ours. What accounts, then, for the better municipal development in their case and for the miserable results in our own? My answer is this: we are attempting to govern our cities upon a theory which has never been found to work practically in any part of the world. Various forms of it were tried in the great cities of antiquity and of the middle ages, especially in the mediaeval republics of Italy, and without exception they ended in tyranny, confiscation, and bloodshed. The same theory has produced the worst results in various countries of modern Europe, down to a recent period.

What is this evil theory? It is simply that the city is a political body; that its interior affairs have to do with national political parties and issues. My fundamental contention is that a city is a corporation; that as a city it has nothing whatever to do with general political interests; that party political names and duties are utterly out of place there. The questions in a city are not political questions. They have reference to the laying out of streets; to the erection of buildings; to sanitary arrangements, sewerage, water supply, gas supply, electrical supply; to the control of franchises and the like; and to provisions for the public health and comfort in parks, boulevards, libraries, and museums. The work of a city being the creation and control of the city property, it should logically be managed as a piece of property by those who have created it, who have a title to it, or a real substantial part in it, and who can therefore feel strongly their duty to it. Under

---

"City Affairs Are Not Political"; originally titled "The Government of American Cities." *Forum* (December 1890): 213–216. Copyright © 1890.

our theory that a city is a political body, a crowd of illiterate peasants, freshly raked in from Irish bogs, or Bohemian mines, or Italian robber nests, may exercise virtual control. How such men govern cities, we know too well; as a rule they are not alive even to their own most direct interests. . . .

The difference between foreign cities and ours, is that all these well-ordered cities in England, France, Germany, Italy, Switzerland, whether in monarchies or republics, accept this principle—that cities are corporations and not political bodies; that they are not concerned with matters of national policy; that national parties as such have nothing whatever to do with city questions. They base their city governments upon ascertained facts regarding human nature, and upon right reason. They try to conduct them upon the principles observed by honest and energetic men in business affairs. We, on the other hand, are putting ourselves upon a basis which has always failed and will always fail—the idea that a city is a political body, and therefore that it is to be ruled, in the long run, by a city proletariat mob, obeying national party cries.

What is our safety? The reader may possibly expect me, in logical consonance with the statement I have just made, to recommend that the city be treated strictly as a corporate body, and governed entirely by those who have a direct pecuniary interest in it. If so, he is mistaken. I am no doctrinaire; politics cannot be bent completely to logic—certainly not all at once. A wise, statesmanlike view would indicate a compromise between the political idea and the corporate idea. I would not break away entirely from the past, but I would build a better future upon what we may preserve from the past.

To this end I would still leave in existence the theory that the city is a political body, as regards the election of the mayor and common council. I would elect the mayor by the votes of the majority of all the citizens, as at present; I would elect the common council by a majority of all the votes of all the citizens; but instead of electing its members from the wards as at present—so that wards largely controlled by thieves and robbers can send thieves and robbers, and so that men who can carry their ward can control the city—I would elect the board of aldermen on a general ticket, just as the mayor is elected now, thus requiring candidates for the board to have a city reputation. So much for retaining the idea of the city as a political body. In addition to this, in consideration of the fact that the city is a corporation, I would have those owning property in it properly recognized. I would leave to them, and to them alone, the election of a board of control, without whose permission no franchise should be granted and no expenditure should be made. This should be the rule, but to this rule I am inclined to make one exception; I would allow the votes of the board of control, as regards expenditures for primary education, to be overridden by a two-thirds majority of the board of aldermen. I should do this because here alone does the city policy come into direct relations with the general political system of the nation at large. The main argument for the existence of our public schools is that they are an absolute necessity to the existence of our Republic; that without preliminary education a republic simply becomes an illiterate mob, that if illiterate elements control, the destruction of the Republic is sure. On this ground, considering the public-school system as based upon a national political necessity, I would have an exception made regarding the expenditures for it, leaving in this matter a last resort to the political assembly of the people.

A theory resulting in a system virtually like this, has made the cities of Europe, whether in monarchies or republics, what they are, and has made it an honor in many foreign countries for the foremost citizens to serve in the common councils of their cities. Take one example: It has been my good fortune to know well Rudolf Von Gneist, councilor of the German Empire. My acquaintance with him began when it was my official duty to present to him a testimonial, in behalf of the government of the United States, for his services in settling the north-west boundary between the United States and Great Britain. The Emperor William was the nominal umpire; he made Von Gneist the real umpire—that shows Von Gneist's standing. He is also a leading professor of law in the University of Berlin, a member of the Imperial Parliament and of the Prussian Legislature, and the author of famous books, not only upon law, but upon the constitutional history of Germany and of England. This man has been, during a considerable time, a member of what we should call the board of aldermen of the city of Berlin, and he is proud to serve in that position. With him have been associated other men the most honored in various walks of life, and among these some of the greatest business men, renowned in all lands for their enterprise and their probity. Look through the councils of our cities, using any microscope you can find, and tell me how many such men you discern in them. Under the system I propose, it is, humanly speaking, certain that these better men would seek entrance into our city councils. Especially would this be the case if our citizens should, by and by, learn that it is better to have in the common council an honest man, though a Republican, than a scoundrel, though a Democrat; and better to have a man of ability and civic pride, though a Democrat, than a weak, yielding creature, though a Republican.

Some objections will be made. It will be said, first, that wealthy and well-to-do people do not do their duty in city matters; that if they should, they would have better city government. This is true to this extent, that even well-to-do men are in city politics strangely led away from their civic duties by fancied allegiance to national party men and party issues. But in other respects it is untrue; the vote of a single tenement house, managed by a professional politician, will neutralize the vote of an entire street of well-to-do citizens. Men in business soon find this out; they soon find that to work for political improvement under the present system is time and labor and self-respect thrown away. It may be also said that the proposal is impracticable. I ask, why? History does not show it to be impracticable; for we have before us, as I have shown, the practice of all other great civilized nations on earth, and especially of our principal sister republics.

But it will be said that "revolutions do not go backward." They did go backward in the great cities of Europe when these rid themselves of the old bad system that had at bottom the theory under which ours are managed, and when they entered into their new and better system. The same objection, that revolutions do not go backward, was made against any reform in the tenure of office of the governor and of the higher judiciary in the State of New York; and yet the revolution did go backward, that is, it went back out of doctrinaire folly into sound, substantial, common-sense statesmanship. In 1847 the State of New York so broke away from the old conservative moorings as to make all judge-ships elective, with short terms, small pay, and wretched accommodations, and the same plan was pursued as regards the governor and other leading officials; but the State, some years since, very wisely went back to much of its former system—in short, made a revolution backward, if any one chooses to call it so—resuming the far better system of giving our governor and higher judges longer terms, larger salaries, better accommodations, and dignified surround-ings. We see, then, that it is not true that steps in a wrong direction in a republic cannot be retraced. As they have been retraced in State affairs, so they may be in municipal affairs.

But it will be said that this change in city government involves a long struggle. It may or it may not. If it does, such a struggle is but part of the price which we pay for the maintenance of free institutions in town, State, and na-tion. For this struggle, I especially urge all men of light and leading to prepare themselves. As to the public at large, what is most needed in regard to munici-pal affairs, as in regard to public affairs generally, is the quiet, steady evolution of a knowledge of truth and of proper action in view of it. That truth, as regards city government, is simply the truth that municipal affairs are not political; that political parties as such have nothing to do with cities; that the men who im-port political considerations into municipal management are to be opposed. This being the case, the adoption of some such system as that which I have sketched would seem likely to prove fruitful of good.

9

Samuel P. Hays

THE POLITICS OF REFORM IN MUNICIPAL GOVERNMENT IN THE PROGRESSIVE ERA

In order to achieve a more complete understanding of social change in the Pro-gressive Era, historians must now undertake a deeper analysis of the practices of economic, political, and social groups. Political ideology alone is no longer satisfactory evidence to describe social patterns because generalizations based upon it, which tend to divide political groups into the moral and the immoral, the rational and the irrational, the efficient and the inefficient, do not square

"The Politics of Reform in Municipal Government in the Progressive Era," by Samuel P. Hays, as printed in *Pacific Northwest Quarterly*, Vol. 55, 1964, pp. 157–169. Reprinted by per-mission of Pacific Northwest Quarterly.

with political practice. Behind this contemporary rhetoric concerning the nature of reform lay patterns of political behavior which were at variance with it. Since an extensive gap separated ideology and practice, we can no longer take the former as an accurate description of the latter, but must reconstruct social behavior from other types of evidence.

Reform in urban government provides one of the most striking examples of this problem of analysis. The demand for change in municipal affairs, whether in terms of over-all reform, such as the commission and city-manager plans, or of more piecemeal modifications, such as the development of the city-wide school boards, deeply involved reform ideology. Reformers loudly proclaimed a new structure of municipal government as more moral, more rational, and more efficient and, because it was so, self-evidently more desirable. But precisely because of this emphasis, there seemed to be no need to analyze the political forces behind change. Because the goals of reform were good, its causes were obvious; rather than being the product of particular people and particular ideas in particular situations, they were deeply imbedded in the universal impulses and truths of "progress." Consequently, historians have rarely tried to determine precisely who the municipal reformers were or what they did, but instead have relied on reform ideology as an accurate description of reform practice.

The reform ideology which became the basis of historical analysis is well known. It appears in classic form in Lincoln Steffens' *Shame of the Cities.* The urban political struggle of the Progressive Era, so the argument goes, involved a conflict between public impulses for "good government" against a corrupt alliance of "machine politicians" and "special interests."

During the rapid urbanization of the late 19th century, the latter had been free to aggrandize themselves, especially through franchise grants, at the expense of the public. Their power lay primarily in their ability to manipulate the political process, by bribery and corruption, for their own ends. Against such arrangements there gradually arose a public protest, a demand by the public for honest government, for officials who would act for the public rather than for themselves. To accomplish their goals, reformers sought basic modifications in the political system, both in the structure of government and in the manner of selecting public officials. These changes, successful in city after city, enabled the "public interest" to triumph.[1]

Recently, George Mowry, Alfred Chandler, Jr., and Richard Hofstadter have modified this analysis by emphasizing the fact that the impulse for reform did not come from the working class.[2] This might have been suspected from the rather strained efforts of National Municipal League writers in the "Era of Reform" to go out of their way to demonstrate working-class support for commission and city-manager governments.[3] We now know that they clutched at straws, and often erroneously, in order to prove to themselves as well as to the public that municipal reform was a mass movement.

The Mowry-Chandler-Hofstadter writings have further modified older views by asserting that reform in general and municipal reform in particular sprang from a distinctively middle-class movement. This has now become the prevailing view. Its popularity is surprising not only because it is based upon faulty logic and extremely limited evidence, but also because it, too, emphasizes the analysis of ideology rather than practice and fails to contribute much to the understanding of who distinctively were involved in reform and why.

Ostensibly, the "middle-class" theory of reform is based upon a new type of behavioral evidence, the collective biography, in studies by Mowry of California Progressive party leaders, by Chandler of a nationwide group of that party's leading figures, and by Hofstadter of four professions—ministers, lawyers, teachers, editors. These studies demonstrate the middle-class nature of reform, but they fail to determine if reformers were distinctively middle class, specifically if they differed from their opponents. One study of 300 political leaders in the state of Iowa, for example, discovered that Progressive party, Old Guard, and Cummins Republicans were all substantially alike, the Progressives differing only in that they were slightly younger than the others and had less political experience.[4] If its opponents were also middle class, then one cannot describe Progressive reform as a phenomenon, the special nature of which can be explained in terms of middle-class characteristics. One cannot explain the distinctive behavior of people in terms of characteristics which are not distinctive to them.

Hofstadter's evidence concerning professional men fails in yet another way to determine the peculiar characteristics of reformers. For he describes ministers, lawyers, teachers, and editors without determining who within these professions became reformers and who did not. Two analytical distinctions might be made. Ministers involved in municipal reform, it appears, came not from all segments of religion, but peculiarly from upper-class churches. They enjoyed the highest prestige and salaries in the religious community and had no reason to feel a loss of "status," as Hofstadter argues. Their role in reform arose from the class character of their religious organizations rather than from the mere fact of their occupation as ministers.[5] Professional men involved in reform (many of whom—engineers, architects, and doctors—Hofstadter did not examine at all) seem to have come especially from the more advanced segments of their professions, from those who sought to apply their specialized knowledge to a wider range of public affairs.[6] Their role in reform is related not to their attempt to defend earlier patterns of culture, but to the working out of the inner dynamics of professionalization in modern society.

The weakness of the "middle-class" theory of reform stems from the fact that it rests primarily upon ideological evidence, not on a thoroughgoing description of political practice. Although the studies of Mowry, Chandler, and Hofstadter ostensibly derive from behavioral evidence, they actually derive largely from the extensive expressions of middle-ground ideological position, of the reformers' own descriptions of their contemporary society, and of their expressed fears of both the lower and the upper classes, of the fright of being ground between the millstones of labor and capital.[7]

Such evidence, though it accurately portrays what people thought, does not accurately describe what they did. The great majority of Americans look upon themselves as "middle class" and subscribe to a middle-ground ideology, even though in practice they belong to a great variety of distinct social classes. Such ideologies are not rationalizations of deliberate attempts to deceive. They are natural phenomena of human behavior. But the historian should be especially sensitive to their role so that he will not take evidence of political ideology as an accurate representation of political practice.

In the following account I will summarize evidence in both secondary and primary works concerning the political practices in which municipal reformers were involved. Such an analysis logically can be broken down into three parts, each one corresponding to a step in the traditional argument. First, what was the source of reform? Did it lie in the general public rather than in particular groups? Was it middle class, working class, or perhaps of other composition? Second, what was the reform target of attack? Were reformers primarily interested in ousting the corrupt individual, the political or business leader who made private arrangements at the expense of the public, or were they interested in something else? Third, what political innovations did reformers bring about? Did they seek to expand popular participation in the governmental process?

There is now sufficient evidence to determine the validity of these specific elements of the more general argument. Some of it has been available for several decades; some has appeared more recently; some is presented here for the first time. All of it adds up to the conclusion that reform in municipal government involved a political development far different from what we have assumed in the past.

Available evidence indicates that the source of support for reform in municipal government did not come from the lower or middle classes, but from the upper class. The leading business groups in each city and professional men closely allied with them initiated and dominated municipal movements. Leonard White, in his study of the city manager published in 1927, wrote:

> The opposition to bad government usually comes to a head in the local chamber of commerce. Business men finally acquire the conviction that the growth of their city is being seriously impaired by the failures of city officials to perform their duties efficiently. Looking about for a remedy, they are captivated by the resemblance of the city-manager plan to their corporate form of business organization.[8]

In the 1930s White directed a number of studies of the origin of city-manager government. The resulting reports invariably begin with such statements as, "the Chamber of Commerce spearheaded the movement," or commission government in this city was a "businessmen's government."[9] Of thirty-two cases of city-manager government in Oklahoma examined by Jewell C. Phillips, twenty-nine were initiated either by chambers of commerce or by community committees dominated by businessmen.[10] More recently James Weinstein has presented almost irrefutable evidence that the business community, represented largely by chambers of commerce, was the overwhelming force behind both commission and city-manager movements.[11]

Dominant elements of the business community played a prominent role in another crucial aspect of municipal reform: the Municipal Research Bureau movement.[12] Especially in the larger cities, where they had less success in shaping the structure of government, reformers established centers to conduct research in municipal affairs as a springboard for influence.

The first such organization, the Bureau of Municipal Research of New York City, was founded in 1906; it was financed largely through the efforts of Andrew Carnegie and John D. Rockefeller. An investment banker provided the crucial support in Philadelphia, where a Bureau was founded in 1908. A group of wealthy Chicagoans in 1910 established the Bureau of Public Efficiency, a research agency. John H. Patterson of the National Cash Register Company, the leading figure in Dayton municipal reform, financed the Dayton Bureau, founded in 1912. And George Eastman was the driving force behind both the Bureau of Municipal Research and city-manager government in Rochester. In smaller cities data about city government [were] collected by interested individuals in a more informal way or by chambers of commerce, but in larger cities the task required special support, and prominent businessmen supplied it.

The character of municipal reform is demonstrated more precisely by a brief examination of the movements in Des Moines and Pittsburgh. The Des Moines Commercial Club inaugurated and carefully controlled the drive for the commission form of government.[13] In January, 1906 the Club held a so-called "mass meeting" of business and professional men to secure an enabling act from the state legislature. P. C. Kenyon, president of the Club, selected a Committee of 300, composed principally of business and professional men, to draw up a specific proposal. After the legislature approved their plan, the same committee managed the campaign which persuaded the electorate to accept the commission form of government by a narrow margin in June, 1907.

In this election the lower-income wards of the city opposed the change, the upper-income wards supported it strongly, and the middle-income wards were more evenly divided. In order to control the new government, the Committee of 300, now expanded to 530, sought to determine the nomination and election of the five new commissioners, and to this end they selected an avowedly businessman's slate. Their plans backfired when the voters swept into office a slate of anticommission candidates who now controlled the new commission government.

Proponents of the commission form of government in Des Moines spoke frequently in the name of the "people." But their more explicit statements emphasized their intent that the new plan be a "business system" of government, run by businessmen. The slate of candidates for commissioner endorsed by advocates of the plan was known as the "businessman's ticket." J. W. Hill, president of the committees of 300 and 530, bluntly declared: "The professional politician must be ousted and in his place capable businessmen chosen to conduct the affairs of the city." I. M. Farle, general counsel of the Bankers Life Association and a prominent figure in the movement, put the point more precisely: "When the plan was adopted it was the intention to get businessmen to run it."

Although reformers used the ideology of popular government, they in no sense meant that all segments of society should be involved equally in municipal decision-making. They meant that their concept of the city's welfare would be best achieved if the business community controlled city government. As one businessman told a labor audience, the businessman's slate represented labor "better than you do yourself."

The composition of the municipal reform movement in Pittsburgh demonstrates its upper-class and professional as well as its business sources.[14] Here the two principal reform organizations were the Civic Club and the Voters' League. The 745 members of these two organizations came primarily from the upper class. Sixty-five percent appeared in upper-class directories which contained the names of only 2 percent of the city's families. Furthermore, many who were not listed in these directories lived in upper-class areas. These reformers, it should be stressed, comprised not an old but a new upper class. Few came from earlier industrial and mercantile families. Most of them had risen to social position from wealth created after 1870 in the iron, steel, electrical equipment, and other industries, and they lived in the newer rather than the older fashionable areas.

Almost half (48 percent) of the reformers were professional men: doctors, lawyers, ministers, directors of libraries and museums, engineers, architects, private and public school teachers, and college professors. Some of these belonged to the upper class as well, especially the lawyers, ministers, and private school teachers. But for the most part their interest in reform stemmed from the inherent dynamics of their professions rather than from their class connections. They came from the more advanced segments of their organizations, from those in the forefront of the acquisition and application of knowledge. They were not the older professional men, seeking to preserve the past against change; they were in the vanguard of professional life, actively seeking to apply expertise more widely to public affairs.

Pittsburgh reformers included a large segment of businessmen; 52 percent were bankers and corporation officials or their wives. Among them were the presidents of fourteen large banks and officials of Westinghouse, Pittsburgh Plate Glass, U.S. Steel and its component parts (such as Carnegie Steel, American Bridge, and National Tube), Jones and Laughlin, lesser steel companies (such as Crucible, Pittsburgh, Superior, Lockhart, and H. K. Porter), the H. J. Heinz Company, and the Pittsburgh Coal Company, as well as officials of the Pennsylvania Railroad and the Pittsburgh and Lake Erie. These men were not small businessmen; they directed the most powerful banking and industrial organizations of the city. They represented not the old business community, but industries which had developed and grown primarily within the past fifty years and which had come to dominate the city's economic life.

These business, professional, and upper-class groups who dominated municipal reform movements were all involved in the rationalization and systematization of modern life; they wished a form of government which would be more consistent with the objectives inherent in those developments. The most important single feature of their perspective was the rapid expansion of the geographical scope of affairs which they wished to influence and manipulate, a scope which was no longer limited and narrow, no longer within the confines of pedestrian communities, but was now broad and city-wide, covering the whole range of activities of the metropolitan area.

The migration of the upper class from central to outlying areas created a geographical distance between its residential communities and its economic institutions. To protect the latter required involvement both in local ward affairs and in the larger city government as well. Moreover, upper-class cultural institutions, such as museums, libraries, and symphony orchestras, required an active interest in the larger municipal context from which these institutions drew much of their clientele.

Professional groups, broadening the scope of affairs which they sought to study, measure, or manipulate, also sought to influence the public health, the educational system, or the physical arrangements of the entire city. Their concerns were limitless, not bounded by geography, but as expansive as the professional imagination. Finally, the new industrial community greatly broadened its perspective in governmental affairs because of its new recognition of the way in which factors throughout the city affected business growth. The increasing size and scope of industry, the greater stake in more varied and geographically dispersed facts of city life, the effect of floods on many business concerns, the need to promote traffic flows to and from work for both blue-collar and managerial employees—all contributed to this larger interest. The geographically larger private perspectives of upper-class, professional, and business groups gave rise to a geographically larger public perspective.

These reformers were dissatisfied with existing systems of municipal government. They did not oppose corruption per se—although there was plenty of that. They objected to the structure of government which enabled local and particularistic interests to dominate. Prior to the reforms of the Progressive Era, city government consisted primarily of confederations of local wards, each of which was represented on the city's legislative body. Each ward frequently had its own elementary schools and ward-elected school boards which administered them.

These particularistic interests were the focus of a decentralized political life. City councilmen were local leaders. They spoke for their local areas, the economic interests of their inhabitants, their residential concerns, their educational, recreational, and religious interests—i.e., for those aspects of community life which mattered most to those they represented. They rolled logs in the city council to provide streets, sewers, and other public works for their local areas. They defended the community's cultural practices, its distinctive languages or national customs, its liberal attitude toward liquor, and its saloons and dance halls which served as centers of community life. One observer described this process of representation in Seattle:

> The residents of the hill-tops and the suburbs may not fully appreciate the faithfulness of certain downtown ward councilmen to the interests of their constituents. . . .
> The people of a state would rise in arms against a senator or representative in Congress who deliberately misrepresented their wishes and imperiled their interests, though he might plead a higher regard for national good. Yet people in other parts of the city seem to forget that under the old system the ward elected councilmen with the idea of procuring service of special benefit to that ward.[15]

In short, pre-reform officials spoke for their constituencies, inevitably their own wards which had elected them, rather than for other sections or groups of the city.

The ward system of government especially gave representation in city affairs to lower- and middle-class groups. Most elected ward officials were from these groups, and they, in turn, constituted the major opposition to reforms in municipal government. In Pittsburgh, for example, immediately prior to the changes in both the city council and the school board in 1911 in which citywide representation replaced ward representation, only 24 percent of the 387 members of those bodies represented the same managerial, professional, and banker occupations which dominated the membership of the Civic Club and the Voters' League. The great majority (67 percent) were small businessmen—grocers, saloonkeepers, livery-stable proprietors, owners of small hotels, druggists—white-collar workers such as clerks and bookkeepers, and skilled and unskilled workmen.[16]

This decentralized system of urban growth and the institutions which arose from it reformers now opposed. Social, professional, and economic life had developed not only in the local wards in a small community context, but also on a larger scale had become highly integrated and organized, giving rise to a superstructure of social organization which lay far above that of ward life and which was sharply divorced from it in both personal contacts and perspective.

By the late 19th century, those involved in these larger institutions found that the decentralized system of political life limited their larger objectives. The movement for reform in municipal government, therefore, constituted an attempt by upper-class, advanced professional, and large business groups to take formal political power from the previously dominant lower- and middle-class elements so that they might advance their own conceptions of desirable public policy. These two groups came from entirely different urban worlds, and the political system fashioned by one was no longer acceptable to the other.

Lower- and middle-class groups not only dominated the pre-reform governments, but vigorously opposed reform. It is significant that none of the occupational groups among them, for example, small businessmen or white-collar workers, skilled or unskilled artisans, had important representation in reform organizations thus far examined. The case studies of city-manager government undertaken in the 1930s under the direction of Leonard White detailed in city after city the particular opposition of labor. In their analysis of Jackson, Michigan, the authors of these studies wrote:

> The *Square Deal,* oldest Labor paper in the state, has been consistently against manager government, perhaps largely because labor has felt that with a decentralized government elected on a ward basis it was more likely to have some voice and to receive its share of privileges.[17]

In Janesville, Wisconsin, the small shopkeepers and workingmen on the west and south sides, heavily Catholic and often Irish, opposed the commission plan in 1911 and in 1912 and the city-manager plan when adopted in 1923.[18] "In Dallas there is hardly a trace of class consciousness in the Marxian sense," one investigator declared, "yet in city elections the division has been to a great extent along class lines."[19] The commission and city-manager elections were no exceptions. To these authors it seemed a logical reaction, rather than an embarrassing fact that had to be swept away, that workingmen should have opposed municipal reform.[20]

In Des Moines working-class representatives, who in previous years might have been council members, were conspicuously absent from the "businessman's slate." Workingmen acceptable to reformers could not be found. A workingman's slate of candidates, therefore, appeared to challenge the reform slate. Organized labor, and especially the mineworkers, took the lead; one of their number, Wesley Ash, a deputy sheriff and union member, made "an astonishing run" in the primary, coming in second among a field of more than twenty candidates.[21] In fact, the strength of anticommission candidates in the primary so alarmed reformers that they frantically sought to appease labor.

The day before the final election they modified their platform to pledge both an eight-hour day and an "American standard of wages." They attempted to persuade the voters that their slate consisted of men who represented labor because they had "begun at the bottom of the ladder and made a good climb toward success by their own unaided efforts."[22] But their tactics failed. In the election on March 30, 1908, voters swept into office the entire "opposition" slate. The business and professional community had succeeded in changing the form of government, but not in securing its control. A cartoon in the leading reform newspaper illustrated their disappointment; John Q. Public sat dejectedly and muttered, "Aw, What's the Use?"

The most visible opposition to reform and the most readily available target of reform attack was the so-called "machine," for through the "machine" many different ward communities as well as lower- and middle-income groups joined effectively to influence the central city government. Their private occupational and social life did not naturally involve these groups in larger citywide activities in the same way as the upper class was involved; hence they lacked access to privately organized economic and social power on which they could construct political power. The "machine" filled this organizational gap.

Yet it should never be forgotten that the social and economic institutions in the wards themselves provided the "machine's" sustaining support and gave it larger significance. When reformers attacked the "machine" as the most visible institutional element of the ward system, they attacked the entire ward form of political organization and the political power of lower- and middle-income groups which lay behind it.

Reformers often gave the impression that they opposed merely the corrupt politician and his "machine." But in a more fundamental way they looked upon the deficiencies of pre-reform political leaders in terms not of their personal shortcomings, but of the limitations inherent in their occupational, institutional, and class positions. In 1911 the Voters' League of Pittsburgh wrote in its pamphlet analyzing the qualifications of candidates that "a man's occupation ought to give a strong indication of his qualifications for membership on a school board."[23] Certain occupations inherently disqualified a man from serving:

> Employment as ordinary laborer and in the lowest class of mill work would naturally lead to the conclusion that such men did not have sufficient education or business training to act as school directors. . . . Objection might also be made to small shopkeepers, clerks, workmen at many trades, who by lack of educational advantages and business training, could not, no matter how honest, be expected to administer properly the affairs of an educational system, requiring special knowledge, and where millions are spent each year.

These, of course, were precisely the groups which did dominate Pittsburgh government prior to reform. The League deplored the fact that school boards contained only a small number of "men prominent throughout the city in business life . . . in professional occupations . . . holding positions as managers, secretaries, auditors, superintendents and foremen" and exhorted these classes to participate more actively as candidates for office.

Reformers, therefore, wished not simply to replace bad men with good; they proposed to change the occupational and class origins of decision-makers. Toward this end they sought innovations in the formal machinery of government, which would concentrate political power by sharply centralizing the processes of decision-making rather than distribute it through more popular participation in public affairs. According to the liberal view of the Progressive Era, the major political innovations of reform involved the equalization of political power through the primary, the direct election of public officials, and the initiative, referendum, and recall. These measures played a large role in the political ideology of the time and were frequently incorporated into new municipal charters. But they provided at best only an occasional and often incidental process of decision-making. Far more important in continuous, sustained, day-to-day processes of government were those innovations which centralized decision-making in the hands of fewer and fewer people.

The systematization of municipal government took place on both the executive and the legislative levels. The strong-mayor and city manager types become the most widely used examples of the former. In the first decade of the 20th century, the commission plan had considerable appeal, but its distribution of administrative responsibility among five people gave rise to a demand for a form with more centralized executive power; consequently, the city-manager or the commission-manager variant often replaced it.[24]

A far more pervasive and significant change, however, lay in the centralization of the system of representation, the shift from ward to city-wide election of councils and school boards. Governing bodies so selected, reformers argued, would give less attention to local and particularistic matters and more to affairs of city-wide scope. This shift, an invariable feature of both commission and city-manager plans, was often adopted by itself. In Pittsburgh, for example, the new charter of 1911 provided as the major innovation that a council of twenty-seven, each member elected from a separate ward, be replaced by a council of nine, each elected by the city as a whole.

Cities displayed wide variations in this innovation. Some regrouped wards into larger units but kept the principle of areas of representation smaller than the entire city. Some combined a majority of councilmen elected by wards with additional ones selected at large. All such innovations, however, constituted steps toward the centralization of the system of representation.

Liberal historians have not appreciated the extent to which municipal reform in the Progressive Era involved a debate over the system of representation. The ward form of representation was universally condemned on the grounds that it gave too much influence to the separate units and not enough attention to the larger problems of the city. Harry A. Toulmin, whose book, *The City Manager,* was published by the National Municipal League, stated the case:

> The spirit of sectionalism had dominated the political life of every city. Ward pitted against ward, alderman against alderman, and legislation only effected by "long-rolling" extravagant measures into operation, molding the city, but gratifying the greed of constituents, has too long stung the conscience of decent citizenship. This constant treaty-making of factionalism has been no less than a curse. The city manager plan proposes the commendable thing of abolishing wards. The plan is not unique in this for it has been common to many forms of commission government. . . [25]

Such a system should be supplanted, the argument usually went, with city-wide representation in which elected officials could consider the city "as a unit." "The new officers are elected," wrote Toulmin, "each to represent all the people. Their duties are so defined that they must administer the corporate business in its entirety, not as a hodge-podge of associated localities."

Behind the debate over the method of representation, however, lay a debate over who should be represented, over whose views of public policy should prevail. Many reform leaders often explicitly, if not implicitly, expressed fear that lower- and middle-income groups had too much influence in decision-making. One Galveston leader, for example, complained about the movement for initiative, referendum, and recall:

> We have in our city a very large number of negroes employed on the docks; we also have a very large number of unskilled white laborers; this city also has more barrooms, according to its population, than any other city in Texas. Under these circumstances it would be extremely difficult to maintain a satisfactory city government where all ordinances must be submitted back to the voters of the city for their ratification and approval.[26]

At the National Municipal League convention of 1907, Rear Admiral F. E. Chadwick (USN Ret.), a leader in the Newport, Rhode Island, movement for municipal reform, spoke to this question even more directly:

> Our present system has excluded in large degree the representation of those who have the city's well-being most at heart. It has brought, in municipalities . . . a government established by the least educated, the least interested class of citizens.
>
> It stands to reason that a man paying $5,000 taxes in a town is more interested in the well-being and development of his town than the man who pays no taxes. . . .

It equally stands to reason that the man of the $5,000 tax should be assured a representation in the committee which lays the tax and spends the money which he contributes. . . . Shall we be truly democratic and give the property owner a fair show or shall we develop a tyranny of ignorance which shall crush him?[27]

Municipal reformers thus debated frequently the question of who should be represented as well as the question of what method of representation should be employed.

That these two questions were intimately connected was revealed in other reform proposals for representation, proposals which were rarely taken seriously. One suggestion was that a class system of representation be substituted for ward representation. For example, in 1908 one of the prominent candidates for commissioner in Des Moines proposed that the city council be composed of representatives of five classes: educational and ministerial organizations, manufacturers and jobbers, public utility corporations, retail merchants including liquor men, and the Des Moines Trades and Labor Assembly. Such a system would have greatly reduced the influence in the council of both middle- and lower-class groups. The proposal revealed the basic problem confronting business and professional leaders: how to reduce the influence in government of the majority of voters among middle- and lower-income groups.[28]

A growing imbalance between population and representation sharpened the desire of reformers to change from ward to city-wide elections. Despite shifts in population within most cities, neither ward district lines nor the apportionment of city council and school board sets changed frequently. Consequently, older areas of the city, with wards that were small in geographical size and held declining populations (usually lower and middle class in composition), continued to be overrepresented, and newer upper-class areas, where population was growing, became increasingly underrepresented. This intensified the reformers' conviction that the structure of government must be changed to give them the voice they needed to make their views on public policy prevail.[29]

It is not insignificant that in some cities (by no means a majority) municipal reform came about outside the urban electoral process. The original commission government in Galveston was appointed rather than elected. "The failure of previous attempts to secure an efficient city government through the local electorate made the business man of Galveston willing to put the conduct of the city's affairs in the hands of a commission dominated by state-appointed officials."[30] Only in 1903 did the courts force Galveston to elect the members of the commission, an innovation which one writer described as "an abandonment of the commission idea," and which led to the decline of influence of the business community in the commission government.[31]

In 1911 Pittsburgh voters were not permitted to approve either the new city charter or the new school board plan, both of which provided for city-wide representation; they were a result of state legislative enactment. The governor appointed the first members of the new city council, but thereafter they were elected. The judges of the court of common pleas, however, and not the voters, selected members of the new school board.

The composition of the new city council and new school board in Pittsburgh, both of which were inaugurated in 1911, revealed the degree to which the shift from ward to city-wide representation produced a change in group representation.[32] Members of the upper class, the advanced professional men, and the larger business groups dominated both. Of the fifteen members of the Pittsburgh Board of Education appointed in 1911 and the nine members of the new city council, none were small businessmen or white-collar workers. Each body contained only one person who could remotely be classified as a blue-collar worker; each of these men filled a position specifically but unofficially designed as reserved for a "representative of labor," and each was an official of the Amalgamated Association of Iron, Steel, and Tin Workers. Six of the nine members of the new city council were prominent businessmen, and all six were listed in upper-class directories. Two others were doctors closely associated with the upper class in both professional and social life. The fifteen members of the Board of Education included ten businessmen with city-wide interests, one doctor associated with the upper class, and three women previously active in upper-class public welfare.

Lower- and middle-class elements felt that the new city governments did not represent them.[33] The studies carried out under the direction of Leonard White contain numerous expressions of the way in which the change in the structure of government produced not only a change in the geographical scope of representation, but also in groups represented. "It is not the policies of the manager or the council they oppose," one researcher declared, "as much as the lack of representation for their economic level and social groups."[34] And another wrote:

> There had been nothing unapproachable about the old ward aldermen. Every voter had a neighbor on the common council who was interested in serving him. The new councilmen, however, made an unfavorable impression on the less well-to-do voters. . . . Election at large made a change that, however desirable in other ways, left the voters in the poorer wards with a feeling that they had been deprived of their share of political importance.[35]

The success of the drive for centralization of administration and representation varied with the size of the city. In the smaller cities, business, professional, and elite groups could easily exercise a dominant influence. Their close ties readily enabled them to shape informal political power which they could transform into formal political power. After the mid-1890s the widespread organization of chambers of commerce provided a base for political action to reform municipal government, resulting in a host of small-city commission and city-manager innovations. In the larger, more heterogeneous cities, whose subcommunities were more dispersed, such community-wide action was extremely difficult. Few commission or city-manager proposals materialized here. Mayors became stronger, and steps were taken toward centralization of representation, but the ward system or some modified version usually persisted. Reformers in large cities often had to rest content with their Municipal

Research Bureaus through which they could exert political influence from outside the municipal government.

A central element in the analysis of municipal reform in the Progressive Era is governmental corruption. Should it be understood in moral or political terms? Was it a product of evil men or of particular sociopolitical circumstances? Reform historians have adopted the former view. Selfish and evil men arose to take advantage of a political arrangement whereby unsystematic government offered many opportunities for personal gain at public expense. The system thrived until the "better elements," "men of intelligence and civic responsibility," or "right-thinking people" ousted the culprits and fashioned a political force which produced decisions in the "public interest." In this scheme of things, corruption in public affairs grew out of individual personal failings and a deficient governmental structure which could not hold those predispositions in check, rather than from the peculiar nature of social forces. The contestants involved were morally defined: evil men who must be driven from power, and good men who must be activated politically to secure control of the municipal affairs.

Public corruption, however, involves political even more than moral considerations. It arises more out of the particular distribution of political power than of personal morality. For corruption is a device to exercise control and influence outside the legal channels of decision-making when those channels are not readily responsive. Most generally, corruption stems from an inconsistency between control of the instruments of formal governmental power and the exercise of informal influence in the community. If powerful groups are denied access for formal power in legitimate ways, they seek access through procedures which the community considers illegitimate. Corrupt government, therefore, does not reflect the genius of evil men, but rather the lack of acceptable means for those who exercise power in the private community to wield the same influence in governmental affairs. It can be understood in the Progressive Era not simply by the preponderance of evil men over good, but by the peculiar nature of the distribution of political power.

The political corruption of the "Era of Reform" arose from the inaccessibility of municipal government to those who were rising in power and influence. Municipal government in the United States developed in the 19th century within a context of universal manhood suffrage which decentralized political control. Because all men, whatever their economic, social, or cultural conditions, could vote, leaders who reflected a wide variety of community interests and who represented the views of people of every circumstance arose to guide and direct municipal affairs. Since the majority of urban voters were workingmen or immigrants, the views of those groups carried great and often decisive weight in governmental affairs. Thus, as Herbert Gutman has shown, during strikes in the 1870s city officials were usually friendly to workingmen and refused to use police power to protect strikebreakers.[36]

Ward representation on city councils was an integral part of grass-roots influence, for it enabled diverse urban communities, invariably identified with particular geographical areas of the city, to express their views more clearly through councilmen peculiarly receptive to their concerns. There was a direct, reciprocal flow of power between wards and the center of city affairs in which voters felt a relatively close connection with public matters and city leaders gave special attention to their needs.

Within this political system the community's business leaders grew in influence and power as industrialism advanced, only to find that their economic position did not readily admit them to the formal machinery of government. Thus, during strikes, they had to rely on either their own private police, Pinkertons, or the state militia to enforce their use of strikebreakers. They frequently found that city officials did not accept their views of what was best for the city and what direction municipal policies should take. They had developed a common outlook, closely related to their economic activities, that the city's economic expansion should become the prime concern of municipal government, and yet they found that this view had to compete with even more influential views of public policy. They found that political tendencies which arose from universal manhood suffrage and ward representation were not always friendly to their political conceptions and goals and had produced a political system over which they had little control, despite the fact that their economic ventures were the core of the city's prosperity and the hope for future urban growth.

Under such circumstances, businessmen sought other methods of influencing municipal affairs. They did not restrict themselves to the channels of popular election and representation, but frequently applied direct influence—if not verbal persuasion, then bribery and corruption. Thereby arose the graft which Lincoln Steffens recounted in his *Shame of the Cities.* Utilities were only the largest of those business groups and individuals who requested special favors, and the franchises they sought were only the most sensational of the prizes which included such items as favorable tax assessments and rates, the vacating of streets wanted for factory expansion, or permission to operate amid antiliquor and other laws regulating personal behavior. The relationships between business and formal government became a maze of accommodations, a set of political arrangements which grew up because effective power had few legitimate means of accomplishing its ends.

Steffens and subsequent liberal historians, however, misread the significance of these arrangements, emphasizing their personal rather than their more fundamental institutional elements. To them corruption involved personal arrangements between powerful business leaders and powerful "machine" politicians. Just as they did not fully appreciate the significance of the search for political influence by the rising business community as a whole, so they did not see fully the role of the "ward politician." They stressed the argument that the political leader manipulated voters to his own personal ends, that he used constituents rather than reflected their views.

A different approach is now taking root, namely, that the urban political organization was an integral part of community life, expressing its needs and its goals. As Oscar Handlin has said, for example, the "machine" not only fulfilled specific wants, but provided one of the few avenues to success and public recognition available to the immigrant.[37] The political leader's arrangements with businessmen, therefore, were not simply personal agreements between conniving individuals; they were far-reaching accommodations between powerful sets of institutions in industrial America.

These accommodations, however, proved to be burdensome and unsatisfactory to the business community and to the upper third of socioeconomic groups in general. They were expensive; they were wasteful; they were uncertain. Toward the end of the 19th century, therefore, business and professional men sought more direct control over municipal government in order to exercise political influence more effectively. They realized their goals in the early 20th century in the new commission and city-manager forms of government and in the shift from ward to city-wide representation.

These innovations did not always accomplish the objectives that the business community desired because other forces could and often did adjust to the change in governmental structure and reestablish their influence. But businessmen hoped that reform would enable them to increase their political power, and most frequently it did. In most cases the innovations which were introduced between 1901, when Galveston adopted a commission form of government, and the Great Depression, and especially the city-manager form which reached a height of popularity in the mid-1920s, served as vehicles whereby business and professional leaders moved directly into the inner circles of government, brought into one political system their own power and the formal machinery of government, and dominated municipal affairs for two decades.

Municipal reform in the early 20th century involves a paradox: the ideology of an extension of political control and the practice of its concentration. While reformers maintained that their movement rested on a wave of popular demands, called their gatherings of business and professional leaders "mass meetings," described their reforms as "part of a world-wide trend toward popular government," and proclaimed an ideology of a popular upheaval against a selfish few, they were in practice shaping the structure of municipal government so that political power would no longer be broadly distributed, but would in fact be more centralized in the hands of a relatively small segment of the population. The paradox became even sharper when new city charters included provisions for the initiative, referendum, and recall. How does the historian cope with this paradox? Does it represent deliberate deception or simply political strategy? Or does it reflect a phenomenon which should be understood rather than explained away?

The expansion of popular involvement in decision-making was frequently a political tactic, not a political system to be established permanently, but a device to secure immediate political victory. The prohibitionist advocacy of the referendum, one of the most extensive sources of support for such a measure, came from the belief that the referendum would provide the opportunity to outlaw liquor more rapidly. The Anti-Saloon League, therefore, urged local option. But the League was not consistent. Towns which were wet, when faced with a county-wide local-option decision to outlaw liquor, demanded town or township local option to reinstate it. The League objected to this as not the proper application of the referendum idea.

Again, "Progressive" reformers often espoused the direct primary when fighting for nominations for their candidates within the party, but once in control they often became cool to it because it might result in their own defeat. By the same token, many municipal reformers attached the initiative, referendum, and recall to municipal charters often as a device to appease voters who opposed the centralization of representation and executive authority. But, by requiring a high percentage of voters to sign petitions—often 25 to 30 percent—these innovations could be and were rendered relatively harmless.

More fundamentally, however, the distinction between ideology and practice in municipal reform arose from the different roles which each played. The ideology of democratization of decision-making was negative rather than positive; it served as an instrument of attack against the existing political system rather than as a guide to alternative action. Those who wished to destroy the "machine" and to eliminate party competition in local government widely utilized the theory that these political instruments thwarted public impulses, and thereby shaped the tone of their attack.

But there is little evidence that the ideology represented a faith in a purely democratic system of decision-making or that reformers actually wished, in practice, to substitute direct democracy as a continuing system of sustained decision-making in place of the old. It was used to destroy the political institutions of the lower and middle classes and the political power which those institutions gave rise to, rather than to provide a clear-cut guide for alternative action.[38]

The guide to alternative action lay in the model of the business enterprise. In describing new conditions which they wished to create, reformers drew on the analogy of the "efficient business enterprise," criticizing current practices with the argument that "no business could conduct its affairs that way and remain in business," and calling upon business practices as the guides to improvement. As one student remarked:

> The folklore of the business elite came by gradual transition to be the symbols of governmental reformers. Efficiency, system, orderliness, budgets, economy, saving, were all injected into the efforts of reformers who sought to remodel municipal government in terms of the great impersonality of corporate enterprise.[39]

Clinton Rodgers Woodruff of the National Municipal League explained that the commission form was "a simple, direct, businesslike way of administering the business affairs of the city. . . . An application to city administration of that type of business organization which has been so common and so successful in the field of commerce and industry."[40] The centralization of decision-making which developed in the business corporation was now applied in municipal reform.

The model of the efficient business enterprise, then, rather than the New England town meeting, provided the positive inspiration for the municipal reformer. In giving concrete shape to this model in the strong-mayor, commission, and city-manager plans, reformers engaged in the elaboration of the processes of rationalization and systematization inherent in modern science and technology. For in many areas of society, industrialization brought a gradual shift upward in the location of decision-making and the geographical extension of the scope of the area affected by decisions.

Experts in business, in government, and in the professions measured, studied, analyzed, and manipulated ever wider realms of human life, and devices which they used to control such affairs constituted the most fundamental and far-reaching innovations in decision-making in modern America, whether in formal government or in the informal exercise of power in private life. Reformers in the Progressive Era played a major role in shaping this new system. While they expressed an ideology of restoring a previous order, they in fact helped to bring forth a system drastically new.[41]

The drama of reform lay in the competition for supremacy between two systems of decision-making. One system, based upon ward representation and growing out of the practices and ideas of representative government, involved wide latitude for the expression of grass-roots impulses and their involvement in the political process. The other grew out of the rationalization of life which came with science and technology, in which decisions arose from expert analysis and flowed from fewer and smaller centers outward to the rest of society. Those who espoused the former looked with fear upon the loss of influence which the latter involved, and those who espoused the latter looked only with disdain upon the wastefulness and inefficiency of the former.

The Progressive Era witnessed rapid strides toward a more centralized system and a relative decline for a more decentralized system. This development constituted an accommodation of forces outside the business community to the political trends within business and professional life rather than vice versa. It involved a tendency for the decision-making processes inherent in science and technology to prevail over those inherent in representative government.

Reformers in the Progressive Era and liberal historians since then misread the nature of the movement to change municipal government because they concentrated upon dramatic and sensational episodes and ignored the analysis of more fundamental political structure, of the persistent relationships of influence and power which grew out of the community's social, ideological, economic, and cultural activities. The reconstruction of these patterns of human relationships and of the changes in them is the historian's most crucial task, for they constitute the central context of historical development. History consists not of erratic and spasmodic fluctuations, of a series of random thoughts and actions, but of patterns of activity and changes in which people hold thoughts and actions in common and in which there are close connections between sequences of events. These contexts give rise to a structure of human relationships which pervade all areas of life; for the political historian the most important of these is the structure of the distribution of power and influence.

The structure of political relationships, however, cannot be adequately understood if we concentrate on evidence concerning ideology rather than practice. For it is becoming increasingly clear that ideological evidence is no safe guide to the understanding of practice, that what people thought and said about their society is not necessarily an accurate representation of what they did. The current task of the historian of the Progressive Era is to quit taking the reformers' own description of political practice at its face value and to utilize a wide variety of new types of evidence to reconstruct political practice in its own terms. This is not to argue that ideology is either important or unimportant. It is merely to state that ideological evidence is not appropriate to the discovery of the nature of political practice.

Only by maintaining this clear distinction can the historian successfully investigate the structure of political life in the Progressive Era. And only then can he begin to cope with the most fundamental problem of all: the relationship between political ideology and political practice. For each of these facets of political life must be understood in its own terms, through its own historical record. Each involves a distinct set of historical phenomena. The relationship between them for the Progressive Era is not now clear; it has not been investigated. But it cannot be explored until the conceptual distinction is made clear and evidence tapped which is pertinent to each. Because the nature of political practice has so long been distorted by the use of ideological evidence, the most pressing task is for its investigation through new types of evidence appropriate to it. The reconstruction of the movement for municipal reform can constitute a major step forward toward that goal.

Notes

1. See, for example, Clifford W. Patton, *Battle for Municipal Reform* (Washington, D.C., 1940), and Frank Mann Stewart, *A Half-Century of Municipal Reform* (Berkeley, 1950).
2. George F, Mowry. *The California Progressives* (Berkeley and Los Angeles, 1951), pp. 86–101; Richard Hofstadter, *The Age of Reform* (New York, 1955), pp. 131–260; Alfred D. Chandler, Jr., "The Origins of Progressive Leadership," in Elting Morrison et al. (eds.), *Letters of Theodore Roosevelt* (Cambridge, 1951–1954), VIII, Appendix III, pp. 1462–64.
3. Harry A. Toulmin, *The City Manager* (New York, 1915), pp. 156–168; Clinton R[odgers] Woodruff, *City Government by Commission* (New York, 1911), pp. 243–253.
4. Eli Daniel Potts, "A Comparative Study of the Leadership of Republican Factions in Iowa, 1904–1914," M.A. thesis (State University of Iowa, 1956). Another satisfactory comparative analysis is contained in William T. Kerr, Jr., "The Progressives of Washington, 1910–12," *PNQ 55* (1964): 16–27.
5. Based upon a study of eleven ministers involved in municipal reform in Pittsburgh, who represented exclusively the upper-class Presbyterian and Episcopal churches.
6. Based upon a study of professional men involved in municipal reform in Pittsburgh, comprising eighty-three doctors, twelve architects, twenty-five educators, and thirteen engineers.
7. See especially Mowry, *The California Progressives*.
8. Leonard White, *The City Manager* (Chicago, 1927), pp. ix–x.
9. Harold A. Stone et al., *City Manager Government in Nine Cities* (Chicago, 1940); Frederick C. Mosher et al., *City Manager Government in Seven Cities* (Chicago, 1940); Harold A. Stone et al., *City Manager Government in the United States* (Chicago, 1940). Cities covered by these studies include: Austin, Texas; Charlotte, North Carolina; Dallas, Texas; Dayton, Ohio; Fredericksburg, Virginia; Jackson, Michigan; Janesville, Wisconsin; Kingsport, Tennessee; Lynchburg. Virginia; Rochester, New York; San Diego, California.

10. Jewell Cass Phillips, *Operation of the Council-Manager Plan of Government in Oklahoma Cities* (Philadelphia, 1935), pp. 31–39.

11. James Weinstein, "Organized Business and the City Commission and Manager Movements," *Journal of Southern History* XXVIII (1962): 166–182.

12. Norman N. Gill, *Municipal Research Bureaus* (Washington, [D.C.] 1944).

13. This account of the movement for commission government in Des Moines is derived from items in the Des Moines *Register* during the years from 1905 through 1908.

14. Biographical data constitutes the main source of evidence for this study of Pittsburgh reform leaders. It was found in city directories, social registers, directories of corporate directors, biographical compilations, reports of boards of education, settlement houses, welfare organizations, and similar types of material. Especially valuable was the clipping file maintained at the Carnegie Library of Pittsburgh.

15. *Town Crier* (Seattle), Feb. 18, 1911, p. 13.

16. Information derived from the same sources as cited in n. 14.

17. Stone *et al., Nine Cities,* p. 212.

18. *Ibid.,* pp. 3–13.

19. *Ibid.,* p. 329.

20. Stone *et al., City Manager Government,* pp. 26, 237–241, for analysis of opposition to city manager government.

21. Des Moines *Register and Leader,* March 17, 1908.

22. *Ibid.,* March 30, March 28, 1908.

23. Voters' Civic League of Allegheny County, "Bulletin of the Voters' Civic League of Allegheny County Concerning the Public School System of Pittsburgh," Feb. 14, 1911, pp. 2–3.

24. In the decade 1911 to 1920, 45 percent of the municipal charters adopted in eleven home rule states involved the commission form and 35 percent the city manager form; in the following decade the figures stood at 6 percent and 71 percent respectively. The adoption of city manager charters reached a peak in the years 1918 through 1923 and declined sharply after 1933. See Leonard D. White, "The Future of Public Administration," *Public Management* XV (1933): 12.

25. Toulmin, *The City Manager,* p. 42.

26. Woodruff, *City Government,* p. 315. The Galveston commission plan did not contain provisions for the initiative, referendum, or recall, and Galveston commercial groups which had fathered the commission plan opposed movements to include them. In 1911 Governor Colquitt of Texas vetoed a charter bill for Texarkana because it contained such provisions; he maintained that they were "undemocratic" and unnecessary to the success of commission government. *Ibid.,* pp. 314–315.

27. *Ibid.,* pp. 207–208.

28. Des Moines *Register and Leader,* Jan. 15, 1908.

29. Voters' Civic League of Allegheny County, "Report on the Voters' League in the Redistricting of the Wards of the City of Pittsburgh" (Pittsburgh, n.d.).

30. Horace E. Deming, "The Government of American Cities," in Woodruff, *City Government,* p. 167.

31. *Ibid.,* p. 168.

32. Information derived from the same sources as cited in n. 14.

33. W. R. Hopkins, city manager of Cleveland, indicated the degree to which the new type of government was more responsive to the business community: "It is undoubtedly easier for a city manager to insist upon acting in accordance with the business interests of the city than it is for a mayor to do the same thing." Quoted in White, *The City Manager,* p. 13.

34. Stone *et al., Nine Cities,* p. 20.
35. *Ibid.,* p. 225.
36. Herbert Gutman, "An Iron Workers' Strike in the Ohio Valley, 1873–1874," *Ohio Historical Quarterly* LXVIII (1959): 353–370: "Trouble on the Railroads, 1873–1874: Prelude to the 1877 Crisis," *Labor History,* II (1961): 215–236.
37. Oscar Handlin, *The Uprooted* (Boston, 1951), pp. 209–217.
38. Clinton Rodgers Woodruff of the National Municipal League even argued that the initiative, referendum, and recall were rarely used. "Their value lies in their existence rather than in their use." Woodruff, *City Government,* p. 314. It seems apparent that the most widely used of these devices, the referendum, was popularized by legislative bodies when they could not agree or did not want to take responsibility for a decision and sought to pass that responsibility to the general public, rather than because of a faith in the wisdom of popular will.
39. J. B. Shannon, "County Consolidation," *Annals of the American Academy of Political and Social Science* 207 (1940): 168.
40. Woodruff, *City Government,* pp. 29–30.
41. Several recent studies emphasize various aspects of this movement. See, for example, Loren Baritz, *Servants of Power* (Middletown, 1960); Raymond E. Callahan, *Education and the Cult of Efficiency* (Chicago, 1962); Samuel P. Hays, *Conservation and the Gospel of Efficiency* (Cambridge, 1959); Dwight Waldo, *The Administrative State* (New York, 1948), pp. 3–61.

CHAPTER 4

RACIAL POLITICS AND THE CRISIS OF THE CITIES

The Crisis of the Cities

After World War II, the fate of downtown became an abiding concern. Historically, downtowns had been the lifeblood of their metropolitan areas and the economic engines of the national economy. Before the industrial city, everyone lived crowded together in or close to the center. In the industrial era, rail lines converged on the factories and workforces concentrated in the dense, thriving cities. Some affluent families had begun moving to the suburbs as early as the 1890s and the pace of suburban movement picked up in the prosperous 1920s. Still, the cities did not seem threatened. But in the years during the Great Depression and the war, the physical condition of the cities deteriorated. The fate of downtown became a chronic worry.

In the selection from Robert M. Fogelson's book, *Downtown,* the author notes that "Many office buildings were old and dingy. No new ones had been erected in a decade." But the problems went beyond mere physical dilapidation. Though there were "signs the downtowns were holding their own" because people still flocked downtown to work and shop there, property values were sagging and mass transit systems were in decline. Increasingly, people took cars into the cities and made a quick exit back to the growing suburbs. Retail sales were falling. Two momentous developments in the suburbs were especially threatening to the future of downtown: the emergence of regional shopping centers, and the decentralization of office space. Attitudes toward the downtown were changing as well. To many urban residents, it no longer seemed to serve their needs. Los Angeles, more than any other city, seemed to be the harbinger of the urban future: a sprawled metropolis without a center.

Rising racial tensions were the second dramatic indicator that the cities were in trouble. Abundant jobs in the industrial cities during the war drew black workers to northern cities, but once the war was over the migration picked up even more steam. In 1940, blacks made up just 9.3 percent of Detroit's population; by 1970 the proportion had increased to 63 percent. As the selection from Thomas J. Sugrue's book about Detroit shows, whites reacted to the presence of blacks by organizing homeowners and citizens' associations, and by resorting to violence, to keep them from moving into white neighborhoods. Sugrue shows that racial exclusion provided the primary motivation for the formation of these kinds of organizations. White homeowners felt economically vulnerable, and they projected onto blacks their insecurities. The growing slums that blacks were forced to crowd into projected a real-life image of the problems that whites feared. As Sugrue explains, the resistance to black movement into white neighborhoods assumed some of the aspects of war. Blacks who moved close to or into white neighborhoods were subjected to violence and harassment. Racial change in the neighborhoods occurred in block-by-block skirmishes, with whites making an uneven, slow retreat.

The basic pattern of the twentieth-century metropolis remains intact. Today Detroit is a city where more than three-quarters of the residents are blacks; in the suburbs, blacks comprise less than 10 percent of the population. Although Detroit is an extreme case, the city/suburban racial divide inherited from the past still exists in virtually all older metropolitan areas in the United States. Things are changing, however. Downtowns are on the rebound, and new immigrants are moving to the suburbs in large numbers. Patterns of racial and ethnic segregation will undoubtedly continue, but the old city/suburban divide may be disappearing.

10

Robert M. Fogelson

DOWNTOWN IN THE MID TWENTIETH CENTURY

In April 1950 the *St. Louis Post-Dispatch* published an article about downtown St. Louis, the eighth in a series about Greater St. Louis entitled "Progress or Decay? St. Louis Must Choose." Downtown St. Louis was ailing, wrote reporter Richard G. Baumhoff. Many office buildings were old and dingy. No new ones had been erected in a decade. And a few department stores were establishing branches in Clayton and other rapidly growing outlying business districts. Downtown's property values were on the rise, but its assessed value was lower than in 1930. Only 375,000 people, roughly one of every five, entered the central business district on weekdays, but as more than half of them came by car, traffic was congested and parking hard to find. While residential construction was booming on the periphery, the center was "encircled by a rotting ring of slums." But "downtown is not dying," Baumhoff declared. It is still "the center, the core, the heart that pumps the blood of commerce through the area's arteries." Efforts to revitalize it were under way. Downtown businessmen were

Robert M. Fogelson, "Just Another Business District? Downtown in the Mid Twentieth Century" from *Downtown: Its Rise and Fall, 1880-1950*. Yale University Press, 2001, pp. 381-394 (text only), and notes on pp. 471-474. Corresponding notes on pp. 339-344, 349-350, 355-357, 359-360.

renovating department stores and office buildings. Local officials were planning to build a system of expressways and provide additional off-street parking. And business and political leaders were mounting a campaign to redevelop the blighted areas adjacent to the central business district. What would come of these efforts was not clear. What was clear, wrote Baumhoff, was that the well-being of downtown and the well-being of the metropolitan area were synonymous. "Without a vigorous Downtown, St. Louis loses its chief economic reasons for existence; without a vigorous St. Louis, the whole metropolitan district falters and fails—economically, culturally, physically."[1]

As Baumhoff pointed out, St. Louis was not unique. Although the country was out of the depression, downtown was still in the doldrums. And there it would stay, the downtown business interests believed, unless the cities could slow down decentralization. But could they build the limited-access highways, off-street parking facilities, and rapid transit lines needed to enhance the accessibility of the central business district and make it competitive with the outlying business districts? Could they transform the slums and blighted areas into middle- and upper-middle-class neighborhoods and create new markets for downtown goods and services? To put it another way, was it possible to reverse the long-term trends indicating that downtown's daytime population was increasing very little, if at all, that retail trade was growing much more slowly in the central business district than in the outlying business districts, and that property values were rising much less rapidly in the center than on the periphery? Downtown, most Americans realized, would never again be the business district, the place to which virtually everybody went every day to work, shop, do business, and amuse themselves. But whether it would retain its position as the central business district or, as a Los Angeles traffic engineer put it, turn into "just another" business district, and not necessarily the most attractive or most prosperous, remained to be seen.[2]

There were some signs that downtown was holding its own in the immediate postwar years. Millions of Americans still poured into it on weekdays. "There are lots of people downtown," *Business Week* declared in 1951. After a decade and a half in which more office buildings had been torn down than put up, scores of new skyscrapers were erected in urban America, notably in midtown Manhattan, downtown San Francisco, and the Chicago Loop. From 1945 to 1950 roughly thirty million square feet of new office space came on the market, an increase of about 14 percent, most of it in the central business district. And occupancy rates were over 95 percent. According to the National Association of Building Owners and Managers, the central business districts were "maintaining, if not strengthening, their hold on [the] volume of office space." And in 1952 James C. Downs, a Chicago real estate analyst, assured the association's members that they need have no fear that the "downtown areas" would one day become "ghost towns." Many of the leading department stores were undergoing costly renovations too. According to *Business Week*, Jordan Marsh (Boston) was putting $11 million into its downtown store. Gimbel's (New York) was investing $5 million, Halle Bros. (Cleveland) $8 million, Neiman-Marcus (Dallas) $5 million, and Marshall Field (Chicago) $19 million. No "top drawer [department] store" had left the central business district, Richard C. Bond, president of Philadelphia's Wanamaker's, pointed out. Despite the growing decentralization of retail trade, "it is still much too soon to count the urban center out of the picture," a Marshall Field executive insisted in 1952. "Our own experience over nearly a quarter-century indicates beyond any doubt that there remains now and for the predictable future a great retailing opportunity in the familiar downtown."[3]

In the meantime the campaign to curb decentralization was gathering momentum. Even before Congress created the interstate highway system in 1956, New York, Chicago, Los Angeles, and other cities were building huge limited-access highways running from the outlying residential sections to the central business district. These freeways, wrote journalist Hal Burton, "permit the motorist to skim above city streets or to whiz along below them" at speeds that would once have been inconceivable. Although some warned that the freeways would promote decentralization, many held that they might well be "the salvation of the central business district." To accommodate the heavy traffic generated by the freeways, Boston, Pittsburgh, Detroit, and other cities were also building large garages and parking lots. "The time is not likely to come when everybody who wants to park downtown can find a space, on or off the street," wrote Burton. "Yet, year by year, progress is being made." Moreover, even before Congress passed the Housing Act of 1949, several cities were moving ahead on plans to redevelop the slums and blighted areas adjacent to the central business district as well as the blighted commercial areas inside it. They ran into political obstacles, bureaucratic red tape, and legal challenges, but before long many projects were under way; and some, like Pittsburgh's Gateway Center and Chicago's Lake Meadows, were done—though whether these projects would lure the well-to-do from the periphery to the center was far from clear. "A firm start has been made to save the rotting core of America's biggest communities," wrote Chalmers M. Roberts, a *Washington Post* reporter, in 1952. "Downtown is coming back," said Sylvia Porter, a syndicated columnist, five years later.[4]

But there were other signs that downtown was not holding its own, much less coming back. Millions of Americans were moving to the suburbs, which grew more than four times as fast as the central cities, some of which lost population, in the 1940s. And many of them were no longer going downtown, even in the few cities with a fairly robust central business district. A case in point is Chicago, where between 1948 and 1952, a period of steady growth in the metropolitan area, the number of people entering the Loop fell by nearly 200,000, or about 20 percent. Fewer people went to the Loop in 1952 than in any year since 1926 (except 1935). Property values were rising more slowly in the central business districts, if they were rising at all, than in the outlying business districts. In the San Francisco Bay area, for example, values increased much more rapidly after the war in the San Mateo and Hayward business districts than in downtown San Francisco or downtown Oakland. Indeed, property values there were no higher in the early 1950s than in the late 1920s; adjusted for inflation, they were lower. After a brief respite during the war, the mass transit systems—the streetcars, els, and subways that had been so vital to the growth of downtown—resumed their long decline. The riding habit fell sharply in the few cities that had a rapid transit system. It fell even more sharply in the many cities that had only streetcars and motorbuses. In Detroit, for instance, the riding habit plunged from 238 in 1945 to 126 in 1951, a drop of nearly 50 percent in just six years, which was lower than it had been at any time since the depths of the depression.[5]

The proliferation of motels, nearly all of which were located outside the central business district, was another ominous sign. A relatively recent phenomenon, the motel—or, as it was originally known, the motor court or roadside inn—had first appeared in the 1920s, mostly in the South and West. But before the depression it had not posed much of a threat to downtown hotels. After World War II, however, the number of motels soared. Between 1948 and 1958, a decade during which the number of hotels, most of which were located inside the central business district, fell slightly, the number of motels rose by almost 60 percent. For every four hotels, there were now three motels. Another ominous sign was the seemingly inexorable decentralization of retail trade. Between 1948 and 1954 retail sales went down in many central business districts—by 10 percent in St. Louis, by 11 percent in Detroit, and by 16 percent in Pittsburgh, a city that had one of the country's most ambitious urban redevelopment programs. Where retail sales went up in the central business district, they went up more elsewhere in the metropolitan area—more than six times as much in New York, more than seven times as much in Cleveland, more than eight times as much in Seattle, and more than twenty times as much in Atlanta. Overall, the central business district's share of the metropolitan area's retail trade declined from 16 percent to 12 percent in the five largest cities and from 23 percent to 18 percent in the thirteen next largest ones.[6]

Even more ominous were two momentous developments, both of which got under way in the immediate postwar period. One was the emergence of the regional shopping center. For decades retailing had been moving away from downtown. Shopkeepers opened up hardware, clothing, and other stores in the outlying business districts. Developers built a few small shopping centers in the suburbs. Chains set up large stores in the outlying areas, proving that retail outlets offering standardized merchandise and ample parking could do a high volume even if they were located miles from the central business district. And department stores established branches in the suburbs. (They had no choice, wrote one journalist. They did not create the problems downtown. "They can and should help [solve them]; but in the meantime they had best roll with the punch and head for the suburbs.") But none of these developments had prepared Americans for the regional shopping centers that were built in the late 1940s and early 1950s. They were "quite unlike any other retail development in the nation," writes historian Richard Longstreth, referring to the first of them, the Crenshaw Center, which opened in southwest Los Angeles in late 1947.[7]

Among their many distinctive features, by far the most striking was size. They were immense. Some covered dozens of acres, housed fifty to a hundred stores, with half a million to a million square feet of floor space, and provided parking for several thousand automobiles. Each regional shopping center was anchored by a large branch of a major department store—Detroit's Northland by J. L. Hudson, Seattle's Northgate by Bon Marché, and Boston's Shoppers' World by Jordan Marsh. New York's Cross County Center, which was located in Westchester County, a booming suburban area north of the city, was anchored by two, Wanamaker's and Gimbel's. Besides a department store, the regional shopping centers usually included chain stores, like Woolworth and W.T. Grant, apparel, hardware, drug, and furniture stores, a small bank, a supermarket, and perhaps a movie theater and one or more restaurants. "In effect," wrote Larry Smith, a Seattle real estate economist and shopping center consultant, "they are downtown business communities transferred to the residential areas."[8] Owned by real estate syndicates or major department stores, the regional shopping centers had strong competitive advantages. Located along one or more major highways, they were highly accessible to motorists. They provided ample parking, a wide selection of merchandise, and the much-touted "one-stop" shopping. Designed, developed, and managed as a unit, the regional shopping centers were also in a good position to respond swiftly to changes in the market.

Although a strong sign of the ongoing decentralization of retail trade, the regional shopping centers were not "a serious threat" to the central business district, Smith argued in 1952. Max S. Wehrly, executive director of the Urban Land Institute, agreed, pointing out that thus far these centers had not depressed business downtown (and might well have stimulated it). So did Philip M. Talbott, a vice president of Woodward & Lothrop, a Washington, D.C., department store, who held that regional shopping centers represented "additional business—not competition." Other Americans disagreed. There was only so much business to be done, insisted John Galbreath, a Columbus, Ohio, realtor; and as more was done in the regional shopping centers, less would be done in the central business district. Some observers also feared that as the shopping centers spread throughout the suburbs, the downtown stores would be forced to resort to "'bargain basement retailing' for whatever customers emerge from the encroaching slums." Whether things would get that bad was hard to say. But by the mid 1950s—by which time several well-known firms had closed their downtown department stores, something that had not happened even during the Great Depression—they were bad enough. The regional shopping centers had made "startling inroads" on downtown business, wrote the Buffalo City Planning Commission in 1956. If this trend continued, which seemed likely, the commission forecast the "economic collapse of the central business district."[9]

The other momentous development that got under way in the immediate postwar period was the incipient decentralization of office space—or, to be more precise, corporate office space. This development was even more unexpected than the emergence of the regional shopping center. For corporate offices had not followed the lead of the factories, wholesale houses, department stores, and other enterprises that had moved to the outlying business districts. Neither had most of the banks and investment banks, stock and commodity exchanges, insurance companies, law firms, accounting firms, and advertising agencies on which corporate America relied so heavily. Through World War II they had stayed in the central business district, and in the central business district they would remain, Americans believed. According to the conventional wisdom, they could not function anywhere but in a highly compact, extremely concentrated, and centrally located business district that brought together all the administrative, financial, legal, and technical expertise required to run the nation's economy.[10]

Starting in the late 1940s and early 1950s, however, a handful of small insurance companies moved their offices from Manhattan to Westchester County—one to White Plains, another to Port Chester, and yet another to Harrison. So did several large corporations, including General Foods and Standard Oil. A few others, among them General Electric and Union Carbide, were thinking about moving out of Manhattan, most to Westchester, some to New Jersey, Long Island, and southern Connecticut. And a few had already bought large tracts of land to build on. Offices were moving to the suburbs in other cities too. To give a couple of examples, MacManus, John & Adam, an advertising agency, left downtown Detroit for Bloomfield Hills, and Cargill, the country's largest grain trader, went from downtown Minneapolis to the shores of Lake Minnetonka. According to observers, many firms were moving because they needed more space and could not find it in the central business district except at exorbitant prices, often two and three times as much as they were paying. As one insurance company executive wrote, "Our prospective rent bill was staggering [if we remained in Manhattan]." Some firms were also fed up with downtown's noise and dirt, its traffic congestion and parking shortage. A bucolic setting, they believed, would make it easier to attract and retain qualified workers. Some firms might have moved in order to reduce the commuting time of their chief executives, many of whom lived in wealthy suburbs a short drive from their new offices. And though most executives were unwilling to admit it, a few firms might have moved out of fear that the central business district would be a prime target in the event of atomic war.[11]

Most observers downplayed the importance of this development. Only a tiny fraction of New York's many corporations had moved out of Manhattan, they pointed out. For every firm that left for the suburbs, noted the New York State Department of Commerce, "others have eagerly sought the space left behind." Despite a great surge of construction in the postwar period, the vacancy rate in New York's office buildings was only 2 percent. Many firms that had considered moving to the suburbs decided instead to stay put and modernize their quarters or erect new buildings. A few firms that had moved to the suburbs returned to the city. If there was not much of a trend to suburban offices in New York, wrote the Wall Street Journal, there was even less of one in other cities. There was no evidence that management was heading out of downtown in Boston, Chicago, Pittsburgh, and San Francisco.[12] But there was a trend, albeit a weak one. At least a few corporate executives no longer took it for granted that their firms had to be located in the central business district. And that was cause for alarm. For the central business district could survive the decentralization of industry and wholesaling. Some Americans held that it might even be better off without these messy and noisy activities. It might even survive the decentralization of retailing and entertainment. What it could not survive was the decentralization of office space, the loss of which would be disastrous not only for the downtown property owners but also for the downtown retailers and other businessmen whose well-being had come to depend more heavily than ever on the downtown workforce.

As downtown changed, so did the way Americans thought about it. Employing metaphors that were almost a century old, some still spoke of downtown as the "heart" and "hub" of the city and metropolitan area. As they saw it, there were some economic activities that could only be carried on in the central business district—which would always be home to the large department stores, tall office buildings, and grand hotels. There were other economic activities that could be carried on in the outlying business districts but had to be supervised from the central business district—which, said a department store executive, was the "nerve center" of the economy. Downtown, these Americans acknowledged, was no longer the only business district. But it was still the main one. And the main one it would always be. As two midwestern economists wrote in 1953, "There is nothing to indicate that the Loop—the world's greatest concentration of business establishments—will not continue as the economic mainspring of the Chicago metropolitan area." A Boston planner agreed. "No vision of the 'city of tomorrow[,]' no matter how decentralized or how dispersed, can conceive of no downtown," he declared two years later.[13]

Downtown, these Americans believed, was still as vital to the city as the heart was to the body and the hub to the wheel. "Like the human heart, it pumps life into the entire trading [area]," said a department store executive. Without it, wrote Baumhoff, the *St. Louis Post-Dispatch* reporter, the city is doomed. Downtown was a major source of revenue, too. Indeed, a Dayton realtor pointed out, the central business district generates so much more in taxes than it consumes in services that it subsidizes the residential property owners. Downtown was also the city's most striking feature, the feature, noted Walter S. Schmidt, "by [which] the city is judged and evaluated, not only by the visitors to it, who frequently see little else, but by the citizens themselves." Downtown was vital to the outlying sections as well, these Americans believed. The suburbs could not survive without the city, and the city could not survive without the central business district. "Even the largest, the most prosperous and best operated suburban communities in Greater Cleveland would dry up and blow away were it not for Cleveland in general and downtown Cleveland in particular," declared the *Lakewood Post,* a suburban Cleveland newspaper. "[What would] New York [be] without Fifth Avenue; Chicago without the Loop; or Philadelphia without Market, Chestnut and Walnut Streets?" asked a Philadelphia realtor. "Destroy these business areas, and you destroy the city." And if you destroy the city, "there would be no reasons for [its] sub-centers."[14]

But other Americans were less sanguine about the future of the central business district. Some doubted that it could hold its own against the outlying business districts. In time, wrote two Florida economists, downtown businesses will find it easier to move to their customers than to bring their customers to them. As that happens, the suburbs may well "absorb major portions of what used to be considered downtown commerce and industry, professional services, and commercialized recreation." It was too late to attempt to restore downtown to its "former unchallenged preeminence," a traffic expert pointed out shortly before the United States entered World War II. All that could be done was to try to create a balance between the central business district and the outlying business districts. Others thought that the central business district could hold its own—but only if the local authorities and downtown businessmen worked together to improve mass transit, build limited-access highways, provide off-street parking, and turn the inner-city slums and blighted areas into middle- and upper-middle-class neighborhoods. Even these measures might not be enough unless retailers stopped spending millions in the outlying areas and used the money to renovate their downtown stores. Downtown stores could compete with suburban stores, wrote Hal Burton, but not if they are "crippled by inertia, old-fashioned methods, or plain bad merchandising."[15]

As revealing as what these Americans said was what they did. During the early and mid 1950s the Urban Land Institute, whose official position was that downtown was "the vital hub" of the metropolitan area, sent panels to a dozen cities to figure out how to revitalize their central business districts. At the same time periodicals convened roundtables at which merchants, realtors, planners, and engineers shared their thoughts about its plight, and trade and professional groups devoted parts of their annual meetings to a discussion of its problems. In one city after another downtown businessmen and property owners also established voluntary associations to promote the interests of the central business district—something they had been disinclined to do when downtown was in its heyday. By the mid 1950s virtually every city had at least one organization that was devoted exclusively to the well-being of the central business district. Los Angeles had two—the Downtown Businessmen's Association and the Central Business District Association. There were so many of these associations that in 1954 delegates from thirty cities formed the International Downtown Executives' Association, a group of downtown associations from the United States and Canada.[16] As much as anything, this proliferation revealed how deeply concerned downtown business interests were about the future.

The proliferation also revealed that many downtown businessmen and property owners no longer believed in spatial harmony. After more than two decades of rampant decentralization, during which time the central business district steadily lost ground to the outlying business districts, some still adhered to the traditional notion that rivalry between the center and the periphery was unnatural. But many now believed that rivalry within cities, especially between the central business district and the outlying business districts, was as natural as rivalry among cities. Some Americans went even further, arguing that the cities and the suburbs were locked in "mortal combat," to quote Edmond H. Hoben, assistant director of the National Association of Housing Officials. Perhaps no one made this point more forcefully than William Zeckendorf, the flamboyant president of Webb & Knapp, a leading New York real estate firm, and one of the most outspoken supporters of urban redevelopment. "Satellite cities, which are the product of decentralization, are parasites," he wrote in 1952. "Every satellite town saps off the buying power, the taxing power, and the vital factors that make for a cohesive, comprehensive, healthy city."[17]

Not everyone was concerned, let alone deeply concerned. Downtown, some believed, was no longer necessary. It was no longer true that "every city must have one large central business district," wrote E. E. East, chief engineer of the Automobile Club of Southern California. "We find in the metropolitan area of Los Angeles more than a hundred trading areas where every commodity and service essential to daily life may be obtained." East also pooh-poohed the idea that a business district "must be closely built-up to attract business." "This is a tradition handed down from the days of mass rail transportation," he explained. "It ignores the fact that an almost countless number of establishments are today doing a thriving business in locations far removed from closely built-up business centers."[18] Speaking at the national conference of planners in 1948, Hans Blumenfeld, a Philadelphia planner, took a similar position. Downtown, he insisted, was anachronistic. It was time for the advocates of urban redevelopment, "these modern King Canutes," to realize that decentralization was irreversible. "The densely crowded agglomeration of the 19th Century with its concomitant, the fantastic skyrocketing of urban land values, was a short-lived passing phenomenon." A product of an outdated transportation system, "it was bound to disappear forever; and I, for one say; good riddance!"

These Americans believed that a compact and highly congested central business district served only the interests of downtown businessmen and property owners. They agreed with Los Angeles planner Gordon Whitnall that the cities would be better off organized around a group of "well-balanced, self-contained community sub-centers" than around one central business district and many outlying residential sections. Decentralization, they conceded, had done severe damage. But it had in it "the seeds of a better urban existence for the mass of suffering humanity," said T. Ledyard Blakeman, executive director of the Detroit Metropolitan Area Regional Planning Commission. Provided it was "properly planned," decentralization would improve living and working conditions on the periphery and in the center. Novelist Louis Bromfield took this argument one step further. It was not just the central business district that was anachronistic; it was also the huge metropolitan area of which it was the most visible symbol. Bromfield, too, favored decentralization—but not so much the shift from the center to the periphery as the movement from big cities to small towns and rural areas and from the most developed regions to the least developed.[19]

The belief that the central business district had outlived its usefulness was heightened by the growing fear of atomic warfare. Less than a year after the United States obliterated Hiroshima and Nagasaki, some Americans were wondering whether the modern city was doomed. As early as 1948 Tracy B.

Augur, past president of the American Institute of Planners, declared that the only defense against atomic weapons was dispersal. "We cannot afford *not* to disperse our cities," he said. "If we delay too long," he warned, "we may wake up some morning and find that we haven't any country, that is, if we wake up at all that morning." Although some skeptics argued that dispersal would be impractical and ineffective, Augur and others made a strong impression on many Americans, even many who had a substantial stake in the well-being of the central business district. A good example is Albert D. Hutzler, president of Hutzler Brothers, Baltimore's leading department store. Asked at the 1948 Businessmen's Conference on Urban Problems, a conference sponsored by the U.S. Chamber of Commerce, "Isn't decentralization inevitable? Aren't we wasting money and energy in trying to delay it?" he replied:

> If you would have asked me that a few years ago, I would have been extremely hot in saying it was not inevitable. I would have been tremendously strong in saying that our best course was redevelopment, spending all the money necessary for it. However, I have wavered a little bit since the atomic bomb. I am quite serious. I wonder whether, from a military standpoint, it might be better to save this money to develop additional subsidiary sections and to let the central business district remain fairly stationary.[20]

Hutzler had more to worry about than atomic warfare. For decades downtown Baltimore's department stores and other retailers had been losing ground, and there was no reason to think they would regain it. Between 1948 and 1954, during which time retail trade rose 25 percent in metropolitan Baltimore, it fell 2 percent in downtown Baltimore. And downtown's share of the metropolitan area's retail trade declined from over 20 percent to under 16 percent. Equally disquieting, the assessed value of the central business district dropped from $175 million in 1931 to $128 million in 1947—a decrease of 27 percent that occurred at the same time the assessed value of the city increased by 2 percent and the assessed value of the periphery by 26 percent. As late as the mid 1920s experts had predicted that downtown Baltimore would be so busy in 1950 that it would be necessary to double- and triple-deck the streets and to build subways and els to accommodate the hundreds of thousands of commuters. But when 1950 arrived, downtown was no busier than it had been in the mid 1920s. All this Hutzler knew. But one thing in particular puzzled him. According to the conventional wisdom, a busy downtown was vital to the well-being of the city. But if things were slow in downtown Baltimore, they were even slower in downtown Los Angeles. Yet Los Angeles, Hutzler pointed out, was "the fastest growing city in the country" and by no means the "poorest."[21]

The growth of Los Angeles was phenomenal, as phenomenal as the growth of New York and Chicago. From a nondescript town of 11,000 in 1880, Los Angeles had grown by 1930 into the nation's fifth largest city, with more than 1.2 million people, and its fourth largest metropolitan area, with upward of 2.3 million. A major commercial entrepôt and industrial center, the ninth largest manufacturer in the country, it was already the metropolis of the Southwest and would in time replace San Francisco as the metropolis of the West Coast. The growth of Los Angeles slowed during the 1930s. But with the end of the Great Depression and the outbreak of World War II, it picked up again—and at a pace that astonished observers, one of whom called it "one of the most spectacular of all municipal growths." "People are swarming into Los Angeles at the rate of 3,000 per week," he wrote in 1949, "and they have not come to see [actor] Van Johnson's house. They have come to stay." By 1950 the city had nearly 2 million people, making it the fourth largest in the nation, and the metropolitan area had almost 4 million, making it the third largest after New York and Chicago. With a booming and highly diversified economy, an economy, reported *Newsweek,* "undergoing its greatest period of industrial expansion," Greater Los Angeles was also second among metropolitan areas in construction and auto production, third in employment, income, retail sales, wholesale trade, and banking, and fourth in manufacturing.[22]

Los Angeles was also the nation's—possibly, wrote *Newsweek,* the world's —most decentralized metropolis. The signs were visible everywhere, in the sprawling residential subdivisions, in the growing outlying business districts, and in the booming regional shopping centers. But nowhere were they more striking then in the sorry state of the central business district. From its heyday in the mid 1920s, downtown had gone steadily downhill. Things were very bad during the Great Depression and not much better afterward. Between the mid 1920s and early 1950s, during which time the population of Los Angeles County more than tripled, the number of people who went downtown rose less than 10 percent. On a typical weekday in 1953 only 15 percent of the population entered the central business district, down from 41 percent in 1926. Construction downtown, which had come to a halt in the 1930s and 1940s, was still dormant. The central business district's share of the metropolitan area's retail trade fell sharply too, from 30 percent in 1930 to 11 percent in 1948. And after the Crenshaw and other regional shopping centers opened, it plummeted to 6 percent in 1954. "It looks as though the fate of the downtown stores in that city has been sealed," wrote *Business Week* in 1951. "There hasn't been a lick of expansion in the downtown stores since the war. The trend is all outward."[23]

Los Angeles was not, as *Business Week* put it, "one of a kind," just the first of its kind—"the first modern, widely decentralized industrial city in America," journalist Carey McWilliams wrote.[24] As such, it revealed that a city could grow and prosper without a vibrant downtown. It also revealed that the dispersal of residences might well be incompatible with the centralization of business, a possibility raised by John A. Miller in the early 1940s. In Los Angeles, as in other cities, it was no longer true that no matter where people lived, no matter how far from the center, they would travel downtown every day, that the more they went to the periphery to live, the more they would come to the center to work, shop, do business, and amuse themselves. Los Angeles also revealed that the efforts to curb decentralization might well be doomed. There was reason to think that people were not going to downtown L.A. because they did not want to. If so, more limited-access highways would not do much good. Nor would additional off-street parking, of which Los Angeles already had more than any other city. There was also reason to think that the well-to-do had no desire to move from the periphery to the center. If so, urban redevelopment would not do much good either. If the metropolis of the future was unfolding in Los Angeles, as many Americans believed, it did not bode well for Hutzler and other businessmen and property owners that downtown L.A. was or would soon be "just another" business district.

Notes

1. *St. Louis Post-Dispatch,* April 23, 1950.
2. Scott L. Bottles, *Los Angeles and the Automobile: The Making of the Modern City* (Berkeley, 1987), page 195.
3. *Business Week,* October 6, 1951, page 138; *Reduction of Urban Vulnerability: Part V of the Report on Project East River* (New York, 1952), page 60b; *Architectural Forum,* June 1952, page 59; Richard C. Bond, "Apropos—Any City," *Urban Land,* October 1953, page 4; *Proceedings of the Annual National Planning Conference: 1952,* pages 42–43.
4. Bernard J. Frieden and Lynne B. Sagalyn, *Downtown, Inc.: How America Rebuilds Cities* (Cambridge, 1989), pages 20–25; Hal Burton, *The City Fights Back* (New York, 1954), chapters 5, 6, 11; Jon C. Teaford, *The Rough Road to Renaissance: Urban Revitalization in America, 1940–1985* (Baltimore, 1990), pages 93–99, 107–113; *Architectural Forum,* June 1953, pages 46–47; Chalmers M. Roberts, "How Other Cities Fight 'Downtown Blight,' " in Washington Post Company, *Progress or Decay? 'Downtown Blight' in the Nation's Capital* (1952), page 4; Cleveland Rapid Transit System, *The Future of Metropolitan Cleveland Depends on the Subway* (1957), page 36.
5. W. L. C. Wheaton, "Is Economic Disaster Ahead for Our Cities?" *National Real Estate and Building Journal,* May 1953, page 39; "How to Rebuild Cities Downtown," *Architectural Forum,* June 1955, page 123; Chicago Department of Streets and Electricity, Bureau of Street Traffic, "Cordon Count Data on the Central Business District" (1949), page 2; Paul F. Wendt, "Urban Land Value Trends," *Appraisal Journal,* April 1958, pages 260–262; Teaford, *Rough Road to Renaissance,* pages 104–105; William J. Watkins, *Parking as a Factor in Business: Part 3. Relationship Between Downtown-Automobile Parking Conditions and Retail-Business Decentralization* (Washington, D.C., 1953), page 103.
6. Warren James Belasco, *Americans on the Road: From Autocamp to Motel, 1910–1945* (Cambridge, 1979), chapter 6; Harris, Kerr, Forster & Company, *Trends in the Hotel-Motel Business: Twenty-seventh Annual Review* (1962), pages 2–3; U.S. Bureau of the Census, *1954 Census of Business: Central Business District Statistics Summary Report* (Washington, D.C., 1958), pages 10–11; Murray D. Dessel, "Central Business Districts and Their Metropolitan Areas: A Summary of Geographic Shifts in Retail Sales Growth, 1948–1954," U.S. Department of Commerce, Office of Area Development, *Area Trend Series, No. 1* (Washington, D.C., 1957), pages 10–11.
7. Meredith L. Clausen, "Northgate Regional Shopper Center—Paradigm from the Provinces," *Journal of the Society of Architectural Historians,* May 1984, page 146; *City Planning,* January 1931, page 40; "Suburban Shopping Centers," *National Real Estate Journal,* December 1938, pages 30–32; *Architectural Record,* September 1940, pages 32–42; Dero A. Saunders, "Department Stores: Race for the Suburbs," *Fortune,* December

1951, pages 99, 173; Richard Longstreth, *City Center to Regional Mall: Architecture, the Automobile, and Retailing in Los Angeles, 1920–1950* (Cambridge, 1997), page 230.

8. Larry Smith, "The Economic Base of the Community," in U.S. Chamber of Commerce, *Business Action for Better Cities: A Complete Report of the Businessmen's Conference on Urban Problems* (Washington, D.C., 1952), page 45. See also "Suburban Retail Districts," *Architectural Forum*, August 1950, pages 106–109; Clausen, "Northgate Regional Shopping Center," pages 150–156; "Regional Shopping Centers," *American City*, May 1954, pages 126–127; "Shoppers' World," *Architectural Forum*, December 1951, pages 186–187; C. D. Palmer, "The Shopping Center Goes to the Shopper," *New York Times Magazine*, November 29, 1952, page 37.

9. Smith, "Economic Base," pages 45–48; "Will Today's Shopping Centers Succeed?" *National Real Estate and Building Journal*, February 1953, pages 23–24; J. Gordon Dawkins, "Solving the Downtown Problem," *Stores*, August 1955, page 6; Arthur Rubloff, "Regional Shopping Centers and Their Effect on the Future of Our Cities," in Harlean James, ed., *American Planning and Civic Annual* (Washington, D.C., 1953), page 49; "Marshall Field's New Shopping Center," *Architectural Forum*, December 1954, pages 186–187; Mabel Walker, "The Impact of Outlying Shopping Centers on Central Business Districts," *Public Management*, August 1957, page 173; Buffalo City Planning Commission, "A Proposed Shopping and Transportation Concourse for Downtown Buffalo" (1956), page 2.

10. Larry Smith, "Maintaining the Health of Our Central Business Districts," *Traffic Quarterly*, April 1954, pages 116–117; H. W. Lochner & Co. and DeLeuw, Cather & Co., *Highway and Transportation Plan [for] Knoxville, Tennessee* (Chicago, 1948), page 4.

11. "Offices Move to Suburbs," *Business Week*, March 17, 1951, pages 79–83; "Big Business Going Rural," ibid., June 28, 1952, pages 88–90; *Architectural Forum*, June 1953, page 43; "Should Management Move to the Country?" *Fortune*, December 1952, pages 142–143, 164–170; "Office Decentralization," *Urban Land*, October 1950, page 3.

12. "Should Management Move to the Country?" page 143; *Architectural Forum*, January 1953, pages 43–45; Cleveland Rapid Transit System, *The Future of Metropolitan Cleveland*, page 36; *American Society of Planning Officials Newsletter*, December 1955, page 98; George J. Eberle, "Metropolitan Decentralization and the Retailer," *Journal of Retailing*, December 1946, page 93.

13. Richard J. Seltzer, "Where Shall I Shop?" *Appraisal Journal*, January 1949, pages 118–119; *Detroit News*, February 25, 1955; Burton, *The City Fights Back*, pages 10, 24–25: Philip M. Talbott, "Rescuing 'Downtown' and Its Transit," *Public Utilities Fortnightly*, December 8, 1955, page 942; Eberle, "Metropolitan Decentralization," page 93; Smith, "Our Central Business Districts," page 117; *Urban Land*, March 1950, page 4; Morton Bodfish and Ralph J. Lueders, "Forces of Decentralization in Chicago," *Savings and Homeownership*, July 1953; William H. P. Smith, "Greater Boston's Big Headache," *Greater Boston Business*, August 1955, pages 7–8.

14. Talbott, "Rescuing 'Downtown,'" page 942; *St. Louis Post-Dispatch*, April 23, 1950; Cleveland Rapid Transit System, *The Future of Metropolitan Cleveland*, pages 37–38: "How to Rebuild Cities Downtown," page 236; J. Ross McKeever, "A View of the Year," *Urban Land*, January 1955, page 4; L. P. Cookingham, "Introductory Remarks," in Harlean James, ed., *American Planning and Civic Annual* (Washington, D.C., 1954), page 12; Seltzer, "Where Shall I Shop?" page 119.

15. Reinhold P. Wolff and Frederich H. Bair, Jr., "Are We Reaching City Limits?" *Dun's Review*, April 1951, page 78; Theodore T. McCrosky, "Decentralization and Parking,"

Proceedings [of the] Annual Meeting [of the] Institute of Traffic Engineers: 1941, page 63; McKeever, "A View of the Year," page 4; Jay D. Runkle, "A Downtown Merchant Looks at the Future of Downtown Shopping Areas," *Stores,* November 1947, pages 68–70; Henry A. Barnes, "Downtown Baltimore: Prosperity or Doom?" *Baltimore,* June 1956, page 21; Burton, *The City Fights Back,* page 155.

16. *Detroit News,* February 25, 1955; Burton, *The City Fights Back,* pages 11–15; 223–224, 260; "How to Rebuild Cities Downtown," page 122; Alan A. Altshuler, *The City Planning Process: A Political Analysis* (Ithaca, 1965), page 202; Teaford, *Rough Road to Renaissance,* pages 49–50; Longstreth, *City Center to Regional Mall,* chapter 8; Donald C. Hyde, "Transit Isn't *That* Sick," *Public Utilities Fortnightly,* September 29, 1955, page 460.

17. William Zeckendorf, "Cities Versus Suburbs," *Atlantic Monthly,* July 1952, page 24. See also *Urban Land,* March 1950, page 3; U.S. Chamber of Commerce, *Better Cities . . . Better Business: A Complete Report on the Businessmen's Conference on Urban Problems* (Washington, D.C., 1948), page 155; Sy Adler, "Why BART and No LART? The Political Economy of Rail Rapid Transit Planning in the Los Angeles and San Francisco Metropolitan Areas, 1945–1957," *Planning Perspectives,* May 1957, pages 149–157; *Proceedings [of the] National Conference on Planning: 1941,* page 231.

18. E. E. East, "Los Angeles' Street Traffic Problem," *Civil Engineering,* August 1942, page 436. See also Hans Blumenfeld, "Alternative Solutions for Metropolitan Development," *Proceedings of the Annual National Planning Conference: 1948,* page 20.

19. T. Ledyard Blakeman, "Regional Planning and Decentralization," in U.S. Chamber of Commerce, *Better Cities . . . Better Business,* pages 162–163; Louis Bromfield, "The Flight from the Cities," *Town and Country Planning,* Summer 1949, pages 110–111.

20. U.S. Chamber of Commerce, *Your City Is Your Business: A Complete Report on the Businessmen's Conference on Urban Problems* (Washington, D.C., 1947), pages 222–223. See also Louis Wirth, "Does the Atomic Bomb Doom the Modern City?" *New Jersey Municipalities,* April 1946, pages 25–29; Tracy B. Augur, "Decentralization Can't Wait," *Proceedings of the Annual National Planning Conference: 1948,* pages 27–35; Charles B. Merriam, "Problems of Reorganizing Our Great Cities," ibid., pages 35–42; Paul Boyer, *By the Bomb's Early Light* (New York, 1954), pages 148–152, 175–176, 320–321, 327–328.

21. U.S. Chamber of Commerce, *Your City Is Your Business,* page 223. See also Dessel, "Central Business Districts and Their Metropolitan Areas," page 11; Albert D. Hutzler, "Decentralization and the Central District," in U.S. Chamber of Commerce, *Your City Is Your Business,* pages 192–193; *Baltimore Sun,* June 14, 1925.

22. Robert M. Fogelson, *The Fragmented Metropolis: Los Angeles, 1850–1930* (Cambridge, 1967), chapters 4 and 6; Sam Boal, "Los Angeles Has It, But What Is It?" *New York Times Magazine,* September 14, 1949, page 37; "City of the Angels: It's Still an Age of Miracles," *Newsweek,* August 3, 1953, pages 64–66.

23. "City of the Angels," page 66; Coverdale and Colpitts, *Report of the Los Angeles Metropolitan Transit Authority on a Monorail Rapid Transit Line for Los Angeles* (1954), page 62; Longstreth, *City Center to Regional Mall,* pages 199–201, 221–226; Dessel, "Central Business Districts and Their Metropolitan Areas," page 11; "There Are Lots of People Downtown," *Business Week,* October 6, 1951, page 140.

24. Carey McWilliams, "Look What's Happened to California," *Harper's,* October 1949, page 28. See also "There Are Lots of People Downtown," page 140; John A. Miller, "Cities on the Toboggan," *Transit Journal,* February 1941, page 46; James W. Rouse, "Will Downtown Face Up to Its Future?" *Urban Land,* February 1957, pages 3–4.

11

Thomas J. Sugrue

RACIAL CONFRONTATION IN POST-WAR DETROIT

The Rise of the Homeowners' Movement

Between 1943 and 1965, Detroit whites founded at least 192 neighborhood organizations throughout the city, variously called "civic associations," "protective associations," "improvement associations," and "homeowners' associations."[1] Few scholars have fully appreciated the enormous contribution of this kind of grassroots organization to the racial and political climate of twentieth-century American cities.[2] Their titles revealed their place in the ideology of white Detroiters. As civic associations, they saw their purpose as upholding the values of self-government and participatory democracy. They offered members a unified voice in city politics. As protective associations, they fiercely guarded the investments their members had made in their homes. They also paternalistically defended neighborhood, home, family, women, and children against the forces of social disorder that they saw arrayed against them in the city. As improvement associations, they emphasized the ideology of self-help and individual achievement that lay at the very heart of the American notion of homeownership. Above all, as home and property owners' associations, these groups represented the interests of those who perceived themselves as independent and rooted rather than dependent and transient.

The surviving records of homeowners associations do not, unfortunately, permit a close analysis of their membership. From the hundreds of letters that groups sent to city officials and civil rights groups, from neighborhood newsletters, and from improvement association letterheads, it is clear that no single ethnic group dominated most neighborhood associations. Names as diverse as Fadanelli, Csanyi, Berge, and Watson appeared on the same petitions. Officers of the Greater Detroit Homeowners' Association, Unit No. 2, in a blue-collar northwest Detroit neighborhood, included a veritable United Nations of ethnic names, among them Benzing, Bonaventura, Francisco, Kopicko, Sloan, Clanahan, Klebba, Beardsley, Twomey, and Barr. Groups met in public-school buildings, Catholic and Protestant churches, union halls, Veterans of Foreign Wars clubhouses, and parks. Letters, even from residents with discernibly "ethnic" names, seldom referred to national heritage or religious background.

Excerpts from Thomas J. Sugrue, *The Origins of the Urban Crisis: Race and Inequality in Postwar Detroit*. Princeton University Press, 1996, pp. 211-218, 231-234, 246-249, 256-258, and corresponding notes on pp. 339-344, 349-350, 355-357, 359-360.

Organizational newsletters and neighborhood newspapers never used ethnic modifiers or monikers to describe neighborhood association members—they reserved ethnic nomenclature for "the colored" and Asians (and occasionally Jews). The diversity of ethnic membership in neighborhood groups is not surprising, given that Detroit had few ethnically homogeneous neighborhoods by midcentury. But the heterogeneity of Detroit's neighborhoods only partially explains the absence of ethnic affiliation in remaining records. Homeowners and neighborhood groups shared a common bond of whiteness and Americanness—a bond that they asserted forcefully at public meetings and in correspondence with public officials. They referred to the "white race," and spoke of "we the white people." Some called for the creation of a "National Association for the Advancement of White People," and others drew from the "unqualified support of every white family, loyal to white ideas."[3]

Detroit was a magnet for southern white migrants, but there is no evidence of a distinctive southern white presence in neighborhood organizations. "Hillbillies," as they were labeled, were frequently blamed for racial tension in the city, but their role was greatly exaggerated. Most of them dispersed throughout the metropolitan area, and quickly disappeared into the larger white population. There were a few concentrations of poor white southerners in the city, like the Briggs neighborhood near Tiger Stadium. Even in these neighborhoods, however, they tended not to form civic or political organizations. Scattered evidence from voter surveys suggests that they tended to vote solidly Democratic; indeed, in 1949 and 1951 they were more likely to support liberal candidates than were Italians and Poles. In addition, as historical anthropologist John Hartigan has shown, southern whites often lived in close proximity to blacks with little long-term resistance. Most importantly, a 1951 public opinion survey found that "Southerners who now live in Detroit express no more negative attitudes about Negroes and are no more in favor of segregation than are people from other parts of the country." The racial politics of Detroit's neighborhood associations were thoroughly homegrown.[4]

Racial exclusion had not always been the primary purpose of neighborhood associations. Real estate developers had originally created them to enforce building restrictions, restrictive covenants and, later, zoning laws. Their members served as watchdogs, gathering complaints from neighbors and informing the City Plan Commission of zoning violations. Frequently, they lobbied city officials for the provision of better public services such as street lighting, stop signs, traffic lights, and garbage pickup. Improvement associations were also social clubs that welcomed new neighbors and brought together residents of adjacent streets for events such as block parties, dinner dances, and excursions to local amusement parks or baseball games. They sponsored community cleanup and home improvement competitions. Their newsletters included admonitions to association members to drive safely, announcements of local dinner dances, neighborhood gossip, and home improvement and homemaking tips.[5]

During and after World War II, these organizations grew rapidly in number and influence, as hundreds of thousands of working-class whites became homeowners for the first time. Detroit's industrial workers had used their relatively high wages, along with federal mortgage subsidies, to purchase or build modest single-family houses on the sprawling Northeast and Northwest sides. The proportion of owner-occupied homes in the city rose from 39.2 percent in 1940 to 54.1 percent in 1960.[6] Yet the working-class hold on affluence was tenuous. Many city residents had spent a large part of their life savings to buy a home, and they usually had little else to show for their work. Most Detroiters viewed homeownership as a precarious state, always under siege by external forces beyond their control. Even those who held steady employment found that mortgage or land contract payments stretched family budgets to the breaking point. In a comprehensive survey of Detroit residents conducted in 1951, Wayne University sociologist Arthur Kornhauser found that white Detroiters ranked housing needs as the most pressing problem in the city. Homeownership required a significant financial sacrifice for Detroit residents: the most frequent complaint (voiced by 32 percent of respondents) was that the cost of housing was too high.[7] To a generation that had struggled through the Great Depression, the specter of foreclosure and eviction was very real. For working Detroiters, the vagaries of layoffs, plant closings, and automation jeopardized their most significant asset, usually their only substantial investment—their homes.

Homeownership was as much an identity as a financial investment. Many of Detroit's homeowners were descendants of immigrants from eastern and southern Europe, for whom a house and property provided the very definition of a family. They placed enormous value on the household as the repository of family values and the center of community life. In addition, for many immigrants and their children, homeownership was proof of success, evidence that they had truly become Americans. A well-kept property became tangible evidence of hard work, savings, and prudent investment, the sign of upward mobility and middle-class status.[8]

To white ethnics, homeownership was more than the product of individual enterprise. Detroiters, by and large, lived in intensely communal neighborhoods. In Detroit's working-class districts, houses were close together on small lots. Day-to-day life was structured by countless small interactions among neighbors; little was private. Property maintenance, behavior, and attitudes seldom escaped the close scrutiny of neighbors. Reinforcing the ties of proximity were the common bonds of religion. In the mid-1950s, about 65 percent of Detroit's population was Roman Catholic; the white population was probably closer to 75 or 80 percent Catholic. Catholic familial and institutional bonds ordered urban life in ways that cannot be underestimated. Paul Wrobel, a third-generation Polish American, recalled that life in the heavily Catholic East Side neighborhood of his youth "centered around three separate but related spheres: Family, Parish, and Neighborhood." In largely Catholic neighborhoods, improvement associations grew out of parish social organizations, frequently held meetings in church halls, and often got material and spiritual support from pastors. Improvement associations in largely Polish neighborhoods on Detroit's East Side, reported the Mayor's Interracial Committee (MIC), "conform to the bounds of Catholic Church parish lines rather than subdivisions." Although many Catholic clergy supported civil rights, priests at some Detroit-area churches encouraged their parishioners to support homeowners' associations, for fear that black "invasions" would hurt parish life. Parishioners at Saint Andrew and Saint Benedict, a large Catholic church in a racially changing southwest Detroit neighborhood, were active in the Southwest Civic Improvement League. MIC officials reported a "prevailing sentiment of antagonism and fear" and a "feeling that this investment [in a new parish school building] and the social life of the church will be affected by the movement out . . . of large numbers of church members."[9] Catholic parishes were not the only bases for homeowners' groups, however. White civic associations also found religious and political support among evangelical Protestants. Many white fundamentalist churches, such as the Temple Baptist Church and the Metropolitan Tabernacle, fostered racial prejudices and often sponsored neighborhood association meetings.[10]

The homeowners' movement, then, emerged as the public voice of proud homeowners who defined themselves in terms of their tightly knit, exclusive communities. But the simultaneous occurrence of economic dislocation and black migration in postwar Detroit created a sense of crisis among homeowners. Both their economic interests and their communal identities were threatened. They turned to civic associations to defend a world that they feared was slipping away. Increasingly, they blamed blacks for their insecurity. In the era of open housing, responding to the threat of black movement into their neighborhoods became the raison d'être of white community groups. One new group, the Northwest Civic Association, called its founding meeting "So YOU will have first hand information on the colored situation in this area," and invited "ALL interested in maintaining Property Values in the NORTHWEST section of Detroit." The Courville District association gathered together residents of a northeast Detroit neighborhood to combat the "influx of colored people" to the area, and rallied supporters with its provocatively entitled newsletter, *Action!* When a black family moved onto Cherrylawn Street on the city's West Side, between six hundred and a thousand white neighbors attended an emergency meeting to form a neighborhood association. The founders of the Connor-East Homeowners' Association promised to "protect the Area from undesirable elements." Members of the San Benardo Improvement Association pledged to keep their neighborhood free of "undesirables"—or "Niggers"—as several who eschewed euphemism shouted at the group's first meeting. Existing organizations took on a new emphasis with the threat of black "invasion." In 1950, Orville Tenaglia, president of the Southwest Detroit Improvement League, recounted his group's history: "Originally we organized in 1941 to promote better civic affairs, but now we are banded together just to protect our homes." The league was engaged in a "war of nerves" over the movement of blacks into the community.[11]

The issues of race and housing were inseparable in the minds of many white Detroiters. Economically vulnerable homeowners feared, above all, that an influx of blacks would imperil their precarious investments. "Stop selling houses to the colored," advocated one white Detroiter. "Where would we move? No place—poor people have no place to move," he added. "What is the poor people to do?" Speaking for homeowners who felt threatened by the black migration, a self-described "average American housewife" wrote: "What about us, who cannot afford to move to a better location and are surrounded by colored? . . . Most of us invested our life's savings in property and now we are in constant fear that the neighbor will sell its property to people of different race.[12] Kornhauser found that race relations followed a close second to housing in Detroiters' ranking of the city's most pressing problems. Only 18 percent of white respondents from all over the city expressed "favorable" views toward the "full acceptance of Negroes" and 54 percent expressed "unfavorable" attitudes toward integration. When asked to discuss ways in which race relations "were not as good as they should be," 27 percent of white respondents mentioned "Negroes moving into white neighborhoods." 22 percent answered that the "Negro has too many rights and privileges; too much power; too much intermingling." Another 14 percent mentioned "Negroes' undesirable characteristics." Only 14 percent mentioned the existence of discrimination as a problem in race relations.[13]

Whites in Detroit regularly spoke of the "colored problem" or the "Negro problem."[14] In their responses to open-ended questions, Kornhauser's informants made clear what they meant by the "colored problem." Of blacks: "Eighty percent of them are animals," stated one white respondent. "If they keep them all in the right place there wouldn't be any trouble," responded another. "Colored treat the whites in an insolent way," added a third white, "They think they own the city." A majority of whites looked to increased segregation as the solution to Detroit's "colored problem."[15] When asked, "What do you feel ought to be done about relations between Negroes and whites in Detroit?" a remarkable 68 percent of white respondents called for some form of racial segregation—56 percent of whites surveyed advocated residential segregation. Many cited the Jim Crow South as a model for successful race relations.[16]

Class, union membership, and religion all affected whites' attitudes toward blacks. Working-class and poor whites expressed negative views toward blacks more frequently than other respondents to Kornhauser's survey. 85 percent of poor and working-class whites supported racial segregation, in contrast to 56 percent of middle-income and 42 percent of upper-income whites. Union members were slightly "less favorable than others towards accepting Negroes." CIO members were even more likely than other white Detroiters to express negative views of African Americans—65 percent—although more CIO members were also likely to support full racial equality (18 percent) than ordinary white Detroiters. And finally, Catholics were significantly more likely than Protestants to express unfavorable feelings toward blacks.[17]

Neighborhood groups responded to the threat of "invasion" with such urgency because of the extraordinary speed of racial change. Most blocks in changing neighborhoods went from being all-white to predominantly black in a period of three or four years. They also reacted viscerally against the tactics of blockbusting real estate brokers, whose activities fueled their sense of desperation. Whites living just beyond "racially transitional" areas witnessed the rapid black movement into those areas. They feared that without concerted action, their neighborhoods would turn over just as quickly.

White Detroiters also looked beyond transitional neighborhoods to the "slum," a place that confirmed all of their greatest fears. Whites saw in the neighborhoods to which blacks had been confined in the center city area, such as Paradise Valley, a grim prophecy of their own neighborhoods' futures. The rundown, shabby appearance of inner-city housing, the piles of uncollected garbage, and the streets crowded with children and families escaping tightly packed apartments seemed confirmation of whites' worst fears of social disorder. To them, the ghetto was the antithesis of their tightly-knit, orderly communities. They also noticed the striking class difference between blacks and whites. The median family income of blacks in Detroit was at best two-thirds of that of whites between the 1940s and the 1960s. Although the poorest blacks were seldom the first to move into formerly white neighborhoods (in fact black "pioneers" were often better off than many of their white neighbors), whites feared the incursion of a "lowerclass element" into their neighborhoods.[18]

To white Detroiters, the wretched conditions in Paradise Valley and other poor African American neighborhoods were the fault of irresponsible blacks, not greedy landlords or neglectful city officials. Because housing was such a powerful symbol of "making it" for immigrant and working-class families, many Detroit whites interpreted poor housing conditions as a sign of personal failure and family breakdown. Wherever blacks lived, whites believed, neighborhoods inevitably deteriorated. "Let us keep out the slums," admonished one East Side homeowners' group. If blacks moved into white neighborhoods, they would bring with them "noisy roomers, loud parties, auto horns, and in general riotous living," thus depreciating real estate values and destroying the moral fiber of the community. A middle-aged Catholic woman living in a racially changing Detroit neighborhood offered a similar view. Blacks "just destroy the whole neighborhood," she told an interviewer. "They neglect everything. Their way of life is so different from ours."[19] A Northwest Side neighborhood association poster played on the fears of white residents afraid of the crime that they believed would accompany racial change: "Home Owners Can You Afford to . . . Have your children exposed to gangster operated skid row saloons? Phornographic [sic] pictures and literature? Gamblers and prostitution? You Face These Issues Now!"[20]

As black joblessness rates rose in the 1950s, such fears were not totally without basis. As more and more young African American men faced underemployment or unemployment, many spent time hanging out on street-corners, a scene that whites found threatening. And as the city's economy began its downward spiral in the mid-1950s, rates of burglary, robbery, and murder began to rise. In the city's poorest black neighborhoods, an alternative economy of gambling, drugs, and prostitution flourished. Even though whites were seldom the victims of black-initiated crimes, Detroit's white-owned daily newspapers paid special attention to black-on-white crimes, giving prominent billing to murders and rapes. Often sensationalistic accounts mentioned the race of a black perpetrator, but seldom, if ever, mentioned that of whites.[21]

Whites also commonly expressed fears of racial intermingling. Black "penetration" of white neighborhoods posed a fundamental challenge to white racial identity. Again and again, neighborhood groups and letter writers referred to the perils of rapacious black sexuality and race mixing. The politics of family, home, and neighborhood were inseparable from the containment of uncontrolled sexuality and the imminent danger of interracial liaisons. Neighborhood newsletters ominously warned of the threat of miscegenation. One Northwest Side newspaper praised a Common Council candidate with a banner headline: "Kronk Bucks Mixing Races." Members of the Courville District association discussed "interracial housing," "interracial marriage," and "interracial dancing in our schools and elsewhere." Proximity to blacks risked intimacy. "Do you want your children to marry colored?" asked one woman at an improvement association rally in 1957. At a meeting at Saint Scholastica Catholic Church in northwest Detroit nine years later, fears of racial intermarriage remained the most pressing concern. Parishioners expressed concerns about the supposed sexual potency of black men.[22]

The undistilled sentiments of youth offer a revealing glimpse into the racial attitudes that undergirded Detroit's battles over housing. In the mid-1940s, a teacher at the all-white Van Dyke School in northeast Detroit asked students in a sixth-grade class to write essays on "Why I like or don't like Negroes." The students frequently mentioned cleanliness, violence, and housing conditions as grounds for disliking blacks, and often offered pejorative comments about blacks' living habits. Several students expressed concerns about black neighbors. "They are durty fighters and they do not keep their yardes clean," wrote one sixth-grader. In the words of another student, "they try to mix in with white people when they don't want them." A classmate stated that "they wanted to live out on Van Dyke and we didn't want them to." Another argued (in words that must have come right from his parents), that "if you give them a inch they take a mile and they are sneaky." Mary Conk drew up a list which encapsulated most of her classmates' sentiments:

1. Because they are mean
2. And they are not very clean.
3. Some of them don't like white people
4. They leave garbage in the yard and it smells
5. And in the dark the skare you
6. And they pick you up in a car and kill you. at nite
7. And they start riots

Most of the students at the Van Dyke School had never lived near a black person. Few spoke from experience. But the children, fearful of the prospect of blacks as neighbors, expressed attitudes that they had heard again and again from their parents and friends. As white Detroiters continued to fight against black movement throughout the city, they ensured that subsequent generations of children and adults would share Mary Conk's fears about blacks.[23]

. . .

Life was good for Easby Wilson in the spring of 1955. The city was in a recession, but Wilson was still steadily employed on the day shift at the Dodge Main plant. At a time when many of his fellow black workers were being laid off, Wilson was lucky. He had saved enough money so that he, his wife, and their five-year-old son could move from the crowded and run-down Paradise Valley area to the quiet, leafy neighborhood around the Courville School on Detroit's Northeast Side. The Courville area was popular with Dodge Main workers because it was affordable, attractive, and only three miles from the plant. Wilson could drive from his house to the factory gate in about ten minutes, or take a fifteen-minute bus ride down Dequindre Avenue.[24]

After looking at a few houses in March 1955, the Wilsons chose a modest frame house on Riopelle Street. They knew that the neighborhood was predominantly white and had heard rumors of racially motivated violence in changing Detroit neighborhoods. But their real estate agent reassured him that "the situation" (a euphemism for race relations) "was fine." What the broker failed to tell them was that they were breaching an invisible racial boundary by buying a house west of Dequindre Avenue. The neighborhood to the east of Dequindre had a rapidly growing black population, but only one other black family lived on the blocks to the west. The Wilsons also did not know that over the preceding decade, white residents of the surrounding neighborhood had formed a powerful homeowners' association to resist the black "invasion" of their area, had harassed whites who offered their houses to blacks, and had driven out several black newcomers. Less than two years before the Wilsons bought their house, neighbors in the same block had threatened a white family who put their house on the market with a black broker.[25]

Shortly after the Wilsons closed on the real estate deal, their new house became a racial battleground. Indignant white neighbors launched a five-month siege on 18199 Riopelle. In late April, just before the Wilsons moved in, someone broke into the house, turned on all the faucets, blocked the kitchen sink, flooded the basement, and spattered black paint on the walls and floors. Later that day, after the Wilsons cleaned up the mess and left, vandals broke all the front windows in the house. Despite the noise, no neighbors reported the attack to the police. On Tuesday, April 26, the Wilsons moved in. The onslaught escalated. White members of the Cadillac Improvement Association approached the Wilsons and demanded that they sell the house. That evening, someone threw a stone through the bathroom window. For two straight nights, the phone rang with angry, anonymous calls.

On Friday, after dinner, a small crowd gathered on Riopelle Street in front of the Wilsons' house. They were soon joined by more than four hundred picketing and chanting whites, summoned by young boys who rode their bikes up and down the street, blowing whistles. The crowd drew together a cross-section of neighborhood residents: as Mrs. Wilson reported, "it was children; it was old people; it was teen-agers; in fact all ages were there." Demonstrators screamed epithets. "You'd better go back where you belong!" shouted an angry neighbor. A rock shattered the dining room window. Trapped inside, Easby

Wilson could barely contain his rage. "He lost his head" before he was calmed by his wife and a police officer. The following evening, more protesters filled the street in front of the Wilson house; despite police surveillance, someone threw a large rock toward the house so hard that it stuck in the asbestos siding.

In the aftermath of the demonstrations, some of Wilson's friends from UAW Local 3 stood guard occasionally on the Wilsons' porch. The police stationed a patrol car near the house twenty-four hours a day. Gradually the pickets subsided, but over the next two months, hit-and-run vandals launched eggs, rocks, and bricks at the Wilsons' windows, splashed red, black, and yellow paint on the facade of the house, and put several snakes in the basement. An older white woman who lived next door threatened the family and was caught one evening pouring salt on the Wilsons' lawn. "At night," reported Mrs. Wilson, "when the lights are out, you can expect anything." Despite the police protection, the attacks went unabated; in fact many of the attacks occurred while police officers sat in their car nearby. At the end of the second month of the siege, Mrs. Wilson was exasperated. "I don't know whether it's worthwhile. I believe in Democracy; I believe in what my husband fought for [in World War II]. . . . They fought for the peace and I wonder if it's worthwhile. I have a question in my mind: where is the peace they fought for—where is it?"

The beleaguered Wilsons reported a "terrific strain" because of the incidents. Easby Wilson suffered from a mild heart condition that was aggravated by the stress of constant harassment. Their son Raymond, a five-year-old, began having "nervous attacks," waking up in the middle of the night complaining that he felt like "something was crawling over him, maybe ants." Raymond's affliction proved to be the last indignity the Wilsons would suffer. They moved out of their Riopelle Street house when a psychologist warned the Wilsons that Raymond risked "becoming afflicted with a permanent mental injury" because of the relentless attacks. The siege on the Wilsons, and other attacks on black newcomers to the area, served as an effective deterrent to black movement onto the streets west of Dequindre Avenue, between McNichols and Seven Mile Roads. In 1960, almost five years after the Wilsons were driven out, only 2.9 percent of the area's residents were black.[26]

Violent incidents like the attacks on the Wilsons' home were commonplace in Detroit between the Second World War and the 1960s. The postwar era, as a city race relations official recalled, was marked by many "small disturbances, near-riots, and riots." The city "did a lot of firefighting in those days." White Detroiters instigated over two hundred incidents against blacks moving into formerly all-white neighborhoods, including harassment, mass demonstrations, picketing, effigy burning, window breaking, arson, vandalism, and physical attacks. Most incidents followed improvement association meetings. The number of attacks peaked between 1954 and 1957, when the city's economy was buffeted by plant closings, recession, and unemployment, limiting the housing options of many white, working-class Detroiters. Incidents accelerated again in the early 1960s, reaching a violent crescendo in 1963, when the Commission on Community Relations reported sixty-five incidents. A potent mixture of fear, anger, and desperation animated whites who violently defended their neighborhoods. All but the most liberal whites who lived along the city's racial frontier believed that they had only two options. They could flee, as vast numbers of white urbanites did, or they could hold their ground and fight.[27]

The violence that whites unleashed against blacks was not simply a manifestation of lawlessness and disorder. It was not random, nor was it irrational. In the arena of housing, violence in Detroit was organized and widespread, the outgrowth of one of the largest grassroots movements in the city's history. It involved thousands of whites, directly affected hundreds of blacks, mainly those who were among the first families to break the residential barriers of race, and indirectly constrained the housing choices of tens of thousands of blacks fearful of harassment and physical injury if they broke through Detroit's residential color line. The violent clashes between whites and blacks that marred the city were political acts, the consequence of perceptions of homeownership, community, gender, and race deeply held by white Detroiters. The result of profound economic insecurities among working- and middle-class whites, they were, above all, desperate acts of neighborhood self-determination, by well-organized community groups, in response to an array of social and economic changes over which they had little control.

Racial incidents encoded possession and difference in urban space. Residents of postwar Detroit carried with them a cognitive map that helped them negotiate the complex urban landscape. In a large, amorphous twentieth-century city like Detroit, there were few visible landmarks to distinguish one neighborhood from another. But residents imposed onto the city's featureless topography all sorts of invisible boundaries—boundaries shaped by intimate association, by institutions (like public-school catchment areas or Catholic parish boundaries), by class, and, most importantly, by race. As the city's racial demography changed in the postwar years and as blacks began to move out of the center city, white neighborhood organizations acted to define and defend the invisible boundaries that divided the city. Their actions were, in large part, an attempt to mark their territory symbolically and visibly, to stake out turf and remind outsiders that to violate those borders was to risk grave danger.[28]

The sustained violence in Detroit's neighborhoods was the consummate act in a process of identity formation. White Detroiters invented communities of race in the city that they defined spatially. Race in the postwar city was not just a cultural construction. Instead, whiteness, and by implication blackness, assumed a material dimension, imposed onto the geography of the city. Through the drawing of racial boundaries and through the use of systematic violence to maintain those boundaries, whites reinforced their own fragile racial identity. Ultimately, they were unsuccessful in preventing the movement of blacks into many Detroit neighborhoods, but their defensive measures succeeded in deepening the divide between two Detroits, one black and one white. On one side of the ever-shifting, contested color line were insecure white workers who expressed their racial sentiments politically and depended on the most extreme among them to patrol racial borders. On the other side of the line were blacks, initially optimistic about the prospects of residential integration, but increasingly unwilling to venture into territory they justifiably considered hostile.

. . .

Territoriality

For those white Detroiters unwilling or unable to flee, black movement into their neighborhoods was the moral equivalent of war. As the racial demography of Detroit changed, neighborhood groups demarcated racial boundaries with great precision, and, abetted by federal agencies and private real estate agents, divided cities into strictly enforced racial territories. In the postwar years, white urban dwellers fiercely defended their turf. They referred to the black migration in military terms: they spoke of "invasions" and "penetration," and plotted strategies of "resistance." White neighborhoods became "battlegrounds" where residents struggled to preserve segregated housing. Homeowners' associations helped whites to "defend" their homes and "protect" their property.[29]

In defended neighborhoods, white organizations served as gatekeepers by diplomacy and by force. Their goal was nothing short of the containment of Detroit's black population, a domestic Cold War to keep the forces of social disorder, represented by blacks, at bay.[30] White community organizations served the double function of social club and neighborhood militia. On the Lower West Side, homeowners formed the "Property Owners Association" in 1945 to combat the expansion of the black West Side into their neighborhood with "every means at our command."[31] "United Communities are Impregnable," noted founders of the National Association of Community Councils, a grandiosely named "protective, vigilant, American organization" on the West Side.[32]

Most neighborhood improvement associations that battled black newcomers assumed a paramilitary model of organization. The Courville District Association divided the neighborhood into "danger spots," that were "in the process of disintegration by an influx of colored families in the past year." Each section had "captains" and "supervisors" who would lead residents to "retard and diminish this influx, and prevent our white families from exodus."[33] Residents of the De Witt–Clinton area adapted the civil defense system from World War II to their new racial battleground. They formed as "Unit Number 2" of the Greater Detroit Neighbors Association (later renamed the De Witt–Clinton Civic Association) in 1949, a full seven years before the first black family attempted to move into the area. "Block wardens" were responsible for the defense of every street in the area. Residents of other Wyoming Corridor neighborhoods invited De Witt–Clinton officials to help them organize in 1955, 1956, and 1957. They formed a tightly knit network of neighborhood groups that covered every subdivision along the West Side's racial frontier and that shared leadership and passed on information about black movements in the area.[34]

One of the most important roles of improvement associations was to mark the city's racial borders. Frequently, groups used signs to make visible the invisible boundaries of race. In November 1945, for example, white residents of a neighborhood that was beginning to attract blacks to its low-rent apartments posted a sign on a building: "Negroes moving here will be burned, Signed Neighbors."[35] Residents of a West Side street posted "Whites Only" and "KKK" on a house sold to a black family.[36] Blacks seeking homes on American Street in Saint Luke's parish could not miss two large signs at each end of the block that boldly proclaimed "ALL WHITE."[37] Protesters in front of a new house built for an African American in the "white section" of the Seven Mile–Fenelon area carried signs reading, "If you're black, you'd better go back to Africa where you belong."[38] Signs often greeted the first black families who crossed invisible racial lines, warning them of their proper place in the city. The first black family to cross into the Northeast Side neighborhood surrounding Saint Bartholomew's parish in 1963, for example, was greeted with a sign that read "Get back on the other side of 7 Mile."[39] And countless variations on the theme "No Niggers Wanted" (posted on a West Side house in 1957) appeared throughout the city. Signs sometimes conveyed a more subtle message. Some whites in neighborhoods threatened by racial change attempted to stake their turf and deter "blockbusting" real estate agents by posting signs declaring "This House is Not for Sale."[40]

Often protesters chose boundaries as the site of demonstrations. In the Seven Mile–Fenelon area, in November 1948, two men burned an effigy at the corner of Nevada and Conley, only a block from the Sojourner Truth site, on the edge of their threatened white neighborhood. Their ominously simple symbolic act made clear to blacks the risks of crossing racial barriers. When private developers announced plans to construct homes in a formerly all-white section of the area to be sold "on a non-restricted basis," Seven Mile–Fenelon residents tore down signs advertising the new homes and vandalized the houses that breached the racial divide.[41] In the Courville area, residents of Nevada and Marx Streets joined a "car parade," for the purpose of "keeping undesirables out." Led by a sound truck, the paraders ritualistically marked the line that they did not want breached.[42]

In the crucible of racial change, white protesters targeted and stigmatized outsiders whom they believed threatened their communities. The consummate outsiders were blockbusting real estate agents, who violated community boundaries and acted as the catalyst of racial "invasions." In 1948, a coalition of homeowners' organizations published a list of brokers who sold homes to blacks and encouraged members to "Get busy on the phone." Even though the pamphlet asked members to "Never threaten or argue," whites in defended neighborhoods regularly called and harassed offending brokers. Especially galling to white groups was the prominence of blacks and Jews in real estate firms conducting business in changing neighborhoods. Both suffered relentless abuse from members of community groups. When Nathan Slobin, a Jewish real estate agent working in the Lower West Side, sold a home on Poplar Street to a black family, unnamed women barraged him with over a hundred phone calls, many with "obscene and menacing language." Area residents carrying anti-Semitic signs picketed his office and his home. Members of the Seven Mile–Fenelon Association threatened Charles Taylor, a black real estate broker who worked with contractors in the area, and warned him that any new homes for blacks constructed north of Stockton Street "will be burned down as fast as you can build them."[43] In the Courville area, white residents made death threats to a real estate agent who sold a house to a black family. On Woodingham, a crowd catcalled James Morris, a black real estate agent showing a house to a black family. In another incident on Woodingham, the police demonstrated their solidarity with protesting whites when they arrested Morris, after he had requested police intervention to quell the hostile mob that had gathered. On nearby Tuller and Cherrylawn Streets, gangs of youths harassed black real estate agents and their clients.[44]

Equally galling to residents of defended communities were white neighbors who listed their homes with known blockbusting real estate agents. Protesters reserved special venom for white "race traitors" who sold their homes to African Americans. Frequently, threats were ominous. Whites hid behind the cloak of anonymity "to intimidate and terrify white people who might sell to Negroes." In one case, Mrs. Florence Gifford, a Lower West Side white woman who offered her house with a black real estate agent, received a hundred phone calls over a ten-day period in early 1948. All the calls came from women, but only three were willing to identify themselves, all members of the neighborhood improvement association. Callers threatened property damage and offered more vague warnings like "It will be too bad if you sell to Negroes." Protesters also followed blockbusting white sellers to their new neighborhoods and tried to poison their relations with their new neighbors. Lower West Side picketers tracked Edward Brock to his new house on Detroit's far West Side, and circulated copies of his business card to his new neighbors along with a handbill that read: "WATCH ED BROCK . . . IS ATTEMPTING TO PUT COLORED IN OUR *WHITE* NEIGHBORHOOD 3420 HARRISON. HE WOULD DO THE SAME TO YOU!!" In 1956, white residents of Ruritan Park followed Mr. and Mrs. Peter Hays to their new suburban Livonia home after they sold their Detroit house to a family suspected to be black. They warned the Hays' Livonia neighbors that the couple was "just the type who would sell a home to Negroes.[45]

Occasionally, community groups sought reprisals in the workplace. In 1955, the president of one neighborhood association gleefully reported that his group "had taken care of the white seller on his job." The owner of the chain store where the seller worked "asked us not to boycott [his] business because of this man." In 1957, protesters on Cherrylawn Street tried a similar tactic, threatening officials at Federals Department Store with a boycott if they did not fire Stella Nowak, a white woman who had sold her house to an African American family. Such threats deterred many whites from being the first on a block to sell to blacks.[46]

Threats were most effective when combined with diplomacy. In well-organized neighborhoods, delegations from improvement associations approached parties involved in the sale of a house to offer them alternatives. Often, community groups offered to purchase the house, usually for a sum greater than the asking price. If they lacked the financial resources, delegations often simply approached buyers and sellers and warned them of the dire consequences of breaching the residential color line. By approaching the offending seller or customer, whites presented a united community front, making clear their determination to preserve the neighborhood's racial homogeneity.[47]

. . .

Black resisters were the exception rather than the norm. White-initiated violence or the threat of it was a powerful deterrent to black pioneers. The effect of white resistance was to create a sieve through which a relatively small number of black Detroiters passed. The Seven Mile–Fenelon Association's activity did not fully preserve the racial status quo in the area, but it severely limited the residential options open to black home buyers, and slowed black residential movement. 26 percent of the population in the area was black in 1940, and only 35 percent was black in 1950. Considering that 250 black families had moved into the Sojourner Truth project, black movement to other parts of the neighborhood was at best incremental. 1960 census data make more clear the dynamics of racial transition in the area. Blacks were confined to the section of the neighborhood sandwiched between Conant Gardens and Sojourner Truth and to certain blocks immediately to the east.[48] Whites maintained the invisible boundary of race along Dequindre Avenue and slowed black movement further west. In 1960, the section of Courville west of Dequindre was only 2.7 percent black.[49] The De Witt–Clinton area also preserved its racial homogeneity for nearly fifteen years. Although the neighborhoods to the east steadily gained black population, from 1949, when they formed an association, to 1963, not a single black family successfully moved into the neighborhood.[50] The one exception to the norm was the Lower West Side. The number of blacks living in the area increased between 1940 and 1950, but relatively slowly. Of the entire area, only 11.2 percent of the population was black in 1950; and over one-third of the black population was concentrated in the one census tract closest to the Tireman–Grand Boulevard area. By 1960, however, all but one of the tracts in the former turf covered by the Property Owners Association had a black population of at least 30 percent, but the western part of the district attracted more blacks and fewer whites.[51]

By preoccupying blacks in block-by-block skirmishes, and hastily retreating when blacks finally "broke a block," residents of defended neighborhoods offered a small safety valve to residents of the overcrowded inner city. The rearguard actions of the defended neighborhoods essentially preserved—indeed strengthened—the principle of racial segregation in housing. They protected the homogeneity of all-white neighborhoods beyond the contested blocks. Over the long run, most of the defended neighborhoods became majority black communities. Whites, as one observer noted, "hold 'til the dam bursts, then run like hell." Those whites who remained were, with a few exceptions, older people who could not afford to move.[52]

Detroit was not alone in its pattern of racial violence. Urban whites responded to the influx of millions of black migrants to their cities in the 1940s, 1950s, and 1960s by redefining urban geography and urban politics in starkly racial terms. In Chicago and Cicero, Illinois, working-class whites rioted in the 1940s and 1950s to oppose the construction of public housing in their neighborhoods. White Chicagoans fashioned a brand of Democratic party politics, especially under mayors Martin Kennelly and Richard Daley, that had a sharp racial edge. In Newark, New Jersey, in the 1950s, blue-collar Italian and Polish Americans harassed African American newcomers to their neighborhoods. And in the postwar period, white Philadelphians and Cincinnatians attacked blacks who moved into previously all-white enclaves, and resisted efforts to integrate the housing market.[53] Countless whites retreated to suburbs or neighborhoods on the periphery of cities where they prevented black movement into their communities with federally sanctioned redlining practices, real estate steering, and restrictive zoning laws.[54]

Racial violence had far-reaching effects in the city. It hardened definitions of white and black identities, objectifying them by plotting them on the map of the city. The combination of neighborhood violence, real estate practices, covenants, and the operations of the housing market sharply circumscribed the housing opportunities available to Detroit's African American population. Persistent housing segregation stigmatized blacks, reinforced unequal race relations, and perpetuated racial divisions.

A visitor walking or driving through Detroit in the 1960s—like his or her counterpart in the 1940s—would have passed through two Detroits, one black and one white. Writing in 1963, sociologists Albert J. Mayer and Thomas Hoult noted that blacks in Detroit "live in essentially the same places that their predecessors lived during the 1930s—the only difference is that due to increasing numbers, they occupy more space centered around their traditional quarters."[55] Segregation in housing constrained black housing choices enormously. Whole sections of the city and the vast majority of the suburbs were entirely off limits to blacks. Racial discrimination and the housing market confined blacks to some of Detroit's oldest and worst housing stock, mainly that of the center-city area, and several enclaves on the periphery of the city.[56] Through sustained violence, Detroit whites engaged in battle over turf, a battle that had economic and social as well as political and ideological consequences.

But more than that, it added to Detroit blacks' already deep distrust of whites and white institutions. Speaking to an open housing conference in 1963, the Reverend Charles W. Butler, a prominent African American minister and civil rights advocate, reminded his audience of the anger that seethed among Detroit's blacks. "The desire and ability to move without the right to move," he argued, "is refined slavery." Butler summed up his remarks with a warning that racial segregation "spawned and cultivated the spirit of rebellion. . . . This rebellion is evident in many forms, from nonviolent resistance to vandalism. This rebellion is proof positive that the Negro has grown weary of being the eternal afterthought of America." Racial violence left blacks in neighborhoods increasingly bereft of capital, distant from workplaces, and marginalized politically. In a city deeply divided by racial violence, it was only a matter of time before blacks retaliated. The results of housing segregation, in combination with persistent workplace discrimination and deindustrialization, were explosive.[57]

Notes

1. Joseph Coles, a prominent Democratic activist and an appointee to the Detroit Mayor's Interracial Committee (MIC), stated that 155 homeowners' associations existed in Detroit during the Cobo administration. Joseph Coles, Oral History, 15. Blacks in the Labor Movement Collection, ALUA. Coles slightly underestimated the number of associations. At least 171 organizations existed during the Cobo administration and at least 191 organizations thrived in Detroit from the end of World War II to 1965. This figure undoubtedly understates the number of such associations, for many were ephemeral and kept no records. The most important source is: "Improvement Associations of Detroit, List From Zoning Board of Appeals," July 12, 1955, DUL, Box 43, Folder A7–13, which includes names and addresses of 88 improvement associations. Through a detailed survey of letters and petitions on matters of housing and expressway construction sent to Mayor Albert Cobo, and especially through careful examination of letters in Cobo's separate files of correspondence from "civic associations," I was able to identify another 83 neighborhood groups not included in the 1955 list. See Mayor's Papers (1950) Boxes 2, 3, 5; (1951) Boxes 2, 3; (1953) Box 1, 3, 4; (1954) Box 2; (1955) Boxes 2, 4. The remaining associations were identified in a number of sources: a list of property owners' associations that joined the amicus curiae brief for the plaintiff in *Sipes v. McGhee* before the Michigan Supreme Court in Clement Vose. *Caucasians Only: The Supreme Court, the NAACP, and the Restrictive Covenant Cases* (Berkeley: University of California Press, 1959), 272, n. 41; Richard J. Peck, Community Services Department, Detroit Urban League, "Summary of Known Improvement Association Activities in Past Two Years 1955–1957," 6, in VF, Pre-1960, Folder: Community Organization 1950s; *Michigan Chronicle,* December 4, 1948, August 6, 1955, September 9, 1961; *Detroit News,* July 21, 1962; *Brightmoor Journal,* May 3, 1956, October 29, 1964, June 2, 1966, October 19, 1967, November 16, 1967; letters and brochures in SLAA; MIC, Incident Reports 1949, CCR, Part I, Series 1, Box 6, Folder 49–37; "A Study of Interracial Housing Incidents," January 20, 1949, ibid., Folder 49–3; CCR, Field Reports December 18, 1961, in RK, Box 2, Folder 4.

2. In 1955, housing activist Charles Abrams noted the importance of improvement associations in major cities and the dearth of studies of their activities. See Charles Abrams, *Forbidden Neighbors: A Study of Prejudice in Housing* (New York: Harper, 1955), 181–90. Abrams's call for research has remained largely unheeded, with the important exception of the brilliant discussion of Los Angeles' powerful grassroots homeowners' association movement in Mike Davis, *City of Quartz: Excavating the Future in Los Angeles* (London: Verso, 1990), 153–219.

3. Quotes from *Action!* the Newsletter of the Courville District Improvement Association, vol. 1 (February 15, 1948), attached to Mayor's Interracial Committee Minutes, April 4, 1948, CCR, Part I, Series 1, Box 10; *The Civic Voice,* the newsletter of the Plymouth Manor Property Owners Association, vol. 2, no. 9 (September 1962), in CCR, Part III, Box 25, Folder 25–128. For examples of ethnic diversity in Detroit, letters to Mayor Edward Jeffries, regarding the Algonquin Street and Oakwood defense housing projects, in Mayor's Papers (1945), Box 3, Folder: Housing Commission. See also Exhibit A, October 22, 1945, 1–2, attached to Memorandum to Charles S. Johnson et al. from Charles H. Houston, NAACP, Group II, Box B133, Folder: Michigan: *Swanson v. Hayden: Neighborhood Informer,* Greater Detroit Neighbors Association—Unit No. 2 (December 1949), 2, UAW-CAP, Box 4, Folder 4–19. The editor of the *Informer,* it should be mentioned, was a James Sugrue, a first cousin once removed of the author. For derogatory references to Jews, see "Demonstrations Protesting Negro Occupancy of Homes, September 1, 1945–September 1, 1946: Memorandum J," 31, CCR, Part I, Series 1, Box 3; and

"Activities of the East Outer Drive Improvement Association," February 8, 1947, ibid., Part III, Box 25, Folder 25–49. For a reference to "niggers, chinamen, and russians," see William K. Anderson to Herbert Schultz, October 17, 1958, SLAA. For housing incidents involving an Indian family, a Chinese family, and a Filipino family moving into white neighborhoods, see Chronological Index of Cases, 1951 (51–31) and (51–58), CCR, Part I, Series 1, Box 13; Detroit Police Department Special Investigation Bureau, Summary of Racial Activities, April 30, 1956–May 17, 1956, DUL, Box 38, Folder A2–26. On the ethnic heterogeneity of Detroit neighborhoods, see Olivier Zunz, *The Changing Face of Inequality: Urbanization, Industrial Development and Immigrants in Detroit, 1880–1920* (Chicago, 1982), 340–51. In his examination of arrest records for whites arrested in anti-public housing riots in Chicago, Arnold Hirsch also found great diversity in ethnic affiliations. See Hirsch, *Making the Second Ghetto: Race and Housing in Chicago, 1940–1960* (New York: Cambridge University Press, 1983), 81–84.

4. See Dominic J. Capeci, Jr. and Martha Wilkerson, *Layered Violence: The Detroit Rioters of 1943* (Jackson: The University Press of Mississippi, 1991); on Briggs, see John M. Hartigan, Jr., "Cultural Constructions of Whiteness: Racial and Class Formations in Detroit" (Ph.D. diss., University of California, Santa Cruz, 1995); Arthur Kornhauser, *Detroit as the People See It: A Survey of Attitudes in an Industrial City* (Detroit: Wayne University Press, 1952), 104. On Southern whites and their organizational affiliations, see Cleo Y. Boyd, "Detroit's Southern Whites and the Store-Front Churches," Department of Research and Church Planning, Detroit Council of Churches, 1958, in DUL, Box 44, Folder A8–25; on their voting patterns, see Handwritten Vote Counts [1949], UAW-PAC, Box 63, Folder 63–2; "Degree of Voting in Detroit Primary," September 11, 1951, and "Indexes of Group Voting for Selected Councilmanic Candidates," September 11, 1951, ibid., Box 62, Folder 62–25. In 1956, Mrs. Cledah Sundwall, a Northwest Side resident and possibly a southern white migrant, called for the creation of a White Citizens Council in Detroit, calling it a "modern version of the old-time town meeting called to meet any crisis by expressing the will of the people. The primary aim of the council is to combat the NAACP and to preserve the upkeep of neighborhoods" (*Brightmoor Journal*, May 3, 1956). There is no evidence that the organization attracted any significant number of adherents in the city, perhaps because of the strength and ubiquity of improvement associations.

5. The South Lakewood Area Association had its humble origins in a protest against a proposal to expand off-street parking for stores on Jefferson Avenue: *East Side Shopper,* April 28, 1955. The SLAA papers offer evidence of the role of the homeowners' association in matters of zoning, traffic control, and parking. The South Lakewood area, on the Southeast Side of the city, was far enough removed from Detroit's black population that race seldom became an issue for the organization. The neighborhood association was concerned about what appeared to be a boarding house at 670 Lakewood, and noted "One colored" among the many boys who played in front of the house. ("Report—July 14, 1958," SLAA, Folder: 1957–1960). For a group concerned with city services, zoning enforcement, and streets and traffic, as well as racial transition, see Interoffice Correspondence, Subject: Meeting of the Burns Civic Association, April 1, 1963, CCR, Part III, Box 25, Folder 25–40. For concern about recreation, garbage pickup, and city services, see "Report on Puritan Park Civic Association Meeting," September 20, 1956, ibid., Folder 25–101. On the role of neighborhood associations in zoning enforcement, planning, and cleanups, see Detroit City Plan Commission, *Planner,* January 1945, 3–4, in the author's possession. Robert J. Mowitz and Deil S. Wright, *Profile of a Metropolis: A Case Book* (Detroit: Wayne State University Press, 1962), 426–29, describe the role of Northwest Side civic associations in battling the construction of the Lodge Freeway extension. For an excellent discussion of civic associations in Queens, New York (which, because of its distance from black populations, did not organize around racial issues in the 1950s), see

Sylvie Murray, "Suburban Citizens: Domesticity and Community Politics in Queens, New York, 1945–1960" (Ph.D. diss., Yale University, 1994), esp. 78–131, 181–261.

For an example of the combination of civic uplift and racist rhetoric, see *Action!* vol. 1 (February 15, 1948). The Northwest Home Owners, Inc., met to discuss threats to the community including a city incinerator and "possible Negro residence in the neighborhood." Richard J. Peck, Community Services Department, Detroit Urban League, "Summary of Known Improvement Association Activities in Past Two Years 1955–1957," 6, VF, Pre-1960, Box 2, Folder: Community Organization 1950s. For a discussion of the role that improvement associations played in upholding restrictive covenants, see Herman H. Long and Charles S. Johnson, *People vs. Property: Race Restrictive Covenants in Housing* (Nashville, Tenn.: Fisk University Press, 1947), 39–55; for examples of similar associations in Chicago, Baltimore, Washington, D.C., Los Angeles, Houston, Miami, and San Francisco, see Abrams, *Forbidden Neighbors,* 181–90.

6. U.S. Department of Commerce, Bureau of the Census, *U.S. Census of Population and Housing, 1940, Census Tracts Statistics for Detroit, Michigan and Adjacent Area* (Washington, D.C.: U.S. Government Printing Office, 1942), Table 4; U.S. Department of Commerce, Bureau of the Census, *U.S. Census of Population and Housing: 1960, Census Tracts, Detroit, Michigan Standard Metropolitan Statistical Area* (Washington, D.C.: U.S. Government Printing Office, 1962), Table H-1.

7. Kornhauser, *Detroit as the People See It,* 68–69, 75, 77–82. Kornhauser's team interviewed 593 adult men and women randomly selected from all sections of the city. For an elaborate discussion of the survey's methodology, see ibid., Appendix B, pp. 189–96.

8. Kenneth T. Jackson, *Crabgrass Frontier: The Suburbanization of the United States* (New York: Oxford University Press, 1985), 49–52, 117–18; on the desire of immigrants to own their own homes, see John Bodnar, Roger Simon, and Michael P. Weber, *Lives of Their Own: Blacks, Italians, and Poles in Pittsburgh, 1900–1960* (Urbana: University of Illinois Press, 1982), 153–83; a succinct synthesis of literature on homeownership and mobility can be found in Eric H. Monkkonen, *America Becomes Urban: The Development of U.S. Cities and Towns* (Berkeley: University of California Press, 1989), 182–205. On high rates of homeownership among ethnic Detroiters, see Zunz, *The Changing Face of Inequality,* 152–61.

9. The National Council of Churches conducted a census of church membership by county in the mid-1950s. It estimated that 65.9 percent of residents of Wayne County, Michigan, were Roman Catholics. Because so few African Americans were Catholic, the percentage of Wayne County whites who were Catholic was probably significantly higher. See National Council of Churches, Bureau of Research and Survey, "Churches and Church Membership in the United States: An Enumeration and Analysis by Counties, States, and Regions," series C, no. 17 (1957), Table 46; Paul Wrobel, "Becoming a Polish-American: A Personal Point of View," in *Immigrants and Migrants: The Detroit Ethnic Experience: Ethnic Studies Reader,* ed. David W. Hartman (Detroit: New University Thought Publishing Company, 1974), 187. "Survey of Racial and Religious Conflict Forces," Interviews with Father Constantine Djuik, Bishop Stephen Wozniak, Father Edward Hickey, in CRC, Box 70; Dominic J. Capeci, Jr., *Race Relations in Wartime Detroit: The Sojourner Truth Housing Controversy of 1942* (Philadelphia: Temple University Press, 1984), 77–78, 89–90; Memorandum Dictated by Major Jack Tierney, October 17, 1945, in NAACP, Group II, Box A505, Folder: Racial Tension, Detroit, Mich., 1944–46; Edward J. Hickey to Edward Connor, May 9, 1944, CHPC, Box 41. In April 1948, the pastors of Saint Louis the King Catholic Church and Saint Bartholomew's Catholic Church reportedly urged parishioners to attend City Council meetings to opposed the construction of houses for blacks on a Northeast Side site: See CCR, Part I, Series 1, Box 4, Folder 48–80. Quote on Polish parishes from Mayor's Interracial Committee Minutes, February 19, 1947, 3, ibid., Box 10. On Saints Andrew and Benedict Parish, see Mayor's Interracial Committee Minutes, April

17, 1950, ibid., Part III, Box 25, Folder 25–114. John T. McGreevy, "American Catholics and the African-American Migration, 1919–1970" (Ph.D. diss., Stanford University, 1992) 56–58, 119–20, 159–160; also on the importance of Catholicism in Detroit, see Gerhard Lenski, *The Religious Factor: A Sociological Study of Religion's Impact on Politics, Economics, and Family Life* (Garden City, N.Y.: Doubleday, 1961).

10. See Report on Meeting, Temple Baptist Church, October 25, 1956, and States-Lawn Civic Association, February 14, 1957, DUL, Box 43, Folder A7–13; Metropolitan Tabernacle pamphlets, MDCC, Part I, Box 9, Folder: Civil Rights Activity Feedback and Box 10, Folder: Housing—Homeowners' Ordinance, Friendly; Jim Wallis, "By Accident of Birth: Growing Up White in Detroit," *Sojourners,* June–July 1983, 12–16.

11. Poster, "OPEN MEETING . . . for Owners and Tenants," n.d. [c. 1945], CRC, Box 66, Folder: Property Owners Association; *Action!,* vol. 1 (Feb. 15, 1948), 2; Guyton Home Owners' Association and Connor-East Home Owners Association, leaflets, in SLAA, Folder: 1957–1960; Peck, "Summary of Known Improvement Association Activity;" *Southwest Detroiter,* May 11, 1950, copy in Mayor's Papers (1950), Box 5, Folder: Housing Commission.

12. Kornhauser, *Detroit as the People See It,* 62; "Integration Statement," anonymous letter, n.d., in MDCC, Part I, Box 9. For another example of economically vulnerable workers' insecurity about homeownership, see Bill Collett, "Open Letter to Henry Ford II," *Ford Facts,* September 15, 1951.

13. Kornhauser, *Detroit as the People See It,* 95; quotations from Kornhauser's analysis of survey response patterns.

14. The term "colored problem" was used most frequently by whites to describe black movement into their neighborhoods. See, for example, Property Owners Association flyer, 1945, in CRC, Box 66; *Action!,* vol. 1 (Feb. 15, 1948).

15. Kornhauser, *Detroit as the People See It,* 85, 185.

16. Ibid., 100. It should be recalled that there was already virtually complete residential segregation in Detroit when Kornhauser conducted his survey. In 1950, the index of dissimilarity between blacks and whites (a measure of segregation calculated on the percentage of whites who would have to move to achieve complete racial integration) was 88.8; the index of dissimilarity in 1940 had been 89.9. Respondents to the survey then supported even stricter racial segregation than already existed. Figures from Karl E. Taeuber and Alma F. Taeuber, *Negroes in Cities: Residential Segregation and Neighborhood Change* (Chicago: Aldine, 1965), 39.

17. Kornhauser, *Detroit as the People See It,* 87, 90, 91. For findings on the racial conservatism of Detroit Catholics that confirm Kornhauser's data, see Lenski, *The Religious Factor,* 65. On the importance of Catholic parish boundaries in preserving the racial homogeneity of a neighborhood and in shaping Catholic attitudes toward blacks, see McCreevy, "American Catholics and African-American Migration" and Gerald Gamm, "Neighborhood Roots: Institutions and Neighborhood Change in Boston 1870–1994," (Ph.D. diss., Harvard University, 1994).

18. Detroit Housing Commission and Work Projects Administration, *Real Property Survey of Detroit, Michigan,* vol. 3 (Detroit: Bureau of Government Research, 1939), maps and data for Area K. As Northwest Side resident Alan MacNichol complained: "I have watched the area within the Boulevard deteriorate into slums as the character of the neighborhood changed, restrictions were broken, and multiple flats came in," *Brightmoor Journal,* December 22, 1949.

19. Outer–Van Dyke Home Owners' Association, "Dear Neighbor," [1948], CCR, Part III, Box 25, Folder 25–94; Interview with Six Mile Road—Riopelle area neighbors in Incident Report, August 30, 1954, DUL, Box 43, Folder A7–13; William Price, "Factors Which Mili-

tate against the Stabilization of Neighborhoods," July 3, 1956, ibid., Box 38, Folder A2–17; woman quoted in Lenski, *The Religious Factor,* 66.

20. Longview Home Owners Association poster, n.d., MDCC, Part I, Box 10, Folder: Housing—Homeowners Ordinance—Friendly. Ellipsis in original.

21. For statistics on crime in Detroit, see Robert Conot, *American Odyssey* (New York: William Morrow, 1974), Statistical Appendix.

22. Alex Csanyi and family to Mayor Jeffries, February 20, 1945, Mayor's Papers (1945), Box 3, Folder: Housing Commission 1945. Ellipsis in original. *Home Gazette,* October 25, 1945: copy in CAH; Gloster Current, "The Detroit Elections: A Problem in Reconversion," *Crisis* 52 (November 1945): 319–21; "Program: General Meeting Courville District Improvement Association," April 2, 1948, CCR, Part III, Box 26, Folder 26–4; *Action!* vol. 1 (February 15, 1948); "Report on Formation of Area B Improvement Association," DUL, Box 38, Folder A2–22; Detroit Urban League Housing Committee, Quarterly Report, April–June 1966, ibid., Box 53, Folder A17–1. For other examples of fears of racial mixing, see John Bublevsky, Tom Gates, Lola Gibson, Victor Harbay, and Sally Stretch, "A Spatial Study of Racial Tension or 'The Walls Come Tumbling Down,' " CCR, Part III, Box 13, Folder 13–20; "Report on the Improvement Association Meeting at Vernor School," September 13, 1955, DUL, Box 43, Folder A7–13; Kornhauser, *Detroit as the People See It,* 28, 37, 101–2.

23. The original essays and a complete typescript are in "Compositions—6B Grade—Van Dyke School," CCR, Part I, Series 1, Box 3, Folder: Community Reports—Supplementing. Accompanying the essays cited were drawings and responses to another assignment, intended to foster racial harmony, on "Why Little Brown Ko-Ko is My Friend," based on a short story about a black child. The name Mary Conk is a pseudonym.

24. All quotes and details regarding the Easby Wilson case are drawn from the following sources (unless otherwise noted): "Summary of Facts of Case Involving Mr. Easby Wilson," UAW Press Release, July 25, 1955; and "Interview: Housing Discrimination" (Mrs. Easby Wilson and Harry Ross), all in UAW-FP, Box 14, Folder 14–8; *Pittsburgh Courier,* June 18, 1955; *Michigan Chronicle,* July 30, 1955; report on racial incident, in DUL, Box 43, Folder A7–13.

25. See, for example, George Schermer, "Re: Case 52–16, Petition—Courville Improvement Association Members," July 25, 1952, 1, CCR, Part I, Series 1, Box 9, Folder 52–16CP. When a white neighbor on the same section of Riopelle Street had offered his house for sale in the fall of 1953, a crowd of five hundred had gathered on the street to protest. See Incident Report, 18176 Riopelle, October 31, 1953, ibid., Folder 53–38; *Pittsburgh Courier,* October 31, 1953; Incident Report, November 7, 1954, DUL, Box 43, Folder A7–13.

26. U.S. Department of Commerce, Bureau of the Census, *U.S. Census of Population and Housing: 1960, Census Tracts, Detroit, Michigan Standard Metropolitan Statistical Area,* Final Report PHC(1)–40 (Washington: U.S. Government Printing Office, 1962) (hereafter cited as *1960 Census*), data for tract 606.

27. "A lot of firefighting": John G. Feild, oral history, December 28, 1967 (Katherine Shannon, interviewer), 11, Civil Rights Documentation Project, MSRC. The finding guide and interview transcript mistakenly spell Feild as Fields. John Feild, "A Study of Interracial Housing Incidents," January 20, 1949, 4, CCR, Part I, Series 1, Box 6, Folder 49–3, identified five "techniques employed" by improvement associations in the 1940s: warnings, street demonstrations, anonymous threats, picketing, and property damage. I have calculated the number of racial incidents through a comprehensive survey of records in CCR, DNAACP, DUL, and Detroit's African American newspapers, *Michigan Chronicle, Detroit Tribune,* and *Pittsburgh Courier* (Detroit edition). The number of reported incidents ranged

from seven in 1953 to sixty-five in 1963. Unfortunately the Commission on Community Relations only kept complete data for a limited number of years.

28. An important discussion of territoriality is Gerald D. Suttles, *The Social Construction of Communities* (Chicago: University of Chicago Press, 1972). Suttles's discussion of defended neighborhoods is rich in its theoretical implications for studies of neighborhood change. But by building on the ecological model of Chicago School sociology, Suttles offers too deterministic a model of "invasion" and "succession," ignoring the political and economic determinants of urban transformation. An important revision that has strongly influenced my own work is Gerald Gamm, "City Walls: Neighborhoods, Suburbs, and the American City" (paper presented to the American Political Science Association, New York, September 1994).

29. *Brightmoor Journal,* October 11, 1945; *Neighborhood Informer,* December 1949, 1, 3, copy in UAW-CAP, Box 4, Folder 4–19; Handbill, "Emergency Meeting, March 11, 1950," CCR, Part III, Box 25, Folder 25–107; Ruritan Park Civic Association, "Dear Neighbor," ibid., Folder 25–101.

30. Detroit race relations official Richard Marks used the term "containment" (to describe white resistance to housing integration) in his testimony in the school desegregation case, *Milliken v. Bradley.* See Dimond, *Beyond Busing,* 43–44. For a development of the notion of "domestic containment" (though not applied to race), see Elaine Tyler May, "Cold War, Warm Hearth: Politics and the Family in Postwar America," in *The Rise and Fall of the New Deal Order, 1930–1980,* ed. Steve Fraser and Gary Gerstle (Princeton, N.J.: Princeton University Press, 1988), 153–81.

31. "Demonstrations, 1945–1946," 4.

32. National Association of Community Councils, "To Make a Long Story Short," CCR, Part III, Box 20, Folder 20–37.

33. *Action! The Newsletter of the Courville District Improvement Association,* vol. 1, February 15, 1948, 5–6, CCR, Part I, Series 1, Box 10.; *Michigan Chronicle,* March 6, 1948.

34. *Neighborhood Informer,* December 1949, March 1951, copies in UAW-CAP, Box 4, Folder 4–19; *Brightmoor Journal,* February 10, 1955, March 24, 1955; Richard J. Peck, "Summary of Known Improvement Association Activities in Past Two Years, 1955–1957," 1–2, VF—Pre-1960, Box 2, Folder: Community Organization 1950s; "Report on Ruritan Park Civic Association Meeting," 3, September 20, 1956, DUL, Box 43, Folder A7–13; Richard J. Peck, "Report on Formation of Area E Improvement Association," 9, ibid., Box 38, Folder A2–22; "Activities Report, February 1–March 1, 1957, Current Status of Property, Cherrylawn Case," 4, ibid., Folder A2–23.

35. Detroit Police Department, Special Investigation Squad, Memo from Detective Sergeant Leo Mack and Detective Bert Berry to Commanding Officer, Special Investigation Squad, November 7, 1945, CCR, Part I, Series 1, Box 3, Folder: Incidents Housing 1945.

36. *Michigan Chronicle,* November 6, 1948.

37. Memo, n.d. [c. 1955], DUL, Box 43, Folder A7–13.

38. John Feild, "Special Report, Subject: Opposition to Negro Occupancy in Northeast Detroit," April 28, 1950, 3–4, CCR, Part I, Series 1, Box 7, Folder 50–18.

39. Commission on Community Relations, Field Division, Case Reports, January 21, 1963, CCR, Part I, Series 4, Box 4; see also Memo, Classification: Housing, September 27, 1954, DUL, Box 38, Folder A2–13.

40. *Southwest Detroiter,* May 11, 1950, copy in Mayor's Papers (1950), Box 5, Folder: Housing Commission (2); *Michigan Chronicle,* July 16, 1955; Commission on Community Relations, Minutes, June 17, 1957, CCR, Part I, Series 4, Box 2; Commission on Community Relations, Field Division Report, February 20, 1961, ibid., Box 3; McGreevy, "American Catholics and the African American Migration," 122.

41. See "Chronological Summary of Incidents in the Seven Mile-Fenelon Area," attached to John Feild, "A Study of Interracial Housing Incidents," January 20, 1949, CCR, Part I, Series 1, Box 6, Folder 49–3, ALUA.

42. Commission on Community Relations, Minutes, September 21, 1959, ibid., Part I, Series 4, Box 3. Nevada marked the boundary of Saint Rita's parish. See Saint Rita's Parish Boundary File, AAD.

43. *Michigan Chronicle,* December 4, 1948; "Demonstrations, 1945–1946": Memorandum J, 31. John Feild, "Special Report, Subject: Opposition to Negro Occupancy in Northeast Detroit," April 28, 1950, 3–4, CCR, Part I, Series 1, Box 7, Folder 50–18.

44. Thomas H. Kleene, "Report of Incident, Subject: Opposition to Negro Occupancy of Dwelling at 4227 Seventeenth Street (Continued)," ibid., Box 5, Folder 48–124H. On Courville, see Incident Report, November 7, 1954, DUL, Box 43, Folder A7–13. James Morris, the real estate broker who had originally called the police to the scene on Woodingham Street, was charged with driving with an expired license. The police, who did nothing to disperse the crowd, responded with remarkable efficiency to a neighbor's complaint that Morris's car was obstructing a driveway, the offense that gave occasion to ask Morris for his license. Another black realtist, John Humphrey, testified in the Detroit school desegregation case *Milliken v. Bradley* that he had suffered harassment by the police when he showed houses in predominantly white neighborhoods. See Dimond, *Beyond Busing,* 50–51. CCR Field Division, Case Reports, September 18, 1961, in RK, Box 2, Folder 4; on Tuller and Cherrylawn, see CCR Field Division, Case Reports, August 11, 1961, October 23, 1961, ibid. See also *East Side Shopper* clipping, n.d. [September 1952], in CCR, Part I, Series 1, Box 9, Folder 52–30; *Michigan Chronicle,* December 4, 1948; "9423 Meyers," Case Reports for Period August 27–September 23, 1957, CCR, Part I, Series 4, Box 2.

45. John Feild and Joseph Coles, "Report of Incident, Subject: Protest to Negro Occupancy at 3414 and 3420 Harrison Street, August 23, 1948," in CCR, Part I, Series 1, Box 5, Folder 48–124; included in the file are Brock's card and the attached notice; see also "Buyer Beware," *Time,* April 16, 1956, 24.

46. Richard J. Peck, "Summary of Known Improvement Association Activity in Past Two Years 1955–1957," 3, in VF—Pre-1960, Box 2, Folder: Community Organization 1950s; see also Report of Second Meeting of Ruritan Park Civic Association, Fitzgerald School, November 29, 1956, DUL, Box 43, Folder A7–13; Commission on Community Relations Minutes, February 18, 1957, CCR, Part I, Series 4, Box 2.

47. Successful purchases include Yorkshire and Evanston (1948), ibid., Series 1, Box 5, Folder 48–120; 7745 Chalfonte and Tracy and Chippewa in 1955, DUL, Box 38, File A2–15; 15550 Robson, *Detroit Free Press,* May 7, 1956; Richard J. Peck, "Summary of Known Improvement Association Activities in the Past Two Years, 1955–1957," pp. 1, 4, in VF—Pre-1960, Box 2, Folder: Community Organization 1950s. Attempts include "Report of Incident: Intimidation of Henry Lyons (Negro) by a White Group at 18680 Caldwell," September 22, 1947, CCR, Part I, Series 1, Box 4, Folder 47–59H; "Protest of Negro Occupancy at 18087 Shields," 1949, ibid., Box 6, Folder 49–33; Detroit Police Department Interoffice Memorandum, Subject: Racial Disturbance at 2966 Greyfriars, August 31, 1953, DSL, Box 20, Folder: Racial—Gang Activities and Complaints (2).

48. 1950 *Census,* tract 603; 1960 *Census,* tracts 603A, 603B.

49. Ibid., data for tracts 604, 605, 606.

50. *Michigan Chronicle,* September 10, 1955; Incident Report, DUL, Box 38, Folder A2–15. *1960 Census,* tract 261; tracts to the east, 170, 171, 172, 173.

51. *1950 Census* and *1960 Census,* tracts 9, 10, 35, 36, 37, 38, 39, 41.

52. *Detroit News,* October 4, 1961.

53. Hirsch, *Making the Second Ghetto,* 40–99.

54. Kenneth T. Jackson, *Crabgrass Frontier: The Suburbanization of the United States* (New York, 1985), esp. 190–218; Patricia Burgess Stach, "Deed Restrictions and Subdivision Development in Columbus Ohio, 1900–1970," *Journal of Urban History* 15 (November 1988): 42–68.

55. Albert Mayer and Thomas F. Hoult, *Race and Residence in Detroit* (Detroit: Urban Research Laboratory, Institute for Urban Studies, Wayne State University, 1962), 2.

56. A superb overview of patterns of racial segregation in Detroit is Donald R. Deskins, Jr., *Residential Mobility of Negroes in Detroit, 1837–1965* (Ann Arbor: Department of Geography, University of Michigan, 1972). For a perceptive discussion of similar patterns nationwide, see Douglas S. Massey and Nancy A. Denton, *American Apartheid: Segregation and the Making of the Underclass* (Cambridge: Harvard University Press, 1993).

57. Reverend Charles W. Butler, "Message to the Open Occupancy Conference," in *A City in Racial Crisis: The Case of Detroit Pre- and Post- the 1967 Riot.* ed. Leonard Gordon (n.p.: William C. Brown Publishers, 1971), 33. For an earlier statement of black suspicion of white homeowners, vandals, and the police, see *Michigan Chronicle,* September 24, 1955.

CHAPTER 5

SUBURBIA AND THE
DIVIDED METROPOLIS

The Politics of Suburban Development

The urban crisis of the twentieth century emerged from two interrelated developments: the migration of blacks and other minorities to the central cities, and the
flight of middle-class families to the suburbs. Suburbanization had started earlier
in the century, but it took on a different character in the years following World
War II because, increasingly, it represented an escape from the cities and their
problems. Rising incomes meant that more families could afford newer and
more spacious housing available in new housing developments outside the
cities. For its part, Congress assisted the trek to suburbia through a bevy of new
programs. The federal government ensured and subsidized affordable mortgages
for buyers of new suburban homes, provided tax benefits to help homeowners
pay their housing bills, and undertook ambitious highway programs—including
the vast interstate network—that enabled faster and easier commutation between home and job. Other federal programs frequently induced businesses to
seek suburban locations for expansion or for new investments. A movement to
the suburbs probably was inevitable, but these powerful forces greatly accelerated the process.

It could be said that the families who were moving to the suburbs were pursuing the American dream. But there was another side, too. The new suburban
residents took measures to keep blacks and the poor from making the same
move. The move to the suburbs was irresistible, but the pattern that emerged—in
which the suburbs became a segregated white middle-class bastion—was not at
all inevitable. In Western Europe suburbanization happened at almost the same
time as it did in America, but hardly any British or continental metropolitan areas are highly segregated. European central cities continued to attract wealthy
residents who often preferred the older neighborhoods while newer suburbs
drew people of all social classes. In America, the development of suburbia has
been strongly shaped by political decisions that created the divide between city
and suburb.

At every stage, suburban development in America involved the construction
of enclaves, where those who were affluent enough could segregate themselves

from the people and problems of the cities and maintain lower taxes, higher property values, and superior amenities. The key to preserving such advantages was local control of the suburban "gates." We have reprinted a selection from Michael N. Danielson's book, *The Politics of Exclusion,* to convey an impression of the political process by which the social segregation of the suburbs was accomplished. In an effort to protect the privileges that residential segregation bestowed on them, suburban residents sought control over the land use regulations that state legislatures commonly delegated to municipalities. Once in place, land-use powers could be used to keep poorer people from moving in by prescribing minimum lot sizes and building regulations and forbidding multiunit dwellings. To gain control of the regulations, the only act necessary was incorporation. According to Danielson, suburban autonomy was the ultimate prize. It enabled people who made it to the suburbs to use public power to close the door to others. The exclusionary policies enforced by suburban jurisdictions helped to create the great divide separating suburbs from central cities, and richer suburbs from poorer ones.

Political decisions have also played a key role in creating some of the problems associated with the suburbs. Suburbs are not occupied only by people; there are also retail malls, business parks, office strips, retail outlets and other uses. The multitudes of political jurisdictions in the suburbs compete vigorously for businesses that might help to reduce taxes for homeowners and help pay the bills for schools and other expensive services. Developers are skilled at playing off one suburb against another. Often it seems like a free-for-all in which new commercial developments, malls, business parks, and other so-called edge nodes or business enclaves pop up helter-skelter in suburban landscapes.

The selection from Dolores Hayden's book, *Building Suburbia,* describes how this style of suburban sprawl is actually planned by political wheeling and dealing among developers, local governments and other promoters of commercial building projects. By taking advantage of subsidies and tax breaks as well as laws interpreted in their favor, such projects are made viable. Hayden describes how this process has often led to fast-paced growth of low-quality and poorly conceived projects on small and large scale, from vast retail malls, hodgepodge commercial strips, big box stores, office parks, to even stand-alone "edge cities" that quickly tend to become obsolete. This commercialization of suburban space often has devastating effects on existing businesses that are threatened by the flight of tenants and shoppers to whatever is new in nearby areas. Hayden concludes that, "For the most part, edge nodes are uncomfortable and ugly places. Building is cheap; depreciation is accelerated; obsolescence is rapid. . . . developers . . . design for rapid turnover." Although most of these enclaves of commerce and industry have few defenders and many critics, the political system of suburbia is poorly equipped to change things. Yet the hand of the public sector helps make this style of development possible.

12

Michael N. Danielson

SUBURBAN AUTONOMY

Suburbia is essentially a political phenomenon. Political independence is the one thing the increasingly diversified settlements beyond the city limits have in common. Local autonomy means that suburban communities seek to control their own destiny largely free from the need to adjust their interests to those of other local jurisdictions and residents of the metropolis. Since local governments in the United States bear the primary responsibility for the provision of basic public services such as education, police and fire protection, as well as the regulation of housing and land use, independence provides suburbs with considerable control over the vital parameters of community life, including the power to exclude unwanted neighbors. In the differentiated and fragmented metropolis, these powers are exercised by suburban governments which are usually responsive to the interests of their relatively homogeneous constituencies. The result, as Robert C. Wood notes, is the division of the metropolitan population into "clusters homogeneous in their skills and outlook which have achieved municipal status and erected social and political barriers against invasion."[1]

With few exceptions, political autonomy affords suburbanites a potential for exclusion which exceeds that usually available to the resident of the central city. Through zoning, building codes, and other planning powers, suburban communities to a far greater degree than city neighborhoods are able to protect the local turf from undesirable housing and residents. Independence also means that the formal consent of local government must be obtained before most state or federal housing programs for the poor can be initiated, a power rarely delegated by city hall to its neighborhoods. In addition, exclusionary policies are more easily pursued in small and relatively cohesive political systems than in large ones with diverse constituency interests. To protect itself from unwanted developments, a city neighborhood must keep an eye on a variety of agencies and possess substantial clout in complex political arenas.

By living in a smaller, more homogeneous, and less complex polity, the resident of an autonomous suburb tends to be insulated from unwanted change. Local actions are far less likely to threaten him with lower-income neighbors or other disturbing developments in a jurisdiction where both fellow citizens and public officials share his frame of reference. As a consequence, political independence reduces the chances that suburban dwellers will face the sorts of issues concerning race, status, property values, and community character that frequently confront blue-collar and middle-class neighborhoods in the central city. When suburbanites cannot avoid such challenges, they are more likely to enlist the support of a local government that is closely tuned to their interests and values than is commonly the case in the large and heterogeneous central city.

Because of these considerations, the use of local powers over land, housing, and urban development to promote local social values and protect community character are widely viewed as the most important functions of local governments in suburbia. Residents of upper- and middle-class suburbs in the Philadelphia area ranked maintenance of their community's social characteristics—defined in terms of keeping out "undesirables" and maintaining the "quality" of residents—as a more important objective for local government than either the provision of public services or maintenance of low tax rates. In suburbs of lower social rank, maintenance of social characteristics was considered more important than the provision of local services and amenities, and almost as important as keeping down local tax rates.[2]

Exclusionary considerations, of course, are neither the sole nor the most important factor underlying the exodus to the suburbs. Most urban Americans have moved outward in search of better housing, nicer surroundings, social status, and separation from the inner city and its inhabitants. Increasingly, however, political separation has come to be an essential element of the appeal of the suburbs. In the words of a local leader in a blue-collar suburb in the Detroit area, "the most important thing to many people in Warren is just the simple fact that it isn't Detroit."[3] Speaking of the blacks who flocked to East Cleveland during the 1960s, the suburb's black city manager notes that "they feel that at least they are not living in the inner city."[4] Regardless of their reasons for

Table 5.1 Attitudes of Residents of 16 Suburbs in the Philadelphia Area Toward the Importance of Various Objectives of Local Government

Attitude	Social Rank Grouping of Municipalities (percent judging objective very important)		
	Upper	Middle	Lower
Keep undesirables out	62.0	79.5	75.0
Maintain "quality" of residents	69.0	47.0	43.0
Maintain improved public services	44.8	41.2	35.7
Provide aesthetic amenities	50.0	38.2	32.1
Acquire business and industry	8.6	23.5	50.0
Keep tax rate down	56.9	79.5	82.0

Source: Oliver P. Williams, *et al., Suburban Differences and Metropolitan Policies: A Philadelphia Story* (Philadelphia: University of Pennsylvania Press, 1965), pp. 217–219.

moving outward, most suburbanites quickly discover the utility of local autonomy as a means of protecting their neighborhood, their social standing, their
property values, and the racial integrity of the local schools from outside
threats. As Daniel J. Elazar notes: "People sought *suburbanization* for essentially
private purposes, revolving around better living conditions. The same people
sought *suburbs* with independent local governments of their own for essentially public ones, namely the ability to maintain these conditions by joining
with like-minded neighbors to preserve those life styles which they sought in
suburbanization."[5] In the process, local autonomy and exclusion have become
closely intertwined. Political independence greatly strengthens the suburban
community's ability to exclude, while the desire to exclude both enhances the
attractions of local autonomy and reinforces the suburban commitment to the
preservation of local control over the vital parameters of community life.

The Scope of Local Autonomy

In its simplest form, suburban autonomy involves a ring of unincorporated
communities lying beyond the city limits, with local governmental services
provided by town or county governments. The largest of these "doughnut"
types of metropolitan political systems is found in the Baltimore area. Baltimore County, whose 610 square miles and 616,000 inhabitants surround the
city of Baltimore and its 895,000 residents, has no incorporated municipalities
or elected local officials except for a county executive and a seven-member
council.[6] While approximately half of all suburbanites in the United States live
in unincorporated areas, arrangements typically are more complex than those
in Baltimore County. Rarely does the entire suburban portion of a metropolitan
area consist of unincorporated territory. Instead, municipalities are usually
scattered amidst the unincorporated neighborhoods. Public services for unincorporated areas tend to be provided by a melange of authorities, school districts, county governments, and state agencies. Regulatory and planning activities affecting land use and housing normally are the responsibility of county
governments in unincorporated areas.

Greater control over land, housing, and other key local functions is exercised by suburban communities which have incorporated as municipalities under state law. Municipal governments have more extensive authority than local
governments in unincorporated areas to tax, to borrow, to provide services,
and to regulate urban development. Another attraction of incorporation is the
protection it provides a suburb against absorption into other local jurisdictions.
In most states, incorporation guarantees the political independence of a community, since territory in a municipality cannot be annexed by another local
government. On the other hand, incorporation usually means more extensive
and expensive local services. As a result, many suburbanites prefer unincorporated status, particularly when essential public services are available from
other public agencies and when state law protects unincorporated areas from
the territorial ambitions of adjacent municipalities.

Incorporation also provides suburbanites with a local government more responsive to community desires than is the case with unincorporated areas. Responsiveness results primarily from size and spatial differentiation. Most suburban municipalities are quite small. In 1967, two-thirds of all incorporated local jurisdictions in metropolitan areas had fewer than 5,000 inhabitants. And half of all suburban municipalities encompassed less than a square mile of land area.[7] Superimposing these small governmental units on the spatially differentiated population of the metropolis commonly results in relatively homogeneous local constituencies. Within these jurisdictions, local government tends to be highly responsive to the wishes of residents, particularly on sensitive issues such as housing and community development. By contrast, constituencies are larger and more diverse in most unincorporated areas in suburbia. In these larger local units, governments generally are less concerned about particular neighborhoods than is the typical small-scale incorporated suburban government.

The desire to secure local control over land use, housing, and urban development has been a common motivation for the incorporation of suburban municipalities. Local land owners, builders, and developers have employed incorporation to secure control over planning and zoning in order to advance or protect their economic interests. On the other hand, residents, particularly in newly suburbanizing areas, have frequently sought to incorporate their communities in order to transfer planning responsibilities and land-use controls from the hands of county and township officials to those of local residents, elected to office by their neighbors. Often with good reason, these larger units of suburban local government are considered to be too sympathetic to development interests and insufficiently concerned with the interests of individual communities. As the leader of a homeowner's group seeking to incorporate a suburban neighborhood in the Chicago area explains: "Our main goal in trying to incorporate is to protect our residents from improper zoning. Present restrictions by the county, which . . . controls zoning within our boundaries, is rather loose."[8]

Another common but usually unvoiced concern which has stimulated incorporation efforts is the desire to exclude blacks and subsidized housing. In the San Francisco area, John H. Denton believes "that one of the principal purposes (if not the entire purpose) of suburban incorporations is to give their populations control of the racial composition of their communities."[9] Municipal status substantially enhances the capability of a suburban community to exclude subsidized housing, and the blacks who might live in such units. Incorporation permits local officials to decide whether the community will participate in subsidized housing programs. It also provides local residents with control over zoning and other powers which can prevent the construction of subsidized housing.

An illustration of the creation of a suburban municipality to foreclose the construction of subsidized housing is provided by the incorporation of Black Jack, a community of 2,900 in the St. Louis area.[10] Late in 1969, a nonprofit group organized by church organizations in the St. Louis area took an option on a twelve-acre site in an unincorporated section of St. Louis County known as Black Jack. The land in question was part of 67 acres which had been zoned by the county government for multiple-family dwellings; and over 300 apartments already had been constructed by private developers on fifteen of the acres. The church group planned to construct 210 apartments for rental to families earning between $5,700 and $10,200 under the federal government's Section 236 program for moderate-income housing. The site was chosen by the church groups because they "wanted to determine the feasibility of providing subsidized housing for people—black and white—just beginning to climb above the poverty line but still too poor to move to the suburbs."[11]

For residents of the area, almost all of whom were white, middle-income, and living in single-family homes costing between $25,000 and $45,000, the notion of subsidized and integrated housing for lower-income families in their community was not at all feasible. Their reaction was vehement and their actions swift. With local neighborhood associations leading the opposition, circulars were distributed, mass meetings held, and public officials contacted. In addition, a delegation was dispatched to Washington to present petitions to top officials of the Department of Housing and Urban Development. In opposing the project, residents emphasized the lack of public services, overcrowded local schools, poor transportation links with the rest of the metropolis, and the absence of jobs in Black Jack's portion of St. Louis County. Concern also was expressed over the impact on property values and community character if lower-income families, and particularly poor blacks, were to live in Black Jack.

Dissatisfaction with county housing and land-use policies in the Black Jack area had stirred thoughts of incorporation before the subsidized housing project materialized. With the announcement of the project, local residents moved quickly to seek incorporation in order to deny the development of the site for apartments. Two weeks after the federal government agreed to finance the project, over 1,400 residents of the area petitioned the St. Louis County Council for incorporation of 265 square miles encompassing the proposed housing. At the request of the county council, the incorporation proposal was evaluated by the county planning department, which opposed the creation of a new municipality "on fiscal, planning, and legal grounds."[12] Far more influential with the county council, however, was the strong local support for incorporation. Black Jack's advocates successfully linked opposition to incorporation with support for subsidized housing. Suburbanites throughout the northern portion of the county were warned by the Black Jack Improvement Association that approval of the project "could open the door to similar projects being located almost anywhere in the North County area. By stopping this project, you would lessen the chance of one perhaps appearing in your neighborhood."[13] Obviously, the way to stop the project was to permit incorporation. Framing the issue in these terms, as one observer notes, rendered the council members "powerless. The housing issue which precipitated the incorporation was too politically sensitive to allow the council to turn down the petition, and thus indirectly sanction" the construction of subsidized housing.[14]

The result was approval by the county council of the creation of the city of Black Jack, the first new municipality in St. Louis County in over a decade. With incorporation, control over land use within Black Jack was transferred from the county to the new municipality. Less than three months after incorporation, Black Jack's City Council enacted a zoning ordinance which prohibited the construction of apartments within the municipality, thus blocking the proposed subsidized housing.[15]

While the powers available to independent local governments provide suburban communities such as Black Jack with the capability to exclude, local autonomy is relative rather than absolute. Local control over land use, housing, and related matters, like all local powers in the United States, is derived from state governments. Autonomy of suburban governments is limited by municipal charters which are granted by the state and by delegation of responsibilities to other units of local government, such as townships and counties by the state constitution or legislature. The states oversee a wide range of local activities and provide local governments with substantial financial assistance, particularly for public education. They also construct most of the major roads and regulate sewer development, a pair of activities which greatly influence the accessibility of land for development. State actions may constrain suburban autonomy, as in the establishment of public agencies empowered to supersede local land-use controls, such as New Jersey's Hackensack Meadowlands Development Commission or New York's Urban Development Corporation.[16] On the other hand, the state may expand the powers of residents of independent suburbs, as have those states which require that public housing proposals be approved by local voters in a referendum.

Local autonomy in the suburbs also is affected by activities of metropolitan and federal agencies, as well as by intervention from the courts. A wide variety of metropolitan agencies exercise responsibility for area-wide planning, major public works, and other activities which affect housing and development patterns within local jurisdictions in the metropolis. The federal government supports housing, highway, water, sewer, planning, and other programs which influence the ability of suburban governments to shape the nature and timing of development within their boundaries. The federal government also has substantial powers to prevent local governments from discriminating against minorities in the development, sale, and rental of housing. In addition, all local authority is subject to review in state courts, and the exercise of many local powers raise issues which fall within the jurisdiction of federal courts.

In the policy areas of greatest importance for exclusion, however, local autonomy tends to be particularly broad. As Richard F. Babcock notes: "Local control over use of private land has withstood with incredible resilience the centripetal political forces of the last generation."[17] State governments typically have delegated virtually all responsibility for planning, zoning, building codes, and related activities to local governments. Few states even maintain an administrative machinery to oversee local land-use and housing controls. Only in response to environmental problems and pressures have states begun to develop plans and regulatory mechanisms which seek to guide or supercede the land-use activities of local governments. Almost all of these state efforts, however, are limited to areas of critical ecological concern, such as coastal zones and floodplains.[18]

Most states also have done little to enlarge the scale of land-use control in suburbia. County governments usually are limited to regulating unincorporated areas, with few states providing counties with a significant land-use role within suburban municipalities. When states provide for county agencies or regional bodies to review local zoning actions, the review power typically, as Coke and Gargan note, "is advisory only; the reviewing agency has no authority unilaterally to overrun the zoning action."[19] Nor have states necessarily permitted metropolitan governments, in the few areas where they have been created, to exercise land-use controls throughout their jurisdiction. In Miami, as the National Commission on Urban Problems pointed out, "the metropolitan government has zoning authority only in unincorporated territory. In Nashville-Davidson County, several small suburban municipalities continued in existence after the creation of the metropolitan government and retained their zoning powers."[20] The state law creating Unigov in the Indianapolis area also permitted suburban municipalities to continue to control land use.

Local autonomy over housing and land use is bolstered further by the absence of a direct federal role in zoning and other development controls. Moreover, local rather than federal officials determine the location of housing units supported by national subsidy programs.[21] A final factor enhancing the ability of suburban governments to use their autonomy to foster exclusion has been the reluctance of most courts to impose significant constraints on the exercise of local land-use powers.[22]

As a result of these developments, suburban governments have been able to use their autonomy to influence housing opportunities with relatively little outside interference. And because land-use patterns strongly affect local taxes and public services, community character, and the quality of local schools, zoning has become the essence of local autonomy for most suburbanites.

Using Local Autonomy

Local autonomy, of course, does not guarantee success to suburbanites in their efforts to control development. Great variations exist in the use of local controls. A few suburbs permit almost any kind of development, others seek to exclude practically everything. Most, however, pursue more selective policies which result from the concerns and values of local residents, fiscal realities, environmental constraints, and the pressures for growth and change which constantly test the effectiveness of local controls. Some suburbs are highly skilled in their use of the means available to influence settlement patterns, employing sophisticated planning techniques and acting in a timely fashion to shape the forces of change. Others are far less skillful, and their tardy and piecemeal efforts tend to be overwhelmed by private developers.

Size is a major barrier to the acquisition of planning and zoning expertise in many suburbs. In his analysis of suburban land development in three northeastern metropolitan areas, Marion Clawson emphasizes that:

> Most of these local governments are . . . too small in most instances to engage any full-time employees for any of these functions. Those which do hire usually pay low wages. Only the largest of the local governments have top-ranking jobs that pay enough to attract and hold well-trained professional or technical people. Staffing levels in planning and land-use-related activities are low in relation to numbers of persons engaged in the construction activities affected by their work.[23]

Many suburbs, however, have overcome the handicaps posed by small size and limited resources. Mounting suburban concern over the implications of unregulated development during the 1960s increased local willingness to invest in the acquisition of sophisticated planning capabilities. The financial burdens imposed by these activities were eased by assistance from federal and state planning programs. And the shortage of skilled local employees was offset by the availability of advice from private planning consultants.

Acquisition of planning skills, however, cannot insure that local efforts will strongly influence development. Accessibility, topography, land values, and other physical and market factors play a major role in shaping settlement patterns in suburbs. So do the decisions of metropolitan, state, and federal agencies concerning roads, water supply, sewers, and other major public facilities. Control over land use, the primary power available to local government, is essentially negative. Zoning, subdivision regulation, building codes, and other planning devices may prevent undesirable development, but by themselves cannot induce desired change. Zoning vacant land in a working-class suburb for two-acre estates may foreclose the construction of more tract houses on small lots. In the absence of excellent schools, attractive surroundings, and separation from lower-status neighbors, however, such local action is unlikely to result in construction of expensive housing for an upper-income clientele. Similarly, creation of a commercial or industrial district within a suburb will not attract developers unless the site is desirable in terms of the availability of an adequate tract of land at a competitive price, its proximity to highways and other transportation facilities, and its accessibility to markets, suppliers, and labor force.

The ability of suburban governments to shape urban development is frequently undermined by the very factors which afford growing suburbs an opportunity to influence settlement patterns. Having vacant land and being in the path of development in the decentralizing metropolis often means that growth overwhelms the capacity of small and amateur local governments to cope with the complexities of suburbanization. For some fiscally hard-pressed suburban jurisdictions, the perceived tax benefits of growth outweigh the advantages of effective controls, at least during the crucial initial phases of the development process. Local planning controls often fail to check the private sector because of the dominant influence in newly developing areas of large land owners, real estate operators, bankers, and related interests. Local officials frequently are closely tied to those who are profiting from suburbanization. In Santa Clara County in California, as in many rapidly developing areas, local "officials and the greedy land speculators and developers . . . were never really opposing interests. With few exceptions the local officials were also involved in real estate speculation, had other vested interests in the rapid development of the valley, or . . . simply were unable to make a strong stand against the powerful development interests and their allies in local government."[24]

Outright corruption also subverts the suburban plans and zoning regulations. The high financial stakes of land development combines with the importance of local land-use controls to produce offers which some suburban officials cannot resist. Illustrative is the experience of Hoffman Estates, a suburb in the Chicago area where three officials were convicted of bribery, conspiracy, and tax evasion in 1973 after taking bribes from Kaufman & Broad Homes, one of the nation's largest homebuilding firms. As Ed McCahill has pointed out, the rewards in this instance were high for both local officials and the developer:

> For about $90,000 in bribes, Kaufman & Broad nearly were able to plop an entire town of 25,000 residents right in the middle of a community which had no hospital or industry to speak of, an inadequate transportation system, and schools filled to capacity. The rezoning proposal allowed 33 housing units per acre when Hoffman Estates had no zoning specifications other than "residential." The $90,000 in bribes was paid during the 1960s, when the village had only recently been incorporated and was unaccustomed to planning for subdivisions. One of the incidents that tipped off Hoffman Estates homeowners that something was amiss was when their showers went dry in 1970, as 2,500 new neighbors started tapping into the inadequate water system.[25]

As more and more people move to suburbs residential interests are less likely to be compromised by local governments in contests involving developers. With growth constantly augmenting the ranks of those who seek to use local autonomy to preserve and protect their local community from unwanted change, residents have become increasingly active participants in the politics of suburban development. Doubts, often well founded, concerning the ability or desire of local officials to withstand the pressures and other blandishments of developers has stimulated a great deal of political activity at the grass roots. Neighborhood organizations have been created or politicized to bring pressure to bear on local governments, and to fight adverse land-use actions in the courts.[26] An official of a neighborhood civic organization opposed to more apartment construction in East Brunswick, New Jersey, explains the evolution of his group's political activities as follows: "We were a loose social organization that met for July 4 neighborhood picnics before this zoning dilemma blew up. That action pulled us into legal action, with each of the families contributing money to legally fight the variance before the Zoning Board."[27] To check the discretionary power of local officials, suburbanites in some jurisdictions have sought direct public participation in land-use questions. Voters in Eastlake, a suburb in the Cleveland area, approved an amendment to the local charter in 1971 which required approval of all rezoning sections by 55 percent of those voting in a public referendum. Residential interests supporting the provision "wanted to get the power back to the people" by making it necessary for "a developer to convince the voters he's bringing something good into the city."[28]

Local officials who fail to respond to these residential pressures increasingly face retribution at the polls. In many suburbs, a new generation of office holders is emerging dedicated to using local autonomy to protect residential interests rather than to facilitate developers and land owners. As Fred P. Bosselman notes:

> The most important manifestation of the new mood is the changing character of suburban political leaders. Traditionally suburban governments have been dominated by the local businessmen, especially real estate brokers, many of whom owned substantial tracts of vacant land. They naturally saw growth as good for business—as long as it didn't attract "undesirables," of course.
>
> This is changing . . . . [In] many parts of the country in the past few years . . . voters have ousted the incumbents and replaced them with a new type of local official. They are housewives, junior executives, engineers, mechanics, truck drivers—in short, typical suburban homeowners who's only contact with the community is to live in it, not to make money off it. This might be characterized . . . as "suburbia for the suburbanites."[29]

As a consequence of these developments, more and more public officials in suburbia reflect the values of the relatively homogenous constituencies which elect them or hire them. Zoning and planning boards increasingly are composed of members sympathetic to the interests of local residents. In Greenwich, Connecticut, as in thousands of suburbs, "no one can get elected unless he swears on the Bible, under the tree at midnight, and with a blood oath to uphold zoning."[30] Suburban city managers, planning directors, and the consultants who provide much of the technical and planning advice in many suburbs commonly adjust their attitudes, proposals, and actions to the limited horizons of the suburban jurisdiction which hires them. As a former suburban mayor emphasizes, "the officials they elect understand that their responsibility is to keep the community the way the people here want it."[31]

Of course, the growing influence of residents in suburban politics does not mean that local controls over housing and land use always are employed to advance residential interests. Residents are not cohesive on every development issue, especially in the larger and more heterogeneous suburban jurisdiction. Moreover, landowners and developers retain considerable influence, particularly in areas in the path of suburbanization where residents often are outnumbered by those who seek to profit from development. Nor does local autonomy protect residents of suburbs from losing battles with state highway departments and other outside agencies which are able to alter the pattern of suburban development without the consent of the affected localities.

Despite these limitations, local autonomy constitutes an effective shield against social change in many suburban jurisdictions. As residential influence mounts, autonomy offers most suburbanites local governmental institutions responsive to their interests. Equally important, political independence provides the legal means to pursue these objectives through the exercise of local planning, land-use, and housing controls. In the typical community, the purposes of local autonomy tend to be defined by the widespread suburban preoccupation with home and school, class and status concerns, racial separation, and the desire to be insulated from the problems of the inner city. Internal consensus on the uses of local autonomy, particularly in smaller and relatively homogeneous suburban jurisdictions, is likely to be high when property values, educational quality, community character, or the influx of blacks or lower-income residents are at issue. The result, in the words of one suburban political leader, is "the politics of the territorial imperative . . . [which] means opposing new housing and new people, anything that might change the status quo."[32]

Notes

1. *Suburbia: Its People and Their Politics* (Boston: Houghton Mifflin, 1958), p. 128.
2. See Oliver P. Williams et al., *Suburban Differences and Metropolitan Policies: A Philadelphia Story* (Philadelphia: University of Pa. Press, 1965), pp. 217–219.
3. See Walter S. Mossberg, "A Blue Collar Town Fears Urban Renewal Perils Its Way of Life," *Wall Street Journal*, Nov. 2, 1970.
4. Gladstone L. Chandler, Jr., city manager, East Cleveland, Oh., quoted in Paul Delaney, "The Outer City: Negroes Find Few Tangible Gains," *New York Times*, June 1, 1971; reprinted as "Negroes Find Few Tangible Gains," in Louis H. Masotti and Jeffrey K. Hadden, eds., *Suburbia in Transition*, (New York: Franklin Watts, 1974), p. 278. East Cleveland had no black residents in the mid-1950s; by 1970, 60 percent of its population was black.
5. "Suburbanization; Reviving the Town on the Metropolitan Frontier," *Publius 5*, (Winter, 1975), p. 59.
6. The Baltimore standard metropolitan statistical area contains four additional counties— Anne Arundel, Carroll, Harford and Howard—which lie beyond Baltimore County.
7. See Allen D. Manvel, "Metropolitan Growth and Governmental Fragmentation," in A. E. Kier Nash, ed., *Governance and Population: The Governmental Implications of Population Change*, Vol. 4, Research Reports, U.S. Commission on Population Growth and the American Future (Washington: U.S. Government Printing Office, 1972), p. 181.
8. Robert Poltzer, Prospect Heights Improvement Association, quoted in Dan Egler, "Prospect Heights Seeks to Incorporate," *Chicago Tribune*, Oct. 1, 1972.
9. "Phase I Report" to the National Committee Against Discrimination in Housing. U.S. Department of Housing and Urban Development Project, No. Cal. D-8 (n.d.), pt. 3, p. Jc–11.
10. For a summary of the events leading to the incorporation of Black Jack, see Ronald F. Kirby, Frank de Leeuw, and William Silverman, *Residential Zoning and Equal Housing Opportunities: A Case Study in Black Jack, Missouri* (Washington: Urban Inst., 1972), pp. 17–27.
11. See B. Drummond Ayres, "Bulldozers Turn Up Soil and Ill Will in a Suburb of St. Louis," *New York Times*, Jan. 18, 1971.
12. See *Park View Heights Corporation v. City of Black Jack*, 467 F.2d 1208 (1972) at 1211.

13. See William K. Reilly, ed., *The Use of Land: A Citizens' Policy Guide to Urban Growth*, A Task Force Report Sponsored by The Rockefeller Brothers Fund (New York: Thomas Y. Crowell Company, 1973), p. 90.

14. Jerome Pratter, "Dispersed Subsidized Housing and Suburbia: Confrontation in Black Jack," *Land-Use Controls Annual* (Chicago: American Society of Planning Officials, 1972), p. 152.

15. Black Jack's actions were challenged in court by the sponsors of the project, other organizations, and the federal government; see *United States v. City of Black Jack, Missouri*, 372 F. Supp. 319 (1974); *United States v. City of Black Jack, Missouri*, 508 F.2d 1179 (1974); *Park View Heights Corporation v. City of Black Jack*, 467 F.2d 1208; and the discussion of the Black Jack litigation in chapter 7.

16. Suburban opposition to this grant of power to the Urban Development Corporation led the New York legislature to rescind it in 1973; see chapter 10 for a discussion of the New York Urban Development Corporation's turbulent efforts to open the suburbs.

17. *The Zoning Game: Municipal Practices and Policies* (Madison: University of Wis. Press, 1966), p. 19.

18. State land-use activities and their impact on suburban exclusion are discussed in detail in chapter 10.

19. James G. Coke and John I. Gargan, *Fragmentation in Land-Use Planning and Control*, Prepared for the consideration of the National Commission on Urban Problems, Research Report No. 18 (Washington: U.S. Government Printing Office, 1969), p. 6.

20. *Building the American City*, Report of the National Commission on Urban Problems to the Congress and President of the United States. 91st Cong., 1st sess., House Doc. No. 91-34 (Washington: U.S. Government Printing Office, 1968), p. 209.

21. The federal role in suburban exclusion is examined in chapter 8.

22. Judicial attitudes concerning exclusionary zoning and housing policies began to shift in the late 1960s; see chapter 7 for an analysis of the role of the courts in opening the suburbs.

23. *Suburban Land Conversion in the United States: An Economic and Governmental Process* (Baltimore: Johns Hopkins University Press, 1971), pp. 65–66.

24. Leonard Downie, Jr., *Mortgage on America* (New York: Praeger Publishers, 1974), p. 111.

25. "Stealing: A Primer on Zoning Corruption," *Planning* 39 (Dec., 1973), p. 6.

26. For a discussion of suburban neighborhood associations, and their role in land-use politics, see R. Robert Linowes and Don T. Allensworth, *The Politics of Land Use: Planning, Zoning and the Private Developer* (New York: Praeger Publishers, 1973), pp. 114–142.

27. George Post, vice president, Prides Wood Civic Association, East Brunswick, N.J., quoted in Ruth Ann Burns, "Apartment Proposal Stirs a Dispute in East Brunswick," *New York Times*, Oct. 8, 1972.

28. See "Eastlake is Upheld on Requiring Vote in Rezoning Cases," *Cleveland Plain Dealer*, Oct. 31, 1972, Eastlake's ordinance was overturned four years later by the Supreme Court of Ohio; see *Forest City Enterprises, Inc., v. City of Eastlake*, 41 Ohio St. 2d 187, 324 N.F.2d, 740 (1975).

29. "The Right to Move, the Need to Grow," *Planning* 39 (Sept., 1973), pp. 10–11.

30. See Ralph Blumenthal, "Pressures of Growth Stir Zoning Battles in Suburbs," *New York Times*, May 29, 1967.

31. Harry J. Butler, Wayne, N.J., quoted in Richard Reeves, "Land Is Prize in Battle for Control of Suburbs," *New York Times*, Aug. 17, 1971; reprinted as "The Battle Over Land," in Masotti and Hadden, *Suburbia in Transition*, p. 310.

32. John F. English, former chairman of the Democratic Party, Nassau County, N.Y., quoted in *ibid.*, p. 304.

13

Dolores Hayden

PLANNING SUBURBAN-STYLE DEVELOPMENT

"Planned Sprawl" and the Rise of the Mall

The greatest beneficiaries of federal highway programs and commercial real estate subsidies were the developers of shopping malls. Well-designed, small shopping areas had been part of earlier elite picturesque enclaves, such as Lake Forest, Illinois, Roland Park, Maryland, and the Country Club Plaza in Kansas City. Small strip shopping areas had also emerged on many suburban arterials in the 1920s. By the 1940s architects such as Victor Gruen were promoting "shopping towns" with anchor stores and smaller stores surrounded by parking.[1] Gruen was a Viennese émigré who worked on luxury boutiques in Manhattan before developing a firm in Southern California. Gruen designed the first fully enclosed mall at Southdale, near Minneapolis, in 1956, and prospered as a specialist in retail malls.[2]

Malls in the late forties and early fifties were risky. Suburban customers still believed in making major purchases in the central business districts of cities and towns, where they expected to find the greatest selection of merchandise and the most competitive prices. After the tax laws of 1954, this changed. Shopping mall developers were among the biggest beneficiaries of accelerated depreciation, and they most often located projects where the older strips met the new interchanges of major highways. With the new tax write-offs, over 98 percent of malls made money for their investors.[3] Together, the tax breaks and the new roads explain the orgy of commercial real estate built in automotive configurations after the mid-1950s. According to Hanchett, tax incentives helped spur the construction of many more shopping centers than would otherwise have been started.[4] Frequently state and local governments also subsidized malls with "economic development" grants, infrastructure such as local access roads, and abatements of local taxes.[5] The culture of land use planning became very corrupt in many places, with both elected officials and paid staff in local governments receiving handouts from speculators, builders, and bankers in exchange for tens of millions in subsidies.

In a landmark study of the late 1970s, *Planned Sprawl*, sociologist Mark Gottdiener looked at the largest township in Suffolk County, Long Island, to analyze the planning behind roadside suburban development. He challenged observers who called the landscape chaotic, showing that physical disorder

Excerpt from Dolores Hayden, *Building Suburbia: Green Fields and Urban Growth, 1820-2000*. Pantheon Books, 2003, pp. 168-180 (text only), and corresponding notes on pp. 274-276.

resulted from planned and systematic profit-seeking by builders, developers, and banks. He documented one case where a developer sought and received rezoning for a project called Dollarhaven Mall from local politicians. In general, Gottdiener noted many ways for developers to promote deals: "buying blocks of tickets to party functions," "purchasing a service from a business" (such as a local newspaper, construction firm, or car dealership associated with a political boss, his associates, or a councilman), and making campaign contributions.[6] Other writers railed against *The Great Land Hustle* and the *Mortgage on America*.[7] Although some academics and politicians advocated more effective regional planning, metropolitan government, and environmental regulation, little was done to halt the federal, state, and local subsidies for growth channeled to real estate developers.

Between the mid-1950s and the late 1970s about 22,000 suburban shopping centers were built. By the late 1990s there were 43,000.[8] They included thousands of strip malls, euphemistically called "neighborhood or community shopping centers," with one large store such as a supermarket, drugstore, or low-cost department store and a line of little stores facing parking. There were hundreds of "regional malls" like the Connecticut Post Mall in Milford, Connecticut. Regional malls were sited on at least thirty acres, usually enclosed, with multiple shops and at least one big anchor store including 100,000 square feet of leasable space. And there were the superregional malls, totaling over 1,400,000 square feet of leasable space. At one place in New Jersey, citizens renamed their municipality "Cherry Hill" after the mall developed by James Rouse in 1961. Other localities were not so delighted. Malls eroded the economic base of older downtown department stores as well as stores on Main Streets in small towns and older suburbs, leaving empty storefronts. They privatized and commercialized public space. As historian Lizabeth Cohen has documented, mall owners were often anxious to restrict public access, and one of the ways of achieving this was to make access by public transit minimal, or to organize bus routes to reinforce market segmentation and racial segregation by race and class. Cohen suggests that malls also feminized public space: "they enhanced women's claim on the suburban landscape but also empowered them more as consumers than producers."[9]

By 2000, Americans had built almost twice as much retail space per citizen as any other country in the world: over nineteen square feet per person.[10] Most of it was in malls. A superregional such as the South Coast Mall in Orange County, California, claimed to do more retail business every day than all of downtown San Francisco.[11] The Mall of America (MOA) in Bloomington, Minnesota, is even more gigantic. A project of the Ghermezian brothers, with Melvin Simon and Associates as developer and managing partner, it opened in 1992. The largest superregional mall in the United States, in 2002 MOA included four anchor department stores and over 520 stores, 51 restaurants, 8 nightclubs, 14 theater screens, and theme park attractions. Its Camp Snoopy offers twenty-eight rides on seven acres, a virtual NASCAR speedway, a bowling alley, and 1.2-million-gallon aquarium with three thousand marine animals, including sharks and stingrays. With a gross building area of 4.2 million square feet and leasable space of 2.5 million square feet, it draws between six hundred thousand and nine hundred thousand visitors weekly. Attractions include hair-coloring demonstrations, children's fashion shows, cheerleader tryouts, mall walks for seniors, and a show of red, white, and blue flowers called "Great American Backyard." At 42.5 million visitors per year, the Mall of America claims to top Disney World, Graceland, and the Grand Canyon as the most popular tourist destination in the United States.[12]

From the Mall to the Edge Node

Edge nodes expanded with the rise of malls, especially the superregionals with their surrounding seas of parking. In edge nodes, site plans are scaled to the truck or car, never to the pedestrian. Edge nodes have assumed different forms in various parts of the country since the 1970s, but many of them are in unincorporated areas rather than politically bounded towns. Many have a maze of overlapping jurisdictions such as county, town, and special service districts. Most nodes are "boomers" like Tysons Corner, exploding out of strip commercial areas on older arterials near freeway interchanges, where loose zoning and automotive uses have prevailed since the 1920s, and a new mall brought development to the area. Garreau uses the term "pig in the python" to describe the way some boomers are formed as big nodes within a linear strip.[13] Edge nodes can also be "uptown," that is, on the site of an older downtown, perhaps one that has been razed by urban redevelopment, with land then sold on favorable terms to new private investors. Such is the case in Stamford, Connecticut, where an industrial city making Yale locks gave way to a mall and corporate offices.[14] A third kind of edge node is "greenfield," located in open, undeveloped land, usually near a freeway exit.

The privately planned new towns and Title VII communities founded in the 1960s provide an exception to Garreau's typology. Urban planner Ann Forsyth notes that all were "highly designed—and designed with parking seen as 'landbank' for future expansion."[15] The developers, planners, architects, and landscape architects who worked on these projects saw themselves as providing an alternative to the sprawling suburbs of the 1950s. Columbia, Maryland, was developed by James Rouse beginning in 1963. With about fourteen thousand acres, Columbia held eighty-eight thousand residents in 2000. About one-fifth were African-American because Rouse had emphasized achieving racial integration. The Woodlands, outside of Houston, Texas, was developed by George Mitchell, beginning in 1964. He hired Ian McHarg to develop an ecological focus for the planning of 15,000 acres (now 27,305 acres). The Woodlands reached 55,649 inhabitants by 2000. The Irvine Company began to develop a new town in 1960 and hired William Pereira as master planner for more than ninety-three thousand acres in Southern California. The city of Irvine holds one hundred and thirty thousand people. These three planned developments included regional retail as well as neighborhood retail centers serving both single-family houses and apartments. All three managed to create long-term job development, including office parks, and by 1991 they appeared on Joel Garreau's list of edge cities, although they derived from consistent attempts to plan and develop large new suburban communities.

For the most part, edge nodes are uncomfortable and ugly places. Building is cheap; depreciation is accelerated; obsolescence is rapid. Money might be spent on a corporate headquarters when a corporation intends to stay, but developers of speculative office parks design for rapid turnover. There is little site design beyond inexpensive buildings with big signs and parking lots, although private security services and building maintenance services are often provided to tenants. Developers of industrial parks also build minimal buildings. Clustered around malls, offices, and industry are office services, such as lawyers, accountants, and printing, and other services, such as fast food, chain motels, cineplexes, and freeway churches. When geographer Peter Muller documented the growth of King of Prussia, Pennsylvania, in 1976, his diagram showed the Pennsylvania Turnpike, Interstate 76, and U.S. 202 wrapping a series of pods, with a mall, office parks, industrial parks, hotels, fast food, a freeway church, and a music fair.[16] It lacked the pedestrian structure of a traditional downtown, where sidewalks allowed pedestrians to walk from office to restaurant or from church to shopping. Despite Muller's optimism about the upscale King of Prussia mall providing "prestige" addresses for adjoining businesses, there was little public space. His diagram showed an edge node that could grow but could not improve with time. Each new single-use pod was surrounded by its own sea of parking.

The older building types that had been on the strips of the 1920s were replaced by newer facilities as the nodes grew, but they did not produce places with a pedestrian presence. Fast-food franchises disrupted sidewalks with drive-throughs that encouraged people to eat on the road. They also displaced public playgrounds with private ones to attract children and parents to fast food. Chain hotels and motels supplanted older hotels and tourist courts. Cineplexes, multiple-screen theaters housed in big, warehouselike buildings without sidewalks, replaced art deco single-screen Main Street theaters, whose slogan had been "the show starts on the sidewalk." Freeway churches drew large congregations to locations near offramps, surrounded by seas of parking, replacing churches on downtown corners. Over time, many evangelical freeway churches added sports facilities, fitness centers, and food courts to their sanctuaries. They were designed to look more like malls than churches.[17]

By the 1990s planner Robert Cervero noted that most edge nodes were being built at densities too low for the effective provision of public transport, yet high enough to cause traffic gridlock. Each new pod added to an edge node might be designed for internal traffic circulation, but the parcels tended to agglomerate with no consistent land use planning or traffic circulation beyond the property line.[18] "Suburbia may be paved with good intentions, but mainly it is paved," said architect Douglas Kelbaugh.[19] Introducing new urban design guidelines is uphill work; renovation of existing spaces is even harder.

Big Boxes, Category Killers, and Outlet Malls

In the 1990s big-box discount stores of fifty thousand to two hundred thousand square feet began to undercut the older shopping malls that had been at the heart of the edge nodes. The largest big-box stores like Wal-Mart sell almost everything—drugs, hardware, linens, furniture, stationery, toys, clothing, electronics, plants, and eyeglasses. Their supercenters also include a full supermarket. Wal-Mart had over nine hundred thousand employees in 1999, which makes it the largest private employer in America, surpassing General Motors. Wal-Mart has claimed that 93 million Americans shop there every week. It also operates in many other countries, exporting American-style big-box retailing.[20] Category killers—slightly smaller big-box discount stores of twenty-five thousand to one hundred thousand square feet—attempt to dominate (or kill) a particular sales category. Toys "R" Us specializes in toys, Staples in office supplies, Home Depot in building supplies and hardware.

In the face of the big boxes' aggressive expansion, local drugstores, stationery stores, clothing stores, and hardware stores have disappeared by the tens of thousands, changing the shape of older suburbs and small towns.[21] In the ten years between 1983 and 1993, the state of Iowa lost 7,326 small retail businesses. Making the case against sprawl, activist Al Norman contended, "There's one thing you can't buy in a Wal-Mart. That's small town quality of life. And once you lose it, you can't get it back at any price."[22] Through the 1990s the big boxes "killed" older malls, chain supermarkets, chain drugstores, and small department stores, as well as little markets, pharmacies, and clothing stores. The scale of roadside commercial development became overwhelming. Less and less was local. Warehouselike buildings were dictated by management rules about "facilities" of twenty-five thousand to two hundred thousand square feet, with no interior columns, no windows, and parking for thousands of cars.[23] Most of these buildings had no relationship in siting or style to the character of the towns where they were located, although occasionally local planners were able to persuade chains to insert their operations into older structures.

Big boxes were tied to national or international chains, part of an expanding global economy often requiring port and airport access as well as access by truck. Ports such as Long Beach, near Los Angeles, were restructured to accommodate vast containers filled with manufactured goods headed to American discount stores from foreign farms and factories. Airports expanded their cargo areas. Highways were jammed with trucks hauling fifty-three-foot-long containers to speed four billion tons of "just-in-time" merchandise to retail outlets every year.[24] The trucking firms demanded wider arterials and bigger intersections. Trucks shook the foundations of older buildings when they tore into towns.

A few attempts have been made to disguise the bloated architectural scale of big boxes and outlet malls. Developers may present them as villages by decorating one facade of the warehouse or by putting a veneer of Victorian trim on the central public circulation, leaving the rear for the trucks. Sometimes old-fashioned items designed at the human scale, such as sailboats or train coaches, have been added to an outlet mall's design. Their purpose is to serve as "memory points," landmarks to keep thousands of customers from getting lost in rows of warehouses. More common is a lineup of two or three big boxes as a "power center" with no access designed for pedestrians at all. The trucks find this best. One big-box retailer, Target, has emphasized aesthetics in its advertising, hiring noted architects and industrial designers to create its lamps and tea kettles and bring order to store interiors. Unfortunately, they have not yet campaigned for better exterior and site design to modify the scale of the big boxes and parking lots.

Defenders of the big boxes and outlet malls argue that they attract customers. Wal-Mart underwear is cheap, and so is Home Depot's plastic paneling, and so are McDonald's hamburgers.[25] Outlets do beat smaller stores' prices, but quality is often low. Even if quality is the same for mass-produced products, such as flashlight batteries, the customer is missing the local experience the old neighborhood stores used to provide. The customer's time and the customer's automobile replace a neighborhood store's clerk and personal service. Once in the big box, self-service is usually the rule, as customers fill carts and lug purchases. Labor costs are low, compared with traditional department stores, hardware stores, or restaurants, because often workers are part-time and working at the minimum wage without benefits. Many big-box employers discourage unionization. However, Wal-Mart workers who claimed they were frequently forced to put in overtime without pay organized class-action suits across the country in 2002.[26]

Many of the giants are now under close scrutiny for their effects on American towns. Companies may argue that they compete to serve "the market," but federal subsidies for roads and commercial overbuilding have supported the rise of the giants and contributed to the demise of thousands of small local businesses. It is hard to find a small town or older suburb that has not been disrupted. Not only local restaurants but also family farms and small ranches which used to provide vegetables and meat have been displaced from the American landscape by the rise of gigantic global businesses purveying fast food. But not every transaction in the edge nodes is about making a profit on inexpensive goods and services. In a heavily franchised landscape, many calculations cycle back to real estate, and the rise of mass investments in Real Estate Investment Trusts (REITs). The Teachers Insurance and Annuity Association (TIAA) handles pension funds for professors and teachers across the United States. While researching malls I was disconcerted to discover that my own retirement savings helped to build the Mall of America.

Legacies of Accelerated Depreciation

Although it has become the most visible of American suburban landscapes, the edge node has few architectural defenders. Even developers despair: "Shopping centers built only in the 1960s are already being abandoned. Their abandonment brings down the values of nearby neighborhoods. Wal-Marts built five years ago are already being abandoned for superstores. We have built a world of junk, a degraded environment. It may be profitable for a short-term, but its long-term economic prognosis is bleak."[27] Those who do speak in favor of edge nodes, like Joel Garreau, tend to idealize them as a temporary, rough "frontier" of economic growth. He admits most nodes are "as ugly as poison ivy."[28]

No one has yet done a definitive economic study of how much edge nodes have been subsidized by federal tax concessions and local government subsidies. Because of federal, state, and local giveaways, government has encouraged very large businesses to cannibalize smaller businesses, wiping out many Main Streets and older suburban commercial areas, but few Americans understand how their tax dollars have supported this destructive process. The end result has been a mall glut. About four thousand dead malls were empty or abandoned in the United States in 2002.[29] More failures are expected. Older big boxes and outlet malls have also been abandoned. Some developers and designers are working on plans for adding housing to retail in dying malls in order to redevelop older complexes. Meanwhile, the edge node has replaced Main Street, and both shoppers and workers are stuck in traffic.

Few Americans can describe the physical form or financial underpinnings of edge nodes like Tysons Corner or King of Prussia. Even scholars and design professionals are often unaware how complex, hidden subsidies have boosted their growth. Jobs and commerce have moved to edge nodes, but few people want to live in them. The presence of housing in edge nodes is often the result of spot builders filling in leftover sites with "affordable" housing units. Nearby freeways make many of these units undesirable. Occasionally expensive apartments for households without children are added near upscale mall areas, such as the Houston Galleria or the new Southdale Mall in Edina, near Minneapolis, but most affluent families prefer to live elsewhere. Ugly environments, cheap gas, and subsidized freeways mean that workers commute to residences far outside the edge nodes, scattering into less dense areas, creating one more suburban pattern, the rural fringes.

Notes

1. Victor Gruen and Larry Smith, *Shopping Towns USA: The Planning of Shopping Centers* (New York: Reinhold, 1960); also see Howard Gillette, Jr., "The Evolution of the Planned Shopping Center in Suburb and City," *American Planning Association Journal* 51 (Autumn 1985): 449–60.

2. Mark Jeffrey Hardwick, *The Mallmaker: Cities, Suburbs, and Architect Victor Gruen* (Philadelphia: University of Pennsylvania Press, forthcoming).

3. Margaret Crawford, "The World in a Shopping Mall," in *Variations on a Theme Park: The New American City and the End of Public Space,* ed. Michael Sorkin (New York: Hill and Wang, 1992), 3–30. On market segmentation and characterizations of malls, see Michael J. Weiss, *The Clustered World: How We Live, What We Buy, and What It All Means About Who We Are* (Boston: Little, Brown, 2000).

4. Hanchett, "U.S. Tax Policy," 1108.

5. A comic example of this is described in William Fulton, *The Reluctant Metropolis: The Politics of Urban Growth in Los Angeles* (Point Arena, Calif.: Solano Press, 1997), 255–82.

6. Mark Gottdiener, *Planned Sprawl: Private and Public Interests in Suburbia* (Beverly Hills, Calif.: Sage, 1977), 103.

7. Morton Paulson, *The Great Land Hustle* (Chicago: Henry Regnery, 1972); Leonard Downie, *Mortgage on America* (New York: Praeger, 1974).

8. International Council of Shopping Centers, http://www.icsc.com (March 23, 2002); William Leach, *Country of Exiles: The Destruction of Place in American Life* (New York: Pantheon, 1999), 55. On the design of malls and how they can work in Main Street situations, especially in Australia, see Ann Forsyth, "Variations on a Main Street; When a Mall is an Arcade," *Journal of Urban Design* 2 (Fall 1997): 297–307.

9. Lizabeth Cohen, "From Town Center to Shopping Center: The Reconfiguration of Community Marketplaces in Postwar America," *American Historical Review* 101 (October 1996): 1050–81; Lizabeth Cohen, A Consumers' *Republic:* The Politics of Mass-Consumption in Postwar America (New York: Knopf, 2003), 257–344.

10. Frank Jossi, "Rewrapping the Big Box," *Planning* 64 (August 1998): 16–18.

11. Benfield, Raimi, and Chen, *Once There Were Greenfields,* 15.

12. "Mall of America," http://www.mallofamerica.com (March 23, 2002).

13. Garreau, *Edge City,* 113–16.

14. Bettina Drew, *Crossing the Expendable Landscape* (Minneapolis: Graywolf, 1998), 11–31.

15. Ann Forsyth, personal communication, August 2002; Ann Forsyth, *Reforming Suburbia: Building New Communities in Irvine, Columbia, and The Woodlands* (Berkeley; University of California Press, forthcoming). She notes that The Woodlands was "the only one of the thirteen 'Title VII' new towns to be largely completed."

16. Muller, *Contemporary Suburban America,* 164.

17. Patricia Leigh Brown, "Megachurches as Minitowns," *New York Times,* May 9, 2002, F1. This recalls attempts around 1900 to make churches resemble urban settlement houses, with spaces for sports and meetings.

18. Benfield, Raimi, and Chen, *Once There Were Greenfields,* 36–40.

19. Douglas Kelbaugh, article in *Urban Land,* June 1999, quoted in Konsoulis and Sies, *Metropolitan Perspectives,* n.p.

20. Al Norman, *Slam-Dunking Wal-Mart* (Atlantic City, N.J.: Raphael Marketing, 1999); Bill Saporito and Jacqueline M. Graves, "And the Winner is Still . . . Wal-Mart," *Fortune* 129 (May 2, 1994): 62ff.

21. Constance E. Beaumont, *How Superstore Sprawl Can Harm Communities and What Citizens Can Do About It* (Washington, D.C.: National Trust for Historic Preservation, 1994); Constance E. Beaumont, *Better Models for Superstores* (Washington, D.C.: National Trust for Historic Preservation, 1997).

22. Al Norman, "The Case Against Sprawl," www.sprawlbusters.com (May 10, 2002).

23. Keller Easterling, *Organization Space: Landscapes, Highways, and Houses in America* (Cambridge, Mass.: MIT Press, 1999).

24. Leach, *Country of Exiles,* 32–35.

25. Schlosser, *Fast Food Nation,* 6–10, condemns McDonald's massive monopoly of beef and potatoes, processed according to the rules of headquarters, who freeze a standard product complete with flavor additives and "mouthfeel" texture.

26. *Ibid.,* 59–88; Steven Greenhouse, "Suits Say Wal-Mart Forces Workers to Toil Off the Clock," *New York Times,* June 25, 2002, A18.

27. Robert Davis, "Postscript," in Congress for the New Urbanism, *Charter of the New Urbanism* (New York: McGraw-Hill, 2000), 182.

28. Garreau, *Edge City,* 14–15.

29. Timothy Egan, "Retail Darwinism Puts Old Malls in Jeopardy," *New York Times* (January 1, 2000), A20.

CHAPTER 6

THE MULTIETHNIC METROPOLIS

Political Conflict in the New Metropolis

Recent decades have witnessed flows of immigration that are paralleled only by the immigrant floodtides of the late nineteenth and early twentieth centuries. The volume of immigration to the United States in the 1990s exceeded the previous peak of immigration from 1900 to 1910, with the decade of the 1980s close behind (although the proportion of immigrants in the population was far less than a century earlier). A larger number of immigrants lived in the United States by 1990—17 million—than in any previous period in the nation's history. And much more than in the earlier period, recent immigration is truly global, originating from many nations of eastern Europe, Latin America, Asia, and the Caribbean.

Immigrants are establishing an uneven but growing political presence in America's urban politics. Early in the last century some immigrants—in particular, the Irish—were able to find a voice in the party machines. That avenue is no longer available, but the ballot box still gives them powerful leverage. But this leverage may be reduced because immigrant groups do not have identical interests nor do they vote as a bloc. Reuel Rogers focuses on coalition-building in cities where new and old minority immigrant groups compete for power. He wonders whether the newcomers will forge coalitions with their native-born counterparts, particularly African Americans. In the past, many believed that race-based alliances between nonwhite immigrants and African Americans were likely since both have experienced racial discrimination and frequently share other group characteristics that give them common cause. Using the case of Caribbean- and American-born blacks in New York City, he describes the absence of alliances between these groups over many years. Having common racial interests has not been sufficient to overcome a pattern of inter-minority tensions and political competition. Rogers explores why race alone is not a satisfactory foundation for alliance-building between these two groups. He finds that competition for political turf frequently divides Caribbean and American blacks. Entrenched African-American elites have an interest in resisting the mobilization and inclusion of newer Carribean blacks in order to preserve their hold on jobs and power. For their part, Caribbean minorities seek political recognition and their leaders give priority to constituency-building within their own enclave.

Rogers also believes that governmental institutions play a part in dividing these two groups. In particular, he says that New York City's highly decentralized political system rewards mobilization of ethnic groups and targeted appeals that become divisive. In addition, the city's one-party politics and lack of rich networks of community-based organizations encourages political faction. Reuel Rogers concludes that race is unlikely to form a very stable foundation for governance in big cities like New York for some time, if ever.

The essay by Harvey Newman, "Race and the Tourist Bubble," asserts that urban inequality and racial discrimination are sometimes created by urban policies, even in cities with governments run by minorities. Tourism has become a big business in many cities struggling to find a niche in the global economy. As jobs in the old economy dry up or leave town, city after city has looked to make itself into tourist destinations and to attract business travelers seeking meeting places for conferences. Looking at Atlanta, Harvey describes such efforts and finds them wanting as a way of providing benefits to the city's black community.

He describes how the remaking of Atlanta's downtown for tourism has created a "tourist bubble" of segregated enclaves where pedestrians have little contact with the city's ordinary folk who happen to be predominantly black. Sealed skywalk systems that connect hotels, conference centers, restaurants and other buildings isolate visitors from the people outside, ensuring little contact with black neighborhoods, businesses, and commercial areas. The city avoids supporting projects that might integrate the economy, as do white investors. A succession of black administrations has hardly wavered from sponsoring tourist bubble projects like those created by white politicians in the past even though most of the economic benefits bypass black neighborhoods and commercial areas. It is likely that the social effects of Atlanta's tourist bubble strategy are similar to the experience in many other cities.

When assessing the ability of immigrants to exert political influence, it is essential to keep in mind the complexity of the recent immigrant streams. Many recent immigrants are focused on just getting by; it is thus their children and grandchildren who will enter the social and political mainstream. The selection from *Picture Windows*, a book by Rosalyn Baxandall and Elizabeth Ewen, describes the social changes in the suburbs of Long Island. There, recent immigration has exerted immense pressures on housing, schools, and social services. Many of the immigrants work in what Baxandall and Ewen term an "underwater economy" of low-pay, informal jobs where they work as day-laborers, maids, gardeners, babysitters, and the like. The consequences of the low-wage economy are becoming increasingly apparent in the suburbs where the immigrants live. Workers hang out at corners where contractors and other employers drive by to select them as day laborers. To find affordable housing many of the immigrants crowd into substandard housing. Local health clinics and schools are overcrowded. In these and in other ways, the social consequences of ethnic division and inequality have come to the suburbs of Long Island, and increasingly to suburbs everywhere in the nation.

14

Reuel R. Rogers

MINORITY GROUPS AND COALITIONAL POLITICS

The current wave of non-White immigrants to American cities has prompted a range of important empirical and normative questions for political scientists to ponder. One of the most widely considered is how these newcomers will alter coalition dynamics in demographically diverse cities such as New York and Los Angeles, where alliances are a do-or-die fact of political life. Some researchers have speculated that the non-White racial status of the immigrants and their vulnerability to discrimination will lead them to forge coalitions with native-born minorities, specifically African-Americans (Jennings 1997; Marable 1994; Henry and Munoz 1991). Combating racial discrimination has long been a central political preoccupation for American-born Blacks. Scholars who subscribe to the "minority group" view believe that it will also be a chief concern for the new, non-White immigrants. Their conclusion is that this shared interest will become a powerful basis for interminority alliances, unifying African-Americans and their foreign-born counterparts. In short, this perspective anticipates a grand rainbow coalition among native-born Blacks and recent non-White immigrants from Latin America, Asia, and the Caribbean.[1]

But in cities with significant numbers of African-Americans and non-White newcomers, race-based alliances among these groups generally have proven to be an elusive political goal. Stable coalitions between native-born Blacks and their foreign-born counterparts have not been much in evidence in cities around the country. In New York, for instance, political figures as varied as Al Sharpton and Fernando Ferrer have tried to foster an alliance between African-Americans and Latinos with only the most limited results (Falcon 1988; Mollenkopf 2003). At the other end of the Atlantic seaboard in Miami, African-Americans and Cubans have been at odds for decades (Warren and Moreno 2003). Tensions also have simmered between African-Americans and Asians in Los Angeles (Sonenshein 2003b). In short, political relations between Blacks and recent non-White immigrants have been marked more often by conflict than by cooperation. Although race-based coalitions among native-born Blacks and foreign-born minority groups are widely expected, it turns out that they are actually quite rare.

URBAN AFFAIRS REVIEW. Vol. 39, No. 3, January 2004 283–317
DOI: 10.1177/1078087403258960

The rarity of such alliances has led some researchers to speculate that African-Americans are more likely to find themselves in grim political isolation than in any grand rainbow coalition with non-White immigrants (Mollenkopf 2003). A few observers even dismiss the idea of race-based alliances altogether as a misguided and losing electoral strategy in increasingly diverse, multiracial cities, where immigration has scrambled the old Black-White, biracial political calculus (Sleeper 1993). Whatever their future prospects, race-based coalitions between African-Americans and non-White immigrants have not had much success to date.

. . .

Why have such race-based alliances been difficult to foster? A number of studies have noted the political conflicts between Blacks and non-White immigrants, to be sure. But very few have provided detailed analyses of why the racial commonalities they share have not been enough to override differences and produce stable alliances between them. . . .

The Case Study

This article takes up that question with a case study analysis of political relations between African-Americans and Afro-Caribbean immigrants in New York City.[2] These two groups of Black New Yorkers—one native and the other foreign born—together furnish a highly instructive case for exploring why the race-based alliances anticipated by the minority group view have not come to fruition. By the logic of the minority group perspective, rainbow alliances among non-Whites should be most likely when the racial commonalities between them are strong and the racial divisions separating them from Whites are pronounced and politically salient. The strategy for this analysis, then, was to identify a case that fully meets those conditions to give the minority group hypothesis a favorable test.

African-Americans and Afro-Caribbean immigrants living in New York City do just that. As Blacks, the two groups share the same ascriptive racial category, encounter similar forms of discrimination and disadvantage, and have a number of political and economic interests in common. True enough, they also have a history of occasional intergroup tensions, which could undermine any potential for a race-based political alliance between them. Yet the minority group perspective would maintain that racial commonalities, shared interests, and the potential benefits of a race-based coalition should override the intermittent interethnic conflicts.

The analysis reveals, however, that Afro-Caribbeans and African-Americans in New York—like non-White groups elsewhere—have not had much success at fostering a sturdy race-based coalition. I find that relations between Afro-Caribbean and African-American leaders typically have deteriorated in the face of interest conflicts over descriptive representation. The critical role that interest convergence plays in coalition building has been well established by scholars (Sonenshein 2003a). When interests are at odds, alliances crumble, or fail to develop for that matter. But rather than leaving the analysis at that conventional wisdom, the article explores why the racial commonalities the two groups share have not compelled them to settle these differences, as the minority group perspective would predict. It would be simplistic not to expect divisions of some kind among non-White groups. The challenge of any coalition is to overcome the inevitable intergroup differences and emphasize commonalities and compromises. Scholars who subscribe to the minority group view believe that race provides much of the incentive to do so.

I offer evidence from a series of interviews with Afro-Caribbean political leaders, however, that race is not always the unifying category that minority group scholars expect it to be. My analysis of the interview data shows that race, despite its potential as a rallying point, has serious limits as a linchpin for coalitions among non-Whites. In fact, it actually may heighten divisions among racial minority groups by emphasizing some interests over others. The analysis specifies and traces the conditions under which such differences tend to manifest, even in the face of strong racial affinities such as the ones shared by Afro-Caribbean and African-American New Yorkers.

I then turn from the internal dynamics between these two groups to consider whether any external factors may also help to explain why they have been unable to capitalize on their commonalities to forge a stable alliance. I argue that two key New York City political institutions—its parties and elections—have tended to undermine the intraracial commonalities between these two constituencies; these institutions, in fact, often have exacerbated the interethnic conflicts over descriptive representation between them. I also speculate that the lack of an institutional vehicle to bring African-American and Afro-Caribbean elites together to emphasize shared racial interests, address disagreements, and find compromises has also made it difficult for them to sustain a coalition. In sum, the article draws two major conclusions from the case study. First, race has serious limits as a site for coalition building among non-White groups. Second, whatever potential it does hold may be undermined by a city's political institutions. More generally, the article suggests that the literature on coalition building among non-White minorities in cities should be more attentive to how the complexities of race play out in intergroup relations and how institutions shape these dynamics.

. . .

The Minority Group Theoretical Perspective

With so few cases of successful race-based alliances between non-White immigrants and African-Americans in the literature, the question is why they are expected to develop at all. Why would scholars who advance the minority group perspective predict such a coalition in light of such limited empirical evidence? First, their expectations rest on the bedrock of dominant historical patterns in

American politics. Race has been a long-standing and stubborn dividing line in local, state, and national politics in the United States. "Indeed, throughout American politics, the racial barrier redefined opinions, attitudes, and alignments" (Sonenshein 2003b, 334). In urban politics, race has been a key axis for the ideological divisions and interest conflicts that dominate campaigns, make and break political alliances, and shape voting preferences. For much of that history, Blacks and Whites have been on opposite sides of the dividing line. But even when groups of Blacks and Whites have managed to forge alliances, racial issues often have been the touchstone for interest and ideological convergence between the two (Browning et al. 2003).

Although some observers believe that the new non-White immigrants will blur and diminish the significance of the racial divide in urban politics, minority group scholars predict that it will hold. Only instead of pitting Whites against Blacks, it will divide Whites and non-Whites. Even with limited empirical evidence to date of race-based coalitions between Blacks and the new immigrants, minority group scholars infer from the long history of racial division in this country that such alliances are still likely to develop. They reason that as non-White newcomers meet racial barriers such as the ones African-Americans have encountered, the probability of their making political common cause with their native-born Black counterparts will increase.

Beyond the dominant patterns of racial division in this country, minority group scholars also take their analytic cues from theories of African-American politics. More specifically, the minority group view draws much of its inspiration from the literature on "linked racial fate" in African-American politics (Dawson 1994a; Tate 1993). Scholars have found that African-Americans remain a unified voting bloc in many cities, despite growing class divisions within the population (Stone and Pieranunzi 1997; Reed 1988). Dawson and others contend that the persistence of the racial divide and anti-Black discrimination in American life are what keep middle- and low-income African-Americans in relatively close political step. African-Americans, the argument goes, share a "linked fate" insofar as they all inevitably confront racial disadvantages. Race is, in short, a powerful political common denominator among African-Americans, trumping the divisions between the middle class and the poor. It is essentially the linchpin unifying middle- and low-income Blacks in an intraracial coalition. Similarly, minority group scholars predict that race will override the differences between African-Americans and the new immigrants and encourage them to forge political alliances.

The Prima Facie Case for an Afro-Caribbean and African-American Alliance

There are good reasons to expect this prediction to hold for non-white groups in New York City, particularly African-Americans and Afro-Caribbean immigrants. First, racial division and inequality have long been salient features of life in the city. Immigration has increased New York's demographic diversity in recent decades, to be sure: Foreign-born minority groups from Latin America, Asia, and the Caribbean have proliferated, while the numbers of native-born Whites and Blacks have declined. But even in the face of these new patterns of population diversity, familiar racial divisions remain. The city's political and economic sectors are marked by a pronounced racial divide, with well-off Whites often on one side and relatively disadvantaged non-White minorities on the other.

New York's Racial Divisions

New York's racial minorities have made significant advances in the past few decades, to be sure. Blacks, Latinos, and Asians have gone from having virtually no presence on the city council in the 1970s to a level of representation now almost proportionate to their numbers in the population. Racial minorities likewise have elected their own representatives to the state legislature and Congress, as well as to three of the city's five boroughs presidencies (Mollenkopf 2003). There are also signs of minority progress in the economy. Among the more notable trends from the past decade are the increases in Black incomes, Asian educational progress, and Latino business growth (Lewis Mumford Center for Comparative Urban and Regional Research 2002).

But the picture is not altogether sanguine. Even with these advances by racial minorities, Whites continue to enjoy a disproportionate share of the power, influence, and rewards in both the economic and political spheres of New York life. Table 6.1 indicates that significant disparities remain between the city's White and minority populations on key indicators of economic well-being. White New Yorkers outpace their minority counterparts by a substantial margin in median income. One recent study also uncovered a wide racial gap in neighborhood quality among New York residents (Lewis Mumford Center for Comparative Urban and Regional Research 2002). Whites tend to live in areas of the city with higher incomes, more homeowners, greater numbers of degree holders, and lower poverty rates than their minority counterparts.

Similarly, although New York's minorities have enjoyed considerable political gains in the past two decades, they nonetheless have much less substantive policy influence than Whites do. That is, they have less access to the political levers that actually control policy outcomes. Mollenkopf (2003) noted,

Table 6.1 Median Income by Groups in New York City

Year	All Groups	Non-Hispanic Whites	Non-Hispanic Blacks	Hispanics	Asians
2000	38,293	50,920	35,629	27,881	41,338
1990	38,706	47,325	31,955	20,402	41,350

Source: Data are from Lewis Mumford Center for Comparative Urban and Regional Research (2002).
Note: Median income for both years adjusted for 2000 dollars.

With the exception of Congressman Charles Rangel . . . none of the city's minority legislators . . . wields great influence within their legislative bodies. . . . The city's minority legislators can and do extract rewards from the White leaders of their bodies, but they do not exert a strong and independent influence on the overall allocation of public benefits. (Pp. 121–22)

At the mayoral level, minorities largely have been at the margins or outside of the electoral and governing coalitions assembled by New York's chief executive. Several of the elections for the top office have been racially divisive. What is more, the mayoralty has been occupied by a succession of White politicians. Aside from the short-lived administration headed by African-American David Dinkins, minorities have not played a leading role in the city's mayoral regimes. Although several have relied on a modicum of minority support, they have been dominated largely by Whites. Blacks, Latinos, and Asians mostly have occupied subordinate positions, if any at all.

Racial Commonalities between Afro-Caribbeans and African-Americans

Although the divisions separating Whites and non-Whites in New York are pronounced and politically salient, there is no reason to believe that they alone would compel a race-based alliance among the city's minority constituencies. The minority group view holds that such divisions are necessary but not sufficient to produce the predicted coalition. According to this perspective, alliances among non-Whites are probable, not only when there is a sharp racial divide in the political system but also when there are strong commonalities among the minority groups. By that logic, minority group scholars perhaps would not be surprised to find that African-Americans have not been able to forge a sustained alliance with the city's Latino or Asian constituencies (Falcon 1988; Mollenkopf 2003).[3]

After all, there are notable cultural, ideological, economic, and even racial differences between native-born Blacks and these immigrant groups. Many Latinos, for instance, do not identify as non-Whites or racial minorities, unlike African-Americans who largely do. In short, the racial commonalities between African-American New Yorkers and their Asian and Latino counterparts are limited; the differences among these groups arguably match or outweigh the similarities.

For African-Americans and Afro-Caribbean immigrants, however, there is a much stronger argument to be made for racial commonalities. The two groups of Black New Yorkers appear to have considerable mutual interests and incentives for forging a race-based alliance. Consider the prima facie case. First, Afro-Caribbeans and African-Americans obviously share the commonality of Black skin color in a country where discrimination against Blacks has a long history. . . .

The two groups experience higher levels of residential segregation than any other population in New York (Lewis Mumford Center for Comparative Urban and Regional Research 2003). Put another way, both Afro-Caribbeans and African-Americans are confined to overwhelmingly Black sections of the city.[4] The neighborhoods where the two groups live tend to be more economically distressed than majority-White areas. Afro-Caribbeans and African-Americans are exposed to the same neighborhood problems, whether they be failing schools, concentrated poverty, or crime. These two groups thus often have overlapping interests in contests over the distribution of public services and resources to city neighborhoods.

Both Afro-Caribbeans and African-Americans also have had their share of neighborhood-level tensions with Whites. Quite a few of New York's most serious cases of interracial conflict from the past two decades have involved either Afro-Caribbeans or African-Americans and White residents. In the late 1980s and early 1990s, the city was convulsed by a series of violent attacks against Blacks by groups of Whites. All but one of these incidents involved an Afro-Caribbean victim (Waters 1996). The two groups also have had turbulent relations with the city's mostly White police force. There is no need to rehearse individual instances of conflict here. But suffice it to say that there have been complaints about police brutality and misconduct from both the African-American and Afro-Caribbean communities.

Finally, Afro-Caribbean immigrants and African-Americans have similar partisan attachments. The two groups are more heavily Democratic than any other constituency—White or non-White—in the New York City electorate. Although first-generation Afro-Caribbean immigrants do not have the same long-standing, historical ties to the party as their native-born counterparts, they nonetheless have favored the Democratic line almost as much as African-Americans in their voting and registration patterns.

This shared party allegiance does not necessarily mean that Afro-Caribbeans and African-Americans have identical ideological outlooks. Indeed, Afro-Caribbean election districts are consistently several points less Democratic than African-American districts. Although both groups tend to be fairly liberal in their political outlooks, there are shades of difference between them on particular policy questions. Afro-Caribbeans, for instance, are supportive of liberal immigration policies, whereas African-Americans are more ambivalent (Fuchs 1990; Rogers 2000). A few case studies also have suggested that Afro-Caribbeans may be a little less supportive than their native-born counterparts of government solutions to social problems (Rogers 2000; Waters 1999). Still, there is no evidence of deep ideological divisions between these two overwhelmingly Democratic constituencies.

Support for the party has led to gains for African-Americans and Afro-Caribbean immigrants at the elite level. African-Americans have secured leadership positions in the Democratic county organizations. The party also has incorporated a handful of Afro-Caribbean elites in recent years. Even with these gains, both groups have less power within the party than Whites do. In Queens and the Bronx, Whites continue to control a disproportionate share of the leadership positions and influence within the Democratic Party; only in Manhattan, and in Brooklyn to a lesser extent, have African-Americans been able to wield a decisive share of power in the party organization. After many decades of unwavering allegiance to the Democratic Party, then, native-born Blacks still do not match their White counterparts in their level of influence over the organization. Afro-Caribbeans, on the other hand, are marginal players, as the party continues to ignore the vast majority of these immigrants.

All in all, the racial commonalities between African-Americans and Afro-Caribbean immigrants are more than skin deep. The two groups have a number of experiences, interests, and partisan viewpoints in common. They also boast a solid cadre of leaders who regularly interact within New York's Democratic Party. All these factors—common interests, shared ideology, and familiar leadership, coupled with the pronounced racial divide in New York City politics—would appear to pave the way for a race-based alliance between Afro-Caribbean immigrants and African-Americans. This is not to say that there are no potential divisions between the two groups. Yet the minority group view would argue that their commonalities and the strategic appeal of a race-based coalition should override such divisions. This perspective recognizes a clear imperative for these two groups of Blacks to "close racial ranks" and forge a stable political alliance (Kasinitz 1992; Carmichael and Hamilton 1967).

Race-based mobilization represents an alternative route into politics for the thousands of Afro-Caribbean immigrants who have been neglected by the Democratic Party. Outnumbered by African-Americans, these newcomers might find it hard to resist the strategic benefits of combining with their native-born counterparts to build a larger Black constituency and thereby achieve incorporation. Likewise, such mobilization could also serve as a potent source of political leverage for African-Americans seeking to enlarge their share of government resources and influence on the direction of public policy. With their combined numbers, the two groups could comprise a powerful minority bloc of voters with the potential to decide election outcomes.

The Empirical Case: A Coalition that Never Came

Yet Afro-Caribbean and African-American New Yorkers thus far have been unable to establish a stable coalition. For all their prima facie commonalities, the two groups have been no more successful at fostering a race-based alliance than their non-White counterparts in other cities. There have been instances of political cooperation and common cause between them, to be sure. In 1989, for example, Afro-Caribbean and African-American voters lined up solidly behind Dinkins in his successful first bid for the mayoralty. Together, the two groups were the single largest bloc of voters to support Dinkins in the election (Arian et al. 1991). Since then, these two groups of Black ethnics have also joined together at the voting booth to support high-profile Democratic candidates for state- and citywide office, such as Senator Hillary Clinton and unsuccessful mayoral candidate Mark Green.

Similarly, the episodes of police brutality in Black neighborhoods in the late 1990s galvanized hundreds of Afro-Caribbeans and African-Americans to take to the streets and demand greater police accountability. Both the Dinkins election and the protests against police brutality appealed to the sense of racial solidarity among African-Americans and Afro-Caribbeans. The two instances might well have been viewed as promising precursors to the race-based coalition anticipated by minority group scholars. But these cases of mutual support were episodic and short lived.

Patterns of Conflict

Relations between Afro-Caribbean immigrants and African-Americans over the past two decades more often have been marked by a stubborn undercurrent of tension. My interviews with Afro-Caribbean elites reveal a pattern of friction in the political relationship between the two groups. The conflicts have not extended to rank-and-file Afro-Caribbean and African-American constituents. Nor have they revolved around anything such as competing economic interests, substantive policy differences, or ideological disagreements. Rather, the conflicts typically have been confined to the elite level and have centered mostly on matters of political turf. More specifically, African-American and Afro-Caribbean leaders have clashed over attempts by the latter group to secure descriptive representation and carve out political influence for a distinct Caribbean constituency. African-American leaders have resisted these efforts, whereas their Afro-Caribbean counterparts have complained about the opposition from their fellow Black leaders.

My interview respondents noted that African-American politicians have long been resistant or lukewarm to the prospect of Afro-Caribbean mobilization. One interviewee (November 22, 1996) conjectured that African-American opposition to Caribbean participation was one impediment to greater electoral representation for the immigrant group. As he explained, Afro-Caribbeans have yet to achieve a level of representation proportionate to their numbers, "partially because there has been opposition from African-American leaders." Caribbean Action Lobby (CAL) member and former state senator Waldaba Stewart (interview, May 2, 1997) recalled that many African-American politicians were either slow or unwilling to acknowledge the emergence of an Afro-Caribbean ethnic constituency in the 1980s.

> Ten, fifteen years ago, African-Americans—many of them—took the position that the only relevant issues were African-American issues, and in many respects ignored the growing Caribbean bloc. . . . In the 1980s, they didn't even want us to run for political office.

Indeed, as Kasinitz (1992) has recounted in his study, African-American politicians consistently opposed or refused to support Afro-Caribbean candidates for elective office in the 1980s.

The pattern continued into the 1990s. Consider former city councilwoman Una Clarke's account of her 1991 bid for a legislative seat. Clarke was seeking to represent a heavily Caribbean district in Brooklyn; her victory made her the first Caribbean-born member of the city council. Her account of the campaign underscores her perception that African-American leaders have often resisted

Afro-Caribbean mobilization. The Jamaican-born politician (interview, December 13, 20, 1996) recalled,

> I helped to elect almost every African-American in central Brooklyn, and when my time came to run they were far and few in between that supported me. . . . There was not a single African-American that considered themselves "progressive" that did not come to me and did not ask for my support, and for whom I gave it. So when my time came, I thought that everybody was gonna rally around me, that there would not even be a campaign. . . . "Look your time has come.". . . Nothing of the sort happened.

In a 1999 interview, the former city councilwoman lamented, "I never saw bias until I ran in 1991. When I entered office the street talk was 'Why do these West Indians feel they have to be in politics?' " (Dao 1999). To be fair, Clarke did have the support of African-American Congressman Major Owens, who perhaps recognized that backing her would carry important symbolic value in his own increasingly Caribbean district. But staunch opposition to Clarke's campaign came from African-American Clarence Norman, Brooklyn's Democratic county leader. Norman ran his own candidate, fellow African-American Carl Andrews, for the council seat and led an ultimately aborted legal challenge to Clarke's victory in the aftermath of the election. Clarke and Norman have managed to build a cordial, if somewhat delicate, relationship since then (*New York Carib News* 1996a).

The former city councilwoman and other elite respondents also noted that African-American leaders generally have been slow to court Afro-Caribbeans as a distinct constituency. When asked whether African-American politicians reach out to Caribbean-American voters, one campaign organizer (interview, November 24, 1996) replied tersely, "Not enough. And when they do, they reach out half-heartedly." Another respondent (interview, July 5, 1997) offered,

> [Clarence] Norman has enormous political clout because he is the head of the Democratic Party in Brooklyn. From time to time, I've heard Caribbean leaders, including Una Clarke, that he would support other people than them. I'm not sure if that's the case. But I would like to see him in more [Caribbean] events. I would like to see him reach out more to the community.

Clarke rated White politicians slightly higher than African-Americans on outreach to the Caribbean population. She (interview, December 13, 20, 1996) elaborated, "I think White politicians [unlike their Black counterparts] feel compelled to do that kind of outreach. Yes. Marty Markowitz is a well-known example. And I can give other examples too."

More recently, some African-American leaders—Dinkins, Owens, Sharpton, and Rangel—have begun to make their own appeals to the immigrant community. Owens and Sharpton have been particularly vocal about incidents of police brutality involving immigrants from the Caribbean, Latin America, and Africa. Their efforts are clearly intended to acknowledge the growing numbers of foreign-born newcomers to the city and perhaps to prevent conservative interests from pursuing divide-and-conquer tactics among New York's minority constituencies. But some of my respondents still characterize these efforts by African-American leaders as begrudging or lukewarm. One (interview, November 22, 1996) recalled Dinkins's early outreach to Caribbean-Americans. "Oh, we had a rough time getting Dinkins out into the Caribbean community. . . . They say that there were some people in Dinkins's camp who were very anti-Caribbean—African-American people." In sum, many Afro-Caribbean elites remain convinced that some African-American politicians still regard the prospect of Caribbean mobilization with ambivalence or resistance.

Key historical episodes in the relations between Afro-Caribbean and African-American political elites tend to support the views of these respondents. One of the most well known instances of conflict between the two groups came during former mayor Ed Koch's 1985 bid for reelection. A group of approximately 150 politically active Afro-Caribbeans established "Caribbeans for Koch" to back the incumbent mayor's campaign. Support for Koch in the Afro-Caribbean immigrant community was hardly widespread or deep. But the group's aim was largely symbolic. That is, to secure greater access to the mayor and City Hall for Afro-Caribbean immigrants—especially since Koch would likely be reelected. Caribbeans for Koch was thus an early attempt by Afro-Caribbean elites to signal the emergence of their immigrant community as a distinctive ethnic constituency with its own aspirations to political power (Kasinitz 1992, 253).

Whatever the motivation, Caribbeans for Koch was met with a torrent of angry criticism from African-American political leaders. Their outrage was fueled by two major concerns. First, anti-Koch sentiment was pervasive in the African-American community. African-American leaders accused the mayor of fomenting anti-Black racism and exacerbating the city's racial problems with his incendiary rhetoric. In their view, then, Caribbeans for Koch showed complete disregard for the mayor's troubling record on race relations; that insensitivity was perhaps all the more incensing to African-American leaders because it came from a group of Black immigrants, who were expected to be equally as outraged by the mayor's record on race as their native-born counterparts.

Second, Caribbeans for Koch was established at the same time that African-American leaders were attempting to "close ranks" and mount an independent political initiative to replace Koch with a Black mayor. The Coalition for a Just New York brought together scores of Black politicians and activists to identify a candidate and support his campaign. The expectation by organizers was that the group would mobilize Blacks and other minority New Yorkers to help ensure electoral victory. The coalition was riven by internal division, though; their African-American candidate ran a poor campaign and lost. Yet many African-Americans strongly criticized Caribbeans for Koch for working at cross-purposes with the coalition, flouting the goals of African-American political leadership, and undermining the larger struggle for Black empowerment. As one of my elite respondents recalled, the African-American leader of the Coalition for a Just New York, Al Vann, publicly reproached Afro-Caribbean leaders for pursuing divisive strategies. "They were not happy with us [Caribbean American leaders]. Al Vann called our attempts to organize on our own tribalism" (interview, November 22, 1996). The supporters of the

Coalition for a Just New York essentially saw this attempt at independent Caribbean mobilization as a strain against the tether of racial solidarity.

There have been more recent political conflicts between the two groups involving issues of racial unity and representation. In fact, the tensions have become more palpable as growing numbers of Caribbean politicians run for elective office in the name of a distinct Afro-Caribbean ethnic constituency. As the numbers of Afro-Caribbean New Yorkers have increased steadily over the past two decades, so too has the political viability and likelihood of such ethnically targeted campaigns by Caribbean politicians. These attempts by Afro-Caribbean political entrepreneurs to organize their fellow immigrants into a distinct voting bloc still engender occasional criticism and resistance from some African-American leaders.

A number of Afro-Caribbean candidates joined the fray in the last round of New York City elections by making direct appeals to their coethnics. The most notable instance was the 2000 race for Brooklyn's Eleventh Congressional District seat between nine-term incumbent Owens and former city councilwoman Clarke. Blacks comprise 55% of the district population; more than two-thirds of them trace their roots to the Caribbean. The large numbers of Afro-Caribbeans in the district is a striking example of how immigration has transformed this stretch of central Brooklyn over the past few decades. Despite these demographic shifts, African-American Congressman Owens had held on to his seat since 1982 without a serious electoral challenge. That is, until he faced a fierce test from Clarke in the 2001 Democratic primary. Although Owens won the primary and went on to retain the seat in a lopsided general election victory, the race was one of the most bitter of the campaign season.

Practically none of the rancor between the two candidates was driven by actual issue disagreements. Rather, it was fueled by two very emotionally charged factors. First, there was the underlying tableau of political betrayal. The two were long-time political allies before Clarke announced her candidacy. Owens described himself as a former mentor to the councilwoman (Hicks 2000b). He thus saw her bid to replace him as an act of political betrayal. Clarke, on the other hand, dismissed the talk of betrayal as a distraction from her true motivation for mounting her campaign: that is, to serve the district's constituents. As she put it, "Too much has been made of friendship. It's about leadership and effectiveness. I don't think he's kept up with the needs of the changing community" (Hicks 2000a). Note that Clarke's mention of the "changing community" might be taken as a thinly veiled reference to the increasing numbers of Caribbean immigrants in the district. Her allusion hints at the other factor that fueled the rancor of the contest between these two candidates.

Even more significant than this personal tableau was the pall of interethnic conflict that hung over the race. Clarke made a point of trumpeting her Caribbean roots, appealing directly to her coethnics, and painting her opponent as anti-immigrant. Her goal clearly was to announce the presence of a distinct Caribbean constituency within the majority Black Eleventh District. Even more critically, she sought to emphasize her affinity with these immigrant voters while at the same time raising doubts about the incumbent's sensitivity to their concerns. Owens, in turn, condemned Clarke for couching her campaign in what he described as a divisive ethnic chauvinism (Hicks 2000a). His complaint was echoed by a number of African-American leaders who sent Clarke a letter urging her to abandon her candidacy. The congressman lamented that Clarke's tactics would split Brooklyn's Black community and undermine the larger cause of Black empowerment. His complaints practically echoed those directed against Caribbeans for Koch by African-American leaders more than 15 years earlier.

Case Study Analysis

The conflicts over descriptive representation between Afro-Caribbean and African-American leaders are striking for how often the question of racial unity is invoked. The fact that racial solidarity has not provided the incentive for the two groups to overcome these differences belies the predictions of the minority group view. The steady recurrence of such conflicts suggests that even racial commonality has its limits as a potential coalition linchpin.

The Limits of Racial Solidarity

The interviews and historical evidence indicate that African-American politicians have had one prevailing criticism against their Afro-Caribbean counterparts in the conflicts over descriptive representation. They complain that the immigrants' efforts to appeal to a separate Afro-Caribbean constituency are divisive and antithetical to the cause of racial solidarity and greater Black empowerment.[5] This lament typically greets electoral campaigns by Caribbean politicians seeking to rally, mobilize, or acknowledge their coethnics as a distinct constituency. The logic behind this line of criticism is straightforward. Appealing separately to Afro-Caribbean immigrants, the complaint goes, is tantamount to splitting apart Black New Yorkers, which in turn undermines Black political power. African-American political leaders have grown increasingly concerned about these potential divisions over the past decade, as the numbers of non-White immigrants in the city have expanded. Their worry is that conservative political interests will look to exploit or even sow divisions between African-Americans and these new immigrant constituencies, thereby dousing any potential for a liberal rainbow coalition led by Blacks. It is the classic divide-and-conquer strategy. Divisions between native- and Caribbean-born Black New Yorkers, they contend, might be put to those very political designs. In short, some African-Americans argue that the mobilization of Afro-Caribbeans as a distinct constituency is ultimately a threat to Black racial solidarity and empowerment.

Afro-Caribbeans, on the other hand, insist that the opposition from African-American leaders is unfair and that appeals to racial unity are beside the point. More precisely, Afro-Caribbean politicians note that the immigrant community is large enough to warrant its own representatives and has distinctive concerns that cannot be taken for granted or glossed over with appeals to Black racial solidarity. My elite respondents were emphatic on this point. One (interview, December 14, 1996) offered,

> I think because we [Caribbean-Americans] have some separate interests, we have a responsibility to be a distinct bloc, be it around immigration and immigration reform, be it around trade with the Caribbean. I think that we can play a pivotal role. . . . We have that obligation. And I think it's a mistake to use skin color to be the only criterion. To use skin color as the only criterion stifles both African-Americans and Caribbean-Americans.

Another respondent gave a more concise reply to the same question. He (interview, November 23, 1996) explained, "Caribbean-Americans are a distinct bloc. Of course, we share many of the same concerns of African-Americans. But we have our own needs and concerns that you just can't dismiss or take it for granted that they [African-Americans] will understand." A community activist answered the charge that Afro-Caribbean mobilization promotes divisiveness within New York's Black population this way.

> Our comment is that you have different Caucasian or White groups, you have the Irish, the Italian, the this and that. What's wrong with us? Why can't we have that too? Just because we're originally, say from Africa, does that mean we have to think and act the same way? Don't we [Caribbean-Americans] have our own needs and issues? (interview, May 2, 1997)

Furthermore, many resent what they perceive to be African-American leaders' implicit assumption that Afro-Caribbeans will be relegated to junior status in any alliance between the two groups. In a 1996 interview, for example, Clarke bristled when she was asked about African-American county leader Norman's aim to consolidate Black political power in the heavily Caribbean 43rd AD. "There are over 300,000 Caribbean Americans in Central Brooklyn. What consolidation are we talking about here? Nobody will relegate us to second class status" (*New York Carib News* 1996b). It is clear that Clarke's objection is not necessarily to the prospect of a unified Black political bloc; in fact, she and many of the Caribbean-American leaders I interviewed were supportive of the notion of a coalition between the two groups. But her worry is that the political goals and interests of Afro-Caribbean immigrants will be subordinated in any such alliance.

Clarke's concern illuminates an important analytic point about alliances built around the idea of racial solidarity. The former city councilwoman noted that African-American leaders insist on serving as racial agents on behalf of Afro-Caribbean immigrants by appealing to the notion of group unity,[6] but in doing so, they often diminish or ignore the distinctive ethnic interests of their foreign-born counterparts. Appeals to racial group unity or collective racial interests—such as the ones made by Vann, Norman, and Owens more recently—are almost always articulated in an effort to advance very specific agendas, which ultimately favor some interests over others. Vann's Coalition for a Just New York, for instance, invoked the goal of racial group unity to criticize and discourage independent mobilization by Afro-Caribbean politicians. The coalition's expectation was that all Black New Yorkers, native- and foreign-born alike, should fall in line with their hand-picked candidates and issue positions. Their notion of group unity, then, was one in which their agenda took precedence over other interests within New York's Black community, such as Afro-Caribbeans' desire for their own share of political influence.

Of course, racial solidarity in politics does not necessarily prescribe or authorize a particular agenda, set of positions, or slate of candidates. Indeed, calls to racial unity might well be seen as an invitation to discuss and reach negotiated stances on such issues. Yet appeals to racial solidarity often implicitly privilege one set of interests over others without any open debate. Even worse, the resulting bias takes cover beneath the rhetorical gloss of "natural" or "collective" racial interests that benefit the population as a whole. Consequently, interests that ought to be debated or evaluated for how they affect different constituents are instead deemed to be settled and beyond question. The case of African-Americans and Afro-Caribbeans in New York demonstrates that the group that happens to have more influence—whether by virtue of numbers, longer political history, or whatever—has the advantage of framing the agenda in this way. African-American elites in New York thus have often taken the lead in prescribing what is required for a race-based alliance or minority empowerment, even if that agenda is not necessarily conducive to the interests of Afro-Caribbeans or other non-White groups.

Furthermore, the case demonstrates that the notion of racial group unity not only favors specific interests and agendas but also can be used to impose discipline and gatekeeping. Appeals to racial group solidarity are often made in the service of mobilization efforts. But the tensions between African-American and Afro-Caribbean politicians show that racial group unity is a two-edged sword that can also be used to discourage mobilization by particular interests within the Black population, or any minority constituency for that matter. To discipline specific constituencies within the population, dominant elites often stake out certain positions and label them as the ones most in keeping with the aims of racial empowerment and the political preferences of Blacks as a whole.[7] Any interests that appear to deviate from those positions are then conveniently challenged for threatening group unity, the "true" preferences of Blacks, or the cause of empowerment. The criticisms lodged against Caribbeans for Koch by the leaders of the Coalition for a Just New York are an obvious example of this tactic.

Owens employed a similar strategy against Clarke in their 2000 primary battle. The congressman tried to portray the city councilwoman as a supporter of Mayor Rudolph Giuliani, who was notoriously unpopular among Blacks during his tenure in office. He also charged that Clarke had been silent on the issue of police brutality, about which the vast majority of Black New Yorkers were acutely concerned. In contrast, he noted that he had engaged in demonstrations to protest incidents of brutality and had even been arrested (Hicks 2000a). Owens essentially waved his civil rights credentials in support of Blacks, while implying that Clarke had none to show. The strategy served to brand the Caribbean-born candidate as a kind of race traitor, a politician out of step with Black interests and the goal of Black empowerment. Tactics such as these are likely to play a role in the conflicts between Afro-Caribbean and African-American leaders, precisely because questions of racial unity so often come into play.[8]

Why Interest Conflicts Over Descriptive Representation

The analysis demonstrates why race is not the ultimate unifying category that minority group scholars expect it to be, even for two groups of Blacks. Yet the question that remains is why the interest conflicts between Afro-Caribbean and African-American elites have focused on descriptive representation. African-Americans have achieved higher levels of influence in New York City politics than have Afro-Caribbeans and other non-White groups. As the dominant minority group in the Democratic Party, in fact, African-Americans have been able to control a significant share of the material rewards. Mobilization by Afro-Caribbean newcomers, or any other minority group for that matter, could potentially threaten their hold on these political prizes. Entrenched African-American elites thus have a rational interest in maintaining the status quo and resisting Afro-Caribbean mobilization.

Afro-Caribbeans and African-Americans are concentrated in many of the same election districts. The ascension of an Afro-Caribbean to political office could mean the displacement of an African-American incumbent. Several respondents explained this competitive intergroup dynamic.

> There definitely is competition and conflict between the two groups sometimes, especially in politics. Part of the problem is, if you want to call it, we are fighting for the same political offices in the same election districts. We're fighting for the same piece of the pie. And African-Americans probably think if Caribbean people get elected they will lose out on their share. (interview, November 28, 1996)

The result is often African-American resistance to Caribbean political initiative and organization. As Clarke (interview, December 13, 20, 1996) put it, "The [African-American] attitude is 'don't try passing me. I've been here.' "

Battles over political turf and representation between the two groups thus devolve into zero-sum struggles. The conflicts are not simply over political office but also access to the government jobs and other prizes that come with it. For some African-American politicians, then, the interest in political self-preservation trumps any vision for race-based mobilization and coalition building between them and their Caribbean-born counterparts. Afro-Caribbean elites, on the other hand, worry that their interest in greater descriptive representation and policy influence will be trumped by African-American political prerogatives.

The competition between African-Americans and Afro-Caribbeans is arguably reminiscent of earlier historical conflicts among White ethnic groups. There were, for example, fierce battles over patronage and positions within the Democratic Party between Jewish and Italian New Yorkers. But there is an important distinction between those earlier interethnic conflicts and the current tensions between African-American and Afro-Caribbeans. The earlier competition for patronage and public jobs among Irish, Italian, and Jewish ethnics was diminished, or at least moderated, as one or the other group moved into private-sector employment and up the socioeconomic ladder. Italian politicians, for instance, had less of a stake in holding on to government jobs when their coethnics began to find success in private-sector professions. They were thus gradually inclined to relinquish patronage positions in government to their Jewish rivals.

Today's African-American political elites, however, are much more reluctant to concede public-sector jobs and positions to their Caribbean-born counterparts. Their determination to hold on to these forms of public patronage is not surprising. Discrimination historically has made it difficult for African-Americans to find jobs and move up the career ladder in the private sector. Government, in contrast, has long furnished them with fair and ample employment opportunities. Indeed, public-sector jobs have helped foster the expansion of a stable African-American middle class in New York and other cities. The incentive to hold on to these public-sector jobs is thus much greater for African-Americans than it was for White ethnics in the past century. To put it more bluntly, the stakes are higher.

African-Americans thus arguably have legitimate reason to worry about Afro-Caribbean political mobilization. Their concern is likely compounded by the widespread perception that Whites often view these foreign-born Blacks more favorably than African-Americans (Waters 1999).[9] Any potential advancement by Afro-Caribbeans essentially raises the specter not only of political displacement but also economic backsliding for African-Americans. By this light, Afro-Caribbeans look less like a racial in-group and potential coalition partner for native-born Blacks and more like a competing out-group that could threaten African-Americans' share of political power and public-sector resources. That threat of competition and displacement calls into question a key assumption of the minority group perspective: that is, that non-White groups are likely to find common cause and grounds for coalition building in their shared racial experiences. For all the galvanizing power that race carries, this has not been the case with African-American and Afro-Caribbean New Yorkers. Clearly, even presumed common racial interests have their limits.

Electoral Institutions

Another weakness of the minority perspective is a failure to consider how institutional factors might influence the way groups perceive and frame their interests. Racial inequalities and divisions in the political system provide considerable impetus for African-Americans, Afro-Caribbeans, and other non-Whites to forge a race-based alliance, to be sure. But whether groups opt to coalesce and capitalize on common interests—racial or otherwise—or go it alone depends to some degree to the incentive structure of the political system. The prospects hinge on how political institutions frame group perceptions about interests, competition, rewards, and so on. In the case of Afro-Caribbeans, the interviews make it clear that the immigrants are inclined to elect their own co-ethnics to political office rather than having African-Americans serve as their racial agents. The question is how the immigrants came to value ethnic over racial representation.

It turns out that New York's elective institutions may very well dispose them to do so. The city's electoral structure encourages groups to organize and think of themselves primarily as ethnic cohorts, rather than as racial constituents. Electoral jurisdictions in New York City closely follow the outlines of ethnic neighborhoods. The scores of community board, city council, and state assembly seats in New York are based on districts that often track the boundaries of residential enclaves bearing the unmistakable stamp of particular ethnic groups. It is not too much of an exaggeration, then, to conclude that the basic political jurisdiction in the minds of New York politicians and perhaps its voters is the ethnic neighborhood. It is the fundamental unit of the city's political cartography. New York's "city trenches," to borrow Katznelson's (1981) famous phrase, are its ethnic neighborhoods.

Consider the 40th city council district seat, formerly held by Caribbean-born Una Clarke and now occupied by her daughter. The city created this district in 1991 specifically to accommodate the proliferation of Caribbean immigrant enclaves in central Brooklyn. Most of the pressure to establish the seat came from Afro-Caribbean politicians. The new district essentially gave the ethnic group an opportunity to garner its own share of political representation. As Stewart of CAL (interview, May 2, 1997) put it, "We [Caribbean politicians] noticed that other groups had districts to represent their people, we felt we should have some too." His remark suggests that the decision to push for a heavily Caribbean city council district was not merely the result of constituent pressure or elite initiative. Rather, it was encouraged by politicians' perceptions of the institutional logic of the city's electoral districts. Once institutional arrangements are in place, they tend to influence how elites understand their interests, their ties to constituents, and their relations with other groups. Sure enough, the 40th city council seat has come to be held perpetually and predictably by a Caribbean politician, fulfilling the logic of the district's original design.

More generally, the city's electoral battles are waged from these ethnic neighborhood trenches. The most obvious way for an aspiring politician to build a constituent base in New York is to rally and mobilize voters in ethnic neighborhoods. If a politician can put together a sizable, cohesive bloc of ethnic votes at the neighborhood level, he or she essentially can become a serious player in New York's political game. Politicians are thus often encouraged to make ethnic group appeals. Ethnic politics has long been a staple of political life in American cities, to be sure. The ethnic and immigrant enclaves across New York City are a hard-to-miss source of votes. But the close continuity between the design of the city's electoral institutions and the pattern of its ethnic neighborhoods reinforces this ethnically conscious form of political organization and mobilization. Ethnic appeals are practically dictated by the logic of the city's political jurisdictions.

Some researchers have argued convincingly that this neighborhood-based system of representation serves to regulate and perhaps mute interethnic tensions (Skerry 1993; Mollenkopf 1999). On this view, the system channels interethnic conflicts that might otherwise spill over into the streets and translates them to the bargaining table of the political process where they can be managed or resolved. That may explain why cities like New York and San Antonio, which both boast this kind of neighborhood-based system, have been less susceptible to volatile intergroup clashes than Los Angeles, where no such system exists. Nevertheless, this electoral institutional design simply transfers the potential for interethnic tension from the neighborhood to the elite level, where leaders are often encouraged to position themselves and relate to each other as representatives of particular ethnic groups. The interethnic conflicts thus move from the neighborhood level to the party system, the campaign trail, and the legislature.

It is no wonder, then, that relations between Afro-Caribbean and African-American political elites have been plagued by interethnic tensions over descriptive representation. The potential for interethnic conflict between these two groups of Black leaders is fairly telegraphed in the pattern of Black neighborhood settlement across New York City. Recall that African-Americans and Afro-Caribbean immigrants often live in adjoining neighborhoods or even share the same ones. When these areas are carved up into electoral jurisdictions, they easily become arenas for ethnically tinged, intraBlack bickering over descriptive representation. When a district that was predominantly African-American is somehow redrawn to give growing numbers of Afro-Caribbean immigrants a numerical advantage, the strategic incentive for Caribbean political entrepreneurs to make targeted ethnic appeals is hard to resist.

There are a few who avoid playing the ethnic card in campaigns. State Senator John Sampson is a good example. This second-generation Afro-Caribbean New Yorker has largely refrained from making exclusive appeals to his coethnics.[10] He instead campaigns to Blacks generally and scrupulously avoids the interethnic schisms that have erupted among the city's Black leaders. But most other Afro-Caribbean politicians have followed the ethnic strategy. The price of giving into the temptation is the danger of engendering interethnic conflict with African-American political elites faced with the specter of electoral displacement. The primary battle between Clarke and Owens is just one of the more well-known recent examples. But several cases fit this predicted pattern.

A simple historical comparison helps to demonstrate how the institutional design of New York's electoral districts shapes intergroup dynamics. It is no coincidence that the tensions over descriptive representation between Afro-Caribbean and African-American political elites have emerged only in the past two decades. Prior to 1989, the city council was not composed of the 51 neighborhood-based seats it boasts today. Rather, it consisted of 10 at-large districts, with 2 designated for each of the five boroughs (Macchiarola and Diaz 1993). Council members were elected on a borough-wide basis. Unlike the current neighborhood-based system, the at-large configuration compelled officeholders and candidates to make broad appeals beyond the boundaries of the city's ethnic enclaves.

An Afro-Caribbean politician with aspirations to the city council, for instance, could hardly afford to target only Caribbean voters in select neighborhoods. Minority candidates could win only by making wide cross-ethnic and sometimes cross-racial appeals. Earlier generations of Afro-Caribbean politicians thus refrained from marketing themselves as ethnic representatives of a distinct Caribbean constituency or appealing exclusively to their coethnics. Rather, they attempted to speak for Blacks at large and did not draw a distinction between themselves and their African-American counterparts (Kasinitz 1992; Watkins-Owens 1996). Consequently, there were almost no interethnic tensions over descriptive political representation between the two groups in that earlier era. This is not to say that there were no conflicts at all between Afro-Caribbeans and African-Americans. There were the inevitable cultural clashes and occasional conflicts over jobs when the immigrants first began migrating to New York (Vickerman 1999; Watkins-Owens 1996; Foner 1985; Hellwig 1978; Reid 1939).

Yet the friction between the two groups did not have much of a political dimension.[11] Ethnicity was simply not a major source of division or conflict among Blacks in the electoral sphere. With the shift to neighborhood-based city council seats, however, there is greater electoral incentive for Afro-Caribbean politicians to engage in the kind of ethnically targeted appeals that lead to tensions with African-American leaders. The past two decades have thus seen a marked increase in political conflicts between the two groups. Although this historical shift is not conclusive evidence, it does suggest indirectly that institutional configurations have some casual impact on intergroup racial and ethnic dynamics.

A brief comparison across cities also makes the point. The city of Hartford, like New York, is home to a sizable minority population of American- and Caribbean-born Blacks. Both groups, in fact, comprise roughly similar proportions of the minority population in both cities, although New York fairly dwarfs Hartford in absolute numbers. African-Americans in Hartford, like their counterparts in New York, also have enjoyed greater levels of electoral representation and influence than the city's other minority constituencies. But in the past decade, the other groups have started to make their own serious bids for political power. Afro-Caribbean leaders in Hartford have begun to organize their coethnics to participate in politics, much like their fellow Black immigrants in New York have been doing for the past two to three decades.

Yet these efforts by Hartford's Caribbean-born residents have generated considerably less friction and resistance from African-American leaders there than have the attempts by their counterparts in New York. A number of factors may explain this difference in intergroup dynamics, to be sure. But one important variable may be the design of Hartford's electoral institutions. Unlike New York's neighborhood-based city council districts, Hartford's legislature is composed of at-large seats. By the logic of the at-large electoral design, ethnically targeted campaigning must be balanced by broader appeals to other constituencies, which ultimately may serve to moderate or minimize interethnic conflict. It bears noting that the Hartford comparison is also not conclusive support for the casual impact of electoral institutions on intergroup dynamics, but it is certainly suggestive.

In the New York case, it should be emphasized that the interethnic tensions between these two groups of Black leaders took shape as Afro-Caribbean ethnic enclaves have developed and expanded to proportions large enough to leave an imprint or have an impact on the pattern of neighborhood-based electoral districts in boroughs such as Brooklyn and Queens. Prior to the 1980s, Caribbean settlements in these areas were too small to have much of an influence on the design of the city's system of elective representation or stand alone as a politically viable ethnic constituency. What is more, African-American and Afro-Caribbean political leaders could talk of representing the city's Blacks without drawing any further ethnic distinctions. Representing Blacks essentially meant African-Americans by and large. With the dramatic growth of the Caribbean immigrant population over the past few decades, however, intra-Black ethnic distinctions have taken on political salience. The potential for intergroup conflict is now reinforced by the city's electoral institutions.

The Absence of an Institutional Mechanism

Still, a final question remains: Why have the two groups been unable to resolve these interethnic differences over descriptive representation to build a coalition around their intraracial common interests and shared policy concerns? If New York's electoral institutions have encouraged or exacerbated the interethnic conflicts between Afro-Caribbean and African-American political leaders, the absence of certain other kinds of institutions have made those differences difficult to bridge. Sonenshein (2003b) was correct that shared interests, ideological compatibility, personal ties, and strong leadership are all essential for forging sturdy intergroup alliances. But his formulation overlooks one other important building block. Institutions are equally as important as interests, ideology, personal relations, and leadership for cultivating and sustaining coalitions. Viable institutions provide a framework for groups to engage in social learning, that is, articulate shared interests, acknowledge distinct ones, reinforce ideological commitments, solidify personal ties, and identify promising leaders.[12]

Race-based alliances among non-White groups do not simply spring from some essential racial viewpoint or presumptive group interest. Rather, such coalitions require an institutional mechanism for expressing and mobilizing substantive, shared racial interests—a point that proponents of the minority group view sometimes miss or overlook. Blacks in Chicago, for instance, developed a network of community organizations in the early 1980s that proved crucial to the election of the city's first Black mayor in 1983 (Grimshaw 1992). This institutional framework allowed Black Chicagoans to negotiate internal divisions, identify a strong mayoral candidate in Harold Washington, and muster the voter mobilization necessary to win the election. Similarly, institutional networks have been critical to successful intergroup coalition building in cities such as Atlanta (Stone 1989). The absence of such an institutional vehicle for New York's Afro-Caribbean and African-American political leaders largely explains their failure to override interethnic tensions and build an enduring race-based alliance.

The Democratic Party may appear, at first blush, to be a potentially viable institutional site for Afro-Caribbean and African-American elites to organize a race-based movement. By virtue of their combined numbers inside the party, the two groups have the makings of a powerful caucus capable of a reform. The overwhelming attachment of African-American and Afro-Caribbean voters to the Democratic Party also gives these leaders the electoral clout necessary for mounting such a challenge. In fact, a Black reform impulse surfaced in the party's Brooklyn organization in the mid-1970s. But it faded as infighting erupted and many of the erstwhile insurgents made peace with the regular Democratic machine. Since then, there has been no major, viable movement for insurgency by Blacks in Brooklyn or the other borough party organizations.

The failure of African-Americans and Afro-Caribbeans to mount an insurgent movement from within the Democratic Party confirms the long-standing common sense of V.O. Key's (1949) 50-year-old observation about one-party systems. Key argued that one-party systems tend to be breeding grounds for factionalism. Factions, he noted, give rise to personality-driven politics that focus on invidious status or group distinctions and drown out substantive policy issues. Hence, one-party systems, such as New York's Democratic organization, are notoriously unsuitable institutions for launching and sustaining reform movements. It is no wonder then that African-American and Afro-Caribbean leaders have been unable to put together an insurgent coalition from within New York's dominant Democratic party. Their relations within the party show all the symptoms of Key's diagnosis: squabbles over turf between individual politicians and disagreements over descriptive representation that deteriorate into interethnic schisms. Congruent with Key's predictions, tensions between Afro-Caribbean and African-American political leaders in the party tend to obscure the substantive issues in which they may share a common racial interest or mutual understanding.

Despite the dominance of the Democratic Party in New York City politics, there is a modest Republican organization that conceivably could serve as site for establishing a reformist coalition. Mollenkopf (1992, 89) reminds us that the Republican Party played this role in New York politics for many decades, uniting "discontented elements of the city electorate into potent, if short-lived, fusion movements." But it no longer does so today. The Republican Party has lost much of its organizational muscle and has transformed into a more conservative institution. As Mollenkopf (1997, 105) noted, "The Republican party has forsaken its traditional role as the organizational kernel of reform." Even more significantly, the party has made virtually no effort to court African-American and Afro-Caribbean voters. There is thus little chance that African-Americans and Afro-Caribbeans will mount a race-based movement for reform from either the Republican or Democratic Party.

Parties, however, hardly exhaust the list of potential institutional sites from which Afro-Caribbean and African-American New Yorkers could cultivate and sustain a reformist alliance. In fact, minority group scholars note that insurgent movements for greater racial inclusion typically begin from bases outside the conventional party system. Movements for African-American political empowerment and racial reform, for example, historically have begun in churches, civic groups, and neighborhood-based service organizations. These institutions provide a critical site for African-Americans to delineate their interests, clarify ideology, groom leaders, and strike alliances with other groups (Dawson 1994a).[13] In cities such as Chicago and Atlanta, African-Americans used these sites to forge reformist alliances with liberal Whites (Grimshaw 1992; Kleppner 1985; Stone 1989).

In New York, African-Americans attempted to sustain reform movements from a network of community-based organizations in the 1970s and early 1980s. The short-lived insurgent movement led by Al Vann in the 1970s took root in this network (Green and Wilson 1989). Vann's race-based alliance, the Coalition for Community Empowerment (CCE), brought together African-American politicians with ties to Brooklyn's Black churches and the community action programs spawned by President Johnson's War on Poverty and Mayor John Lindsay's liberal neighborhood government policies. The alliance included figures such as Congressman Owens and Assemblyman Norman, who traced their political beginnings to this network of community-based institutions. A handful of Afro-Caribbeans were also involved in the coalition, although none in leadership positions. Most of them had ties to community-based institutions, particularly school and community boards.

In the context of this institutional network, alliance members united around a shared vision for greater Black political empowerment, community control, and racial reform. As members were elected to the state and city legislatures, the alliance became a virtual party within Brooklyn's Democratic Party. The movement collapsed in the early 1980s, however, as its institutional base began to decay. The network of community-based agencies that had furnished an organizational framework for the movement was absorbed by the local city government and lost much of its political independence. Many of these agencies fell into disarray in the face of fiscal retrenchment and federal funding cutbacks. The African-American churches that had also supplied leaders for the movement remained an important part of some Brooklyn neighborhoods, but they struggled to attract younger parishioners. Consequently, they were no longer a leading source of leadership for Black politics in Brooklyn. Bereft of its independent institutional base, the CCE began to lose its way. Internal divisions surfaced, former insurgents were absorbed into the regular party organizations, and the push for reform ebbed.

Just as the movement was deteriorating in the 1980s, the CCE came into conflict with Afro-Caribbean elites who were seeking to win seats on the state assembly. Most of these Afro-Caribbean candidates had no ties to the institutional network that had spawned the African-American-led CCE movement. They were largely entrepreneurial lone wolves, such as Trinidadian-born Anthony Agard, or endorsees of immigrant organizations, such as Panamanian-born Stewart of the CAL. In short, they had no institutional ties to the African-American politicians involved in the CCE. The organization fiercely opposed the Afro-Caribbean candidates in their races for the state legislature. Without a shared institutional framework to build trust and dialogue, African-American politicians in the CCE and Afro-Caribbean elites were unable to resolve their differences in the interest of their shared racial goals.

The Future of Race-Based Coalitions

Not much has changed since then. The absence of an institutional mechanism for uniting and building trust between Afro-Caribbean and African-American elites diminishes the prospects of race-based mobilization. Of course, there have been small pockets of mutual cooperation and attempts at shared institution building in parts of Brooklyn and Queens—in political clubs and elsewhere. Recently, for example, native and foreign-born Black New Yorkers established a citywide organization to ensure that their numbers in the population are accurately reflected in the decennial census (John Flateau, personal communication, June 16, 2000). It is too early, however, to tell if the organization will last, especially since it has yet to face the difficult challenges posed by the city's electoral politics; reapportionment, for instance, could easily trigger the usual conflicts over descriptive representation. All in all, then, none of these recent organizational efforts have quite taken firm root; most have been ad hoc and short lived.

One potential institutional network that already has the benefit of longevity is New York's constellation of public unions. Emerging research on labor union activity in cities such as New York and Los Angeles over the past decade suggests that these institutions are beginning to serve a key role in the political adjustment of new immigrants to the United States (Wong 2000). This marks a radical break with a long, notorious history of anti-immigrant activity among American labor unions. Scholars speculate that changing demographic and economic realities have precipitated this shift. The growing numbers of non-White immigrants in American manufacturing and service-sector jobs, coupled with the overall decline in union membership, has compelled labor leaders to recruit these newcomers (Greenhouse 2000).

What is more, the new generation of labor union leaders are drawn largely from the ranks of native-born racial minority groups. African-Americans, for example, are at the helm of several active unions in New York. These native-born Blacks and their Caribbean-born counterparts, in fact, comprise a significant share of the membership in two of the city's most powerful public employee unions, Local 1199 of hospital workers and District Council 37 of city workers. By sharing these institutional vehicles, the two groups can engage in the kind of social learning and mutual search for shared interests that make coalition building easier. It may turn out that these unions prove to be the most promising institutional site for identifying leaders skilled in bridging the intergroup divisions among Afro-Caribbeans, African-Americans, and other racial minority populations. Still, there is an important caution to bear in mind. Much like local party machines, unions historically have been prone to internal wars of ethnic and racial succession (Mink 1986). Whether these union organizations can navigate those potential pitfalls well enough to become a stable site for a race-based alliance remains to be seen.

Some observers speculate that the ideological fervor for race-based mobilization has diminished, with the successes of the civil rights movement and the measurable minority group progress of the past few decades (Sleeper 1993). Simply put, the claim is that race-based movements are politically passé. Post-civil rights concerns, the argument goes, do not generate the same sense of urgency and consensus among minorities that fueled the civil rights movement. The conclusion is that race-based mobilization will be unlikely or difficult to foster in the current ideological climate. Yet Afro-Caribbean and African-American outrage over issues such as police brutality suggests that there are still grounds for race-based mobilization.

This study, however, shows that racial commonalities are not enough to generate an alliance of minority groups; indeed, appeals to racial unity actually may privilege some interests over others and thus heighten divisions among non-White groups. What is more, the institutional design of a city's electoral system may exacerbate these differences. To avoid these perverse effects, political leaders looking to foster race-based alliances must turn to neighborhood and community institutions. Without an institutional framework to identify shared issue concerns, acknowledge distinct interests, and generate dialogue, stable coalitions between African-Americans and Afro-Caribbeans or other racial minority newcomers will be difficult to generate.

Notes

1. I use *non-White* and *minority* interchangeably throughout this article to refer to Blacks, Latinos, and Asians. I distinguish these three groups from Whites, who remain the majority racial population in this country. It should be noted that Latinos, unlike the other groups, are not classified as a distinct racial group by the census. In fact, they may identify as Black, White, or other under the census classification scheme. Most opt for White or other. Yet urban scholars typically define Latinos as a minority group by virtue of their numbers and cultural distinctiveness. This article follows that convention.

2. I use *Afro-Caribbean* to refer to Black immigrants from the Anglophone Caribbean region and to distinguish them from their counterparts from the French- and Spanish-speaking Caribbean. Anglophone Caribbean immigrants are the focus of this study. Although I use the term *Afro*-Caribbean, most of these Black newcomers refer to themselves as *Caribbean American* or *West Indian*. New York's Afro-Caribbean immigrants hail from throughout the Caribbean region, but the largest numbers come from Jamaica, Trinidad, and Guyana.

3. Scholars have puzzled over the absence of a strong minority coalition in New York. The city would seem to be fertile soil for this kind of alliance. The fact that one has yet to take root makes New York a "great anomaly" in the urban politics literature (Mollenkopf 2003).

4. Afro-Caribbean immigrants living in these overwhelmingly Black areas have carved out their own distinctive residential niches, often of marginally higher socioeconomic quality than surrounding African-American neighborhoods (Crowder and Tedrow 2001). Yet this modest economic advantage has not won them access to more integrated neighborhoods, a predicament they share with their middle-class African-American counterparts.

5. The obvious irony of this complaint is that African-Americans view attempts by a group of Black immigrants to achieve political influence as a threat to Black empowerment, rather than a step in that direction.

6. I borrow the term *racial agents* from a conversation with Jack Citrin.

7. The essentialist behavioral notions of racial identity that pervade everyday, commonsense thinking in this country follow the same perverse logic. That is, racial groups are deemed to "behave" or "act" in keeping with an identifiable mold. Blacks, say, are expected to be good dancers, or Asians good students. When group members deviate from the behavioral mold, they are labeled racially inauthentic. For a useful discussion of how this essentialist conflation of racial identity and behavior nonetheless allows for an antiessentialist critique of racial categories, see Jackson (2001).

8. Challenging the racial credentials or commitments of a fellow Black politician in electoral competition is a strategy that surfaces even among African-Americans themselves. The famously acrimonious 2002 race between Newark mayoral incumbent Sharpe James and young upstart Cory Booker is a recent example. Although both men are African-American, questions of racial solidarity and authenticity emerged nonetheless. The James camp took the tactic to bizarre extremes when they began circulating rumors that Booker was actually White and passing as Black to win the support of Newark's mostly Black voters. Such strategies likely will become even more common as the Black population becomes more diverse in cities around the country.

9. For a thoughtful discussion on how White perceptions can engender conflict among subordinate minority groups, see Kim (1999, 2000).

10. Sampson's avoidance of the ethnic strategy may be due to his socialization in the United States. Born to Caribbean parents in New York, his ties to African-Americans run deep. His second-generation experiences and how they influence his political choices may be a precursor to the future of Black politics in New York. He is part of a new, expanding population of second-generation Caribbean New Yorkers. These children of Black immigrants likely will have a significant influence on the city's political future, as they become increasingly involved in the electoral process. It remains to be seen whether they will identify mostly as second-generation Caribbean ethnics or as African-Americans. But whatever the case, they may find coalition building with African-Americans easier than their parents have if they interact regularly with their counterparts in institutional settings.

11. African-American leaders at the time accused White party leaders of playing ethnic favorites by doling out the choicest patronage jobs to Afro-Caribbeans, who tended to be better educated than their native-born counterparts (Watkins-Owens 1996; Hellwig 1978; Holder 1980). But this was more job competition than political conflict, as the party structure was one of the few avenues of social mobility open to Black New Yorkers.

12. Social learning refers to the process by which potential coalition partners acquire knowledge and understanding of each other's interests (Stone 1989).

13. Taken together, these institutions comprise what Dawson (1994b) called the African-American counterpublic.

References

Arian, A., A. Goldberg, J. Mollenkopf, and E. Rogowsky. 1990. *Changing New York City politics.* New York: Routledge.

Browning, R., D. Marshall, and D. Tabb, eds. 2003. *Racial politics in American cities.* 3rd ed, New York: Longman.

Carmichael, S., and C. Hamilton. 1967. *Black power: The politics of liberation in America.* New York: Random House.

Crowder K., and L. Tedrow. 2001. West Indians and the residential landscape of New York. In *Islands in the city: West Indian migration to New York,* edited by Nancy Foner. Berkeley: Univ. of California Press.

Dao, J. 1999. Immigrant diversity slows traditional political climb. *New York Times.* December 28.

Dawson, M. 1994a. *Behind the mule: Race and class in African-American politics.* Princeton, NJ: Princeton Univ. Press.

———. 1994b. A Black counterpublic? Economic earthquakes, racial agenda(s), and Black politics. *Public Culture* 7:195–223.

Falcon, A. 1988. Black and Latino politics in New York City: Race and ethnicity in a changing urban context. In *Latinos and the political system,* edited by F. Chris Garcia. Notre Dame, IN: Note Dame Univ. Press.

Foner, N. 1985. Race and color: Jamaican immigrants in London and New York. *International Migration Review* 19:284–313.

Fuchs, L. 1990. *The American kaleidoscope: Race, ethnicity, and civic culture.* Hanover, NH: Wesleyan Univ. Press.

Green, C., and B. Wilson. 1989. *The struggle for Black empowerment in New York City: Beyond the politics of pigmentation.* New York: Praeger.

Greenhouse, S. 2000. Despite defeat on China bill, labor is on rise. *New York Times,* April 28.

Grimshaw, W. 1992. *Bitter fruit: Black politics and the Chicago machine,* Chicago: Univ. of Chicago Press.

Hellwig, D. 1978. Black meets Black: Afro-American reactions to West Indian immigrants in the 1920s. *South Atlantic Quarterly* 72:205–25.

Hicks, J. 2000a. Bitter primary contest hits ethnic nerve among Blacks. *New York Times,* August 31.

———. 2000b. Term limits turn old allies into opponents; protege against mentor, backer against incumbent. *New York Times,* March 22.

Holder, C. 1980. The rise of the West Indian politician in New York City. *Afro-Americans in New York Life and History* 4:45–59.

Henry, C., and C. Munoz Jr. 1991. Ideological and interest linkages in California rainbow politics. In *Racial and ethnic politics in California,* edited by B. Jackson and M. Preston. Berkeley, CA: IGS Press.

Jackson, J. 2001. *Harlemworld: Doing race and class in contemporary Black America.* Chicago: Univ. of Chicago Press.

Jennings, J. 1997. *Race and politics: New challenges and responses for Black activism.* London: Verso.

Kasinitz, P. 1992. *Caribbean New York: Black immigrants and the politics of race.* Ithaca, NY: Cornell Univ. Press.

Katznelson, I. 1981. *City trenches: Urban politics and the patterning of class in the United States.* New York: Pantheon.

Key, V.O. 1949. *Southern politics in state and nation.* New York: Vintage.

Kim, C. 1999. The racial triangulation of Asian Americans. *Politics and Society* 27(1): 105–38.

———. 2000. *Bitter fruit: The politics of Black-Korean conflict in New York City.* New Haven, CT: Yale Univ. Press.

Kleppner, P. 1985. *Chicago divided: The making of a Black mayor.* Dekalb: Northern Illinois Press.

Lewis Mumford Center for Comparative Urban and Regional Research. 2002. *Separate and unequal: The neighborhood gap for Blacks and Hispanics in metropolitan America.* Albany, NY: Univ. at Albany Press.

Lewis Mumford Center for Comparative Urban and Regional Research. 2003. *Black diversity in metropolitan America.* Albany, NY: Univ. at Albany Press.

Macchiarola, F., and J. Diaz. 1993. Minority political empowerment in New York City: Beyond the Voting Rights Act. *Political Science Quarterly* 108 (1): 37–57.

Marable, M. 1994. Building coalitions among communities of color. In *Blacks, Latinos, and Asians in urban America,* edited by J. Jennings. New York: Praeger.

Mink, G. 1986. *Old labor and new immigrants in American political development.* Ithaca. NY: Cornell Univ. Press.

Mollenkopf, J. 1992. *A phoenix in the ashes: The rise and fall of the Koch coalition in New York City.* Princeton, NJ: Princeton Univ. Press.

———. 1997. New York: The great anomaly. In *Racial politics in American cities,* 2nd ed., edited by R. Browning, D. Marshall, and D. Tabb. New York: Longman.

———. 1999. Urban political conflicts and alliances: New York and Los Angeles compared. In *The handbook of international migration: The American experience,* edited by C. Hirschman, P. Kasinitz, and J. DeWind. New York: Russell Sage Foundation.

———. 2003. New York: The great anomaly. In *Racial politics in American cities,* 3rd ed., edited R. P. Browning, D. R. Marshall, and D. H. Tabb, New York: Longman.

New York Carib News. 1996a. April 23.

New York Carib News. 1996b. October 1.

———. 1988. Black urban regime: Structural origins and constraints. *Comparative Urban and Community Research* 1:138–89.

Reid, I. 1939. *The Negro immigrant: His background characteristics and social adjustments, 1899–1937.* New York: AMS Press.

Rogers, R. 2000. Between race and ethnicity: Afro-Caribbean immigrants, African Americans, and the politics of incorporation, Ph.D. diss., Princeton University.

Skerry, P. 1993. *Mexican Americans: The ambivalent minority.* Cambridge, MA: Harvard Univ. Press.

Sleeper, J. 1993. The end of the rainbow. *New Republic,* November 20–25.

Sonenshein, R. 1993. *Politics in black and white: Race and power in Los Angeles.* Princeton, NJ: Princeton Univ. Press.

———. 2003a. Post-incorporation politics in Los Angeles. In *Racial politics in American cities,* 3rd ed., edited by R. P. Browning, D. R. Marshall, and D. H. Tabb. New York: Longman.

———. 2003b. The prospects for multiracial coalitions: Lessons from America's three largest cities. In *Racial politics in American cities,* 3rd ed., edited by R. P. Browning, D. R. Marshall, and D. H. Tabb. New York: Longman.

Stone, C. 1989. *Regime politics: Governing Atlanta, 1946–1988.* Lawrence: University Press of Kansas.

Stone, C., and C. Pierannunzi. 1997. Atlanta and the limited reach of electoral control. In *Racial politics in American cities,* 2nd ed., edited by R. Browning, D. Marshall, and D. Tabb. New York: Longman.

Tate, K. 1993. *From protest to politics: The new Black voters in American elections.* Cambridge, MA: Harvard Univ. Press.

Vickerman, M. 1999. *Crosscurrents: West Indian immigrants and race.* New York: Oxford Univ. Press.

Warren, C., and D. Moreno. 2003. Power without a program: Hispanic incorporation in Miami. In *Racial politics in American cities,* 3rd ed., edited by R. Browning, D. Marshall, and D. Tabb. New York: Longman.

Waters, M. 1996. Ethnic and racial groups in the USA: Conflict and cooperation. In *Ethnicity and power in the contemporary world,* edited by K. Rupesinghe and V. Tishkov. London: U.N. University.

Waters, M. 1999. *Black identities: West Indian immigrant dreams and American realities.* Cambridge, MA: Harvard Univ. Press.

Watkins-Owens, I. 1996. *Blood relations: Caribbean immigrants and the Harlem community, 1900–1930,* Bloomington: Indiana Univ. Press.

Wong, J. 2000. Institutional context and political mobilization among Mexican and Chinese immigrants. Paper presented at the Immigrant Political Participation in New York City Working Conference, New York, June.

15

RACE AND THE TOURIST BUBBLE IN DOWNTOWN ATLANTA

Harvey K. Newman

The downtown area of most U.S. cities once functioned as a central business district where a majority of employment and economic activity for the entire city took place. One of the important changes since World War II is the declining significance of these downtowns as cities became sprawling metropolises.

URBAN AFFAIRS REVIEW. Vol. 37, No. 3, January 2002 301–321 © 2002 Sage Publications

Local leaders scrambled to try a variety of strategies that would revitalize the core of their central cities. They constructed expressways to make downtown more accessible to an increasingly suburbanized population, and they used urban renewal funds to clear land of unwanted slum housing and small businesses to make way for new uses. However, finding new economic activities to replace manufacturing, retail, and other types of jobs that were leaving central cities was a challenge for elected public officials and business leaders.

Since the 1960s, the leaders of many cities have adopted tourism as a strategy to attract investment in downtowns and construct space for the enjoyment of visitors. Even cities that lacked natural attractions for tourists could become what Judd and Fainstein (1999, 266–67) described as "converted cities" by carving out space for tourism. Judd's chapter in this volume suggests that many cities constructed what he calls a "tourist bubble"—that is, a well-defined part of town designed to envelop the traveler and to shield the visitor from the unpleasant aspects of urban living.

In this study, I examine two questions: (1) how the partnership between Atlanta's business and political leaders worked together to create the components of a downtown tourist bubble and (2) how the issue of race affected this tourist space. Stone (1989) described the decision making by Atlanta's coalition of civic leaders as a regime. Although many components of the tourist bubble were created during the tenure of business-oriented white mayors, these officials were willing to sacrifice the residences and small businesses of black Atlantans to convert space for tourism. Another important issue is how this largely segregated white tourist space fared after 1973, when the city elected African-American mayors.

The Tourist Bubble

The link between downtown regeneration and tourism is an important theme in the research of scholars such as Frieden and Sagalyn (1989), Zukin (1991), Sorkin (1992), and Judd and Fainstein (1999). All these works suggest that city leaders selected tourism as a growth strategy to restore the economic base of downtown areas where decline was evident. If a city could attract tourists, these visitors would bring money to spend in the local economy and create demand for new facilities that would contribute to the improvement of the area. Local residents accepted this process because their leaders promised to produce jobs and taxes as well as improve the image of the city to potential investors (Shaw and Williams 1994).

One city that typifies the "success" of this strategy is Baltimore, where city leaders turned an area of urban decay into the convention and tourism space known as Harborplace. The Harborplace area shelters the 30 million tourists who visit Baltimore each year and protects them from seeing other parts of the city beyond this redeveloped "economic island" that is unconnected to the deteriorating neighborhoods around it (Levine 1987, 118). Judd described this secured, protected, and normalized environment for visitors as a "tourist bubble." Inside this space is an artificial, segregated environment devoted to consumption and play, whereas substantial areas of the city outside the bubble are left to deal with the problems of the loss of industrial employment in the restructuring of the city's economy toward the service sector (Judd and Fainstein 1999).

Frieden and Sagalyn (1989) indicated that the components of downtown tourist spaces are similar in cities throughout the United States. The center of a city's downtown tourist space is usually its convention center. In the competition with other cities to attract the lucrative convention business, cities of all sizes built convention centers. Between 1970 and 1985, U.S. cities constructed more than 100 such centers, and by 1995, there were at least 434 in operation as part of what was a "virtual arms race" of competition among cities for the convention business. Most of these convention centers require annual subsidies for the repayment of bond debt used for their construction and for operating expenses. Local convention and visitors bureaus also spend heavily to promote the advantages of their city to lure large meetings. Yet, despite these costs, cities keep investing in larger and more elaborate facilities just to stay competitive with other places (Judd and Fainstein 1999).

Other expensive items that cities provide for visitors and residents are professional sports franchises. City leaders consider stadiums and sports arenas as essential for downtown regeneration, so despite their enormous costs, these facilities are an essential signifier of "big league" status. Indeed, the major benefit of professional sports teams to a city may be the intangible quality of the image they provide for civic boosters, as the stadiums and sports arenas are among the most expensive components of a city's tourism infrastructure. The battle to get and keep sports franchises is another aspect of the interurban competition within the tourist industry. Owners are skillful in playing one city off against another with the threat of moving their teams in efforts to extract concessions in the form of new facilities, luxury boxes, and other subsidies. Much of the revenue generated from professional sports flows to wealthy owners, making public subsidies for the facilities a questionable economic investment for cities. The powerful symbolism of "big league sports" keeps the leaders of cities such as Cleveland eager to maintain their town's status despite the limited economic benefits of professional sports to most urban residents (Keating 1997).

Festival malls are another component of the downtown tourist bubble. These are self-contained shopping areas that are promoted to help reverse the long-term decline of downtown retailing. Projects developed in cities throughout the country by James Rouse and Atlanta's John Portman attempt to lure recreational shoppers rather than a resident population seeking mundane necessities. Most are the result of public subsidies and private investments funneled through special authorities created to foster these public-private partnerships. The malls segregate the process of consumption from the routine aspects of daily life in the city in a process influenced by the success of the Disney Corporation's projects. As Zukin (1991, 232) suggested, the festival mall is probably more important than any other component of the standardized tourist space in establishing the atmosphere and context of a "utopian visual consumption" that has the potential to make every city, whatever its past function or present condition, a tourist attraction.

The most recent component of the tourist bubble in many cities is casino gambling. Once confined to Las Vegas, casinos have spread rapidly as cities such as Atlantic City, Kansas City, St. Louis, Detroit, and New Orleans sought the revenues available from this form of tourism. Despite questions about the social and economic impacts of casino gambling as well as considerable political opposition, municipal leaders are scrambling to add these facilities as attractions for tourists to come and spend money in their cities rather than elsewhere. Despite well-documented negative impacts of casino gambling on cities as diverse as Atlantic City and Central City, Colorado, elected public officials still press for casinos as they search for ways to regenerate urban economies (Hannigan 1998).

Faced with declining financial support from the federal and state governments, leaders in U.S. cities look to tourism revenues to support their fragile local economies. As amusement park operators learned long ago that new rides and attractions keep visitors coming back, city leaders also try to add new baubles to their downtown tourist spaces that will keep visitors returning. Despite enormous costs and intense competition among cities for tourists, business and public leaders feel they cannot be complacent with their tourist areas. However, as Keating (1997) described Cleveland's comeback, a city may promote an image of success in its downtown regeneration by investing in tourist space but fail to provide substantial economic benefits outside the central business district. Atlanta is a city that has likewise attempted to use the components of a tourist bubble to restructure its downtown area.

Atlanta's Downtown Tourist Bubble

Built along the intersection of rail lines in the Southeast, Atlanta established itself as a crossroads town during the mid-nineteenth century. The transportation connections by train, automobile, bus, and, later, airplane brought a steady stream of visitors to Atlanta. In a region noted for its hospitality, local leaders quickly recognized the commercial importance of tourism as a way of attracting visitors to come and invest in the young town (Newman 1999). By 1895, the partnership of business and political leaders hosted a national convention and a series of three expositions designed to promote their city. Early in the twentieth century, this partnership began shaping the elements of an early tourist bubble. At the urging of white business leaders, local public officials prepared the city to host conventions by constructing a municipal auditorium-armory building that opened in 1909. In November of that year, Atlanta welcomed the National Association of Automobile Manufacturers as it met for the first time in the South.

Preparations for this event showed how Atlanta's business and political partners worked cooperatively to showcase their downtown for visitors. After providing the convention facility as the centerpiece of an early twentieth-century tourist space, the city government also illuminated the sidewalks along the major thoroughfare, Peachtree Street, to form what was called "the Great White Way." Designers of this project attempted to make people feel more secure as they strolled downtown streets to patronize stores, theaters, and hotels. The Great White Way was a public space set aside to appeal to upper-class whites, whereas others were excluded from the amenities offered by the area. With the creation of the Great White Way in 1909, Atlanta's leaders carved out a segregated environment devoted to consumption and play for those white visitors and residents who could afford it. For the next 50 years, the tourist space along Peachtree formed the center of an important convention industry for the city. Typical of the private-sector components of this tourist space was the Weincoff Hotel that opened on Peachtree Street in 1913 and remained a family-operated business until after World War II, appealing to visitors with its proximity to theaters, shopping, and dining.

The partnership between the public and private sectors functioned to make Atlanta an early national leader in the convention business. Local government provided meeting facilities and paid for the illumination of Peachtree Street, and businesses such as hotels, restaurants, theaters, and stores thrived from the visitors attracted to the area. Business leaders in the Atlanta Chamber of Commerce organized a Convention Bureau in 1912 that aggressively solicited groups to hold their meetings in the city. Public officials such as the mayor and the governor further assisted the process by writing letters of invitation extending the warmth of southern hospitality to groups thinking of meeting in Atlanta. The city council's Committee on Auditorium and Conventions provided money to prepare the city for the event, especially if the group brought delegates from throughout the nation in a meeting that meant potential investment in the city. The mayor and council members also offered an official welcome to Atlanta for convention visitors. This pattern of public and private cooperation to shape a downtown tourist space would persist throughout the twentieth century despite many changes in the city.

For more than half of the twentieth century, laws reinforced regional cultural patterns of racial segregation to keep blacks separate from whites. Within this Jim Crow system, the public-private partnership to promote the city's convention industry hosted segregated conventions for African-Americans. In August 1906, for instance, the city welcomed a three-day meeting of the National Negro Business League, led by Booker T. Washington of Tuskegee, Alabama. The city's black hotels, restaurants, bars, and amusements eagerly received the convention delegates, who were greeted by the mayor and president of the all-white Chamber of Commerce. Financial support for the event came from white and black businesses that expected to gain from the money spent by the more than 1,000 visiting delegates. The city's largest black church hosted the meeting, and city government provided the use of a municipal park that was desegregated for the visitors but then closed again to African-Americans following the convention. The requirements of segregation were not allowed to stand in the way of opportunities to attract business and growth with displays of Atlanta's warm hospitality. As Peachtree Street formed the tourist space for whites, segregation pushed African-American tourist businesses into restricted areas, primarily along Auburn Avenue and Decatur Street.

Atlanta's African-Americans promoted their convention business with the same enthusiasm as their white counterparts. Even though the city served as the national headquarters for a revived Ku Klux Klan, blacks advertised for their brothers and sisters to hold meetings in Atlanta and compared the attractions of Auburn Avenue with the bright spots of New York and Chicago. This separate tourist space for African-Americans continued to attract conventions and tourists until after the passage of the 1964 Civil Rights Act that desegregated the city's tourist businesses and facilities. Atlanta's white leaders made political decisions that would also have a dramatic impact on this segregated tourist space.

By 1950, there was a growing awareness among white business and political leaders that the physical condition of downtown Atlanta was deteriorating. First the Depression and then World War II brought the construction of new buildings to a halt. In the years immediately following the war, builders focused their efforts on meeting the demand for suburban housing. The lack of development in downtown Atlanta troubled the city's white power structure. When Hunter (1953, 214–15) conducted his study of "Regional City," he found this elite group most concerned about the issues of growth and development as well as traffic and the "Negro question." The city's leaders made plans to deal with all of these issues at once. Prior to the federal interstate highway program, the city began construction in 1950 on an expressway that curved around downtown, giving whites living in northern and southern suburbs easy access to the central city. White civic leaders designed the expressway not only to relieve traffic congestion but also to serve as a buffer between the central business district and the African-American neighborhood to the east.

The federal urban renewal program provided the Atlanta public-private partnership with the means of clearing the land within the curve in the expressway by relocating black residents and businesses outside the downtown area. The Butler Street urban renewal district provided space for 1,300 new hotel rooms in the downtown area within the curve of the expressway. As initially proposed, this district would have eliminated all of the commercial area of Auburn Avenue, but protests from the black newspaper, the *Daily World*, and African-American leaders succeeded in protecting "Sweet Auburn" (Bayor 1996). The land cleared for the Butler Street area provided space for the Downtown Marriott (now operated as the Sheraton) that opened in 1966. This hotel reflected significant change taking place in the city's hospitality businesses as national corporate ownership replaced local businesses.

The decisions made by the partnership of white business and political leaders during the 1960s guided the redevelopment of Atlanta's downtown tourist bubble. The city still depended on its transportation connections to bring people to the downtown area that was a commercial center of regional and increasingly national importance. Ivan Allen, Jr., a business owner and president of the Chamber of Commerce, campaigned successfully for mayor in 1961 by promising to build a new convention center to replace the outdated

Municipal Auditorium. He used the urban renewal program to clear more space for tourism at the site of a new facility known as the Civic Center. A third urban renewal area provided land for the construction of the city's major league sports facility known as the Atlanta-Fulton County Stadium, where a relocated baseball team and a new National Football League franchise played their games.

The local partnership of white business and political leaders used the combination of expressway construction and three urban renewal areas to transform the city's earlier downtown tourist space. The new facilities enabled Atlanta to continue its success as a convention city, but at considerable cost to more than 55,000 African-American residents whose homes were destroyed in the process of reshaping Atlanta's tourist bubble (Eric Hill Associates 1966). Tourists could enjoy the 1,300 new hotel rooms, the Civic Center, and the stadium, but the once-thriving center of African-American commerce along Auburn Avenue was left to deteriorate as a result of the policies pursued by the local regime.

In 1996, Mayor Allen announced that Atlanta was ready to take its place as more than a regional capital and become a city of national importance. As proof, he cited the city's new jet-age airport, a major league stadium, a new convention center under construction, and a doubling of the number of downtown hotel rooms since 1945. In addition, voters approved a referendum for liquor by the drink sales, and plans were under way for a rapid transit system (Pomerantz 1996).

Another important contributor to the development of Atlanta's tourist space was an ambitious young architect, John Portman, who opened a downtown merchandise mart in 1961 to serve as a wholesale shopping center for store owners from throughout the region. The success of the mart in attracting crowds to Atlanta created demand for an adjacent hotel. Portman envisioned the two buildings forming the core of a "Rockefeller Center-type complex" to redevelop an entire section of downtown along Peachtree Street (Crown 1964, 40–41). Portman not only designed the new hotel but also developed the project, which became known as Peachtree Center. When the Hyatt Regency opened in 1967, its blue glass revolving cocktail lounge served as a landmark in the Atlanta skyline. At the time, architects considered the hotel a revolution in design with a huge atrium of 3 million square feet extending 22 stories high. Exposed tear-shaped glass elevators provided visitors with a ride similar to an amusement park. The Hyatt Corporation and other national chains replicated these novel features, creating a class of atrium hotels in cities throughout the United States ("Downtown Is Looking Up" 1976).

John Portman's Hyatt Regency was a financial success as well, boasting a 95% occupancy rate within three months of its opening. The Hyatt Corporation wanted more rooms, so Portman added 200 more in a cylindrical glass tower built on top of the hotel's ballroom. This design would be replicated in 1976 on a larger scale for the Westin Peachtree Plaza, which became the second hotel in Peachtree Center. The success of the hotel led Portman in 1968 to double the size of the merchandise mart and to construct the first office tower in his

Rockefeller Center-type complex. Eventually, Portman added a third hotel, the Marriott Marquis, to Peachtree Center as it occupied all or part of 17 city blocks, making it one of the largest private developments in the world.

John Portman's investments had enormous impact in updating Atlanta's downtown tourist bubble. Peachtree Center reshaped a major portion of downtown, spurring growth northward along Peachtree Street and away from the traditional center of the business district at Five Points. Although Portman gave Atlanta's downtown some of its most distinctive architecture, he also changed the way many tourists experience the city by enclosing a section of downtown. As Judd (1999, 47) observed,

> Atlanta has moved indoors, and the city streets have been almost deserted by pedestrian traffic. Shops, hotels and their lobbies, offices, food courts, and atriums are connected by a maze of escalators, skytubes and arcades. The glassed-in skywalks of Peachtree Center isolate its inhabitants from the streets below. A similar isolation characterizes Portman's other developments as well—the Renaissance Center in Detroit, the Hyatt at Embarcadero Center in San Francisco, the Bonaventure Hotel in Los Angeles, and Marriott Marquis in Manhattan's Times Square.

The skywalk system connecting the buildings and the interior space of the Peachtree Center complex was the most controversial aspect of the project. Called "honkey tubes" by many local African-Americans, the skywalks tend to segregate the mostly white visitors within the buildings rather than encouraging them to experience the life of the city outside the buildings. One critic called this design "anti-urban" since the space isolates occupants within the megastructure complex rather than having the buildings relate to the city around them. Travel writer Arthur Frommer (1987, D-1) criticized the exterior design of Peachtree Center's buildings as "fortresses with forbidding walls, opaque exteriors making no contribution and adding no color or light to their city streets, confining guests 'inside the moat,' so to speak, excluding them from Atlanta instead of introducing them to it."

Portman was not the only developer reshaping Atlanta's tourist space. The city's historic preservation commission, organized in 1966, issued a resolution that year calling attention to the downtown area near the railroad tracks under the city's viaducts. The old storefronts and warehouses of late nineteenth-century Atlanta were left behind as a home for derelicts but could be restored for use by tourists as New Orleans did with its French Quarter and St. Louis with its Gas Light Square. By 1969, two young entrepreneurs formed a company, leased space under the viaducts, and called the area Underground Atlanta. The attraction opened that year with 22 tenants providing tourists with a mixture of restaurants, clubs, museums, and shops. Within two years, Underground Atlanta was the best-known and most-visited tourist attraction in the city, offering 65 establishments to appeal to a variety of tastes. Conventioneers and out-of-town visitors were not the only ones who made Underground popular. The location was within walking distance of downtown business and government offices, attracting lunch, happy hour, and evening crowds of residents as well as visitors. The legal drinking age in the state was 18, and the surrounding jurisdictions were legally dry so that Underground Atlanta also attracted large crowds of young people.

Although Underground Atlanta was initially successful, problems soon developed. Souvenir shops charged high prices for cheap goods, and public safety and crime problems from the large crowds of teenage drinkers began to scare off older local residents. Fewer patrons caused a steady decline in the number of businesses in Underground, with the last closing its doors in 1982. The loss of this tourist attraction led hospitality business leaders to begin immediately calling for a revival of Underground Atlanta as an essential component in the city's convention trade.

Atlanta's convention facility, known as the Civic Center, was less than five years old when city leaders realized its size was inadequate to host the meetings of large national organizations such as civic clubs and political parties. Planning began in 1971 for a convention center to keep the city competitive in attracting major events. Fearing a lack of support among voters for the expense of a new facility, Atlanta's business leaders turned to the state government, asking Georgia to create a special authority to build and operate the $20 million building. After intensive lobbying by business leaders and support from a pro-business governor, a reluctant general assembly in 1974 agreed to fund the project whose price had risen to $35 million. When the Georgia World Congress Center opened two years later, its 640,000 square feet of exhibition space made it the "world's largest hall." Chamber of Commerce boosters noted that the new building featured meeting rooms with built-in simultaneous translation facilities so that the city could host meetings of 60,000 or more with delegates from all over the world. This was regarded as an important step in Atlanta's aspirations to become known as an international city. Trade shows such as the textile industry's "bobbin show" became regular events attracting thousands of domestic and international tourists. With the new facility, more than 10,000 downtown hotel rooms, and the city's transportation connections, local business leaders hoped Atlanta could overtake New York and Chicago to become "America's Convention Capital" (Galphin 1975, 74).

Atlanta's aspirations as a "major league" city came true in 1966 when the National League Braves relocated from Milwaukee to occupy the new stadium. Later that year, the city welcomed the new National Football League expansion franchise known as the Atlanta Falcons. Despite fan support for the two teams, gate receipts did not cover the principal and interest on the $18 million debt used to finance the stadium, forcing the city and county to pay almost $500,000 to reduce the debt in 1967 and more than $900,000 the following year (Martin 1987). This type of revenue shortfall is common among cities that are financing expensive sports facilities, leading many urban scholars to question the wisdom of the investment (see Rosentraub 1997). For local boosters in Atlanta, however, the stadium and its two major league teams were a validation of the claim that the city had attained national prominence. They serve as important elements in the city's tourist bubble because professional sports provide a diversion for visitors, attract media coverage, and provide intangible benefits such as an increase in civic pride, community spirit, and collective self-image (Law 1993).

Although public officials in Atlanta liked to take credit for the addition of components to the city's tourist bubble such as the stadium and its professional sports teams (see Allen and Hemphill 1971), private-sector developers made most of the decisions that created space for the tourist industry. Atlanta's largest real estate developers sometimes made investments based on their personal competition with one another. For example, the success of Portman's Peachtree Center caused rival developer, Tom Cousins, to build another project in a different section of downtown. In 1968, Cousins purchased the National Basketball Association's St. Louis Hawks and persuaded the city to construct an arena called the Omni as their home. Four years later, he purchased another sports franchise to play in the Omni, the Atlanta Flames of the National Hockey League. Cousins also began construction of another multifunction megastructure known as the Omni complex adjacent to the sports arena. It contained the Omni International Hotel, restaurants, shops, an ice skating rink, and a $17 million indoor amusement park called the World of Sid and Marty Krofft. The plan was to lure investment away from Portman's Peachtree Street development toward the Marietta Street location of Cousins's project. After its opening in the spring of 1976, the amusement park closed within six months.

Although given elaborate promotional efforts, the hockey franchise failed to sell out its games or to attract widespread local enthusiasm for a sport that was new to the region. After several years of declining revenues, the team moved to the cooler climate of Calgary in 1980. The hotel and entire complex struggled financially for several years until they were purchased in 1985 by communications mogul Ted Turner, who converted the Omni into CNN Center, which functioned as the studios and headquarters of his media companies. Cousins eventually sold the Atlanta Hawks to Turner, who also bought the Atlanta Braves in order to televise games as part of his nationwide "superstation."

The personal competition between two developers spurred construction of the Omni Complex and additions to Peachtree Center, causing significant impact on downtown Atlanta's tourist bubble. Both megastructures tended to seal visitors within the complexes, reducing pedestrian activity on the city's sidewalks. In 1988, as the city prepared to host the Democratic National Convention and again in anticipation of the 1996 Summer Olympic Games, Atlanta spent millions of dollars in public funds to improve sidewalks by making them more attractive with improved lighting, trees, and art. The enclosed space of the city's two megastructures made the creation of a pleasant outdoor pedestrian environment more difficult.

Despite changes in Atlanta's political leadership, support for tourism as an economic development strategy for downtown remained strong within the longstanding coalition of business and political leaders. Three business groups—the Atlanta Convention and Tourist Bureau, Central Atlanta Progress, and the Chamber of Commerce—were well organized to promote tourism. They also supported a policy research group known as Research Atlanta to analyze policies of importance to the business community. No sooner had the last business in Underground Atlanta closed its doors than business leaders began calling for more entertainment for convention visitors. Research Atlanta published reports in 1982 and 1983 citing the need for downtown entertainment as the greatest weakness in the city's convention business (Research Atlanta 1982, 1983).

Eager to show his cooperation with business leaders, newly elected mayor Andrew Young embraced the proposal to revitalize Underground Atlanta. In a well-coordinated effort, the city joined with Fulton County, the state of Georgia, and the business organization Central Atlanta Progress to fund a $400,000 feasibility study on the revitalization of Underground Atlanta. The American City Corporation (owned by James Rouse, the developer of Harborplace and other festival marketplaces throughout the country) conducted the study that recommended the redevelopment of the Underground area with a mix of restaurants, nightclubs, specialty shops, and public spaces. Many small property owners in the area and some members of the city council were skeptical about the need for the revitalization that reminded them of the old urban renewal program.

In contrast to the rebuilding of Faneuil Hall in Boston (an earlier Rouse project), which required less than 21% public-sector support, the redevelopment of Underground Atlanta was a different kind of partnership, with more than 80% of the $144 million investment coming from a variety of public sources. Although downtown business leaders wanted the project, they were unwilling to assume a large share of the financial risk. There was no doubt that this project carried considerable risk because both the earlier version of Underground and the Omni's entertainment park, the World of Sid and Marty Krofft, failed.

The expectations for the revived Underground Atlanta were great. The mayor regarded the project as a legacy to the city that would provide jobs and tax revenues as well as the potential financial gains from the city's role as entrepreneur. The city council hoped the project would provide opportunities for minority businesses in the construction and operation of the marketplace and stimulate the renewal of the southern edge of downtown through increased economic activity in the area. Tourism officials and other business leaders anticipated that crowds of conventioneers would visit the new attraction.

The celebration of the reopening took place in 1989, and during the first year of operation, an estimated 13 million people visited Underground Atlanta. Only 40% of these patrons were visiting tourists, and the rest were local area residents. Convention delegates came in smaller numbers than anticipated. The major convention hotels were at a considerable distance from the complex, and there was little of the historic Underground left for visitors to experience. As a consequence, the site lacked the authentic qualities to set it apart from similar festival marketplaces in other cities. The original Underground Atlanta was popular in part because it was a historical and architectural signifier of the city's nineteenth-century railroad-era past. With the proliferation of festival marketplaces in cities throughout the country, the new Underground had little novelty to offer visitors.

Rouse Company projections said that Underground Atlanta would generate 3,000 new jobs. Three years after its opening, there were only 969 new jobs in the complex, including 552 full-time and 417 part-time positions. Although the city collected almost a million dollars in additional property, sales, and beverage taxes during 1991, it had the additional expense of providing public safety for the project (Sjoquist and Williams 1992). The fear of crime in the complex caused the city to open a police precinct station in Underground Atlanta that functioned in addition to the private security force of 30 officers. These precautions did not prevent a black gang-related killing in 1990, followed by several other crimes that diminished the number of white suburban visitors to Underground. The result was a $28 million loss during the first five years of operation. In 1994, the Rouse Company's subsidiary, Underground Festival, Inc., which operated the marketplace, asked for and received a restructuring of its debt to the city to continue operations. Shortly after the departure of the crowds of Olympic visitors in 1996, Rouse's management company canceled its contract, forcing the city to hire new managers and raising doubt about the continued viability of Underground Atlanta.

Among the first tenants to close in the new Underground Atlanta were undercapitalized minority-owned businesses that had comprised 27% of the project's tenants at the time of opening. National chain businesses replaced many of these smaller merchants (mostly African-American females), causing racial tensions among the remaining tenants. The presence of the national corporations added to the homogenization of the tourist experience at Underground because the same fudge, T-shirt, and other shops could be found in the festival marketplaces of other cities.

An additional goal of the project was to provide an economic stimulus to downtown and to encourage the revitalization of the south side of the central business district. One year after Underground's reopening, the Coca-Cola Company opened a pavilion known as the World of Coca-Cola, where people could learn about the history of the soft drink in its hometown. From the outset, the Coke exhibit was extremely popular and made its way onto the list of "must-see" attractions in the city, but only a few hundred yards away from its entrance, Underground Atlanta was far less crowded.

With convention delegates avoiding Underground Atlanta, both attendance and revenues were lower than anticipated. This situation provoked a lively debate in the city council over the future of the complex. During 1999, Underground needed a new manager, providing the city council with an opportunity to explore a variety of options. One council member proposed casino gambling as a solution, but a majority voted to give the contract to a company promising to make the complex more attractive to families with children. Meanwhile, Mayor Bill Campbell proposed adding another attraction to the area by investing $75 million in an aquarium located next to Underground Atlanta. No business or foundation stepped forward to provide support for the aquarium project. This portion of Atlanta's tourist space remains without a casino or an aquarium, proving it is often difficult to add new attractions to the theme park city (Sorkin 1992).

Race and Atlanta's Tourist Bubble

The issue that did not surface in the debate on the future of Underground Atlanta but that affects the project as well as other parts of the downtown tourist bubble is race. Atlanta became a majority African-American city in 1970, and low-income black neighborhoods surround much of the central business district. According to 1990 statistics, the 23 census tracts that form a "U" to the east, south, and west of downtown have a poverty rate more than 35%, and more than 90% of the 50,000 residents in this area are African-American (City of Atlanta 1993). Life for these residents is quite different from the experience of convention delegates and office workers downtown. Like Baltimore, Atlanta's downtown tourist space segregates visitors and office workers inside a bubble that is secured, protected, and normalized (Judd and Fainstein 1999).

Although the convention bureau aggressively recruits as many African-American groups as possible, most of the convention visitors to Atlanta are white. The cultural symbols displayed at Underground Atlanta reflect this dilemma. The original Underground offered tourists a mixture of the real and imagined heritage of southern whites, reaching its nadir in the shop operated by former governor Lester Maddox, who sold autographed pickaxe handles similar to the ones used in 1964 to prevent the integration of his restaurant. This made the other stores selling confederate flags and caps as well as *Gone with the Wind* paraphernalia seem tame.

When the rebuilt Underground project opened in 1989, its cultural symbols were biracial. Although it was still possible to buy confederate flags, there were also pictures and symbols of the civil rights era and black pride T-shirts for sale. This cultural ambiguity contributed to Underground Atlanta's difficulty finding its niche as a tourist attraction. The more white convention visitors perceived Underground as catering to African-American tastes, the less attractive it became to them. On the other hand, Underground lacked authentic cultural experiences of regional cooking, offering fast food and chain operations that catered to mass tastes. Further complicating these cultural issues involving race were concerns over public safety frequently voiced by Underground's management in terms of "loitering" by young black males. The location of a police precinct and the hiring of a private security force discourage this practice, resulting in the privatization of public space described by Sorkin (1992).

If the issue of race played a role in determining the fate of Underground Atlanta, it was the decisive issue in discussions about another of the city's tourist attractions. In the era of segregation, Auburn Avenue was the most important street for Atlanta's African-American cultural institutions, businesses, and entertainment. The combination of expressway construction, urban renewal, and the desegregation of tourist businesses plunged the commercial area of Auburn Avenue into a spiral of decay and neglect. The building of the downtown connector cut a swath through the street, closing many small businesses in its path and separating the largely residential area on the east side of the expressway from the commercial district on the west. The Butler Street urban renewal area destroyed more homes and businesses in the area but created space for new hotels serving the convention trade. After the passage of the Civil Rights Act, blacks were free to eat, sleep, and drink in businesses open to all, but few whites patronized the previously African-American businesses along Auburn Avenue. Small hotels catering to a previously African-American clientele closed first, followed by the gradual decline in the number of restaurants, clubs, and other businesses on the street.

Among the numerous African-American cultural institutions that remain on Auburn Avenue is Ebenezer Baptist Church, where Dr. Martin Luther King, Jr. and his father served as ministers. Also located on the eastern end of the residential portion of this historic street is the house in which Dr. King was born. Near the birth home and church are Dr. King's tomb and the MLK Center for Non-Violent Social Change. Much of this area became a national park providing funds for the restoration of the houses in the neighborhood. The area draws more than 3 million visitors annually, making the site the most heavily visited tourist attraction in the city. Despite the crowds of tourists and several revitalization efforts, the commercial area of Auburn Avenue located to the west of the expressway continued to deteriorate. A Main Street program attempted to renovate the facades of the storefronts along the avenue. Preparations for the 1996 Olympics included replacing the sidewalks, planting trees, improving the street lighting, and placing interpretive signs along a path designated as the "Freedom Walk" on the entire length of Auburn Avenue. Despite these efforts, the commercial area of the street received no additional private-sector investment. Merchants complain that visitors arrive at the national park area in tour buses, get off, visit the sites, and leave without exploring the historic district's commercial section. Their frustration is much like that resulting from efforts to make Harlem a more important destination for tourists in New York City (Hoffman 1999). The national park area of Auburn Avenue certainly figures as an important element of Atlanta's tourist bubble; however, the issue of race makes the revitalization of the entire avenue a more complicated process. Although public-sector policies have invested in the streets and sidewalks of Auburn Avenue, white business leaders have avoided investments in what is regarded as a black area, leaving it neglected and decaying.

Tourist Bubble Politics

In 1970, Atlanta became a majority black city, enabling residents to elect the city's first African-American mayor, Maynard Jackson, three years later. Prior to Jackson's election, the partnership between white public officials and business leaders reshaped the city's downtown tourist bubble to provide for the needs of convention visitors at the expense of black neighborhoods and small businesses. How did the change in Atlanta's political leadership affect the longstanding partnership between city government and business leaders to support the city's downtown convention business?

During his initial term as mayor, Maynard Jackson frequently took policy positions that antagonized white business leaders. Jackson argued that the new airport be located on the same site as the old one, providing a symbolic gesture to south-side black voters. He also insisted that airport construction contracts include joint-venture minority partners and affirmative action requirements for companies doing business with the city. After a public dispute with the Constitution and the leadership of Central Atlanta Progress, Jackson made great efforts to restore relationships with the business elite (Newman 2000). This was particularly important in light of the three major hotels (the Peachtree Plaza, Omni, and Downtown Hilton) and the new state-funded convention center scheduled to open in 1976. As part of his efforts, Jackson and the head of the Chamber of Commerce launched a national tour of other cities promoting investment and painting a picture of harmony between the mayor and the Atlanta business community. Addressing an audience in Chicago, Jackson said, "Atlanta can't prosper without city hall and business in bed together" (Teasley 1974, A–1). Adolph Reed (1987) suggested that this accommodation between Mayor Jackson and white business leaders was necessary because of the private-sector control of investments in the city. Many of the largest investments were in the downtown tourist bubble's megastructures and hotels.

To cement his cooperative relationship with the business community during his second term in office, Jackson established an economic development corporation to create public-private partnerships and with its allied organization, the Downtown Development Authority, to finance projects in the city. Among its first efforts was a $9 million industrial development bond financing for the construction of the French-owned Ibis Hotel in downtown. This project was one of many that would enhance the city's tourist bubble. Thus, despite racial change in city government, support for tourism investments in downtown Atlanta continued. This confirms Reed's (1987, 168) observation that black urban regimes are "by and large only black versions of the progrowth regimes that they have replaced."

If Jackson tried to revive the coalition of city government and business leaders, his successor, Andrew Young, fully restored the partnership to promote downtown tourism. His administration worked closely with Central Atlanta Progress to rebuild Underground Atlanta and joined with Fulton County and state government to build a new indoor stadium known as the Georgia Dome for the use of the Falcons of the National Football League. The construction of the Georgia Dome and its parking lots involved displacing a small black neighborhood known as Lightning as well as several African-American churches. As initially proposed, there were no relocation funds for area residents or the churches; however, protests by the city's black clergy finally won $25 million from the state for assistance to those affected.

The building of the Georgia Dome was similar to the city's earlier use of the urban renewal program to expand the downtown tourist bubble at the expense of blacks living near downtown. In this instance, local government support for the development came from the city's African-American mayor. Andrew Young also took an active role in promoting tourism, helping business leaders raise funds for a new promotional campaign to attract conventions. He used his diplomatic skill and international contacts to attract major events to

Atlanta such as the 1988 Democratic National Convention and the Olympics. These high-profile events attracted additional international investment in downtown tourist facilities such as hotels and restaurants.

The pattern of decision making in Atlanta throughout most of the twentieth century reflected a close partnership between business and government. Stone (1993) indicated that Atlanta maintained a development regime with tourism as an important strategy to attract attention and promote investment in the city. Incumbent mayor Bill Campbell has attempted to continue this process with the addition of a new sports arena, which opened in 1999 to replace the Omni as the home for the Atlanta Hawks basketball team and an expansion hockey club, the Thrashers. The sports franchises and media empire owned by Ted Turner were purchased by Time Warner, which subsequently merged with America Online (AOL). This conglomerate signed a 30-year lease on the new sports arena, guaranteeing the repayment on the construction debt and that the teams will play downtown. Continuing the partnership with local government, the city and county financed public improvements around the arena with a new tax on car rentals. The corporate owner of the sports teams also received the right to sell the name of the new arena to Philips, the Dutch electronics firm. The naming rights are reported to be worth $180 million with another $20 million per year from other sponsorship agreements. This more than covers the cost of the sports facility, leaving gate receipts, parking, concessions, and rent from sky boxes as additional sources of profit for AOL–Time Warner (Unger and Poole 1999).

In other efforts, Mayor Campbell has been less successful than his predecessors in promoting private-sector investment in downtown's tourist bubble. For example, he has not attracted investors in a proposed aquarium to be located near Underground Atlanta. With the city of Atlanta representing less than 10% of the metropolitan area's population, business leaders are increasingly focused on suburban areas outside the city. Also, businesses are often owned by international corporations that have little concern for the central city, so in may ways, city government is relegated to the position of a junior partner in the once-flourishing relationship with business leaders.

Yet, despite these changes in the city, Atlanta continues to attract convention visitors. Meeting planners describe the city as convenient because of its airport and rapid rail system. Atlanta also receives high marks for its convention facilities, supply of hotel rooms, and restaurants but is criticized for its safety and lack of interesting sights (Saporta 1990). The issues of crime and the lack of interesting attractions are both related to the city's construction of an enclosed space for tourists in the downtown area. Small businesses and residences were cleared to make way for megastructures such as Peachtree Center and CNN Center. With few people living downtown, the area lacks the 24-hour population as office workers depart for their suburban homes at 5:00 p.m., leaving empty streets and sidewalks. With little regard for historic preservation, older buildings were demolished to make space for newer structures, and the area lacks the character and charm that older buildings would have contributed. Instead, the downtown tourist bubble has been described as "dull and excessively devoted to business and finance" (Frommer 1987, D-1).

Despite these drawbacks, visitors still come to Atlanta because of the city's accessibility, facilities, and relentless promotional efforts. In 1998, the Atlanta Convention and Visitors Bureau reported that the city hosted 3,057 meetings attended by more than 3,423,000 people. This badge-wearing army of convention delegates is an important component of the city's basic economy. Atlanta, along with other cities such as Orlando, Las Vegas, Anaheim, and Phoenix, has fueled its growth with service and leisure-oriented activities instead of more traditional primary and secondary industries. Although older manufacturing centers have declined, these tourism-oriented cities are part of a new emerging hierarchy of urban places. According to Zelinsky (1994), hosting conventions is one of several economic functions that sets the postmodern city apart from its antecedents.

In the case of Atlanta, the city's leaders have used tourism to promote its economic development with expositions and conventions since the nineteenth century. Local business and public officials began constructing the elements of a consumption-oriented tourist space along Peachtree Street in 1909. Economic restructuring in Atlanta did not mean a major shift from manufacturing to service activities such as tourism but did involve rebuilding the downtown tourist space during the 1960s. There were also changes in ownership patterns within the hospitality industry. Smaller family-owned hotels and tourist businesses gave way during the postwar era to national chains and, more recently, to international corporate ownership.

Atlanta's extensive space constructed by private businesses and the public sector for a tourist bubble certainly puts the city among the vanguard of places with downtown areas transformed for purposes of spectacle and consumption. With the hosting of major events such as the 1988 Democratic National Convention, two National Football League "Superbowls," and the 1996 Summer Olympic Games, Atlanta used its tourist space to promote the city as a place worthy of global attention and investment. The only components of the tourist bubble that Atlanta has not added to its theme park downtown are an aquarium and casino gambling. Both have been proposed by public officials but not promoted by business leaders.

The partnership between local government and business that produced Atlanta's tourist bubble still functions to promote downtown convention industry despite racial change at city hall. Nevertheless, the issue of race is evident in the failure of Underground Atlanta and the unrevived commercial section of Auburn Avenue. Although one was built as a $144 million tourist destination that has failed to lure convention visitors, the other has not attracted commercial investment despite the presence of more than 3 million tourists who visit the area each year. The past decisions of the city's public-private partnership created a tourist space that isolates and encloses visitors, giving them little contact with downtown Atlanta outside the hotels and the convention center. As a result, many visitors find Atlanta dull and uninteresting, so they tend not to bring spouses and other family members, nor do convention delegates stay extra days after their meetings (Saporta 1990).

Atlanta's pro-growth regime has used tourism as a strategy to attract investment in downtown. The partnership between business and local government has produced an area devoted to a business-oriented form of tourism, the convention industry. In contrast to New York, Boston, San Francisco, and, especially, European cities where tourist spaces are not isolated from the daily fabric of urban life, Atlanta has a downtown tourist space that is devoted to sports, consumption, and spectacle but encloses its visitors within a secured and protected environment. Within this bubble, business travelers do not mix with a resident population to create an interesting, around-the-clock city (Judd and Fainstein 1999). To the contrary, business and political leaders have not hesitated to move black residents living near downtown. The transition from white to black political leadership did not bring change that benefited African-Americans. As Reed (1988) observed, black urban regimes usually continue the pro-growth policies of their white predecessors. In Atlanta, this meant support for the continued expansion of the downtown tourist bubble. As the examples of Underground Atlanta, the Georgia Dome, and other projects show, black businesses and residents were moved to make way for an enlarged tourist space. Rather than learn from mistakes made during the urban renewal program, Atlanta continues to repeat them.

References

Allen, I., Jr., and P. Hemphill. 1971. *Mayor: Notes on the sixties*. New York: Simon & Schuster.

Bayor, R. H. 1996. *Race and the shaping of twentieth-century Atlanta*. Chapel Hill: Univ. of North Carolina Press.

City of Atlanta, 1993. *Creating an urban village: Atlanta's community driven vision for the empowerment zone: Vol. I, Strategic development*. Atlanta, GA: Author.

Crown, J. 1964. After forty years: A new hotel. *Atlanta* 3 (February): 40–41.

Downtown is looking up. 1976. *Time*, 5 July, 54–62.

Eric Hill Associates. 1966. *City of Atlanta, Georgia, report on the relocation of individuals, families, and businesses*. Atlanta, GA: Community Improvement Program.

Frieden, B. J., and L. B. Sagalyn. 1989. *Downtown Inc. How America builds cities*. Cambridge, MA: MIT Press.

Frommer, A. 1987. Key to Atlanta's future lies in its past. *Constitution*, 18 January, D-1, D-6.

Galphin, B. 1975. Atlanta's $35 million salesman. *Atlanta* 14 (January): 60–74.

Hannigan, J. 1998. *Fantasy city: Pleasure and profit in the postmodern metropolis*. London: Routledge Kegan Paul.

Hoffman, L. 1999. Tourism and the inner city: Marketing diversity. Paper presented at the annual meeting of the Urban Affairs Association, April, Louisville, KY.

Hunter, F. 1953. *Community power structure: A study of decision makers*. Chapel Hill: Univ. of North Carolina Press.

Judd, D. R. 1999. Constructing the tourist bubble. In *The tourist city*, edited by D. R. Judd and S. S. Fainstein, 35–53. New Haven, CT: Yale Univ. Press.

Judd, D. R., and S. S. Fainstein, eds. 1999. *The tourist city*. New Haven, CT: Yale Univ. Press.

Keating, W. D. 1997, Cleveland: The "comeback" city: The politics of redevelopment and sports stadiums amidst urban decline. In *Reconstructing urban regime theory: Regulating urban politics in a global economy*, edited by M. Lauria, 189–205. Thousand Oaks, CA: Sage.

Law, C. M. 1993. *Urban tourism: Attracting visitors to large cities*. London: Mansell.

Levine, M. V. 1987. Downtown redevelopment as an urban growth strategy: A critical appraisal of the Baltimore renaissance. *Journal of Urban Affairs* 9 (2): 103–23.

Martin, H. H. 1987. *Atlanta and environs: A chronicle of its people and events.* Vol. 3. Atlanta: Atlanta Historical Society and Univ. of Georgia Press.

Newman, H. K. 1999. *Southern hospitality: Tourism and the growth of Atlanta.* Tuscaloosa: Univ. of Alabama Press.

———. 2000. Hospitality and violence: Contradictions in a southern city. *Urban Affairs Review* 35 (4): 541–58.

Pomerantz, G. 1996. *Where Peachtree meets Sweet Auburn: The saga of two families and the making of Atlanta.* New York: Scribner.

Reed, A. L., Jr. 1987. A critique of neo-progressivism in theorizing about local development policy: A case from Atlanta. In *The politics of urban development,* edited by C. Stone and H. Sanders, 199–215. Lawrence: University Press of Kansas.

———. 1988. The black urban regime: Structural origins and constraints. In *Power, community and the city,* edited by M. P. Smith, 138–89. New Brunswick, NJ: Transaction Books.

Research Atlanta. 1982. *The convention industry in Atlanta.* Atlanta, GA: Author.

———. 1983. *Atlanta tourism and convention market: A synopsis of several studies.* Atlanta, GA: Author.

Rosentraub, M. S. 1997. *Major league losers: The real cost of sports and who's paying for it.* New York: Basic Books.

Saporta, M. 1990. GWCC tops list of meeting sites. *Constitution,* 13 March, A-1, A-7.

Shaw, G., and A. M. Williams. 1994. *Critical issues in tourism: A geographical perspective.* Oxford, UK: Blackwell.

Sjoquist, D. L., and L. Williams. 1992. *The Underground Atlanta project: An economic analysis.* Atlanta: Policy Research Center, Georgia State University.

Sorkin, M., ed. 1992. *Variations on a theme park: The new American city and the end of public space.* New York: Hill & Wang.

Stone, C. N. 1989. *Regime politics: Governing Atlanta, 1946–1988.* Lawrence: University Press of Kansas.

———. 1993. Urban regimes and the capacity to govern: A political economy approach. *Journal of Urban Affairs* 15 (1): 1–28.

Teasley, C. 1974. Mayor, Currey deny rift, seek business in Chicago. *Constitution,* 21 November, A-1.

Unger, H., and S. Poole. 1999. Philips arena creating a look: Corporate club. *Constitution,* 12 September, P-13.

Zelinsky, W. 1994. Conventionland USA: The geography of a latterday phenomenon. *Annals of the Association of American Geographers* 84 (1): 68–86.

Zukin, S. 1991. *Landscapes of power: From Detroit to Disney World.* Berkeley: Univ. of California Press.

16

Rosalyn Baxandall and Elizabeth Ewen

SUBURBAN CHANGE AND THE "UNDERWATER ECONOMY"

New Immigrants

Beginning in the 1980s many older white residents began leaving Long Island suburbs for more rural places or warmer climes. At the same time, a mosaic of

---

"New Immigrants" (Chapter 17) from Rosalyn Baxandall and Elizabeth Ewen, *Picture Windows: How the Suburbs Happened.* Basic Books, 2000, pp. 239–250, and endnotes on pp. 287–288.

immigrants, mainly from Central America but also from South America, the subcontinent of India, Asia, and the Middle East, were moving to Long Island. Japanese, Iranians, Koreans, Cubans, Haitians, and Vietnamese, as well as Indians, Pakistanis, Guatemalans, and Salvadorans, were part of a national trend in immigration. No one knows exactly how many new immigrants live on Long Island. Even the Immigration and Naturalization Service cannot estimate the number. Some experts point to the growth of the Salvadoran population as an indication of the extent of the surge: "In 1979 before civil war broke out in El Salvador, there were as few as 5,000 Salvadorans living on the island. Today according to immigrant groups and outreach workers, the number is well over 100,000."[1]

Unlike their turn-of-the-century predecessors, these immigrants were not of one class. They were wealthy, educated, middle class, working class, uneducated, and poor. Traditionally families moved to suburbs to escape metropolitan exigencies and acquire a private house, with a car in the garage and a yard on a quiet, uncluttered street where children can roam freely. For poor immigrants this is not the case; they live and work in situations that rival the worst turn-of-the-century sweatshops and tenements, exposed by muckrakers like Jacob Riis and Lewis Hines. Few muckrakers today expose the suburban underbelly. Omar Enriquez, organizer for the Workplace Project, suggested, "The problem is much bigger on Long Island than most people will admit. We have a dirty secret here."[2]

Generally poor and unacculturated, the new immigrants challenge the suburban image while their labor helps to preserve and enhance it.[3] "With unemployment at 2.8 percent in Nassau and 3.7 percent in Suffolk, experts and local officials say many of these [low-paying] jobs would not get done without immigrant labor."[4] Nonetheless, some older residents—especially those who live near the immigrants—just don't want them in their backyards. As Vincent Bullock, seventy-five, of Farmingdale, Long Island, said, "[The] long and short of it [is], they're knocking down my property values and I'll be damned if I'm paying a dime to help them do it."[5]

Part of the problem is that many suburbanites and public officials see the issue as cultural rather than economic. Older residents, white and black, complain about men hanging out in groups on suburban street corners, talking and listening to loud music until late at night; yet none of them bother to ask why these new residents are out on the street.

One of the factors that had always differentiated suburbs from cities is the absence of street culture. Front porches and stoops rarely were found. Street life for new suburban immigrants, however, is a result of cultural traditions and overcrowding. As one longtime Freeport resident explains, "Suburbia does not like the idea of people congregating fifteen to twenty of them on suburban street corners, sitting on top of their cars blaring their big radios."[6]

Long Island villages need to both familiarize immigrants with the tacit customs of the suburbs and get longtime residents to accept the different mores of their new neighbors. The village of Glen Cove issued a short flier explaining what is and is not considered acceptable: public drinking is against the law, but outdoor gatherings are not illegal, unless they block the street.[7]

Another striking difference is that most newer immigrants bypass the city and go directly from the airport to the suburbs, a pattern that had begun in the late 1950s, when the majority of suburban immigrants were Puerto Ricans. Cubans joined them in the 1960s and 1970s; in the 1980s Dominicans, Haitians, Jamaicans, Salvadorans, and others arrived from the Caribbean. Jennifer Gordon, organizer of the Workplace Project in Hempstead, makes the point that, "Long Island has become a center for Central Americans in the New York Metropolitan area and is home to more of them than New York City or any other urban area."[8]

Advertisements promising cheap property, jobs in farms, greenhouses, nurseries, factories, and domestic service brought many rural Central Americans to the United States. Others, mainly from El Salvador and Guatemala, came because of political oppression and violent civil wars. Rural families tended to be attracted to Suffolk, while those from cities came to work in the non-unionized light industries of the South Shore of Nassau County, to towns such as Freeport, Rockville Center, Westbury, Glen Cove, and Hempstead.[9]

By the late 1980s pressures began to mount over issues related to the new immigrant presence in schools, housing, jobs, and suburban culture. Long Island, like other suburban areas, had little experience in dealing with newly arrived, diverse immigrant populations. Recession, budget cuts, a skyrocketing real estate market, and anti-immigrant sentiment all conspired against integration into the existing culture. Unlike large cities, suburbs have few local governmental agencies, social services, or homeless shelters to accommodate immigrants. Since many are not eligible to vote, politicians have no motivation to help these groups. Nonprofit advocacy organizations such as the Community Advocates in Nassau, the Central American Refugee Center, and the Workplace Project in Hempstead—an impressive center that assists immigrants with legal problems, holds classes in English and legal rights, and helps Hispanic residents in organizing labor co-ops—along with many churches have attempted, sometimes successfully, to fill the void. Like other pioneers to suburbia, immigrants rely on each other, their extended families, and informal networks.

Central American immigrants depend on an unconventional, illegal, and mostly informal economy—so hidden and secret that "Salvadorans call it by the Spanish phrase, *baja del agua* [underwater]. . . . In this economic underwater of Long Island there is nothing extraordinary about a suburban home doubling as a dental office or a restaurant, or a makeshift pharmacy in a bodega."[10] Most immigrants have to make use of this underwater economy. Sara Mahler, anthropologist, describes why: "You cannot survive on Long Island with the wages they are earning. In El Salvador, they hear they can make six dollars an hour and translate the worth to their home country. When they get here, they are shocked by the cost of living." In Hempstead, Westbury, and Brentwood,

a licensed dentist charges about $55 dollars for tooth extraction, in the underwater, the bill comes to $25 dollars. A Main Street restaurant asks $1.25 for Salvadoran pupusas [made of thick tortillas and meat] but underwater cooks charge 75 cents. You can get your laundry done for two dollars and pharmaceuticals for about a dollar a pill.[11]

Although such networks offer the advantages of familiarity, language, and costs, they have disadvantages, too. Consumers have no legal recourse if service is shoddy or deleterious. Sometimes you get what you pay for, sometimes you don't.

The only work available to recent immigrants, who speak little English and sometimes are undocumented, is badly paid and erratic, with long hours and poor conditions. Immigrants often work as day workers doing landscaping or construction for local contractors. Some have more regular jobs in light manufacturing, building, cleaning, maintenance, and restaurants, or work as cashiers, stockroom clerks, gas station attendants, and domestics. Most of these jobs place immigrants at a disadvantage, because "They often take place outside the realm of the law. Employers are rarely registered with the appropriate authorities: many of them neither comply with labor laws nor pay taxes to the government and often, they fail to participate in mandatory insurance programs such as workers compensation or disability."[12]

Maria Luisa Paz (who used a pseudonym because she feared giving her own name) was undocumented and worked in a commercial laundry with 300 other Central American workers. Their work consisted of disinfecting, washing, pressing, and folding mounds of hospital linen. Her job was to fold the sheets that came off the presses. The damp sheets were scalding hot and seldom was she given anything to protect her hands. After a recent Occupational Health and Safety Organization (OSHA) inspection, the company was forced to hand out a few pairs of thin uninsulated gloves.

In the room where Paz worked the temperature was often 100 degrees. After a few weeks Paz's gloves had holes burned in every finger and her fingers were covered with large, watery blisters. Her shirt was splattered with blood from frequent heat-related nosebleeds, and her arms and legs were flecked with white chemical stains. She was not alone. Other workers had been injured as well: one man lost half a finger, another was severely burned on the chest by chemical water that had boiled over, and a woman fainted on the job from heat and fumes. When Paz complained, the owners responded, "We didn't do anything wrong; those health problems are your fault." She then was asked to produce work authorization and was fired when she couldn't. Paz then contacted OSHA about filing a discrimination complaint, but was discouraged because the OSHA investigator told her he couldn't do much for illegals like her.[13]

Suburbia would like simply to ignore these new faces, but often they become all too visible. One way they obtain work is by lining up along major thoroughfares in the morning so that work trucks can fetch them. This creates a problem for local residents, who resent this unsightly practice and gripe to the police, who then try to enforce local ordinances against loitering. In Glen Cove one policeman warned a group of men who had strayed into the street, "It's against the law to hang out in the street in groups, that's from the Mayor himself. We'll have to give you an appearance ticket or jail at worst, if we see you hanging around." When this message had been translated into Spanish, the full meaning sank in. Francisco Martinez, a Hempstead resident from El Salvador, "raised his hand and spoke, 'One question! We don't have the right to buy a coffee? If we go to buy a coffee, they are going to think we are hanging around'."[14] After much ruckus Glen Cove resolved the visibility issue by creating an unobtrusive location for the shape-up (work truck pickup). There are at least five other similar shape-up stops scattered throughout Nassau and Suffolk counties.

In another Long Island town, Inwood, residents in 1994 attempted to remove workers from the corner where they were lined up waiting for employment. The residents complained that the workers were disrupting the neighborhood. Workers were videotaped, verbally harassed, and physically threatened by townspeople who eventually had the police blockade the street. With the help of the Workplace Project, the workers negotiated a settlement for a better place to wait. If towns see these gatherings as disruptive, organizers find them useful for making workers aware of their rights and helping them set new wage standards.[15]

Another hazard immigrant workers face is being cheated out of their wages by fly-by-night companies. Raoul Melendez (a pseudonym) waited on a street corner in the town of Franklin Square with sixty other Latino men at six in the morning. Melendez thought himself lucky to find a job with a landscape company that employed him at first for a few days, then for two weeks. He began to relax waiting for his first paycheck.

Unfortunately, his hand was badly cut by a lawn mower. His employer drove him to the hospital promising to return, but never did. Melendez was not paid for any of his work and was sorely in need of Workers' Compensation—but the company that hired him was not listed in the phone book and not registered with the Chamber of Commerce. Melendez was never paid.[16]

One of Raoul's friends at the Franklin Square street corner, Miguel Gueverra (also an assumed name) was not paid for nine days of work with another landscape company. He tried to confront the boss, who told him that the owner of the house didn't pay him and "when I don't get paid, you don't get paid." Gueverra, along with other workers and the Workplace Project, devised a strategy. They figured out where the landscape boss was working and went to the job site to confront him. Disturbed by the noise, the owner of the house came out and witnessed the confrontation. The home owner was horrified and the landscaper embarrassed by being caught. The boss agreed to pay the money because the home owner said to Gueverra, "If he doesn't pay you the rest like he promised, I won't be paying him what I promised either." The next week the debt was paid in full.[17]

In order to circumvent these irresponsible employment practices, the Workplace Project has set up a landscaping cooperative. The Cooperative Landscaping Innovation Project (CLIP) serves over fifty private clients and a church. Workers are responsible for both the administration of the business and the landscaping itself. Everyone votes on the issues and owns a part of everything. They make $12 an hour, far more than the going wage. As Jose Martinez, who fled the war in El Salvador, where he worked as an electrician, exclaimed, "The miracle is happening. After nine years as a day laborer, I have become my own boss."[18] Another sign of the Workplace Project's success is the passage of the Unpaid Wages Prohibition Act in New York State. This bill creates penalties for nonpayment or payment under the minimum wage. Enforcement remains spotty.[19]

Even when there are laws and redress agencies, enormous problems remain. The Hempstead office of the New York State Department of Labor

> seems designed to discourage immigrants from filing claims of non-payment of wages. A Spanish speaking interviewer is only available for three hours once every two weeks. Moreover because no one who answers the phone—if it is answered at all—speaks Spanish, it is impossible for Spanish-speaking workers to learn the hours of the Spanish-speaking interviewer.[20]

Also, many wage claims that are filed are not investigated for long periods of time, sometimes as long as eighteen months.

The New York State Division of Human Rights, charged with enforcing antidiscrimination laws, takes up to five years to investigate and decide discrimination cases. These practices, combined with requests for documentation concerning taxes, witnesses, and authorization of work "effectively turn a blind eye to the entire underground economy, the arena of the greatest labor abuses."[21]

Another often invisible occupation taken by immigrants is domestic work. In the hierarchy of domestic work, living with an employer is considered the lowest rung of the ladder. Women are isolated without transportation and often are compelled to work hours without defined limits. Hidden in the homes of upper-middle-class suburbs are immigrant women who work up to fifteen-hour shifts six days a week for wages amounting to $2 an hour. The popular Spanish term for this job, encerrado, "gets to the heart of the matter—locked up."[22]

Some domestics work by the day cleaning, doing laundry, and taking care of children. These female workers face problems similar to those of their male counterparts: working long hours for less than minimum wage, being subjected to the whims of employers, and having little guarantees of payment or benefits. Dina Aguirre worked for three weeks for a family in Garden City without getting paid. "I worked from seven in the morning until seven at night and sometimes until 11. I asked the woman to pay me and she said, 'I don't owe you anything, because you ruined my blouse.' She said, 'Give me your address and I will send you a bill for all that you owe me.'" Aguirre was finally paid, but only after suing in small claims court. Even when domestic workers go to court for back wages, often they remain unpaid. Yanira Juarez worked for an employer in Bellport, where she won her claim in court for more than $2,000 in back wages, but she was never actually paid. "I returned and returned again, with a friend who spoke English to tell her that I needed the money. She took my address and said, I will send it, I'm still waiting."[23] Other employers deny even having employed the worker, or falsely accuse them of stealing.[24]

The Workplace Project is organizing domestic workers by circulating an advice book about scornful bosses and their overworked maids, as well as forming Justice Committees of domestic workers who will appear at employers' homes to show their court orders and demand back wages. They plan to follow this up with a cooperative for domestic workers.

These low-paid, tenuous employment practices make decent housing for immigrants hard to find, especially in suburbia, where there is little inexpensive housing and a market that favors single-family homes. Most communities have laws limiting the number of unrelated people sharing a home. Town and village officials do not have nearly enough inspectors to handle even a fraction of the hundreds of thousands of illegal apartments believed to exist on Long Island.[25]

Often then, immigrants are forced to live in substandard, illegal makeshift housing with five or six other families who share a single kitchen and bathroom. The situation is even worse for undocumented immigrants, who have no legal recourse and sometimes are forced into renting beds by the day or night. Often "an extra bed in someone's home is rented in shifts to day and night laborers who pay $300 dollars a month and call them hot beds because they are rarely without a warm body."[26] Landlords frequently let small rooms at inflated rents, from $250 to $500 a month; they can get as much as $5,000 a month leasing a house. In 1988 the Long Island Regional Planning Board estimated that there were at least 90,000 illegal apartments, "which is obviously an underestimation considering the massive new immigration and the difficulty in detection."[27]

Suburban neighborhoods by day present a tidy picture. By nightfall, when residents come home from work, the streets change to reveal telltale cracks in the suburban facade. Cars on lawns, groups of people walking because they can't speak enough English to get a driver's license, loud music, cookouts on the street, and general noise are signs that homes meant to house a family have now become rental tenements. Only catastrophe makes this situation fully apparent: a fire, a raid, or a fight.

In May 1999 in Huntington Station a fire engulfed a single-family house crowded with thirty-three Salvadoran immigrants, killing three people and leaving sixteen injured and thirty homeless.[28] Jose Santos Fuentes died of exposure in 1997, after falling into a creek next to his bed under a Glen Cove overpass.[29] Another fire, in Freeport in 1996, revealed twenty-two people, most of them Central American immigrants, crammed into makeshift cubicles of plywood and cardboard on every floor, from the basement up to the third-floor attic. A raid by police and building inspectors in Hicksville turned up nearly 100 immigrants living in a hodgepodge of one- and two-story buildings. The building's residents all worked, but they were living on the edge. Some, like the Delgado family, had pooled their income to pay $2,700 a month to house fifteen people in an office suite that had been converted into seven tiny bedrooms, two small kitchens, two bathrooms, and a tattered former reception area that served as a living room. The Delgado family still lives in this office suite, but now their bags are always packed in case of a raid.[30]

Even when inspections are made, there is no guarantee that living conditions will improve. Huntington's public safety director, Bruce Richards, said that in 1994,

"inspectors found men living in outdoor sheds on property, and more people living in two apartments carved illegally out of the garage. The sheds were removed and the owner, Estrella Martinez, paid $375 in fines." In 1997 Mr. Richards checked out a report of an overflowing cesspool on the same property and discovered at least 15 people—all of them, apparently undocumented, living on the property: in a camper parked next to the garage; in four rooms in the cellar, two of which he likened to crawl space; and in an upstairs attic.[31]

The house was declared unfit for occupants and Ms. Martinez fined $1,100, but in January 1998 inspectors returned to investigate another complaint and found people again occupying illegal apartments and the cellar. She was given a summons and told to report to court. This situation is not unusual. Landlords calculate the fines in their cost of doing business.

As Marge Rogatz, president of the nonprofit Community Advocates in Nassau County, explained, "We are turning our backs on the low income people working in our communities. We need them to run all kinds of enterprises, but we are perfectly willing to have them come to work from living in a place we don't want to know about."[32]

The black market in housing is a result of the unwillingness to build low-income housing, or to change the zoning regulations that only allow single-family dwellings. The situation persists because of "the extraordinary collusion of landlords, tenants, real estate brokers and contractors tacitly abetted by judges and bureaucrats who are partly unwilling and partly unable to stop it."[33] Without new laws and protections, safety and health conditions cannot be assured.

The integration of this new population into the schools has also been difficult. Since 1990 Long Island has the highest level of students with limited English in New York State. Most of these limited-English districts are on the South Shore of Long Island. Some Long Island districts report that students speak thirty or more languages and dialectics.[34] Non-English-speaking students are expensive to educate; they need bilingual classes. Some school districts have tried to incorporate bilingual education into their curricula, at least for Hispanic students. The financial strain is greatest in poor districts that already are underfunded.

One solution is to place non-English-speaking students into special education classes, intended officially for the learning disabled. A 1994 special education report on teaching English as a second language noted that "the over representation of minorities and the foreign born in special education classes was not restricted to . . . Long Island. It reflects the failure of suburban school systems nationwide to adapt as their populations have changed." The report indicated that in many schools there is only "forty-five minutes of English instruction daily for students expected to master high school level mathematics, biology and history."[35]

One science teacher in Westbury, Long Island, taught twenty Haitian Creole-speaking students with no assistance. Eventually he became so frustrated that he slammed the door on a fourteen-year-old boy's finger, severing the tip. He landed in jail. The Haitian community then pressed school officials for Creole-speaking teachers and aides, but the Westbury school did not respond. Creole-speaking teachers were available, but the Haitian parents hadn't enough clout to ensure that their children's needs were met.[36]

Stringent residency requirements make it difficult for immigrant students to attend school. In many Long Island schools and other suburban districts in the country, one needs to prove residency by showing "lease contracts, mortgage statements and notarized letters from absentee landlords." Nine-year-old Daniel Amaya, whose family did not have these precious documents because they lived in a doubled-up dwelling, where such documents are difficult to attain, was barred from a Hempstead public school. Mrs. Amaya stated, "I have no idea who the owner is. I live with my two sisters." A meeting was arranged for immigrant women and children to explain the requirements. Unfortunately the Salvadoran group spoke no English and no official came to translate. Daniel Amaya captured the essence of this frustration when he said, "I don't understand anything they are saying, but they are really angry at all of us."[37]

In spite of these cultural skirmishes, the new immigrants have had an impact on Long Island. Street signs in a town such as Brentwood are in Spanish and English. In a delicatessen in Patchogue, a sign advertises a *cerveza light*. "The nearby mainstreet market sells baccaloo (dried cod fish) as well as t-bone steaks. Across the street at La Vida Christiana children receive religious instruction and adults learn English."[38] You can buy *platanos* (bananas used for cooking), Jamaican meat patties, curries of all varieties, and *Kim Chee* (Korean pickled cabbage). Video stores carry films in Indian dialects, Spanish, and Chinese.

> In Hicksville, a little India has developed encompassing a five block area offering food markets, restaurants, an Indian-owned hair salon and a duplex movie theatre showing only Indian films. The two biggest annual events [in Brentwood] . . . are the St. Patrick's Day Parade in March and the Adelante Day Parade, which celebrates Hispanic struggle, in June.[39]

There is such variety now that ethnic neighbors don't automatically bond. "Twenty years ago, if you saw a Hispanic person, you held him and said, 'I'm Spanish,'" Roberto Portal explained. "Now we are so many that if we see a Hispanic, we go across the street."[40]

Suburbs are now becoming—albeit not always willingly—multiclass, multiethnic, and multiracial. This assimilation continues to be knotty and remains in flux. Can older suburbs accommodate these new ethnic groups, or will outmoded decentralized government structures and prejudice keep them hidden *baja del agua*—underwater? Will these new populations revitalize the dream and energize suburbia to change once again?

Notes

1. Charlie LeDuff and David Halbfinger, "Wages and Squalor for Immigrant Workers," *New York Times,* 5 May 1999.
2. *New York Times,* 24 July 1997.
3. Sara Mahler, "First Stop Suburbia," *NACLA* [North American Committee on Latin America] *Report on the Americas* 26, 1 (July 1992): 19.
4. LeDuff and Halbfinger, "Wages and Squalor."
5. Ibid.

6. Norman Appelton, interview by authors, January 1991.
7. Doreen Carvajal, "New York Suburbs Take on a Latin Accent," *New York Times,* 29 July 1993.
8. Jennifer Gordon, "We Make the Road by Walking: Immigrant Workers, the Workplace Project and the Struggle for Social Change," *Harvard Civil Rights Civil Liberties Law Review* (Summer 1995): 411.
9. Mahler, "First Stop Suburbia," 20–48.
10. Doreen Carvajal, "Making Ends Meet in a Nether World," *New York Times,* 13 December 1994.
11. Mahler, "First Stop Suburbia," 20–24.
12. Gordon, "We Make the Road by Walking," 412–13.
13. Ibid., 408, 418, 419.
14. Doreen Carvajal, "Out of Sight, Out of Mind, But Not Out of Work," *New York Times,* 8 July 1995.
15. Ibid.
16. Gordon, "We Make the Road by Walking," 408–9.
17. Ibid., 432.
18. Evelyn Nieves, "Day Laborer Stakes Out His Own Patch," *New York Times,* 10 May 1998.
19. *New York Times,* 24 July 1997; *New York Times* editorial, 31 August 1997; *New York Times,* 19 September 1997.
20. Gordon, "We Make the Road by Walking," 420–21.
21. Ibid., 418–21. See also Kenneth C. Crowe, "The Big Payback," *Newsday,* 7 January 1996.
22. Doreen Carvajal, "For Immigrant Maids, Not a Job But Servitude," *New York Times,* 25 February 1996.
23. Ibid.
24. *New York Times,* 24 July 1997.
25. LeDuff and Halbfinger, "Wages and Squalor."
26. Doreen Carvajal, "Making Ends Meet"; idem, "A Mayor Asks Help on Illegal Tenancies," *New York Times,* 11 October 1996.
27. Ibid., "A Mayor Asks Help"; LeDuff and Halbfinger, "Wages and Squalor."
28. Robert McFadden, "Fire in a Crowded Home of Immigrants Kills 3 and Injures 16 on L.I.," *New York Times,* 2 May 1999.
29. LeDuff and Halbfinger, "Wages and Squalor."
30. McFadden, "Fire in a Crowded Home."
31. Ibid.
32. Bruce Lambert, "Raid on Illegal Housing, Shows the Plight of Suburbs Working Poor," *New York Times,* 7 December 1996.
33. Frank Bruni, with Debra Sontag, "Behind a Suburban Facade in Queens, A Teeming Angry Urban Arithmetic," *New York Times,* 8 October 1996.
34. John Rather, "New Immigrants Transforming the Population," *New York Times,* 17 March 1996, Long Island edition.
35. Diana Jean Schemo, "Education as a Second Language," *New York Times,* 25 July 1994.
36. Doreen Carvajal, "Cultures Clash in Suburbs, Schools Struggle to Cope With Influx of Immigrant Students," *New York Times,* 8 January 1995.
37. Doreen Carvajal, "Immigrants Fight Residency Rules, Blocking Students in Long Island Schools," *New York Times,* 7 June 1995.
38. Sylvia Moreno, "Long Island Census Shows 3.9% Hispanic," *Newsday,* 27 April 1981.
39. Patrick Boyle, "Brentwood's a Melting Pot of Promise," *Newsday,* 1 December 1996; Lyn Dobrin, "The Spice Root in Hicksville." *Newsday,* 16 October 1995.
40. Ibid. New York Suburbs Take on a Latin Accent.

CHAPTER 7

CITIES IN THE INTERNATIONAL MARKETPLACE

City Politics and the New Economy

In some ways the imperatives that influence urban economic development to-day differ from the past. Internationalization has made cities, suburbs, and even whole regions part of a global marketplace marked by rapid communication, transnational business activities, and complex linkages to workers, managers, and cultures all over the world. American capitalism has become less dependent upon industry and hard goods production because growth in business activities has shifted decidedly into services, taking cities, towns and villages along in the process. The economic function of cities is changing as they become enmeshed in this revolutionary transformation; where cities once pursued smokestack industries, they now are converting old warehouse, seaport, and industrial districts to tourist destinations, downtown malls, and office centers. Where once the armies of blue-collar workers working in factories fueled city growth, today it is more likely to be driven by white-collar managers and technicians meeting face-to-face in downtown offices, business parks, and upscale restaurants.

Despite these new changes, the contemporary urban political economy also displays important similarities to the past. Economic globalization has been accompanied by the disengagement of the federal government from the cities. These cities are engaged in economic rivalry with one another that in some ways resembles the fierce competition of the nineteenth century. As in the first decades of the Republic, today's cities participate in place wars for economic survival. The new mobility of capital extends urban competition to a vast international marketplace in which the future is dominated by uncertainty and intense intercity rivalry. Within the cities this has triggered contests over growth policies and over the distribution of public benefits. In a sense, urban development politics has the competitive features of the early days of capitalism.

The readings in this chapter describe the strategies used by urban governments to compete for economic growth; each selection also raises questions about who benefits from these policies. There is evidence that citizens often end up empty handed and public officials give up far too much in the deal-making that goes on between business and government.

Richard Foglesong's brief story on the coming of Disney World to Winter Park, Florida, describes how the transformation of that community by one of America's most famous entertainment giants was dominated by private purposes and unexpected public consequences. Although Disney promised to build a model city for people to live in, what eventually materialized was a megacomplex entertainment center run purely as a business. This was possible in part because the Disney Corporation won the legal right to incorporate as a virtual city-state controlled by the company, but enjoying regulatory powers and privileges normally reserved by law for elected local governments. Without a resident citizen population, the government of Epcot became—to use Foglesong's phrase—"a Vatican with mouse ears." As such, company executives could make key decisions without having to answer to local residents.

The last two readings in this chapter probe the opportunities for city governments to gain greater leverage in the urban development process and describe the costs of alternative policy strategies. Elizabeth Strom points out that as the traditional economic base of cities has weakened, culture and the arts have became increasingly important for urban revitalization. She points out that a major advantage of many older large cities is their wealth of historic districts, museums, concert halls, opera houses, art galleries, and other "high culture" assets. Strom describes how an interesting confluence of private and public interests has occurred. Promoters of culture and the arts now seek opportunities to market their "products" to the mass public and obtain public funds in order to preserve what they have and possibly grow even bigger. To do so successfully, however, means taking a much greater interest in urban development than ever before. For its part, city government officials perceive cultural and art institutions as virtual industries with the potential for adding much to their plans for revitalization. The result: cultural institutions and public development agencies become major stakeholders in one another. Strom believes questions should be raised about the public consequences of having art and culture so dependent on generating revenue-producing activities in the cities. Does the commercialization of culture exclude supporting artistic endeavors that have public or aesthetic value but cannot draw crowds and long lines? Does it bias public support for the arts in favor of events that have quick audience potential, but diminish sustained support for museums and concert halls after they are built? Ultimately, is the quality of life in cities improved or degraded by the new culture-development alliance?

Paul Kantor and H. V. Savitch show how local officials can sometimes gain considerable influence in the urban development process despite the pressures to compete. Cities are sometimes depicted as junior partners with business in the global development game. After all, in theory business investors have many cities and regions to choose from; cities are often desperate to attract their money and employees. In their comparative analysis of cities in the United States and Western Europe, Kantor and Savitch show that the real world is not always so one-sided. The authors describe how city bargaining advantages relative to business are not uniform; sometimes business is the junior partner. In their theory they describe how the bargaining advantages of cities can be enhanced by market conditions, local political systems, and national urban policies.

For example, some city governments possess the advantage of a favorable market environment for attracting or keeping business, and not all are desperate to chase every dollar investors offer. This may be because some businesses have large sunk costs not easily moved elsewhere; an example is entertainment parks. Alternatively, some cities, such as London, Tokyo, and New York, are global cities that serve as anchors for industries like financial services; this limits the economic competition they face from smaller cities. Still others may have highly diversified economies so that lost jobs are easily replaced. In all these circumstances, economic advantages can favor cities, not investors. This, in turn, makes it possible for these city governments to act with greater independence and promote development policies that generate more community benefits than others can.

As the authors note, bargaining advantages are not always economic in nature. Cities that have highly democratic political systems are better able to resist business demands. Cities having access to assistance from national governments that take an active role in urban affairs are also better able to extract concessions from the private sector and limit business power. In fact, the role of nations in supporting their cities may be pivotal. U.S. cities tend to have fewer bargaining advantages than their counterparts in Western Europe—largely because of the exceptionally limited role the national government plays in supporting and regulating local economic development policy activity.

17

Richard Foglesong

WHEN DISNEY COMES TO TOWN

"It was as though they'd put a gun to our head," said the director of tri-county planning. "They were offering to invest $600 million. And there was the glamour of Disney. You could hardly say no to that. We were all just spellbound."

They had come from around the state to hear, finally, what Disney's new East Coast theme park would look like. The new Republican governor and most of his cabinet were there. So was half the legislature. Bankers, developers and a planeload of reporters filled out the audience. Everyone was clamoring to hear Disney's proposal, but the politicians, in particular, were anxious to know what the giant entertainment company would demand of the state legislature.

The project was Walt Disney World; the year was 1967; the place was Winter Park, Fla., outside Orlando, where the pooh-bahs had gathered to hear Disney's

"When Disney Comes to Town," by Richard Foglesong, as appeared in *The Washington Post Magazine*, May 15, 1994. Richard Foglesong is Professor of Politics at Rollins College in Florida. Reprinted by permission of the author.

plans for a regional theme park. There are significant differences between 1960s Florida and 1990s Virginia, of course—Floridians were relatively untutored in the consequences of urban growth, while Virginians today are not so naive—yet the odd familiarity of the Winter Park scene highlights some of the more striking parallels between Disney's Orlando project and its present-day plans for a park in Haymarket. Then, as now, Disney's proposal was accompanied by hardball lobbying from the company, hoopla from business interests, enthusiastic support from a Republican governor and a struggle over the financing of roads. Then—as now—the Walt Disney Co. proved more powerful than local critics or media skeptics, hiring the right lobbyists and nurturing the right legislators. Then—as now—Disney got what it wanted from the state.

Given these similarities, it's instructive to consider the disparity between the plan that Disney laid out on that heady day in Winter Park and what actually transpired in Central Florida. Simply put, the California company proposed one kind of development, which it used to gain special governmental powers, and then built something else. And yet Floridians, blinded by the pixie dust, hardly noticed. Then—as now?—people were mesmerized by the Disney mystique.

The big news about the Florida project, initially, was its much-vaunted plan for a model city where ordinary people would make their homes and go about their lives in an idealized setting. This was a concept that had been brewing for some time: Two years before the Winter Park presentation, Walt Disney, speaking at a Florida press conference, rhapsodized about building a "City of Tomorrow." In the following months, the City of Tomorrow became an obsession with Walt, according to Disney biographer Bob Thomas. The company already knew how to build an amusement park, Walt insisted; so he focused his attention on what he was soon calling "an experimental prototype community of tomorrow"—or Epcot.

But the company's commitment to Epcot depended on the creative leadership of one man—Walt himself. In the fall of 1966, Orlando banker and power broker Billy Dial flew to California to meet with the 64-year-old Disney. Worried about the showman's health, he asked over lunch: "Mr. Disney, if you walked out of this restaurant and were hit by a truck, what would happen to the Orlando project?" Walt responded: "Absolutely nothing. My brother runs this company, I just piddle around."

Dial was unpersuaded, and with good reason: Three weeks later, he was in New York at the Bankers Trust Co. when he received a hurried phone call from Disney executive Donn Tatum, who said simply, "Walt is dead." It was December 15, 1966, and Walt Disney had died from lung cancer before almost anyone realized he was ill. His death left the company directionless—creatively at least—and Epcot, which had existed mostly in his head, in a state of flux. Roy Disney, the company's financial mastermind and Walt's older brother, was 73 and had already announced his plans to retire.

Roy agreed to stay on and, after polling senior executives, gave the East Coast project his blessing and directed that it be called *Walt* Disney World as a tribute to his brother. Disney execs knew little of Walt's Epcot plans, however, so they focused instead on building a Disneyland-type amusement park; as Disney Vice President Card Walker would later observe, "It was the thing we knew best."

Indeed, Walt's comments on a May 23, 1966, memo suggest that he himself had privately backed away from the model city vision before he died. In the memo, which was found in Walt's desk and is now kept at the Disney Archives in Burbank, Calif., Florida attorney Paul Helliwell sketched out the problem of allowing permanent residents at Epcot. If people lived there, they would vote there, diluting the company's political control of the property. It seems that Walt's thoughts were headed in a similar direction: On the memo, every time Helliwell referred to "permanent residents," Walt crossed it out and substituted "temporary residents/tourists."

Yet the company persisted in hyping Epcot as the centerpiece of Walt Disney World. When, shortly after Walt's death, Roy addressed that SRO crowd in Winter Park, he touted Epcot. The highlight of the press conference was a 25-minute color film, Walt's last screen appearance, in which he described Epcot as the "heart" of the Florida project, a vibrant community where people would "live and work and play." In the film and in the accompanying press release, the company said Epcot would "serve a new population of 20,000."

Following the Winter Park press conference, Roy and Republican Gov. Claude Kirk flew to Jacksonville, where they filmed a joint presentation that was shown along with the Epcot film on statewide television. Floridians thus saw Walt, in a posthumous appearance, describing Epcot as a working community that would always be on the cutting edge of technology and urban design. The film was unequivocal in this depiction; yet, a decade later, a Disney spokesman would state that the model city concept was "only one visual presentation of one way to go." The film was likewise shown to the Florida legislature as it began work on the Disney legislation.

If, after Walt's death, the company was uncommitted to building a true residential community, why did company officials present this as the crux of their proposal? In part it was because the Epcot film was so visually compelling—with Walt alive on screen, offering his futuristic vision of Epcot and appealing for lawmakers' support. But it was also for legal reasons best explained in the Helliwell memo.

In that memo, Helliwell expressed concern about state and local laws that might limit the company's "freedom of action" in developing its 43-square-mile property. He proposed a Disney-controlled government with regulatory powers "superseding to the fullest extent possible under law state and county regulatory authorities." There was just one hitch: Under Florida law, as Helliwell explained, planning and zoning authority could only be exercised by a popularly elected government. To escape external land-use controls, the company had to submit to control by voters. Disney attorneys, however, found a clever way to avoid this fate.

Their proposed legislation called for a two-tier system of government. The top tier, embracing an area twice the size of Manhattan, was the Reedy Creek Improvement District. It would be controlled by the landowner, its board of supervisors elected on the principle of one acre equals one vote. Since Disney owned the land, Disney would elect the board. The bottom tier consisted of two municipalities, Bay Lake and Lake Buena Vista, each having a handful of residents who would be trusted Disney employees living in company housing. Officially, planning and zoning authority was vested in these two municipalities. Their residents would elect a government and then—ingeniously—transfer administrative responsibility for planning and zoning to the Reedy Creek District.

By this legal magic, the company was able to comply with the law and still enjoy regulatory immunity. The charter made it possible for the Reedy Creek government to regulate land use, provide police and fire services, license the manufacture and sale of alcoholic beverages, build roads, lay sewer lines, construct waste-treatment plants, carry out flood projects—even build an airport or nuclear plant, all without local or state approval. The company was creating a sort of Vatican with Mouse ears: a city-state within the larger state of Florida, controlled by the company yet enjoying regulatory powers reserved by law for popularly elected governments.

To acquire such powers, the company had to convince the Florida legislature that Epcot would be a bona fide community. Paul Helliwell, acting as lobbyist, frequently used the term "resident" in describing the company's plans. Disney lobbyists also told lawmakers that Disney would include "public school sites and other public needs in their two cities," according to an April 22, 1967, article in the Orlando Sentinel-Star. And Helliwell told legislators, few of whom had read the thick Reedy Creek charter, that the company was not asking for anything "that had not been done before." At best the statement was half-true: The charter combined the powers available in three kinds of special districts. But Florida had not combined those powers in one district before.

In persuading the legislature to adopt this legislation, the California company ably plied the old-boy system. A good example is a meeting between J. J. Griffin, a former state representative who became a Disney lobbyist, and the powerful president of the Senate, Verle Pope. Griffin had started a long-winded explanation of the weighty Reedy Creek charter when Pope stopped him. "J. J.," he said, "I just have one question. Is this good for Florida?" Griffin answered, "Yes, sir, I believe it is." Whereupon Pope said, "Well, that's good enough for me." (The anecdote is recounted by Griffin in the film "Florida's Disney Decade," produced by Disney.)

With Pope's blessing, the legislation sailed through the Senate, passing unanimously and without debate. In the House there was one dissenting vote, from Miami. Less than an hour after the vote, the State Road Board approved emergency funding for Disney's road requests. And finally, the Florida Supreme Court ruled in 1968 that the Reedy Creek District was legally entitled to issue tax-free municipal bonds. The bonding power would "greatly and Disney interests" but would nevertheless benefit the "numerous inhabitants of the district," the court ruled.

What about those "numerous inhabitants" today? How fares the city where 20,000 would "live and work and play"? Sure enough, in 1982, 11 years after the turnstiles began spinning at Disney World, the company opened something called Epcot. Yet today, there are more hotels than homes on Disney property. Between the two cities of Bay Lake and Lake Buena Vista, there are 43 residents living in 17 mobile homes—all nonunion Disney supervisors and their families, who safeguard the company's political control of its property.

Disney is also designing a huge mixed-use development called "Celebration," billed as a further realization of Walt's urban vision. While some permanent housing is scheduled for Celebration, it will be de-annexed from the Reedy Creek District—making it impossible for homeowners to vote in Disney elections. Celebration will also have time-share units, whose temporary occupants will not have voting rights. The model city described by Walt, promoted by Roy and dangled before Florida lawmakers by Disney lobbyists has never come about; the promises of 1967 are the stuff of history.

18

Elizabeth Strom

CULTURAL INSTITUTIONS AND DOWNTOWN DEVELOPMENT

American cities have rediscovered their cultural resources. During the past two decades, city officials have learned to value the historic communities that their predecessors have been eager to raze; have dubbed desolate, derelict warehouses "arts districts"; and have committed local tax dollars to their museums and performing arts complexes, many newly built or recently expanded. A survey of 65 U.S. cities (those with populations of 250,000 and above) finds that 71 major performing arts centers and museums have been either built or substantially expanded since 1985.[1] From Charlotte's Blumenthal Hall, to Los Angeles' Getty Museum, to Seattle's Benaroya Hall, a cultural building boom is clearly under way.

Of course, cultural facilities have always concentrated in urban areas. What is new and interesting, first, is that so many new facilities have been built in a relatively short time span, and so many have been built outside traditional cultural centers such as New York, Boston, Chicago, and San Francisco.[2] Second, whereas once the arts were considered a luxury, supported by philanthropy and enjoyed by an elite group of connoisseurs, today's cultural institutions are constructed as an explicit part of a city's economic revitalization program. This shift reflects changes both in the political economy of cities and in the organization and mission of highbrow cultural institutions. This article examines these changes and

Elizabeth Strom, "Converting Pork into Porcelain: Cultural Institutions and Downtown Development," *Urban Affairs Review,* Vol. 38, No. 1, September 2002, pp. 3–21, excluding the table.

shows how they have led to an increasingly close and mutually beneficial relationship between urban political, economic, and cultural entrepreneurs.

The urban cultural building boom, this article maintains, represents a confluence of three related trends. First, cities seeking to attract businesses with quality-of-life amenities are eager to support the development of cultural institutions, especially in their once moribund centers. They believe that these institutions will increase the city's symbolic capital and catalyze other, unsubsidized commercial activities. Second, cultural institutions are drawn by their own economic needs and by the imperatives of their funding sources to seek broader audiences and exploit more commercial, income-generating strategies. They are able to achieve these goals without completely sacrificing their aesthetic legitimacy because, third, the boundaries between high culture—once their dominant domain—and popular culture have blurred. Cultural institutions today are thus better positioned than those of 100 years ago to become active stakeholders in urban growth politics.

Culture in the Growth Coalition: Why Business and Political Leaders Need the Arts

Business elites have long recognized that the prestige of high arts institutions could bring economic benefit to their hometowns, but policies explicitly drawing on the arts to achieve economic development goals have only recently become common. The urban renewal projects of the 1950s and 1960s occasionally included cultural institutions—landmarks such as New York's Lincoln Center and Washington's Arena Stage were built on sites cleared of tenement housing with the support of city development officials, business elites, and the cultural institutions that would inhabit them (Toffler 1964, 1973). However, during this period, most city planners and business-people still saw investments in culture as incidental to the main city development goals of industrial retention and office and housing development.

By the 1980s, the dominant urban development policy paradigm had shifted away from "smokestack chasing" in which cities competed for investment by offering lower costs (Bailey 1989). Competing for corporate headquarters and producer service firms, economic development practitioners realized, required more than just abating taxes and improving infrastructure. Clark (2000) maintains that today's educated workers are more likely to choose appealing locations, most notably those with attractive natural and cultural resources, and then consider their employment options. In this model, firms that rely on highly skilled labor have greater incentive than ever to either choose amenity-rich locations or to strive to improve the quality of life in their headquarters city. As cities compete for mobile, skilled workers and the firms that employ them, low taxes may be less important than riverfront parks, sports arenas, and historic districts. Moreover, city officials have become ever more aware of the economic importance of tourism and have put a great deal of energy into building and enlarging convention centers (Sanders 1998), subsidizing new hotels, and attracting major retailers (Friedan and Sagalyn 1989; Hannigan 1998; Judd 1999).

Cultural institutions represent an important element of the recreational infrastructure thought to make a city more appealing to tourists and investors (Eisinger 2000; Hannigan 1998). Corporations have come to see the presence of local arts institutions as a business asset, and their support for such organizations represents good business sense as much as philanthropy. Ford Motor's marketing director, who was asked why his company has nearly single-handedly kept Detroit's opera company solvent, noted that the presence of such an institution made it easier to recruit white-collar employees (Bradsher 1999). Donors to the New Jersey Performing Arts Center made this point as well (Strom 1999).

City governments and place-based business elites have become more intent on marketing their cities. Local boosterism, of course, is hardly new, but today professionals with large budgets have replaced the well-intentioned amateurs of an earlier era (Ward 1998; Holcomb 1993). Moreover, as is true throughout the business world, city promoters have moved from a model of *selling*, where one tries to persuade the buyer to purchase what one has, to *marketing*, where one tries to have what the buyer wants (Holcomb 1993). Marketers do not merely come up with a catchy jingle; they seek to remake the city, or at least the most visible part of the city, to conform to the expectations of the affluent consumers they want to attract. Cultural institutions, associated with beauty, good taste, and higher purpose, become singularly important symbolic assets for image-conscious marketers.

At the same time, development practitioners and scholars began to appreciate that the arts comprise a wealth-generating economic sector, one in which urban areas retain a competitive advantage. Since the 1980s, the economic impact of the arts has received considerable attention. In major cultural capitals like New York, the "culture industry," as the production and consumption of the arts is called, comprises an important economic sector (National Endowment for the Arts 1981; the Port Authority of New York and New Jersey 1993). Even in less obvious places, the culture industry plays a measurable economic role (Perryman 2000).

Cultural projects are valued for more than their direct economic impact. They are built in locations well situated to transform waning downtowns, obsolete factory districts, and disregarded waterfronts. New museums and performing arts centers now feature architectural designs that embrace and enhance their surroundings, rather than isolate their audiences from the city around them, as had been the case in an earlier generation (Russell 1999). And the new projects have been seen as a means of bringing life—and economic impulse—to central cities that are too often deserted after business hours. Philadelphia's Kimmel Center for the Performing Arts, it is hoped, will anchor new economic activity in Center City, where until recently check-cashing businesses and nude dance halls were as common as restaurants and theaters. During the past decade, Seattle has built two major arts facilities downtown: a new home for the Seattle Art Museum, opened in 1991, and Benaroya Hall, a performing arts complex built primarily for the Seattle Symphony, which opened in 1998. Seattle business leaders credit these cultural institutions with a downtown revival that includes the development of several major retail complexes and a 40% increase in the number of people living downtown since 1990 (Byrd 1997).

The arts can also lend greater legitimacy to other urban development efforts. One hundred years ago, urban arts patrons were quite clear about their hope that cultural institutions would serve to placate a growing immigrant working class (Horowitz 1976). As Boston entrepreneur Henry Lee Higginson wrote in 1886, "Educate and save ourselves and our families and our money from mobs!" (Quoted in Levine 1988, 205). The social control function of urban arts institutions today is far subtler. To David Harvey (1989), the contemporary urban spectacle—which includes ephemera like street fairs and festivals, as well as more institutionalized cultural facilities and entertainment districts—has become a way of co-opting the oppositional politics of the 1960s. To others, the presence of culture, especially serious, nonprofit culture, can serve to legitimize urban redevelopment among those who would not normally see themselves as its beneficiaries. Large-scale urban renewal projects can be made more palatable to voters and opinion shapers (if not always to those displaced in their wake) when they are packaged as new cultural centers or filled with public art (Miles 1998). In the words of a National Endowment for the Arts official,

> The arts . . . are like Mom and apple pie; they're consensus-makers, common ground. People can easily focus on the arts activities in a new project, instead of dwelling on the complicated costs and benefits public support for private development activity usually entails. (Quoted in Clack 1983, 13)

Arts organizations therefore represent a significant and unique component of the amalgam of downtown consumption palaces Judd (1999) has labeled the "tourist bubble." Urban scholars have analyzed the actors in the urban tourism and entertainment infrastructure, including retail mall developers, convention center operators, and major-league sports franchises, to understand why they are drawn to participate in downtown real estate projects (Friedan and Sagalyn 1989; Rosentraub 1997; Danielson 1997; Sanders 1998). Cultural institutions, however, have not received similar attention from urban political economists, even though their incorporation into urban growth politics begs explanation. Urban scholars have not asked why an elite cultural institution, whose legitimacy has long been based on its ability to showcase the most serious, academically sanctioned art, might join with those seeking to develop and market the city to the widest possible audience. Today's cultural institutions, however, have been affected by some of the same pressures as city governments. Living in a more competitive environment in which entrepreneurship and marketing are held to be the key to their survival, arts organizations have themselves been transformed.

Culture, Consumption, and Revitalization: Why Arts Institutions Need Urban Development

Cultural institutions are not just the objects of urban development schemes: They have themselves become active promoters of revitalization and place marketing activities, and they have done so to realize their own institutional goals. Cultural facilities, especially art museums, must expand to remain "competitive" in the art world, and their expansion needs often place them at the center of local development plans. They have at least five important reasons for wanting to be part of the area's revitalization.

First, some of their concerns about the city's economic health may derive from the interests of their trustees (Logan and Molotch 1987). In nearly every city, there is considerable overlap between those who are prominent in the city's highest business circles and those who are active on cultural boards. One study found that 70% of the members of Louisville's most prestigious development organizations also served on the boards of cultural organizations. (In contrast, those active in peak economic development groups were far less likely to be found on human service agency boards, suggesting the unique importance of arts organizations to those most concerned with the city's development) (Whitt and Lammers 1991). It would be a mistake, however, to assume that major cultural organizations are mere extensions of profit-seeking trustees. Cultural board members usually grant the arts professionals a great deal of autonomy in running the institution's operations. Nominations to the most prestigious nonprofit institution boards are coveted; those invited to join are unlikely to jeopardize the hard-earned esteem of their peers by asserting a self-serving agenda (Ostrower 1998).[3] The business interests of board members provide a context for institutional decision making, but they are unlikely to be the primary imperative pushing cultural organizations toward a development agenda.

Second, cultural institutions need to bring their customers—the cultural audiences—to them. People are unlikely to visit a place if the surrounding community is thought to be dangerous. Many cultural consumers are not arts aficionados willing to go anywhere to see, say, a particular Rembrandt, but rather those for whom arts events are part of an entertainment experience. Not only will high crime and extensive physical deterioration put a cultural institution at a disadvantage, but so also will a dearth of amenities like good restaurants.

Third, numerous studies indicate the extent to which cultural institutions depend on tourist visits (the Port Authority of New York and New Jersey 1993; McDowell 1997). New York's Museum of Modern Art estimates that two-thirds of its visits are from out-of-towners, and half of those come from overseas.[4] Of those who visited the Los Angeles County Museum of Art Van Gogh exhibition in 1999, 56% came from outside Los Angeles (Morey and Associates 1999). Cultural institutions therefore have a strong interest in the city's overall appeal to tourists.

Fourth, cultural institutions are heavily dependent on the availability of local volunteers (there are 2.5 volunteers for every paid museum staff member, according to the American Association of Museums). Location in an impoverished city or in a declining neighborhood may make it more difficult to recruit volunteers. Fifth, wealthy individuals and corporations, which provide the program funds for many cultural organizations, usually focus their giving in their hometowns. When a corporation fails or relocates, local arts organizations lose an important source of support.

In sum, arts organizations in thriving areas will have more visitors, more volunteers, and greater fund-raising success than those in depressed areas.

It is clear that arts organizations benefit when their cities are economically healthy. Moreover, cultural groups are learning that they can benefit when they are perceived as one of the sources of that economic health. Today, preparing a study of one's economic impact seems to be a staple of large arts organizations and local arts councils. Such studies are of questionable economic merit (Cwi and Lyall 1977)—as Eisinger (2000, 327) notes, "Consultants hired by project proponents often seem to pull their multipliers out of thin air." But their purpose is not rigorous cost-benefit analysis; rather, they are tools used by arts groups in their efforts to gain funding and political support. The claim that flourishing arts institutions are important to the urban economy has given arts advocates a rationale to appeal for government support even when tight budgets and political controversies might make public arts funding difficult to obtain (Wyszomirski 1995).

By emphasizing their importance to local revitalization, arts administrators have also been able to gain access to new funding sources. The construction of the New Jersey Performing Arts Center (NJPAC) was supported by $106 million in state contributions, mostly from funds earmarked for economic development activities. Such a large sum would not have been made available for a cultural project had it not been able to claim an important regional economic impact—New Jersey's entire annual cultural budget has never been higher than $20 million (Strom 1999). Arts projects in Louisville, Seattle, and Philadelphia all received generous capital grants from state governments, grants that were clearly tied to the economic mission of these institutions. Similarly, major arts institutions are receiving support from private sources that are more interested in urban revitalization than in art. New Jersey financier Ray Chambers, a man who had never shown much interest in cultural activities but who was deeply committed to the future of Newark, spearheaded the development of NJPAC. Clothing manufacturer Sidney Kimmel made clear in remarks broadcast on local radio that his $15 million donation to Philadelphia's new performing arts center was in support of the center's urban revitalization promises. Arts institutions can show funders that their contributions are not mere charity but rather serve as investments in the city's economic future.

New Audiences, New Patrons: Why Today's Cultural Institutions Are Well Positioned to Participate in Urban Development

Funding and Organizing High Culture

Cultural institutions may have long had a clear interest in the city's economic health, but only recently have they emerged as ideal partners for the sorts of growth-oriented coalitions described in Mollenkopf (1983), Logan and Molotch (1987), and Stone (1989). The participation of cultural institutions in urban development coalitions has been facilitated by far-reaching changes in arts patronage and arts management ongoing at least since the 1960s. If nineteenth-century institutions looked to wealthy families for financial support, since that time the private collector/patron has been largely eclipsed by more institution-alized forms of funding.[5] Many wealthy families now route their donations through foundations, the largest of which have professional staffs. Since the mid-1960s, the single most important patron of high culture has been the government. The National Endowment of the Arts will have a budget of about $115 million in 2001–2002, and the 50 state governments have allocated $447.5 million for arts and cultural programs in fiscal year 2001 (National Association of State Arts Agencies 2001). During the 1970s, corporate funding became an increasingly significant source of support. According to the Business Committee for the Arts, corporate support for culture increased from $22 million in 1967 to $1.16 billion in 1997,[6] and corporate arts funding tripled during the 1975–1985 period (DiMaggio 1986).

Changes in arts funding affect arts programming in ways that have implications for economic development policies. More so than private patrons, government agencies and corporate donors seek programs with broad audience appeal (Zolberg 1983; Alexander 1996). The National Endowment for the Arts (NEA) and the state arts councils are eager to associate with programs whose popularity can translate into political support for their efforts. For businesses, cultural donations are a "highbrow form of advertising" (Alexander 1996, 2), as corporations seek to attach their names to programs that are highly visible and prestigious. A well-placed, $200,000 cultural donation, according to one corporate foundation official, can have the same impact as $50 million in paid advertising.[7] Government and corporate funding influence the form of cultural offerings as well as the content. Few corporations want to fund a museum's operations; they prefer to attach their name to special, traveling exhibitions that attract large crowds in a number of cities. Alexander (1996) correlates the growth of government and corporate funding with the increasing number of special, "blockbuster" exhibits mounted by museums (and there may well be similar parallels in others kinds of arts institutions). Museum managers see such events as opportunities to attract large, paying audiences (many museums charge for such special exhibits) and generate new members who will continue to support the museum once the special exhibit has moved on.[8]

If such big-ticket events bring benefits for museum managers, they also fit well into the marketing strategies of urban development and tourism officials. Indeed, arts advocates, economic development officials, and the tourism industry have, since the mid-1990s, consciously sought to promote "cultural tourism." An estimated 50 cultural tourism programs have been founded in state, county, and local convention and visitors bureaus, and two national networks, Partners in Tourism (which is sponsored by American Express) and the Cultural Tourism Alliance, hold conferences and publish newsletters on cultural tourism. The Los Angeles County Museum of Art Van Gogh exhibition that drew so many out-of-town visitors had been promoted heavily by the Los Angeles Convention and Visitors Bureau, which advertised "Van Gogh weekend packages" in such upscale publications as *The New Yorker*. The convergence

of interests is clear: City marketing officials, arts funders, and ultimately pub-
licity-conscious cultural administrators all find benefit in mounting large, well-
publicized exhibits or performances that attract big audiences.[9]

The Shifting Brows

Highbrow arts institutions would have limited value as economic development catalysts, however, if they were catering to a narrow stratum of social
elites and art connoisseurs. But a dramatic shift in the way culture is framed
and classified has made an expansion of art audiences possible. Boundaries between serious and popular art, and between the audiences who enjoy them,
have become increasingly blurred. Of course, even the high-low distinctions
that seemed so secure at midcentury were hardly inevitable; rather, scholars
have shown them to be largely a product of the mid- to late nineteenth century
(DiMaggio 1982, Levine 1988). In the earlier part of the nineteenth century, concerts might include pieces by Bach or Haydn as well as popular fare; an
evening of Shakespeare might be interspersed with acrobatic performances;
and fledgling museums displayed works of established, serious artists next to
curios (DiMaggio 1982). Even in the late nineteenth century, museums such as
Philadelphia's Pennsylvania Museum unapologetically celebrated industrial
design alongside European painting (Conn 1998). Such catholic sensibilities
soon vanished in favor of more rigid classification schemes that made some
cultural artifacts the exclusive terrain of those with education and money. Cultural objects that had once been universally enjoyed, including Shakespearean
plays and Italian operas, were reinterpreted so that their more accessible elements were abandoned, and they became the property of the possessors of cultural capital (Levine 1988). That this reclassification took place in the decades
surrounding the turn of the century was not accidental: It represented a response on the part of the upper classes to the growing presence and political
strength of an increasingly vocal and politically mobilized working class.
Defining an elite culture created a safe haven for the upper classes, who could
rely on their association with high cultural goods to legitimize their class position (Horowitz 1976; Bourdieu 1984).

High art and popular culture also became institutionally segregated. Earlier
in the nineteenth century, high culture had been marketed through the same
commercial mechanisms as popular fare. The Swedish opera singer Jenny Lind
made a wildly popular American tour in the 1850s under the sponsorship of P.
T. Barnum, and European ballerina Fanny Ellsler, who toured the United States
from 1840 to 1842, managed to become the darling of economic and cultural
elites while still acquiring a mass following and making good profits selling
Fanny Ellsler brand garters, stockings, corsets, and shaving soap (Levine 1988).

By the late nineteenth century, however, high and low art forms each had
their own institutional home. Profit-driven entrepreneurs disseminated popular culture. The newly created nonprofit corporation, on the other hand, become the vehicle for disseminating high culture. Museums and orchestras so

organized had a mix of public and private purposes that suited their patrons. As private corporations, they remained under the control of their appointed trustees. Because they relied on charitable donations, and not on popular political support, they could maintain high standards of elite culture. And because they were nonprofit, they could make claims to have a broader public purpose than a fully private, profit-seeking operation, thus justifying appeals for public support (DiMaggio 1982). Disseminated through the nonprofit corporation, the artifacts of serious culture could maintain their distance from the marketplace.

Today, however, the distinctions so carefully honed in the nineteenth century have become blurred. Rigid classifications fell under attack from several fronts. Gans (1974, 1999) notes a convergence of tastes dating back to the 1920s. The emergence of the middlebrow provided middle classes with more accessible versions of elite art, and today you do not need highbrow credentials to visit a blockbuster event at an art museum or enjoy a foreign film. At the same time, there was a "gentrification" of lowbrow arts, as elite artists and musicians explored jazz and folk art (Peterson 1997). Today, more modern and accessible art forms like jazz, modern dance, film, and photography can be created and consumed in many different venues and at many different levels, challenging the sorts of hierarchies described by Bourdieu (1984). Moreover, theoretical and empirical evidence suggests that the typical upper-class cultural consumer is no longer the snob, whose consumption of elite culture was linked to his or her rejection of other cultural forms, but the "omnivore," who consumes traditional high culture but also partakes of a variety of popular genres (Peterson and Kern 1996). The possibilities for mixing audiences of different classes and art of different genres are far greater today than they were at the turn of the nineteenth century.

The boundaries separating the organization of elite and popular culture have shifted as well. High culture remains the domain of elite, nonprofit institutions, but it is increasingly marketed with reference to the symbols and presentations of popular culture and supported by commercial market mechanisms. Museum shops no longer merely sell postcards and art books. They now feature a whole range of merchandise, some replicas of objects in their collections, some using motifs from objects in their collection (e.g., famous paintings printed on scarves and umbrellas), and some having little to do with their collections but presumably gaining value just by their association with great art. Museums and performing arts centers boast full-scale, four-star restaurants that become part of a city's lure to tourists, and their staffs include people with the business skills needed to help such enterprises run profitably (Alexander 1996).

The obscuring of cultural boundaries has important implications for the value of culture as an element of urban revitalization. Not only can cultural institutions take advantage of the market for arts-associated products. They can also broaden their programmatic offerings without losing their core constituencies. Today's arts organization trustees, apparently mindful of the need to appeal to broader audiences, are able to accept the use of popularizing techniques and commercial marketing without feeling that their elite status is compromised (Ostrower 1998). The Metropolitan Museum features Hollywood cos-

tumes; the Guggenheim showcases motorcycles and the work of fashion designer Armani. They do this while displaying their collections of European
paintings and Greek sculpture, retaining their base of upscale donors and remaining highly desirable conveyers of status for those fortunate enough to be
named to their boards.

Performing arts institutions have exhibited an even greater eclecticism
than museums. Because performances are very time limited, a theater's programming can simultaneously appeal to diverse audiences. Indeed, many of
today's performing arts centers, built with the goal of having maximum economic impact, contain multiple performance spaces, so that radically different
types of performances can take place on the same evening (Rothstein 1998).
One need only peruse the calendars of America's leading performing arts centers to find intriguing juxtapositions, as Broadway shows share the theater
complex with symphony orchestras, country fiddlers, and travel lectures. In
November 2000, just to offer one example, the Tulsa Performing Arts Center's
calendar included the Broadway musical Showboat, Brahms Oratorio music,
the Moscow String Quartet, the U.S. Marine Band, and a pops concert of Frank
Sinatra hits. On one very busy Saturday in February 1998, West Palm Beach's
Kravis Center for the Performing Arts hosted singers Steve Lawrence and Ey-
die Gorme, the Gospel Gala, and the Emerson String Quartet. This is exactly
the mix we might expect given the new relationship between the brows. On
one hand, distinctions are maintained—these performances all took place in
different halls, most likely attracting different audiences who probably conducted themselves according to different codes of behavior. On the other hand,
these audiences apparently did not feel that their enjoyment of their brand of
art was compromised by their proximity to others enjoying a different kind of
performance. A few may have even come back another night to attend one of
the other shows.

As long as cultural institutions could not easily cut across genres, their usefulness as vehicles of economic development was limited. They could function
as elite establishments, bringing prestige to their city and perhaps attracting a
few well-heeled tourists and an occasional amenity-oriented business. However, they would seldom draw large enough crowds or identify with broad
enough consumption opportunities to be considered commercial catalysts. On
the other hand, organizations offering popular fare might bring in the crowds
but would be less likely to earn the support of political and social elites or serve
to improve a city's symbolic capital. But this has changed, as we can see when
we observe those performing arts center calendars. The Broadway musicals
pay the bills. The ethnically diverse programming assures broader political legitimacy. The European art, the symphonic music, the elegant galas affirm an
institution's highbrow bona fides to social and economic elites. Institutions of
high culture fulfill their unique role within today's urban growth coalitions
precisely because they can catalyze profit-generating activities, while bringing
their nonprofit, noncommercial credentials with them.

DiMaggio and Powell have theorized that organizations working together
in the same "organizational field" come to share structural characteristics to fa-

cilitate their relations in a process that is shaped by resource dependencies as well as shared professional norms (DiMaggio and Powell 1983). Peterson has applied this theory to the study of cultural institutions and arts patrons, noting that arts organizations have become more professionalized (there are now 40 graduate programs in arts administration) and specialized as arts funding has shifted from private patronage to bureaucratic support (Peterson 1986). The organizational field of cultural production and consumption can perhaps today be expanded to include not just arts organizations and their funders but also the local officials who are involved in developing and marketing the city's cultural offerings. The marriage of culture and development is thus facilitated by the shared goals and norms of their advocates, and increasingly it is institutionalized through cultural tourism offices, arts district promotional agencies, or national collaboratives like the Institute for Community Development and the Arts, a project uniting the advocacy group Americans for the Arts with the United States Conference of Mayors. All are involved in selling an image of an urbane place of cultural sophistication, in which the museum or performance hall lends its panache to the city around it, which reciprocates by creating an atmosphere that promotes the consumption of culture.

Art and the Economy: A Changing Relationship

The cultural life of American cities has always had a complex relationship to the local political economy. Local cultural landscapes were shaped by social rivalries and boosterist regional competition. Such revered institutions as New York's Metropolitan Opera, for example, were created to display the wealth of newly rich industrialists (Burrows and Wallace 1999); the patrons of Chicago's now renowned art museum and symphony sought to assert their cultural parity with Boston and New York (Horowitz 1976). If late-nineteenth- and early-twentieth-century patrons could appreciate the potential benefits that accrued to those who built cultural centers, however, for those founding nineteenth-century museums and concert halls—in contrast to today's cultural entrepreneurs—economic gain remained subtext. Cultural institutions of their era were built to show off wealth, not to generate it. Reporting on the opening of the (at that time very modestly housed) Newark Museum in 1909, the local press proclaimed, "The city is rich! A part of the wealth of its citizens should be invested in paintings, sculpture and other art objects" (Newark Museum 1959, 7). Businessman and arts patron Joseph Choate, speaking at the Metropolitan Museum's opening, stressed the museum's function as an uplifting source of beauty and urged men of wealth to "convert pork into porcelain, grain and produce into priceless pottery, the rude ores of commerce into sculpted marble, and railroad shares and mining stocks ... into the glorified canvas of the world's masters" (Tomkins 1970, 23). Today, the relationship between the city's economy and its cultural institutions is understood very differently. Kicking off a fund-raising drive for the expansion of the Newark Museum—the same museum celebrated as a symbol of local prosperity in 1909—New Jersey Governor

Tom Kean touted the museum and other urban cultural assets as "catalysts of rebirth," "creating the kind of public image needed for growth and new jobs" (Courtney 1984). Countless public officials and donors have similarly proclaimed their support for culture as a means of spurring an economic revival (Byrd 1997; Davies 1998).

The association of economic development and culture has by now become commonplace, and commentary on this new relationship is largely laudatory. There have been a few cautionary voices: Some urban scholars have expressed concern that an urban development strategy whose primary goal is to attract outsiders to privatized entertainment spaces can be undemocratic and exclusionary (Eisinger 2000; Judd 1999), diverting public funds from projects of more direct benefit to most urban residents (Strom 1999). Even those cultural facilities deemed successful will never generate the tax revenue and employment to make them appear to be good investments in a cost-benefit analysis (National Endowment for the Arts 1981),[10] giving rise to the same critiques that have been leveled against subsidized sports and convention venues (Sanders 1998; Rosentraub 1997). Of course, unlike convention center and sport stadium proponents, cultural advocates have never argued that they could justify public subsidy purely through their production of direct economic benefits. Rather, the arts are said to increase the value of other products and deliver noneconomic benefits as well. Many museums and performing arts centers have effective outreach and education programs that make them genuinely accessible, Surely no other "tourist bubble" institution can make such a claim.

Cultural institutions themselves may face conflicts when they adapt their mission to that of the city's economic development strategists. Hoping for the biggest possible impact on their central city areas, economic development proponents are eager to build new museums and concert halls, and less concerned with sustaining these institutions once they are built. Individual and corporate donors also like to contribute to capital campaigns, where their largesse can be rewarded with wall plaques and naming opportunities. As a result, bricks and mortar investments may be favored over support for cultural programs; smaller arts organizations may be overlooked in favor of the larger groups better able to document their economic clout.

The need to prove their economic mettle to political allies and funders becomes yet one more pressure on cultural institutions already hard-pressed to disseminate great art while paying their bills. The fine arts can certainly be "popular," drawing large audiences. There is also art that is unlikely to play to full houses or attract long lines because it is difficult or challenging or cutting-edge. If arts institutions are primarily seen as mechanisms for urban revitalization and are valued for their ability to draw large numbers of people to city hotels and restaurants, they may be less willing or able to realize the scholarly or educational aspects of their work. To be sure, urban development stakeholders are hardly the only ones pushing arts institutions toward a more commercial, less scholarly mission. And museum curators have often been clever at mounting the kinds of shows that will draw the crowds and pay the bills to gain resources to support more esoteric or challenging programs (Alexander 1996). However, too much focus on the arts institutions' economic role may obscure the fact that making money for the city can never be their primary purpose.

Notes

1. Major performing arts centers are defined as those with 1,000 seats or more. Major museums are those with annual attendance of 50,000 or more. Because this survey looks only at large cultural facilities, it understates the full extent of cultural building.
2. No doubt cultural institution capital campaigns have been aided by the unusually prosperous 1990s. States and cities had budget surpluses, and wealthy individuals could gain prestige and tax benefits by donating stock market gains to nonprofit arts institutions. Many of these projects, however, originated years before the economic boom.
3. Similar comments were made by cultural trustees of cultural organizations interviewed by the author as part of an ongoing study of Newark- and Philadephia-based organizations.
4. Comments of museum administrator made at the Art of the Deal conference, Rutgers University, New Brunswick, 27 March, 2001.
5. Arts administrators report that individual patrons have gained in importance in the late 1990s; individual giving has been fueled by the strong stock market (comments of museum administrator made at the Art of the Deal conference, 2001).
6. Whitt (1987) has questioned the methods by which the Business Committee for the Arts collects its data; as an advocacy group, it could well be inclined to inflate the importance of business contributions.
7. Comments of corporate foundation executive made at the Art of the Deal conference, 2001.
8. This strategy seems to be successful: Many museums point to big jumps in membership during blockbuster exhibits (Dobrzynski 1998).
9. The media play a role in cementing this convergence of interests. A study of newspaper arts coverage found that visual arts get short shrift in most newspapers, except when blockbuster exhibits come to town. Local media, then, become part of the system making highly visible and popular exhibits useful for arts institutions and local development officials (Janeway et al. 1999).
10. The National Endowment for the Arts studied the arts institutions of six cities and found that only in three did they generate as much or more local revenue than they cost the city in subsidies and services. Had these calculations included the costs of state and federal subsidies, the balance sheet would have even looked less favorable.

References

Alexander, V.D. 1996. *Museums and money*. Bloomington: Indiana Univ. Press.

American Association of Museums. 1999. *The official museum directory*. New Providence, NJ: National Register Publishing.

Bailey, J.T. 1989. *Marketing cities in the 1980s and beyond*. Rosemont, IL: American Economic Development Council.

Bourdieu, P. 1984. *Distinction*. Cambridge, MA: Harvard Univ. Press.

Bradsher, K. 1999. A horn of plenty for opera in Detroit. *New York Times*, 28 October, E1, 10.

Burrows, E. G., and M. Wallace. 1999. *Gotham: A history of New York City to 1898*. New York and Oxford, UK: Oxford Univ. Press.

Byrd, J, 1997. Culture at the core. *Seattle Post-Intelligencer*, 9 February, J1.

Clack, G. 1983. Footlight districts. In *The city as stage*, edited by K. W. Green. Washington, DC: Partners for Livable Places.

Clark, T. N. 2000. Old and new paradigms for urban research: Globalization and the Fiscal Austerity and Urban Innovation Project. *Urban Affairs Review* 36 (1): 3–45.

Conn, S. 1998. *Museums and American intellectual life, 1876–1926.* Chicago: Univ. of Chicago Press.

Courtney, M. 1984. Newark museum revives growth plans. *New York Times*, 8 April, B1, 4.

Cwi, D. and K. Lyall. 1977. *Economic impact of arts and cultural institutions: A model for assessment and a case study for Baltimore.* Washington, DC: National Endowment for the Arts.

Danielson, M. N. 1997. *Home team*, Princeton, NJ: Princeton Univ. Press.

Davies, P. 1998. Philadelphia could make big gains from Performing Arts Center visitors. *Philadelphia Daily News*, 17 April.

DiMaggio, P. J. 1982. Cultural entrepreneurship in nineteenth-century Boston: The creation of an organizational base for high culture in America. *Media, Culture and Society* 4:33–50.

———. 1986. Can culture survive the marketplace? In *Nonprofit enterprise in the arts*, edited by P. J. DiMaggio, 65–92. New York and Oxford, UK: Oxford Univ. Press.

DiMaggio, P.J., and W.W. Powell, 1983. The iron cage revisited: Institutional isomorphism and collective rationality in organizational fields. *American Sociological Review* 48:147–60.

Dobrzynski, J. 1998. Blockbuster shows and prices to match. *New York Times*, 10 November, E1, 13.

Duncan, C. 1995. *Civilizing rituals: Inside art museums.* London, New York: Routledge.

Eisinger, P. 2000. The politics of bread and circuses. *Urban Affairs Review* 35 (3): 316–33.

Friedan, B. J., and L. B. Sagalyn. 1989. *Downtown Inc.* Cambridge, MA: MIT Press.

Gans, H. J. 1974. *Popular culture and high culture.* New York: Basic Books.

———. 1999. *Popular culture and high culture.* Rev. ed. New York: Basic Books.

Hannigan, J. 1998. *Fantasy city.* London: Routledge.

Harvey, D. 1989. *The condition of postmodernity.* Oxford, UK: Basil Blackwell.

Holcomb, B. 1993. Revisioning place: De- and re-constructing the image of the industrial city. In *Selling places: The city as cultural capital, past and present*, edited by G. Kearns and C. Philo. Oxford, UK: Pergamon.

Horowitz, H. L. 1976. *Culture and the city.* Lexington: Univ. Press of Kentucky.

Janeway, M., D. S. Levy, A. Szanto, and A. Tyndall, 1999. *Reporting the arts: News coverage of arts and culture in America.* New York: Columbia Univ., National Arts Journalism Program.

Judd, D. 1999. Constructing the tourist bubble. In *The tourist city*, edited by D. Judd and S. Fainstein, 35–53. New Haven, CT: Yale Univ. Press.

Levine, L. W. 1988. *Highbrow/lowbrow: The emergence of cultural hierarchy in America.* Cambridge, MA: Harvard Univ. Press.

Logan, J. R., and H. L. Molotch, 1987. *Urban fortunes.* Berkeley: Univ. of California Press.

McDowell, E. 1997. Tourists respond to lure of culture. *New York Times*, 24 April, D1, 4.

Miles, M. 1998. A game of appearance: Public art and urban development—Complicity or sustainability? In *The entrepreneurial city*, edited by T. Hall and P. Hubbard, 203–24. Chichester, UK: Wiley.

Mollenkopf, J. M. 1983. *The contested city*, Princeton, NJ: Princeton Univ. Press.

Morey and Associates, Inc. 1999. Economic impact analysis of the Los Angeles County Museum of Art and the Van Gogh exhibition. Unpublished report.

National Association of State Arts Agencies. 2001. Retrieved 11 April 2001, from www.nasaa-arts.org.

National Endowment for the Arts. 1981. *Economic impact of arts and cultural institutions.* Washington, DC: National Endowment for the Arts.

Newark Museum. 1959. *The Newark Museum: A fifty-year survey.* Newark: Newark Museum.

Ostrower, F. 1998. The arts as cultural capital among elites: Bourdieu's theory reconsidered. *Poetics* 26:43–53.

Perryman, M. R. 2000. The arts, culture, and the Texas economy. Retrieved 15 April 2001, from www.perrymangroup.com.

Peterson, R. A. 1986. From impresario to arts administrator. In *Nonprofit enterprise in the arts*, edited by P.J. DiMaggio, 161–83. New York and Oxford, UK: Oxford Univ. Press.

———. 1997. The rise and fall of highbrow snobbery as a status marker. *Poetics* 25:75–92.

Peterson, R. A., and R. M. Kern. 1996. Changing highbrow taste: From snob to omnivore. *American Sociological Review* 61:900–907.

The Port Authority of New York and New Jersey and the Cultural Assistance Center. 1993. *The arts as indus-try: Their economic importance to the New York—New Jersey metropolitan region.* New York: The Port Authority of New York and New Jersey.

Rosentraub, M. S. 1997. *Major league losers.* New York: Basic Books.

Rothstein, E. 1998. Arts centers are changing the face of culture. *San Diego Union-Tribune,* 6 December, E10.

Russell, J. S. 1999. Performing arts centers: Using art to revive cities. *Architectural Record,* May, 223–28.

Sanders, H. T. 1998. Convention center follies. *Public Interest* (summer): 58–72.

Stone, C. N. 1989. *Regime politics.* Lawrence: University Press of Kansas.

Strom, E. 1999. Let's put on a show: Performing arts and urban revitalization in Newark, New Jersey. *Journal of Urban Affairs* 21:423–36.

Toffler, A. 1964. *The culture consumers.* New York: Random House.

———. 1973. *The culture consumers.* Rev. ed. New York: Random House.

Tomkins, C. 1970. *Merchants and masterpieces.* New York: E. P. Dutton.

Ward, S. V. 1998. *Selling places.* New York and London: Routledge.

Whitt, J. A. 1987. Mozart in the metropolis: The arts coalition and the urban growth machine. *Urban Affairs Quarterly* 23:15–36.

Whitt, J. A., and J. C. Lammers. 1991. The art of growth. *Urban Affairs Quarterly* 26 (3): 376–93.

Wyszomirski, M. J. 1995. The politics of arts policy: Subgovernment to issue network. In *America's commit-ment to culture: Government and the arts,* edited by K. Mulcahy and M. J. Wyszomirski. Boulder, CO: Westview.

Zolberg, V. 1983. Changing patterns of patronage in the arts. In *Performers and performances,* edited by J. B. Kamerman and R. Martorella, 251–68. New York: Praeger.

19

Paul Kantor and H. V. Savitch

CAN POLITICIANS BARGAIN WITH BUSINESS? A THEORETICAL AND COMPARATIVE PERSPECTIVE ON URBAN DEVELOPMENT

In the summer of 1989, United Air Lines announced it was planning a new maintenance hub that would bring nearly a billion dollars in investment and generate over 7,000 jobs for the region lucky enough to attract it. Within a few short months, officials in over 90 localities were competing for the bonanza and were tripping over one another in an effort to lure United. Denver offered $115 million in incentives and cash, Oklahoma City sought to raise $120 million, and localities in Virginia offered a similar amount. The competition for United was so keen that cities began to bid against one another and asked that their bids be kept secret.

United was so delighted at the level of bidding that it repeatedly delayed its decision in anticipation the offers would get even better. Nearly two years

"Can Politicians Bargain with Business?" by Paul Kantor and H. V. Savitch in *Urban Affairs Quarterly.* December 1993, pp. 230–255. Copyright © 1992 by Paul Kantor and H. V. Savitch. Reprinted by permission of Sage Publications.

later, city officials in nine finalists were enhancing their incentives, courting United executives, and holding their breaths. Reflecting on the competition, Louisville Mayor Jerry Abramson quipped, "We haven't begun to offer up our firstborn yet, but we're getting close. Right now we are into siblings."[1]

Except for the extremity of the case, there is nothing new about cities questing for private capital. Cities compete with one another for tourism, foreign trade, baseball franchises, and federal grants. Yet, there is another side to this behavior. Although 93 cities competed for the United hub, many others did not, and some cities would have resisted the corporate intrusion (Etzkowitz and Mack 1976; Savitch 1988). When United stalled and raised the ante, Kentucky's governor angrily withdrew, complaining that he would "not continue this auction, this bidding war. There is a point at which you draw the line" ("Governor turns down UAL," *Courier-Journal*, 18 October 1991). In Denver, the legislature's majority leader protested, saying, "United has a ring and is pulling Colorado by the nose." With those remarks and heightening resentment, public opinion began to pull the state away from the lure of United ("UAL bidding goes on," *Courier-Journal*, 22 October 1991).

Such cases do not seem uncommon. Although many cities are willing to build sports stadia, others have turned down the opportunity. For instance, when Fort Wayne, Indiana, declined to go beyond its offer of a short-term low-interest loan to obtain a minor-league baseball team, the franchise was taken elsewhere (Rosentraub and Swindell 1990). Although officials in some cities trip over one another in efforts to attract business by lowering taxes, officials in others raise them. Over the last three years, Los Angeles, New York, and Denver have increased business taxes. Notwithstanding high taxes and locational costs, business continues to seek out such cities as San Francisco, Tokyo, London, Toronto, and Frankfurt.

Nevertheless, the literature on urban politics has not systematically examined such "nondecisional" cases (Bachrach and Baratz 1962) to probe the precise circumstances under which local governments can influence the capital investment process. . . .

. . .We propose that questions of how, when, and why local government can influence economic development are best answered by treating political control as something that springs from bargaining advantages that the state has in political and economic exchange relationships with business. Variations in local-government influence are strongly tied to the ways in which the larger political economy distributes particular bargaining resources between the public and private sectors.

Following Lindblom (1977), we find that it is useful to regard this context as a liberal-democratic system in which there is a division of labor between business and government (Kantor 1988; Elkin 1987). The private sector is responsible for the production of wealth in a market system in which choices over production and exchange are determined by price mechanisms. For its part, the public sector is organized along polyarchal lines (Dahl 1971; Dahl and Lindblom 1965) in which public decisions are subject to popular control. Public officials may be viewed as primarily responsible for the management of political support for governmental undertakings; business leaders can be considered essentially managers of market enterprises.

This perspective suggests that even though public and private control systems are theoretically separate, in reality they are highly interdependent. So far as government is concerned, the private sector produces economic resources that are necessary for the well-being of the political community—including jobs, revenues for public programs, and political support that is likely to flow to public authorities from popular satisfaction with economic prosperity and security. For business, the public sector is important because it provides forms of intervention into the market that are necessary for the promotion of economic enterprise but that the private sector cannot provide on its own. Such interventions include inducements that enable private investors to take risks (tax abatements and tax credits), the resolution of private conflicts that threaten social or economic stability (courts, mediation services), and the creation of an infrastructure or other forms of support (highways, workforce training).

Configuring Bargaining Advantages

Conceptualized in this manner, business and government must engage in exchange relationships (bargaining) to realize common goals. This is done by using bargaining advantages that derive from three dimensions or spheres of interdependence: market conditions, popular-control systems, and public-intervention mechanisms.

Market conditions consist of the circumstances or forces that make cities more or less appealing to private investors. The market position that results is a source of bargaining advantages or disadvantages for government. Market conditions may be site specific, as when localities find they are desirable because of innate features that have become critical (e.g., Washington, D.C., as an important organizational locale or Singapore as a gateway for investment in Asia). Market conditions are also reflected in larger economic fluctuations that put urban investment at a premium (e.g., the office-building boom of the 1980s) or put urban investment at risk (e.g., the savings-and-loan bust of the 1990s). We posit that cities with strong market positions obtain influence over the capital investment process.

Popular-control systems are the polyarchal processes through which public-sector decisions that affect urban development are legitimized. Such processes may vary along several dimensions, including the scope of public participation, the extent to which participation is organized, and the effectiveness of electoral mechanisms in ensuring accountability in the process of legitimization. We posit that popular-control systems that motivate and enable elected political leaders to exercise influence over the process of legitimizing economic development decisions enhance local-government control over business investment.

Public-intervention mechanisms are relationships and methods used by state institutions to regulate the marketplace. The kinds of policy instruments available to government and the way in which it uses them can affect the distribution of bargaining advantages between business and government. We posit that governmental systems that centralize or coordinate power as well as financial support are better able to regulate economic development and shape the marketplace. These systems enhance local governmental influence over investment.

Although we are unable to test all of these propositions systematically, we seek to illustrate their reality in the pages that follow. Our analysis suggests that there is substantial variation among local governments in their ability to bargain. We also suggest that bargaining advantages tend to be cumulative—that is, the more advantages a city holds, the greater its ability to bargain. Finally, we suggest that because bargaining is a product of political and economic circumstance, so is urban development. Although it may not be possible for a city to manipulate all the variables affecting its bargaining position, most cities can manipulate some and thereby shape its own future.

Table 7.1 describes how differences in market conditions, popular-control systems and public-intervention mechanisms furnish bargaining advantages or disadvantages to cities. Each of these bargaining components are examined here. In our analysis, public-sector influence over capital investment is indicated by distinct kinds of outcomes. When bargaining relationships put local government at a persistent disadvantage, the public sector tends to absorb

Table 7.1 System Characteristics

	Characteristics Determining Governmental Bargaining Advantages	
Sphere of Activity	Low	High
Market condition	Competitive	Noncompetitive
	Nondiversified	Economic diversity
	Company towns	Economics of agglomeration
	Flexible capital	Fixed capital
	Mobile investment	Sunk investments
Popular control	Low party competition	Competitive parties
	Unstable partisanship	Stable partisanship
	Low ideological cohesion	High ideological cohesion
	Nonprogrammatic parties	Programmatic parties
	Fragmented party organization	High party discipline
	Few channels for citizen participation	Multiple channels for citizen participation
Public intervention	Particularistic policies	General market regulation
	Side payments	Spending on infrastructure, subsidies
	Decentralized	Centralized
	Local borrowing	National borrowing
	Finance: dependence on private investment	Finance: autonomous investment

greater costs and risks of private enterprise (Jones and Bachelor 1986). Cities in a weak position also are more inclined to accommodate private-sector demands, even at the cost of maintaining or expanding programs that serve non-business groups.

When bargaining relationships put local governments at a persistent advantage, an altogether different set of outcomes are likely (Logan and Molotch 1987; Capek and Gilderbloom 1992). Public actors tend to impose costs for the privilege of doing business in the locality or to place other demands on the private investor. They may levy differential taxes on businesses located in high-density commercial districts, charge linkage fees on downtown development (which can be invested elsewhere), demand amenity contributions that are applied toward the enhancement of city services, or impose inclusionary zoning, requiring developers to set aside a number of low- or moderate-income rental units in market-rate housing. More often than not, cities will be somewhere between such bipolar situations of a weak or strong bargaining position. Table 7.2 indicates the kinds of outcomes that are related to the three kinds of bargaining components.

Table 7.2 Bargaining Components

	Bargaining Yields
Market conditions	
Unfavorable	Inducement to business:
	Cash outlays, tax exemptions, aid to capital projects, loan guarantees, free land, large-scale condemnation
Favorable	Demands on business:
	Development fees (linkage), public amenities (refurbished train stations, bus shelters, pedestrian walkways), higher business taxes, stiffer architectural (building setbacks), restrictive zoning requirements
Mixed	Negotiations with business:
	Extent of tax abatements, public-private contributions to capital projects, payments for land, capital improvements to land
Popular control	
Weak	Acquiescent, uninvolved public—bargaining takes place exclusively between elites—increasing number of side payments, low accountability, exclusionary zoning
Strong	Institutionalized land-use review policies, employment concessions for local residents and minorities, contract set-asides for local firms or minority contractors, rent control or stabilization laws, inclusionary zoning
[Public] intervention	
Dispersed	Absence of zoning or loose zoning laws, tax code enforcement, intense competition between localities, significant sublocal disparities
Integrated	Highly restrictive zoning laws, strict code enforcement, extensive infrastructure investments, frequent public-private compacts

Markets and Public Control of Urban Development

There is little doubt that businesses' greatest bargaining resource in urban development is its control over private wealth in the capital investment process. It is this dimension of business-government relations that Peterson's (1981) market-centered model of local politics describes. The logic of this model is that cities compete for capital investment by seeking to attract mobile capital to the community; failure to meet the conditions demanded by business for investment leads to the "automatic punishing recoil" (Lindblom 1982) of the marketplace as business disinvests. This notion has been variously interpreted to suggest that business inherently holds a dominant position (Fainstein et al. 1986; Mollenkopf 1983; Logan and Molotch 1987; Jones and Bachelor 1986; Kantor 1988).

Although the market-centered model is a powerful tool for analyzing development politics, it does not fully capture the bargaining relationships that logically derive from it. Specifically, the market perspective tends to highlight only those advantages that accrue to business. Yet, the marketplace works in two directions, not one. If we look at specific market conditions and bargaining demands, it becomes apparent that government also can use the market to obtain leverage over business. Thus we will present a number of common market-centered arguments and show their other side.

The Cities-Lose-If-Business-Wins Argument

In the market model, public and private actors represent institutions that compete to achieve rival goals. Business pursues public objectives only insofar as they serve private needs; if important business needs are not met, local government experiences the discipline of the marketplace as capital and labor seek alternative locations.

Yet, in this description of market dynamics, cases in which local government and business may also share the same goals (as distinct from the same interests) are ignored; in such instances the market model no longer indicates business advantage in the development process. Thus a local government may have an interest in raising public revenue by increasing retail sales while shopkeepers and investors have an interest in maximizing profits. Though their interests are different, they may share the common goal of bringing about higher sales through expanded development. When this happens, bargaining between government and business shifts from rivalry over competing goals to settling differences over how to facilitate what already has been agreed on. This kind of scenario enhances the value of bargaining resources that are mostly owned by the public sector. Development politics focuses on such things as the ability to amass land, grant legal privileges and rights, control zoning, provide appropriate infrastructure, and—not least—enlist public support. Because alternative means of promoting growth are important choices (Logan and Swanstrom 1990), substantial bargaining leverage over development outcomes is placed in the hands of those who manage the governmental process, a point that Mollenkopf (1983) underscored in his study of urban renewal politics.

Yet, this partial escape from the market often is not recognized. Peterson (1981) considered the sharing of interests and goals to be one and the same. Other scholars have often assumed that there is an inherent conflict between private and public goals (Stone and Sanders 1987; Logan and Swanstrom 1990; Swanstrom 1986). However, a strong case can be made that business and government often share common goals. Although they cannot logically share interests, public officials, motivated by different stakes, frequently choose to pursue economic objectives that are also favored by business (Cummings 1988). Although some critics reject progrowth values, these values tend to be supported broadly by local electorates (Logan and Molotch 1987, 50–98; Vaughn 1979; Crenson 1971).

To take a different tack on former head of General Motors Charles Wilson's aphorism, scholars may be too anxious to suggest that if it is good for General Motors, it must be bad for Detroit. Yet, local officials and their publics do not always share this logic. When government and business perceive common goals, such perceptions can have a powerful effect on opportunities for political control over the urban economy. Under these conditions, the ability of political authorities to create political support for specific programs and their willingness to use public authority to assist business can become important bargaining resources for achieving their own interests. At the very least, the extent to which agreement between business and local government is a byproduct of political choice rather than of economic constraint should be a premise for empirical investigation instead of an a priori conclusion.

The Capital Mobility Argument

This argument encompasses an assumption that bargaining advantages accrue to business as it becomes more mobile. Historically, private capital was more dependent on the local state than it is today (Kantor 1988). Technological advances in production, communications, and transportation have enhanced the ability of business to move more easily and rapidly. Changes in the organization of capital, especially the rise of multilocational corporations, have increased business mobility and made urban locations interchangable. Automation, robotics, and the postindustrial revolution are supposed to enhance capital mobility. Fixed capital has been nudged aside by a new postindustrial technology of flexible capital (Hill 1989; Parkinson, Foley, and Judd 1989).

It would seem to follow that increasing capital mobility must favor business interests. Yet, this conclusion does not always follow, if one considers specific cities and businesses that are caught up in this process of economic globalization. Capital is, in fact, not always very portable. Although cities are frequently viewed as interchangeable by some corporations, many cities retain inherent advantages of location (e.g., Brussels), of agglomeration (e.g., New York), of technological prowess (e.g., Grenoble), or of political access (e.g., Washington, D.C.). The dispersion of capital has triggered a countermovement to create centers that specialize in the communication, coordination, and support of far-flung corporate units. Larger global cities have captured these roles.

Much of postindustrial capital has put enormous sunk costs into major cities. One of the more conspicuous examples is the Canadian development firm of Olympia and York, which has invested billions of dollars in New York, London, Ontario, and a host of other cities. As Olympia and York teeters on the edge of collapse, banks, realty interests, and mortgage brokers are also threatened. It is not easy for any of these interests to pull up stakes.

There has been a fairly stable tendency for corporate headquarters operations, together with the ancillary services on which headquarters depend, to gravitate to large cities that have acquired the status of world business centers (Sassen 1988; Noyelle and Stanback 1984). New York's downtown and midtown, London's financial district and its docklands, Paris's La Defense, and Tokyo's Shinjuku are some outstanding examples of postindustrialism that [have] generated billions in fixed investments. Movement by individual enterprises away from such established corporate business centers is unlikely for various reasons, including that this kind of change imposes costs on those owning fixed assets in these locations and disrupts established business networks.

Cities that have experienced ascendant market positions have not been reluctant to cash in on this. When property values and development pressures rose in downtowns, local politicians used the advantage to impose new planning requirements and demand development fees. In San Francisco, a moratorium on high-rise construction regulates the amount and pace of investment (Muzzio and Bailey 1986). In Boston and several other large cities, linkage policies have exacted fees on office development to support moderate-income housing (Dreier 1989). In Paris, differential taxes have been placed on high-rise development and the proceeds used to support city services (Savitch 1988). One should also recognize that market conditions are not immutable.

Local governments may be subject to the blandishments of business at an early stage of development, when there is great eagerness for development and capital has wide investment choices. However, once business has made the investment, it may be bound for the long term. Thus bargaining does not stop after the first deal is struck, and the advantages may shift.

This occurred in Orlando, Florida, where Disney World exacted early concessions from the local governments, only to be faced with new sets of public demands afterward (Foglesong 1989). Prior to building what is now a vast entertainment complex near Orlando, Disney planners capitalized on their impending investment and won huge concessions from government (including political autonomy, tax advantages, and free infrastructure). However, as Disney transformed the region into a sprawling tourist center, local government demanded that the corporation relinquish autonomy and pressured it to pay for physical improvements. Disney struggled to defeat these demands but eventually conceded. With huge sunk investments, Disney executives had little choice but to accommodate the public sector.

So although some industries have grown more mobile, others have not. The issue turns on the relative costs incurred by business and by government when facilities, jobs, and people are moved. How relative costs are assessed and the likelihood that businesses will absorb them influence the respective bargaining postures of business and government.

The City-Cannot-Choose Argument

In the market model, business makes investment choices among stationary cities; because cities cannot move, powerful bargaining advantages accrue to business in the urban development process and supposedly this enables them to exact what they want from local governments. Although this is sometimes the case, it is also true that local communities may have investment choices as well. Some local governments can make choices among alternative types of business investment. In particular, economic diversification enables local political authorities to market the community in a particular economic sector (e.g., as a tourist city, as a research or technical center, or as a sound place in which to retire). Further, economic diversification enhances a locality's ability to withstand economic pressure from any particular segment of the business community. This has occurred in cities as far ranging as Seattle, Singapore, and Rome, enabling them to maintain powerful market positions for years, despite profound changes in the world and national economies.

Experience teaches city officials to sense their vulnerabilities and develop defenses against dominance by a single industry. Through diversification, these cities can gain a good deal of strength, not only in weathering economic fluctuations but in dealing with prospective investors. Houston's experience after oil prices crashed moved city leaders to develop high-technology and service industries (Feagin 1988). Pittsburgh's successful effort to clean its air gave that city a new economic complexion. Louisville's deindustrial crisis was followed by a succession of new investments in health services, a revival in the transportation industry, and a booming business in the arts (Vogel 1990). Diversification, which was so instrumental in strengthening the public hand, was actually made possible by government coalitions with business.

The advantages of diversification are most apparent when these cities are compared to localities that are prisoners of relatively monopolistic bargaining relations with business. Officials in single-industry towns are strongly inclined to accommodate business demands on matters of development because they lack alternative sources of capital investment. Crenson (1971) found this pattern in Gary, Indiana, where local officials resisted proposals for pollution control because they feared that U.S. Steel would lay off workers. Similarly, Jones and Bachelor (1986) described how Detroit leaders weakened their market position when they sought to preserve the city's position as a site for automobile manufacturing. When worldwide changes in the auto industry eroded Detroit's traditional competitive advantages, political leaders fought to subsidize new plants and to demolish an otherwise viable residential neighborhood.

Neither Gary's steel-centered strategy nor Detroit's auto-centered strategy has stemmed their economic decline. The lesson for urban politicians is clear:

Instead of vainly hanging on to old industry, go for new, preferably clean business. More than most politicians, big-city mayors have learned well and are fast becoming major economic promoters (Savitch and Thomas 1991).

The City-Maximizes-Growth Argument

Although the market model is built on the supposition that it is in the interest of cities to promote economic growth, not all localities seek to compete in capital markets. To the extent that communities ignore participation in this market, they do not have to bargain with business over demands that they might choose to bring to the bargaining table. Santa Barbara, Vancouver, and Stockholm are cities that have insisted growth and instituted extensive land-use controls. These cities are in enviable positions as they deal with business and developers.

Aside from major cities, there are smaller communities that do not seek to compete for capital investment such as suburban areas and middle-size cities that after years of expansion, now face environmental degradation. Even if these localities have a stake in maintaining competitive advantages as bedroom communities or steady-state mixed commercial/residential locales, their bargaining relationship with business is more independent than in relatively growth-hungry urban communities (Danielson 1976). University towns, in which a self-sustaining and alert population values its traditions, have managed to resist the intrusions of unwanted industry. Coastal cities, which seek to preserve open space, have successfully acquired land or used zoning to curtail development.

Moreover, there are cities in which governmental structures reduce financial pressure and are able to resist indiscriminate development. Regionalism and annexation have enabled cities to widen their tax nets, so that business cannot easily play one municipality off against another. Minneapolis-St. Paul, Miami-Dade, and metro Toronto furnish examples of localities banding together to strengthen their fiscal positions and turn down unwanted growth. In Western European and other non-American nations, cities are heavily financed by central government, thereby reducing and sometimes eliminating the pressure to attract development. For these cities, growth only engenders liabilities.

Popular-Control Systems and Urban Development

Democratic political institutions not only provide means of disciplining public officials, but they constrain all political actors who seek governmental cooperation or public legitimation in the pursuit of their interests. The reality of this is suggested by the fact that business development projects frequently get stopped when they lack a compelling public rationale and generate significant community opposition. This has occurred under varying conditions and in different types of cities. In Paris, neighborhood mobilization successfully averted developers (Body-Gendrot 1987); in London, communities were able to totally redo urban renewal plans (Christensen 1979); in Amsterdam and Berlin, local squatters defied property owners by taking over abandoned buildings; after the recent earthquake in San Francisco, public opinion prevailed against the business community in preventing the reconstruction of a major highway. The existence of open, competitive systems of elections and other polyarchal institutions affords a means by which nonbusiness interests are able to influence, however imperfectly, an urban development process in which business power otherwise looms large.

But do institutions of popular control afford political authorities with a valuable bargaining resource in dealing with business? Are democratic institutions loose cannons that are irrelevant to political bargaining over economic development? From our bargaining perspective, it would appear that these institutions can provide a resource upon which political leaders can draw to impose their own policy preferences when the three conditions described in the following paragraphs are satisfied.

First, public approval of bargaining outcomes between government and business must be connected to the capital-investment process. This is often not the case because most private-sector investment decisions are virtually outside the influence of local government. Even when the characteristics of private projects require substantial public-sector cooperation, many decisions are only indirectly dependent on processes of political approval. Economic-development decisions have increasingly become insulated from the mainstream political processes of city governments as a result of the proliferation of public-benefit corporations (Walsh 1978; Kantor 1993). As power to finance and regulate business development has been ceded to public-benefit corporations, the ability of elected political leaders to build popular coalitions around development issues has shrunk because it makes little sense to appeal to voters on matters that they cannot influence.

On the other hand, the importance of this bargaining resource increases as issues spill over their ordinary institutional boundaries and into public or neighborhood arenas. When this occurs, elected political authorities gain bargaining advantages by putting together coalitions that can play a vital role in the urban development game. Consequently, even the most powerful public and private developers can be checked by politicians representing hostile voter coalitions.

In New York, Robert Moses's slide from power was made possible by mounting public discontent with his later projects and by the intervention of a popular governor who capitalized on this to undercut Moses's position (Caro 1974); Donald Trump's plans for the Upper West Side of Manhattan incurred defeats by a coalition of irate residents, local legislators, and a hostile mayor (Savitch 1988); a major highway (Westway) proposal, sponsored by developers, bankers, and other business interests, was defeated by community activists who skillfully used the courts to question the project's environmental impact.

Second, public authorities must have the managerial capability to organize and deliver political support for programs sought by business. Credible bargaining requires organizing a stable constituency whose consent can be offered to business in a quid pro quo process. However, political authorities clearly differ enormously in their capacity to draw on this resource. In the United States, the decline of machine politics, the weakening of party loyalties and organizations, and the dispersal of political power to interest groups have weakened the capacity of elected political authorities. To some extent, this has been counterbalanced by grassroots and other populist-style movements that have provided a broad base for mayors and other political leaders (Swanstrom 1986; Dreier and Keating 1990; Savitch and Thomas 1991; Capek and Gilderbloom 1992).

In contrast, in Western European cities, the stability and cohesion displayed by urban party systems more frequently strengthen political control of development. In Paris, extensive political control over major development projects is related to stable and well-organized political support enjoyed by officials who dominated the central and local governments (Savitch 1988). In London, ideological divisions between Conservative and Labour parties at the local and national levels limit the ability of business interests to win a powerful role, even in cases involving massive redevelopment such as Covent Garden, the construction of motorways, and the docklands renewal adjacent to the financial city. For example, changes in planning the docklands project were tied to shifts in party control at both the national and local levels. Given the political significance of development issues to both major British parties, it was difficult for nonparty interests to offer inducements that were capable of splitting politicians away from their partisan agendas (Savitch 1988).

Similarly, even highly fragmented but highly ideological political party systems seem capable of providing a powerful bargaining resource to elected governmental authorities. In Italy, many small parties compete for power at the national and local levels. Although this is sometimes a source of political instability, the relatively stable ideological character of party loyalties means that elected politicians are assured of constituency support. Consequently, this base of political power offers substantial bargaining advantages in dealing with business. According to Molotch and Vicari (1988), this enables elected political authorities to undertake major projects relatively free from business pressure. In Milan, officials planned and built a subway line through the downtown commercial district of the city with minimal involvement of local business.

Third, popular-control mechanisms are a valuable bargaining resource when they bind elected leaders to programmatic objectives. If political authorities are not easily disciplined for failure to promote programmatic objectives in development bargaining, business may promote their claims by providing selective incentives (side payments), such as jobs, campaign donations, and other petty favors, to public officials in exchange for their cooperation. When this happens, the bargaining position of city governments is undermined by splitting off public officials from their representational roles—and the process of popular control becomes more of a business resource.

In America, where partisan attachments are weak and where ethnic, neighborhood, and other particularistic loyalties are strong, political leaders are inclined to put a high value on seeking selective benefits to the neglect of pro-grammatic objectives. Although populist mayors have sometimes succeeded in overcoming these obstacles (Swanstrom 1986; Dreier and Keating 1990), the need to maintain unstable political coalitions that are easily undermined by racial and ethnic rivalries limits programmatic political competition. For exam-ple, in Detroit and Atlanta, black mayors have relied heavily on economic de-velopment to generate side payments that are used to minimize political oppo-sition; this is facilitated by the symbolic importance that these black mayors enjoy among the heavily black electorates in the two cities. Consequently, they have been able to hold on to power without challenging many business de-mands (Stone 1989; Hill 1986). In contrast, in Western Europe, where political-party systems more frequently discipline public officials to compete on programmatic grounds, bargaining with business is less likely to focus on side payments. As suggested earlier, in France, Italy, and Britain, votes are more of-ten secured by partisan and ideological loyalties and reinforced by progam-matic competition than by generating selective incentives for followers.

In sum, city governments vary enormously in their capacity to draw on the popular-control process in bargaining over development. The proximity of electoral competition to development, the capability of officials to organize voter support, and the extent of competition over programmatic objectives are crucial factors that weaken or enhance the resources of city governments.

State Intervention and Urban Development

From our bargaining perspective, public policy can be a valuable resource in dealing with business as long as two conditions are present: (1) Government proposals are either desired by business or can be imposed without choking off business performance, and (2) public authorities can threaten to withhold the benefits of public intervention to secure other demands. In reality, it is not al-ways easy for local governments to meet these two conditions. Tax abatements, loans, grants, and other business incentives often are not sufficiently enticing to influence investment behavior. Further, such subsidies may be easily replaced by competing local and state governments (Eisinger 1989).

Still, there are valuable resources that politicians can use to enhance their bargaining posture. Most valuable are forms of public intervention that are not easily replaceable by the private sector, programs that arise from market fail-ure, particularly land-use regulations and investments in public works that support or enhance private-sector activities, such as highways and bridges.

The history of zoning suggests how government can shape private invest-ment via land-use regulation. In New York City, the rise of zoning legislation occurred in response to the needs of businesses to find a means of preventing land values from plummeting. In 1916, retail merchants along New York's fash-ionable Fifth Avenue were threatened by encroachments from factories and warehouses in the nearby garment district, and reformers capitalized on business needs by promoting a zoning ordinance. At the same time, reformers went a step beyond business and seized the opportunity to build public support for a broader zoning law. They adopted a system that protected residential, as well as commercial, areas and initiated a system of public scrutiny of commercial, industrial, and residential land-use changes (Makielski 1966).

Ironically, integrated national governmental systems appear to enhance local governmental control of urban development, and political structures that decentralize the regulation of market failures afford less local governmental influence. Political systems that accord a powerful urban regulatory role for the national government limit local political authority in urban planning, of course. Yet, these more centralized systems can often work to enhance local governmental bargaining power with the private sector; they do this by making it easier for governments to contain capital movement (overriding private decision making), as well as by permitting localities to draw on the resources, regulatory apparatus, and political support of higher levels of government.

Contrasts between American and some Western European cities illustrate the different bargaining implications of each system. The United States is unique in the degree to which urban public capital investment is highly decentralized. Although the national government provides grants to support highway and other capital projects, this aid is spotty and unconnected to any system of national urban planning. Most important, responsibility for financing most local infrastructure is highly decentralized. Consequently, local and state governments have little choice but to find an administrative means of extracting revenues from the private sector that gives priority to satisfying investor confidence. To market long-term debt, public corporations must contend with investor fears that borrowed funds might be diverted to satisfy political pressures, rather than used for debt repayment. Consequently, major urban infrastructure development is in the hands of public corporations that are only indirectly accountable to urban electorates. These corporations are well known for courting private investors and treating them as constituents rather than as bargaining rivals (Caro 1974; Walsh 1978).

The European experience is quite different. There, most capital expenditures are supported by the central government. In France, upwards of 75% of local budgets are financed by central government; in Holland, the figure is 92%. This relieves some of the pressure on local authorities to compete with one another for capital investment to finance basic services. Local governments in Europe are capable of dealing with business from a position of greater strength. Beyond this, national government is not as dependent on private capital as local government is and can turn to vast financial and regulatory powers to reinforce public bargaining on the part of national and local governmental authorities.

The case of La Defense, just outside of Paris, is instructive of how state-business relations have been managed in Western Europe. During the 1960s, the national government planned to build another central business district for Paris on the vacant fields of La Defense. Despite skepticism by private investors, funds were allocated by the national government. Just as the project was launched, it was confronted by a fiscal crisis. French business looked on as La Defense reeled from one difficulty to another, and the enterprise was mocked as a "white elephant." The national government responded quickly, infusing the project with funds from the treasury, from nationalized banks, and from pensions. To buttress these efforts, the government clamped down on new office construction within Paris and used other carrots and sticks to persuade corporations that La Defense was the wave of the future. The effort worked, and La Defense became a premier site as an international business headquarters.

La Defense was not built in unique circumstances. To the contrary, it demonstrates the cumulative effect of centralized policy intervention on urban development. It is not unusual for governments throughout Western Europe to pour infrastructure into a particular development area, to freeze the price of surrounding land to prevent speculation, to construct buildings in the same area by relying on public corporations, and to design all the structures in the development site. The last public act is usually to invite private investors to compete for the privilege of obtaining space. Only then does bargaining begin. . . .

Comparison of . . . two antipodal cities [—Amsterdam and Detroit—] permits us to illustrate the cumulative consequences of differences in bargaining resources for political control of business development. To begin with market conditions, Amsterdam has a highly favorable market position because it is at the center of Holland's economic engine—a horseshoe shaped region called the Randstad. The cities of the Randstad (Amsterdam, Utrecht, Rotterdam, and the Hague) form a powerful and diversified conurbation that drives Holland's economy, its politics, and its sociocultural life. Amsterdam itself is the nation's political and financial capital. It also holds light industry, is a tourist and historic center, and is one of northern Europe's transportation hubs. Although Amsterdam has gone through significant deindustrialization (Jobse and Needham 1987) and has lost 21% of its population since 1960, it has transformed its economy to residential and postindustrial uses and is attractively positioned as one of the keystones of a united Europe.

Detroit's market conditions are dramatically less favorable. It is situated in what was once America's industrial heartland and what is now balefully called the Rustbelt. Known as America's Motor City, its economy revolved around automobile manufacture. Deindustrialization and foreign competition have taken a devastating toll. In just three decades, Detroit lost more than half its manufacturing jobs and 38% of its population (Darden et al. 1987). Nearly half the population lives below the poverty line, and one quarter is unemployed (Nethercutt 1987). Detroit has tried to come back to its former prominence by rebuilding its downtown and diversifying its economy for tourism and banking. But those efforts have not changed the city's market posture. Jobs and the middle class continue to move to surrounding suburbs, and any possible conversion of the Rustbelt economy appears slim when viewed against more attractive opportunities elsewhere.

The differences in popular control of these two cities are equally stark. Amsterdam is governed by a 45-member council that is elected by proportional representation (the council also elects a smaller body of aldermen) and is well organized and easily disciplined by the voters. Political parties have cohesive programs geared to conservative, social democratic, centrist, and leftwing orientations. Political accountability is reinforced by a system of elected district councils that represent different neighborhoods of the city. These councils participate in a host of decentralized services including land use, housing, and development.

In contrast, Detroit's government is poorly organized in respect to promoting popular control of economic development. A nine-member city council is elected at large and in nonpartisan balloting. Detroit's mayor [in 1993], Coleman Young, has held power for 16 years and has based his administration on distributing selective benefits, especially city jobs and contracts, while focusing on downtown project development (Hill 1986; Rich 1991). The system affords scant opportunity for neighborhood expression, and the city's singular ethnic composition (Detroit is 75% black) is coupled to a politics of black symbolism that impedes programmatic accountability and pluralist opposition. Indeed, one scholar has described Detroit as ruled by a tight-knit elite (Ewen 1978); two other researchers believed that the city's power was exercised at the peaks of major sectors within the city (Jones and Bachelor 1986).

The two cities also differ dramatically in respect to modes of policy intervention. Like many European cities, Amsterdam is governed within an integrated national planning scheme. The Dutch rely on three-tier government, at the national, regional, and municipal levels. Goals are set at the uppermost levels, master plans are developed at the regional level, and allocation plans are implemented at the grass roots. A municipalities fund allocates financial support based on population, and over 90% of Amsterdam's budget is carried by the national treasury.

By contrast, Detroit stands very much alone. While "golden corridors" (drawn from Detroit's former wealth) have sprung up in affluent outskirts, the suburbs now resist the central city. Attempts at creating metropolitan mechanisms to share tax bases or to undertake planning have failed (Darden et al. 1987). Over the years, federal aid has shrunk and now accounts for less than 6% of the city's budget (Savitch and Thomas 1991). State aid has compensated for some of Detroit's shortfalls, but like most states, Michigan is at a loss to do anything about the internecine struggles for jobs and investment.

Given the cumulative differences along all three dimensions, the bargaining outcomes for each city are dramatically opposite. Under the planning and support of national and regional authorities, Amsterdam has managed its deindustrialization—first by moving heavy industry to specific subregions (called *concentrated deconcentration*) and later by locating housing and light commerce in abandoned wharves and depleted neighborhoods. The Dutch have accomplished this through a combination of infrastructure investment, direct subsidies, and the power to finance and build housing (Levine and Van Weesop 1988; Van Weesop and Wiegersma 1991). Amsterdam's capacity to construct housing is a particularly potent policy instrument and constitutes a countervailing alternative to private development. Between 50% and 80% of housing in Amsterdam is subsidized or publicly built. This puts a considerable squeeze on private developers, who face limitations of land availability as well as zoning, density, and architectural controls. As a condition of development, it is not uncommon for commercial investors to agree to devote a portion of their projects toward residential use (Van Weesop and Wiegersma 1991).

Indeed, the bargaining game in Holland is tilted toward the public sector in ways that seem unimaginable in the United States. Freestyle commercial development in Amsterdam has been restricted, so that most neighborhoods remain residential. Because of massive housing subsidies, neighborhoods have lacked the extremes of wealth or poverty. Even squatting has been declared legal. Abandoned buildings have been taken over by groups of young, marginal, and working-class populations—thus leading to lower-class gentrification (Mamadouh 1990).

All this compares very differently to the thrust of development outcomes in Detroit. The case of Poletown provides a stark profile of Detroit's response to bargaining with the private sector (Fasenfest 1986). When General Motors announced that it was looking for a new plant site, the city invoked the state's "quick take" law, allowing municipalities to acquire property before actually reaching agreement with individual owners. To attract the plant and an anticipated 6,000 jobs, the city moved more than 3,000 residents and 143 institutions (hospitals, churches, schools, and businesses) and demolished more than 1,000 buildings. To strike this bargain, Detroit committed to at least $200 million in direct expenditures and a dozen years of tax abatements. In the end, the bargaining exchange resulted in one lost neighborhood and a gain of an automobile plant—all under what one judge labeled as the "guiding and sustaining, indeed controlling hand of the General Motors Corporation" (Jones and Bachelor 1986).

In many respects, Poletown reflects a larger pattern of bargaining. The city is now trying to expand its airport. At stake are 3,600 homes, more than 12,000 residents, and scores of businesses. The city and a local bank also have their sights set on a venerable auditorium called Ford Hall. The arrangement calls for razing Ford Hall and granting the developers an $18 million no-interest loan, payable in 28 years. When citizen protests stalled the project, developers threatened to move elsewhere. Since then, Detroit's city council approved the project (Rich 1991).

The polar cases of Amsterdam and Detroit reveal something about the vastly different development prizes and sacrifices that particular cities experience as a result of their accumulated bargaining advantages. Amsterdam is able to use public investment to extract concessions from investors and enforce development standards in a process conducted under public scrutiny. Detroit offers land, money, and tax relief to attract development in a process managed by a tight circle of political and economic elites.

Political Control of Urban Development

By examining urban development from a state-bargaining perspective, we are able to identify some critical forces that influence local governmental control over this area of policy. From this vantage point, public influence over urban development appears to be tied to differences in market conditions, popular control mechanisms, and public policy systems because these interdependent spheres powerfully affect the ability of politicians to bargain with business. . . .

By using our bargaining perspective, future researchers may be able to overcome the limitations of extant theory and better understand the actual political choices of local communities in economic development.

Note

1. Urban Summit Conference, New York City, 12 November 1990.

References

Almond, G. 1988. The return to the state. *American Political Science Review* 82:853–874.

Bachrach, P., and M. Baratz. 1962. The two faces of power. *American Political Science Review* 56:947–952.

Body-Gendrot, S. 1987. Grass roots mobilization in the Thirteenth Arrondissment: A cross national view. In *The politics of urban development,* edited by C. Stone and H. Sanders, 125–143. Lawrence: University Press of Kansas.

Capek, S., and J. Gilderbloom. 1992. *Community versus commodity.* Albany: State University of New York Press.

Caro, R. 1974. *The power broker.* New York: Vintage.

Christensen, T. 1979. *Neighborhood survival.* London: Prism Press.

Crenson, M. 1971. *The un-politics of air pollution.* Baltimore, MD: Johns Hopkins University Press.

Cummings, S., ed. 1988. *Business elites and urban development.* Albany: State University of New York Press.

Dahl, R. 1971. *Polyarchy.* New Haven, CT: Yale University Press.

Dahl, R., and C. E. Lindblom. 1965. *Politics, economics, and welfare.* New Haven, CT: Yale University Press.

Danielson, M. 1976. *The politics of exclusion.* New York: Columbia University Press.

Darden, J., R. C. Hill, J. Thomas, and R. Thomas. 1987. *Race and uneven development.* Philadelphia: Temple University Press.

Dreier, P. 1989. Economic growth and economic justice in Boston, In *Unequal partnerships,* edited by G. Squires, 35–58. New Brunswick, NJ: Rutgers University Press.

Dreier, P., and W. D. Keating. 1990. The limits of localism: Progressive housing policies in Boston, 1984–1989. *Urban Affairs Quarterly* 26:191–216.

Eisinger, P. 1989. *Rise of the entrepreneurial state.* Madison: University of Wisconsin Press.

Elkin, D. 1987. State and market in city politics: Or, the real Dallas. In *The politics of urban development,* edited by C. Stone and H. Sanders, 25–51. Lawrence: University Press of Kansas.

Etzkowitz, H., and R. Mack. 1976. Emperialism in the First World: The corporation and the suburb. Paper presented at the Pacific Sociological Association meetings, San Jose, CA, March.

Ewen, L. 1978. *Corporate power and the urban crisis in Detroit.* Princeton, NJ: Princeton University Press.

Fainstein, S. S., N. I. Fainstein, R. C. Hill, D. Judd, and M. P. Smith. 1986. *Restructuring the city*. 2nd ed. New York: Longman.

Fasenfest, D. 1986. Community politics and urban redevelopment. *Urban Affairs Quarterly* 22:101–123.

Feagin, J. 1988. *Free enterprise city*. New Brunswick, NJ: Rutgers University Press.

Foglesong, R. 1989. Do politics matter in the formulation of local economic development policy: The case of Orlando, Florida. Paper presented at the annual meeting of the American Political Science Association, Atlanta, GA, September.

Governor turns down UAL. 1991. *Courier-Journal*, 18 October, 1.

Hill, R. C. 1986. Crisis in the motor city: The politics of urban development in Detroit. In *Restructuring the city*, 2d ed., by S. S. Fainstein, N. I. Fainstein, R. C. Hill, D. Judd, and M. P. Smith. New York: Longman.

———. Industrial restructuring, state intervention, and uneven development in the United States and Japan. Paper presented at conference: The tiger by the tail: Urban policy and economic restructuring in Comparative perspective. State University of New York, Albany, October.

Jobse, B., and B. Needham. 1987. The economic future of the Randstad, Holland. *Urban Studies* 25: 282–296.

Jones, B., and L. Bachelor. 1986. *The sustaining hand*. Lawrence: University Press of Kansas.

Kantor, P. 1993. The dual city as political choice. *Journal of Urban Affairs* 15 (3): 231–244.

Kantor, P. (with S. David). 1988. *The dependent city*. Boston, MA: Scott, Foresman/Little, Brown.

Levine, M., and J. Van Weesop. 1988. The changing nature of urban planning in the Netherlands. *Journal of the American Planning Association* 54:315–323.

Lindblom, C. 1977. *Politics and markets*. New Haven, CT: Yale University Press.

———. 1982. The market as a prison. *Journal of Politics*. 44:324–336.

Logan, J., and H. Molotch. 1987. *Urban fortunes*. Berkeley: University of California Press.

Logan, J., and T. Swanstrom, eds. 1990. *Beyond the city limits*. Philadelphia: Temple University Press.

Makielski, S. 1966. *The politics of zoning*. New York: Columbia University Press.

Mamadouh, V. 1990. Squatting, housing, and urban policy in Amsterdam. Paper presented at the International Research Conference on Housing Debates and Urban Challenges, Paris, July.

Mollenkopf, J. 1983. *The contested city*. Princeton, NJ: Princeton University Press.

Molotch, H., and S. Vicari. 1988. Three ways to build: The development process in the United States, Japan, and Italy. *Urban Affairs Quarterly* 24:188–214.

Muzzio, D., and R. Bailey. 1986. Economic development, housing, and zoning. *Journal of Urban Affairs* 8:1–18.

Nethercutt, M. 1987. *Detroit twenty years after: A statistical profile of the Detroit area since 1967*. Detroit, MI: Center for Urban Studies, Wayne State University.

Noyelle, T., and T. M. Stanback. 1984. *Economic transformation of American cities*. New York: Conservation for Human Resources Columbia University.

Parkinson, M., B. Foley, and D. Judd. 1989. *Regenerating the cities*. Boston, MA: Scott, Foresman.

Peterson, P. 1981. *City limits*. Chicago: University of Chicago Press.

Rich, W. 1991. Detroit: From Motor City to service hub. In *Big city politics in transition*, edited by H. V. Savitch and J. C. Thomas, 64–85. Newbury Park, CA: Sage Publications.

Rosentraub, M., and D. Swindell. 1990. "Just say no"? The economic and political realities of a small city's investment in minor league baseball. Paper presented at the 20th annual meeting of the Urban Affairs Association, Charlotte, NC, April.

Sassen, S. 1988. *The mobility of capital and labor*. Cambridge: Cambridge University Press.

Savitch, H. V. 1988. *Post-industrial cities: Politics and planning in New York, Paris, and London*. Princeton, NJ: Princeton University Press.

Savitch, H. V., and J. C. Thomas, eds. 1991. *Big city politics in transition*. Newbury Park, CA: Sage Publications.

Stone, C. 1989. *Regime politics*. Lawrence: University Press of Kansas.

Stone, C., and H. Sanders, eds. 1987. *The politics of urban development*. Lawrence: University Press of Kansas.

Swanstrom, T. 1986. *The crisis of growth politics*. Philadelphia: Temple University Press.

UAL bidding goes on. 1991. *Courier-Journal*, 22 October, 1.

Van Weesop, J., and M. Wiegersma. 1991. Gentrification in the Netherlands. In *Urban housing for the better-off: Gentrification in Europe* edited by J. Van Weesop and S. Musterd, 98–111. Utrecht, Netherlands: Bureau Stedellijke Netwerken.

Vaughn, R. 1979. *State taxation and economic development*. Washington, DC: Council of State Planning Agencies.

Vogel, R. 1990. The local regime and economic development. *Economic Development Quarterly* 4:101–112.

Walsh, A. 1978. *The public's business*. Cambridge: MIT Press.

CHAPTER 8

DEFENDED SPACE AND THE
POLITICS OF FEAR

The Politics of Fear

The geography and politics of cities in the twenty-first century will be shaped by perceptions of safety and security. If people feel secure, neighborhoods will become less segregated and racial and ethnic differences will lose their divisive force. If, on the other hand, people do not feel secure, the lessons from the past are clear. In the twentieth century, affluent citizens escaped the problems of the city by moving to the suburbs. In the twenty-first century, attempts to escape from urban problems will be expressed in a different way. In city and in suburb, people will move into walled-off spaces such as gated communities, condominium towers, and fortress office buildings.

In a selection from Mike Davis's book, *City of Quartz*, the author asserts that urban inequalities and social tensions have resulted in the militarization of space in Los Angeles. The construction of corporate fortresses downtown and the spread of defended residential enclaves, are a means by which the affluent respond to urban tensions. In Davis's rendering the militarization of space has taken various forms. There has been, first, the destruction of public spaces where people are able to freely mingle. Second, "mean streets" have become sharply segregated from the privatized spaces hidden behind facades and walls. Third, minority populations and the poor have been subjected to high-tech policy enforcement and a pervasive surveillance, creating a "carceral city"—by this phrase Davis means to compare the city inhabited by the poor to a prison. For those readers who bridle at Davis's metaphor, it may be helpful to remember that the movie *Bladerunner* portrays Los Angeles in an even more negative light than does Davis.

The selection from Kristen Hill Maher treats an interesting, generally hidden phenomenon: the connection between the household service economy of the suburbs and the anxieties felt by suburban residents about safety and security. In her study of Ridgewood, a neighborhood located in Orange County, California, she finds that service workers who come into the neighborhood to tend gardens, take care of children, do laundry, fix and repair homes, and engage in other jobs are expected to abide by implicit rules and tacit understandings that will make the limited purpose of their presence in the neighborhood clear. At the time of Maher's study, Ridgewood was going through a debate about whether to "gate" the neighborhood, and the residents she interviewed expressed anxiety about crime and about strangers coming through the neighborhood. She found that "the strangers that residents in this community read as most threatening tended to be of other races and classes than those living in Ridgewood." In fact, many of the Latinos working in Ridgewood appeared to fit the descriptions that residents gave of potential criminals, but residents made a sharp distinction between the two groups. To make this distinction, residents looked for indicators such as a Latina with a group of white children, and they looked for active signs of work. For their part, the workers were aware of these concerns and went to some pains to make the purpose of their presence obvious. The overall result, in the author's view, is that the presence of Latinos is not likely to reduce stereotypes enough to eliminate the tendency of suburban residents to "fort up."

Terrorism adds still another dimension to concerns about security and urban life. Terrorism is new to American cities, deriving from globalization. U.S. cities are becoming potential targets of violent international organizations trying to gain political influence abroad by sending messages through terrorist attacks. In the selection by Peter Eisenger, the author explores the degree to which the attacks of 9/11 continue to harm urban economies. The selection also assesses the degree to which people feel fear of future terrorist attacks. Although cities suffered from declines in tourist visits, businesses do not appear to have changed their attitudes toward investing in the central cities. Eisenger also found that the effects on urban residents was temporary; only a small percentage of urban residents express a continuing anxiety about terrorist attacks. He concludes that cities are affected by large-scale events such as 9/11, but for the most part "they are shaped. . .by much larger change agents" such as immigration, the business cycle, and other influences. Thus, international terror has not yet altered urban politics in fundamental ways even though other forces of globalization are already doing so. In particular, American cities are not becoming garrison states in the wake of the 9/11 attack.

20

Mike Davis

FORTRESS LOS ANGELES: THE MILITARIZATION OF URBAN SPACE

The city bristles with malice. The carefully manicured lawns of the Westside sprout ominous little signs threatening "*ARMED RESPONSE*!" Wealthier neighborhoods in the canyons and hillsides cower behind walls guarded by gun-toting

---

private police and state-of-the-art electronic surveillance systems. Downtown, a publicly subsidized "urban renaissance" has raised a forbidding corporate citadel, separated from the surrounding poor neighborhoods by battlements and moats. Some of these neighborhoods—predominately black or Latino—have in turn been sealed off by the police with barricades and checkpoints. In Hollywood, architect Frank Gehry has enshrined the siege look in a library that looks like a Foreign Legion fort. In Watts, developer Alexander Haagen has pioneered the totally secure shopping mall, a latter-day Panopticon, a prison of consumerism surrounded by iron-stake fences and motion detectors, overseen by a police substation in a central tower. Meanwhile in Downtown, a spectacular structure that tourists regularly mistake for a hotel is actually a new federal prison.

Welcome to post-liberal Los Angeles, where the defense of luxury has given birth to an arsenal of security systems and an obsession with the policing of social boundaries through architecture. This militarization of city life is increasingly visible everywhere in the built environment of the 1990s. Yet contemporary urban theory has remained oddly silent about its implications. Indeed, the pop apocalypticism of Hollywood movies and pulp science fiction has been more realistic—and politically perceptive—in representing the hardening of the urban landscape. Images of prison-like inner cities (*Escape from New York, Running Man*), high-tech police death squads (*Bladerunner*), sentient skyscrapers (*Die Hard*), and guerrilla warfare in the streets (*Colors*) are not fantasies, but merely extrapolations from the present.

Such stark dystopian visions show how much the obsession with security has supplanted hopes for urban reform and social integration. The dire predictions of Richard Nixon's 1969 National Commission on the Causes and Prevention of Violence have been tragically fulfilled in the social polarizations of the Reagan era.[1] We do indeed now live in "fortress cities" brutally divided into "fortified cells" of affluence and "places of terror" where police battle the criminalized poor. The "Second Civil War" that began during the long hot summers of the late 1960s has been institutionalized in the very structure of urban space. The old liberal attempts at social control, which at least tried to balance repression with reform, have been superseded by open social warfare that pits the interests of the middle class against the welfare of the urban poor. In cities like Los Angeles, on the hard edge of post-modernity, architecture and the police apparatus are being merged to an unprecedented degree.

The Destruction of Public Space

The universal consequence of the crusade to secure the city is the destruction of any truly democratic urban space. The American city is being systematically turned inward. The "public" spaces of the new megastructures and supermalls have supplanted traditional streets and disciplined their spontaneity. Inside malls, office centers, and cultural complexes, public activities are sorted into strictly functional compartments under the gaze of private police forces. This architectural privatization of the physical public sphere, moreover, is complemented by a paralleled restructuring of electronic space, as heavily guarded, pay-access databases and subscription cable services expropriate the invisible *agora*. In Los Angeles, for example, the ghetto is defined not only by its paucity of parks and public amenities, but also by the fact that it is not wired into any of the key information circuits. In contrast, the affluent Westside is plugged—often at public expense—into dense networks of educational and cultural media.

In either guise, architectural or electronic, this polarization marks the decline of urban liberalism, and with it the end of what might be called the Olmstedian vision of public space in America. Frederick Law Olmsted, the father of Central Park, conceived public landscapes and parks as social safety-valves, *mixing* classes and ethnicities in common (bourgeois) recreations and pleasures: "No one who has closely observed the conduct of the people who visit [Central] Park," he wrote, "can doubt that it exercises a distinctly harmonizing and refining influence upon the most unfortunate and most lawless classes of the city—an influence favorable to courtesy, self-control, and temperance."[2]

This reformist ideal of public space as the emollient of class struggle is now as obsolete as Rooseveltian nostrums of full employment and an Economic Bill of Rights. As for the mixing of classes, contemporary urban America is more like Victorian England than the New York of Walt Whitman or Fiorello La Guardia. In Los Angeles—once a paradise of free beaches, luxurious parks, and "cruising strips"—genuinely democratic space is virtually extinct. The pleasure domes of the elite Westside rely upon the social imprisonment of a third-world service proletariat in increasingly repressive ghettos and barrios. In a city of several million aspiring immigrants (where Spanish-surname children are now almost two-thirds of the school-age population), public amenities are shrinking radically, libraries and playgrounds are closing, parks are falling derelict, and streets are growing ever more desolate and dangerous.

Here, as in other American cities, municipal policy has taken its lead from the security offensive and the middle-class demand for increased spatial and social insulation. Taxes previously targeted for traditional public spaces and recreational facilities have been redirected to support corporate redevelopment projects. A pliant city government—in the case of Los Angeles, one ironically professing to represent a liberal biracial coalition—has collaborated in privatizing public space and subsidizing new exclusive enclaves (benignly called "urban villages"). The celebratory language used to describe contemporary Los Angeles—"urban renaissance," "city of the future," and so on—is only a triumphal gloss laid over the brutalization of its inner-city neighborhoods and the stark divisions of class and race represented in its built environment. Urban form obediently follows repressive function. Los Angeles, as always in the vanguard, offers an especially disturbing guide to the emerging liaisons between urban architecture and the police state.

Forbidden City

Los Angeles's first spatial militarist was the legendary General Harrison Gray Otis, proprietor of the *Times* and implacable foe of organized labor. In the 1890s, after locking out his union printers and announcing a crusade for "industrial freedom," Otis retreated into a new *Times* building designed as a fortress with grim turrets and battlements crowned by a bellicose bronze eagle. To emphasize his truculence, he later had a small, functional cannon installed on the hood of his Packard touring car. Not surprisingly, this display of aggression produced a response in kind. On October 1, 1910, the heavily fortified *Times* headquarters—the command-post of the open shop on the West Coast—was destroyed in a catastrophic explosion, blamed on union saboteurs.

Eighty years later, the martial spirit of General Otis pervades the design of Los Angeles's new Downtown, whose skyscrapers march from Bunker Hill down the Figueroa corridor. Two billion dollars of public tax subsidies have enticed big banks and corporate headquarters back to a central city they almost abandoned in the 1960s. Into a waiting grid, cleared of tenement housing by the city's powerful and largely unaccountable redevelopment agency, local developers and offshore investors (increasingly Japanese) have planted a series of block-square complexes: Crocker Center, the Bonaventure Hotel and Shopping Mall, the World Trade Center, California Plaza, Arco Center, and so on. With an increasingly dense and self-contained circulation system linking these superblocks, the new financial district is best conceived as a single, self-referential hyperstructure, a Miesian skyscape of fantastic proportions.

Like similar megalomaniacal complexes tethered to fragmented and desolate downtowns—such as the Renaissance Center in Detroit and the Peachtree and Omni centers in Atlanta—Bunker Hill and the Figueroa corridor have provoked a storm of objections to their abuse of scale and composition, their denigration of street life, and their confiscation of the vital energy of the center, now sequestered within their subterranean concourses or privatized plazas. Sam Hall Kaplan, the former design critic of the *Times*, has vociferously denounced the antistreet bias of redevelopment; in his view, the superimposition of "hermetically sealed fortresses" and random "pieces of suburbia" onto Downtown has "killed the street" and "dammed the rivers of life."[3]

Yet Kaplan's vigorous defense of pedestrian democracy remains grounded in liberal complaints about "bland design" and "elitist planning practices." Like most architectural critics, he rails against the oversights of urban design without conceding a dimension of foresight, and even of deliberate repressive intent. For when Downtown's new "Gold Coast" is seen in relation to other social landscapes in the central city, the "fortress effect" emerges, not as an inadvertent failure of design, but as an explicit—and, in its own terms, successful—socio-spatial strategy.

The goals of this strategy may be summarized as a double repression: to obliterate all connection with Downtown's past and to prevent any dynamic association with the non-Anglo urbanism of its future. Los Angeles is unusual among major urban centers in having preserved, however negligently, most of its Beaux Arts commercial core. Yet the city chose to transplant—at immense public cost—the entire corporate and financial district from around Broadway and Spring Street to Bunker Hill, a half-dozen blocks further west.

The underlying logic of this operation is revealing. In other cities, developers have tried to harmonize the new cityscape and the old, exploiting the latter's historic buildings to create gentrified zones (Faneuil Market, Ghirardelli Square, and so on) as supports to middle-class residential colonization. But Downtown Los Angeles's redevelopers considered property values in the old Broadway core as irreversibly eroded by the area's status as the hub of public transportation primarily used by black and Mexican poor. In the wake of the 1965 Watts Rebellion, whose fires burned to within a few blocks of the old Downtown, resegregated spatial security became the paramount concern. The 1960–64 "Centropolis" masterplan, which had envisioned the renewal of the old core, was unceremoniously scrapped. Meanwhile the Los Angeles Police Department (LAPD) abetted the flight of business from the Broadway–Spring Street area to the fortified redoubts of Bunker Hill by spreading scare literature about the "immigrant gang invasion" by black teenagers.[4]

To emphasize the "security" of the new Downtown, virtually all the traditional pedestrian links to the old center, including the famous Angels' Flight funicular railroad, were removed. The Harbor Freeway and the regraded palisades of Bunker Hill further cut off the new financial core from the poor immigrant neighborhoods that surround it on every side. Along the base of California Plaza (home of the Museum of Contemporary Art), Hill Street functions as the stark boundary separating the luxury of Bunker Hill from the chaotic life of Broadway, now the primary shopping and entertainment street for Latino immigrants. Because gentrifiers now have their eye on the northern end of the Broadway corridor (redubbed Bunker Hill East), the redevelopment agency promises to restore pedestrian access to the Hill in the 1990s. This, of course, only dramatizes the current bias against any spatial interaction between old and new, poor and rich—except in the framework of gentrification. Although a few white-collar types sometimes venture into the Grand Central Market—a popular emporium of tropical produce and fresh foods—Latino shoppers or Saturday *flaneurs* never ascend to the upscale precincts above Hill Street. The occasional appearance of a destitute street nomad in Broadway Plaza or in front of the Museum of Contemporary Art sets off a quiet panic, as video cameras turn on their mounts and security guards adjust their belts.

Photographs of the old Downtown in its 1940s prime show crowds of Anglo, black, and Mexican shoppers of all ages and classes. The contemporary Downtown "renaissance" renders such heterogeneity virtually impossible. It is intended not just to "kill the street" as Kaplan feared, but to "kill the crowd," to eliminate that democratic mixture that Olmsted believed was America's antidote to European class polarization. The new Downtown is designed to ensure a seamless continuum of middle-class work, consumption, and recreation, insulated from the city's "unsavory" streets. Ramparts and battlements, reflective glass and elevated pedways, are tropes in an architectural language warning off the underclass Other. Although architectural critics are usually blind to this militarized syntax, urban pariah groups—whether young black men, poor Latino immigrants, or elderly homeless white females, read the signs immediately.

Extreme though it may seem, Bunker Hill is only one local expression of the national movement toward "defensible" urban centers. Cities of all sizes are rushing to apply and profit from a formula that links together clustered development, social homogeneity, and a perception of security. As an article in *Urban Land* magazine on "how to overcome fear of crime in downtowns" advised:

> A downtown can be designed and developed to make visitors feel that it—or a significant portion of it—is attractive and the type of place that "respectable people" like themselves tend to frequent.... A core downtown area that is compact, densely developed and multifunctional, [with] offices and housing for middle- and upper-income residents ... can assure a high percentage of "respectable," law-abiding pedestrians. Such an attractive redeveloped core area would also be large enough to affect the downtown's overall image.[5]

Mean Streets

This strategic armoring of the city against the poor is especially obvious at street level. In his famous study of the "social life of small urban spaces," William Whyte points out that the quality of any urban environment can be measured, first of all, by whether there are convenient, comfortable places for pedestrians to sit. This maxim has been warmly taken to heart by designers of the high corporate precincts of Bunker Hill and its adjacent "urban villages." As part of the city's policy of subsidizing the white-collar residential colonization of Downtown, tens of millions of dollars of tax revenue have been invested in the creation of attractive "soft" environments in favored areas. Planners envision a succession of opulent piazzas, fountains, public art, exotic shrubbery, and comfortable street furniture along a ten-block pedestrian corridor from Bunker Hill to South Park. Brochures sell Downtown's "livability" with idyllic representations of office workers and affluent tourists sipping cappuccino and listening to free jazz concerts in the terraced gardens of California Plaza and Grand Hope Park.

In stark contrast, a few blocks away, the city is engaged in a relentless struggle to make the streets as unlivable as possible for the homeless and poor. The persistence of thousands of street people on the fringes of Bunker Hill and the Civic Center tarnishes the image of designer living Downtown and betrays the laboriously constructed illusion of an urban "renaissance." City hall has retaliated with its own version of low-intensity warfare.

Although city leaders periodically propose schemes for removing indigents *en masse*—deporting them to a poor farm on the edge of the desert, confining them in camps on the mountains, or interning them on derelict ferries in the harbor—such "final solutions" have been blocked by council members' fears of the displacement of the homeless into their districts. Instead the city, self-consciously adopting the idiom of cold war, has promoted the "containment" (the official term) of the homeless in Skid Row, along Fifth Street, systematically transforming the neighborhood into an outdoor poorhouse. But this containment strategy breeds its own vicious cycle of contradiction. By condensing the mass of the desperate and helpless together in such a small space, and denying adequate housing, official policy has transformed Skid Row into probably the most dangerous ten square blocks in the world. Every night on Skid Row is Friday the 13th, and, unsurprisingly, many of the homeless seek to escape the area during the night at all costs, searching safer niches in other parts of Downtown. The city in turn tightens the noose with increased police harassment and ingenious design deterrents.

One of the simplest but most mean-spirited of these deterrents is the Rapid Transit District's new barrel-shaped bus bench, which offers a minimal surface for uncomfortable sitting while making sleeping impossible. Such "bumproof" benches are being widely introduced on the periphery of Skid Row. Another invention is the aggressive deployment of outdoor sprinklers. Several years ago the city opened a Skid Row Park; to ensure that the park could not be used for overnight camping, overhead sprinklers were programmed to drench un-suspecting sleepers at random times during the night. The system was imme-diately copied by local merchants to drive the homeless away from (public) storefront sidewalks. Meanwhile Downtown restaurants and markets have built baroque enclosures to protect their refuse from the homeless. Although no one in Los Angeles has yet proposed adding cyanide to the garbage, as was suggested in Phoenix a few years back, one popular seafood restaurant has spent $12,000 to build the ultimate bag-lady-proof trash cage: three-quarter-inch steel rods with alloy locks and vicious out-turned spikes to safeguard moldering fishheads and stale french fries.

Public toilets, however, have become the real frontline of the city's war on the homeless. Los Angeles, as a matter of deliberate policy, has fewer public lavatories than any other major North American city. On the advice of the Los Angeles police, who now sit on the "design board" of at least one major Downtown project, the redevelopment agency bulldozed the few remaining public toilets on Skid Row. Agency planners then considered whether to in-clude a "free-standing public toilet" in their design for the upscale South Park residential development; agency chairman Jim Wood later admitted that the decision not to build the toilet was a "policy decision and not a design deci-sion." The agency preferred the alternative of "quasi-public restrooms"—toi-lets in restaurants, art galleries, and office buildings—which can be made available selectively to tourists and white-collar workers while being denied to vagrants and other unsuitables. The same logic has inspired the city's trans-portation planners to exclude toilets from their designs for Los Angeles's new subway system.[6]

Bereft of toilets, the Downtown badlands east of Hill Street also lack out-side water sources for drinking or washing. A common and troubling sight these days is the homeless men—many of them young refugees from El Sal-vador—washing, swimming, even drinking from the sewer effluent that flows down the concrete channel of the Los Angeles River on the eastern edge of Downtown. The city's public health department has made no effort to post warning signs in Spanish or to mobilize alternative clean-water sources.

In those areas where Downtown professionals must cross paths with the homeless or the working poor—such as the zone of gentrification along Broad-way just south of the Civic Center—extraordinary precautions have been taken to ensure the physical separation of the different classes. The redevelopment agency, for example, again brought in the police to help design "twenty-four-hour, state-of-the-art security" for the two new parking structures that serve the *Los Angeles Times* headquarters and the Ronald Reagan State Office Building. In contrast to the mean streets outside, both parking structures incorporate beautifully landscaped microparks, and one even boasts a food court, picnic area, and historical exhibit. Both structures are intended to function as "confidence-building" circulation systems that allow white-collar workers to walk from car to office, or from car to boutique, with minimum exposure to the public street. The Broadway-Spring Center, in particular, which links the two local hubs of gentrification (the Reagan Building and the proposed Grand Central Square) has been warmly praised by architectural critics for adding greenery and art to parking. It also adds a considerable dose of menace—armed guards, locked gates, and ubiquitous security cameras—to scare away the homeless and the poor.

The cold war on the streets of Downtown is ever escalating. The police, lobbied by Downtown merchants and developers, have broken up every attempt by the homeless and their allies to create safe havens or self-governed encampments. "Justiceville," founded by homeless activist Ted Hayes, was roughly dispersed; when its inhabitants attempted to find refuge at Venice Beach, they were arrested at the behest of the local council member (a renowned environmentalist) and sent back to Skid Row. The city's own brief experiment with legalized camping—a grudging response to a series of deaths from exposure during the cold winter of 1987—was abruptly terminated after only four months to make way for the construction of a transit maintenance yard. Current policy seems to involve perverse play upon the famous irony about the equal rights of the rich and poor to sleep in the rough. As the former head of the city planning commission explained, in the City of the Angels it is not against the law to sleep in the street per se—"only to erect any sort of protective shelter."[7] To enforce this proscription against "cardboard condos," the police periodically sweep the Nickel, tearing down shelters, confiscating possessions, and arresting resisters. Such cynical repression has turned the majority of the homeless into bedouins. They are visible all over Downtown, pushing their few pathetic possessions in stolen shopping carts, always fugitive, always in motion, pressed between the official policy of containment and the inhumanity of Downtown streets.

Sequestering the Poor

An insidious spatial logic also regulates the lives of Los Angeles's working poor. Just across the moat of the Harbor Freeway, west of Bunker Hill, lies the MacArthur Park district—once upon a time the city's wealthiest neighborhood. Although frequently characterized as a no-man's-land awaiting resurrection by developers, the district is, in fact, home to the largest Central American community in the United States. In the congested streets bordering the park, a hundred thousand Salvadorans and Guatemalans, including a large community of Mayan-speakers, crowd into tenements and boarding houses barely adequate for a fourth as many people. Every morning at 6 A.M. this Latino Bantustan dispatches armies of sewing *operadoras*, dishwashers, and janitors to turn the wheels of the Downtown economy. But because MacArthur Park is midway between Downtown and the famous Miracle Mile, it too will soon fall to redevelopment's bulldozers.

Hungry to exploit the lower land prices in the district, a powerful coterie of developers, represented by a famous ex-councilman and the former president of the planning commissions, has won official approval for their vision of "Central City West": literally, a second Downtown comprising 25 million square feet of new office and retail space. Although local politicians have insisted upon a significant quota of low-income replacement housing, such a palliative will hardly compensate for the large-scale population displacement sure to follow the construction of the new skyscrapers and yuppified "urban villages." In the meantime, Korean capital, seeking *lebensraum* for Los Angeles's burgeoning Koreatown, is also pushing into the MacArthur Park area, uprooting tenements to construct heavily fortified condominiums and office complexes. Other Asian and European speculators are counting on the new Metrorail stations, across from the park, to become a magnet for new investment in the district.

The recent intrusion of so many powerful interests into the area has put increasing pressure upon the police to "take back the streets" from what is usually represented as an occupying army of drug-dealers, illegal immigrants, and homicidal homeboys. Thus in the summer of 1990 the LAPD announced a massive operation to "retake crime-plagued MacArthur Park" and surrounding neighborhoods "street by street, alley by alley." While the area is undoubtedly a major drug market, principally for drive-in Anglo commuters, the police have focused not only on addict-dealers and gang members, but also on the industrious sidewalk vendors who have made the circumference of the park an exuberant swap meet. Thus Mayan women selling such local staples as tropical fruit, baby clothes, and roach spray have been rounded up in the same sweeps as alleged "narcoterrorists."[8] (Similar dragnets in other Southern California communities have focused on Latino day-laborers congregated at streetcorner "slave markets.")

By criminalizing every attempt by the poor—whether the Skid Row homeless or MacArthur Park vendors—to use public space for survival purposes, law-enforcement agencies have abolished the last informal safety-net separating misery from catastrophe. (Few third-world cities are so pitiless.) At the same time, the police, encouraged by local businessmen and property owners, are taking the first, tentative steps toward criminalizing entire inner-city communities. The "war" on drugs and gangs again has been the pretext for the LAPD's novel, and disturbing, experiments with community blockades. A large section of the Pico-Union neighborhood, just south of MacArthur Park, has been quarantined since the summer of 1989; "Narcotics Enforcement Area" barriers restrict entry to residents "on legitimate business only." Inspired by the positive response of older residents and local politicians, the police have subsequently franchised "Operation Cul-de-Sac" to other low-income Latino and black neighborhoods.

Thus in November 1989 (as the Berlin Wall was being demolished), the Devonshire Division of the LAPD closed off a "drug-ridden" twelve-block section of the northern San Fernando Valley. To control circulation within this largely Latino neighborhood, the police convinced apartment owners to finance the construction of a permanent guard station. Twenty miles to the south, a square mile of the mixed black and Latino Central-Avalon community has also been converted into Narcotic Enforcement turf with concrete roadblocks. Given the popularity of these quarantines—save amongst the ghetto youth against whom they are directed—it is possible that a majority of the inner city may eventually be partitioned into police-regulated "no-go" areas.

The official rhetoric of the contemporary war against the urban underclasses resounds with comparisons to the War in Vietnam a generation ago. The LAPD's community blockades evoke the infamous policy of quarantining suspect populations in "strategic hamlets." But an even more ominous emulation is the reconstruction of Los Angeles's public housing projects as "defensible spaces." Deep in the Mekong Delta of the Watts-Willowbrook ghetto, for example, the Imperial Courts Housing Project has been fortified with chainlink fencing, RESTRICTED ENTRY signs, obligatory identity passes—and a substation of the LAPD. Visitors are stopped and frisked, the police routinely order residents back into their apartments at night, and domestic life is subjected to constant police scrutiny. For public-housing tenants and inhabitants of narcotic-enforcement zones, the loss of freedom is the price of "security."

Security by Design

If the contemporary search for bourgeois security can be read in the design of bus benches, megastructures, and housing projects, it is also visible at the level of *auteur*. No recent architect has so ingeniously elaborated or so brazenly embraced the urban-security function as Los Angeles's Pritzker Prize laureate Frank Gehry. His strongest suit is his straightforward exploitations of rough urban environments, and the explicit incorporation of their harshest edges and detritus as powerful representational elements. Affectionately described by colleagues as an "old socialist" or "street-fighter with a heart," Gehry makes little pretense at architectural reformism or "design for democracy." He boasts instead of trying "to make the best with the reality of things."[9] With sometimes chilling effect, his work clarifies the underlying relations of repression, surveillance, and exclusion that characterize the fragmented landscape of Los Angeles.

An early example of Gehry's new urban realism was his 1964 solution of the problem of how to insert luxurious spaces—and high property values— into decaying neighborhoods. His Danziger Studio in Hollywood is the pioneer instance of what has become an entire species of Los Angeles "stealth houses," which dissimulate their opulence behind proletarian or gangster fa-cades. The street frontage of the Danziger is simply a massive gray wall, treated with a rough finish to ensure that it would collect dust from the passing traffic and weather into a simulacrum of the nearby porn studios and garages. Gehry was explicit in his search for a design that was "introverted and fortresslike," with the silent aura of a "dumb box."[10]

Indeed, "dumb boxes" and screen walls form an entire cycle of his work, ranging from the American School of Dance (1968) to his Gemini GEL (1979)—both in Hollywood. His most seminal design, however, was his walled town center for Cochiti Lake, New Mexico (1973): here ice-blue ramparts of awesome severity enclose an entire community, a plan replicated on a smaller scale in his 1976 Jung Institute in Los Angeles. In both of these cases architectural drama is generated by the contrast between the fortified exteriors, set against "unap-pealing neighborhoods" (Gehry) or deserts, and the opulent interiors, opened to the sky by clerestories and lightwells. Gehry's walled-in compounds and cities, in other words, offer powerful metaphors for the retreat from the street and the introversion of space that has characterized the design backlash to the urban insurrections of the 1960s.

Gehry took up the same problem in 1984 in his design for the Loyala Law School in MacArthur Park district. The inner-city location of the campus con-fronted Gehry with an explicit choice: to create a genuine public space, extend-ing into the community, or to choose the security of a defensible enclave, as in his previous work. Gehry's choice, as one critic explained, was a neoconserva-tive design that was "open, but not *too* open. The South Instructional Hall and the chapel show solid backs to Olympic Boulevard, and with the anonymous street sides of the Burns Building, form a gateway that is neither forbidding nor overly welcoming. It is simply there, like everything else in the neighbor-hood."[11] This description considerably understates the forbidding qualities of the campus's formidable steel-stake fencing, concrete-block ziggurat, and stark frontage walls.

But if the Danziger Studio camouflages itself, and the Cochiti Lake and Loyala designs are dumb boxes with an attitude, Gehry's baroquely fortified Goldwyn Branch Library in Hollywood (1984) positively taunts potential tres-passers "to make my day." This is probably the most menacing library ever built, a bizarre hybrid of a drydocked dreadnought and a cavalry fort. With its fifteen-foot-high security walls of stuccoed concrete block, it's anti-graffiti bar-ricades covered in ceramic tile, its sunken entrance protected by ten-foot-high steel stakes, and its stylized sentry boxes perched precariously on each side, the Goldwyn Library (influenced by Gehry's 1980 high-security design for the U.S. Chancellery in Damascus) projects nothing less than sheer aggression.

Some of the Gehry's admirers have praised the Library as "generous and inviting,"[12] "the old-fashioned kind of library," and so on. But they miss the point. The previous Hollywood library had been destroyed by arson, and the Samuel Goldwyn Foundation, which endows this collection of filmland mem-orabilia, was understandably preoccupied by physical security. Gehry's com-mission was to design a structure that was inherently vandalproof. His innovation, of course, was to reject the low-profile high-tech security systems that most architects subtly integrate into their blueprints, and to choose instead a high-profile, low-tech approach that foregrounds the security function as the central motif of the design. There is no dissimulation of function by form here—quite the opposite. How playful or witty you find the resulting effect depends on your existential position. The Goldwyn Library by its very structure conjures up the demonic Other—arsonist, graffitist, invader—and casts the shadow of its own arrogant paranoia onto the surrounding seedy, though not particularly hostile streets.

These streets are a battleground, but not of the expected kind. Several years ago the *Los Angeles Times* broke the sordid story of how the entertainment conglomerates and a few large landowners had managed to capture control of the local redevelopment process. Their plan, still the focus of controversy, is to use eminent domain and higher taxes to clear the poor (increasingly refugees from Central American) from the streets of Hollywood and reap the huge windfalls from "upgrading" the area into a glitzy theme-park for international tourism.[13] In the context of this strategy, the Goldwyn Library—like Gehry's earlier walled compounds—is a kind of architectural fire-base, a beachhead for gentrification. Its soaring, light-filled interiors surrounded by barricades speak volumes about how public architecture in America is literally turning its back on the city for security and profit.

The Panopticon Mall

In other parts of the inner city, however, similar "fortress" designs are being used to recapture the poor as consumers. If the Goldwyn Library is a "shining example of the possibilities of public- and private-sector cooperation," then developer Alexander Haagen's ghetto malls are truly stellar instances. Haagen, who began his career distributing jukeboxes to the honkytonks of Wilmington, made his first fortune selling corner lots to oil companies for gas stations—sites since recycled as minimalls. He now controls the largest retail-development empire in Southern California, comprising more than forty shopping centers, and has become nationally acclaimed as the impresario of South-Central Los Angeles's "retail revival."

Haagen was perhaps the first major developer in the nation to grasp the latent profit potential of abandoned inner-city retail markets. After the Watts Rebellion in 1965, the handful of large discount stores in the South-Central region took flight, and small businesses were closed down by the banks' discriminatory redlining practices. As a result, 750,000 black and Latino shoppers were forced to commute to distant regional malls or adjacent white neighborhoods even for their everyday groceries. Haagen reasoned that a retail developer prepared to return to the inner city could monopolize very high sales volumes. He also was well aware of the accumulating anger of the black community against decades of benign neglect by City Hall and the redevelopment agency; while the agency had moved swiftly to assemble land for billionaire developers

Downtown, it floundered in Watts for years, unable to attract a single super-market to anchor a proposed neighborhood shopping center. Haagen knew that the Bradley regime, in hot water with its South-Central constituents, would handsomely reward any private-sector initiative that could solve the an-chor-tenant problem. His ingenious solution was a comprehensive "*security-oriented* design and management strategy."[14]

Haagen made his first move in 1979, taking title to an old Sears site in the heart of the ghetto. Impressed by his success there, the redevelopment agency transferred to him the completion of its long-delayed Martin Luther King, Jr., Center in Watts. A year later Haagen Development won the bid for the $120 million renovation of Crenshaw Plaza (a pioneer 1940s mall on the western fringe of the ghetto), as well as a contract from Los Angeles County to build an-other shopping complex in the Willowbrook area south of Watts. In each case Haagen's guarantee of total physical security was the key to persuading retail-ers and their insurers to take up leases. The essence of security, in turn, was a site plan clearly derived from Jeremy Bentham's proposed Panopticon—the eighteenth-century model prison to be constructed radially so that a single guard in a central tower could observe every prisoner at all times.

The King Shopping Center in Watts provides the best prototype of this commercial Brave New World for the inner city:

> The King Center site is surrounded by an eight-foot-high, wrought-iron fence com-parable to security fences found at the perimeters of private estates and exclusive residential communities. Video cameras equipped with motion detectors are posi-tioned near entrances and throughout the shopping center. The center, including parking lots, can be bathed in bright [lights] at the flip of a switch.
>
> There are six entrances to the center: three entry points for autos, two service gates, and one pedestrian walkway. . . . The service area . . . is enclosed with a six-foot-high concrete-block wall; both service gates remain closed and are under closed-circuit video surveillance, equipped for two-way voice communications, and operated by remote control from a security "observatory." Infrared beams at the bases of light fixtures detect intruders who might circumvent video cameras by climbing over the wall.[15]

The observatory functions as both eye and brain of this complex security system. It contains the headquarters of the shopping-center manager, a substa-tion of the LAPD, and a dispatch operator who both monitors the video and audio systems and maintains communication "with other secure shopping cen-ters tied into the system, and with the police and fire departments." At any time of day or night, there are at least four security guards on duty—one at the observatory, and three on patrol. They are trained and backed up by the regu-lar LAPD officers operating from the observatory substation.[16]

The King Center and its three siblings (all variations on the Panopticon theme), as expected, have been bonanzas, averaging annual sales of more than $350 per leasable square foot, as compared to about $200 for their suburban equivalents.[17] Moreover, Haagen has reaped the multiple windfalls of tax breaks, federal and city grants, massive free publicity, subsidized tenants, and sixty- to ninety-year ground leases. No wonder he has been able to boast,

"We've proved that the only color that counts in business is green. There are huge opportunities and huge profits to be made in these depressed inner-city areas of America that have been abandoned."[18]

High-Rent Security

The security-driven logic of contemporary urban design finds its major "grass-roots" expression in the frenetic efforts of Los Angeles's affluent neighborhoods to physically insulate their real-estate values and life-styles. Luxury developments outside the city limits have often been able to incorporate as "fortress cities," complete with security walls, guarded entries, private police, and even private roadways. It is simply impossible for ordinary citizens to enter the "cities" of Hidden Hills (western San Fernando Valley), Bradbury (San Gabriel Valley), Rancho Mirage (low desert), or Palos Verdes Estates (Palos Verdes Peninsula) without an invitation from a resident. Indeed Bradbury, with nine hundred inhabitants and ten miles of gated private roads, is so obsessed with security that its three city officials will not return phone calls from the press, since "each time an article appears, . . . it draws attention to the city, and the number of burglaries increases."[19]

Recently, Hidden Hills, a Norman Rockwell painting behind walls, has been bitterly divided over a Superior Court order to build forty-eight units of seniors' housing on vacant land outside the city gates. At meetings of the city's powerful homeowners' association (whose members include Frankie Avalon, Neil Diamond, and Bob Eubanks) opponents of compliance have argued vehemently that the old folks "will attract gangs and dope."[20]

Meanwhile, older high-income cities like Beverly Hills and San Marino have restricted access to their public facilities, using byzantine layers of regulations to build invisible walls. San Marino, which may be the richest and most Republican city in the country (85 percent), now closes its parks on weekends to exclude Latino and Asian families from adjacent communities. An alternative plan, now under discussion, would reopen the parks on Saturdays, but only to those with proof of residence or the means to pay daunting use fees. Other upscale areas (including thirty-seven Los Angeles neighborhoods) have minted similar residential privileges by restricting parking to local homeowners. Predictably such preferential parking ordinances proliferate mainly neighborhoods with three-car garages.

Affluent areas of the City of Los Angeles have long envied the autonomy of fortress enclaves like Hidden Hills and Palos Verdes. Now, with the cooperation of a pliant city council, they are winning permission to literally wall themselves off from the rest of the city. Since its construction in the late 1940s, Park La Brea has been Los Angeles's most successful experiment in mixed-income, high-rise living. Its urbane population of singles, young families, and retirees has always given a touch of Manhattan to the La Brea Tarpits area of Wilshire Boulevard. But its new owners, Forest City Enterprises, hope to "upgrade" the project image by sealing it off from the surrounding neighborhoods with security fencing and NO TRESPASSING signs. As a spokesperson for the owners blandly observed, "It's a trend in general to have enclosed communities."[21]

A few miles north of Park La Brea, above the Hollywood Bowl, the wealthy residents of Whitley Heights have won the unprecedented privilege of withdrawing their streets from public use. Eight high-tech gates will restrict access to residents and approved visitors using special electronic codes. An immediate byproduct of "gatehood" has been a dramatic 20 percent rise in local property values—a windfall that other residential districts are eager to emulate. Thus in the once wide-open tractlands of the San Fernando Valley—where a decade ago there were virtually no walled-off communities—homeowners are rushing to fortify their equity with walls and gates. Brian Weinstock, a leading local contractor, proudly boasts of the Valley's more than one hundred newly gated neighborhoods, and reports insatiable demand for additional security. "The first question out of [every buyer's] mouth is whether there is a gated community. The demand is there on a three-to-one basis."[22]

Meanwhile the very rich are yearning for unassailable high-tech castles. Where gates and walls will not suffice, the house itself is redesigned to incorporate state-of-the-art security. An important if unacknowledged motive for the current "mansionizing" mania on the city's Westside—the tearing down of $3 million houses to build $30 million supermansions—is the search for "absolute security." To achieve it, residential architects are borrowing design secrets from overseas embassies and military command posts. For example, one of the features currently in high demand is the "terrorist-proof security room" concealed in the houseplan and reached by hidden sliding panels or secret doors. Merv Griffin and his fellow mansionizers are hardening their palaces like banks or missile silos.

But technology is not enough. Contemporary residential security in Los Angeles—whether in the fortified mansion or the average suburban bunker—depends upon the extensive deployment of private security services. Through their local homeowners' associations, virtually every affluent neighborhood from the Palisades to Silver Lake contracts its own private policing; hence the thousands of lawns displaying the little ARMED RESPONSE warnings. A recent *Times* want-ads section contained over a hundred ads for guards and patrolmen, mostly from firms specializing in residential protection. Within greater Los Angeles, the security-services industry is a Cinderella sector that has tripled its sales and workforce—from 24,000 to 75,000 guards—over the last decade. "It is easier to become an armed guard than it is to become a barber, hairdresser, or journeyman carpenter," reports Linda Williams in the *Times*. Although the patrolmen are mostly minority males earning close to minimum wage, their employers are often multinational conglomerates offering a dazzling range of security products and services. As Michael Kaye, president of burgeoning Westec, a subsidiary of Japan's Secom, Ltd., explains: "We're not a security-guard company. We sell a *concept* of security."[23]

What homeowners' associations contract from Westec—or its principal rival, Bel-Air Patrol (part of Borg-Warner's family of security companies, which include Burns and Pinkerton)—is a complete "systems package": alarm hardware, monitoring, watch patrols, personal escorts, and, of course, "armed response" as necessary. Although law-enforcement experts debate the efficiency of such systems in foiling professional criminals, there is no doubt that they are brilliantly successful in deterring unintentional trespassers and innocent pedestrians. Anyone who has tried to take a stroll at dusk through a neighborhood patrolled by armed security guards and signposted with death threats quickly realizes how merely notional, if not utterly obsolete, is the old idea of "freedom of the city."

The LAPD as Space Police

This comprehensive urban security mobilization depends not only on the incorporation of the police function into the built environment, but also on the growing technopower of the police themselves. Undoubtedly the LAPD's pioneering substitution of technology for manpower was in part a necessary adaptation to the city's dispersed form; but it also expresses the department's particular relationship to the community. Especially in its self-representation, the LAPD appears as the progressive antithesis to the traditional big city police department with its patronage armies of patrolmen grafting off their beats. The LAPD, as reformed in the early 1950s by the legendary Chief Parker (who admired, above all, the gung-ho elitism of the Marines), would be incorruptible because unapproachable, a "few good men" doing battle with a fundamentally evil city. *Dragnet's* Sergeant Friday precisely captured the Parkerized LAPD's prudish alienation from a citizenry composed of fools, degenerates, and psychopaths.

Technology helped foster this paranoid esprit de corps, and virtually established a new definition of policing, where technologized surveillance and response supplanted the traditional patrolman's intimate folk knowledge of a specific community. Thus back in the 1920s the LAPD had pioneered the replacement of the flatfoot or mounted officer with the radio patrol car—the beginning of dispersed, mechanized policing. Under Parker, ever alert to spin-offs from military technology, the LAPD introduced the first police helicopters for systematic aerial surveillance. After the Watts Rebellion of 1965, this airborne effort became the cornerstone of a policing strategy for the entire inner city. As part of its Astro program LAPD helicopters maintain an average nineteen-hour-per-day vigil over "high-crime areas." To facilitate ground-air coordination, thousands of residential rooftops have been painted with large, identifying street numbers, transforming the aerial view of the city into a huge police grid.

The fifty-pilot LAPD airforce was recently updated with French Aerospatiale helicopters equipped with futuristic surveillance technology. Their forward-looking infrared cameras are extraordinary night eyes that can easily form heat images from a single burning cigarette a mile away, while their 30-million-candle-power spotlights, appropriately called "Night Suns," can turn night into day. Meanwhile the LAPD retains another fleet of Bell Jet Rangers capable of delivering SWAT units anywhere in the region. Their training, which sometimes includes practice assaults on Downtown high-rises, anticipates some of the spookier Hollywood images—as in *Blue Thunder* or *Running Man*—of airborne police terror.

But the decisive element in the LAPD's metamorphosis into a Technopolice has been its long and successful liaison with the military aerospace industry.[24] Just in time for the opening of the 1984 Los Angeles Olympics, the department acquired ECCCS (Emergency Command Control Communications Systems), the most powerful police communications system in the world. First conceptualized by Hughes Aerospace between 1969 and 1971, ECCCS's design was refined and updated by NASA's Jet Propulsion Laboratory, incorporating elements of space technology and mission-centered communication.

Bunkered in the earthquake-proof security-hardened fourth and fifth sublevels of City Hall East (and interconnecting with the police pentagon in Parker Center), the Central Dispatch Center coordinates all the complex itineraries and responses of the LAPD using digitalized communication to eliminate voice congestion and guaranteed the secrecy of transmission. ECCCS, together with the LAPD's prodigious information-processing assets, including ever-growing databases on suspect citizens, have become the central neural system for the vast and disparate security operations, both public and private, taking place in Los Angeles.

The Carceral City

All these technologically advanced policing strategies have led to an invisible Haussmannization of Los Angeles. No need to clear fields of fire when you control the sky; no need to hire informers when surveillance cameras ornament every building. But the police have also reorganized space in far more straightforward ways. We have already seen their growing role as Downtown urban designers, indispensable for their expertise in "security." In addition they lobby incessantly for the allocation of more land for such law-and-order needs as jail space for a burgeoning inmate population and expanded administrative and training facilities for themselves. In Los Angeles this has taken the form of a *de facto* urban-renewal program, operated by the police agencies, that threatens to convert an entire section of Downtown and East LA into a vast penal colony.

Nearly 25,000 prisoners are presently held in six severely overcrowded county and federal facilities within a three-mile radius of City Hall—the largest single incarcerated population in the country. Racing to meet the challenge of the "war on drugs"—which will double detained populations within a decade—authorities are forging ahead with the reconstruction of a controversial state prison in East Los Angeles as well as a giant expansion of County Jail near Chinatown. The Immigration and Naturalization Service, meanwhile, has been trying to shoehorn privatized "microprisons" into unsuspecting innercity neighborhoods. Confronting record overcrowding in its regular detention centers, the INS has commandeered motels and apartments for operation by private contractors as auxiliary jails for detained aliens— many of them Chinese and Central American political refugees.

The demand for more law-enforcement space in the central city, however, will inevitably bring the police into conflict with developers. The plan to add two high-rise towers with 2,400 new beds to County Jail on Bauchet Street, Downtown, has already raised the ire of developers hoping to make nearby Union Station the hub of a vast complex of skyscraper hotels and offices. One solution to the increasing conflict between carceral and commercial redevelopment is to use architectural camouflage to insert jail space into the skyscape. Ironically, even as buildings and homes become more like prisons or fortresses, prisons are becoming aesthetic objects. Indeed, carceral structures are the new frontier of public architecture. As an office glut in most parts of the country reduces commissions for corporate highrises, celebrity architects are designing jails, prisons, and police stations.

An extraordinary example, the flagship of the emergent genre, is Welton Becket Associates' new Metropolitan Detentions Center in Downtown Los Angeles. Although this ten-story Federal Bureau of Prisons facility is one of the most visible new structures in the city, few of the hundreds of thousands of commuters who pass by every day have even an inkling of its function as a holding center for what has been officially describe[d] as the "managerial elite of narco-terrorism." This postmodern Bastille—the largest prison built in a major U.S. urban center in decades—looks instead like a futuristic hotel or office block, with artistic flourishes (for example, the high-tech trellises on its bridge-balconies) that are comparable to Downtown's best-designed recent architecture. In contrast to the human inferno of desperately overcrowded County Jail a few blocks away, the Becket structure appears less a detention center than a convention center for federal felons—a "distinguished" addition to Downtown's continuum of security and design.

The Fear of Crowds

In actual practice, the militarization of urban space tends to race far ahead of its theoretical representations. This is not to say, however, that the fortress city lacks apologists. Charles Murray, ideologue *par excellence* of 1980s antiwelfarism, has recently outlined ambitious justifications for renewed urban segregation in the 1990s. Writing in the *New Republic* (increasingly, the theoretical journal of the backlash against the urban poor), Murray argues that *landlords*—"one of the greatly maligned forces for social good in this country"—*not cops* are the best bet for winning the war on drugs.[25] Given the prohibitive cost of building sufficient prison space to warehouse the country's burgeoning population of inner-city drug users, Murray proposes instead to isolate them socially and spatially. In his three-prong strategy, employers would urine-test and fire drug-tainted workers at will; parents would use vouchers to remove their children from drug-ridden public schools; and, most importantly, landlords would maintain drug-free neighborhoods by excluding the "wrong kind of person."

Murray advocates, in other words, the restoration of the right of employers and landlords to discriminate—"without having to justify their arbitrariness." Only by letting "like-minded people . . . control and shape their small worlds," and letting landlords pursue their natural instinct "to let good tenants be and to evict bad ones," can the larger part of urban America find its way back to a golden age of harmonious, self-regulating communities. Murray is undoubtedly proud of all the Los Angeles suburbanites rushing to wall off their tract-home *gemeinschafts*.

At the same time, he unflinchingly accepts that the underclass—typified, in his words, by the "pregnant teenage[r] smoking crack" and the "Uzi-toting young male"—will become even more outcast: "If the result of implementing these policies is to concentrate the bad apples into a few hyperviolent, antisocial neighborhoods, so be it." Presumably it will be cheaper to police these pariah communities—where *everyone*, by definition, is a member of the dangerous class—than to apprehend and incarcerate hundreds of thousands of individuals. "Drug-free zones" for the majority, as a logical corollary, demand social-refuse dumps for the criminalized minority. Resurrected Jim Crow legislation, euphemistically advertised as "local self-determination," will insulate the urban middle classes (now including the Cosby family as well) from the New Jack City at their doorstep.

In this quest for spatial discrimination, the aims of contemporary architecture and the police converge most strikingly around the problem of crowd control. Cothinkers of Murray doubtless find the heterogeneous crowd a subversive anathema to their idyll of "like-mindedness." As we have seen, the designers of malls and pseudopublic space attack the crowd by homogenizing it. They set up architectural and semiotic barriers that filter out the "undesirables." They enclose the mass that remains, directing its circulation with behaviorist ferocity. The crowd is lured by visual stimuli of all kinds, dulled by Muzak, sometimes even scented by invisible aromatizers. This Skinnerian orchestration, if well conducted, produces a veritable commercial symphony of swarming, consuming nomads moving from one cash-point to another.

Outside in the streets, the task is more difficult. The LAPD continues to restrict the rights of public assembly and freedom of movement, especially of the young, through its mass sweeps and "Operation Hammer," selective juvenile curfews, and regular blockades of popular "cruising" boulevards. Even gilded white youth suffer from the strict police regulation of personal mobility. In the former world capital of adolescence, where millions overseas still imagine Gidget at a late-night beach party, the beaches are now closed at dusk, patrolled by helicopter gunships and police dune buggies.

A watershed in the local assault on the crowd was the rise and fall of the "Los Angeles Street Scene." Launched in 1978, the two-day annual festival at the Civic Center was intended to publicize Downtown's revitalization as well as to provide Mayor Bradley's version of the traditional Democratic barbecue. The LAPD remained skeptical. Finally in 1986, after the failure of the Ramones to appear as promised, a youthful audience began to tear up one of the stages. They were immediately charged by a phalanx of 150 police, including mounted units. In the two-hour melee that followed, angry punks bombarded the police cavalry with rocks and bottles; fifteen officers and horses were injured. The producer of the Street Scene, a Bradley official, suggested that "more middle-of-the-road entertainment" might attract less "boisterous crowds." The prestigious *Downtown News* counterattacked: "The Street Scene gives Downtown a bad name. It flies in the face of all that has been done here in the last thirty years." The paper demanded "reparations for the wounded 'reputation of Downtown.' " The Mayor canceled the Scene.[26]

The demise of the Scene suggested the consolidation of an official consensus about crowds and the use of space in Los Angeles. Once the restructuring of Downtown eliminated the social mixing of groups in normal pedestrian circulation, the Street Scene (ironically named) remained one of the few occasions or places (along with redevelopment-threatened Hollywood Boulevard and the Venice boardwalks) where Chinatown punks, Glendale skinheads, Boyle Height lowriders, Valley Girls, Marina designer couples, Slauson rappers, Skid Row homeless, and gawkers from Des Moines could still mingle together in relative amity. Moreover, in the years since the Battle of the Ramones, relentless police intimidation has ignited one youthful crowd after another into pandemonium, producing major riots in Hollywood on Halloween night in 1988, and in Westwood Village in March 1991 (during the premiere of *New Jack City*). Each incident, in turn, furnishes new pretexts for regulating crowds and "preventing the invasion of outsiders" (as one Westwood merchant explained in a TV interview). Inexorably, Los Angeles moves to extinguish [its] last public spaces, with all of their democratic intoxications, risks, and undeodorized odors.

Notes

1. National Committee on the Causes and Prevention of Violence. *To Establish Justice, to Ensure Domestic Tranquility* (Final Report. Washington D.C.: USGPO, 1969).
2. Quoted in John F. Kasson, *Amusing the Millions* (New York: Hill and Wang, 1978), p. 15.
3. *Los Angeles Times*, Nov. 4, 1978.
4. Ibid., Dec. 24, 1972.
5. N. David Milder, "Crime and Downtown Revitalization," *Urban Land*, Sept. 1987, p. 18.
6. Tom Chorneau, "Quandary over a Park Restroom," *Downtown News*, August 25, 1986.
7. See "Cold Snap's Toll at 5 as its Iciest Night Arrives," *Los Angeles Times*, Dec. 29, 1988.
8. Ibid., June 17, 1990.
9. "The old socialist" quote is from Michael Rotundi of Morphosis. Gehry himself boasts: "I get my inspiration from the streets. I'm more of a street fighter than a Roman scholar." (Quoted in Adele Freedman, *Progressive Architecture*, Oct. 1986, p. 99.)
10. The best catalogue of Gehry's work is Peter Arnell and Ted Bickford, eds., *Frank Gehry: Buildings and Projects* (New York: 1985).
11. Milfred Friedman, ed., *The Architecture of Frank Gehry* (New York: 1986), p. 175.
12. Pilar Viladas, "Illuminated Manuscripts," *Progressive Architecture*, Oct. 1986, pp. 76, 84.
13. See David Ferrell's articles in the *Los Angeles Times*, Aug. 31 and Oct. 16, 1987.

14. Ibid., Oct. 7, 1987.
15. Jane Bukwalter, "Securing Shopping Centers for Inner Cities," *Urban Land*, Apr. 1987, p. 24.
16. Ibid.
17. Richard Titus, "Security Works," *Urban Land*, Jan. 1990, p. 2.
18. Buckwalter, "Securing," p. 25.
19. *Los Angeles Daily News*, Nov. 1, 1987.
20. Interview, Fox News, Mar. 1990.
21. *Los Angeles Times*, July 25, 1989.
22. Jim Carlton, quoted in *Los Angeles Times*, Oct. 8, 1988.
23. Quoted in *Los Angeles Times*, Aug. 29, 1988.
24. Interviews with LAPD personnel; also Don Rosen, "Bleu Thunder," *Los Angeles Herald Examiner*, May 28, 1989.
25. Charles Murray, "How to Win the War on Drugs," *New Republic*, May 21, 1990, pp. 19–25.
26. *Los Angeles Times*, Sept. 22 and 25, 1986.

21

Kristen Hill Maher

THE LANDSCAPE OF SUBURBAN FEAR

A Tale of Two Cities

This study examines the social relations and anxieties about crime in a single neighborhood that I will call "Ridgewood" in Irvine, California. Understanding this research site requires some introduction to Orange County—located between Los Angeles and San Diego—and particularly to its cities of Irvine and Santa Ana.

Within the mental maps of developers and many residents, Orange County divides into a north and a south with a veritable Mason-Dixon line cutting across the middle (Dodson 1989). North and South County differ in their historical development, the physical layout of their residential and business areas, and their demographics in terms of socioeconomic status and racial-ethnic distribution. These differences have come to represent fundamental differences in identity. South County is reputed as wealthy and white, a collection of orderly, planned developments. In contrast, North County is reputed as middle and working class and nonwhite, a "chaotic" extension of urban Los Angeles (Till 1993). Neither of these representations is entirely accurate, although they do reflect real patterns of racial segregation. The geography of Latino residences is

Kristen Hill Maher, "Workers and Strangers: The Household Service Economy and the Landscape of Suburban Fear," *Urban Affairs Review*, Vol. 38, No. 6, July 2003, pp. 751–786. Excerpts from pp. 757–759, 764–774, 774–779, and corresponding notes and references on pp. 780–786.

particularly striking. [There is] a concentration of Latinos in North County and their virtual absence in South County—a spatial division so clear, it appears almost as a wall or border demarcating racialized territories. Because household services in South County are performed almost exclusively by Latinos, one might imagine the daily commute for workers from North to South County as a type of "border crossing" that blurs social boundaries and binds North to South in an economic interdependence.

Irvine, in South County, is one of the fastest-growing small cities in the United States, part of the mass suburbanization and development of Orange County since the 1950s. Irvine was centrally planned and strategically developed from private ranch lands in the garden city model, marketed to potential home buyers as a decentralized suburban utopia (Schiesl 1991). With a population of 143,072 in 2000, Irvine is ethnically diverse, although that diversity primarily spans ethnicities that are white (61%) and Asian (30%). Alongside its residential development grew a strong high-tech industrial base, such that Irvine is now one of four "major technopoles" in the greater Los Angeles area (Scott and Soja 1996, 13). Given the centrality of high-tech industries in Irvine's economic base, the city's labor market has largely bifurcated into jobs for high-skilled, high-wage professionals and for low-skilled, low-wage workers in the service economy. Latino labor forms the backbone of Irvine's low-skilled service sector; however, Irvine's zoning regulations and expensive housing market discourage these workers from local residence. Instead, most service workers commute to Irvine from Latino residential enclaves such as those in Santa Ana in North County, roughly 10 miles away.

In contrast to the recent planning behind Irvine's incorporation (1971) and growth, Santa Ana was incorporated in 1886 and has long served as the administrative center of the county, with a relatively dense urban population that comprised more than a quarter of the county's residents earlier in the century (between 1930 and 1950). Although Santa Ana's population has increased six-fold since 1950,[1] this growth has not kept up with the much more rapid development elsewhere in the county. Santa Ana remains the administrative center of the county, but it is no longer the population or commercial hub.

The other historical process that marks contemporary Santa Ana's position in the county is a significant Latino in-migration and a simultaneous out-migration of other racial-ethnic groups, particularly whites. In 1960, only 15% of Santa Ana's residents were Latino;[2] by 2000, the proportion of Latinos had grown to 76%, comprising roughly 40% of all the Latinos in Orange County.[3] Like areas of Los Angeles that have become Latino immigrant enclaves over the past several decades,[4] the process of transformation in Santa Ana has been rooted in the restructuring of the economy. The loss of blue-collar manufacturing jobs weakened Santa Ana's economic base and spurred former blue-collar workers to move elsewhere. Given relatively low housing costs, Latino immigrants then found this area an attractive point of entry. At the same time, low-paying jobs that remained attractive opportunities for immigrants proliferated in textile and food production as well as services,[5] including many service jobs in nearby South County. In the 1970s, Latino merchants revived Santa Ana's languishing downtown area, reinventing it as a commercial and cultural center that continues to flourish.[6]

In the emerging postindustrial economy, Orange County has become another place where "yuppies and poor migrant workers depend upon each other" (Caldeira 1996, 310). Like global cities (Sassen 1991), suburban areas are becoming another place where we see economies of service and support growing alongside a transnational, high-tech, information-based economy. Part of what this study documents, then, are interdependencies between the peoples and residential spaces of this bifurcated economy, divisions that largely fall along the lines of class, racial-ethnic identity, and—to some extent—migrant status. However, none of the divisions organizing the social relations in Orange County are merely "given"; they are also subject to continuing negotiation. Although this study captures only a moment in an ongoing process, it illustrates some of the possible sociopolitical dynamics of the emerging household service economy in suburban areas. . . .

The Threat of the Random Stranger

In discussing past and potential crime, residents raised several categories of potential criminals: "renters" from neighboring communities who trespassed to use Ridgewood's private park or pool illicitly, "neighborhood kids" who either lived in Ridgewood or who were friends with resident teens, service workers, and strangers from the "outside." Of these categories, there was no expectation that the gate would eliminate potential crime by anyone but strangers. Trespassers from neighboring communities entered by walking, and a gate would not eliminate pedestrian access. Local teenagers—who were identified both by residents and by periodic Irvine police bulletins as the likely perpetrators of most burglaries—would also continue to have unrestricted access to community space were a gate installed. For these reasons, it became clear that the key target of gating would be the category of "strangers." The strangers who were feared were defined as either nonresidents of a "different element" who randomly wandered into the neighborhood or burglars who selectively targeted neighborhoods like Ridgewood because of their relative affluence.[7]

The category of "strangers" raises an interesting question. Ridgewood's residents did not personally know all their neighbors or all those present in the community, such that there were in fact many strangers present at all times. How, then, did they decide which strangers were threatening? For the most part, residents described those they deemed threatening only according to the car they were driving. The cars that were most often described as anxiety producing were the "bad" ones: "if this gross-looking, funky-looking, beat-up truck is sitting there . . . you are aware, and you kind of keep an eyeball on them, because you don't know if they're scoping. You don't know what they're doing" (Cheryl). Another resident described the vehicles that make her suspicious as follows: "You know, is it a van? Is it a pickup truck? Is it kind of rusty and scruffy-looking, as opposed to being a Mercedes or something? I mean, real estate agents certainly drive around a lot" (Nancy). Part of this identification of bad cars certainly had something to do with the identification of working-class people as more likely criminals. But it also had to do with the availability of potential explanations for what the drivers might be doing there. If there was an unfamiliar BMW in the neighborhood, it could belong to a friend of a neighbor, a real estate agent, a business contact, a potential home buyer, and so forth. If there was an unfamiliar "bad car" in the neighborhood, there were fewer possible explanations for it: "You see people driving along going slowly looking at everything. If they're in a fancy car, you figure they're looking for a new house. If they're in an old car, you figure they're scoping it out" (Gerry).

Talk about cars appeared to be not only the result of a cue-taking about potential criminals but also a coded language in which people could talk about class and race in a context in which explicit discussion of these topics is widely thought to be impolite.[8] Many of the residents' descriptions about what kinds of cars made them nervous involved clear class references encoded in the descriptions of cars as "broken-down" or not fitting "the Irvine mold." More subtle were the racial overtones of some observations, such as the woman who said she became nervous when drivers were not any of the housekeepers or gardeners she personally knew. Clearly, these drivers were Latinos because she compared them to service workers rather than to neighbors or others she might have personally known. Others were slightly more obvious about the racial content of their observations about bad cars, identifying the cars that made them most suspicious more specifically as "lowriders," augmented Chevrolets often associated with working-class Chicano culture. These kinds of descriptions suggest that it was not necessarily the cars themselves but rather the kinds of people driving them that elicited anxiety from Ridgewood residents.

There was some agreement among those who favored the gate that it would help reduce the random presence of bad cars in the community more than it would eliminate the possibility of strategic burglary by experienced criminals. Although a few people suggested that a gate would be "just one more deterrent" that would encourage a "professional burglar" to go elsewhere instead, most said that there is nothing you can do about that kind of crime. They suggested that someone who made a habit of burglary could get in anywhere he wanted, such that no neighborhood was completely safe. To illustrate this point, even those who supported the gate gave examples of break-ins they had heard about *within* gated communities elsewhere. Instead, the gate was more often estimated to keep out the random stranger in a bad car who might just straggle in to the community.

Santa Ana and the Imagined Future

As references to bad cars and low-riders above suggest, the strangers that residents in this community read as most threatening tended to be of other races and classes than those living in Ridgewood. This section more explicitly addresses the social geography of feared strangers. It suggests that the pervasive fears about security relate to macroeconomic shifts that residents discussed and interpreted using the language of crime and social decline, adopting working-class Latinos living in areas like Santa Ana as the central characters in a dystopic narrative about change.

In discussions about where dangerous strangers might come from, some residents remained vague about social geography, suggesting that the danger came from the freeway, where people from all sorts of places drive by in close proximity to Irvine. They apparently imagined the freeway as a connection to the world, and especially to urban areas, that made an otherwise insulated area vulnerable to crime. Others more explicitly identified Santa Ana and other regions north of Irvine as the source of their insecurities. For instance, Cheryl mentioned at the beginning of her interview that she did not fear crime at all and in fact had not had the security system on her house engaged for months. Yet, she wanted to have Ridgewood add gates because of a threat she perceives as spreading soon to Irvine. "They're coming in from Santa Ana," she explained, and later added the following:

> Cheryl: In the last two years—I haven't seen it but I hear it from other people, that the gangs are coming down this way.
> KHM: From?
> Cheryl: Santa Ana, and wait . . . what's above Santa Ana? What is it, Stanton? It's something to think about. But you know they're going to be everywhere.

This interview excerpt is revealing about the insecurity that makes Cheryl want to install a gate around her community. In part, the relevant question was "Where is the danger?" insofar as she feared an invasion of gangs and minorities from Santa Ana and other places north of Irvine. But the more critical question might instead be "*When* is the danger?" insofar as it was something that Cheryl had not yet experienced in her daily life but feared will happen in the future: "You know they're going to be everywhere."

Cheryl was not the only one who seemed to fear the future more than anything in the present. Consider the following excerpt from the interview with Jeff, who presented the problem in terms of changing "demographics" not just in Santa Ana but also over the past century in Los Angeles:

> Jeff: The demographics are changing here. When I moved here back in the early seventies, I was a typical person here in Orange County. And, as you well know, now . . . Costa Mesa and Santa Ana have declined in their social structure. Or, I don't know if that's the proper terminology, but the bottom line is their crime rates have risen, and that type of person has moved down and started to encroach on Irvine. . . . The best way to look, I guess—go to Los Angeles. Fifty years ago or, you know, ninety years ago, downtown Los Angeles was the place to be. And I guarantee you wouldn't walk there at night now.
> KHM: So your perception, or people around here perceive that that's the future for Irvine as well . . .?
> Jeff: It's a possibility. . . . I absolutely see change in this neighborhood. I've seen it! Go to the schools and look at the change in where the kids are coming from and what their background is. I mean, what do their parents do? . . . All of a sudden I'm looking around and saying. "Gosh, everything's connected here."

Although Jeff was careful not to say so explicitly, shifts in the racial composition of the greater Los Angeles area were clearly at the center of his concerns. Although he—as a white man—used to be the "typical person here in Orange County," there had been a "decline" in the "social structure" of Santa Ana and Costa Mesa (the two closest areas experiencing significant Latino immigration), much like in Los Angeles.[9] And this "type of person has moved down and started to encroach on Irvine," as was evidenced by simply looking at the "background" of the kids in nearby schools. Jeff seemed to fear the ways that Irvine would eventually be subject to racial and class shifts like those occurring in nearby cities and to what he saw as a concurrent rise in crime.

Similarly, in the excerpt below, Tom very colorfully identifies a rise in crime in Santa Ana and Los Angeles as the primary reason why so many communities in South Orange County have been gating:

> Tom: All of the new communities that have opened in Newport [Beach] in the last three or four years, every single one of them has been gated. Because people are seeing crime on the rise. And they perceive that it may eventually get to them, whether it's in the safest city in the U.S., in Irvine, or in the rich city, in Newport Beach.
>
> KHM: So the place that they're seeing crime on the rise is not amongst their own neighbors?
>
> Tom: No! But it's in *anticipation* of what could happen.
>
> KHM: Where do they get it [this idea], do you think?
>
> Tom: Well, the press, We get a constant diet of it through the press. Christ, turn the 6:00 news on. What is it? Rape, pillage and plunder. They're not talking about the Boy Scouts having a campout.
>
> KHM: But they're talking about Los Angeles most of the time.
>
> Tom: It doesn't matter. Los Angeles is Orange County. We still have awful things happen here. . . . Listen, we've got a very serious gang problem over in Santa Ana. It's almost out of control, the police there are just—they're beside themselves. And is that going to move our way? I don't know, but people are doing things in anticipation of the fact that maybe it could. And if it is, I want to be behind a gated wall. It's real simple.

Tom emphasized throughout his interview that Irvine was an exceptionally safe city, but here he qualified that observation, raising the specter of Los Angeles and Santa Ana as places that for him represented the future. Whatever was coming was moving south with the unforgiving destiny of a glacier, bringing urban races and urban ills all at once. And when it happened, he wanted to "be behind a gated wall."

A common theme throughout the interviews cited above (as well as others not cited here) was that the urban ills of Los Angeles and Santa Ana were not contained within the geography of these cities but were spreading to other areas via mobile urban minorities. This expectation appeared to rest upon an implicit suggestion that urban minorities in Santa Ana and Los Angeles had *caused* problems like poverty and crime rather than being victims of them.[10] There have been a number of significant transformations occurring in these cities: the loss of much of their traditional manufacturing base and scores of stable, unionized jobs with benefits; the concurrent growth in "flexible," part-time, and poorly paid jobs; the influx of new immigrants for whom even inse-cure or poorly compensated jobs remain attractive opportunities; and height-ened poverty among workers earning low-skilled service wages. Despite the macroeconomic nature of these shifts, a number of the participants in this study implicitly attributed the decline in these areas to the influx of Latino immigrants.

In this sense, the narrative about Santa Ana also rested on essentialized no-tions of Latinos as the kind of people who instigate urban problems and who bring poverty, crime, and urban malaise in their wake. The racial anxieties in Ridgewood were certainly not limited to Latinos: Interviews also included sto-ries of racial tensions regarding Persians, Hasidic Jews, and African-Ameri-cans. One resident reported an incident in which she had called the police in re-sponse to a preteen African-American boy simply wandering through the neighborhood. However, in the discussions about crime and decline, local cities like Santa Ana and Costa Mesa, which are home to fast-growing Latino immigrant enclaves, figured most prominently in the perception of threat.

Teresa Caldeira's (2000) study of middle-class residents living in "fortified enclaves" in São Paulo found similar narratives regarding *nordestinos*, migrants from Northeast Brazil. Caldeira suggests that residents commonly character-ized nordestinos as criminals and engaged in the "talk of crime" to represent the range of local changes they found distressing. She argues that all sorts of losses and anxieties can be articulated through the language of crime:

> Crime supplies a generative symbolism with which to talk about other things that are perceived as wrong or bad, but for which no consensus of interpretation or vo-cabulary may exist. It also offers symbolism with which to talk about other kinds of loss, such as downward mobility. Moreover, crime adds drama to the narration of events that themselves may be undramatic—for example, a forty-year process of change in a neighborhood—but whose consequences can be distressing. (P. 34)

The talk of crime reduces a complex, disorderly reality to a few essentialized categories that "elaborate prejudices" at the same time as they give the narrator a means to organize the world and gain a sense of control (pp. 19–41).

Caldeira's (2000) argument is useful for making sense of the contradictions in the talk of crime in Ridgewood. The narratives about crime in Ridgewood certainly did not correlate to any empirical reality: There were few personal ex-periences of crime among those in the neighborhood, and the focus of most anxiety was not about any immediate sense of danger. (Indeed, the kinds of added security under debate in this community such as gated entries were not even targeted at those persons thought to be the most likely perpetrators of ac-tual crime in the neighborhood.) Instead, the talk of crime in Ridgewood ap-peared to be a more general way to articulate fear or unease about a range of other local transformations. Almost every interview included some expression of disquiet about the inevitability of urbanization and the loss of the "rural feel" of Irvine. Even though many residents described community life in

Ridgewood in very positive terms, there was simultaneously a sense of the loss of Eden.[11] They noted that Irvine was increasingly woven into a net of freeways that tied it to more urban centers. They saw evidence of more bad cars around. They observed a greater local presence of minorities they viewed as urban. They observed struggling economies and what they perceived as out-of-control crime in nearby cities. Although these observations could be understood as simple antiurban sentiment, they also reflected a perception of a shifting geography in Orange County in which the "invasion of Latinos" and "Santa Ana" served as potent symbols of a future in which they felt that their accustomed way of life and social status were not secure.

This symbolic language masked the extent to which the transformations in Orange County, and particularly the growth of Latino populations in Santa Ana, had been produced in part by the emerging racialized service economy.[12] The growing consumption of household services in neighborhoods like Ridgewood in South County had generated thousands of new, low-paying service jobs for Latinos living in North County. Workers providing household services must by necessity live nearby, close enough to facilitate a daily commute, so it was no coincidence that a community like Santa Ana that is close to the North/South divide in Orange County had been experiencing a lot of population growth. As the household service economy in suburban areas like Irvine grows, so will the nearby communities in which service workers live, in effect, following those retreating into gated communities. This is one of the two ways that the service economy in Ridgewood itself contributes indirectly to the forting up of its suburban landscape.

Workers and Strangers: Blurred Boundaries

A second connection between the suburban service economy and the tendency toward fortification lies in the daily practices within neighborhood space. Most service workers in Ridgewood strongly resembled those random strangers driving bad cars from places in North County like Santa Ana that many Ridgewood residents wanted to keep out with a gated entry. And yet, with few exceptions, residents did not perceive service workers to constitute any potential criminal threat. This perception rested upon a categorical dichotomy that residents tended to assume between "workers" and "potential criminals," as well as upon unspoken regulations of workers' behavior that made their service role more visible. However, not all of those connected to the service economy could easily be contained by this worker-stranger dichotomy; there was, in fact, blurring between these categories that contributed to popular anxieties about a growing presence of threatening strangers.

Signs of the "Bona Fide Worker"

In general, residents described service workers in very positive terms, as "hard-working, sweet people" (Jeff) or "just people who want a better life for themselves" (Jeanne). Most represented the regular traffic of workers in the neighborhood as normal and unproblematic.

One resident illustrated the normality of Latino service workers with a story about how his 10-year-old daughter coming to Ridgewood to live initially made the mistake of thinking that gardeners were threatening. On her first day of school, she came home from school panicked, saying that there had been a man in a white truck following her. Her father had looked into it and realized that the men working for local landscaping companies were all Latinos driving white trucks:

> And my little Anglo-Saxon daughter coming from Cleveland, Ohio, sees all these dark-looking Mexican guys in these trucks. And they were like following them because they were always driving around as [the children] walked home from school. And it threw her off. I had to explain it to her, so I took her out and I introduced her to them. And I said, you know, these are the people who clean our greenbelt and everything. (Gerry)

Evidently, for Gerry, confusing Latino service workers for other Latinos who might be threatening was a naive error that would only be made by someone who does not understand the social landscape in Orange County.[13] For him, the categories of "service workers" and "potential criminals" appeared to be mutually exclusive.

Only two of those interviewed raised any doubts about this categorical division, suggesting that workers might be engaged in petty theft or tipping off friends who could burglarize. As one explained, there was no real evidence of whether workers were actually stealing things but that one of the first responses when "things go missing" is to blame the gardener: When "someone's garage door is open, if the gardeners are in the neighborhood, it immediately seems to go that people are convinced that *they're* the ones, you know" (Harrison). But most of those interviewed dismissed the possibility of crime by workers, some laughing at the prospect when I raised it.[14] Similarly, no one seriously entertained the possibility that their own neighbors might pose a criminal threat, whereas the residents of surrounding neighborhoods were more often considered suspect. These patterns suggest that the residents in this community had a psychological investment in expecting prosocial behavior from all those who "belonged" within neighborhood space, reserving the expectation of threat for outsiders.

Perhaps for this reason, residents almost always placed service workers in a category separate from potential criminals. These dichotomous categories rested on knowing the difference between a worker "who belongs there" and a stranger they might consider threatening. Most residents expressed certainty about their ability to tell the difference. In some cases, this confidence rested on the familiarity some residents felt with their neighbors and their service workers' routines: "You know who's doing what today; you know who's going where" (Cheryl). In other cases, the confidence seemed to be premised on the clarity of worker's signification. As Mary noted, "You can just tell who is a service worker." Or, as Carolyn elaborated,

> There have only been a couple of occasions when I saw somebody and went, mm, they don't look like they live in the area. They don't look like a gardener. Somebody driving around in a car and . . . circling the neighborhood. . . . There's only been once or twice that I've seen something like that happen. More often than not, the people that we see in the neighborhood appear to be *bona fide* gardeners. Either that, or they've got a real elaborate camouflage scheme.

The distinction between someone just "driving around in a car" and a service worker in this case rested upon the service worker actively demonstrating or performing his credentials as a "bona fide gardener." That might mean, for instance, that he needed to drive a white pickup truck with equipment in it. Once out of the truck, he should not stray far from it or else should have equipment on his person or simply remain actively at work.

One resident noted that she suspected the gardeners were aware that they needed to be careful about how they spent their breaks:

> You know, the guys who are pruning the trees or whatever, and they're taking a rest—I think they try to look . . . not too much like they're just out to have a picnic. . . . Their tools are near, or . . . there might be a much nicer tree that they could go to. But they stay very close to their instruments of work, like their tools. (Anne)

Not just gardeners but all Latino service workers in the neighborhood needed to remain easily legible to the home owners there to remain unthreatening. The primary means of identifying a nanny in this neighborhood involved seeing a Latina with children of some other race, a schema articulated by Margaret as follows: "I see a lot of people with baby strollers with blonde children and South American people pushing them. You know that they're not the parents, so that you can just tell." As in most suburban communities in Southern California, the social distinction between those providing services and those consuming them in Ridgewood was a racialized division, where workers were marked by a "uniform of color," much as in colonial contexts such as South Africa (Kuper 1947). However, this "uniform" alone did not provide cues for distinction between workers and potentially threatening strangers, given that residents also used racialized cues for identifying criminals.

Hence unwritten social norms in the community had developed to regulate worker behavior, norms that were apparent in the almost complete uniformity in what workers did and did not do within Ridgewood and that were confirmed by interviews with the workers themselves.[15] No workers engaged in visible leisure in the community, even during their time off.[16] Gardeners stayed close to their trucks and tools. Domestic workers performed their worker status by being visible only when there was a work-related reason to be outdoors, for instance, by accompanying children who appeared not to be their own. Housekeepers who did not care for children were not visible at all, except when waiting for a ride or walking to or from the bus stop. The informal regulations requiring service workers to actively perform their service roles when visible in community space helped support the dichotomy residents maintained between bona fide workers and strangers whose presence would be cause for alarm.

The Ambiguity of Signification and Indeterminacy of Categories

Despite the pervasive social regulation of service workers, Ridgewood residents' confidence in the dichotomy between workers and strangers was misplaced. In fact, these categories blurred into one another in two ways that contributed to residents' anxieties about security. First, the signs of someone associated with the service economy were ambiguous enough to permit misreadings of workers as strangers (and vice versa). Second, in practice, the categories of workers and strangers were not as clearly delineated as the popular dichotomy among residents presumed. Both kinds of categorical blurring contributed to some residents' sense that their neighborhood was vulnerable to crime and other ills they associated with the seemingly random presence of working-class Latinos in the vicinity.

As discussed above, the signs of a bona fide worker rested largely on race and the active performance of work. Both of these kinds of signification left plenty of room for misreadings. For instance, the racialized schemas residents used to identify nannies were highly imperfect and backfired in some cases in which the formula of a Latina nanny with blonde children did not apply. Middle Eastern and Asian families had recently begun to move into the neighborhood and had also hired Latina nannies, confusing the expected racial schema, as it was less clear that the children were not their own. According to one resident, what happened then was that "you would get some nanny with some black-haired kids in the park, and somebody is saying, you know, 'who are these people coming in and using the park?' " (Nancy). In contrast, Latina nannies from other neighborhoods brought light-haired children to the park and pool in Ridgewood without any suspicion that they were trespassing because they fit the expected formula. The domestic workers employed in Ridgewood were apparently the only ones to perceive that these women were present without authorization. The racialized schema for identifying service workers permitted both of these kinds of misperceptions about who "belonged" within community space.

More important, the performance of work was not a reliable sign of whose presence in the community was related to the service economy. The service sector in this community produced a regular traffic of working-class Latinos, not all of whom were easily marked by their labor, tools, or signification as being there for a reason rather than "randomly" entering the community to scope it out. For instance, some of the discussion about the increase in bad cars in the community (mentioned in the earlier section on security concerns) suggested that those associated with the service economy were not always legible as such.

. . . The worker-stranger dichotomy falsely disembedded service workers from any social context besides that of the service relationship, as if they were a fundamentally separate group of people than the strangers from places like Santa Ana who were a key source of anxiety. This became most apparent in residents' reactions to the family and friends of service workers, who were not always viewed in the same positive terms as the workers themselves. For instance, in answer to my question about whether there was a rule against nannies using the pool for their own leisure, Claire expressed discomfort about the prospect of workers' families coming into the neighborhood:

> I don't know what the feeling of the community would be. It wouldn't bother me personally, unless people were getting out of hand. Or—now this is not very nice— but unless it was attracting some sort of riff-raff into the community. You know, that's another issue, too, that had never occurred to me. That if other family members were coming in, then that would be an issue that I think a lot of people would have a hard time with.

Others affirmed this feeling in relation to general neighborhood sentiment: "If they brought their whole family in, I'm not sure that would . . . go over" (Nancy).

Many of those I asked about whether live-in domestic workers had friends or family members visit them at their workplace responded with considerable surprise or anxiety about this possibility. These reactions suggested that these residents had not thought much about where the workers had come from or what the circumstances of their lives were outside the neighborhood. Other discussions about the service workers affirmed this point; in one case, one resident described watching the domestic worker from next door with her husband and child as she was leaving work and said she found herself thinking, "They look just like a regular family":

> I see them putting their child in, and they have a baby seat. . . . And she was talking to him, I think it must have been, in hushed tones about her day, and stuff like that. It was just very . . . you know, a very usual domestic kind of scene. . . . It was a surprise to my system to see her in that role. (Anne)

Because the workers had such a limited, defined role within the neighborhood as service personnel—and because the residents' relationship to them was generally limited to that of an employer or potential employer—it would have been easy to forget all the other aspects of the workers' lives and particularly how they fitted into other social contexts such as their own family and friendship networks. This perception obscured the extent to which those employed in service occupations were embedded in social networks outside Ridgewood and the extent to which the friends and families of workers had become part of the social landscape within Ridgewood insofar as they offered rides, brought lunch, or came to visit. Like those entering the community to drum up business, workers' friends and family members were associated with the service economy but might not be easily legible as such.

The ambiguities of the legible signs of whose presence was connected to the service economy rather than being random or pernicious in intent almost certainly contributed to the anxieties about security in Ridgewood. Recall that the increasing presence of bad cars was a key factor in residents' decision to try to gate out random strangers. In fact, there must have been a significant amount of automobile traffic associated with all the service labor in the neighborhood. There were the vehicles of the workers themselves but also the cars of those who gave rides to workers without transportation, those who were drumming up business, and friends and family of workers who came to meet them in the neighborhood. Most of these vehicles probably did not fit the profile of those that belonged to community residents, and any of them had the potential to generate anxiety insofar as they carried the races and classes of people that many residents associated with criminality. As residents in this neighborhood increase their consumption of services,[17] they can expect to see a greater proliferation of bad cars in the area.

The growing household service economy is generating new social heterogeneity within and near suburban areas like Ridgewood that have formerly been spatially segregated by race and class. The Ridgewood case suggests that two kinds of "fortressing" or "border" practices may develop in response: first, an interest in the physical fortification of boundaries; and second, social regulations to sharpen the distinctions between workers and strangers. However, neither of these kinds of practices had been fully effective in containing the social complexity of the household service economy in Ridgewood. Much as the residents of this community tried to differentiate between the workers they wanted to keep hiring and the strangers they feared and wanted to keep out, these categories could not be fully disentangled in practice.

Fortressing and the Household Service Economy

The bifurcated, service-oriented economy in the suburbs is creating new interdependencies between those who consume services and those who provide them. To some extent, service workers and their middle-class employers enable each other's well-being, a relationship that Sarah Mahler (1995) characterizes as symbiotic. For instance, employment in neighborhoods like Ridgewood provides workers who are immigrants with a livelihood and work conditions that can be preferable to those in other industries in which many Latino immigrants work in Southern California, such as agriculture or textile manufacturing. In return, service workers make possible the standard of living that suburban residents enjoy. Housekeepers, nannies, and gardeners permit home owners to have large houses and complex landscaping that require a lot of labor for upkeep. They permit the "liberation" of middle-class women from the unpleasant or routine aspects of domestic labor[18] and in so doing provide two-parent households the possibility of a dual-income, dual-career family, as well as the wealth that accompanies it. At a symbolic level, they give their employers the prestige that accompanies having servants and a certain style of house and garden.

Service workers and their employers in the Ridgewood context had developed this kind of interdependent relationship at an individual level. Less obvious but equally important was the interdependency between Santa Ana and Irvine, the communities in which service workers lived and those in which they were employed. Much as residents of Ridgewood wanted to withdraw from Santa Ana's Latino communities, the household service economy bound them economically and even spatially together. The way of life in Ridgewood rested on the existence of a Santa Ana nearby, and vice versa.

These interdependencies are not without their complications, as this study illustrates. The employment of service labor in communities like Ridgewood challenged social geographies in a number of ways that contributed to the anxieties that appeared to underlie the popular desire to fortify neighborhood boundaries with walls and gates. First, residents did not express concern about Latinos entering their community to work, but the category of "workers" was not always static or self-evident. That is, although residents of Ridgewood were confident that they could tell who was a worker by the visible performance of work, they could not identify which people were potential workers, those who transported workers, those who comprised workers' social connections, or even workers in their time off. This indeterminacy contributed to residents' anxieties about the growing number of bad cars in the neighborhood and the permeability of neighborhood boundaries to those whose presence they could not explain.

The other challenge issued from the spatial proximity and growth of nearby working-class Latino residential neighborhoods, trends that Ridgewood residents interpreted as a sign of the decline that might eventually bring crime and lower property values in Irvine as well. An irony about such a vision of the future is that the economic transition from manufacturing to service that has challenged Santa Ana in recent years had not deterred Irvine's economic prosperity and growth in the past several decades at all. On the contrary, Irvine residents had benefited not only from the high-tech, globalized economy but also from the poorly paid labor of workers who lived in Santa Ana. However, those in Ridgewood who understood the transitions occurring around them in racial rather than macroeconomic terms appeared to conclude that any influx of Latinos spelled bad news for a region's economy and social order.

These two challenges to social geography appeared to contribute strongly to Ridgewood residents' anxieties about the future, about the security of their property and their potential to maintain a way of life insulated from urban ills. They responded to these anxieties by "forting up" not only with new forms of border security but also with informal social regulations, both of which might be considered "fortressing institutions" that function to regulate social boundaries.[19]

In short, the Ridgewood case illustrates how the consumption of household services among suburban residents helped *create* those circumstances from which they felt it necessary to defend themselves. What is less apparent from this case study is the strength of the relationship between the household service economy and fortressing. The kinds of anxieties Ridgewood residents felt about security and social heterogeneity developed within a complex context in Southern California in which racial tensions have run high with the demographic transformations of immigration, particularly after the 1992 civil unrest in Los Angeles. It may be impossible to disentangle the fears that appear to accompany the household service economy from more general middle-class white anxieties about race, class, and social order. Similarly, the motivation to add gates in any community has complex social and historical roots, such as historical patterns of suburban segregation, widespread beliefs about the correlation between property values and social homogeneity, and the historical anti-urbanism of the suburbs (as discussed earlier). Although Ridgewood residents often articulated the rationale for gating in terms of security, the actual values and beliefs that made gating appear an attractive option were surely also informed by some of these more general cultural trends.

Can we expect suburban communities to develop into "cities of walls"[20] in response to a bifurcated economy in which household services proliferate? Extrapolating from the findings of this study, there appears to be a possibility that the shifts in social geography that accompany the household service economy will generate more suburban fortressing. The extent to which this occurs will depend on a number of factors, such as the extent to which household services continue to become normalized as part of middle-class suburban life. Not all regions in the United States have developed the same forms or degree of commodified social reproduction as Southern California.[21] The regional variations in how social reproduction is being accomplished may have some relationship to immigrant settlement patterns. That is, household services appear to be most common in coastal or border regions with significant immigrant populations.[22] Immigrant settlement patterns also appear to correlate roughly with the metropolitan regions where Blakely and Snyder (1997) found gated communities to be most prevalent, such as Los Angeles, New York, Miami, Houston, and Chicago; more study is needed to examine this relationship and the potential role that service economies play in it. Finally, whether more suburban communities "fort up" will also depend upon the existence of social and legal obstacles such as those apparent in the Ridgewood community, which has developed some fortressing institutions but has not (to date) actually become a private, gated community. That is, legal obstacles to privatizing spaces that are now public as well as grassroots opposition to gating may hinder the retreat of suburban communities into private fortresses.

Notes

1. Santa Ana had a population of 45,533 in 1950 (Haas 1991) and 305,800 in 1996 (California State Department of Finance).
2. This measurement was based on the proportion of those with Spanish surnames (Haas 1991, 257).
3. U.S. Census 2000.
4. See Rocco (1996) about the economic bases for population shifts in several Los Angeles neighborhoods, which outlines in greater detail the kinds of processes I report here.
5. For instance, the state of California's Labor Market Information Division, "Orange MSA Annual Average Labor Force and Industry Employment" (available at http://www.calmis.ca.gov/) documents that service-sector jobs more than doubled in Orange County from 1983 to 1999 and that textile and food products (nondurable goods) were the only manufacturing divisions to gain jobs during this same time period.
6. Coethnic markets and social networks comprise other important factors in the continuing pattern of immigrant settlement in Santa Ana. Enrico Marcelli (2001) has recently found, however, that job growth is a critical factor in understanding immigrant settlement, a critical piece of the "puzzle" of rapid economic and demographic change.

7. The categories listed here and amalgams of those respondents used during interviews. Many respondents used the phrasing "renters" (with one variation of "apartment dwellers" [Jeff]) to refer to people from nearby neighborhoods that they perceived to be lower class, although high rents in these apartment complexes would not have permitted any genuinely poor residents. "Teenagers" was also a common phrasing, with many respondents clarifying that they thought the "kids" or "teens" responsible for burglaries in the community lived either is the neighborhood or nearby. The category of "strangers" was less commonly articulated in exactly this manner. I have adopted this term to capture a range of descriptions of people of a "different element" (Mary, Cheryl) who are "not from Irvine." (Nancy) who "have no business" being in the neighborhood (Marilyn), who either randomly "straggle" into the neighborhood (Michelle), or who are "hardened burglar types" (Mary) that break in "at night with a mask" (Gerry).

8. I found is very difficult to get people to articulate explicitly their assumptions about race and class as they related to criminality, undoubtedly because there is no polite language available with which to talk about these things among the middle classes. Race and class differentiation are sticky issues in a culture that has mythologized the "color-blind society" in which everyone is part of the all-encompassing middle class. One of the consequences of these myths is the frequent coding or translation of race and class description, or their omission altogether, such that they are only present in the silences.

9. For the record, Los Angeles was historically a "small, largely Hispanic backwater" town (Laslett 1996, 39) and even 90 years ago incorporated substantial ethnic-racial diversity, including native and immigrant Mexicans, native and immigrant Europeans, African-Americans, and Japanese and Chinese immigrants. However, there has been significant growth of the Latino population in recent decades, from 18.3% of the population in 1970 to 37.8% in 1990 (U.S. Census Bureau 1970, 1990).

10. This discourse also appears to rest on an implicit representation of Los Angeles and Santa Ana as places of danger and decline, a representation that simplified the extent to which both cities are in fact socially and economically complex, places of significant racial diversity and great wealth as well as poverty. References to these cities apparently did not attempt literal description as much as they served a symbolic purpose in a narrative about the need to maintain and protect boundaries between "here" and "there," between "us" and "them." This kind of narrative has also emerged as a common theme in several others studies on representations of central cities among suburbanites (Till 1993; Low 2001).

11. See Patricia Zavella (1997, 137) about white citizens' sense of California as "paradise lost"—"one of the cultural undertones of the current racial tensions we are experiencing in the state today, especially regarding Latinos."

12. The recent growth of Santa Ana's immigrant enclave had a number of likely structural causes, including immigration policy reforms, social networks, and coethnic markets, as well as the macroeconomic shift from a manufacturing to a service economy, with a concurrent increase in the consumption of household services.

13. Gerry had been living in Orange County for a number of years before his daughter came to live with him.

14. There is a strong historical precedent for servants to be suspected of property crimes, so I was a bit surprised to find the strength of the faith Ridgewood residents articulated about the moral fiber of the service workers. This may have been another example of something that they did not think socially appropriate to articulate.

15. The perspective of service workers—such as how they perceived social regulation at work and how they strategically negotiated the "rules"—is developed more fully elsewhere (Maher 1999).

16. The only exceptions that I discovered were the few live-in workers who took walks in the evening at about the time that residents would expect day workers to be walking to the

bus stop. However, these workers did not ever swim in the community pool or engage in other activities that would be less ambiguously leisure, despite their full-time residence and the fact that they spent many of their hours off within the neighborhood.

17. I did not formally poll residents about the shifts in their service consumption, although during the interviews, it was repeatedly suggested that it was relatively unusual to hire a housekeeper, nanny, or gardener until the mid-1980s. This information is consistent with census statistics on service-sector employment, as described earlier.

18. Romero (1992) notes that this liberation is one that does not in any way challenge the notion that domestic labor is women's work; instead of challenging patriarchy, it simply shifts the responsibility to working-class women, who are often responsible for the domestic labor in their paid position as well as the unpaid labor in their own homes.

19. I am grateful to an anonymous reviewer for suggesting the concept of *fortressing institutions.*

20. The phrase "a city of walls" comes from Caldeira (2000).

21. For instance, studies from the Bureau of Labor Statistics suggest that the number of people employed in private household services actually decreased in the South and North Central census regions between 1982 and 2000 (Bureau of Labor Statistics 1983, 10; Bureau of Labor Statistics 2002, 13). Although these figures probably undercount the number of immigrant household workers, they do indicate regional variation.

22. The nature of this relationship may not be unidirectional. That is, although some studies have noted that immigrants move where there are jobs, there is also a possibility that different kinds of consumption practices develop in places with a surplus of unskilled labor.

References

Alba, R. D., J. R. Logan, B. J. Stults, G. Marzan, and W. Zhang. 1999. Immigrant groups in the suburbs: A reexamination of suburbanization and spatial assimilation. *American Sociological Review* 64 (3): 446–60.

Baldassare, M. 1992. Suburban communities. *Annual Review of Sociology* 18:475–94.

Blakely, E. J., and M. G. Snyder, 1997. *Fortress America: Gated communities in the United States.* Washington, DC: Brookings Institution Press; Cambridge, MA: Lincoln Institute of Land Policy.

Burawoy, M. 1991. Reconstructing social theories. In *Ethnography unbound: Power and resistance in the modern metropolis,* edited by M. Burawoy, A. Burton, H. A. Ferguson, K. J. Fox, J. Gamson, N. Gartrell, L. Hurst, C. Kutzman, L. Salzinger, J. Schiffman, and S. Ui, 1–8. Berkeley: Univ. of California Press.

———. 2000. Introduction: Reading for the global. In *Global ethnography: Forces, connections, and imaginations in a postmodern world,* edited by M. Burawoy, J. A. Blum, S. George, Z. Gille, T. Gowan, L. Hanen, M. Klawiter, S. H. Lopez, S. O'Riain, and M. Thayer, 1–40. Berkeley: Univ. of California Press.

Bureau of Labor Statistics. 1983. Geographic profile of employment and unemployment, 1982. Bulletin 2170. Washington, DC: U.S. Department of Labor.

———. 2002. Geographic profile of employment and unemployment, 2000. Bulletin 2550. Washington, DC: U.S. Department of Labor.

Caldeira, T.P.R. 1996. Fortified enclaves: The new urban segregation. *Public Culture* 8(2): 303–28.

———. 2000. *City of walls: Crime, segregation, and citizenship in Sao Paulo.* Berkeley: Univ. of California Press.

Colen, S. 1990. Housekeeping for the green card: West Indian household workers, the state, and stratified reproduction in New York City. In *At work in homes: Household workers in world perspective,* edited by R. Sanjek and S. Colen, 89–118. Washington, DC: American Anthropological Society.

Davis, M. 1992. *City of quartz: Excavating the future in Los Angeles.* New York: Vintage.

Dodson, M. 1989. Where is the county's "Mason-Dixon" line? Start at Costa Mesa freeway and meander south. *Los Angeles Times, Orange County Edition,* Metro, 27 August, 2:1.

Glassner, B. 1999. *The culture of fear.* New York: Basic Books.

Glenn, E. N. 1992. From servitude to service work: Historical continuities in the racial division of paid reproductive labor. *Signs: Journal of Women in Culture and Society* 18(1): 1–43.

Gutierrez, D. G. 1995. *Walls and mirrors: Mexican-Americans, Mexican immigrants, and the politics of ethnicity.* Berkeley: Univ. of California Press.

Haas, L. 1991. Grass-roots protest and the politics of planning. In *Postsuburban California: The transformation of Orange County since World War II,* edited by R. Kling, S. Olin, and M. Poster, 254–80. Berkeley: Univ. of California Press.

Hondagneu-Sotelo, P. 1994. Regulating the unregulated: Domestic workers' social networks. *Social Problems* 41:201–15.

———. 2001. *Doméstica: Immigrant women cleaning and caring in the shadows of affluence,* Berkeley: Univ. of California Press.

Jackson, K. 1985. *Crabgrass frontier: The suburbanization of the United States.* New York: Oxford Univ. Press.

Judd, D. R. 1995. The rise of new walled cities. In *Spatial practices,* edited by H. Ligget and D. C. Perry, 144–66. Thousand Oaks, CA: Sage.

Kennedy, D. J. 1995. Residential associations as state actors: Regulating the impact of gated communities on nonmembers. *Yale Law Journal* 105, 3:761–793.

Kuper, H. 1947. *The uniform of colour: A study of white-black relationships in Swaziland.* Johannesburg: Witwatersrand Univ. Press.

Laslett, J. H. M. 1996. Historical perspectives: Immigration and the rise of a distinctive urban region, 1900–1970. In *Ethnic Los Angeles,* by R. Waldinger and M. Bozorgmehr, 39–75. New York: Russell Sage Foundation.

Low, S. 2001. The edge and the center: Gated communities and the discourse of urban fear. *American Anthropologist* 103 (1): 45–58.

Lowe, L. 1996. *Immigrant acts: On Asian American cultural politics.* Durham, NC: Duke Univ. Press.

Maher, K. H. 1999. A stranger in the house: American ambivalence about immigrant labor. Ph.D. diss., University of California, Irvine.

Mahler, S. 1992. First stop: Suburbia. *Report on the Americas* 26 (1): 20–25.

———. 1995. *Salvadorans in suburbia: Symbiosis and conflict.* Needham Heights, MA: Allyn & Bacon.

Marcelli, E. 2001. From the barrio to the "burbs": Immigration and urban sprawl in Southern California. Working paper no. 32, University of California-San Diego, Center for Comparative Immigration Studies.

Marcuse, P. 1997. The enclave, the citadel, and the ghetto: What has changed in the post-Fordist U.S. city. *Urban Affairs Review* 33 (2): 228–64.

Massey, D. S., and N. A. Denton, 1993. *American apartheid; Segregation and the making of the underclass.* Cambridge, MA: Harvard Univ. Press.

McKenzie, E. 1994. *Privatopia: Homeowner associations and the rise of residential private government.* New Haven, CT: Yale Univ. Press.

Parel, R. 2000. *Suburban immigrant communities: Assessments of key characteristics and needs.* Chicago: Fund for Immigrants and Refugees.

Reich, R. B. 1991. Secession of the successful. *New York Times,* 20 January, 6:16, 42.

Rocco, R. A. 1996. Latino Los Angeles: Reframing boundaries/borders. In *The city: Los Angeles, and urban theory at the end of the twentieth century,* edited by A. J. Scott and E. W. Soja, 365–89. Berkeley: Univ. of California Press.

Romero, M. 1992. *Maid in the U.S.A.* New York: Routledge.

Sassen, S. 1990. Economic restructuring and the American city. *Annual Review of Sociology* 16:465–90.

———. 1991. *The global city.* Princeton, NJ: Princeton Univ. Press.

———. 1998. *Globalization and its discontents.* New York: New Press.

Schiesl, M. J. 1991. Designing the model community: The Irvine company and suburban development, 1950–88. In *Postsuburban California: The transformation of Orange County since World War II,* edited by R. Kling, S. Olin, and M. Poster, 55–91. Berkeley: Univ. of California Press.

Scott, A. J., and E. W. Soja, eds. 1996. *The city: Los Angeles and urban theory at the end of the twentieth century.* Berkeley: Univ. of California Press.

Till, K. 1993. Neotraditional towns and urban villages: The cultural production of a geography of "otherness." *Environment and Planning D: Society and Space* 11:709–32.

U.S. Census Bureau, 1970. *California: Characteristics of the population. General social and economic characteristics.* Washington, DC: U.S. Census Bureau.

————. 1980. *California: Characteristics of the population. General social and economic characteristics.* Washington, DC: U.S. Census Bureau.

————. 1990. *California: Characteristics of the population. General social and economic characteristics.* Washington, DC: U.S. Census Bureau.

Uttal, L., and M. Tuominen, 1999. Tenuous relationships: Exploitation, emotion, and racial ethnic significance in paid child care work. *Gender & Society* 13 (6): 758–80.

Waldinger, R. 1989. Immigration and urban change. *Annual Review of Sociology* 15:211–32.

Zavella, P. 1997. The tables are turned: Immigration, poverty, and social conflict in California communities. In *Immigrants out! The new nativism and the anti-immigrant impulse in the United States,* edited by J. F. Perea, 136–61. New York: New York Univ. Press.

22

Peter Eisinger

THE AMERICAN CITY IN THE AGE OF TERROR

The terror attacks of September 11, 2001, on New York and Washington, D.C., were fundamentally challenges to American values, optimism, and global economic dominance, but they must also be seen as assaults on cities as urban places. In targeting these open and unprotected places, populated by a large, socially diverse workforce engaged in the knowledge-intensive occupations of the new cosmopolitan economy in signature buildings that had come to represent some of the most powerful symbols of modern urban achievement, the terrorists took aim at the very essence of American cities. It would hardly be surprising under the circumstances, therefore, if Americans did not begin to wonder in the aftermath of the attacks about the security, role, and importance of urban life and forms in modern society. Yet as the so-called war on terror proceeds, the enduring impacts on cities of those terrible events of September 11 remain unclear.

In the immediate period after the attacks, certain commentators were quick to predict the end of American urban life as we know it. Some believed that fearful cities would respond primarily through strategies of repressive fortification. Peter Marcuse (2002) was among the most emphatic of these pessimists, warning of the erosion of urban democracy, the closing of public spaces, and the emergence of the citadel city, a fortress protected by "pervasive surveillance." Others, however, although just as convinced that there would be deep and lasting effects of the attacks, offered a polar scenario to the so-called hardening of the city, arguing that terrorism would simply hasten patterns of

Peter Eisinger, "The American City in the Age of Terror: A Preliminary Assessment of the Effects of September 11," *Urban Affairs Review,* Vol. 40, No. 1, September 2004, pp. 115–130.

business and residential diffusion that had long been in evidence. No one would build tall buildings anymore, for no one would wish to work or live in them; firms would increasingly move their headquarters and back office functions to suburban locations, joining their out-migrating labor force; business travel and tourism investment would diminish. The terror attacks would simply accelerate the stampede to the far suburbs. Cities would be left struggling for jobs and revenues (Berube and Rivlin 2002; Fainstein 2002; Kantor 2002).

Not everyone believes that American cities were forever altered in profound ways by the 2001 terror attacks. Many observers have long been convinced that the enduring feature of great American urban centers is their resilience. Over half a century ago, E.B. White wrote of New York City that it "is peculiarly constructed to absorb almost anything that comes along" and that New Yorkers survive the myriad challenges and threats of urban life with "a sort of perpetual muddling through" ([1949] 1999, 23, 33). That view is shared by many contemporary social scientists. Although Glaeser and Shapiro (2002) doubt that the commercial neighborhoods below Canal Street in Manhattan will be rebuilt without significant public subsidies, they believe that the more general effects of terror on New York and other U.S. cities will be small. Hank Savitch (2003) acknowledges both short-term economic costs of the attacks in New York and the breadth of fear of future terror among the American public, but in the end, he argues, the impact on cities has been negligible. The American city has not been transformed into a garrison state.

James Harrigan and Phillipe Martin (2002) make a more explicit argument for the resilience of cities in the face of catastrophic events, including terror attacks: Cities exist in the first place because of agglomeration economies. Applying separate simulation models based on labor pooling (where employers derive economic benefits from the proximity of a large and diverse workforce) and core/periphery assumptions (which take account of the desire of firms to be near customers and suppliers to minimize transportation costs), Harrigan and Martin show that the economic advantages derived from concentration of resources are powerful enough to overcome the costs or "tax" of terror events, not only in New York but in other large cities as well.

The effort to assess the impacts of terror on American cities is an on-going enterprise. No examination so far has marshaled much empirical evidence on the matter, however. It is appropriate, therefore, to take stock periodically and to do so from a variety of different angles. This note examines some of the evidence to date relating to the impact on U.S. cities in three broad areas: government and policy, the economy, and what may be called simply the texture of *city life*.

Government and Policy

Within days of the collapse of the World Trade Center towers, the National League of Cities (NLC) polled 456 of its member cities to find out how they were responding to the appearance of massive terror on American soil.

Communities of all sizes and in all parts of the country, it turned out, had set about immediately to secure water supplies, assign guards to critical transportation facilities and government buildings, alert hospitals and public health departments to stand by, and convene officials to discuss emergency plans (Pionke 2001). Mobilization of local public safety resources was not unexpected: Not only did a majority of communities already have terrorism contingency plans in place, but as New Haven Mayor John DeStefano has pointed out, when disaster strikes, "We're the people who show up" (Peirce 2003).

These early responses were simply a foretaste of what have come to be significant new, continuing, and costly burdens borne by municipal governments as they have sought to respond to public demands for security (Wildasin 2002). The emerging institutionalization of these new responsibilities is clear from another survey conducted nearly a year after the attacks by the U.S. Conference of Mayors (USCM). To deal with their concerns about terror attacks, local officials, not just in New York and Washington but in cities of every size in every region (Hoene, Baldassare, and Brennan 2002), began routinely to reassign police officers to guard public buildings and public utilities, conduct vulnerability assessments of likely targets, expand biological and chemical surveillance through increased testing of water supplies and installation of hardware detection devices, increase training of first responders, and switch over to interoperable communications systems among fire and police departments (U.S. Conference of Mayors 2002a).

Because Congress did not appropriate any funds to help state or local governments defray the costs of these new responsibilities until March 2003, cities were reliant entirely on their own resources for nearly two years after September 11. None of this new activity came cheaply. Surveys conducted by the USCM estimate that cities had to spend $2.1 billion of their own funds in 2002 alone for first-responder overtime wages, new equipment, and additional personnel (U.S. Conference of Mayors 2002b). When the Department of Homeland Security raised the terror alert warning from yellow to orange as the war in Iraq began in March 2003, large and small cities all across the country increased their security spending by an estimated nationwide total of $70 million per week (U.S. Conference of Mayors 2003b). These expenditures came on top of existing homeland security outlays. One result of these added burdens is that 42% of the cities contacted in the summer 2002 NLC survey reported that they would be less able to meet their financial needs as a result of the additional security costs after September 11 (Baldassare and Hoene 2002).

By the time Congress finally began to pass federal programs to help defray these locally borne costs, city leaders were already deeply frustrated by the slow pace at which Washington had come to their aid. In the immediate period of shock and resolve after the attacks, there had been an expectation that federal, state, and local governments would come together quickly in a new and tighter partnership to provide security and share the financial burdens. But what has emerged is a nexus of new intergovernmental relationships where the rhetoric of partnership is burdened by feelings of disappointment and neglect.

Mayors complained not only about the complete absence of federal aid but also that the Department of Homeland Security provided no guidelines about how to respond to the terror alert system when it changes from yellow to orange (Sostek 2003). Until January 2004, there were no federal funds to offset these particular added costs, nor are there yet federal guidelines pertaining to different levels of risk that different cities might face and the corresponding steps they might take.

On a broader level, most local officials believed, at least in the early period, that intergovernmental coordination had not improved or had improved only slightly since the attacks. Only a minority of local officials polled by the NLC believed that their local government had increased its coordination with the federal government "a great deal" (8%) or "a good amount" (20%) (Baldassare and Hoene 2002).

At the heart of the new intergovernmental partnership is the issue of federal aid to defray the local costs of increased security. Although President Bush asked Congress in January 2002 for $3.5 billion for training and equipment for local first-responders, no money was actually appropriated until 18 months later, when Congress provided $750 million in direct grants to local firefighters (see Table 8.1). Shortly thereafter, Congress passed a host of programs to finance equipment acquisition, training, personnel costs, and planning by local governments, including the Urban Area Security Initiative, the State Homeland Security Program, and a Wartime Supplemental Appropriation/Critical Infrastructure program.[1]

Except for the Assistance to Firefighters, all these programs provide money to local governments—municipalities, counties, and special authorities— through the states. In most cases, Congress required the states to pass through 80% of their allocation to local government applicants within 45 or 60 days,

Table 8.1 Federal Funding to State and Local Governments for Homeland Security (in millions)

	$ for Fiscal Year 2003	$ for Fiscal Year 2004
Direct aid to local governments	750	750
Assistance of firefighters		
Pass-through aid to local governments[a]		
Urban Area Security Initiative	100	725
Urban Area Security Initiative supplement. FY 2003 budget	700[b]	
State Homeland Security Program	566	1,685
Wartime supplemental appropriation, federal first responder/critical infrastructure	1,500	
Law enforcement terrorism prevention		500
Citizen Corps	35	

[a] In all but one of the cases, 80% of the allocation of the pass-through funds must, by law, be in the hands of local governments within 45 days to 60 days, depending on the program. The one exception is the Critical Infrastructure Program, in which only 50% must be passed through. The state retains the other half.

[b] Of this supplemental sum, $500 million was to be allocated to 30 selected cities, $75 million was for port security, and $65 million was for mass-transit security. Where ports or mass transit systems are run by special authorities, those jurisdictions received the bulk of the funds.

depending on the program. If local political leaders have been angry at the federal government for its perceived tardiness in providing aid, they are even more unhappy with their respective states. They claim in USCM surveys that states routinely miss the pass-through deadlines, Furthermore, mayors contend that they have little or no voice in influencing the allocation process at the state level and that the states favor counties and special authorities over municipalities for emergency response funding (U.S. Conference of Mayors 2003a, 2004).

In sum, the first government impact of the terror attacks on cities has been that municipal governments have taken on new and costly security responsibilities in an intergovernmental environment in which the state and federal partners have often been perceived as both dilatory and unresponsive. Far from drawing the local, state, and federal levels closer together in a common effort to ensure against further terrorist attacks, the intergovernmental funding nexus created new burdens, frustrations, and resentments in cities across the nation.

Economic Effects

In the months immediately following the September 11 catastrophe, New York City lost more than 100,000 jobs, an estimated $3 billion in tax revenues for fiscal year (FY) 2002 and 2003, and approximately $4.5 billion in income—all from diminished business activity and travel (New York City Partnership 2002). Nearly 8,000 jobs in the theater industry alone were lost, as were approximately 12,000 restaurant jobs. The securities industry and retail trade experienced even larger employment losses (Fiscal Policy Institute 2001). Altogether, the attacks in New York cost the city about $83 billion in lost output, wages, business closings, and spending reductions, although these losses are being offset to some degree by roughly $67 billion in insurance and federal assistance, as well as the increased economic activity that resulted from the destruction, such as clean-up and new construction (Government Accounting Office 2002).

Economic impacts have extended far beyond the borders of New York and Washington, D.C., of course, affecting the national and global economies. A review conducted by the Government Accounting Office of studies of the domestic economic impacts of the terror attacks reports a cost to the nation's 315 metropolitan areas in 2001 alone of $191 billion from diminished economic activity (Government Accounting Office 2002, 3). Various analysts have predicted a variety of other economic effects in urban areas around the country, including drastic reductions in tourism and business travel (Fainstein 2002; Berube and Rivlin 2002), an end to unsubsidized office tower construction, and accelerated rates of business and residential dispersal to the suburbs (Mills 2002; Marcuse 2002), and reduced demand for central city office space (PricewaterhouseCoopers 2003). The rising cost of terrorism insurance coverage may also have a chilling effect on financing for high-profile buildings and on business profits.

An analysis of the economic impacts on cities more than two years after the attacks suggests a more nuanced picture than the vision of urban economic desertification. The analysis is complicated by factors in the national economy that have no connection to the events of September 11, including the hangover from the bursting of the Internet stock market bubble and the movement of jobs offshore. Also, the economic downturn that was in process when the terror events occurred, as well as the recovery that has set in since that time have made it difficult to isolate the independent effects of terrorism. Nevertheless, some of the data that follow are suggestive: they indicate on balance that cities—not just the attack sites but all cities—suffered initially but that economic recovery in the subsequent two years has been substantial and widespread. Severe lasting economic effects on cities that can be traced to fear of future terrorist attacks are difficult to discern.[2]

Consider hotel occupancy rates. Table 8.2 reports data on fluctuations in hotel occupancy in the top 25 largest U.S. metropolitan hotel markets for the

Table 8.2 Hotel Occupancy Rates in the 25 Largest Hotel Markets, 1999–2003 (October)

Description	% 1999	% 2000	% 2001	% 2002	% 2003
High-risk metro areas					
New York	90.8	86.7	70.9	80.2	84.1
Los Angeles	71.6	76.0	59.3	69.0	72.8
Chicago	77.1	76.7	62.6	66.4	68.1
San Francisco	85.7	85.8	57.0	67.8	69.1
Washington, D.C.	80.4	81.4	62.9	70.0	76.6
Average	81.1	81.3	62.5	70.7	74.1
Lower-risk metro areas					
Anaheim	63.4	71.3	53.0	61.8	65.3
Atlanta	70.4	67.4	59.2	59.6	59.7
Boston	86.8	87.9	66.9	77.1	74.8
Dallas	68.7	72.4	54.4	58.0	59.3
Denver	66.2	67.1	57.1	58.6	59.1
Detroit	67.5	69.7	59.8	59.3	55.6
Houston	65.4	64.3	63.1	62.6	58.4
Miami	69.6	69.4	49.7	60.6	64.7
Minneapolis	73.6	74.0	61.7	66.3	67.4
Nashville	69.1	67.1	59.2	62.2	62.4
New Orleans	78.5	75.3	64.6	72.7	65.6
Norfolk	60.0	57.8	56.6	58.2	71.8
Oahu	72.6	75.9	54.0	69.4	73.6
Orlando	74.4	70.6	52.9	58.9	62.8
Philadelphia	74.9	74.0	67.5	70.5	73.0
Phoenix	67.7	66.2	57.7	60.2	62.6
San Diego	71.0	73.4	61.5	64.3	68.0
Seattle	67.2	70.3	57.6	63.7	63.0
St. Louis	65.3	67.1	63.4	64.2	63.2
Tampa	59.4	60.4	54.6	56.9	56.5
Average	69.6	70.1	58.7	63.3	64.3

Source: Cornell University School of Hotel Administration (unpublished data, 2003).

years 1999 through 2003. The figures in the table report average occupancy rates for October of each year, first for the five metropolitan areas that might be considered at particularly high risk of terror attacks and then for the remaining twenty lower-risk largest hotel markets.[3] Note that average occupancy rates were highest for both categories of cities in October 2000 and then fell precipitously in October 2001 in the wake of the attacks.[4] Although the drop in occupancy in the high-risk cities was greater than elsewhere (on average, 23% vs. 16%), recovery has been swifter (18.5% vs. 9.5%).[5] Occupancy rates have not returned to their pre-2001 levels in any market, but they have significantly rebounded, particularly among the higher-risk metropolitan areas.[6]

A different set of economic consequences of the terror attacks has to do with business location decisions. In particular, analysts predicted that businesses would be reluctant to seek new locations in densely concentrated downtown buildings and that departures of city firms for suburban sites would accelerate. If business reluctance to locate or stay in the central city has increased significantly, then one should see increasing office vacancy rates in central cities and signs of pressure on suburban office markets, reflected in decreasing vacancy rates or increasing office supply in the form of new construction.

In fact, however, office vacancy rates in central cities and suburbs have both been increasing since the middle of 2000, a trend related not to fear of terror but to speculative building in the 1990s. Furthermore, national data, reported quarterly, show that suburban office vacancy rates were consistently higher than central city rates between the third quarter of 2000 and the third quarter of 2002, that is, from one year before to one year after the terror attacks (CB Richard Ellis 2002). Between the month of the attacks, September 2001 and the end of September 2002, office vacancy rates in central city downtowns went from 10.4% to 12.9%, an increase of 24%. By contrast, suburban vacancy rates went from 13% to 16.5%, an increase of 26.9%. Notably, midtown Manhattan and Washington, D.C., were among the five places in the nation with the lowest downtown office vacancy rates at the end of 2002.

It is true that hundreds of firms in lower Manhattan were displaced by the destruction of the World Trade Center. The city lost about 13 million square feet of office space (PricewaterhouseCoopers 2002). Many firms relocated in the immediate aftermath to midtown and many more went to the suburbs. But the New York City Partnership has concluded that most businesses that were dislocated had actually returned to lower Manhattan a year later (New York City Partnership 2002). Of the 50 companies that had occupied the most office space in and around the World Trade Center at the time of the attack, 54% had returned to downtown locations by September 2002. Another 26% had relocated to midtown Manhattan. These data are consistent with the conclusion of the U.S. General Accounting Office that many of the jobs that left New York City after the attack had returned by May 2002 (Government Accounting Office 2002).

National data on new office construction show declining numbers of new office starts beginning in mid-2001, before the terror attacks, as developers responded to the office surplus (*Wall Street Journal*, January 23, 2004). In each successive quarter of 2002, new starts declined both for central city and suburban sites after September 11 (CB Richard Ellis 2002). If there had been a mass business exodus from dense downtown office concentrations, one should have seen signs of pressure or responses in suburban markets. By 2003, however, PricewaterhouseCoopers saw instead a glut of empty suburban office buildings (PricewaterhouseCoopers 2003). They conclude that although many businesses now believe that it is unwise to concentrate all key decision makers in one place, "no sea change has occurred. Suburbs haven't benefited conspicuously at the expense of cities" (PricewaterhouseCoopers 2002, 12).

If suburbs have not gained significantly in the competition with central cities for business investment, neither do they appear to have gained as locations for federal facilities. The Government Services Administration, responsible for the planning and construction of federal courthouses and office buildings, continues its Good Neighbor program. Begun in 1996, the program promotes, among other things, the use of downtown locations for federal facilities. Periodic e-news bulletins on the GSA Web site indicate that new construction, building renovation, and the hosting of public events in federal buildings continue to take place in downtown locations. A list of capital projects funded by Congress in the period from 2000–2003 shows no tendency to choose suburban rather than downtown sites in metropolitan areas (www.gsa.gov).

Downtown commercial districts nationwide also seem to be thriving since the September 11 attacks. Each year, the National Trust for Historic Preservation surveys approximately 1,400 cities and towns to assess the economic health of historic and older downtown and neighborhood retail areas (National Trust for Historic Preservation 2002). Survey respondents were asked in 2002 to assess changes over the previous year in a variety of economic indicators. About three-quarters of the 370 respondents that answered the survey reported that the attacks had not had significant economic effects on businesses in their so-called Main Street districts. Specifically, almost half said that retail sales had increased over figures in 2001, nearly two-thirds reported an increase in property values, and over four-fifths said that attendance at festivals and special events had increased over the prior year (see Table 8.3). The only negative economic effects that respondents traced to September 11 were a fall-off in

Table 8.3 Main Street District Changes, 2001 to 2002

| | % of Sample Saying: | | |
	Decrease	No Change	Increase
Retail sales	3.1	49.3	47.5
Property values	5.0	30.5	64.5
Storefront occupancy rates	12.6	32.0	55.4
Attendance at festivals and special events	4.6	13.3	82.1

Source: National Trust for Historic Preservation (2002).

business at local travel agencies and greater caution among would-be small business entrepreneurs as they contemplated opening a business.

As the events of September 11 recede in time, other economic forces loom as larger influences on the fortunes of U.S. cities. This is certainly the conclusion of Berube and Rivlin, who point to immigration, globalization, and technological innovation as the more crucial economic factors in urban growth and development (2002, 3, 22). Similarly, the GAO observes that stronger-than-anticipated economic growth as the nation emerged from recession has probably mitigated the economic impacts of the terror attacks on cities (Government Accounting Office 2002).

City Life

In an article titled "Is Density Dangerous?" architect David Dixon worries that the war against terrorism might become "a war against the livability of American cities" (2002, 1). Measures to protect buildings and people, he suggests, could compromise cities' vitality, sense of community, and civic quality. These are hard to measure, of course, but Dixon's concerns evoke visions of closed-off public spaces, fortress-like buildings, constant security screenings in office buildings and mass transit stations, a forest of surveillance hardware, a heavy and constant police presence, and a general sense of dread, constraint, and foreboding.

As early as the mid-1990s, the federal government had begun to undertake some of these measures to protect its property in Washington, D.C. The result, according to the Task Force of the National Capital Planning Commission, was "an unsightly jumble of fences and barriers [that made us] look like a nation in fear" (National Capital Planning Commission 2001, Introduction). The task force called for an integrated design for the capital's monumental core, including landscaping, building setbacks, decorative street furniture, and various traffic and parking modifications. The message of the task force was that Americans must resist the impulse to build garrison cities but rather develop unobtrusive and aesthetically pleasing security measures, while maintaining an open and accessible public environment reflective of democratic values (p. 7).

In Washington, D.C., more security-related construction is under way. In a few vulnerable neighborhoods of New York City, there is also an unusual police presence and a scattering of concrete Jersey barriers. But the casual pedestrian in the American city, including in most parts of Washington, D.C., and New York, in fact, rarely encounters security measures designed to thwart murderous terrorism. The *New York Times* reports that although visitors to office buildings in New York must pass through increased security since September 11, so-called "closed buildings" are rare in other parts of the country. Even in Washington, D.C., most private commercial buildings have free access, except when there are specific terror alerts (*New York Times*, July 9, 2003).

When people gather in public places at high-profile events—a championship football game, New Year's Eve in Times Square—they are searched, and there is a heavy police presence, but people gather, nevertheless. Public political assemblies still take place as they did before terrorism struck American cities. And according to the National Restaurant Association, restaurant patronage has risen nationally every year for 12 straight years and was predicted to rise again in 2004 (www.restaurant.org/trendmapper, January 22, 2004).[7]

Survey data do show signs of public anxiety, it is true, particularly in New York, but it is diminishing. There is little indication that fear has changed the ordinary habits of daily life and entertainment in cities. In a survey conducted by the *New York Times* and CBS News in September 2003, 68% of the respondents said they were "personally very concerned about another terrorist attack in New York City" (*New York Times*, September 8, 2003). This was down from 74% in October 2001. But two-thirds (67%) said their daily routine had gotten back to normal, up from slightly over half (52%) the respondents who gave the same answer in 2001.

In an earlier poll of a national sample of slightly under 1,000 people, this one by Gallup in March 2002, only 8% of people reported being "very worried" and 31% said they were "somewhat worried" that they or members of their family might become victims of a terrorist attack (www.cbsnews.com, June 11, 2002). Gallup also polled samples of 500 people each in New York, Washington, D.C., and Oklahoma City to compare levels of fear in those cities with national patterns. Proportions saying they were very or somewhat worried in Washington, D.C., and Oklahoma City were similar to national levels, but New Yorkers were slightly more afraid.

Other survey evidence reinforces the notion that fear of terrorism among people living outside New York and Washington, D.C., is relatively low. A survey of Californians in the summer of 2002 found that 17% of people in the San Francisco Bay Area and 29% in Los Angeles thought "terrorism and security" were "a big problem" (Baldassare and Hoene 2002). In a statewide survey of Michigan of 773 residents in the summer of 2003, only 10% said that they tend to frequent malls and theaters and parks less often than they had before September 11, whereas 84% said their habits had not changed (Center for Urban Studies 2003).

If the texture and pace of city life are clouded somewhat by public anxieties about terror, the actual changes urban dwellers encounter in their daily lives in most places in the country and at most times are small and relatively unobtrusive. Most cities have not invested heavily in camera surveillance hardware. Retail and entertainment remain vibrant in most places, affected by economic fluctuations to all appearances more than by fears of terror. The urban streetscape has hardly become fortified, except in the official precincts of the nation's capital, nor is the police presence oppressive in these places. There may be threats to civil liberties in the law enforcement methods permitted under the federal Patriot Act, but measures undertaken by cities themselves do not seem to dampen political expression or public assembly, either by design or coincidence.

Conclusions

In certain respects, the September 11 attacks changed America deeply, but the fundamental character of American cities remains much as it was before that day. It would not have been unreasonable to expect that Americans might radically rethink the openness of urban places after such assaults, that security concerns would trump the free-wheeling, increasingly cosmopolitan values that make U.S. cities magnets for people from all over the world who seek opportunity. But the city-as-garrison-state has not taken form. People come and go to the cities, start businesses, stay in hotels and eat in restaurants, rent space and buy property, attend public political and entertainment events, and immigrate from abroad much as they once did before the world changed. Perhaps the biggest lesson so far about the cities in the aftermath of the terror attacks is that they are resilient.

Indeed, the cities seem, if not impervious to change, then at least highly resistant to external shocks like periodic terror events. Cities are shaped instead by much larger change agents. Immigration, global trade and travel, the business cycle, racial competition and conflict, changing tastes for urban living, and the regional and overseas cost of labor all have more to do with the character of cities in America than the fear of future attacks.

This is not to say that there have been no observable effects on cities of the experience of deadly assaults on American soil. A new, but frustrating set of intergovernmental relations is just beginning to take shape, posing new challenges to be navigated by public officials at all levels of the federal system. Local governments face new responsibilities and must develop new capacities, particularly in the area of emergency planning and risk assessment. Local law enforcement personnel must learn new habits of vigilance. Certain economic sectors were badly hurt after September 11 and are only now beginning to recover, particularly those in the travel and hospitality industry, although there is clear evidence that, barring other terrorist attacks, the worst is over. Finally, there is a new appreciation of the need to use architecture, planning, and landscaping not simply in service to efficiency and aesthetic considerations but also for security purposes. But nearly three years after the events of that September, the fundamental character of the American city—open, free-wheeling, striving, competing, diverse—is very much as it was before.

Notes

1. Cities have used funds from the Urban Area Security Initiative, which targets funds to selected high-risk urban areas, and the Wartime Supplemental/Critical Infrastructure for equipment purchases, such as mobile radios and bomb squad robots, and to cover overtime costs for security personnel. The State Homeland Security program is used primarily for equipment acquisition.
2. It is worth noting that PricewaterhouseCoopers' annual report, *Emerging Trends in Real Estate 2004* identifies Washington, D.C., and New York City as two of the top three promising real estate investment markets in the country.

3. The designation of these five metropolitan areas as high-risk is based on the facts that (1) New York and Washington, D.C., have already been attacked, (2) both cities contain other major symbolic targets, such as the White House and Wall Street, and (3) each of the other cities contains highly visible, symbolic targets or targets that have been mentioned in alert bulletins (e.g., the Golden Gate Bridge, the Sears Tower, Los Angeles International Airport).

4. The economic recession had already been cutting into the hotel business before the September attacks, but this does not account for the sharp decline. Data for August 2001 occupancy rates show that average occupancy in hotels in the five high-risk cities had fallen from 2000 levels to 73.8. This dropped after the attacks to 62.5. For the other 20 cities, the August 2001 average occupancy rate was 64.9. After the attacks, the average October rate in these cities was 58.7.

5. These are the average percentage declines from October 2000 to October 2001 and the average percentage increases from October 2001 to October 2003.

6. Analysts suggest that to some undetermined degree, the economic recession has been a brake on hotel recovery from the September 11 shock (Enz and Canina 2002).

7. A telling sign of the way plucky New Yorkers have defied the threat of terror is the appearance of an outdoor cafe in the old taxi pickup area of Grand Central station. Security concerns required barring taxis from driving under the station portico to pick up passengers. So an enterprising cocktail bar has claimed the area and placed handsome tables and chairs there in the warm weather. Where taxis once drew up to the door, drinkers now gather behind Jersey barriers on summer evenings.

References

Baldassare, Mark, and Christopher Hoene. 2002. Coping with homeland security: Perceptions of city officials in California and the United States. Paper presented at the Congress of Cities and Exposition, National League of Cities, Salt Lake City, Utah.

Berube, Alan, and Alice Rivlin. 2002. *The potential impacts of recession and terrorism on U.S. cities.* Washington, DC: Brookings Institution.

CB Richard Ellis. 2002. *Office vacancy index.* www.cbre.com.

Center for Urban Studies. 2003. *Michigan statewide survey.* Detroit, MI: Wayne State University.

Dixon, David. 2002. Is density dangerous? In *Perspectives on preparedness.* Volume 12, Cambridge, MA: Harvard Univ. Press.

Enz, Cathy, and Linda Canina. 2002. The best of times, the worst of times: Differences in hotel performance following 9/11. *Cornell Hotel and Restaurant Administration Quarterly* 43 (October): 41–52.

Fainstein, Susan. 2002. One year on: Reflections on September 11 and the "war on terrorism": Regulating New York City's visitors in the aftermath of September 11th. *International Journal of Urban and Regional Research* 26 (September): 591–95.

Fiscal Policy Institute. 2001. *Economic impact of the September 11 World Trade Center attack, preliminary report.* New York: Author.

Glaeser, Edward, and Jesse Shapiro. 2002. Cities and warfare: The impact of terrorism on urban form. *Journal of Urban Economics* 51:205–24.

Government Accounting Office. 2002. *Review of studies of the economic impact of the September 11, 2001, terrorist attacks on the World Trade Center.* Washington, DC: Author.

Harrigan, James, and Phillipe Martin. 2002. Terrorism and the resilience of cities. *Economic Policy Review* 8 (November): 97–116.

Hoene, Christopher, Mark Baldassare, and Christiana Brennan. 2002. *Homeland security and America's cities: Research brief on America's cities.* Washington, DC: National League of Cities.

Kantor, Paul. 2002. Terrorism and governability in New York City: Old problem, new dilemma. *Urban Affairs Review* 38 (September): 120–27.

Marcuse, Peter, 2002. Urban form and globalization after September 11th: The view from New York. *International Journal of Urban and Regional Research* 26 (September): 596–606.

Mills, Edwin. 2002. Terrorism and U.S. real estate. *Journal of Urban Economics* 51:198–204.

National Capital Planning Commission. 2001. *Designing for security in the nation's capital.* Washington, DC: Interagency Task Force for the National Capital Planning Commission.

National Trust for Historic Preservation. 2002. *National main street trends survey.* www.mainst.org/FrontPage/TrendsSurvey/2002.

New York City Partnership. 2002. *Vital signs: Economic realities and challenges facing New York City one year after 9/11.* New York: NY City Partnership.

Peirce, Neal. 2003. Cities and homeland security spending: As war unfolds, what now? *Government Finance Review* 19 (April): 78–79.

Pionke, John. 2001. *Officials secure cities but resolve to reassess terrorism plans.* National League of Cities' Web site, www.nlc.org.

PricewaterhouseCoopers. 2002. Terror's unsettling legacy. *Emerging Trends in real estate 2003.* New York: Author.

———. 2003. *Emerging trends in real estate 2004.* New York: Author.

Savitch, H. V. 2003. Does 9/11 portend a new paradigm for cities? *Urban Affairs Review* 39 (September): 103–27.

Sostek, Anya. 2003. Orange crush, *Governing* 16 (11): 18–23.

U.S. Conference of Mayors. 2002a. *One year later: A status report on the federal-local partnership on homeland security.* Washington, DC: Author.

———. 2002b. *The cost of heightened security in America's cities: A 192-city survey.* Washington, DC: Author.

———. 2003a. *First mayors' report to the nation: Tracking federal Homeland Security funds to the 50 state governments.* Washington, DC: Author.

———. 2003b. *Survey on cities' direct Homeland Security cost increases related to war/high threat alert.* Washington, DC: Author.

———. 2004. *Second mayors' report to the nation: Tracking Homeland Security funds sent to the 50 state governments.* Washington, DC: Author.

White, E. B. [1949] 1999. *Here is New York.* New York: The Little Book Room.

Wildasin, David. 2002. Local public finance in the aftermath of September 11. *Journal of Urban Economics* 51:225–37.

CHAPTER 9

FACES OF THE NEW FEDERALISM

Urban Responses to Federal Policy

For more than two decades federal policymakers have been shifting responsibilities and burdens to local and state governments. There are several reasons for this: the declining political influence of central-city electorates; the shift of political power to the Sunbelt; and a conservative philosophy opposing an activist federal role in solving social problems. Cities and suburbs are searching for ways of managing their new roles while absorbing the shock waves caused by profound changes in their populations, economies, and political environments.

The selections in this chapter scrutinize this drift in national urban policy and probe its consequences for local communities. Peter Eisinger highlights the complex relationships among local, state, and national governments. He examines the fiscal link between the federal government and municipal governments after years of devolution and concludes that a new federal order has emerged. He argues that changes in intergovernmental relations forced mayors to become preoccupied with managing scarcity; further, he asserts that this priority makes city hall less likely to attend to social, racial, and economic issues. From this context, in very diverse cities like New York, Los Angeles, Philadelphia, Indianapolis, and others, conservative mayors have emerged who stress public order and quality-of-life issues (such as clean streets) that can be addressed with limited government.

Pietro Nivola examines a different aspect of the New Federalism. He points out that the federal government continues to exert a large and growing presence despite declining national financial assistance to localities. He argues that Congress is inclined to pass laws that force local governments to undertake new responsibilities without providing financial help in carrying out these mandates. As a result, the federal government is routinely subjecting the details as well as the policies of local governments to national supervision and regimentation. He describes how national prescriptions frequently deal with the minutia of local affairs, such as requiring bright standard-size yellow lines to separate drivers and passengers on school buses. He concedes that some national prohibitions and regulations are necessary when problems spill over local governmental boundaries, but he asserts that many federal mandates go well beyond that. According to Nivola, one-size-fits-all federal standards are becoming so ubiquitous that they undermine the ability of local officials to find sensible and effective solutions to their problems. Other federal prescriptions have created so many new entitlements that a firestorm of litigation now burdens local officials and taxpayers with costly claims. Nivola concludes that less national government would be better for the cities, especially poorer central cities that are not well positioned to pay the legal bills and compliance costs generated by national regulations.

Taken together, the Eisenger and Nivola selections portray different faces of the New Federalism. One face is the shrinking fiscal presence of the national government in urban affairs; the other face is the expansion of governmental intervention in our cities. Both are happening at the same time.

The capacity of city governments to find their own solutions to pressing problems of poverty is examined in Isaac Martin's essay. At a time of declining federal policy initiative, local governments are generally on their own in devising ways to aid the poor, especially low-income workers. Martin questions the view that local governments cannot pursue egalitarian social welfare programs. He takes issue with Paul Peterson and others who argue that cities must avoid policies that redistribute resources to the poor because it will drive away businesses investors who are free to relocate to other communities. Martin describes how more than a score of city governments have joined the national Living Wage movement by enacting ordinances requiring employers who hold public contracts with the city government or receive public monies to pay a higher wage than the minimum required by federal law. The question is why some cities have joined this movement while others have not.

The author's review of the evidence suggests that local political actors who become linked to successful Living Wage activists in other cities are key factors—indeed, they are more important than the economic conditions of the cities. The author's findings have implications for our understanding of federalism. Martin demonstrates that the federal system may constrain local governments by forcing them to compete to attract capital, but it also *enables* cities to innovate by allowing the diffusion of political ideas from one city to another. Thus, even as the national government cuts back on programs to assist the poor, federalism still provides opportunities for city governments and local activists to expand their role in the area of redistributive social policy.

23

Peter Eisinger

CITY POLITICS IN AN ERA OF FEDERAL DEVOLUTION

The effort that began more than 25 years ago to construct what might be called a New Federal Order is still very much a work in progress. President Clinton

"City Politics in an Era of Federal Devolution" by Peter Eisinger, *Urban Affairs Review*, Vol. 33, No. 3, January 1998, pp. 308–325. Copyright © 1998 by Sage Publications. Reprinted by permission of Sage Publications.

and most members of Congress . . . clearly embraced some of the elements that differentiate this federal arrangement from its New Deal-Great Society predecessor such as diminishing federal intergovernmental aid, block grants, and formal devolution of federal responsibilities. But the scope and details of implementation of this latest iteration of the federal arrangement are not yet fully worked out. The bare walls of the edifice have been erected, but there is little interior decoration.

As members of the tripartite federal partnership that came to its fullest expression in the Great Society and the years immediately following, local governments have a deep interest in the process and outcomes of federal realignment. As the outlines of the New Federal Order of the 1990s have taken shape, it is clear that the implications for urban government are manifold. Nevertheless, even though many of the problems and issues that are reshaping federalism are concentrated in urban areas, much is uncertain about what precise role the cities will play in the emerging intergovernmental environment. Curiously, city representatives and city interests have been, according to Weir (1996, 1), "conspicuously absent from the congressional debate about devolution."

Certain developments in national politics make this an appropriate moment to take stock and to speculate about the future of the cities in the New Federal Order. In summer 1996, Congress passed, and the president signed, the new welfare law, converting cash support for the poor from an open-ended federal entitlement to a fixed block grant to the states. Devolution through block granting is the focus of debate in other areas of public policy, from law enforcement to highway funding and from job training to housing, all policy domains in which the local government role is clearer and more formalized than in the welfare realm. Not only is there now broad interest in devolving power though block grants but the intergovernmental aid reductions put in place in Republican Washington in the 1980s are no longer resisted by deficit-averse Democrats. In this article, then, I explore what is known about cities in the New Federal Order, what their future role might be, and what the effects on cities of the changes in the federal arrangement have been.

I suggest that to the extent that cities are increasingly cut off from federal aid and program initiatives, mayors must focus more and more on making the most of the resources they control. Thus the arts of public management are becoming the primary tasks of local political leadership. This represents an important change in the moral climate of local politics, because city hall is far less likely to be used these days as the bully pulpit from which mayors once sought to exercise leadership on major social, racial, and economic issues.

The New Federal Order

I define the New Federal Order as that rearrangement of federal relationships that began with President Richard Nixon's efforts to devolve authority from Washington to subnational governments through block grants and general revenue sharing and continues today as Congress, the president, and the governors combine to contract the role of the federal government in domestic policy. Although the initial efforts in the 1970s to transform the New Deal-Great Society federal system were seen as partisan attempts to diminish Washington's influence, both parties seem to agree today not only that the era of big government is over but that the proper locus of policy invention and administration is at the state and local level. For example, even before the passage of the welfare reform bill of 1996, the Clinton administration had approved 78 state welfare demonstration projects. More generally, the president's urban policy, according to his assistant secretary of the Department of Housing and Urban Development (HUD) at the time, "recognizes that the most pressing problems facing older cities can no longer be addressed through countercyclical grant-in-aid programs" (Stegman 1996). Where do the cities fit, then, in the New Federal Order?

It is important to begin by distinguishing several different aspects of the process of creating the New Federal Order. One aspect is simply the contraction of federal intergovernmental aid. This trend represents the devolution by default of fiscal responsibility to states and localities. A second aspect is the formal devolution of power from Washington to subnational government, a rearrangement of responsibilities of city governments. A third feature concerns the indirect consequences of devolution to the states. These spin-off fiscal and political effects are manifold, and they affect the cities in important ways.

Fiscal Contraction

Federal assistance to cities is much diminished since the late 1970s. The contraction of aid has been so dramatic that the federal government's loss of interest in urban affairs is one of the signal stories of the great transformation to the New Federal Order. Yet a focus on the big picture alone may be somewhat misleading: Cities have not been entirely cut adrift fiscally to live on their own resources.

In 1977, the year before federal aid contraction began, municipal governments looked to Washington for 15.9% of their total revenues. By 1992, federal assistance had decreased to only 4.7% of local revenues. (Chernick and Reschovsky 1997; see also Wallin 1996). In 1991, combined federal grants in aid to state and local governments regained their high watermark of 1978 (in constant dollar terms), but the functional distribution of intergovernmental fiscal assistance had changed in ways particularly disadvantageous to the cities. Although grants for education, job training, and social services, many of which are allocated to local governments, accounted for 23.9% of federal intergovernmental aid in 1980, the figure had decreased to 15.8% by 1994. Community development assistance decreased during this period from 7.1% to 2.9% of federal aid, and grants for sewer and water construction and environmental cleanup went from 5.9% to 2.0%. Meanwhile, health-related grants, mainly Medicaid, which is channeled through the states to individuals, rose from

17.2% of all federal inter-governmental assistance to 42.1% (Advisory Commission on Intergovernmental Relations 1994, 31). In short, a much smaller proportion of federal aid is devoted to urban programs than was true just a decade and a half ago.

An analysis by the U.S. Conference of Mayors ([USCM] 1994) of funding of key urban programs shows how severe the cuts have been from the perspective of the cities. Between 1981 and 1993, funding of community development block grants, urban development action grants, general revenue sharing, mass transit aid, employment and training programs, clean-water construction, assisted housing, and the various programs of the Economic Development Administration decreased by 66.3% in real dollar terms (see Table 9.1).

State governments did little to make up for the evaporation of federal monies for their municipalities. Reeling from the losses of federal aid that they themselves were experiencing, especially with the end of the state portion of general revenue sharing in 1980, state governments significantly reduced the rate of growth of aid to their local governments. Altogether, state aid to local governments as a proportion of local revenues decreased from 25.4% to 21.2% of local revenues between 1977 and 1992 (Chernick and Reschovsky 1997).

Although urban-oriented federal aid had dropped substantially by the mid-1990s, the federal government in the Clinton era has not abandoned the cities. Beginning with fiscal year 1995, the USCM began tracking federal funding of a range of specific "municipal programs."[1] Of the 80 programs tracked over the three-year period by the USCM, 27 showed decreases, 8 were unchanged, and 45 received increases in funding. Of those 45, however, only 26 received funding increases that equaled or exceeded the inflation rate.

The data indicate, however, that with a few exceptions, municipal programs did not experience the huge cuts in the middle Clinton years that they had suffered in the earlier decade. Federal funding of programs that benefit cities could be described as approaching a steady state, with substantial changes only at the tails of the distribution. One implication for the cities is that although they do not stand to lose even more federal dollars, it is unlikely that

Table 9.1 Federal Funds for Cities, 1981–1993 (in billions of constant 1993 dollars)

Program	FY 1981 ($)	FY 1993 ($)	% Real Cut
Community Development Block Grant	6.3	4.0	− 36.5
Urban Development Action Grant	0.6	0.0	− 100.0
General revenue sharing	8.0	0.0	− 100.0
Mass transit	6.9	3.5	− 49.3
Employment and training	14.3	4.2	− 70.6
Economic Development Administration	0.6	0.2	− 66.7
Assisted housing	26.8	8.9	− 66.8
Clean-water construction	6.0	2.6	− 56.7

Source: U.S. Conference of Mayors (1994).

a return to the patterns of the pre-Reagan era will occur. Nothing in the patterns of federal aid in the 1990s suggests that city governments will be able to relax their habits of fiscal self-reliance.

Formal Devolution

The principal definition of the term devolution in the context of U.S. federalism is the reallocation of specific responsibilities and authority from Washington to subnational governments. Since 1980, devolution has primarily involved a shift from national to state government. Such a rearrangement lay at the heart of President Reagan's New Federalism, one of the elements of which involved a failed proposal to carry out the so-called Great Swap: Washington would assume full responsibility for Medicaid in return for complete state takeover of the Aid to Families with Dependent Children (AFDC) and Food Stamps programs.

Reagan's effort to shape the New Federal Order was not entirely in vain, however: He did succeed in persuading Congress to consolidate 77 categorical grants-in-aid into 10 broad block grants to the states. The consequence was to strip Congress of the authority to designate specific uses of federal assistance for a variety of mainly health and education programs. State governments could now establish their own priorities within the broad boundaries of these new block grants. As in the current era, however, the interests of cities were scarcely considered in this federal reordering. Indeed, the new state power came directly at the expense of the cities: Of the categorical programs consolidated into block grants to the states, 47 had previously delivered funds directly to local governments (Ladd 1994, 219).

The Reagan federalism reforms failed to stem the growth of categorical grants, the number of which had reached an all-time high of 618 by 1995. Yet, contrary to the legislative trend, interest in devolution has remained high, both in Washington and in the state houses, fueled by the increasingly bipartisan conviction that in most matters of domestic policy, government closest to the people governs best. For proponents of devolution, the decade of the 1990s began in a promising way with the passage of the Intermodal Surface Transportation Efficiency Act (ISTEA), which greatly expands the ability of state and local governments alike to reallocate transportation funds among specific modes. Thus, in 1995, for example, more than $800 million was shifted by subnational governments from one purpose to another, such as the New York City Transit Authority's transfer of money initially designated for highways to mass transit projects, including station upgrades and signal modernization.[2]

Another significant devolutionary initiative during the Clinton years was the 1996 Personal Responsibility and Work Opportunity Reconciliation Act, better known as welfare reform, which created the Temporary Assistance to Needy Families (TANF) block grant. Henceforth, states will receive a fixed amount of funding from which to provide income support and work programs. State governments will now be responsible for establishing eligibility requirements and time limits. The shift of welfare responsibility to the states creates no formal local role, however, although there are clearly indirect implications for the cities that will be discussed later.

In no analysis of the urban implications of the changing distribution of responsibilities and authority in the federal system can one ignore two other initiatives of the mid-1990s: the Empowerment Zone and Enterprise Cities Act of 1993 and the Unfunded Mandates Reform Act of 1995. Neither devolves specific powers to subnational governments that they did not have before, but unlike most earlier devolutionary reforms, they both promise to expand the scope of local self-determination.

Along with providing some tax and regulatory relief, the Empowerment Zone and Enterprise Cities Program offers selected communities grants under the Title XX Human Services block grant program that may be used for an expanded range of social services and economic development. The Title XX block grant is made to the states, which in turn pass the funds onto their winning communities. In the first round, the few big winners received grants of $100 million each over a 10-year period, and a larger number of cities won smaller grants.

The program does not represent a devolution of new programmatic authority and responsibility in the field of economic and community development; these already rest primarily at the subnational level. Rather, the empowerment zone program devolves additional *capacity* to facilitate initiatives devised at the local level. Indeed, HUD is explicit in its implementation guidelines that programs are to be the product of strategic plans developed in the neighborhoods rather than in Washington (U.S. Government Accounting Office 1996, 3, 5).

The Unfunded Mandates Reform Act of 1995 has less obvious consequences but holds out the potential for curbing the growth rate of federal intergovernmental regulation and oversight and the imposition on states and localities of enforceable duties, as they are called in the act. The relief from mandates provided by Congress is oblique: The purpose of the act is to "assist congress in its consideration of proposed legislation . . . containing Federal mandates . . . by providing for development of information about the nature and size of mandates, [by promoting] informed and deliberate decisions by Congress on the appropriateness of Federal mandates in any particular instance, [and by requiring] that Congress consider whether to provide funding" to help subnational governments comply with the mandates (Unfunded Mandate Reform Act of 1995, P.L. 104-4). Members of Congress may be called upon to vote explicitly to include a mandate in a new program. The act is thus designed not so much to bar unfunded mandates as to discourage Congress by making the decision to impose a new mandate a thoroughly self-conscious and transparent action. If the intent of the act is realized, state and local governments may find over time that they may exercise unregulated governance over a slightly larger range of functions.

Although it is evident that little formal devolution from Washington to the cities has yet occurred, there are various proposals on the political agenda that would expand the urban role in the New Federal Order. During his term as the head of HUD, Secretary Henry Cisneros recommended creating a block grant through the consolidation of existing programs that would go to local governments to serve the homeless. Cisneros was said to believe that "homelessness is a local problem that is best solved . . . at the local level. . . . The most Washington can do is show the way" (Rapp 1994, 80). There has also been talk in Washington of consolidating 60 current HUD programs into three block grants for housing assistance, housing production, and community development. Another proposal, put forth by congressional Republicans after they won control of the House in the 1994 elections, was to eliminate the Community Oriented Policing Services program and substitute a $10 billion block grant to localities for law enforcement purposes, but President Clinton vetoed the appropriations bill that threatened to transform this signature program.

As these examples make clear, devolution is increasingly a shared goal of both political parties. Unlike the devolution of the Reagan years, the expansion of state authority is not the sole focus of federal reform. Although little formal authority has yet been transferred to local governments, some of the groundwork has been laid by forcing city governments to rely more heavily on their own resources. City governments may anticipate playing an even more central role in the federal rearrangement in the future.

Indirect Consequences of Devolution

As federal devolution proceeds at the end of the century, cities are increasingly subjected to a variety of indirect effects. Some of these are a function of the increased burdens on state governments; others stem from the cities' growing fiscal self-reliance. There are at least three categories of indirect consequences. First, there are the looming fiscal effects of welfare devolution. Second, there will be some shifting of burdens in a variety of functional areas as federal aid reductions force cities to provide services now supported by shared funding. Finally, there are a number of consequences, already evident, for the nature of local politics and political leadership. In particular, political reputation and success increasingly rest on public management skills rather than on the ability to exercise moral suasion on matters of social policy or to promote a racial agenda. These latter effects, already strongly in evidence, are signs of a deep change in the texture of urban politics.

Fiscal Effects Weir (1996) offered the general prediction that states will adjust to reductions in federal funding by poaching on local revenue sources, although how widespread this might become and the particular forms it might take are not yet apparent. There is one modest fiscal challenge to local government revenues, however, and it derives from the new welfare law. Certain provisions of the bill are likely to reduce municipal tax collections, increase local government costs by creating greater demand for local public service jobs and education, and harm the consumer economy in high-poverty neighborhoods by reducing the disposable income of the poor.

The new law provides that after a maximum of two years on TANF, recipients must leave the welfare rolls and engage in some sort of work. Some will succeed, finding unsubsidized jobs in the private sector. Others, however, will not. Indeed, this outcome is the more likely in many cities, because there are simply not enough entry-level jobs to absorb the number of adults that will come off the welfare rolls. For example, if all the unemployed adults in Chicago—those on public assistance as well as those who are not—were to look for work, there would be six workers for every available entry-level job (Weir 1996, 4). In New York City, there are currently approximately 470,000 able-bodied adults on welfare. They will join the roughly 271,000 unemployed people not on welfare in the job search. These roughly three-quarters of a million people will be competing for employment in a local economy that is producing about 20,000 new jobs per year, and many of these require substantial skills and education (Finder 1996).

Of those who do not find work in the private sector, some will migrate from the state and others will fall back on relatives or friends. In either case, they will no longer have the steady, even if modest, spending power provided by cash welfare assistance. Pagano, Lobenhofer, and Dudas (1996) argued that one result of this loss of cash assistance by people otherwise not gainfully employed will be to lower the city's property and sales taxes and the local excise tax base by reducing both rental housing demand and consumer spending. With less cash—and fuel or food stamp benefits—flowing into poor urban communities, retail sales and employment dependent on welfare clients will suffer. Using an economy-wide model developed at the U.S. Department of Agriculture, Smallwood et al. (1995, 10) found that even a modest cut in food assistance will lead to more than 100,000 lost jobs in food processing, retail, and non-food sectors.[3]

Those who exhaust their welfare eligibility but who cannot find work in the private sector and who do not vanish from administrative view by moving in with relatives or leaving the state have several options, according to the law. They may seek subsidized employment in either the public sector or community service programs; they may seek job skills training directly related to employment; or, for high school dropouts, they may return to high school.[4] Although the block grant to the states may fund some of these options, it is also likely that local government resources may be called into play to create public service jobs or classroom training and education. This is so in large part because the new law does not provide enough funding to finance subsidized work and training. The Congressional Budget Office estimates the shortfall in support of the work requirement at $12 billion over the next six years (Super et al. 1996, 14). States may pick up some of these costs, but they are likely to push some of them onto the cities. The 1996 welfare reform, then, will not be free of cost for the cities.

Service Shifting of Burdens Some welfare recipients who reach their time limits will find neither work nor shelter with relatives or friends. Some will no doubt find themselves literally on the streets. Homeless programs that are funded locally will certainly feel the impact. Other unsuccessful job seekers will resort to crime, increasing the burden on the local criminal justice system.

Although anyone who would have been eligible for welfare on 16 July 1996 remains eligible for Medicaid, there is no guarantee that congress will not change the entire Medicaid program. The House and the Senate were near agreement late in 1995 to create a Medicaid block grant to the states that would have provided reduced funding over the next seven years. If such a proposal is successfully revived, one effect on cities will surely be an increase in demand on public hospital emergency services (see Center on Budget and Policy Priorities 1996).

Public Management as Urban Politics The most important impact on the cities of the shifting balance in the federal arrangement has been to change what could be called the moral tenor of urban politics. In short, good public administration has displaced the urban social and racial agendas that had dominated local politics since the 1960s. By increasingly forcing local leaders to make do with less intergovernmental aid and by making them husband what resources can be raised locally, the New Federal Order has placed a premium on local public management skills and discouraged grand visions of social and racial reform. As an official from the USCM explained, "In the last few years, our attention has shifted from trying to increase aid to cities in any form to trying to streamline it and make it more effective. *Let's talk about how we can make better use of what we're getting*" (Stanfield 1996, 1802, emphasis added).

Some scholars see this simply as part of a broad national trend toward conservatism, one that, as Sonenshein, Schockman, and DeLeon (1996, 1) put it, reaches down "even into the generally safe Democratic and minority reaches of urban leadership." Others see a more complex phenomenon taking place; for example, Clark (1994, 23) argued that a New Political Culture has emerged in the cities, one that features lifestyle and consumption concerns (especially lower taxes) rather than redistribution and material issues like housing and community development for the disadvantaged. He traced the crystallization of this middle-class urban politics to the decline of federal and state grants, many of which were targeted to poverty clienteles. Thus the contraction of federal aid has not only meant less money for the cities, but less policy guidance.

In a political climate in which the fear of taxpayer revolts is always present and the continuing flight of the middle class is a constant threat to urban health, leaders must first and foremost demonstrate skills in managing scarce resources. Social issues may or may not be present on current mayoral agendas, but if they are a matter of concern, the new mayors make clear that they can best be addressed by better management. This set of management tasks contrasts significantly with the mayoral challenge of the 1960s and 1970s, the dimensions of which were laid out most clearly by the Kerner Commission (National Advisory Commission on Civil Disorders 1968, 298): "Now, as never before, the American city has need for the personal qualities of strong democratic leadership" to address racial polarization, slum clearance, housing, police misconduct, poverty, and unemployment.

The prototype mayors of this earlier period were people like John Lindsay of New York, Jerome Cavanagh of Detroit, Kevin White of Boston, and Richard

Lee of New Haven. They excelled in grantsmanship, and they understood how to use city hall as a bully pulpit in their efforts to bridge racial and class divisions. As Sonenshein, Schockman, and DeLeon (1996, 5) described, "Sympathetic to the urban poor, supported by private philanthropy and federal aid, seeking redevelopment, these liberal mayors redefined the mayoral role." In the political climate of the 1990s, however, mayors seek guidance to accomplish their leadership tasks not first by reference to the moral compass of liberal reform but rather from the more neutral market. According to Gurwitt (1994, 26), Mayor Steven Goldsmith of Indianapolis, who exemplifies the new mayoral type, argues that market forces and competition ultimately serve the citizens of his city better than the government monopoly. Mastery of the market, he believes, requires the ingenuity of the entrepreneur and the management skills of a corporate executive officer (CEO).

The new mayors seem at ease with their fiscal self-reliance. The mayor of Nashville, quoted in an editorial in *The Wall Street Journal* ("Cities Discover Federalism" 1995), professed that "it's not all bad [that] Washington is busy extricating itself from . . . responsibility for well-being [in the cities]." Cities now have more freedom to experiment. John Norquist, mayor of Milwaukee, made a similar point about the freeing effects of federal divestment: Federal grants, he says, "are only costing us more money, because they force us to . . . do things we wouldn't otherwise do" (quoted in Osborne 1992, 63).

The new mayors speak the language of modern public management and run their administrations accordingly. They believe in reinvention, innovation, privatization, competition, strategic planning, and productivity improvements. They favor economic development and low taxes, partnership with the business sector, and good housekeeping. As Mayor Norquist reportedly said ("A Genuine New Democrat" 1996), his success is a function of performance, not ideology.

The issue of privatization illustrates how the commitment to the new public management crosses partisan and racial boundaries. Although Mayor Goldsmith, a Republican who once declared that he wanted to become the CEO of Indianapolis, is noted for his leadership in privatizing public services, the same policies have been pursued with equal fervor by Mayor Richard Daley, Jr. of Chicago, a Democrat, and by successive black mayoral administrations in Detroit (see Smith and Leyden 1996; Jackson and Wilson 1996). Daley has been particularly vigorous in contracting formerly public responsibilities to private firms, including, among others, the parking garage at O'Hare Airport, sewer cleaning, office janitorial services, the management of public golf courses, water customer billing, abandoned automobile collection, parking ticket enforcement, and tree stump removal.

The change in the moral tenor of urban politics is perhaps nowhere more evident than in the cities governed by black mayors. "New black leaders," such as Michael White of Cleveland, Kurt Schmoke of Baltimore, Marc Morial of New Orleans, and others, are characterized as "technopoliticians" in contrast to such "champions of the race" as Coleman Young of Detroit and Marion Barry of Washington (Barras 1996, 20). According to Barras (p. 19), "They have moved beyond rallies and protest marches, replacing talk with action and ushering in a new era of competent, professional stewardship in cities."

Young's successor in Detroit provides an example. Peirce (1993, 3013) wrote that Mayor Dennis Archer's agenda is to fashion a "reinvented" city government "that pays its bills on time," improves its low bond rating, and "picks up garbage on time and keeps the streetlights on all night." Archer, who established close ties to the white business establishment in pursuit of economic development objectives, is contrasted with Young for "rejecting the politics of class and race." Similarly, Barras (1996) compared Bill Campbell, mayor of Atlanta, to the civil rights giants Maynard Jackson and Andrew Young, who preceded him in city hall.[5] Although Campbell is a strong supporter of affirmative action, he reportedly sees himself

> as the vanguard of a new generation of black leaders who embrace a less conspicuous brand of racial politics. . . . His agenda is less about the fight for black empowerment than about paving potholes, encouraging job growth, making neighborhoods safer and building downtown housing. (Sack 1996)

Two decades ago, the social agendas of both black and white mayors captured the attention of the news media and urban observers, but today, the public spotlight is on the new public managers. Eggers (1993) claimed that "America's boldest mayors" were Edward Rendell of Philadelphia, Milwaukee's Norquist, and Indianapolis's Goldsmith. What was bold about these urban leaders was their management initiatives: Rendell's Private Sector Task Force on Management and Productivity, which saved the city more than $150 million; Norquist's strategic budget process; and Goldsmith's introduction of competitive bidding between city service providers and private firms.

Leadership as public management is what urban electorates apparently want in this age of local fiscal self-reliance. In fact, America's boldest mayors hardly stand out from their colleagues in other cities. Mayor Richard Riordan of Los Angeles, a businessman turned politician, runs his city in the style of a CEO—nonideological, managerial, eschewing the "arts of political leadership and public appeals" (Sonenshein, Schockman, and DeLeon 1996, 15). Even Rudolph Giuliani of New York, an aggressive and brash former public prosecutor, came to office promising to "reinvent" city government by cutting and streamlining its massive size (Gurwitt 1995, 23).

The New Federal Order Brings New City Limits

In the New Federal Order, the fiscal links between Washington and the cities have become significantly attenuated. More than at any time since the early Great Society years, city governments can spend only what they can raise. It is possible to imagine several responses to this local fiscal autonomy. One response is to raise taxes to maintain the array of service responsibilities that people have come to expect. To some modest extent, this is what city governments have done. Beginning in 1982 and continuing through the decade, city governments increased per capita tax revenues to offset rising expenditure burdens (Bahl et al. 1991, Table 7). Another response is to engage vigorously in economic development activities, seeking to raise additional revenues by growing the indigenous tax base. There is strong evidence that this has been done in cities too (Clarke and Gaile 1989).

Another response, ever sensitive to citizen resistance to higher taxes, is to husband the resources that cities control through more careful management strategies characterized by contracting out, strategic planning, downsizing, and reorganizing. There is strong evidence that this, too, has been a major response in the cities to the New Federal Order.

The resultant emergence of a public management agenda in place of a social reform platform—what Sonenshein, Schockman, and DeLeon (1996) called the platform of multiethnic liberalism—might be seen as a narrowing of political vision. In a different light, better, more innovative management of the scarce resources under local control may be seen as simply a realistic response to a fiscal world very different from that of a quarter of a century ago. In a sense, the absence of a growing stream of federal dollars has meant that city political leaders cannot afford, fiscally or politically, to push an agenda of social and racial reform financed by local taxpayers alone. Nor can municipal leaders find much encouragement for defying these realities: Left to confront the great urban racial and economic polarities, few elected officials would be so foolhardy as to risk inevitable failure by initiating solutions based solely on the modest and limited resources that they themselves can raise. It is far easier—and the outcome more certain—to lower taxes, reduce government employment, and fill potholes. City limits have never been more in evidence.

Notes

1. The definition of municipal is somewhat broad. In its analysis, the USCM included Food Stamps, AFDC, Headstart, and National Endowment for the Arts grants, none of which, by any account, would be regarded as particularly municipal in character. But it also included various homeless assistance grants, a broad range of assisted housing programs, mass transit, community policing, and other such programs that have a strong urban component. Prior to 1995, the USCM tracked funding for a mix of specific programs and general categories of programs (see Table 9.1).

2. Testimony of Secretary of Transportation Federico Peña in the *Reauthorization of ISTEA* hearings before the Committee on Transportation and Infrastructure, U.S. House of Representatives, 2 May 1996.

3. A $5 billion cut in federal food assistance would reduce food spending by $750 million per year, a .10% decrease. Smallwood et al. (1995) calculated that 3,600 farm jobs would be lost, as well as 14,000 jobs in food processing and another 103,000 jobs that are generated indirectly.

4. An excellent comparison of the features of the new welfare law with the old Aid to Families with Dependent Children program is contained in Burke (1996).

5. In a national survey of 1,211 black Americans conducted in 1992 for the *Detroit News*, researchers found that 94% of the respondents believed that the people who came to power during the civil rights era were out of touch with the real concerns of ordinary

African-Americans. Such leaders continue to cite racism as the most pressing issue facing blacks, but the black citizenry is concerned about crime, employment, and economic prospects (Barras 1996, 19).

Bibliography

Advisory Commission on Intergovernmental Relations. 1994. *Significant features of fiscal federalism, 1994.* Vol. 2. Washington, DC Government Printing Office.

Bahl, R., J. Martinez, D. Sjoquist, and L. Williams, 1991. The fiscal conditions of U.S. cities at the beginning of the 1990s. Paper presented at the Urban Institute Conference on Big City Governance and Fiscal Choices, Southern California University, Los Angeles, June.

Barras, J. R. 1996. From symbolism to substance: The rise of America's new generation of black political leaders. *New Democrat* 8 (November-December): 19–22.

Burke, V. 1996. New welfare law: Comparison of the new block grant program with Aid to Families with Dependent Children. Congressional Research Service Report to Congress, 26 August.

Center on Budget and Policy Priorities. 1996 (22 March). The NGA Medicaid proposal will shift costs onto local governments. Washington, OC: Author.

Chernick, H., and A. Reschovsky, 1997. Urban fiscal problems: Coordinating actions among governments. In *The urban crisis: Linking research to action,* edited by B. Weisbrod and J. Worthy, 131–176. Evanston, IL: Northwestern University Press.

Cities discover federalism, 1995. *The Wall Street Journal,* 8 December.

Clark, T. N. 1994. Race and class versus the New Political Culture. In *Urban Innovation,* edited by T. N. Clark, 21–78. Thousand Oaks, CA. Sage Publications.

Clarke, S., and G. Gaile. 1989. Moving toward entrepreneurial economic development policies: Opportunities and barriers. *Policy Studies Journal* 17 (spring): 574–598.

Eggers, W. D. 1993. City lights: America's boldest mayors. *Policy Review* (summer): 67–74.

Finder, A. 1996. Welfare clients outnumber jobs they might fill. *The New York Times,* 25 August. A genuine new democrat. 1996. *The Wall Street Journal,* 21 March.

Gurwitt, R. 1994. Indianapolis and the Republican future. *Governing* 7 (February): 24–28.

———. 1995. The trials of Rudy Giuliani. *Governing* 8 (June): 23–27.

———. 1996. Detroit dresses for business. *Governing* 8 (April): 38–42.

Jackson, C., and D. Wilson. 1996. Service delivery in Detroit, Michigan. Paper presented at the annual meeting of the Midwest Political Science Association, Chicago, IL, April.

Ladd, H. 1994. Big-city finances. In *Big-city politics, governance, and fiscal constraints,* edited by G. Peterson, 201–66. Washington, DC: Urban Institute.

National Advisory Commission on Civil Disorders, 1968. *Report of the National Advisory Commission on Civil Disorders.* New York: Bantam.

Osborne, D. 1992. John Norquist and the Milwaukee experiment. *Governing* 5 (November); 63.

Pagano, M., J. Lobenhofer, and A. Dudas. 1996. Cities and the changing federal system: Estimating the Impacts of the Contract with America. Department of Political Science, Miami University of Ohio. Typescript.

Peirce, N. 1993. Motor City's "Mayor Realtor." *National Journal,* 18 December, 3013.

Rapp, D. 1994. A program for Billy Yeager. *Governing* 7 (July): 80.

Sack, K. 1996. Mayor finds old issue emerging in new way. *The New York Times,* 15 July.

Smallwood, D. B. Kuhn, K. Hanson, S. Vogel, and J. Blaylock. 1995. Economic effects of refocusing national food-assistance efforts. *Food Review* 18 (January-April): 2–12.

Smith, D., and K. Leyden, 1996. Exploring the political dimension of privatization: A tale of two cities. Paper presented at the annual meeting of the Midwest Political Science Association, Chicago, IL, April.

Sonenshein, R., E. Schockman, and R. DeLeon, 1996. Urban conservatism in an age of diversity. Paper presented at the 1996 annual meeting of the Western Political Science Association, San Francisco, California, March.

Stanfield, R. 1996. Mayors are the soul of the new machine. *National Journal* 28 (24 August): 1801–1802.

Stegman, M. 1996. Speech presented at Rutgers University, Princeton, NJ, 28 February.

Super, D., S. Parrott, S. Steinmetz, and C. Mann. 1996. The new welfare law. Policy brief. Washington, DC: Center on Budget and Policy Priorities.

U.S. Conference of Mayors (USCM), 1994. *The federal budget and the cities.* Washington, DC: Government Printing Office.

———. 1995–1997. Funding levels for key municipal programs. Annual releases. Washington, DC: Author.

U.S. Government Accounting Office. 1996. Community development: Status of urban empowerment zones. Report to the chair of the Subcommittee on Human Resources and Intergovernmental Relations, Committee on Government Reform and Oversight, House of Representatives, Washington, DC, December.

Wallin, B. 1996. Federal retrenchment and state-local response: Lessons from the past. Paper presented at the annual meeting of the American Political Science Association, San Francisco, 30 August.

Weir, M. 1996. Big cities confront the New Federalism. Paper presented at Columbia University, New York, 12 April.

24

FEDERAL PRESCRIPTIONS AND CITY PROBLEMS

Pietro S. Nivola

It would be nice if America's local governments had a consistent history of good conduct. In reality much has gone wrong—at times so wrong any fair observer would have welcomed or at least understood an extensive federal usurpation of local powers. Think about the following episodes from various cities.

On the evening of May 31, 1921, a lynch mob in Tulsa, Oklahoma, descended on the municipal courthouse in search of a black man who had been charged with (and later acquitted of) raping a white woman.[1] After an altercation at the courthouse the mob invaded the city's black neighborhood, destroying thirty-five square blocks and murdering hundreds of residents. At one downtown location 123 blacks were found clubbed to death. How did city and state authorities respond as the bloodbath unfolded? The Tulsa police department deputized large numbers of the white vigilantes and, according to an account citing court records from the time, instructed them to "go out and kill." The state of Oklahoma appointed a Tulsa Race Riot Commission to launch an investigation—more than three-quarters of a century later.

In 1975 a strange thing happened: New York, the biggest city in the world's richest nation, neared bankruptcy. The sources of this fiscal crisis were complex, but at least one root cause was unmistakable: New York had spent beyond its means on redistributive social services.[2] This municipal welfare state could no longer be sustained by its vulnerable local tax base.

Excerpts from Pietro S. Nivola, *Tense Commandments: Federal Prescriptions and City Problems.* The Brookings Institution, 2002, pp. 15–24, 26–31, 32–33, 33–35, 36, 38–41, 45–47, and corresponding notes on pp. 165–176.

More recently the Atlanta metropolitan area has been experiencing a buildup of air pollution.[3] Along the eastern seaboard of the United States no metropolis belches more smog than Atlanta. It has one of the dirtiest coal-fired power plants in the country, and emission levels of nitrous oxides from motor vehicles have regularly exceeded the Environmental Protection Agency's (EPA) caps and projections. The local political establishment, however, has been slow to act. While Draconian steps such as ordering a four-day work week were rightly rejected, so were more modest proposals—like charging for parking spaces and converting to cleaner fuels. The idea of cleaner fuel, which implied a slight increase in energy prices, caused consternation in the Georgia legislature.

In 1989 a well-known journalist, staunchly committed to public education, described a problem his son experienced in a classroom of the public school system of the city in which they resided. "One of my children," the journalist wrote, "spent a year with an elementary school science teacher who had been shifted from teaching English. She was fully 'qualified' to teach, since she had her credentials, but she knew less about science than most of the children did."[4] One of the things this qualified science teacher did not know was how the moon revolved around the earth.

The Trouble with Localism

The derelictions of local government range from the barbaric to the regrettable, the irresponsible, and the merely ridiculous. What they imply, though, is that in the absence of enforced national standards some self-governed communities have proved capable of sinking below the most elementary regard for public competency, environmental safeguards, financial prudence, or even basic human rights.

The account about the public school teacher who did not understand the orbit of the moon was hardly unique. Reports of this sort or worse are sufficiently common to stir calls for national education standards. Nor was the Tulsa race riot of 1921 an isolated incident. In a wave of hysteria about rumored rapes of whites by blacks during the 1920s racial violence erupted in cities across the country.[5] The federal government may not have had at its disposal sufficient statutory powers to quell these atrocities or even to prosecute their perpetrators. Would that it had.

In the case of Atlanta's polluted atmosphere the argument for national "hammers" to compel an end to the local policy paralysis went beyond a need to protect the region's residents from possible health risks. Air pollution crosses boundaries. Concentrations of ozone can drift across hundreds of square miles. One place's foul air pollutes another region's water.[6] Why should people living in other jurisdictions have to inhale or swallow the poisons spewing from a neighboring urban area whose citizens year after year are not curtailing their wide-ranging effluents?

As Madison warned in *Federalist No. 10*, the inertia of local government has to do, at least in part, with the ability of entrenched interests to capture small polities: how can municipal school systems reinvent themselves when their administrations remain in the grip of obstructive teachers' unions? Will a one-company town, whose factory is the local economy's mainstay but also its worst polluter, put in a fix? Localism begets freeloading. When some jurisdictions become welfare magnets, others are tempted to lower their benefits below an acceptable minimum. A city or state whose contaminated air or water flows downstream to neighboring cities or states has little incentive to control the spillover for their sake. Indeed localities competing for business investment and taxable income might reciprocally "dumb down" standards.[7]

Clearly if interjurisdictional competition and externalities arbitrarily enrich certain communities at the expense of others or else draw too many into a "race to the bottom," or if local mismanagement is so endemic it corrupts the commonweal, or mischievous local factions egregiously violate the fundamental freedoms of citizens, the solution seems plain: "extend the sphere" of governance, as Madison recommended, shifting control from the "smaller" jurisdictions to "the Union."[8]

Mandating without Spending

In the past half-century most of this remedial enlargement of the national ambit has been purchased with federal dollars. As of 1990 nearly $120 billion in grants to state and local governments was being disbursed to patch alleged shortcomings of local policies in transportation, environmental protection, economic development, job training, education, public safety, and much more.[9] Because the purpose of this funding has not been to distribute unrestricted handouts but largely to make up for local deficiencies, receipt of the funds has been conditioned on compliance with a plethora of federal requirements. In theory those requirements could be ignored if the grantees simply turned down the money. In practice this became almost impossible. He who pays the piper calls the tune. New federal instructions are often affixed after the grant programs have been institutionalized. By then their constituencies are so well organized the programs have all but ceased to be voluntary. And typically the federal rules remain firmly in place even if congressional appropriations fall far short of authorizations. The local provision of special education for students with disabilities, for instance, is essentially governed by federal law, even though Congress has never even come close to appropriating its authorized share of this $43 billion-a-year mandate.

Federal grants feature these bait-and-switch dynamics because, despite considerable weaning during the past couple of decades, local governments remain dependent on whatever aid they can get. There are far fewer federal aid junkies today than twenty years ago (when more than three-quarters of the revenues in cities such as Detroit came from Washington), but federal aid remains a substantial source of state and local revenue, still exceeding in many places the proceeds from sales taxes or property taxes.

Going Off Budget

Paying the piper, however, is but one way of gaining influence. In recent decades the manner in which Washington exerts control changed. As the national government's deficits grew, and Congress's propensity to throw money at domestic programs bumped against budget caps, a tendency developed for the federal government to regulate local governments more stringently while aiding them less generously.[10] At the end of 1974 some forty federal mandates reflected this pattern. Twenty years later the number had grown by almost 160 percent (figure 9.1).[11] Presidents Ronald Reagan and George Bush put up faint resistance to what the Advisory Commission on Intergovernmental Relations had come to call regulatory federalism, even in the realm of administrative rulemakings. Between 1981 and 1986 Reagan presided over the promulgation of some 140 agency rules that placed nearly six thousand new obligations on states and localities.[12]

To local entities, of course, many of these actions seemed unfair and irrational. To policymakers at the national level, however, there was method in the madness. Before a retrenchment commenced in the 1980s federal grant giving had gotten out of control. Between 1960 and 1980 expenditures increased one

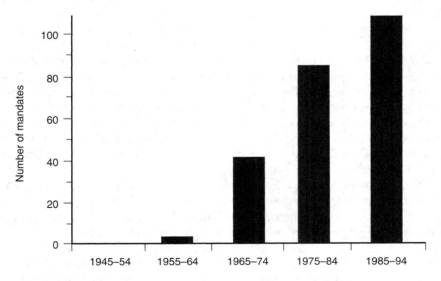

Figure 9.1 Federal Mandates on State and Local Governments, 1955–1994

Source: National Conference of State Legislatures, as cited in Clyde Wayne Crews Jr., *Ten Thousand Commandments: A Policymaker's Snapshot of the Federal Regulatory State* (Washington: Competitive Enterprise Institute, September 1996), p. 17.

and a half times as fast as the growth of the economy. Funds were tossed hither and yon, sponsoring countless questionable "community development" needs—like the construction of a tennis complex in an affluent section of Little Rock, Arkansas, and the expansion of a municipal golf course in Alhambra, California.[13] Gradual curtailment of such waste after 1980 was a positive change regardless of whether a less profligate government might try to extend its influence by means of off-budget regulations.

Indeed, as the federal government applied the brakes to discretionary spending and eventually managed to bring a bloated budget into balance in the 1990s, inflation and interest rates fell, and the national economy surged. Federal austerity yielded by way of economic growth a large net gain for the nation and for the treasuries of most states and municipalities. With plenty of states and many cities now running surpluses there was something to be said for devolving to them more chores and expenses.[14]

Passing responsibilities to local authorities can be fiscally prudent not only for the federal fisc but for society.[15] If local public works are mostly funded by Washington, their costs are harder to contain. States, cities, and counties do not print money; to spend they have to tax. Local resistance to taxation encourages cost consciousness.[16]

Stingy or Just Thriftier?

Local politicians wish Congress would simply shovel them cash and ask no questions. What the same politicians do not always acknowledge is that when Congress declines to write blank checks, and instead subjects state and local governments to uncompensated demands, some of the demands actually conform to local preferences.[17] A federal law that, say, asks states to administer particular licensing procedures for truck drivers using interstate highways is not an oppressive request if almost every state already has adopted, or willingly intends to adopt, essentially those same procedures. Hence, while the locals are often quick to say that, at a minimum, they should be paid back for the cost of meeting federal requirements, an indiscriminate policy of reimbursements would pose a moral hazard. States and municipalities that had been poised to take the desired actions anyhow would acquire an excuse to stop, sit back, and wait for federal payments.

Nor should taxpayers from afar be expected to indulge local governments that get themselves into trouble. In the early 1990s the governor of California, Pete Wilson, repeatedly complained that Washington was leaving his state too many of the burdens of servicing immigrants. In the next breath he insisted that his state had a rightful claim to hundreds of millions of dollars in federal disaster relief for property damage from earthquakes, floods, and mudslides, even in areas in which permissive California building regulations were substantially responsible for the losses.[18] The rotting rubbish at New York City's primary municipal dump discharges into the tri-state region not only one million gallons of polluted water each day but also large quantities of methane, a major contributor to global warming. People residing in

Oregon or Oklahoma—or, for that matter, New Jersey and Connecticut—should not be taxed to detoxify the garbage New Yorkers generate. Efficiency and equity requires that the polluters pay. Most federal environmental regulations operate on that logical principle.

Besides, though federal grants for mandatory pollution abatement have shrunk, other parts of the federal welfare state continued to support the nation's cities. Even during the Reagan years, the social safety net frayed less completely than many observers feared. Measured in constant dollars, federal welfare payments, Food Stamps, Medicaid, child nutrition, and supplemental feeding for women and children—all programs essential to cities—held up reasonably well between 1980 and 1990.[19]

Some would argue that the ability to deduct local property taxes and to exclude interest income earned by state and local debt instruments from the federal income tax represents a $70 billion concession to local control.[20] In 1988 the Supreme Court decided that Congress was free, if it wished, to tax the interest on municipal bonds.[21] Their tax-free status nonetheless has remained intact and continues to favor the beneficiaries with preferential rates of interest. The deductibility of local income and property taxes enables localities to raise more revenue than they otherwise could. Along with these constants at least one other remains in the equation: about half of the billions of dollars in revenues received annually from the sale of minerals, timber, and other commodities on public lands is shared with states and localities.

In sum in the United States as in any other country exactly what the central government "owes" subnational jurisdictions is a debatable matter. And certainly there are times when the Union, in Madisonian terms, has reason to take charge of local affairs—and can legitimately do so even without further indemnifying local governments.

The Yellow Line

But there also can be too much of a good thing.

Consider a small sample of the municipal functions now touched by national regulations. Federal law draws a line, commonly bright yellow, behind which passengers are forbidden to stand when they ride city buses. In many states, federal law may have a say in how firefighters should be deployed when fighting a fire. Federal law has influenced decisions about how long some unruly students in public schools can be suspended. Federal law has a bearing on how much a city pays for everything from snow removal services to contracts for sidewalk ramps. Federal law can affect whether the recruits for a police department are physically fit. Whether your child can walk to school or must commute by bus may depend on federal law. The degree to which a city's vacant industrial land parcels have to be cleared of toxic waste is dictated by federal law. The salary your child's teacher is paid may be affected by federal law that reaches well beyond the national minimum wage. Federal law addresses what protective measures must be taken to secure municipal landfills, school buildings that contain asbestos, and housing units with lead paint. Federal law determines how a city has to purify its drinking water.

None of these examples are flights of fancy.

When charges for basic municipal services rise, personnel costs are typically the reason. In the wake of the Supreme Court's opinion in the 1985 case of *Garcia v. San Antonio Metropolitan Transit Authority* the entire local public sector became liable for retroactive pay to employees filing claims for overtime compensation.[22] Before that time, Congress had moved in 1974 to include state and local governments under the minimum wage and overtime pay provisions of the Fair Labor Standards Act, but two years later this exercise of the commerce clause power had been overturned.[23] *Garcia*, and the subsequent statutory reinstatement of FLSA coverage in the local public sector, can help explain the high cost of operating a fleet of city snowplows during a Sunday night snowstorm.

The Americans with Disabilities Act of 1990 (ADA) tells every municipality to install ramps so that streets and sidewalks can be wheelchair accessible. But when any federal funds help construct these special accommodations (or any other local public works projects) the Davis-Bacon Act, a vestige of the New Deal, requires that the municipal contracts go not to the lowest bidders but to those who pay the "prevailing" (that is, union negotiated) wage of laborers working comparable projects in the geographic vicinity.[24]

Antibias suits brought under the auspices of federal statutes are now so pervasive they shape the employment practices of every municipal agency. Sometimes this litigation appears to have discouraged police departments from testing rigorously for the physical qualifications of the men and women that apply for jobs. For example, after it interrupted such testing in 1986 because of legal challenges, the New York Police Department found itself with some hires who were unfit.[25]

The federally ordained special education program, frequently enforced in painstaking detail by judicial consent decrees, now takes so large a bite out of the budgets of urban school districts that many are unable to raise their regular classroom teachers' salaries, which lag behind those of wealthier suburban districts.

Beginning in the 1960s a number of federal court decisions greatly expanded the rights of students to appeal school suspensions.[26] Despite more modulated opinions by the Supreme Court in later years few teachers or principals can ignore the legal minefield they enter when they contemplate disciplinary actions, especially against students said to be suffering from learning disabilities.[27]

Whether children in a city attend neighborhood schools or are bused sometimes over great distances often hinges on whether and with what methods a federal court order is regulating the racial composition of the city's school system.

As for the instructions to firefighters and the federal pettifogging about where to stand on local public buses, the first fall under standard operating procedures formulated by the Occupational Safety and Health Administration

(OSHA).[28] The second is a Department of Transportation (DOT) regulation, which reads as follows:

> Every bus which is designed and constructed so as to allow standees, shall be plainly marked with a line of contrasting color at least 2 inches wide or equipped with some other means so as to indicate to any person that he/she is prohibited from occupying a space forward of a perpendicular plane drawn through the rear of the driver's seat and perpendicular to the longitudinal axis of the bus. Every bus shall have clearly posted at or near the front, a sign with letters at least one half inch high stating that it is a violation of the Federal Highway Administration's regulations for a bus to be operated with persons occupying the prohibited area.[29]

Crossing the Line

The immersion of the central government in most of these matters seems hard to understand. Why should a national cabinet department or regulatory bureaucracy concern itself with how "standees" ride city buses or with the deployment of firefighters? If local transit authorities or fire departments cannot be left to decide such minutiae, what, if anything, are local governments for? Surely few of the activities in question—putting out fires, riding buses, disciplining troublemakers in schools, hiring police officers, remunerating city workers or contractors—blow fallout across jurisdictions the way some forms of environmental pollution do. . . .

One Size Does Not Fit All

The point of federalizing standards is to set norms for society as a whole and hence ensure uniformity. However, uniform rules of little significance for some jurisdictions can be onerous for others. The reach of the amended Fair Labor Standards Act is illustrative. It extends to public employers the mandatory minimum wage and other provisions that the FLSA originally reserved only for private firms. Not only does this generic regulation of workplaces carry different implications for municipalities than markets, its effects vary from one location to the next. The law would not have for most suburban towns, with no unionized employees, comparatively small payrolls, and bountiful tax bases, the same costly consequences it has had for some major cities.

A federal lawsuit that contests traditional fitness tests can pose difficulties for a big city's police force like New York's, which has to cope with crime-ridden slums. The same suit would be of little consequence for, say, Beverly Hills, a place so affluent and sheltered that, as the joke goes, the police department has an unlisted phone number.[30]

Green Mandates

The unequal impacts of federal environmental regulations are sometimes notorious.[31] In 1987 Congress concluded that every municipality in the United

States would have to treat storm water much the same as discharge of polluted water from industrial plants. This requirement, appropriate for humid climates, was ill-suited to arid regions such as much of the Southwest. Never mind that Phoenix averages only seven inches of rainfall a year. This city nonetheless was required to spend large sums each year monitoring the runoff from extremely infrequent rain storms.

Between 1974 and 1994 American taxpayers poured $213 billion into upgrading their municipal water-treatment plants. Now the EPA predicts that $200 billion more will be needed through the year 2014 to bring local wastewater systems up to newly specified design criteria. To that estimate must be added another $132 billion for the replacement of aging plants. The projected total, therefore, rises to $332 billion—a figure that does not include the soaring increases in operating and maintenance expenses associated with more advanced technologies. If the recent past is prologue, local governments will be expected to come up with more than 90 percent of the funding for these capital improvements, plus 100 percent of annual operating expenses.

And for at least some cities the bill will be needlessly steep. Under the Clean Water Act cities have to install secondary wastewater treatment facilities that remove the remaining organic matter not treated in primary facilities. While secondary treatment is usually necessary for landlocked communities, according to a 1993 study by the National Academy of Sciences, the same precaution may not be essential for many seaport cities. Tides at coastal cities help flush organic residue from water bodies. Although the EPA has granted a number of waivers, arguably more oceanside cities ought to receive dispensations.[32]

So stringent are the federal criteria for cleaning up local land containing toxic wastes, and so unsparing have been the liability provisions, that developers and lending institutions have resisted investing in many abandoned industrial and commercial sites. A recent survey of more than two hundred cities by the U.S. Conference of Mayors reported no fewer than 81,000 acres of brownfields, including some undoubtedly entangled in Superfund suits. These sites continue to languish in the inner cities, costing them possibly as much as $2.4 billion in lost property tax revenue each year and foreclosing opportunities to create as many as 550,000 jobs. Meanwhile policymakers bewail the "sprawl" wrought by businesses that, steering clear of the legal liabilities, opt to locate on virgin acreage in the suburbs.

Under the rules of the Safe Drinking Water Act localities everywhere have been busy examining their water supplies for pesticides and other toxic residues that pose substantial risks only in particular areas. Before it was finally relieved from some of this duty in the mid-1990s Columbus, Ohio, found itself guarding against approximately forty pesticides. Many of them had long since been discontinued in the vicinity, including one product used chiefly on pineapple plantations in Hawaii.[33]

At times the nationalized regulations appear to have created new problems at the regional level. New York, for instance, ran afoul of a national prohibition on ocean dumping of sewage sludge. Banned since 1988 from disposing of any sludge at sea, the city resorted to dewatering and composting its waste. But this practice emits nitrogen-rich effluents that endanger marine life in nearby estuaries. In March 1998 the state of Connecticut filed suit against the city for contaminating Long Island Sound.[34]

Rights and Wrongs

If environmental standards often do not admit enough diversification, latitude, and cognizance of costs at the local level, the federal regulations that fall under the capacious category of civil rights permit even less. For the most part this is as it should be. "Rights tends to be viewed as absolutes," explains Robert A. Katzmann, "overriding considerations of cost effectiveness."[35] But no society can afford to extend "total justice" to an ever-increasing variety of petitioners.[36] What began in the 1960s as a long-awaited effort to secure equality of opportunity for African Americans has expanded into a vast apparatus of federally mandated protections and preferences for many additional groups. Whether every class of claimants has needed maximal compulsory remedies is a good question. So is whether each remedy should be determined from the top down.

Consider the rights of persons with disabilities. The ideal of accommodating the physically impaired is just and desirable, but should every municipality be told how to improve handicapped access in its public facilities? To modernize public buses and retrofit subways, as demanded by the Rehabilitation Act of 1973, New York concluded in 1980 that the requisite capital improvements and annual operating bills would amount to a budget-busting expense. Mayor Edward I. Koch figured, "It would be cheaper for us to provide every severely disabled person with taxi service than make 255 of our subway stations accessible."[37]

Mercifully, after pitched legal battles, the federal planners relented and lowered the costs. New York, with an old and extensive transit system, should never have been sidetracked from opting for alternatives to the federal retrofit policy. For this city it should have been obvious from the outset that investing in advanced paratransit or even subsidizing taxi rides would secure a greater net gain for the seriously disabled and for beleaguered local taxpayers.

In 1973 during the congressional debate on the Rehabilitation Act, the bill's authors seemed to have had no clue that in venues like New York the legislation's burdens might well exceed its blessings. One of the chief sponsors admitted afterward that neither he nor any of his colleagues "had any concept that it would involve such tremendous costs."[38] The deliberations were not altogether different sixteen years later when Congress took up the Americans with Disabilities Act of 1990, an even bolder piece of legislation mandating "fair and just access."[39] Local authorities pleaded for greater leeway or else for federal aid to cushion compliance costs, but Congress seemed untroubled. It wrote into the ADA a raft of requirements and almost no financial assistance.[40]

At congressional hearings on the ADA a representative of the Memphis Area Transit Authority guessed that the measure, if adopted, would force that city to eliminate hundreds of thousands of transit trips annually.[41] Dire warnings like this one about the fiscal havoc the bill portended proved mostly exaggerated. Nevertheless the law's seeming insouciance about local dissimilarities hit some communities hard. Faced with an ultimatum to construct some 65,000 wheelchair ramps by the mid-1990s the city of Phoenix reported that "it would be physically impossible to find enough skilled labor in the Valley to conduct such a massive construction program, even if the deadline were several years away.[42] Ordered to incorporate curb cuts and sidewalk ramps in its plans for downtown street repaving, officials in Philadelphia guessed that more than a third of its planned repavements would be unaffordable.[43] The Washington Metro in the nation's capital is America's most modern and beautifully designed subway system. Nonetheless it was directed to tear up parts of forty-five station platforms and install bumpy tiles along edges to accommodate the sight impaired. Interestingly the two leading organizations representing the blind—the American Council of the Blind and the National Federation of the Blind—disagreed about whether this multimillion dollar effort would protect sight-impaired transit users or perhaps endanger them.

Zero Tolerance

How to handle municipal overtime pay, regulate the town water supply, or resurface city streets and sidewalks used to be judgments that local authorities dispatched. Now, more and more of these daily administrative duties are subject to federal guidance. Whatever the rationale for guiding so many quotidian decisions, however, the government's agenda would be less troublesome for many cities if its specifications sought to set only modest baselines. Alas the specifications are sometimes utopian.

Environmental Perfection

A number of U.S. environmental mandates certainly seem to qualify for that description. Their targets, timetables, and technologies seem specified without regard to whether the perils the rules are meant to diminish are great or small. Indeed policy in important instances proceeds as if risk should be banished at any price. This feverish pursuit of environmental purification, sometimes tolerating virtually no margin of health risk, is unreasonable for many municipalities and thousands of businesses.

When the EPA revised its goals for curbing effluents from municipal incinerators in 1995, for instance, it ordered the virtual elimination of emissions of mercury and lead as well as dioxin.[44] Most of these toxic substances had already dropped dramatically; overall lead emissions, for example, were down 98 percent between 1970 and 1995. The city of Tampa, which had finished building a state-of-the-art incinerator only ten years earlier, now had to refit that modern installation with another round of pollution control equipment costing scores of millions of dollars.[45]

How much the latest incineration standards would improve public health was uncertain. In a review of epidemiological research on the health of persons living near city incinerators in the United Kingdom one study discerned no consistent pattern of ill health.[46] The findings were interesting because the studies surveyed relied primarily on data from the 1970s and 1980s when pollution controls on incinerators were underdeveloped. After at least a decade of stringent regulation it was likely that the remaining health hazards from these facilities would be small—especially in the United States where a person's average exposure to poisons such as mercury is now less than half the average in Europe.[47]

In 1994 the Congressional Budget Office estimated that under the Comprehensive Environmental Response, Compensation and Liability Act the expense of cleaning up the nation's toxic waste dumps would run between $106 billion and a staggering $463 billion.[48] How could this environmental project cost more than twice the entire gross domestic product of Sweden? The excesses of Superfund bear some responsibility. Costs escalate when sites have to be decontaminated so pristinely that a child playing on them could safely eat their dirt for seventy days a year.[49] Thus the program had completed merely 52 of 1,320 designated sites as of 1993. City governments have incurred directly only a fraction of the multibillion dollar Superfund bill. But the persistence of old brownfields, at least partly shadowed by Superfund liabilities, continues to be for inner cities a financial sinkhole. . . .

Hypersensitivity

In bygone days almost anyone joining a big city police force, fire department, sanitation crew, or inner city school system understood that he or she would be entering an often unpleasant, indeed perilous, occupation. The clients of these tough "street-level bureaucracies" were not always polite company, and neither would be some of the supervisors and coworkers. Nasty or boorish encounters would occur; they went with the territory.

Expectations are rather different nowadays. U.S. legal theories have added new meanings to the pursuit of admissible and equitable employment conditions. "Hostile" work environments, unintentional discriminations ("disparate impacts"), even precautions misconstrued as insults or slights—all these imperfections and more are actionable.

Taxpayers, not philanthropists, pay the salaries of municipal employees. One would think that city officials accountable to voters might be permitted to set, say, basic health eligibility criteria and then unceremoniously ask prospective employees for their medical histories, especially if the jobs in question were physically demanding, stressful, or dangerous. Not so fast. To attain a bias-free environment for applicants with disabilities, such queries now have to be conducted with extreme delicacy, if indeed, they can be conducted at all. In one of many revealing vignettes in his 1997 book *The Excuse Factory*, Walter K. Olson relates what happened to a policeman in Boston who was disciplined after his superiors discovered that he had lied under oath about having received inpatient psychiatric care on five occasions. The policeman had to be reinstated, with back pay and damages.[50] What about the subway cleaner in New York who was refused a promotion to train operator because his corpulence prevented him from passing a basic stress test? He had standing to sue for alleged discrimination, did, and got the job.[51]

Sometimes the kinds of pains taken to ensure benign work environments are not without ironies. "A Los Angeles Police Department official," Olson recounts, "said the department was moving against a range of 'inappropriate' male doings even though 'very, very few' of them 'would rise to the level of true sex harassment.'"[52] But some years later misconduct of a different sort was disclosed in the LAPD: some members of the force had trafficked in narcotics and were accused of planting evidence, framing suspects, and shooting some unarmed ones.[53] What had been done to prevent *these* doings? Apparently too little according to newspaper accounts. Some of the officers implicated in the scandal seem to have been hired without adequately checking their backgrounds, which included histories of arrests and alcoholism.[54]

At all levels of government in the United States efforts to protect the civil rights of workers have moved beyond the original mission—to attain basic equality of opportunity for an oppressed minority in the labor force. State and local jurists often have been just as uncompromising as many federal ones in their efforts to sanitize employment procedures. (The Boston policeman took his grievance to a state court, though his could as easily have been a federal case.) The evolution of employment law at the federal level, however, has provided the legal foundation, and the main inspiration, for all concerned. . . .

Adversarial Legalism

Which brings up a third feature of the ubiquitous federal presence: it has helped stoke a firestorm of litigation. Between 1991 and 1995 the cost of routine liability claims in New York City increased 57 percent in constant dollars.[55] By 1992 these legal bills were totaling more than the city's entire budget for its parks and libraries.[56] The trend in some other cities was worse. During the same period Minneapolis experienced a 187 percent increase in liability expenditures.[57]

And that was only one portion of the jagged legal landscape. Alongside the mounting malpractice complaints, traffic accident claims, zoning appeals, slip-and-falls, and countless other petty municipal torts came new causes to sue city governments, now increasingly in the federal courts. Several Supreme Court opinions had widened the general exposure of cities to civil actions.[58] These and other stimulants made themselves felt.

The Long Arm of the Lawsuit

Litigation in the federal courts exploded after 1960. That year there was a total of only 2,483 civil filings under the categories of civil rights-related cases, for example, whereas the number of such cases reached 98,153 by 1995.[59] Of these lawsuits, the ones that targeted the local public sector left virtually no facet of municipal administration undisputed. Major cities found themselves awash in court orders determining everything from the racial balancing of schools to the placement of foster children and the schooling of learning-disabled students, to the provision of shelters for the homeless, the use of city jails, buses, and even public fire alarm boxes.

Fire alarm boxes? In 1996 a federal judge halted the New York City Fire Department's plan to replace 16,300 antiquated alarm boxes with public telephones wired to an emergency system. The rationale: hearing-impaired persons might be unable to use the phones; the new system violated a federal guarantee of "equal access" to public facilities.[60]

For years a federal court had told New York how to run its jails. Conditions in the jails needed reform. But under the terms of its decree, active since 1978, the court-appointed "special masters" became fastidious. No particular was spared—down to the ratio of cups of borax per gallon of water required to mop the bathrooms.[61]

In 1996, at the other end of the country, the Los Angeles Metropolitan Transit Authority (MTA) settled a federal suit in which the MTA was accused of discriminating against minorities because city buses on certain routes were very crowded. One of the plaintiffs characterized the conditions on the MTA's buses as "a brutal violation" of civil rights. The terms of the consent decree got into specifics: there could be no more than an average of fifteen people standing during bus rides for any twenty-minute peak period by the end of 1997; then no more than an average of eleven people by June 2000; then no more than eight by June 2002.[62]

While court orders like those in Los Angeles and New York had delved into details those in some other cities were detailed—and drastic. To relieve overcrowding in Philadelphia's prisons, for instance, a federal judge barred pretrial detention of any suspect not charged with a violent crime. The long-range purpose of this shock treatment was to ameliorate the city's jails, but in the meantime, according to the court's critics, the result was that the number of fugitive drug dealers soared.[63] By one count more than three-quarters of Philadelphia's drug dealers became fugitives within ninety days of their arrests.

To be sure, most legal threats to city authorities would fizzle well short of producing judicial injunctions, usually because the underlying grievances simply could not stand up even by the standards of the world's most accommodating civil justice system. That did not mean, however, that cities could ignore the threats. To limit liabilities millions of dollars have been spent each year paying lawyers, keeping legally bullet-proof records, purchasing insurance, commissioning consultants, administering sensitivity training to personnel, and so forth. . . .[64]

Litigious Workplaces

Employment cases, which already accounted for about a quarter of all civil suits against city governments by the mid-1980s, multiplied as well.[65] A growing number were brought by people expecting to be made whole by one or another of the federal civil rights statutes. Energized by various bold enactments, such as the Age Discrimination in Employment Acts of 1975 and 1986, the Americans with Disabilities Act of 1990, and the Civil Rights Act amendments of 1991, federal antibias suits fanned out to service a lengthening queue of clients. As in environmental advocacy cases plaintiffs acquired new incentives to sue. After 1991, for example, the burden of proof in cases of alleged racial or ethnic discrimination was tilted against defendants. The mere composition by race of an employer's payroll could be used as *prima facie* evidence of racism, leaving the truth to the accused, not the accusers, to establish. The accusers, moreover, could have the fees of their attorneys and expert witnesses recovered in multiples when prejudice was proved. And compensatory and punitive damages became available, with the odds of collecting large sums significantly improved by the use of jury trials.

Novel legal assaults on municipal employment practices also came from federal authorities acting directly. Closely scrutinized by the Equal Employment Opportunity Commission and the Department of Justice's Civil Rights Division have been the testing procedures for city job candidates. In city after city the physical fitness tests conducted by police and fire departments as well as other municipal agencies came under suspicion of victimizing some protected classes (women, for instance), while the pencil-and-paper examinations administered under typical civil service systems risked charges of excluding others (for example, blacks and Hispanics). Statistical discrimination was found even when respectable quotients of minorities ultimately made their way into hiring pools. Minority candidates were 30 percent of those who took a special civil service exam designed to increase minority representation in New York City's police department in the early 1980s. Nearly two thousand blacks and Hispanics reached the final pool. But that was not enough, according to a federal judge, who proceeded to set a standard for the department whereby half of all new hires had to be black or Hispanic until they reached at least 30 percent of the total force. . . .[66]

Suing the Schools

While the municipal workplace became increasingly litigious other sources of legal strife engulfed the delivery of city services, most notably the schools. For decades numerous cities had grappled with court-ordered desegregation plans, many of which had the unwanted consequence of aggravating racial imbalances by accelerating the exodus of white families from urban school systems.[67] These ordeals had finally run their course by the late 1990s, although not everywhere. As of 1995 several major city school districts, including those of Nashville, Buffalo, Indianapolis, and Memphis, were still operating under their original court orders or were still being supervised by a federal court though their original desegregation plans had been revised.[68] And as late as 1998 the DOJ was filing additional briefs requesting continued judicial supervision of the decades-old desegregation case in St. Louis.[69] But even as most of the forced busing experiments receded legal activists pressured school systems to secure other entitlements—such as a right to asbestos-free classrooms and the right of all children with disabilities to receive special educational services.

In 1975 Congress passed the Education of All Handicapped Children Act.[70] The aim of the law was to nationalize standards and procedures by which schools educated the handicapped. Teachers, administrators, and parents were to design jointly "individualized educational programs" for these children. The extensive tests and evaluations needed to prepare the programs could not be "racially or culturally discriminatory." Parents dissatisfied with a program were entitled to appeal up the line, ultimately to the federal courts. Schools would have to mainstream students "to the maximum extent appropriate" and provide for them "related services" such as physical therapy, psychological counseling, and recreational facilities. No school could change the placement of a special education student without parental approval. School districts would be required to identify all possible candidates for special education. This so-called child-find process involved discovering not only the eligible children, but also figuring out which ones were already enrolled but inadequately served.

Enforcing so elaborate a national code stirred legal conflicts as inevitable local infractions pertaining to one provision or another were revealed or perceived. "Every decision you make in special education you ask, 'Am I going to get sued for this?'"[71] That fear, voiced by the principal of an elementary school in Dade Country, Florida, could have been expressed by any number of other school officials around the country in the mid-1980s, at least in districts with sizable special education enrollments. One survey of state and local education boards published in 1987 indicated that more than a quarter of them had been sued.[72]

As the level of disputation rose the Supreme Court tried repeatedly to set boundaries. A decision in 1984 denied parents the ability to recoup attorneys' fees and one in 1989 went so far as to invoke Eleventh Amendment immunity of states from certain federal suits.[73] However, Congress promptly reversed these setbacks. Reauthorizations of the handicapped education act in 1986 and 1990 further enfranchised its citizen litigants, covered their legal expenses (now for administrative hearings as well as trials), and extended the whole program to preschool children.[74]

Predictably the law, presently titled the Individuals with Disabilities Education Act (IDEA), ratcheted the volume of litigation another notch (figure 9.2). As in other spheres of adversarial excess (certain environmental programs, for instance) IDEA raised some bizarre expectations, not just legitimate requests, in the nation's courts of law. The superintendent of one California school district reportedly described confronting plaintiffs' lawyers who demanded such "related services" as karate lessons for a kindergarten child with an immune system disorder, horseback riding lessons as rehabilitation therapy for a child who had had seizures, and school trips to Disneyland for a child who was depressed.[75]

And predictably the distribution of the legal troubles has been uneven: besieged disproportionately have been the districts with large special-ed

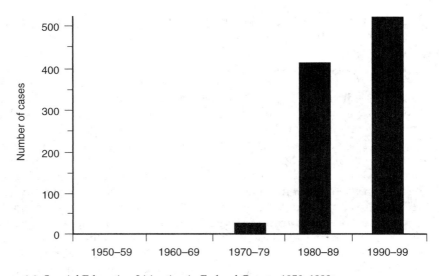

Figure 9.2 Special Education Litigation in Federal Courts, 1950–1999[a]

Source: Perry A. Zirkel, "The 'Explosion' in Education Litigation: An Update," *West's Education Law Reporter*, no. 114 (1997), p. 348.

[a]Data for 1990–99 are a projection that is based on the actual number of cases through December of 1995.

constituencies—the school systems of cities like New York, Baltimore, and Washington, D.C., that would have to cope for years with laborious consent decrees.[76]

Curing or Abetting the Mischiefs of Faction?

The Individuals with Disabilities Education Act is a monument to best intentions gone astray. Back in 1975, when Congress voted almost unanimously to plant this federal foothold in local public education, the lawmakers hardly anticipated what lay ahead. As its original title indicated the legislation was intended to assist the comparatively small number of children who were *handicapped*—that is, blind, deaf, paralyzed, or otherwise gravely impaired. In the ensuing quarter-century, however, definitions of disability widened to include categories of emotional, mental, or behavioral characteristics that had scarcely denoted a "handicap" in years past. Twenty-five years ago, for instance, there was no clinical classification for inattentive pupils. Now, diagnosed as suffering from "attention deficit disorder," they could be eligible for special services.[77] Twenty-five years ago underachieving students were simply called slow learners. Now, they, too, could qualify for special treatment; according to the U.S. Department of Education, "a severe discrepancy between achievement and intellectual ability" could signify that such students were learning disabled.[78] Partly in this fashion, IDEA eventually amassed about 6.1 million clients—and with them, colossal costs.[79]

The lawmakers of 1975 envisioned an expense that might rise to $8 billion nationwide, 40 percent of which would be defrayed by federal grants.[80] By the late 1990s the initiative's annual total was more than five times larger.[81] In the meantime, the federal contribution settled between 8 and 15 percent as congressional appropriators fled the oncoming budgetary behemoth.[82] State and local governments were left to confront it. New York City found itself allocating a quarter of its school budget to special-ed, an obligation so massive it crowded out more than $1 billion of other local priorities, from programs boosting gifted and talented kids to improved street lighting.[83]

Oversubscribed with students in special education, all of whom were entitled to customized "appropriate education" plans and some of whom required extraordinary facilities, many cities resorted to placing substantial percentages in private institutions. The premium for these schools, on top of the rest of the program's lopsided overhead, drove its average per pupil expenditures to twice the average for regular instruction, and in some cities (New York, for instance) to nearly three times the cost of instructing regular students.[84]

No affluent, civilized society can neglect the educational needs of disabled children. In 1975 the decision to assist them with what was supposed to be a large infusion of federal funds was decent and humane. But a responsible government also cannot, in effect, bring forth a blizzard of demands and then renege on its promise, shift the expense to communities that can least afford it, and run the risk of lowering the welfare of the remaining citizens in those communities. It is not too much to say that federal policy for special education has erred in just about all these ways. Its constraints on claims and eligibility are unclear; its appropriated funds have consistently fallen far below authorizations; and it has weighed most heavily on overtaxed cities with weak school systems. . . .

Summary

If each of these federal interventions decidedly improved the quality of urban life, the misgivings expressed in these pages could be shrugged off. But there is a point at which routinely subjecting municipal decisions to national supervision and regimentation risks doing more damage than good.

Federal regulation today reaches into so many details of municipal administration that picayune concerns are nationalized alongside weightier ones. Much of this spectacle is merely a nuisance. A federal court that interferes with the ability of a city to test, say, municipal clerk-typists for grammar, spelling, and punctuation (as the Fifth Circuit ruled a number of years ago) might trifle with the local community's own valued standards but probably does not put it in jeopardy.[85] At times, however, the stakes have been higher. The safety of community residents can be compromised, for example, by rulings that limit the testing of would-be firefighters and police recruits for endurance, strength, or agility (as some of the opinions handed down by the federal courts have done), or by rulings that turn loose hundreds of arrested suspects, including some charged with robbery, stalking, carjacking, drug dealing, and manslaughter (as a federal injunction against pretrial detention did for several years in Philadelphia).

Some federal mandates sock cities with unnecessarily large costs. Costs can soar, for example, amid the national campaigns for risk-free environments—such as perfectly bias-free workplaces, toxin-free tap water, asbestos-free schools, lead-free housing, hazard-free redevelopment sites, and more. The persistence of some 21,000 brownfields languishing in cities is a stark example of the debacle that a zero-risk mentality can create.[86]

Federal law has also enmeshed municipalities in new litigation, some of which manacles their managers, demoralizes their personnel, and ties their budgets in knots. Due in no small part to federal policy, the terms and conditions of municipal employment are cited as the realm most roiled by legal disputes or the threat of them.[87] City schools used to be relatively simple and trusted neighborhood institutions. Since the 1960s, however, they have been buffeted by federal regulatory and judicial directives, leaving many preoccupied with legal bills and compliance issues more than with the quality of instruction for most students.[88]

By the early 1990s New York City's costs of complying with the ten largest court orders and mandates, specifying protocols for various municipal functions, were said to corner 26 percent of the city's tax revenue.[89] Even if every dollar earmarked in this litigious fashion were a dollar well spent (a dubious proposition), local taxpayers could fairly ask whether less adversarial means would have allocated the desired resources better, or at least without as much costly friction. By the early 1990s the cumulative cost of settling New York's liability claims had reached bewildering proportions.[90]

Alongside these considerable vexations lies the fact that some federal regulations are relatively rigid templates, superimposed on cities and towns regardless of their diverse circumstances. In certain locations, therefore, the mandated expenditures are simply a waste of money. (Should Phoenix really be made to spend significant sums to monitor the runoff from practically nonexistent rain storms?) In other instances the costs of meeting a given standard, though not pointless, will vary wildly among localities. For example, all municipalities will have to bring their groundwater treatment up to the nationwide standards of the Safe Drinking Water Act. The charges for households could vary by several thousand percent between small and large cities.[91]

U.S. environmental strictures are hardly the only ones that beget interjurisdictional inequities. Many central cities in the United States continue to contain disproportionate percentages of the low-income residents of metropolitan areas. Hence these cities bear a disproportionate share of poverty-related public expenditures. National regulations can contribute to the imbalance when their costs are not adequately reimbursed and are a function of local poverty rates. The federal special education mandate, as we have seen, falls into this category, but so do quite a few others.[92]

At the end of 1996 the District of Columbia was home to 45 percent of the Washington region's poor.[93] A consequence, as in other cities that have to shoulder comparable concentrations of poverty, is that the expense of administering almost any city service is inherently higher in the District than in the surrounding suburbs.[94] Whatever the other reasons for the District's extraordinary administrative cost structure, the heavy lifting is scarcely alleviated by some thirty-nine federal court decrees, some of which have compelled steep increases in the costliest of municipal items—like overtime compensation for city workers.[95]

Race to the Bottom—or the Top?

It is generally assumed that Washington intervenes in local decisions primarily to prevent intergovernmental rifts and rivalries from degrading basic norms for public health, safety, or welfare. Federal authorities, the theory goes, chiefly step in to set suitable baselines—for Atlanta's air quality, or New York's fiscal practices, or the competence of school teachers in a bunch of cities. But in reality much federal preemption of local policies works the other way around. It subjects state and local governments to national directives even when those governments are emulating, indeed outdoing, one another to run standards up, not down.

In 1986 Congress moved to extend to preschoolers the universal right to special education for handicapped children. But forty-two states already had begun programs of this sort.[96] Similarly, by the time Congress proclaimed that no schoolchild should be exposed to asbestos risks most school districts already had programs to repair dangerous buildings. In 2001 a new administration in Washington proposed to coax the states to start rating the performance of all their local elementary and secondary schools. But less noticed during the national education reform debate was that seventeen states already assigned such ratings, four more were poised to initiate them in 2002, and at least two more planned to do so soon thereafter.[97] The concept of school accountability, in other words, was percolating and spreading at the local level well in advance of any coercive federal measures.

Proponents of central direction, however, frequently seem unimpressed. By their logic, if so many state and local initiatives have already blazed a trail, national standards only complete what the locals have started. The latter, it would appear, are as likely to have their independence shorn when they are proactive and progressive as when they are laggards.

Principled arguments are hard to advance for at least some of the specialized, coerced expenditures that have been pressed upon cities. But worthy or not, federally mandated programs, once established, are not easy to redesign. Program preservationists prevail.[98] The cementing of policies by vested interests was not what the framers of the Constitution had in mind when they sought to enlarge the orbit of national authority. What the founders intended was to check and counterbalance the power of calcified local elites. . . .

Notes

1. For a full account of the Tulsa riot on which this paragraph is based, see Brent Staples, "Unearthing a Riot," *New York Times Magazine*, December 19, 1999, pp. 64–69.
2. See Paul E. Peterson, *City Limits* (University of Chicago Press, 1981), chaps. 10, 11.
3. See David Goldberg, "Heads Up, Atlanta: Cities Are Scrambling to Comply with the Clean Air Act's Strict New Rules," *Planning*, vol. 64 (July 1998), pp. 20–23.
4. James Fallows, *More Like Us* (Houghton Mifflin, 1989), p. 169.
5. Racial violence, sparked by alleged black rapes, exploded in Omaha, Kansas City, Knoxville, Rosewood, Fla., Longview, Tex., and Washington, D.C., among other towns, at about this period.
6. Nearly all the PCBs flowing into the Great Lakes originate from the air. An estimated quarter of the nitrogen in the Chesapeake Bay derives from polluted air drifting from at least four neighboring states. Mary Graham, *The Morning after Earth Day: Practical Environmental Politics* (Brookings, 1999), p. 80.
7. Susan Rose-Ackerman, "Does Federalism Matter? Choice in a Federal public," *Journal of Political Economy*, vol. 49, no. 1 (1981), pp. 152–63. See also John H. Cumberland, "Interregional Pollution Spillovers and Consistency of Environmental Policy," in M. Siebert and others, eds., *Regional Environmental Policy: The Economic Issues* (New York University Press, 1979), pp. 255–81.
8. James Madison, "Federalist No. 10," in Pietro S. Nivola and David H. Rosenbloom, eds., *Classic Readings in American Politics*, 3d ed. (St. Martin's, 1999), p. 34.
9. *Budget of the United States Government, Fiscal Year 1993*, table 12.1, 5, pp. 164–65.
10. This was reflected in the nearly static level of aid to state and local governments between 1980 and 1995, excluding federal assistance for Medicaid, Annothy Conlan, *From New Federalism to Devolution: Twenty-Five Years of Intergovernmental Reform* (Brookings, 1998), pp. 204–06, 219.
11. Conlan, *From New Federalism to Devolution*, p. 204.
12. James Q. Wilson and John J. Dilulio Jr., *American Government: Institutions and Policies*, 7th ed. (Houghton Mifflin Company, 1998), p. 70.
13. Bernard J. Frieden and Marshall Kaplan, *The Politics of Neglect: Urban Aid from Model Cities to Revenue Sharing* (MIT Press, 1977).
14. As early as 1994, the states were enjoying surpluses that totaled more than 7 billion.
15. On how devolution has been a cost-controlling mechanism for social programs such as Medicaid, see James R. Tallon Jr. and Lawrence D. Brown, "Who Gets What? Devolution of Eligibility and Benefits in Medicaid," in Frank J. and John J. Dilulio Jr., *Medicaid and Devolution: A View from the States* [Brookings, 1998], p. 237.
16. See generally, on the efficiency gains from interjurisdictional competition within federal systems, Michael S. Greve, *Real Federalism* (Washington: American Enterprise Institute Press, 1999). For the leading analysis of its disadvantages see Paul E. Peterson, *The Price of Federalism* (Brookings, 1995).
17. Paul C. Light, *The True Size of Government* (Brookings, 1999), p. 32.
18. In 1995, for instance, California collected $1.2 billion in federal disaster relief, much of it to compensate questionable "victims." Dan Morgan, "Governors Bit Helping Hand in Mandates Fight," *Washington Post*, January 1995, pp. A1, A6.
19. Demetrios Caraley, "Washington Abandons the Cities," *Political Science Quarterly*, vol. 107, no. 1 (1992), p. 13.
20. For the subsidy argument, see James R. St. John, "Unfunded Mandates: Financing State and National Needs," *Brookings Review*, vol. 13 (Spring 1995), 12–15.
21. *South Carolina v. Baker*, 485 U.S. 505 (1988).

22. *Garcia v. San Antonio Metropolitan Transit Authority*, 469 U.S. 528 (1985). Nine months later Congress responded by amending the Fair Labor Standards Act (FLSA), extending it again to all public sector employees. Public Law 99-150, November 13, 1985.

23. *National League of Cities v. Usery*, 426 U.S. 833 (1976).

24. On the impact of Davis-Bacon, see U.S. Advisory Commission on Intergovernmental Relations, *The Role of Federal Mandates in Intergovernmental Relations* (January 1996), p. 13.

25. See Walter Olson, *The Excuse Factory: How Employment Law is Paralyzing the American Workplace* (Free Press, 1997), p. 185.

26. For instance, *Tinker v. Des Moines Independent Community School District*, 393 U.S. 503 (1969); *Goss v. Lopez*, 419 U.S. 565 (1975). See Abigail Thernstrom, "Where Did All the Order Go? School Discipline and the Law," in Diane Ravitch, ed., *Brookings Papers on Education Policy, 1999* (Brookings, 1999), p. 213. In a North Carolina school district, for instance, a student who broke a teacher's arm was given a mere two-day suspension.

27. In *Bethel School District No. 403 v. Fraser*, 478 U.S. 675 (1986) and several ensuing decisions, the court sought to nudge the balance of authority back from students to school officials. However, lower courts have tended to restrict removals and even suspensions of special-ed students.

28. According to the so-called "2-in, 2-out" procedure, at least two employees have to remain outside the site of an "interior structural fire" when two go inside (Standard Number 1910.134 (g) (4) (i) through (iii)). OSHA, *Regulations (Standards - 29 (CFR): Standard Number 1910.134*. The rule may apply to many fire departments that have federally approved occupational safety and health (OSH) plans in effect. Section 18(b) of the Occupational Safety and Health Act of 1970 (Public Law 91-596) stipulated that states operating under their own OSH plans are required to provide OSH protection to public as well as private sector workers. And the standards of each state OSH plan have to be at least as stringent as those of the federal OSHA program, which covers all private sector workers. See U.S. Department of Labor, Office of Inspector General, *Evaluating the Status of Occupational Safety and Health Coverage of State and Local Workers in Federal OSHA States* (February 2000). Some two dozen states operate under federally approved OSH plans. Thus, California, as an example, follows the federal OSHA firefighting guideline verbatim. How much, if any, flexibility localities might have in such states is not entirely clear. A note attached to paragraph (g) of the OSHA regulations, however, adds this proviso: "Nothing in this section is meant to preclude firefighters from performing emergency rescue activities before an entire team has assembled."

29. Motor Carrier Safety Administration, Federal Highway Administration, Regulation no. 393.90.

30. I owe the Beverly Hills joke to James Q. Wilson and John J. DiIulio Jr., *American Government: Institutions and Policies* (Boston: Houghton Mifflin Company, 1998), p. 68.

31. The ensuing discussion is drawn from Pietro S. Nivola and Jon A. Shields, *Managing Green Mandates: Local Rigors of U.S. Environmental Regulation* (AEI-Brookings Joint Center for Regulatory Studies, 2001).

32. San Francisco concluded that it was simpler in the long run to build an oceanside secondary treatment plant than to count on obtaining periodic waivers. This city's experience illustrates the kinds of local complications that arise, even under EPA policies intended to increase local flexibility. San Francisco had obtained a waiver in the early 1980s, but it was only good for five years. If, one day, the city would have to build a second treatment plant, a particular site was referred. Rather than risk that subsequent waiver applications might be turned down, and that by then the land at the site might not be available, the city broke ground for the new facility in the late 1980s and opened it in September 1993.

33. At one time, however, the product in question had been in use near Columbus as well. For a breezy account of this and other incidents, see Thomas DiLorenzo, "Federal

Regulations: Environmentalism's Achilles' Heel," *USA Today Magazine*, vol. 123 (September 1994), p. 48.

34. Mike Allen, "Connecticut Joins Lawsuit over Pollution in Sound," *New York Times*, March 24, 1998, p. A24.

35. Robert A. Katzmann, *Institutional Disability: The Saga of Transportation Policy for the Disabled* (Brookings, 1986), p. 189.

36. The phrase is from Lawrence M. Friedman, *Total Justice* (Russell Sage Foundation, 1988).

37. Edward I. Koch, "The Mandate Millstone," *Public Interest*, no. 61 (Fall 1980), p. 45.

38. Representative Charles Vanik, quored in Timothy Clark, "Access for the Handicapped," *National Journal*, October 21, 1978, p. 1673. The Congressional Budget Office estimated that section 504 of the 1973 Rehabilitation Act would require $6.8 billion to equip buses with wheelchair lifts, install elevators in subway systems, and take other measures to expand access to public transit systems for the physically disabled. Congressional Budget Office, *Urban Transportation for Handicapped Persons: Alternative Federal Approaches* (Washington, 1979), p. xi.

39. For a definitive treatment of this initiative see Thomas F. Burke, "On the Rights Track: The Americans with Disabilities Act," in Pietro S. Nivola, ed., *Comparative Disadvantages: Social Regulations and the Global Economy* (Brookings, 1997).

40. Stephen L. Percy, "ADA, Disability Rights, and Evolving Regulatory Federalism," *Publius*, vol. 23 (Fall 1993), p. 87.

41. *Hearings on the Americans with Disabilities Act* before the Subcommittee on Surface Transportation of the House Committee on Public Works and Transportation, 101 Cong. 1 sess. (Government Printing Office, 1989), p. 2721.

42. James H. Matteson, "Americans with Disabilities Act Requirements: Community Sidewalks and Curbs," *City Council Report*, City of Phoenix, January 24, 1997, pp. 1–2.

43. Percy, "ADA," p. 104.

44. Pursuant to the Clean Air Act amendments of 1990, "Standards of Performance for New Stationary Sources and Emissions Guidelines for Existing Sources," *Federal Register*, vol. 60, no. 243 (December 19, 1995), pp. 65378–436.

45. City of Tampa, *Mayor's Strategic Initiatives* (January 1999), pp. 51–52.

46. Medical Research Council, *Health Effects of Waste Combustion Products* (Leicester, UK: Institute for Environment and Health, 1997).

47. U.S. Environmental Protection Agency, *Mercury Study Report to Congress: Volume II* (December 1997).

48. Katherine N. Probst and others, *Footing the Bill for Superfund Cleanup: Who Pays and How?* (Brookings and Resources for the Future, 1995), p. 1995.

49. Cleaning up urban waste sites, rivers, air sheds, and so on, by 90 percent may be practicable, but erasing the remaining 10 percent can be prohibitive. Stephen Breyer, *Breaking the Vicious Cycle: Toward Effective Risk Regulation* (Harvard University Press, 1993), pp. 11–12, 29.

50. Olson, *The Excuse Factory*, p. 17.

51. James Rutenberg, "Long Weight's Over," *New York Daily News*, March 5, 1998, p. 8.

52. Olson, *The Excuse Factory*, p. 253.

53. Rene Sanchez, "LAPD Reeling as Corruption Cases Multiply," *Washington Post*, February 12, 2000, pp. A1, A14.

54. James Sterngold, "Los Angeles Police Officials Admit Widespread Lapses," *New York Times*, February 17, 2000, p. A12.

55. Charles Epp, "Litigation against Local Governments: Expenditures on Legal Services, 1960–1995," paper presented at the annual meeting of the American Political Science Association, 1997, p. 5.

56. Allen R. Myerson, "Soaring Liability Payments Burdening New York," *New York Times*, June 29, 1992, p. B1.

57. Epp, "Litigation against Local Governments," p. 5.

58. See, for instance, *Monell v. New York City Department of Social Services*, 436 U.S. 658, 56 2d 611, 98 S Ct. 2018 (1978); *Owen v. City of Independence*, 445 U.S. 622, 633n., 13m 100 S Ct. 1398, 1406–1407 (1980); and *Maine v. Thiboutot*, 448, 100 S Ct. 2502 (1980).

59. Richard A. Posner, *The Federal Courts: Challenge and Reform* (Harvard University Press, 1996), pp. 57, 60–61.

60. Don Vannatta Jr., "U.S. Judge Says Removing Alarm Boxes Discriminates against the Deaf," *New York Times*, February 14, 1996, pp. B3.

61. Greg B. Smith, "City Asks for End to Jail Regs," *New York Daily News*, May 30, 1996, p. 22.

62. "MTA Officials Admit Violating Federal Court Order to Reduce Overcrowding, Report Says," Associated Press State and Local Wire, September 9, 1998.

63. See Sarah B. Vanderbraak, "Why Criminals Would Rather Be in Philadelphia," *Policy Review*, no. 71 (Summer 1995), pp. 73–75.

64. See Charles R. Epp, "Litigation Stories: Official Perceptions of Lawsuits against Local Government," paper prepared for the 1998 annual meeting of the Law and Society Association, Aspen, Colorado, pp. 9–11.

65. Yong S. Lee, "Civil Liability of State and Local Governments," *Public Administration Review*, vol. 47 (March–April 1987), p. 160.

66. Koch, "Mandate Millstone," p. 53.

67. White student enrollment in Milwaukee stood at 58.9 percent in 1976. After the city's desegregation plan took effect, the percentage dropped to 45.3 percent by 1980. White students had been leaving city schools all along, but the annual rate of departures accelerated by almost 62 percent as the desegregation process unfolded. Paul E. Peterson, Barry G. Rabe, and Kenneth K. Wong, *When Federalism Works* (Brookings, 1986), p. 185. Forced busing in Charlotte-Mecklenburg had been in effect for decades. As of the late 1990s, it had still to achieve racial balance. In fact, forty-two of the district's schools were not in balance as of 1998, compared with only seven in 1979. Busing in Denver began in 1974. Parents responded by moving away to suburban districts, sharply reducing the number of white students in city schools. In 1995 a federal judge finally ordered the busing to stop. "Stopping the School Bus," *Economist*, May 29, 1999, pp. 25–26. Boston's busing program also began in 1974. Today, only 15 percent of the city's public school students are white, compared with 60 percent in the early 1970s. Carey Goldberg, "Busing's Day Ends: Boston Drops Race in Pupil Placement," *New York Times*, July 15, 1999, p. A1.

68. National School Boards Association, *Survey of Public Education in the Nation's Urban Districts* (Alexandria, Va., 1995), pp. 130–32.

69. Clegg, "Lee," p. A19.

70. For an excellent chronicle of this program's evolution, see R. Shep Melnick, *Between the Lines: Interpreting Welfare Rights* (Brookings, 1994), chaps. 7 and 8.

71. Peterson and others, *When Federalism Works*, p. 127.

72. Roberta Weiner and Maggie Hume, *And Education for All: Public Policy and Handicapped Education* (Alexandria, Va.: Capital, 1987), cited in Paul I. Posner, *The Politics of Unfunded Mandates: Whither Federalism* (Georgetown University Press, 1998), p. 132.

73. *Smith v. Robinson*, 468 U.S. 992 (1984); and *Dellmuth v. Muth*, 491 U.S. 223, 230 (1989).

74. See *Congressional Quarterly Almanac* (Washington: Congressional Quarterly, Inc., 1990), p. 616.

75. Lisa Gubernick and Michelle Conlin, "The Special Education Scandal," *Forbes*, February 10, 1997, p. 66.

76. Urban school systems naturally have disproportionate numbers of pupils in special education because learning disabilities are closely correlated with poverty. Jay Gottlieb and others, "Special Education in Urban America," *Journal of Special Education*, vol. 27, no. 4 (1994), pp. 453–65.

77. See Wade F. Horn and Douglas Tynan, "Revamping Special Education," *Public Interest*, no. 144 (Summer 2001), p. 38.

78. Under the wide-ranging category of students said to suffer a "specific learning disability" (SLD) are those who may have trouble listening, speaking, reading basic words, comprehending what they read, expressing themselves in writing, problem solving in mathematics, or doing mathematical calculations. According to the director of the University of Minnesota's National Center on Educational Outcomes, more than 80 percent of all schoolchildren in the United States could qualify as having SLD under one definition or another. Horn and Tynan, "Revamping Special Education," p. 38. See also Joseph P. Shapiro and others, "Separate and Unequal," *U.S. News & World Report*, December 13, 1993. Some diagnosed afflictions seem to have burst onto the scene in epidemic proportions. In the years 1994–99, for instance, the number of children considered autistic increased by 153.6 percent, David Brown, "Autism's New Face," *Washington Post*, March 26, 2000, p. A1.

79. The 6.1 million figure was for 1999–2000 and included children and youth ages three to twenty-one. In 1976–77 the number of children receiving special education services and accommodations had been 3.7 million. Horn and Tynan, "Revamping Special Education," p. 36. Jeffrey L. Katz, "Policy on Disabled is Scrutinized over Discipline Problems, Cost," *Congressional Quarterly Weekly Report*, May 11, 1996.

80. *Congressional Quarterly Almanac*, 1975, vol. 31 (Congressional Quarterly Inc., 1976), p. 651.

81. Tom Loveless and Diane Ravitch, "Broken Promises: What the Federal Government Can Do to Improve American Education," *Brookings Review*, vol. 18 (Spring 2000), p. 20.

82. U.S. Advisory Commission on Intergovernmental Relations, *The Role of Federal Mandates in Intergovernmental Relations* (January 1996). Loveless and Ravitch, "Broken Promises," give a more current 12 percent estimate. See also Jeffrey L. Katz, "Policy on Disabled Is Scrutinized," p. 1297.

83. Norm Fruchter and others, *Focus on Learning: A Report on Reorganizing General and Special Education in New York City*, New York University, Institute for Education and Social Policy, 1995; Sam Illon, "Special Education Absorbs School Resources," *New York Times*, April 7, 1994, p. A1; Scott Miner Brook, "The Cratering of New York," *U.S. News & World Report*, May 27, 1991, p. 31.

84. This distortion in New York was far worse than in the rest of the state. (Spending on special education grew much less rapidly elsewhere in New York State, and did not squeeze the resources available for regular students as badly.) Mark Lankgord and James Wyckoff, "The Allocation of Resources to Special Education and Regular Instruction," in Helen F. Ladd, ed., *Holding Schools Accountable: Performance-Based Reform in Education* (Brookings, 1996), p. 231. In the District of Columbia, as much as $49 million of the city's proposed $125 million special education budget in 1998 may have been claimed by the 17 percent of special education students that had to be sent to private schools. Beset by litigation, the District's program also anticipated paying between $6 million and $8 million in legal fees to plaintiffs' lawyers. Doug Struck and Valerie Strauss, "D.C. Special Ed System Still in Disarray, Report Says," *Washington Post*, July 20, 1998, p. B1.

85. Olson, *Excuse Factory*, p. 181.

86. U.S. Conference of Mayors, *Recycling America's Land: A National Report on Brownfields Redevelopment,* vol. 3 (February 2000), pp. 9–11.

87. Epp, "Litigation Stories," pp. 6–7.

88. Paul T. Hill, "Supplying Effective Public Schools in Big Cities," in Diane Ravitch, ed., *Brookings Papers on Education Policy, 1999* (Brookings, 1999), pp. 422–23.

89. Ross Sandler and David Shoenbrod, "Government by Decree—The High Cost of Letting Judges Make Policy," *City Journal,* vol. 4 (Summer 1994).

90. Allen R. Myerson, "Soaring Liability Payments Burdening New York," *New York Times,* June 29, 1992, sec. B, p. 1.

91. Congressional Budget Office, *Federalism and Environmental Protection: Case Studies for Drinking Water and Ground-Level Ozone* (GPO, November 1997), pp. 25–30.

92. Great variations in the intermediary roles of state governments translate into widely divergent federal impacts. The U.S. special education program does not pose the same financial complexities for the cities of Florida, say, as for the municipalities of New York. (Local districts in Florida are responsible for only 2 to 3 percent of special education spending.) Peterson, *When Federalism Works,* p. 156.

93. Brookings Center on Urban and Metropolitan Government, *A Region Divided: The State of Growth in Greater Washington, D.C.* (Brookings, 1999), p. 3.

94. For a general analysis of this unbalanced pattern in metropolitan areas, see Janet Rothenberg Pack, "Poverty and Urban Public Expenditures," *Urban Studies,* vol. 33, no. 11 (1998), pp. 1995–2020.

95. U.S. General Accounting Office, *District of Columbia Government: Overtime Costs Exceed Those of Neighboring Governments* (September 1997), pp. 21, 32. The GAO found the District paying more in overtime as a percentage of municipal salaries than did any of the city's surrounding counties. For some poverty-related services (corrections, for instance) nearly 18 percent of the District's salary base went to overtime, compared with 0.2 percent in Maryland's Prince George's County.

96. Posner, *Unfunded Mandates,* p. 64.

97. "School Accountability: How Are States Holding Schools Responsible for Results?" *Education Week,* vol. 20 (January 11, 2001), p. 80.

98. See, more generally, the delightfully readable Jonathan Rauch, *Government's End: Why Washington Stopped Working* (New York: Public Affairs, 1999), especially chap. 6.

25

Isaac Martin

LOCAL PROGRESSIVISM AND THE LIVING WAGE

In the past five years, a new form of redistributive policy has emerged in cities across the United States. Following the passage of the first "living wage ordinance" by Baltimore in 1994, 21 other large cities—and at least 17 counties and

Isaac Martin, "Dawn of the Living Wage: The Diffusion of a Redistributive Municipal Policy," *Urban Affairs Review,* Vol. 36, No. 4, March 2001, pp. 470-496. Excerpts from pp. 470-478, 485-490, and corresponding notes and references on pp. 492-493 and 493-496.

other local governments—have passed similar laws that mandate a minimum wage above the poverty line for certain workers in the private sector. By the end of 1999, grassroots campaigns for such ordinances were reportedly under consideration or already underway in at least 50 more cities (American Federation of Labor-Congress of Industrial Organizations [AFL-CIO] 1999a). The sudden emergence, rapid diffusion, and surprising success of these living wage campaigns have attracted the attention of national media and major foundations, prompting several commentators to herald a new "living wage movement" (Kuttner 1997; Pollin and Luce 1998, 1; Nissen 1999, 2).

The demand for a "living wage" is not new; English-speaking labor movements have used the term at least since the nineteenth century (see Glickman 1997). Currently, labor and community activists use it to refer to a narrow set of legislative strategies that are best understood by comparing them to *minimum wage* legislation, on one hand, and *prevailing wage* legislation, on the other. Minimum wage laws establish a standard for wages that applies to all employers within a specified jurisdiction and that is not indexed to market wages. Prevailing wage laws apply only to employers who hold public contracts or receive some form of public subsidy, and they typically require employers to pay the wage that "prevails" in a given market rather than any absolute minimum. Living wage policies share characteristics of both: Like a minimum wage law, they set an absolute minimum standard, but like a prevailing wage law, they apply only to employers who hold public contracts or receive public monies (see Pollin and Luce 1998, chap. 2). There are important differences among living wage policies in the wage level, mandated benefits, and exact scope of coverage (Spain and Wiley 1998), but all of them aim explicitly to raise workers out of poverty. Furthermore, with the exception of policies passed by the states of Maryland and Minnesota, all living wage policies at the time of this writing have been passed by local governments (including municipalities, counties, and public authorities).[1]

What accounts for the emergence and successful passage of living wage policies? According to Paul Peterson's (1981) influential *City Limits*, local governments will tend to avoid policies that redistribute resources to the poor. Peterson argued that city governments in a federal system depend on private investors because a healthy local economy is important to securing revenues and votes. Investors, by contrast, do not depend on any particular local government but are free to relocate their business to another city if they choose. As a consequence of this unequal relationship, cities find themselves competing to attract mobile capital. Cities that pursue egalitarian policies will find themselves at a disadvantage in the competition because such policies benefit the poor by imposing costs on businesses and nonpoor city residents. Peterson concluded that "redistribution is not and cannot ordinarily be a constituent part of local government policy" (p. 210).

In this article, I build on recent scholarship that has contested Peterson's (1981) conclusions, arguing that there is still substantial "space for reform" (Swanstrom 1988) at the local level. First, as economic geographers and others have pointed out, all capital is not equally footloose (Cox 1997; Gertler 1997).

Firms that produce goods or services primarily for local markets, as well as firms that depend on close relationships with local government or other local firms, are likely to be relatively immobile. It follows that even though businesses usually threaten to move when progressive redistribution is proposed at the local level, some of the time they are bluffing (Dreier 1996b, 15). Living wage ordinances call their bluff by targeting employers who depend on city service contracts and who are not likely to move in response to a mandated wage increase.

Second, a growing literature points to variation in the political coalitions that constitute the urban "regime" (Stone 1993; Ferman 1996; Kantor, Savitch, and Haddock 1997). Regime theorists acknowledge that local governments are in an unequal bargaining relationship with private capital, but their work stresses the variability in the bargaining context and resources available to each side. When a local government occupies a commanding market position, whether because state and federal resources insulate it from market pressures or because the city possesses some locational advantage, it will have a greater economic ability to impose conditions on business. Similarly, when politicians form inclusive governing coalitions with labor and community allies, they are in a better political position to enact progressive policies that may antagonize sectors of the business community (DeLeon 1992; Ferman 1996; Kantor, Savitch, and Haddock 1997, 350).

In this article, I draw on this comparative literature, providing empirical evidence that variation in the presence of living wage policies can be explained by the variation in political coalitions across cities. I also echo Peterson's (1981) view that the U.S. federal system shapes local political outcomes, but I argue that it does so in different ways than Peterson proposes. In the argument presented here, the federal system not only constrains but also *enables* redistributive policy making at the city level, by allowing advocates of progressive policies to piggyback on successes in other cities. Because cities are free from strict central government supervision, they look to each other to define appropriate policies and models of governance. As "open systems" (Peterson 1981, 69), cities are sensitive not only to the movements of capital but also to political developments in other cities. If local progressives are to take advantage of this openness, they must have national networks through which policy models and campaign expertise can be shared among cities.

My central argument is thus that both local political coalitions and national networks are important to the explanation of the living wage movement. Before presenting the empirical evidence for this argument, I provide further background on living wage advocacy and review competing explanations for its emergence and success.

The Diffusion of the Living Wage Idea

The first living wage campaign was launched in 1993 by the Solidarity Sponsoring Committee (or Solidarity), an association of low-wage workers in

Baltimore. With the support of the Industrial Areas Foundation (IAF) and a national labor union, the American Federation of State, County, and Municipal Employees (AFSCME), Solidarity sought to organize Baltimore's working poor around a political program that linked social justice concerns to economic development policy. Activists and organizers argued that decades of city subsidies for downtown development had not delivered the promised economic payoff for Baltimore's African-American working-class neighborhoods. Although Solidarity did not ultimately secure a living wage for employees of *all* businesses that received city subsidies, its political influence during the 1994 mayoral race helped it to win the passage of a living wage ordinance that covers businesses holding city service contracts in December of that year.[2]

After the Baltimore ordinance received national media coverage, community organizers began to see the living wage campaign as a replicable model that could be applied in other cities. Organizations affiliated with the IAF and the Association of Community Organizations for Reform Now (ACORN) see the living wage as a winning issue that can both provide concrete improvements in the lives of working poor people and help build a political base for future campaigns (Reynolds 1999). Both the IAF and ACORN are networks of community organizations of low- and moderate-income people that provide their affiliates with access to professional community organizers and tactical expertise. Although the IAF initiated the first living wage campaign, ACORN has positioned itself as a "living wage clearinghouse," cataloguing living wage successes and publicizing them widely, establishing an e-mail list for living wage activists, and organizing national meetings for living wage advocates and researchers (see ACORN 1999). ACORN has assigned national staff to work on the living wage movement full-time and has emerged as an important player in many, though not all, local living wage campaigns (see Conrad 1998, 13; Reynolds 1999).

Many labor unions also find the living wage idea attractive. In Baltimore, AFSCME members employed by the city have benefited from the living wage ordinance, which raises the cost of contracting with the private sector for work that could be done by municipal employees. Other local unions have seen living wage ordinances as a way to aid collective bargaining by raising the prevailing wage for an already-organized sector or as a tool to help organize nonunion workers. Central labor councils (CLCs), which operate as countywide or regional federations of local labor unions within the AFL-CIO, have in many cases actively supported living wage campaigns (see, e.g., Eimer 1999; Nissen 1999).

With recent changes in the leadership of the AFL-CIO, living wage ordinances have also become a part of the strategy of organized labor at the national level. The Baltimore ordinance coincided with a contested election that brought John Sweeney's reform slate to power within the national AFL-CIO, and the new leadership recognized the Baltimore campaign as a way to help labor's program of organizing on a marketwide basis (see Sweeney 1998, 332). In addition to the policy benefits, labor has taken an interest in living wage campaigns as a way to form long-term labor-community coalitions that may help union organizing (see Needleman 1998; but see Bronfenbrenner and Juravich 1998, 32). The AFL-CIO has undertaken a variety of initiatives to encourage its affiliated unions and CLCs to ally with community groups around campaigns, including the living wage. In addition to collecting and disseminating information on living wage ordinances (AFL-CIO 1999a), the AFL-CIO has recently convened national meetings of CLCs to share successful coalition-building strategies (Gapasin and Wial 1998) and has initiated the Union Cities program, which promises additional resources to CLCs that sign an eight-point pledge to act as vehicles for organizing and grassroots coalition building (AFL-CIO 1999b; Eimer 1999; Fine 1998, 126).

Although the living wage idea has spread rapidly, social scientists have been surprisingly slow to follow up with explanations for its success. Between December 1994 and December 1999, 22 large cities passed living wage policies (see Table 9.2). The available literature on these policies consists primarily of policy-oriented surveys (Spain and Wiley 1998; Spain, Tam, and Thomas 1997) and economic studies evaluating the impact of living wage ordinances (Pollin et al. 1996; Weisbrot and Sforza-Roderick 1996; Williams and Sander 1997;

Table 9.2 Large Cities That Had Passed Living Wage Ordinances by December 31, 1999

City	State	Date of Enactment
Baltimore	MD	December 13, 1994
Milwaukee	WI	November 6, 1995
Jersey City	NJ	June 12, 1996
New York	NY	July 11, 1996
St. Paul	MN	January 2, 1997
Minneapolis	MN	March 7, 1997
Los Angeles	CA	March 18, 1997
New Haven	CT	April 24, 1997
Durham	NC	January 20, 1998
Oakland	CA	March 24, 1998
Portland	OR	April 15, 1998
San Antonio	TX	July 2, 1998
Chicago	IL	July 29, 1998
Boston	MA	September 2, 1998
Pasadena	CA	September 14, 1998
Detroit	MI	November 3, 1998
San Jose	CA	November 17, 1998
Madison	WI	March 30, 1999
Hayward	CA	May 3, 1999
Buffalo	NY	July 27, 1999
Tucson	AZ	September 13, 1999
Hartford	CT	October 12, 1999

Source: ACORN (1999), AFL-CIO (1999a), and interviews with city clerks, December 1998.

Niedt et al. 1998). These studies do not explain the emergence of living wage ordinances; instead, they take the living wage ordinance as a causal variable and inquire into its effects. There is also a growing case study literature that describes individual living wage campaigns (Conrad 1998; Fine 1998; Khalil and Hinson 1998; Eimer 1999; Nissen 1999; Reynolds 1999). These narrative case studies describe the mobilization of grassroots coalitions of labor unions and community organizations but offer few explanations for the passage of individual ordinances or for the living wage movement as a whole. They typically attribute the success of living wage campaigns to the ability of each labor-community coalition to outmaneuver the organized business lobby (see Reynolds 1999). This argument begs the question of why labor-community coalitions are able to out-organize business in some cities and not others. Moreover, in the absence of comparisons among cities, the narrative case studies are unable to draw general conclusions about which conditions particularly favor the passage of local living wage ordinances.

Pollin and Luce (1998) presented a plausible explanation for the emergence of local living wage policies in their book *The Living Wage*. First, they argued, the small size of the municipal polity is conductive to grassroots policy initiatives because it inhibits money-dominated politics: "As a matter of strategic politics, living wage campaigns have a greater chance of success in municipalities than at the state or national level since at the municipal level the power of big-money politics is still lower" (p. 54). Second, they argued that living wage campaigns have taken place at the municipal level "because the problem[s] of poverty and low-wage employment are severe in cities" (p. 54). In particular, they emphasized the persistence of poverty despite economic development subsidies that were touted as a means to reverse urban decay. Pollin and Luce argued that living wage campaigns emerged in reaction to the failure of these business subsidies "to reduce urban poverty and reverse the decline of urban communities" (p. 55). They do not provide empirical evidence for these explanations, however, because the main focus of their book is assessing the economic impact of living wage ordinances.

The scholarly literature on linkage fees and other so-called "type II" economic development policies echoes Pollin and Luce's (1998) emphasis on economic explanations. Goetz (1990) coined the label "type II" to refer to a growing category of economic development policies that, like some living wage ordinances, require redistributive concessions from businesses in exchange for government subsidies. The concessions may include requirements such as linkage fees for transportation or housing, contributions to the public schools, or job guarantees (see Goetz 1990; Elkins 1995). In a review of the literature on these policies, Reese (1998) found that most analysts use economic and fiscal variables to explain their passage. Her own analysis showed "residential need" (an index of poverty, unemployment, and low average income) to be a weak but consistent predictor of a city's adoption of type II policies (see also Elkins 1995, 824).

Although plausible, the models that these authors suggest have two principal flaws. First, they assume that the proper place to look for causes of redistributive local policies is within the city itself. But as other scholars have pointed out, a variety of external forces also shape city politics. Local politics are highly dependent on state and federal policies and party alliances (Mollenkopf 1983), and local political actors are often part of national networks that provide resources, expertise, and policy models (Clavel and Kleniewski 1990, 222; Molotch 1993, 37). If the strategies of national organizations influence the passage of local living wage policies, then any explanation of living wage policies that only includes causes internal to the city will miss an important part of the story.

Second, these authors propose economic and fiscal variables—such as urban poverty—as an explanation for the living wage and related policies. But they present no evidence that levels of poverty correlate with the passage of living wage policies. The degree of poverty in a city is not sufficient to explain the presence or timing of a living wage policy. As social movement theorists have argued, economic injustice of one kind or another is relatively constant, but successful grassroots mobilization is more episodic. Political mobilization is best explained not by poverty and injustice but by changing political opportunities and organizational resources (McAdam 1982; Gamson 1990). Moreover, as other scholars have pointed out, there is a range of possible political responses to any set of economic problems (see Bachelor 1994). We are left with the question of why activists and governments in city after city have responded to poverty with living wage policies rather than some other alternative.

Both of these flaws are overcome by so-called "new institutionalist" theories of policy diffusion (DiMaggio and Powell 1991). Theorists in this tradition do not assume that policies are always optimal solutions to economic problems (Meyer and Rowan 1991, 43). Although the economic environment does pose problems for policy makers, it rarely if ever dictates a single solution. Decision makers operate in a world of imperfect information; often, they do not have reliable information about the effectiveness of a policy until after it is implemented and, in many settings, not even then. Under these conditions, the new institutionalists argue, policy makers select policies based on cultural conformity rather than economic imperatives. They will tend to imitate policies that are highly "legitimate," meaning that they have wide currency and are deemed acceptable by other policy makers. Over time, policy makers come to absorb the assumptions of their milieu and take for granted that certain policies are appropriate solutions to common problems, regardless of the actual technical performance of these policies (Zucker 1991).

Knoke (1982) and Tolbert and Zucker (1983) applied this theory to city politics, showing that cities adopting the council-manager form of government early in this century were primarily mimicking other cities rather than responding to local conditions. Clemens (1998) brought the new institutionalist perspective to bear on state politics during the same period, showing that the spread of the "interest group" as a political form occurred through a similar process of imitation. Clemens paid particular attention to the networks through which organizational innovations diffused across the states (chap. 3).

In her account, social movement organizations and voluntary associations with broad geographic reach influenced state politics by taking innovative policy ideas that were successful in one state and campaigning for them in another (p. 62).

Although new institutionalist theory is useful for understanding processes of policy diffusion, it can and should be supplemented by attention to the political struggles that determine whether a policy is ultimately adopted. Scholars associated with the new institutionalism often present a strangely bloodless view of politics. Knoke (1982) and Tolbert and Zucker (1983) depicted cities that dispassionately adopt innovations they perceive to be legitimate. These accounts gloss over the bitter fights that raged over the adoption of the council-manager form in city after city (see Bridges 1997). New institutionalist theory in general tends to omit the contentious politics familiar to participants in and observers of local government. Theorists do not describe struggles over the legitimacy of alternative policies. Instead, they depict the adoption of a policy as a simple function of the familiarity of the policy in question (see Clemens 1998, chap. 2). . . .

The Interaction of Acorn with Local Labor Unions

By most statistical measures, the Twin Cities of Minneapolis and St. Paul are typical of cities that have passed living wage ordinances. They are located in the upper Midwest, and Minneapolis is among the 50 largest cities in the United States by population. The Democratic Farmer Labor Party—its name a legacy of the Progressive Era (Hofstadter 1955, 115)—enjoys broad support in both cities and receives a large percentage of the metropolitan vote in national elections. The cities share a legacy of community-based unionism (Faue 1996), and the militancy of the 1930s and 1960s is still reflected in high rates of union density. The Minneapolis Central Labor Union Council has pledged to become a "Union City." The Twin Cities are also home to a relatively dense field of progressive community organizations—including ACORN chapters in both cities—nourished in part by an unusually generous philanthropic community (Galaskiewicz 1991, 299). All of these factors have a positive association with living wage policy passage; in fact, the first living wage campaign in St. Paul followed closely on the heels of the Baltimore victory, with a ballot initiative proposed by Minnesota ACORN in summer of 1995 (Conrad 1998, 13).

Nonetheless, the first living wage campaign in St. Paul failed. Voters soundly defeated the initiative in November (Lonetree 1995), and it was not until January 1997 that St. Paul passed a living wage policy. Minneapolis followed suit with a policy of its own in March.

What happened between 1995 and 1997 to facilitate the passage of living wage policies in both cities? The crucial difference between 1995 and 1997 was *how* the national networks of living wage advocates interacted with local actors and opportunities. The first campaign was initiated by ACORN after national discussions about the Baltimore living wage ordinance. By circumventing the city council with a ballot initiative, however, Minnesota ACORN avoided the process of coalition building that would have allowed it to work out a policy that had the support of local labor. Organized labor opposed the ordinance, and it failed. The second campaign was shaped by the ability of both ACORN and the CLC to draw lessons from that experience and to share these lessons across city boundaries.

The idea for a St. Paul living wage campaign was sparked in part by national staff discussions within ACORN in early 1995. Following the Baltimore victory, ACORN organizers recognized the possibility of similar campaigns in a number of cities that would tie social justice concerns to economic development policy. Both Chicago ACORN and Minnesota ACORN began planning living wage campaigns in the spring of 1995. By May, Minnesota ACORN members had begun gathering signatures to put a living wage initiative on the ballot.

Minnesota ACORN advanced its first living wage proposal for St. Paul as a ballot initiative to avoid the threat of a veto by the city's Republican mayor. Because it bypassed the city council, however, the living wage campaign failed to engage in the process of interest brokering and compromise that would have been necessary to win the support of organized labor in St. Paul. There were other possible avenues for coalition building: ACORN had ties to some labor unions, which it could have used to gain labor's support. In particular, ACORN had established relationships with several statewide unions through an umbrella lobbying organization called the Minnesota Alliance for Progressive Action (MAPA) and had worked on a common economic development agenda with labor at the state level (Conrad 1998, 11). In part because of this shared history, ACORN's allies in the CLC were at first inclined to support the ballot initiative.

Some powerful unions were not consulted, however, and their opposition to the ballot initiative turned the CLC against it. AFSCME, representing city employees, balked at a provision in the living wage initiative that it believed would establish a St. Paul residence requirement for its members. The building trades unions similarly opposed a provision that they believed would give preference to an ACORN hiring hall over union hiring halls for city-funded construction projects. Although compromise might have been possible on these issues, ACORN had already collected the necessary signatures to put the policy on the ballot; the unions were thus presented with a choice to take it or leave it. The CLC chose to leave it. Labor withdrew its endorsement and acquiesced in the mayor's portrayal of the initiative as a "job killer." The initiative failed in November.

Despite their disagreement, both ACORN and the CLC recognized a potential common interest in a compromise policy. Demonstrating their ability to learn from prior experience—and to reach across the city limits—ACORN and labor lobbied in both Minneapolis and St. Paul for the establishment of a joint living wage task force. Here the progressive political climate of the Twin Cities was decisive. Both labor and ACORN had access to council members, and several council members had a history of associating themselves with progressive efforts. The living wage coalition was thus able to persuade Minneapolis city council member Jim Niland and St. Paul city council president Dave Thune to lead a task force, with additional representation from business, labor, and community organizations, including ACORN (Conrad 1998, 13; Duchschere 1997). Once the task force was created, it became a forum where ACORN and labor could bargain over the terms of a living wage policy *before* another measure was introduced.

The task force deliberated for several months and presented recommendations in favor of a living wage policy to both Minneapolis and St. Paul on November 26, 1996. Both city councils subsequently adopted the recommendations, with some amendments. The critical process that took place on the task force seems to have been the negotiation between ACORN and the unions. Although business representatives sat on the task force, they were less willing to negotiate; a representative from the chamber of commerce cast the lone vote against the task force's recommendations (Smith and Lonetree 1996). Business representatives began negotiating in earnest only after the task force recommendations had been made public, and some sort of living wage policy seemed inevitable.

The city council of St. Paul was the first to endorse the task force's report, by passing a resolution on January 2 establishing standards for companies applying for public aid. The resolution, introduced by Council President Thune, included several exemptions at the insistence of the mayor and the business community.

Minneapolis was slower to adopt the task force's recommendations. Under greater pressure from the business community, the Minneapolis city council opened hearings on the task force report. Labor's clout again proved critical at this stage: Many council members depended on labor's support to get elected, and council races were coming up. Public hearings on the living wage policy coincided with the CLC's council endorsements (Diaz 1997). The council members, anxious to win labor's support, approved the recommendations unanimously in March—albeit with several more exceptions and loopholes than the St. Paul city council had adopted (see Diaz 1997).

By comparing the first and second living wage campaigns in Minneapolis-St. Paul, this case study shows that the living wage policies in the Twin Cities would not have passed if not for the alliance between ACORN and local labor unions. Although Minnesota ACORN had the ability to take campaign ideas, policy models, and legal advice from elsewhere, it still failed in its first attempt to pass a living wage policy because it did not forge a coalition with local labor. Its second attempt was more successful because it did not bypass the process of negotiation and compromise that created a policy able to meet labor's interests and secure labor's active lobbying and campaign support.

Implications for Urban Progressivism

This analysis of living wage campaigns has important implications for the possibilities for progressive city politics. Recent popular and scholarly discourse on city politics has been haunted by the specter of globalization. Mobile capital, so the argument goes, has rendered city governments all but powerless to promote the redistribution of goods and opportunities from the well-off to the poor. Cities that try to pursue "social welfare-oriented" policies will suffer rapid disinvestment, and they will be left without the tax base they need to provide even minimal services to their remaining residents (Rondinelli, Johnson, and Kasarda 1998, 99).

Progressives have hailed the success of living wage campaigns as a promising sign that cities are not as powerless as this received narrative suggests. But under what conditions are cities able to pass redistributive policies without provoking capital flight? This analysis provides support for a bargaining perspective, according to which local governments with greater bargaining advantages will be able to impose more conditions on business (Kantor, Savitch, and Haddock 1997). In the case of living wage ordinances, threats of disinvestment ring hollow. By targeting firms that hold government contracts, living wage policies have focused on relatively immobile capital. Living wage policies have also passed in very large cities such as New York and Los Angeles, which have an advantageous market position and are therefore better able to mandate wage standards for the private sector. Because these large cities command strategic locations in the economy, firms are more willing to tolerate the conditions they impose.

However, these bargaining advantages alone are not sufficient to explain why cities pass living wage laws. The analysis shows that the balance of political forces on the local level matters. Living wage policies have appeared in liberal cities that are more accessible to grassroots pressure and in cities outside the South, a region where labor's political influence has historically been negligible. Local labor unions have taken advantage of the political access they enjoy in liberal, northern cities to campaign successfully for living wage laws. A crucial condition for their success is the political resources they command—in particular, the size of their membership base in the local workforce.

Finally, the analysis shows that explanations that are based only on the local economy and local political forces miss out on the national dynamics of policy diffusion. As the new institutionalists remind us, policy makers and activists choose policy solutions from a limited menu, based on what they perceive to work in other locations. Cities are more likely to pass an ordinance if other cities have passed similar ordinances, and activists are more likely to advocate a policy if they are part of a network with other activists who have done so successfully. As Clemens (1998, 65) noted, reform minded progressives in the early twentieth century regarded the states as "experiment stations," committing their limited resources first to struggles in progressive states where victory was easier and then taking policy models that proved successful and exporting them to other states. Progressive activists today treat cities in much the same way, capitalizing on living wage successes in Minneapolis-St. Paul, for instance, to promote living wage campaigns in Oakland and Hayward, California.

The role of networks in promoting progressive local policies suggests a revaluation of the role of the federal system in explaining urban policy outcomes. In Peterson's (1981, 68) argument, the central features of local government in a federal system are its independent financing and its relative freedom from central government mandates. Peterson argues that these two features predispose cities to defend their tax base by enacting orthodox economic development policies and avoiding redistribution. But the same features of local government may enable cities to function as "experiment stations," which look to each other rather than to the central government to define appropriate economic policy. Innovative, progressive fiscal policies, such as the living wage requirement for service contractors, can make some headway at the local level, especially if activists have connections to other cities where these policies have been successful.

If the decentralization of the federal system permits progressive policies to diffuse across the city limits, progressives must be organized to take advantage of the opportunity that federalism presents. Without active intervention by progressives organized across cities, the same conditions that permit the diffusion of redistributive policies across political boundaries can also facilitate the diffusion of regressive and antilabor policies.[3] For scholars and activists who are concerned with local politics, then, the care and feeding of progressive national (and perhaps international) networks are an important topic for further study. Both local organizing and national networks matter, and neither is likely to be effective at promoting progressive reforms without the other.

Notes

1 For the purposes of this article, I refer to living wage policies and living wage ordinances interchangeably.
2 The ordinance required employers holding contacts for the provision services or other services to the city of Baltimore to pay wage rates of $6.10 per hour in 1996 and legislated annual raises through 1999.
3 At least one national association opposed to living wage ordinances has begun to market "talking points" to local business groups across the United States (see Employment Policies Institute 1998).

References

American Federation of Labor-Congress of Industrial Organizations (AFL-CIO). 1999a. *Living wage table: Updated December 1999*. Washington, DC: Author.
———. 1999b. *The road to Union City: A guide to greatness for local unions and their AFL-CIO Central Labor Councils* [Online]. Available: www.aflcio.org/unioncity
Association of Community Organizations for Reform Now (ACORN). 1999. *Living wage successes: A compilation of living wage policies on the books*. Washington, DC: Author.
Bachelor, L. 1994. Regime maintenance, solution sets, and urban economic development. *Urban Affairs Review* 29:596–616.
Bronfenbrenner, K., and T. Juravich. 1998. It takes more than house calls: Organizing to win with a comprehensive union-building strategy. In *Organizing to win*, edited by K. Bronfenbrenner, S. Friedman, R. W. Hurd, R. A. Oswald, and R. L. Seeber, 19–36. Ithaca, NY: Cornell Univ. Press.

Clavel, P., and N. Kleniewski. 1990. Space for progressive policy: Examples from the United States and the United Kingdom. In *Beyond the city limits*, edited by J. R. Logan and T. Swanstrom. 199–236, Philadelphia: Temple Univ. Press.

Clemens, E. S. 1998. *The people's lobby: Organizational innovation and the rise of interest group politics in the United States, 1890–1925*. Chicago: Univ. of Chicago Press.

Conrad, S. 1998. The campaign for corporate welfare reform in Minnesota. In *Public subsidies, public accountability: Holding corporations to labor and community standards*, edited by Grassroots Policy Project, 18–27. New York: Sustainable America.

Cox, K. R. 1997, Globalization and the politics of distribution: A critical assessment. In *Spaces of globalization: Reasserting the power of the local*, edited by K. R. Cox, 115–36. New York: Guilford.

DeLeon, R. E. 1992. *Left coast city: Progressive politics in San Francisco, 1975–1991*. Lawrence: University Press of Kansas.

Diaz, K. 1997. Minneapolis city council OKs resolution on "living wage." *Minneapolis Star-Tribune*, 8 March, 3B.

Digital Directory Assistance, 1995. *PhoneDisc USA business*. Bethesda, MD: Author.

DiMaggio, P. J., and W. W. Powell. 1991. Introduction. In *The new institutionalism in organizational analysis*, edited by W. W. Powell and P. J. DiMaggio, 1–38. Chicago: Univ. of Chicago Press.

Duchschere, K. 1997. Living-wage concept is gaining attention. *Minneapolis Star-Tribune*, 14 February, 7B.

Eimer, S. 1999. The Milwaukee County labor council and economic development: Fighting for justice beyond the contract. Paper presented at the annual meeting of the University and College Labor Educators Association, April, Atlanta, GA.

Elkins, D. R. 1995. Testing competing explanations for the adoption of type II policies. *Urban Affairs Review* 30:809–39.

Employment Policies Institute. 1998. *The Baltimore Living Wage Study: Omissions, fabrications, and flaws*. Washington, DC: Author.

Faue, E. 1996. Paths of unionization: Community, bureaucracy, and gender in the Minneapolis labor movement of the 1930s. In *"We are all leaders": The alternative unionism of the early 1930s*, edited by S. Lynd, 172–98. Urbana: Univ, of Illinois Press.

Ferman, B. 1996. *Challenging the growth machine: Neighborhood politics in Chicago and Pittsburgh*. Lawrence: University Press of Kansas.

Fine, J. 1998, Moving innovation from the margins to the center. In *A new labor movement for the new century*, edited by G. Mantsios, 119–46. New York: Monthly Review.

Galaskiewicz, J. 1991. Making corporate actors accountable: Institution-building in Minneapolis-St. Paul. In *The new institutionalism in organizational analysis*, edited by W. W. Powell and P. J. DiMaggio, 293–310. Chicago: Univ. of Chicago Press.

Gamson, W. 1990. *The strategy of social protest*. Belmont, CA: Wadsworth.

Gertler, M. S. 1997. Between the local and the global: The spatial limits to productive capital. In *Spaces of globalization: Reasserting the power of the local*, edited by K. R. Cox, 45–64. New York: Guilford.

Glickman, L. B. 1997. *A living wage: American workers and the making of consumer society*. Ithaca, NY: Cornell Univ. Press.

Goetz, E. G. 1990. Type II policy and mandated benefits in economic development. *Urban Affairs Quarterly* 26:170–90.

Hofstadter, R. 1955. *The age of reform; From Bryant to F.D.R.* New York: Knopf.

Kantor, P., H. V. Savitch, and S. V. Haddock. 1997. The political economy of urban regimes: A comparative perspective. *Urban Affairs Review* 32 (3): 348–77.

Khalil, H., and S. Hinson. 1998. The Los Angeles living wage campaign. In *Public subsidies, public accountability: Holding corporations to labor and community standards*, edited by Grassroots Policy Project, 18–27. New York: Sustainable America.

Knoke, D. 1982. The spread of municipal reform: Temporal, spatial, and social dynamics. *American Journal of Sociology* 87 (6): 1314–39.

Kuttner, R. 1997. The living wage movement. *The Washington Post* 20 August, A25.

Lonetree, A. 1995. St. Paul voters kill proposal to tie aid to pay. *Minneapolis Star Tribune*, 8 November, 1B.

McAdam, D. 1982. *Political process and the development of black insurgency, 1930–1970*. Chicago: Univ. of Chicago Press.

Meyer. J. W., and B. Rowan. 1991. Institutionalized organizations: Formal structure as myth and ceremony. In *The new institutionalism in organizational analysis,* edited by W. W. Powell and P. J. DiMaggio, 41–62. Chicago: Univ. of Chicago Press.

Mollenkopf, J. 1983. *The contested city.* Princeton, NJ: Princeton Univ. Press.

Molotch, H. 1993. The political economy of growth machines. *Journal of Urban Affairs,* 15 (1): 29–53.

Needleman, R. 1998. Building relationships for the long haul: Unions and community-based groups working together to organize low-wage workers. In *Organizing to win,* edited by K. Bronfenbrenner, S. Friedman, R. W. Hurd, R. A. Oswald, and R. L. Seeber, 71–86. Ithaca, NY: Cornell Univ. Press.

Nissen, B. 1999. Living wage campaigns from a "social movement" perspective: The Miami case. Paper presented at the annual meeting of the University and College Labor Educators Association, April, Atlanta, GA.

Peterson, P. 1981. *City limits.* Chicago: Univ. of Chicago Press.

Pollin, R., G. Dymski, D. Fairris, M. Weisbrot, M. Brenner, M. Cook, T. Levine, S. Luce, M. Schaberg, M. Sforza-Roderick, and B. Wiens-Tuers. 1996. Economic analysis of the Los Angeles living wage ordinance. Unpublished paper, Department of Economics, University of California. Riverside.

Pollin, R., and S. Luce. 1998. *The living wage: Building a fair economy.* New York: New Press.

Reese, L. A. 1998. Sharing the benefits of economic development: What cities use type II policies? *Urban Affairs Review* 33 (5): 686–711.

Reynolds, D. 1999. Living wage campaigns and beyond: Building labor-community coalitions for the high road. Paper presented at the annual meeting of the University and College Labor Educators Association, April, Atlanta, GA.

Rondinelli, D.A., J.H. Johnson, Jr., and J. D. Kasarda. 1998. The changing forces of urban economic development: Globalization and city competitiveness in the twenty-first century. *Cityscape* 3 (3): 71–106.

Spain, S., T. -M. Tam, and C. Thomas. 1997. *Living wage policies nationwide: An analysis for the city of Oakland.* Oakland, CA: National Economic Development and Law Center.

Spain, S., and J. Wiley. 1998. The living wage ordinance: A first step in reducing poverty. *Clearinghouse Review,* September-October, 252–67.

Stone, C. N. 1993. Urban regimes and the capacity to govern: A political economy approach. *Journal of Urban Affairs* 15 (1): 1–28.

Swanstrom, T. 1988. Urban populism, uneven development, and the space for reform. In *Business elites and urban development: Case studies and critical perspectives,* edited by S. Cummings, 121–52. Albany, NY: SUNY Press.

Tolbert, P. S., and L. G. Zucker. 1983. Institutional sources of change in formal organizations: The diffusion of civil service reform, 1880–1935. *Administrative Science Quarterly* 28:22–39.

Weisbrot, M., and M. Sforza-Roderick. 1996. *Baltimore's living wage law: An analysis of the fiscal and economic costs of Baltimore City Ordinance 442.* Washington, DC: Preamble Center for Public Policy.

Williams, E. D., and R. H. Sander. 1997. An empirical analysis of the proposed Los Angeles living wage ordinance. Unpublished paper, Department of Economics, University of California at Los Angeles.

Zucker, L. G. 1991. The role of institutionalization in cultural persistence. In *The new institutionalism in organizational analysis,* edited by W. W. Powell and P. J. DiMaggio, 83–107. Chicago: Univ. of Chicago Press.

CHAPTER 10

SPRAWL AND THE NEW REGIONALISM

Governing the Twenty-first Century Metropolis

The first years of the twenty-first century finds metropolitan America a sprawling and tangled landscape. Decades of suburban growth accompanied by dispersal of jobs and populations have created massive regions of almost uninterrupted development, but these regions lack governmental coherence. The political fragmentation of metropolitan areas into hundreds of jurisdictions has formed a pattern of checkerboard governance. A few places, such as Miami-Dade county, Florida, and Minneapolis-St. Paul, Minnesota, have forged metropolitan-wide political institutions that help coordinate service delivery. Portland, Oregon, stands alone as a region with a growth boundary and some record of curbing sprawl. Cooperation is commonplace in urban areas as a means of coordinating such services as 911-dialing and county-wide parks and recreation and library services. But except for these arrangements, the governance of metropolitan areas is haphazard.

Effective regional coordination of land use and development is rare. Yet the pressure for improving the governance of regions is building because the consequences of sprawl are becoming severe. The problems are many: traffic congestion; unequal employment opportunities; disparities in fiscal health between poorer central cities and more wealthy suburbs; the loss of open space to sprawled development; lack of investment in mass transit; inequalities in educational resources; waste of energy resources; air and water pollution. These problems require solutions that go beyond the boundaries of particular local governments.

Can regional government really be achieved? In the past, attempts at establishing these institutions have usually failed. They are generally opposed by both suburban local governments fighting threats to their power and citizens wishing to keep the problems of the cities out of their back yards. The essay by Myron Orfield describes how some degree of regional coordination was achieved in the Minneapolis-St. Paul region. Orfield acknowledges that regional reform is difficult and controversial, but he claims it is possible because of the emergence of a new political center of gravity in urban politics. In the past, attempts to build regional political coalitions in Minneapolis-St. Paul were built on weak foundations—notably leaders dedicated to good government ideals. Their initial success in building regional coalitions was short-lived because they neglected to mobilize powerful interests sufficiently. By contrast, practitioners of the New Regionalism persuaded central-city interests to join with older suburbs who shared similar problems of decaying neighborhoods, sagging tax bases, and a retrenching local economy. The Twin Cities' success in building regional cooperation was enabled by this new political coalition—a coalition that potentially exists in other metropolitan areas around the country.

Are there alternatives to regionalism that can successfully address sprawl? The two remaining selections offer contrasting responses. In his essay, Fred Siegel argues that sprawl ". . .is not some malignancy to be summarily excised, but, rather, part and parcel of prosperity." Siegel claims that fragmented government offers abundant advantages. It enables people who live in badly governed central cities to escape to other jurisdictions that provide an array of alternative places to live, shop, and conduct business. Most of all, he believes that fragmented government avoids the dead hand of a single, powerful regional government that restricts choice. Although Siegel concedes that there may be cases of successful regional governments, as in Portland, Oregon, time will tell whether such examples can be copied elsewhere. In the meantime, he prefers to address common regional issues through one-off measures like tax sharing and the prohibition of public policies that actively favor suburbs over cities.

Another approach to sprawl seeks to make it more comfortable despite its flaws. Advocates for the New Urbanism argue that it is possible to nurture a sense of community by redesigning the urban environment. They contend that people increasingly wish to escape the sameness of cookie-cutter housing developments and dull suburban spaces. The developers of New Urbanism projects respond to this impulse by designing enclaves that slow traffic and encourage walking and a sense of community by recreating the look and feel of small-town neighborhoods. In her selection, Dolores Hayden describes the attempt to recapture a slower way of life in the midst of suburban sprawl in the case of Seaside, Florida. Architects Elizabeth Plater-Zyberk and Andres Duany designed a model community that offers a pedestrian-oriented resort of neo-traditional houses set in native landscapes that look like a small southern beach resort of a century ago. Though investors had doubts about its popular acceptance, once it was built Seaside buyers saw it as highly desirable and Seaside housing prices skyrocketed.

The New Urbanists have had growing influence. Projects inspired by their ideas have proliferated in recent years. Hayden describes how their concepts were incorporated on a very large scale in Celebration, Florida, where the Disney corporation built a town for more than 20,000 people. Celebration attempts to recapture the life of front-porch living and pedestrian-centered neighborhoods. Celebration has the outward appearance of a southern small town of one hundred years ago, with traditional houses, quiet streets open to children on bikes, a lake, and even a town hall. But Hayden is skeptical; these creations are more illusion than reality. The developments are accessible only to high-income buyers, and there are few minority residents. They lack a civic life; Seaside and Celebration are actually governed by the developers who built them. A multitude of rules are imposed to ensure that the house exteriors remain intact to maintain an ersatz old-plantation atmosphere. Celebration's town hall is actually the development office since the town has no elected officials. According to Hayden, these developments are essentially quaint residential islands that lack real downtowns, real governments and are economically detached from surrounding urban areas. Indeed, the town of Celebration serves as an anchor for scattered and distant subdivisions and commercial enclaves that also lack a public realm.

These perspectives are important voices in a continuing debate about how to manage the problems of urban regions in the twenty-first century. The debate will continue to be lively because the problems of sprawled growth are not going away.

26

Myron Orfield

CONFLICT OR CONSENSUS?
Forty Years of Minnesota Metropolitan Politics

Skeptics tell me that regional equity reform will never happen in America's metropolitan regions because the suburbs are now in charge of American politics. It may be true that the suburbs are in charge of American politics. But the politics of metropolitan reform is not about cities versus suburbs or, for that matter, about Democrats versus Republicans.

The suburbs are not a monolith, economically, racially, or politically. Surrounding America's central cities, with their high social needs and low per capita tax wealth, are three types of suburbs. First are the older suburbs, which comprise about a quarter of the population of U.S. metropolitan regions. These communities are often declining socially faster than the central cities and often have even less per household property, income, or sales tax wealth. Second are the low tax-base developing suburbs, which make up about 10–15 percent of U.S. metropolitan regions. They are growing rapidly in population, especially among school-age children, but without an adequate tax base to support that growth and its accompanying overcrowded schools, highway congestion, and ground water pollution. Both the central city and these two types of suburbs have small tax bases, comparatively high tax rates, and comparatively low spending. Median household incomes are also comparatively low: $25,000–30,000 in central cities in 1990, $25,000–40,000 in older suburbs, and $35,000–50,000 in low tax-base developing suburbs. Families in these communities are thus extremely sensitive to property tax increases. A third type of suburb is the high tax-base developing community. These affluent communities, with the region's highest median incomes, never amount to more than 30 percent of a region's population. They have all the benefits of a regional economy—access to labor and product markets, regionally built freeways and often airports—but are able to externalize the costs of social and economic need on the older suburbs and the central city.

Suburbs and cities can also be surprisingly diverse in their electoral results. Not all suburbs are Republican—or all cities Democratic. In Philadelphia, Republicans control almost all the suburbs and even the white working-class parts of the city. In Pittsburgh, Democrats control virtually all suburban seats except the highest property-wealth areas. In San Francisco, almost all suburbs are represented by Democrats, while in Los Angeles and Southern California, most of the white suburbs are represented by Republicans. In general, Democrats build their base in central cities, move to the older and low tax-base suburbs, and, if they are very effective, capture a few of the high tax-base suburbs. Republicans do just the opposite. In many states the balance of power rests on electoral contests in a few older suburbs or low tax-capacity developing suburbs.

Minnesota has been engaged in the politics of metropolitan regional reform for almost 40 years. Over the decades, three types of metropolitan coalitions have sought to move policy reforms through the state legislature. The first, a Republican-led bipartisan coalition, engaged in some bitter legislative fights; the second, a consensualist-led coalition, eschewed controversy; the third, a Democratic-driven bipartisan group, revived the real-world reform political style of their Republican predecessors. The following short history of metropolitanism in Minnesota suggests the complexity of coalition politics—and my own conviction that, while compromise and accommodation is the necessary essence of politics, regional reform, like all other real reform movements in U.S. history, necessarily involves some degree of controversy.

The Progressive Republican Vanguard

In the 1960s and 1970s, metropolitan reform efforts in Minnesota's legislature were led by "good government" Rockefeller Republicans and reform Democrats—in a sense the progressives that Richard Hofstader wrote of in his *Age of Reform*. Joined by leaders of local corporations, they took aim at waste in government and set out to plan and shape a more cohesive, cost-effective, efficient, and equitable region. Though they sought rough metropolitan-wide equity in Minnesota's Twin Cities, they were not typical practitioners of class warfare. They valued equity because they knew from hard-headed calculation the costs of inequity and of destructive competition for development among municipalities in a single metropolitan region.

In some ways progressive Republican regionalism was an elegant, direct, limited-government response to growing sprawl and interlocal disparity. Joining Minnesota's Governor LeVander were Oregon's Tom McCall,

Michigan's Miliken and Romney, and the great Republican mayor of Indi-anapolis, Richard Lugar. Had the country heeded their far-sighted strategy, the 1980s and 1990s might have been much different for the central cities and older suburbs.

In Minnesota the progressive Republicans and reform Democrats created regional sewer, transit, and airport authorities for the Twin Cities, as well as a Metropolitan Council of the Twin Cities with weak supervisory powers over these authorities. (Making the Met Council an elected body was a top goal, but it failed in a tie vote in 1967.) They also created a metropolitan land use plan-ning framework and enacted Minnesota's famous tax-base sharing, or fiscal disparities, law, which, since 1971, has shared 40 percent of the growth of our commercial and industrial property tax base among the 187 cities, 49 school districts, and 7 counties in our region of some 2.5 million people.

The battle to pass the fiscal disparities act was brutal. Though the legisla-tion, introduced in 1969, had its origins in the ethereal world of good govern-ment progressivism, its political managers were shrewd vote counters who made sure that two-thirds of the Twin City region's lawmakers understood that the bill would both lower their constituents' taxes and improve their schools and public services. Some of the progressives' key allies were pop-ulists who did not hesitate to play the class card with blue-collar voters in the low property-value suburbs. Probably not coincidentally, the populists col-lected most of the votes. The progressives pragmatically swallowed their compunctions.

The fiscal disparities bill that passed in 1971 was supported by a coalition of Democratic central-city legislators and Republicans from less wealthy sub-urbs—essentially the two-thirds of the region that received new tax base from the act. A few more-rural Republicans who had a strong personal relationship with the bill's Republican sponsor went along. The opposition was also biparti-san—Democrats and Republicans representing areas in the one-third of the re-gion that would lose some of their tax base. Debate over the bill was ugly. Re-publican Charlie Weaver, Sr., the bill's sponsor, was accused of fomenting "communism" and "community socialism" and of being a "Karl Marx" out to take from "the progressive communities to give to the backward ones." One opponent warned that "the fiscal disparities law will destroy the state." "Why should those who wish to work be forced to share with those who won't or can't help themselves?" demanded a representative of the high property-wealth areas. Amid growing controversy, after two divisive failed sessions, the bill would pass the Minnesota Senate by a single vote.

Not until 1975—after court challenges that went all the way to the U.S. Supreme Court (which refused to hear the case)—did the fiscal disparities law finally go into effect. The last legal challenge to the law came in 1981, a decade after passage. High property-wealth southern Twin Cities suburbs were finally rebuffed in the Minnesota Tax Court. But representatives and state senators from high property-wealth Twin Cities suburbs have tried to repeal the statute in virtually every legislative session for the past 25 years.

A New Approach

The tough progressive reformers were followed by consensus-based regional-ists whose preferred approach, it has often been joked, was to convene leaders from across metropolitan Twin Cities in the boardroom of a local bank to hum together the word "regionalism." Highly polished professional policy wonks, the new generation of leaders leaned more to touring the country extolling the virtues of regional reform, which many had no part in accomplishing, than to gritty work in city halls and the legislature to make it happen. To make matters worse, business support for regionalism began to erode. The rise of national and multinational companies created a cadre of rotating, frequently moving ex-ecutives who, facing a more competitive business environment, eschewed con-troversy in favor of political action that would boost the bottom line.

By the 1980s, proponents of the regional perspective in Minnesota had dwindled to the chairman of the Citizens League, a local policy group finan-cially supported by the region's big businesses; a half-dozen legislators; two or three executives of declining power; and the editorial board of the Min-neapolis paper.

Meanwhile, some suburbs, particularly the high property-wealth develop-ing ones that saw no gain but plenty of loss coming from metropolitan action, rebelled. Over the course of the 1980s, as the Twin Cities region rapidly became more like the rest of the nation—more racially and socially segregated—and as fundamental divisions hardened, those suburbs hired high-priced lobbyists and prepared for a fight to dismantle "regional socialism." Metropolitanism's opponents, tough and organized, began to control the regional debate.

During 1980–90, state lawmakers gradually dismantled the metropolitan authority that had been put in place in the 1960s and 1970s. They stripped the Met Council of its authority over major development projects: the downtown domed stadium, a new regional race track, and even the Mall of America—a lo-cal landmark that by its sheer size had a thunderous effect on the retail market in central Minneapolis and St. Paul and the southern suburbs. They severely weakened the land use planning statute by giving supercedence to local zon-ing. They also overturned the Met Council system of infrastructure pricing, abandoned a regional affordable housing system, and shelved well-conceived regional density guidelines. And they took a hard, well-financed run at the fis-cal disparities system.

Sometimes the consensus-based regionalists would oppose the changes, but more often they seemed unable to stomach controversy. Their general re-sponse to the newly assertive high property-wealth suburbs was to seek ac-commodation. Meanwhile, developers in the high property-wealth suburbs and their lawyers obtained coveted seats on the Met Council itself.

The first generation of regionalists had fought bloody fights for land use planning, the consolidation of regional services, and tax equity. A decade later, the consensus-based regionalists were reduced to building regional citizenship through a proposal for a bus that looked like a trolley car to connect the state capital to downtown St. Paul. Times, and tactics, had clearly changed.

The proud legacy of the first-generation regionalists was in shambles. In 1967, the Twin Cities had created a regional transit system with a tax base that encompassed seven regional counties and 187 cities. By 1998, what had been one of the most financially broad-based transit systems in the nation was struggling with below-average funding per capita. The Met Council, now in thrall to developers, allocated virtually all federal resources to its large highway building program. Finally, the Citizens League and the consensus-based regionalists, perhaps to curry favor with the rebellious high property-wealth suburbs, used their influence both to defeat the development of a fixed-rail transit service and to fragment and privatize the transit system. By the early 1980s, the southwestern developing suburbs, the most prosperous parts of the region and those that benefited most from the development of a regional sewer and highway system, were allowed to "opt out" of funding the transit system that served the region's struggling core.

In 1991, the Met Council was on the verge of being abolished. A measure to eliminate the Council passed on the House floor, and the governor opined that the Council should either do something or disappear. The consensus-based regionalists, frustrated after a decade of difficulty, were not even grousing about legislative roadblocks. They had moved on to champion school choice and had joined the business community in an effort to cut comparatively high Minnesota business property taxes.

The Third Generation

Out of this state of affairs emerged a new type of regionalist, of which I count myself one. Most of us were new to politics in the 1990s, and we were spurred to action by worrisome conditions in the Twin Cities, where concentrated poverty was growing—at the fourth fastest rate in the nation.

To address the growing concentration of poverty in the central cities, we began to investigate reforms, particularly in fair housing, at a metropolitan level. We began to wonder, in particular, whether the sprawl at the edge of the Twin Cities area was undermining the stability at the core and whether the older suburbs, adjacent to the city, were having equally serious problems. As we learned more about the region's problems, we came to appreciate the metropolitan structure that had been put in place 20 years before—a structure severely out of fashion and irrelevant in liberal circles. "What does land use planning in the suburbs have to do with us?" asked our central-city politicos. "We need more of a neighborhood-based strategy," they said. We were also received as fish out of water when we went to the Met Council and the Citizens League to discuss our regional concerns. "This is not what the Met Council is about," they said. "It is about land use planning and infrastructure, not about urban issues or poverty."

In addition to the concentration of poverty at the core, we grew interested in the subsidies and governmental actions supporting sprawl. We were inspired by the land use reforms in Oregon and the work of Governor Tom

McCall, Henry Richmond, and 1,000 Friends of Oregon. We read the infrastructure work of Robert Burchell at Rutgers. We became aesthetically attached to New Urbanism and Peter Calthorpe, its proponent of metropolitan social equity and transit-oriented development.

Our third-wave regionalism gradually became broader based. We added environmentalism and the strength of the environmental movement to what had heretofore been a sterile discussion of planning and efficiency. We also brought issues of concentrated poverty and regional fair housing into an equity discussion that had previously been limited to interlocal fiscal equity. The dormant strength of the civil rights movement and social gospel also readied itself for metropolitan action and activism. In only a few years, hundreds of churches joined the movement for regional reform.

We also mobilized the rapidly declining, blue-collar suburbs—angry places unattached to either political party—to advance regional reform. Blue-collar mayors, a few with decidedly hostile views toward social and racial changes in their communities, united with African-American political leaders, environmentalists, and bishops of the major regional churches to advance a regional agenda for fair housing, land use planning, tax equity, and an accountable elected regional governance structure.

In fact, probably the most important element of the new regional coalition was the older, struggling, fully developed suburbs—the biggest prospective winners in regional reform. To them, tax-base sharing means lower property taxes and better services, particularly better-funded schools. Regional housing policy means, over time, fewer units of affordable housing crowding their doorstep. As one older-suburban mayor put it, "If those guys in the new suburbs don't start to build affordable housing, we'll be swimming in this stuff."

Winning over these suburbs was not easy. We had to overcome long-term, powerful resentments and distrust, based on class and race and fueled by every national political campaign since Hubert Humphrey lost the White House in 1968. But after two years of constant cajoling and courting and steady reminders of the growing inequities among the suburbs, the middle-income, working-class, blue-collar suburbs joined the central cities and created a coalition of great political clout in the legislature.

In 1994 this coalition of central-city and suburban legislators passed the Metropolitan Reorganization Act, which placed all regional sewer, transit, and land use planning under the operational authority of the Metropolitan Council of the Twin Cities. In doing so, it transformed the Met Council from a $40-million-a-year planning agency to a $600-million-a-year regional government operating regional sewers and transit, with supervisory authority over the major decisions of another $300-million-a-year agency that runs the regional airport. That same year, in the Metropolitan Land Use Reform Act, our coalition insulated metro-area farmers from public assessments that would have forced them to subdivide farm land for development.

In both 1993 and 1994 the legislature passed sweeping fair housing bills (both vetoed); in 1995 a weakened version was finally signed. In 1995 the legislature passed a measure that would have added a significant part of the residential property tax base to the fiscal disparities pool. While the measure passed strongly, it too was vetoed. In 1996 a statewide land use planning framework was adopted, and a regional brownfields fund created. Throughout the process, we restored to the Council many of the powers and prerogatives that had been removed from it during the 1980s in the areas of land use planning and infrastructure pricing. In each area of reform—land use planning, tax equity, and regional structural reform—we were initially opposed by the consensus-based regionalists as "too controversial," only to have our ideas adopted by them a few years later as the political center of gravity began to change.

Worth Fighting For

Like all real reform, regional reform is a struggle. From the fight against municipal corruption and the fight against the trusts to the women's movement, the consumer movement, the environmental movement, and the civil rights movement, reform has involved difficult contests against entrenched interests who operated against the general welfare. Today, we are told that the Age of Reform is over. We are in an age of consensus politics, when calmer words—"collaboration," "boundary crossing," "win-win" strategies—carry more promise than "assertive" ones.

In every region of this nation, [roughly] 20–40 percent of the people live in central cities, 25–30 percent in older declining suburbs, and 10–15 percent in low tax-base developing suburbs. These communities, representing a clear majority of regional population, are being directly harmed by an inefficient, wasteful, unfair system. Studies indicate that the regions in the nation that have the least economic disparity have the strongest economic growth and those with most disparity are the weakest economically. The social polarization and wasteful sprawl that are common in our nation take opportunity from people and businesses, destroy cities and older suburbs, waste our economic bounty, and threaten our future.

Those who care about these problems must "assert" themselves to reverse these trends. We must engage in a politics that is free of personal attacks and sensationalism, that is conducted with a smile and good manners—like the progressives. At each roadblock, we must seek a compromise that moves equity forward, before we entrench unproductively. We must achieve the broadest possible level of good feeling, gather for our cause as many allies as we can from all walks of life and from all points of the compass. We must educate and persuade. However, if there are those who stand in our path utterly—who will permit no forward movement—we must fight. We must fight for the future of individuals, for the future of communities, and for the future of our country.

In the end, the goal is regional reform, not regional consensus.

27

Fred Siegel

IS REGIONAL GOVERNMENT THE ANSWER?

Suburban sprawl, the spread of low-density housing over an ever-expanding landscape, has attracted a growing list of enemies. Environmentalists have long decried the effects of sprawl on the ecosystem; aesthetes have long derided what they saw as "the ugliness and banality of suburbia"; and liberals have intermittently insisted that suburban prosperity has been purchased at the price of inner-city decline and poverty. But only recently has sprawl become the next great issue in American public life. That's because suburbanites themselves are now calling for limits to seemingly inexorable and frenetic development.

Slow-growth movements are a response to both the cyclical swings of the economy and the secular trend of dispersal. Each of the great postwar booms have, at their cyclical peak, produced calls for restraint. These sentiments have gained a wider hearing as each new upturn of the economy has produced an ever widening wave of exurban growth. A record 96 months of peacetime economic expansion has produced the strongest slow-growth movement to date. In 1998, antisprawl environmentalists and "not-in-my-backyard" slow-growth suburbanites joined forces across the nation to pass ballot measures restricting exurban growth.

Undoubtedly, the loss of land and the environmental degradation produced by sprawl are serious problems that demand public attention. But sprawl also brings enormous benefits as well as considerable costs. It is, in part, an expression of the new high-tech economy whose campus-like office parks on the periphery of urban areas have driven the economic boom of the 1990s. And it's sprawl that has sustained the record rise in home ownership. Sprawl is not some malignancy to be summarily excised but, rather, part and parcel of prosperity. Dealing with its ill effects requires both an understanding of the new landscape of the American economy and a willingness to make subtle trade-offs. We must learn to curb its worst effects without reducing the wealth and freedom that permit sprawl to develop.

Rising incomes and employment, combined with declining interest rates, have allowed a record number of people, including minority and immigrant families, to purchase homes for the first time. Home ownership among blacks, which is increasingly suburban, has risen at more than three times the white

---

rate; a record 45 percent of African Americans owned their own homes in 1998. Nationally, an unprecedented 67 percent of Americans are homeowners.

Sprawl is part of the price we're paying for something novel in human history—the creation of a mass upper middle class. Net household worth has been increasing at the unparalleled annual rate of 10 percent since 1994, so that while in 1970, only 3.2 percent of households had an annual income of $100,000 (in today's dollars), by 1996, 8.2 percent of American households could boast a six-figure annual income. The new prosperity is reflected in the size of new homes, many of whose owners no doubt decry the arrival of still more "McMansions" and new residents, clogging the roads and schools of the latest subdivisions. In the midst of the 1980's boom, homebuilders didn't have a category for mass-produced houses of more than 3,000 square feet: By 1996, one out of every seven new homes built was larger than 3,000 square feet.

Today's Tenement Trail

Sprawl also reflects upward mobility for the aspiring lower-middle class. Nearly a half-century ago, Samuel Lubell dedicated *The Future of American Politics* to the memory of his mother, "who pioneered on the urban frontier." Lubell described a process parallel to the settling of the West, in which families on "the Old Tenement Trail" were continually on the move in search of a better life. In the cities, they abandoned crowded tenements on New York's Lower East Side for better housing in the South Bronx, and from there, went to the "West Bronx, crossing that Great Social Divide—the Grand Concourse—beyond which rolled true middle-class country where janitors were called superintendents."

Today's "tenement trail" takes aspiring working- and lower-middle class Americans to quite different areas. Kendall, Florida, 20 miles southeast of Miami, is every environmentalist's nightmare image of sprawl, a giant grid carved out of the muck of swamp land that encroaches on the Everglades. Stripmalls and mega-stores abound for mile after mile, as do the area's signature giant auto lots. Yet Kendall also represents a late-twentieth-century version of the Old Tenement Trail. Kendall, notes the *New Republic's* Charles Lane, is "the Queens of the late twentieth century," a place where immigrants are buying into America. Carved out of the palmetto wilderness, its population exploded from roughly 20,000 in 1970 to 300,000 today. Agricultural in the 1960s, and a hip place for young whites in the 1970s, Kendall grew increasingly Hispanic in the 1980s, as Cubans, Nicaraguans, and others who arrived with very little worked their way up. Today, it's half Hispanic and a remarkable example of integration. In most of Kendall, notes University of Miami geographer Peter Muller, "You can't point to a white or Latino block because the populations are so intermixed."

Virginia Postrel, the editor of *Reason*, argues that the slow-growth movement is animated by left-wing planners' hostility to suburbia. Others mock slow-growthers as elitists, as in the following quip:

Q: What's the difference between an environmentalist and a developer?
A: The environmentalist already has his house in the mountains.

But, in the 1990s, slow-growth sentiment has been taking hold in middle- and working-class suburbs like Kendall, as development turns into overdevelopment and traffic congestion becomes a daily problem.

Regional Government

One oft-proposed answer to sprawl has been larger regional governments that will exercise a monopoly on land-use decisions. Underlying this solution is the theory—no doubt correct—that sprawl is produced when individuals and townships seek to maximize their own advantage without regard for the good of the whole community. Regionalism, however, is stronger in logic than in practice. For example, the people of Kendall, rather than embracing regionalism, are looking to slow down growth by *seceding* from their regional government. Upon examination, we begin to see some of the problems with regional government.

Kendall is part of Metro-Dade, the oldest major regional government, created in 1957. The largest of its 29 municipalities, Miami, the fourth poorest city in the United States, has 350,000 people; the total population of Metro-Dade is 2 million, 1.1 million of whom live in unincorporated areas. In Metro-Dade, antisprawl and antiregional government sentiments merge. Despite county-imposed growth boundaries, residents have complained bitterly of overdevelopment. The county commissioners—many of whom have been convicted of, or charged with, corruption—have been highly receptive to the developers who are among their largest campaign contributors. As one south Florida resident said of the developers, "It's a lot cheaper to be able to buy just one government." The south Florida secessionists want to return zoning to local control where developers' clout is less likely to overwhelm neighborhood interests.

When Jane Jacobs wrote, in *The Death and Life of Great American Cities,* that "the voters sensibly decline to federate into a system where bigness means local helplessness, ruthless oversimplified planning and administrative chaos," she could have been writing about south Florida. What's striking about Metro-Dade is that it has delivered neither efficiency nor equity nor effective planning while squelching local self-determination.

The fight over Metro-Dade echoes the conflicts of an earlier era. Historically, the fight over regional versus local government was an important, if intermittent, issue for many cities from 1910 to 1970. From about 1850 to 1910, according to urban historian Jon Teaford, suburbanites were eager to be absorbed by cities whose wealth enabled them to build the water, sewage, and road systems they couldn't construct on their own. "The central city," he explains, "provided superior service at a lower cost." But, in the 1920s, well before race became a central issue, suburbanites, who had increasingly sorted themselves out by ethnicity and class, began to use special-service districts and innovative financial methods to provide their own infrastructure and turned away from unification. Suburbanites also denounced consolidation as an invitation to big-city, and often Catholic, "boss rule" and as a threat to "self-government."

In the 1960s, as black politicians began to win influence over big-city governments, they also joined the anticonsolidation chorus. At the same time, county government, once a sleepy extension of rural rule, was modernized, and county executives essentially became the mayors of full-service governments administering what were, in effect, dispersed cities. But they were mayors with a difference. Their constituents often wanted a balance between commercial development, which constrained the rise of taxes, and the suburban ideal of family-friendly semirural living. When development seemed too intrusive, suburban voters in the 1980s, and again in the 1990s, have pushed a slow-growth agenda.

The New Regionalism

In the 1990s, regionalism has been revived as an effort to link the problem of sprawl with the problem of inner-city poverty. Assuming that "flight creates blight," regionalists propose to recapture the revenue of those who have fled the cities and force growth back into older areas by creating regional or metropolitan-area governments with control over land use and taxation.

The new regionalism owes a great deal to a group of circuit-riding reformers. Inspired by the arguments of scholars like Anthony Downs, one of the authors of the Kerner Commission report, and sociologist William Julius Wilson of Harvard, as well as the example of Portland, Oregon's metro-wide government, these itinerant preachers have traveled to hundreds of cities to spread the gospel of regional cooperation. The three most prominent new regionalists—columnist Neil Peirce, former Albuquerque mayor David Rusk, and Minnesota state representative Myron Orfield—have developed a series of distinct, but overlapping, arguments for why cities can't help themselves, and why regional solutions are necessary.

Peirce, in his book *Citistates,* plausibly insists that regions are the real units of competition in the global economy, so that there is a metro-wide imperative to revive the central city, lest the entire area be undermined. Less plausibly, Orfield in *Metropolitics* argues that what he calls "the favored quarter" of fast-growing suburbs on the periphery of the metro area have prospered at the expense of both the central city and the inner-ring suburbs. In order both to revive the central city and save the inner suburbs from decline, Orfield proposes that these two areas join forces, redistributing money from the "favored quarter" to the older areas. Rusk argues, in *Baltimore Unbound,* that older cities, unable to annex the fast growing suburbs, are doomed to further decline. He insists that only "flexible cities"—that is, cities capable of expanding geographically and capturing the wealth of the suburbs—can truly deal with inner-city black poverty. Regionalism, writes Rusk, is "the new civil rights movement."

There are differences among them. Orfield and, to a lesser degree, Rusk operate on a zero-sum model in which gain for the suburbs comes directly at the expense of the central city. Peirce is less radical, proposing regional cooperation as the means to a win-win situation for both city and the surrounding region. But they all share a desire to disperse poverty across the region and, more importantly, recentralize economic growth in the already built-up areas. The latter goal is consistent with both the environmental thrust of the antisprawl movement and the push for regional government. In a speech to a Kansas City civic organization, Rusk laid out the central assumption of the new regionalism. "The greater the fragmentation of governments," he asserted, "the greater the fragmentation of society by race and economic class." Fewer governments, argue the new regionalists, will yield a number of benefits, including better opportunities for regional cooperation, more money for cash-strapped central cities, less racial inequality, less sprawl, and greater economic growth. However, all of these propositions are questionable.

Better Policies, Not Fewer Governments

Consider Baltimore and Philadelphia, cities that the regionalists have studied thoroughly. According to the 1998 *Greater Baltimore State of the Region* report, Philadelphia has 877 units of local government (including school boards)—or 17.8 per 100,000 people. Baltimore has only six government units of any consequence in Baltimore City and the five surrounding counties—or 2.8 per 100,000 people. Greater Baltimore has fewer government units than any other major metro area in the United States. As a political analyst told me: "Get six people in a room, and you have the government of 2,200 square miles, because the county execs have very strong powers." We might expect considerable regional cooperation in Baltimore, but not in Philadelphia. Regionalism has made no headway in either city, however. The failure has little to do with the number of governments and a great deal to do with failed policy choices in both cities.

Rusk does not mention the many failings of Baltimore's city government. He refers to the current mayor, Kurt Schmoke, just once and only to say that Baltimore has had "excellent political leadership." In Rusk's view, Baltimore is "programmed to fail" because of factors entirely beyond its control, namely, the inability to annex its successful suburbs. In the ahistorical world of the regionalist (and here, Peirce is a partial exception), people are always pulled from the city by structural forces but never pushed from the city by bad policies.

Baltimore is not as well financed as the District of Columbia, which ruined itself despite a surfeit of money. But Baltimore, a favorite political son of both Annapolis and Washington, has been blessed with abundant financial support. Over the past decade, Schmoke has increased spending on education and health by over a half-billion dollars. He has also added 200 police officers and spent $60 million more for police over the last four years. "His greatest skill," notes the *Baltimore Sun,* "has been his ability to attract more federal and state aid while subsidies diminished elsewhere." But, notwithstanding these expenditures, middle-class families continue to flee the city at the rate of 1,000 per month, helping to produce the sprawl environmentalists decry.

Little in Baltimore works well. The schools have been taken over by the state, while the Housing Authority is mired in perpetual scandal and corruption. Baltimore is one of the few cities where crime hasn't gone down. That's because Schmoke has insisted, contrary to the experiences of New York and other cities, that drug-related crime could not be reduced until drug use was controlled through treatment. The upshot is that New York, with eight times more people than Baltimore, has only twice as many murders. Baltimore also leads the country in sexually transmitted diseases. These diseases have flourished among the city's drug users partly owing to Schmoke's de facto decriminalization of drugs. According to the Centers for Disease Control and Prevention (CDC), Baltimore has a syphilis rate 18 times the national average, 3 or 4 times as high as areas where the STD epidemic is most concentrated.

Flexible Cities

Rusk attributes extraordinary qualities to flexible cities. He says that they are able to both reduce inequality, curb sprawl, and maintain vital downtowns. Rusk was the mayor of Albuquerque, a flexible city that annexed a vast area, even as its downtown essentially died. The reduced inequality he speaks of is largely a statistical artifact. If New York were to annex Scarsdale, East New York's average income would rise without having any effect on the lives of the people who live there. As for sprawl, flexible cities like Phoenix and Houston are hardly models.

A recent article for *Urban Affairs Review,* by Subhrajit Guhathakurta and Michele Wichert, showed that within the elastic city of Phoenix, inner-city residents poorer than their outer-ring neighbors are subsidizing the building of new developments on the fringes of the metropolis. While sprawl is correlated with downtown decline in Albuquerque, in Phoenix it's connected with what *Fortune* described as "the remarkable rebound of downtown Phoenix, which has become a chic after-dark destination as well as a residential hot spot." There seems to be no automatic connection between regionalism and downtown revival.

Orfield's *Metropolitics* provides another version of an over-determined structuralist argument. According to him, the favored quarter is sucking the inner city dry, and, as a result, central-city blight will inevitably engulf the older first-ring suburbs as well. He is right to see strong pressures on the inner-ring suburbs, stemming from an aging housing stock and population as well as an influx of inner-city poor. But it is how the inner-ring suburbs respond to these pressures that will affect their fate.

When Coleman Young was mayor of Detroit, large sections of the city returned to prairie. But the inner-ring suburbs have done fairly well precisely by not imitating Detroit's practice of providing poor services at premium prices. "Much like the new edge suburbs," explains the *Detroit News,* "older suburbs that follow the proven formula of promoting good schools, public safety and well-kept housing attract new investment." Suburban Mayor Michael Guido sees his city's well developed infrastructure as an asset, which has already been bought and paid for. "Now," says Mayor Guido, "it's a matter of maintenance . . .and we offer a sense of history and a sense of community. That's really important to people, to have a sense of belonging to a whole community rather than a subdivision."

Suburb Power

City-suburban relations are not fixed; they are various depending on the policies both follow. Some suburbs compete with the central city for business. In south Florida, Coral Gables more than holds its own with Miami as a site for business headquarters. Southfield, just outside Detroit, and Clayton, just outside St. Louis, blossomed in the wake of the 1960s' urban riots and now compete with their downtowns. Aurora, with a population of more than 160,000 and to the east of Denver, sees itself as a competitor, and it sees regional efforts at growth management as a means by which the downtown Denver elite can ward off competition.

Suburban growth can also help the central city. In the Philadelphia area, economic growth and new work come largely from the Route 202 high-tech corridor in Chester County, west of the city. While the city has lost 57,000 jobs, even in the midst of national economic prosperity, the fast growing Route 202 companies have been an important source of downtown legal and accounting jobs. At the same time, the suburbs are creating jobs for residents that the central city cannot produce, so that 20 percent of city residents commute to the suburbs while 15 percent of people who live in the suburbs commute to Philadelphia.

The "new regionalists" assume that the prosperity of the edge cities is a function of inner-city decline. But, in many cities, it is more nearly the case that suburban booms are part of what's keeping the central-city economy alive. It is the edge cities that have taken up the time-honored urban task of creating new work.

According to *INC* magazine, the 500 fastest growing small companies are all located in suburbs and exurbs. This is because local governments there are very responsive to the needs of start-up companies. These high-tech hotbeds, dubbed "nerdistans" by Joel Kotkin, are composed of networks of companies that are sometimes partners, sometimes competitors. They provide a pool of seasoned talent for start-ups, where engineers and techies who prefer the orderly, outdoor life of suburbia to the crowds and disorder of the city can move from project to project. Henry Nicholas, CEO of Broadcom, a communications-chip and cable-modem maker, explained why he reluctantly moved to Irvine: "It's hard to relocate techies to L.A. It's the congestion, the expensive housing—and there's a certain stigma to it."

Imagine what the United States would be like if the Bay Area had followed the New York model. In 1898, New York created the first regional government when it consolidated all the areas of the New York harbor—Manhattan, Brooklyn, Queens, the Bronx, and Staten Island—into the then-largest city in the world. The consolidation has worked splendidly for Manhattan, which thrives as a capital of high-end financial and legal services. But over time, the Manhattan-centric economy based on high taxes, heavy social spending, and extensive economic regulation destroyed Brooklyn's once vital shipping and manufacturing economy.

In 1912, San Francisco, the Manhattan of Northern California, proposed to create a unified regional government by incorporating Oakland in the East Bay and San Jose in the South. The plan for a Greater San Francisco was modeled on Greater New York and called for the creation of self-governing boroughs within an enlarged city and county of San Francisco. East Bay opposition defeated the San Francisco expansion in the legislature, and later attempts at consolidation in 1917, 1923, and 1928 also failed. But had San Francisco with its traditions of high taxation and heavy regulation succeeded, Silicon Valley might never have become one of the engines of the American economy. Similarly, it's no accident that the Massachusetts Route 128 high-tech corridor is located outside of the boundaries of Boston, even as it enriches the central city.

The Portland Model

The complex and often ironic history of existing regional governments has been obscured by the bright light of hope emanating from Portland. It seems that in every generation one city is said to have perfected the magic elixir for revival. In the 1950s, it was Philadelphia; today, it's Portland. In recent years, hundreds of city officials have traveled to Portland to study its metropolitan government, comprehensive environmental planning, and the urban-growth boundary that has been credited with Portland's revival and success.

While there are important lessons to be learned from Portland, very little of its success to date can be directly attributed to the growth boundary, which was introduced too recently and with boundaries so capacious as not yet to have had much effect. Thirty-five percent of the land within the boundary was vacant when it was imposed in 1979. And, at the same time, fast growing Clark County, just north of Portland but not part of the urban-growth boundary, has provided an escape valve for potential housing pressures. The upshot, notes demographer Wendell Cox, is that even with the growth boundary, Portland still remains a relatively low-density area with fewer people per square mile than San Diego, San Jose, or Sacramento.

Portland has also been run with honesty and efficiency, unlike Metro-Dade. Blessed with great natural resources, Portland—sometimes dubbed "Silicon forest," because chipmakers are drawn to its vast quantities of cheap clean water—has conserved its man-made as well as natural resources. A city with more cast-iron buildings than any place outside of Manhattan, it has been a leader in historic preservation. Time and again, Portland's leadership has made the right choices. It was one of the first cities to reconnect its downtown with the riverfront. Portland never built a circumferential freeway. And, in the

1970s, under the leadership of mayor Neil Goldschmidt, the city vetoed a number of proposed highway projects that would have threatened the downtown.

In 1978, Portland voters, in conjunction with the state government, created the first directly elected metropolitan government with the power to manage growth over three counties. Portland metro government has banned big-box retailers, like Walmart and Price Club, on the grounds that they demand too much space and encourage too much driving. This is certainly an interesting experiment well worth watching, but should other cities emulate Portland's land-management model? It's too soon to say.

Good government is always important. But aside from that, it's hard to draw any general lessons from the Portland experience. The growth boundaries may or may not work, and there's certainly no reason to think that playing with political boundaries will bring good government to Baltimore.

Living with Sprawl

What then is to be done? First, we can accept the consensus that has developed around preserving open space, despite some contradictory effects. The greenbelts around London, Portland, and Baltimore County pushed some development back toward the city and encouraged further sprawl as growth leapfrogged the open space. The push to preserve open space is only likely to grow stronger as continued growth generates both more congestion and more wealth, which can be used to buy up open land.

Secondly, we can create what Peter Salins, writing in *The Public Interest*[1] described as a "level playing field" between the central cities and the suburbs. This can be done by ending exurban growth subsidies for both transportation as well as new water and sewer lines. These measures might further encourage the revival of interest in old fashioned Main Street living, which is already attracting a new niche of home buyers. State and local governments can also repeal the land-use and zoning regulations that discourage mixed-use development of the sort that produces a clustering of housing around Main Street and unsubsidized low-cost housing in the apartments above the streets' shops.

Because of our strong traditions of local self-government, regionalism has been described as an unnatural act among consenting jurisdictions. But regional cooperation needn't mean the heavy hand of all-encompassing regional government. There are some modest, but promising, experiments already under way in regional revenue sharing whose effects should be carefully evaluated. Allegheny County, which includes Pittsburgh, has created a Regional Asset District that uses a 1 percent sales tax increase to support cultural institutions and reduce other taxes. The Twin Cities have put money derived from the increase in assessed value of commercial and industrial properties into a pot to aid fiscally weaker municipalities. Kansas and Missouri created a cultural district that levies a small increase in the sales tax across the region. The money is being used to rehabilitate the area's most treasured architectural landmark, Kansas City's Union Station.

Cities and suburbs do have some shared interests, as in the growing practice of reverse commuting which links inner-city residents looking to get off welfare with fast growing suburban areas hampered by a shortage of labor. Regionalism can curb sprawl and integrate and sustain central-city populations if it reforms the misguided policies and politics that have sent the black and white middle class streaming out of cities like Baltimore, Washington, and Philadelphia. Regional co-operation between the sprawling high-tech suburbs and the central cities could modernize cities that are in danger of being left further behind by the digital economy. In that vein, the District of Columbia's Mayor Anthony Williams seized on the importance of connecting his welfare population with the fast growing areas of Fairfax County in Northern Virginia. The aim of focused regional policies, argues former HUD Undersecretary Marc Weiss, should be economic, not political, integration.

Sprawl isn't some malignancy that can be surgically removed. It's been part and parcel of healthy growth, and curbing it involves difficult tradeoffs best worked out locally. Sprawl and the movement against sprawl are now a permanent part of the landscape. The future is summed up in a quip attributed to former Oregon Governor Tom McCall, who was instrumental in creating Portland's growth boundary. "Oregonians," he said, "are against two things, sprawl and density."

Reference

1. "Cities, Suburbs, and the Urban Crisis," *The Public Interest,* No. 113 (Fall 1993).

28

Dolores Hayden

THE NEW URBANISM

In 2003 Americans have had almost two centuries of experience with suburban boosters and their growth machines. Living farther and farther from older city centers, Americans spend an increasing proportion of their income on home mortgages and car payments, and purchase freezers, washers, computers, and barbecues as if there will never be a shortage of oil, electricity, water, or air. American movies and television convey the vision of suburban prosperity to other nations. American corporations promote consumption around the world,

Excerpt from Dolores Hayden, *Building Suburbia: Green Fields and Urban Growth, 1820–2000.* Pantheon Books, 2003, pp. 201–203, 205–216 (text only; continuous text, p. 204 is an illustration), and corresponding notes on pp. 280–282.

building highways, shopping malls, and single-family houses. At home, underneath the apparent prosperity lies anxiety. Can the United States sustain growth at the rate of 1.5 million new housing units a year? Is there something inherently shaky about the whole edifice of credit, consumption, and public subsidies for private development?

As environmentalists wrestle with the economic implications of sprawl, architects are tackling its physical symptoms. Many believe better designs can result in better suburbs for the twenty-first century. The "new urbanists" argue for a return to a slower way of life. They elaborate a cozy past, where old-fashioned family life is honored in neo-traditional houses gathered into beautifully landscaped enclaves. The futurist "smart house" advocates prefer a fast-paced world where new digital technologies might bring families freedom from chores and boredom. The "green" architects idealize a connection to nature and design housing to limit the consumption of nonrenewable resources. Designers who grapple with shelter do not always know much history. The nostalgic neo-traditional developments, the science-fiction houses, and the sustainable experiments have all been tried. At the end of the nineteenth century, Ebenezer Howard, founder of the Garden Cities movement, proclaimed a return to the architectural forms of the preindustrial village, and Edward Bellamy, founder of the Nationalist movement, envisioned a world run on electricity and mass communication. Energy conservation was a focus of research during the Depression and World War II. These precedents are rarely cited, but when architects talk about new projects that might be historicist, wired, or green, they often hold a nostalgic, idealized view of affluent families and the picturesque enclaves and borderlands of the American past. Many designers also weaken their visions by trying to fit their projects into "the market" as defined by current real estate development priorities. New forms for model houses never solve major urban problems, but they may be sold as if they can. New real estate developments may demonstrate local solutions to physical problems, but in themselves, they cannot change the national economic and political conditions that underlie sprawl.

Back to The Picturesque Enclave

"No more housing subdivisions! No more shopping centers! No more office parks! No more highways! Neighborhoods or nothing!" is the cry of Andrés Duany and Elizabeth Plater-Zyberk, architects who have created imaginative plans for entire neo-traditional enclaves.[1] The developers who first hired them in the 1980s studied marketing surveys and pitched their projects to middle-class families. While some consumers wanted a house with perfect architectural details, others wanted more sociability and community. And still others wanted to stop worrying about unforeseen development spoiling their views. The designers claimed to have the answer: a new suburban neighborhood with a master plan, tight building codes, narrow streets, attractive public places, and dedicated open spaces, such as parks, beaches, and golf courses.

Seaside, Florida, and the Rise of New Urbanism

Architects interested in historic building patterns have rediscovered the picturesque enclave with its shared parkland—places like Riverside, Illinois, and Palos Verdes, California. One of the most influential new projects of the early 1980s was Seaside, Florida, by developer Robert Davis. Davis had spent vacation time as a child on the fine white beaches of the Florida Panhandle near Alabama with his grandfather, J. S. Smolian. He inherited about eighty acres of land located across from the sand on Route 30-A. As a successful Miami developer, Davis hired architects Elizabeth Plater-Zyberk and Andrés Duany's firm, DPZ, to design a model community for the Seaside property. In a remote location reachable only by car, they developed a master plan for a small, pedestrian-oriented resort of neo-traditional vernacular houses set in indigenous landscaping. The project was specifically designed to recapture a pre-automobile way of life. The developer wanted a place for "extended porch-sitting, leisurely strolling and sharing time with those you care most about, in a way that urban existence rarely allows.[2]

By 2001, over three hundred cottages lined narrow brick streets leading to beach pavilions providing access to the Gulf of Mexico. Neat oyster-shell paths, common parks, and planting strips encouraged walking and bicycling by both adults and children. The DPZ firm developed both a town code and a building code to reconnect designers of houses with the Northwest Florida vernacular building traditions of bungalows and dog-trots. They encouraged wood-frame cottages with deep overhangs, ample porches, windows located for cross-ventilation, and ceiling fans. The combination of porch-sitting and walking fostered by the design helped to re-create the ambiance of a small Southern beach resort of eighty to a hundred years ago, in the era of the horse and buggy. The automobile had pushed families off porches into the relative quiet of the backyard in the 1920s. Air-conditioning and television had drawn them indoors in the 1950s.[3] Seaside promised to draw people back outdoors for casual conversations between family and friends on porch and sidewalk. Seaside also promised environmentally sound landscaping: "The absence of lawns, except in a few public places, does more than spare us the noise of lawnmowers. No lawns means no fertilizer and pesticides to keep them up, and vastly reduces the water usage for irrigation. Native plant species, which predominate here, require no irrigation once they are established."[4]

Architects from all over the world were attracted to Seaside by the chance to design ornament, experiment with colors, and socialize in a convivial setting. Rules stimulated playful formal solutions: all the picket fences on a street had to be different. Next to the Central Square (contoured as an amphitheater) stood a tiny Greek Revival post office, an upscale food market, and several mixed-use buildings with apartments above shops. Across the street, adjoining the beach, was "Per-Spi-Cas-Ity," an outdoor market of small wooden stalls with a "Cinderella Circle" of brightly painted wooden Adirondack chairs.

Because the lots in Seaside were small, the density high, and the architectural constraints very strict, many Florida developers thought Robert Davis would lose a lot of money developing a town center on his small, flat piece of property. They did not believe conventional four-story, beachfront condominiums along the Gulf could be seen as less attractive than small houses a few blocks from the water, located on streets with beach access through community pavilions. Davis proved that building a town center for Seaside made a difference. In 1982 the best lot in Seaside cost $12,000. In March 2001, "Dreamsicle," a 700-square-foot house with 170 square feet of additional porches, located on Rosewalk at the edge of town, was on the market for $475,000 (unfurnished). "Breakaway," a 2,115-square-foot house on Pensacola Street, with a 524-square-foot guest house called "Romance" was priced at $1.1 million (furnished). Waterfront lots cost about $1.7 to 2 million.[5]

Everyone who bought in Seaside had to pay yearly assessments to a Neighborhood Association controlling street and common area maintenance as well as beach access. In addition, most residents joined the Seaside Swim and Tennis Club to have access to swimming pools, tennis courts, and croquet. Owners were identified with painted signs on their houses listing the names of houses, parents, children, and pets, plus their hometown. At 517 Forrest Street, for example, was "Mom's Off Duty" with Rick and Ramelle Forman of Madison, Wisconsin, plus their daughter, Alison, and Freddie, their cat. The personal touch hid a complex system for renting houses and their accessory apartments to tourists as if they were hotel rooms through the Seaside Cottage Rental Agency. Tourism picked up in 1998 after Seaside was chosen as the film location for *The Truman Show*. Actor Jim Carrey starred as Truman Burbank, a young man who has spent his whole life on live television and doesn't realize that his entire "town" is just the set for a reality-TV show. Producers substituted lawns for Seaside's indigenous landscaping to make the place look more conventional. The film implied a critique of Seaside as an overly controlled, cute place, but the location fee helped to pay for the construction of a charter school in 1996 for children in grades six through eight.

Seaside recalled the success of Llewellyn Park, New Jersey, in the 1850s. In both places, common land attracted wealthy residents to a picturesque development in a remarkable landscape. In both places, lifestyle pioneers mingled with millionaires. One was a suburb reached by railroad and the other a community of second homes accessible only by car, but both made their designers famous and led to dozens of imitations. Media attention positioned Seaside as a model for suburban housing in the United States, although architects and planners debated the quality of DPZ's efforts. Some critiqued Seaside as nostalgic, while defenders noted that modernist designers such as Deborah Berke, Steven Holl, Rodolfo Machado, and Jorge Silvetti had all designed buildings in Seaside. Some critiqued Seaside as elitist. Defenders noted the modest size of the houses, if not their prices. Others said Seaside couldn't be a model for how to house Americans, since it was an expensive resort with only three hundred houses and few full-time residents. Defenders replied that rising prices in Seaside persuaded developers that there was money to be made by building walkable neighborhoods around an attractive town center.

In 1993 Duany and Plater-Zyberk joined forces with some West Coast architects to form a loose association called the Congress for the New Urbanism

(CNU). Californian Peter Calthorpe was known for his strong interest in energy conservation and public transit. He and Douglas Kelbaugh argued for "pedestrian pockets" or "transit-oriented development" (TOD). Their work also emphasized mixing housing with commercial space and creating walkable neighborhoods.[6] Others who joined them came from a mix of backgrounds, including solar homes. While all of the CNU architects were in favor of infill (new construction sited within existing neighborhoods), many of their first projects turned out to be affluent greenfield efforts on the suburban fringe. Developers found it easier to assemble raw land and architects found it easier to rezone and recode in unincorporated areas. As the size of projects grew, it was difficult to find a developer wealthy enough to build a very substantial town center or any regional authority able to build light-rail transit. However, CNU's leaders received a lot of press attention for the projects that did get built and they became more credible as both urban and regional planners. By 1996, they were at work on a thoughtful, substantial charter defining new urbanism as "a complex system of policies and design principles that operate at multiple scales," including regions, neighborhoods, and streets.[7] By 2000, the largest firms associated with the movement had hundreds of projects completed, including redevelopments of public housing and old malls, as well as new residential communities.

"Disney's Town of Celebration": Theme Park Meets Enclave

The wit, charm, and modest scale of Seaside, as well as the energy and transit-oriented tone of the charter of the Congress for the New Urbanism were underscored when a much larger development called "Celebration" was established by The Walt Disney Company near Orlando, Florida, in 1994. Unlike Seaside, Celebration was not an incorporated town, although it was advertised as "Disney's Town of Celebration." Thirty years earlier, Walt Disney had purchased 28,000 acres in Osceola County, a citrus and cattle-ranching area in the Florida interior. Disney hoped to build an expanded version of his Southern California theme park, own the surrounding hotels, and build a model town called EPCOT (Experimental Prototype Community of Tomorrow) for 20,000 workers. EPCOT never became a housing development—today it is a theme park. The other ventures thrived. By 1990 Orlando was one of the fastest-growing areas in the United States, home to Walt Disney World Resort and a host of other theme parks focused on everything from sea creatures to the Bible. In 1991 Joel Garreau identified four edge cities there, including one that had taken over the old downtown, so the entire urban region looked a bit like Tysons Corner with scattered office and commercial developments as well as theme parks next to gridlocked freeways.[8] When Orlando's roads literally couldn't handle one more theme park, Disney ventured into real estate development.

Disney's Michael Eisner commissioned Jacquelin Robertson (of Cooper, Robertson and Partners, a New York urban design firm) and Robert A. M. Stern Architects (a New York architecture firm) to draw up a master plan. They proposed a residential area housing 20,000 people on about 4,900 acres in an unincorporated part of Osceola County, a site split off from the Reedy Creek Improvement District (the physical planning entity that included the Disney amusement parks and hotels). The Celebration Company, a subsidiary of The Walt Disney Company, was a developer with deep pockets. Disney poured $2.5 billion into transforming an unpromising wetland into a large and handsome town center—dredging an artificial lake, building roads, parks, and bridges as well as downtown shops. Others built a hotel and schools. An eighteen-hole golf course designed by Robert Trent Jones, Sr., and Robert Trent Jones, Jr., ran through the middle of the site, recalling developer Hugh E. Prather's dictum "The American businessman wants his golf."[9] The links were banded by "Estate Homes" ($600,000 and up). Lesser neighborhoods were handsomely landscaped with parks and playgrounds to serve "Village Homes" ($350,000), "Cottage Homes" ($250,000), townhomes ($250,000), and apartments. Styles included "Classical, Victorian, Colonial Revival, Coastal, Mediterranean, and French." At the edge of the site, next to the freeway, stood "Celebration Health," a 260,000-square-foot "wellness center" (a hospital run by Florida Health, part of the Church of Seventh Day Adventists), and "Celebration Place," a 109-acre office park.[10] Noted architects designed all of the public buildings, but they were not from the younger generation of new urbanists. Robert A. M. Stern's buildings stressed context. Others were more exuberant "signature" buildings in personal styles, including Aldo Rossi's office park. Some worked beautifully, such as Caesar Pelli's art deco theater, sited where its exuberant shapes were reflected in the new lake. Others fell flat, perhaps attempting irony, including Philip Johnson's town hall, with a forest of tall, thin columns and a gigantic door.

I visited Celebration in March 2001. After an hour and a half stuck on crowded freeways within Orlando, I spotted the white three-rail fence that wrapped the exterior of the development, an imitation of the rural fences used on the old horse farms and ranches of central Florida. Once inside, I drove to the Celebration Hotel. Two 1950s Cadillacs permanently parked in the forecourt echoed the theme of Florida plantation culture. In a lobby overlooking the lake, cypress root lamps illuminated ceiling fans, wicker furniture, and large bird cages. Additional props included framed photographs of the horse-and-buggy world of the citrus and cattle towns in central Florida in the 1920s. At the reception desk two women wearing identical white silk blouses and pearls greeted guests. An antique fishing rod and a couple of old brown leather suitcases—the kind often featured in Ralph Lauren ads—were positioned by the desk as if their owner had just arrived. Decor in the hotel room was nostalgic. In case I hadn't decided what to think, memo pads next to the phone read "Celebration Hotel, 'Delightfully Charming.' "

I headed to the dining room past more historical photos. One showed ten African-Americans clearing land with tractors. Next to my table was an image of an African-American crew picking oranges. The old Florida plantation theme was full-blown when I spotted a view of orange groves with two white overseers on horseback. Although Florida is a multiracial state, the only

African-American I saw at the Celebration Hotel that night was standing outside next to the antique Cadiliacs, parking cars.

The next morning I walked over to the Celebration sales center, housed in a
building designed by Charles Moore. I examined the large, well-lit scale model
of Celebration, inquired how large the entire Celebration site was, and asked
about future development, pointing to areas labeled "future residential" or "future multi-family," but I never got a satisfactory answer. Although advertised
on billboards as "Disney's Town of Celebration" and on a website saying "Welcome to Celebration, Florida," Celebration is not a town with political boundaries but a real estate development in Osceola County. My question about
boundaries was not trivial. When I noticed a sign stating that only "cast members" were allowed to handle the lights on the site model, I realized the real estate sales people held the same job title—cast member—as workers in Disney's
amusement parks. Cast members cared for the streets early every morning in
Celebration, just as they did in the theme parks, and the streets were spotless.

I walked around the neighborhoods closest to the center of the project and
the lake, passing small parks planted with flowering trees and traditional beds
of flowers, like well-tended English public parks. This was not indigenous
landscaping, so it felt artificial in central Florida, but I liked the parks and playgrounds and lingered on the perfect sidewalks. The eclectic houses—federal,
Victorian, Greek revival, Spanish colonial revival—were well kept and the cars
were out of sight, in garages accessed from alleys behind the streets. There
were large porches and flourishing private gardens. It was a sunny day, and I
was the only person in sight. Although designed to represent the passage of
time through various architectural styles, everything in Celebration was new,
so I felt as if I had wandered onto the set of a Technicolor movie. I was convinced that I had returned to an affluent moment in the 1920s, before the crash,
to experience a community of middle-class single-family houses, just the way
Herbert Hoover envisioned it.

I returned to the sales office, where I asked if I could visit a model house.
All of Celebration carries the corporate logo of a large tree shading a small
pony-tailed girl on a bicycle riding past a picket fence, trailed by her dog:
CELEBRATION. FLORIDA. EST 1994. In the neighborhoods closest to the center, the
houses were all sold. The salesperson pointed to a map with the locations of
new model houses. "Can I walk?" I asked. "You don't have a car?" she replied
in astonishment. I did have a car, but I had to walk all the way back to the hotel
to get it, and then drive a mile to the open houses.

Writer Alex Marshall has observed that Celebration's designers have
tried to "re-create an urban neighborhood without creating the transportation
network that spawned such neighborhoods. . . . So what you get is a peculiar
thing, an automobile-oriented subdivision dressed up to look like a small
pre-car centered town."[11] There is another ambiguity as well. The presence of
the office park suggests that Celebration is going to become an edge node. Indeed, when I checked public records, I found that in 2002 The Celebration
Company filed a "Master Development Plan" with Osceola County that

showed "Celebration West" across Interstate 4 from "Celebration East." The plan detailed four phases of development through 2020 and included 6,777,033 square feet of retail, commercial, and industrial development. Some residential areas included possible densities as high as forty dwellings to the acre. The height limit on the master plan for Celebration West is twenty-six stories.[12] If this future development occurs, the residential area, including the high-priced golf-course "Estate Homes," will be an adjunct. If many future residents live at very high densities several miles away from the pedestrian center, amid new commercial and industrial projects of Phases 2, 3, and 4, "Celebration" will no longer feel like the upscale picturesque enclaves of the 1920s it now resembles. Only Phase I was visible on Celebration's first plans and models, so some buyers may be in for a shock if it turns out that the expensive picturesque enclave was simply the anchor for a new edge node.

The promotional literature for Celebration that I saw suggested that Disney's salespeople, like many in the real estate world, always straddled the line between life and entertainment, reality and fantasy: "The destination your soul has been searching for," promised one ad. Another crooned: "There was once a place where neighbors greeted neighbors in the quiet of the summer twilight. Where children chased fireflies. . . . The movie house showed cartoons on Saturday. The grocery store delivered. . . . Remember that place? It held a magic all its own. The special magic of an American hometown." The magic flickered like the stream of light from a movie projector. Parts of the development were excellent: the art deco movie house, the charming small parks, the pleasant waterfront. The expansive central area impressed visitors, but the experience of it was undercut by staged interiors such as the banal "plantation" hotel (not run by Disney, as it turned out) and the corny 1940s malt shop. Celebration was unlike a real town in that it housed only the affluent. "Downtown" had schools and apartments, to be sure, but most Disney theme park employees could not afford to live there, even in the least expensive apartments. Most local teachers and firefighters were priced out also. Too many boutiques sold Disney souvenirs. The streetscapes were attractive, but in March 2001 every old-fashioned lamppost held a banner proclaiming "Celebration of Taste," "Celebration of Charm," "Celebration of Style." The notepad people had been busy outdoors.

Behind the real estate sales pitch was a hundred-page "Declaration of Covenants, Conditions, and Restrictions" (CC&R's). As with any Community of Interest Development (CID), a person who purchased a house in Celebration had to sign an agreement giving most of the decision-making power in the community to a management authority representing the developer. The agreement limited what residents could do with their property—no colored curtains, for example. There were restrictions on what they could plant in their yards, where they could park their cars, and how soon they could resell their houses.

When journalists descended on Celebration in its first few years, most were determined to report that it was not "the happiest place on earth." Some builders used crews of illegal immigrants to build houses and many did not deliver a satisfactory "product."[13] Some students and parents were disappointed by the much-advertised model school, leading to lawsuits.[14] Encephalitis-bearing mosquitoes put a cramp on porch-sitting, while residents who planned to play golf found the tee times taken by Japanese tourists.[15] If anyone wanted to protest, the "Town Hall" designed by Philip Johnson housed only the real estate managers hired by The Celebration Company, not elected local government officials, although eventually property owners would have more say.

After a few years, debates about illusion and reality at both Seaside and Celebration wound down. If Seaside could be described as a resort where the theme was Southern rural architecture, Celebration was a community where the theme was pre-1940s Southern small-town living. Yet despite the gibes, both Robert Davis and The Walt Disney Company invested in substantial, attractive public realms intended to shame get-rich-quick developers of edge nodes, malls, and fringe subdivisions. Their message was simple: we sell more houses because we design better public places. As far as the architects were concerned, these developers were exceptional clients, clients to be courted.[16] As far as the developers were concerned, sales prices would validate their investment in neo-traditional design. Their careful attention to the public realm, especially its pedestrian scale, was welcome, but inevitably other developers copied what they liked from these model enclaves without imitating the most expensive investments in site design and architecture.

Gated Enclaves

Neither Seaside nor Celebration had a gate with a guard at the entrance, although both were closely supervised by private real estate developers. The *Charter of the New Urbanism* took a principled position against gated communities, but many critics of new urbanism felt that the design of expensive new suburban areas resembling old-fashioned elite enclaves encouraged exclusivity, whether or not the enclaves had gates. Gates had been part of the appeal in exclusive communities such as Tuxedo Park, and a century later, developers working on projects for almost all income levels found that gates enhanced the sense of security many buyers sought in the sprawling suburban landscape. Evan MacKenzie in *Privatopia* and Ed Blakely and Mary Gail Snyder in *Fortress America* have documented the rapid rise of gated communities in the 1990s.[17] When anthropologist Setha Low interviewed residents in several gated communities, many expressed fear about unsafe neighborhoods, overdevelopment, and uncertain resale values. In order to gain a measure of stability, those who chose to locate in gated communities—perhaps 16 million people by 2002—submitted to arbitrary rules and restrictions, while they enjoyed club-like amenities and private policing of their grounds.[18] Among the gated communities that catered to particular interests were those with golf courses or private beaches. In 2002, new gated communities were also being designed for evangelical churches. Many churches had expanded to offer around-the-clock activities to members including social services, sports, and fast food, as well as religious worship. Journalist Patricia Leigh Brown reported on a visit to the

Community Church of Joy in suburban Phoenix in 2002, where the congregation was planning to add a housing development with a full-time chaplain. This congregation would also include a water park, "part of an Olympic-size aquatic center . . . [on] a Christian theme, with laser shows depicting Jonah and the whale and David and Goliath." Another specialist in religious history called this "Christian cocooning."[19]

Notes

1. Andrés Duany, Elizabeth Plater-Zyberk, and Jeff Speck, *Suburban Nation: The Rise of Sprawl and the Decline of the American Dream* (New York: North Point Press, 2000), 243.
2. "Seaside . . . Still the One, Twenty Years Later," and "Seaside: Environmentally Sound," *Seaside Times,* Extra Special 20th Anniversary Issue, 2001, 7; *A Walking Tour of Seaside* (Seaside, Fla.: Seaside Cottage Rental Agency, n.d.); David Mohney and Keller Easterling, eds., *Seaside; Making a Town in America* (New York: Princeton Architectural Press, 1991).
3. Drummond Buckley, "A Garage in the House," in *The Car and the City: The Automobile, the Built Environment, and Daily Urban Life,* ed. Martin Wachs and Margaret Crawford (Ann Arbor: University of Michigan Press, 1992), 124–40; Raymond Arsenault, "The End of the Long Hot Summer: The Air Conditioner and Southern Culture," *Journal of Southern History* 50 (November 1984): 597–628.
4. "Seaside: Environmentally Sound," *Seaside Times, 7.*
5. Seaside Community Realty, Seaside, Fla., brochure, March 9, 2001. A brochure of March 13, 2002, indicated prices might be down slightly.
6. Congress for the New Urbanism, *Charter of the New Urbanism* (New York: McGraw-Hill, 2000). It was adopted in 1996. The Ahwanee Principles of 1991 are reprinted in Tom Daniels, *When City and Country Collide: Managing Growth in the Metropolitan Fringe* (Washington, D.C.: Island Press, 1999), 91–92. See also Douglas Kelbaugh, ed., *The Pedestrian Pocket Book: A New Suburban Design Strategy* (New York: Princeton Architectural Press, 1989); and Douglas Kelbaugh, *Common Place: Toward Neighborhood and Regional Design* (Seattle: University of Washington Press, 1997). Emily Talen, "The Social Goals of New Urbanism," *Housing Policy Debate* 13 (2002): 165–88, evaluates the aims in the *Charter.*
7. Peter Calthorpe, in Congress for the New Urbanism, *Charter,* 178.
8. Joel Garreau, *Edge City: Life on the New Frontier* (New York: Doubleday, 1991), 433, lists downtown, the Maitland Center area, the airport area, and the University of Central Florida area.
9. Joel Schwartz, "Evolution of the Suburbs," in *Suburbia: The American Dream and Dilemma,* ed. Philip C. Dolce (Garden City, N.Y.: Anchor Press/Doubleday, 1976), 27. Prather was the developer of Highland Park and River Oaks in Texas.
10. Sales information based on Celebration brochures, 1996–2001; "Celebration," http://www.celebrationfl.com (January 2002); *Celebration News* (March 2001); *Celebration Independent* (March 2001); author interview with Robert A. M. Stern, July 2002.
11. Alex Marshall, *How Cities Work: Suburbs, Sprawl, and the Roads Not Taken* (Austin: University of Texas Press, 2000), 6.
12. Osceola County Building and Development, The Celebration Company, "DRI 02-0009 and PD02-00017 Celebration, Map H, Density Map, and Support Document," revised June 26, 2002.

13. Andrew Ross, *The Celebration Chronicles: Life, Liberty, and the Pursuit of Property Value in Disney's New Town* (New York: Ballantine, 1999), 36–44; Douglas Frantz and Catherine Collins, *Celebration, U.S.A.: Living in Disney's Brave New Town* (New York: Marian Wood/ Henry Holt, 1999), 82–101.

14. Marlena Morton, "Class Action Suit Filed Regarding School," *Celebration Independent,* March 2001, I.

15. Andrew Ross, *The Celebration Chronicles,* 13; David L. Kirp, "Pleasantville," *New York Times Book Review,* September 19, 1999, section 7, 22–23.

16. Some of the momentum established in these two enclaves was not to be sustained. DPZ went on to design Rosemary Beach, another Panhandle beach community which abandoned indigenous landscaping and local vernacular architecture for the Dutch Colonial Revival style with lawns.

17. Evan MacKenzie, *Privatopia: Homeowner Associations and the Rise of Residential Private Government* (New Haven: Yale University Press, 1994); Edward J. Blakely and Mary Gail Snyder, *Fortress America: Gated Communities in the United States* (Washington, D.C.: Brookings Institution and Lincoln Institute of Land Policy, 1997).

18. Setha Low, *Behind the Gates: The New American Dream* (New York: Routledge, 2003), 15–16.

19. Patricia Leigh Brown, "Megachurches as Minitowns," *New York Times,* May 9, 2002, F6. The private managers who run all kinds of Community of Interest Developments (CIDs) tend to be conservative. While they believe that they can make rules for their residents as private managers, they have a lot in common with private-property rights activists who dislike federal, state, and local government. The private-property rights advocates—also on the rise in 2000—belong to groups demanding an end to any kind of government regulation of land. Both groups are involved in withdrawing from the public realm. See Harvey M. Jacobs, ed., *Who Owns America? Social Conflict Over Property Rights* (Madison: University of Wisconsin Press, 1998); Charles Geisler and Gail Daneker, eds., *Property and Values: Alternatives to Public and Private Ownership* (Washington, D.C.: Island Press, 2000).